PENGUIN CLASSICS

WILLIAM SHAKESPEARE:
THE SONNETS AND A LOVER'S COMPLAINT

WILLIAM SHAKESPEARE

*

THE SONNETS
AND
A LOVER'S COMPLAINT

EDITED BY
JOHN KERRIGAN

PENGUIN BOOKS

PENGUIN BOOKS

Published by the Penguin Group
Penguin Books Ltd, 27 Wrights Lane, London W8 5TZ, England
Penguin Putnam Inc., 375 Hudson Street, New York, New York 10014, USA
Penguin Books Australia Ltd, Ringwood, Victoria, Australia
Penguin Books Canada Ltd, 10 Alcorn Avenue, Toronto, Ontario, Canada M4V 3B2
Penguin Books (NZ) Ltd, Private Bag 102902, NSMC, Auckland, New Zealand

Penguin Books Ltd, Registered Offices: Harmondsworth, Middlesex, England

This edition first published 1986
Published simultaneously by Viking
Reprinted with minor revisions 1995
Published in Penguin Classics 1999
3 5 7 9 10 8 6 4

Set in Linotron Ehrhardt
Printed in England by Clays Ltd, St Ives plc

CONTENTS

The 'place' of metaphor, its most intimate and final abode, is neither the word, nor the phrase, nor even discourse, but the copula, the couplement [*la copule*] of the verb 'to be'.

Paul Ricœur, *La Métaphore Vive* (1975)

TO.THE.ONLIE.BEGETTER.OF.THESE.INSVING.SONNETS. . . .
Thorpe's dedication in the quarto

That which is creative must create itself –
Keats to J. A. Hessey (8 October 1818)

Adonis, the name of a child, which was son of Cynare, king of Cyprus, whom Venus had for her darling, which was slain with a boar: whom the poets feigned, that Venus turned into a purple flower: some say into a rose.

Thomas Cooper, *Thesaurus Linguae* (1565)

Blindfold he was, and in his cruell fist
A mortall bow and arrowes keene did hold,
With which he shot at random, when him list,
Some headed with sad lead, some with pure gold;
(Ah man beware, how thou those darts behold).
Spenser, *The Faerie Queene* III.xi.48

One, two, three. Time, time!
Cymbeline II.2.51

INTRODUCTION

In the year 1609, when Shakespeare was forty-five and already the author of most of the plays that have made him famous, a slender paperback volume entitled 'SHAKE-SPEARES SONNETS. Neuer before Imprinted' appeared in the London bookshops of William Aspley and John Wright. Those Jacobean Londoners who came off the streets at Christ Church Gate to pay their few pence for this new quarto found themselves in possession of one hundred and fifty-four sonnets and a longish poem in rhyme royal called *A Lover's Complaint*. On the face of it, they would seem to have purchased a heterogeneous collection. The first hundred and twenty-six poems in Shakespeare's book are apparently addressed to a beautiful young man. In almost all of them there is an erotic undertow, but their explicit concerns are exceedingly diverse: nobility; the breeding of children; sexual betrayal; poetry, painting, and cosmetics; the depredations of Time. This group is rounded off by an envoy, a douzain in couplets addressed to the lovely youth. Sonnets 127–52 shift the poetic focus away from the friend to a seductive but treacherous dark-favoured lady. They deal with her charms, with the poet's adulterous passion for her, and with the disgust which envelops him when she proves false. Most readers feel that these sonnets interlock with those written to the young man. Certainly, tone, content, and context all help connect poems like 40, 'Take all my loves, my love, yea, take them all', where the poet ruefully forgives the youth for being seduced by his mistress, with those angrily imploring sonnets in which the dark lady is asked why she must enslave not only the poet but his 'sweet'st friend' as well (133.4). Nevertheless, while Sonnets 127–52 relate to the first group, 1–126, they remain a distinct sub-sequence. And neither set of sonnets seems obviously linked with poems 153–4, both of them imitations of an epigram in the Greek Anthology devoted to Cupid, a maiden votaress of the goddess Diana, and a seething-hot therapeutic spring. These poems form a further group, separating the two longer sets of sonnets from that work in rhyme royal which concludes the quarto, *A Lover's Complaint*.

Inevitably, the question arises: would the diversity of Shakespeare's volume have baffled its early readers? The central claim of this edition is that, no, it would not – though modern critics have neglected to register the point of the collection as a collection. Indeed, it is a standard scholarly ploy to play up the 'mystery' of the Sonnets, and then announce some astonishing 'solution' to the 'problem': the poems are reordered to produce a supposedly coherent narrative, or the youth and dark lady identified with Elizabethans whom Shakespeare might have known. Those critics who most care about poetry sense that this approach is wrong, of course, but, lacking a proper framework for reading the book, they have tended either to construct image patterns at the expense of verbal texture, in the manner of Wilson Knight, or, like Northrop Frye, dissolved the contingencies of the verse in myth, or else, like William Empson, produced brilliant close analyses which, helpful in themselves, do little to illuminate that subtle modulation of material from poem to poem into the form of the whole which makes reading Shakespeare's Sonnets such a concentrated yet essentially cumulative experience.

The continuities are often self-evident. The paired poems on insomnia (27–8), the four elements (44–5), journeying on horseback (50–51), or emotional slavery (57–8) are inseparable; and there are several points at which an initial 'But' or 'Thus' locks a sonnet into the argument of its predecessor. Yet the commonest and most characteristic means to continuity are altogether more secretive. A rhythm, a rhyme, a quirk of syntax, or an echoing image: such minutiae, hardly discernible in conscious reading, knit the poems together. Consider, just at the level of verbal echo, the four famous sonnets 106–9 – a group which happens to cut across the divisions imposed by more than one recent reordering. In the first, Shakespeare confionts a problem central to the 1609 volume: praise. Here the poet breaches the integrity of his text to preserve his text's integrity, invoking medieval annals and romance to praise by indirection. Recalling the 'ladies dead and lovely knights' of antique rhyme, Shakespeare finds in the blazons of their beauty a distant anticipation of the young man's loveliness. It is no wonder, he reflects, that the old texts fall short in their account of mortal beauty, since writers of the present age cannot capture the perfection of the friend. In tone and substance, Sonnet 107 could hardly be more different. It links public and private emotion, remarking a congruence between the poet's love life and (*pace* many editors) the mood of the nation after the accession of James I in 1603. The 'eclipse' of that 'mortal moon' Elizabeth had been dreaded by many, Shakespeare says; but James's coronation has 'crowned' those 'Incertainties' with assurance. The king's peace and declared pacifism here nurture the olive, while the 'time', like its newly anointed sovereign, is dewy with balm. The poet finds his own mood adumbrated in these events: old anxieties fade; his 'love looks fresh'; and though his verse is 'poor', it flourishes. Yet, however different these two sonnets may seem, they are linked by divination and a sense of the present. The 'prophetic soul' of the one derives from the 'prophecies' of the other (107.1, 106.9); in both, great tracts of time revolve around the word 'now' (106.8 and 13, 107.9). Sonnet 108 sets off on another tack. The poet may have 'Nothing' (that very Shakespearian quantity) to add to his old and threadbare verses (the 'poor rhyme' of 107.11); but, he implies, tatty sincerity is better than spruce eloquence. It is noticeable that 'prefiguring' and 'divining eyes' from 106.10–11 become, in 108, 'figured' in line 2 and 'prayers divine' in line 5, while, more subtly, the 'antique pen' of 106 reverberates in 'makes antiquity for aye his page' (108.12) to elicit, in the process, a 'page' of writing, the sonnet itself, from the old but young page-boy of love. These are echoes indeed: resounding and re-sounding words given a new, enlarged significance through their displacement. At the same time, in the contraction of 'My love looks fresh' (107.10) to 'love's fresh case' (at 108.9), we can identify a textual source for that cumulative concentration which is experienced when reading the Sonnets. In 109, finally, the allusive scope is broader: 'my soul, which in thy breast doth lie' evokes earlier, more deliberately artful accounts of interchanged identity (such as 62); 'Like him that travels I return again' itself returns to an old theme (compare 50–51); and 'So that myself bring water for my stain', in line 8, echoes a number of poems lamenting the youth's fickleness: 'Suns of the world may stain when heaven's sun staineth' (33.14). Most resonant of all, however, is the couplet: 'For nothing this wide universe I call | Save thou, my rose; in it thou art my all.' That last 'all' could not be so replete, so total, were it not for the roses of the early sonnets. Yet even here, supporting the grandly symbolic Rose of beauty, local echoes are at work. 'For nothing this wide universe I call' shadows not only the previous line, 'To leave for nothing all thy sum of good', but 'Nothing, sweet boy' at 108.5; while 'this wide universe' is a startling extension of the 'wide world' that dreams in the opening lines of 107.

Links like these – and they recur throughout the sequence, with particular density in 1–126 – suggest that the poems need no reordering. When the words are not echoic, the images are tied, or the argumentative cast is consistent, or the poet's tone of address. Stephen Booth may be too emphatic when he declares 'The continuity of the 1609 sequence is obvious and insistent, but sporadic and inconsistent in the factors by which relationship is perceived', but his hyperbole points us in the right direction. This is not to say, of course, that the poems were composed in their 1609 order, or that Shakespeare knew from the outset what the shape of his collection would be. We have the testimony of Francis Meres that the poet was circulating 'sugared sonnets among his private friends' in or before 1598, and when the versions of 138 and 144 printed in 1599 are taken with the variant material which survives in manuscript (see pages 441–54) the inescapable conclusion is that sonnets or sets of sonnets were quietly made public before the composition of 107. These early texts must have been read or sung as occasional pieces – rather like the lover's poems in *Astrophil and Stella*, where Sidney makes the idea of circulation part of the matter of the sequence itself. The Shakespearian intimacies of 'I' and 'you', the triangle of poet, youth, and dark lady, would thus have stood in one light in the 1590s and in quite another a decade later, when a context would have been provided less by the knowingness of 'private friends' than by the form and ordering of the quarto.

If the poems were lived through, passed about, and then revised before, if not for, publication in 1609, what kind of relationship do they finally have with life? If seventeenth-century history helps us understand Sonnet 107, with its disclosure of personal 'fears' through public ones, might not biographical inquiry solve the 'mystery' of Shakespeare's Sonnets? In 1609, the publisher dedicated his quarto to a 'Mr W.H.' Have we not after all a positive obligation as readers to decide whether this refers to the youth and later friend (if there is only one object of address between 1 and 126) of Shakespeare's sequence, and whether this young man is therefore William Herbert, Henry Wriothesley, William Haughton, Willie Hughes (the seductive boy-player invented by Oscar Wilde), William Hall, William Hathaway, the poet William Himself, or, as some have staunchly maintained, Queen Elizabeth in another guise? And what if the dark lady really was Mary Fitton, or Lucy Negro, Jacqueline Field, Emilia Lanier, or, to back an outsider, Mistress Winifred Burbage?

The answer is that, no, none of this matters much. It's not that the Sonnets are conventional exercises or a mere fiction. Shakespeare is certainly aware of – indeed, he exploits – sonneteering conventions, and literary precursors like Sidney and Daniel intermittently mark his text; but there are so many points in the sequence at which obscurity appears to stem not from failing verbal powers but from an unwillingness to grapple painful emotions into form that it seems reasonable to infer a troubled author behind the poetic 'I'. No editor can tell you – to offer one example – how many Wills the dark lady is supposed to have slept with in Sonnets 135 and 152, and the obsessive wordplay on 'will' seems better calculated to work out an author's anxieties than convey a fiction to the reader. At the same time, biographical reading, as we understand it now, has so little purchase on these poems that criticism directed along such lines soon finds itself spinning off the text into vacuous literary chit-chat. The truth is that the two prevailing approaches, biographical and formalist, are alike anachronistic – incorrigibly post-Romantic. It is no accident that the battle-lines which contemporary critics fight in were drawn up by Wordsworth and Browning. 'With this key Shakespeare unlocked his heart', Wordsworth wrote of the Sonnet; to which Browning replied 'Did Shakespeare? If so, the less Shakespeare he!' We need, temporarily, to forget *My Last Duchess* and *The Prelude* when reading this book of poems. The text is neither fictive nor confessional. Shakespeare stands behind the first person of his sequence as Sidney had stood behind Astrophil – sometimes near the poetic 'I', sometimes farther off, but never without some degree of rhetorical projection. The Sonnets are not autobiographical in a psychological mode.

Nor is this surprising. Autobiography hardly exists in sixteenth-century England, and what there is, like Thomas Hoby's *Travail and Life*, relates deeds and opinions, not inward thought and emotion. It is not until the seventeenth century that the keeping of diaries and the framing of memoirs begin in earnest. And even then, selfhood is in abeyance. It is revealing that astrologers and Calvinists – men seeking less to pursue the vagaries of inwardness than to confirm the working of a metaphysical order in the individual's life – should figure so prominently among our first autobiographers. We read Simon Forman's *Journals* for his sake; he wrote them to trace the influence of the stars upon his actions and opportunities. We read Bampfield's *A Name, an After-One* to see how this particularly interesting dissen-

ter led his life; he wrote it, like so many puritans, to show how closely
a modern life could conform to the paradigm provided by St Paul.
English autobiography developed late, and when it did begin to
flower, new forms were not developed to accommodate it. On the
contrary, received forms were used to exemplify – to make exemplary
– authors' lives. That is why Lodowick Muggleton, the charismatic
sectarian, divided his autobiography into biblical chapter and verse,
making himself an Old Testament prophet, why the courtier Kenelm
Digby modelled his *Loose Fantasies* on Sidney's *Arcadia*, and why the
great *Life* of Clarendon is narrated in a Caesarian third person.
Reading such texts, one is struck not by the inner-directed complex-
ity of post-Romantic autobiography but by an accomplished creative
projection. There is no sense that the literary value of the text in hand
flows through that text from the author. The text is sufficient; its
literary value is inherent; and the author is largely subsumed into the
order of his Life.

But where does this leave us critically? If biography cannot give the
Sonnets depth and resolution, and if reordering is illegitimate, what
can criticism do with these heterogeneous poems? Is there any
principle of coherence at work? A crucial clue is provided here by *A
Lover's Complaint*. Though few indeed have heeded them, the stylis-
tic tests agree that this beautiful and neglected poem – in which a
young woman is overheard lamenting her seduction by a lovely but
heartless youth – was written by Shakespeare after 1600, probably in
1602–5. The text overlaps strongly with several plays composed
in that period. In its source material or founding imagery, it recalls
the secondary, Ophelia plot in *Hamlet*, while connecting with
Desdemona's 'song of willow' in *Othello*. In syntax 'tortive and
errant', like much in *Troilus and Cressida*, it deals with a love affair
resembling that at the centre of *All's Well That Ends Well*, in language
as archly archaic as that deployed in *Pericles*. Given that this is so, and
given that most if not all of the sonnets numbered less than 107 are
Elizabethan in origin (which no one seriously disputes), and given,
too, the evidence of revision in variant sonnets, could it be that
Shakespeare was consciously shaping a collection when he wrote *A
Lover's Complaint* in *c.* 1602–5? The suspicion is confirmed when one
considers the sonnet sequences of the 1590s. Just as, in *Pericles*,
Shakespeare harked back to *The Comedy of Errors*, exploring the tale
of Apollonius which had provided the overplot of that early play, so,
in the 1609 quarto, he looked back admiringly to the sequences

published in his youth. The observation is not implicitly hostile. Nostalgia may have played its part in the creation of Shakespeare's volume, as well as the fulfilment of long-sustained ambition, but no loss of creative force can be detected in this, or indeed the other, recapitulative Jacobean labours – partly because what the poet returned to in them had, in important informing respects, always been with him.

Daniel's *Delia* is a decisive document here. As first published in 1592, the book includes fifty sonnets written to the poet's obdurate mistress, Delia, a short ode in anacreontics (that is, trochaic tetrameters), and a substantial poem in rhyme royal, *The Complaint of Rosamond*. It was this complaint, with its cleverly terraced account of the seduction and enforced suicide of Fair Rosamond, the young mistress of Henry II, which, more than any other in the kind, was to prompt Shakespeare to emulation in his *Lover's Complaint* over a decade later. Meanwhile, as Katherine Duncan-Jones has shown, *Delia* spawned a series of books in which a sonnet sequence is followed by a lyric interlude and a long poem. In 1593, Thomas Lodge published *Phillis*, where a sonnet sequence, divided (rather like Shakespeare's poems to the youth and dark lady) into two distinct groups, precedes a trochaic ode and *The Tragical Complaint of Elstred*. In the same year, Giles Fletcher the Elder's *Licia* appeared: fifty-two sonnets followed by an ode in tetrameters (plus a dialogue between two sea-nymphs, *A Lover's Maze*, three elegies) and the by then predictable concluding complaint, in this case spoken by Richard III. If this tradition is borne in mind, Spenser's *Amoretti* (1595) no longer looks so odd. Those four slight epigrams sandwiched between the eighty-nine sonnets of the *Amoretti* and the concluding *Epithalamion* have puzzled editors; some have denied Spenser's authorship; but they have the same function in Spenser's volume as the odes in *Delia*, *Phillis*, and *Licia* – rather as the *Epithalamion* takes the place of the conventional complaint at the end of the book. The two epigrams on Cupid and the Bee, the frivolous piece on Diana's theft of Cupid's arrow, and the lines on Cupid's mistaking the poet's beloved for Venus are not anacreontic in metre, but they are, in their Cupidic comedy, anacreontic in matter. They give Spenser's book a tripartite Delian structure. Further examples are easily adduced. Richard Barnfield's *Cynthia* appeared in 1595. Its debt to Daniel's format is immediately apparent. After a Spenserian exercise directed at the Queen, Barnfield has twenty sonnets, written (like Shakespeare's first group) to a lovely young man, an ode in anacreontics, and, to end the collection, the tale of Trojan Cassandra. Finally, in Richard Linche's *Diella* (1596), a sonnet takes the place of the ode or epigram, linking a sequence of thirty-seven sonnets to *The amorous poem of Don Diego and Ginevra*; and, despite a final fourteen-line coda, the book's disposition of material is recognizably Delian and tripartite.

The implications of all this are clear. When those first Jacobean readers opened Shakespeare's volume in 1609, they found something perfectly familiar. Here was a sequence of a hundred and fifty-two sonnets in two groups, followed by two sonnets of anacreontic matter (overlapping versions of one fable, like the two epigrams on Cupid and the Bee in Spenser), the whole being brought to a conventional close in *A Lover's Complaint*. Modern critics may be baffled by the heterogeneity of the volume; Shakespeare's audience had a framework for reading it. They could never have thought the pair of Cupid poems 'irrelevant', 'inexplicable', or 'non-Shakespearian', as most recent scholars have. Nor would they have shunned *A Lover's Complaint* for the sake of the hundred and fifty-four short poems. They would have read the volume *as* a volume, and their sense of the parts would have been modified by the whole.

For it is an assumption of the Delian tradition that, in any collection, the sonnets, the anacreontic interlude, and the concluding complaint should be, however diverse in content, mutually illuminating. In *Delia* itself, Daniel goes to great lengths to relate the three parts of his book. The sonnets show Daniel praising Delia's beauty while lamenting her stony, indifferent chastity. In the complaint, by contrast, Rosamond tells how, when a 'seeming Matron' in league with the king praised her beauty, she was prompted to lose her chastity. The linking ode, 'Now each creature joys the other', celebrates the natural world as a place in which beauty is secure and mutual comfort chaste. There adultery can be no trap for beauty, nor can unyielding chastity become the vice of loveliness. Meanwhile, explicit connexions underline the coherence of the volume. Rosamond appears to the poet in a vision because she wants not just the world's but Delia's sympathy. And Daniel agrees to cast her tale in verse for two reasons: 'Because her griefs were worthy to be known, | And telling hers, might hap forget mine own.' So the predicament of the poet in the sonnets finds some resolution in the writing of the complaint. In forging these links, *Delia* is no more than typical. Spenser's *Epithalamion* provides the only possible conclusion to the wooing unfolded in the sonnets of the *Amoretti*; Linche's connecting sonnet urges Diella to consider *The amorous poem of Don Diego and Ginevra* sympathetically because that tale of separation and eventual bliss might (if she so wished) prefigure their own; and so on. Shakespeare's first readers would have come to the quarto with a strong expectation of connectedness. I think they would have found it.

A Lover's Complaint begins with the poet as eavesdropper. Shakespeare has adapted Daniel's frame (which makes the poet see Rosamond in a vision), as though attuning his complaint to the voyeuristic manner of the later, bleaker sonnets to the dark lady. The other main sources (see below, pages 390–94) have been similarly perplexed. Borrowing a scene from Spenser's *Ruines of Time*, Shakespeare landscapes and peoples it involutedly. What seems direct in 'The Willow Song' here becomes reflexive, as though Emilia's echoing Desdemona's mother's maid (IV.3.25–55, V.2.244–9) posed an hermeneutic problem once narrated. 'From off a hill', the complaint starts,

> whose concave womb reworded
> A plaintful story from a sist'ring vale,
> My spirits t'attend this double voice accorded,
> And down I laid to list the sad-tuned tale;
> Ere long espied a fickle maid full pale,
> Tearing of papers, breaking rings a-twain,
> Storming her world with sorrow's wind and rain.
>
> Upon her head a platted hive of straw,
> Which fortified her visage from the sun,
> Whereon the thought might think sometime it saw
> The carcass of a beauty spent and done.
> Time had not scythèd all that youth begun,
> Nor youth all quit, but spite of heaven's fell rage
> Some beauty peeped through lattice of seared age.

The intricacy of the poem is immediately apparent (those fourteen lines of rhyme royal are as densely packed as any sonnet), and so is its artifice. For the images of doubleness – 'reworded', 'sist'ring', 'this double voice', 'breaking rings a-twain' – enacted in the syntax ('wind and rain', 'spent and done', 'Whereon the thought might think', 'all that youth . . . youth all quit'), simultaneously announce the subject and the strategy of the tale. At first, the title *A Lover's Complaint* seems to refer to the poem's female protagonist. But as the text proceeds, and its images of doubleness proliferate, the title 'doubles' in significance, because the Danielesque maiden recounts, within her complaint, the plaint which has wrought her downfall. The primary Jacobean sense of 'Lover' – a male lover – registers as the 'fickle maid' recalls the seductive words of the young man who slept with and then abandoned her. Like the blank and echoing hillside, the girl 'rewords | A plaintful story', communicating to her immediate auditor ('A reverend man that grazed his cattle nigh'), and beyond him the poet (that further 'reworder'), and beyond him the reader, the deceitful pleadings of her duplicitous lover.

For his words are quite as 'double' as hers: indeed, immorally so. Listening to him, or him as she judges the lover to have been, one hears the tones of a Bertram of Rossillion, and the youth of the Sonnets in his colder aspect – beautiful no doubt, accomplished too, but selfish, vain, and callously promiscuous:

> ' "*All my offences that abroad you see*
> *Are errors of the blood, none of the mind;*
> *Love made them not; with acture they may be,*
> *Where neither party is nor true nor kind.*
> *They sought their shame that so their shame did find;*
> *And so much less of shame in me remains*
> *By how much of me their reproach contains . . .*" '

(lines 183–9)

This is moral Doublespeak of the worst, most complacent kind. The youth excuses his affairs by saying that he wasn't really interested in them, not seeing that if he was 'nor true nor kind' (and how can he speak for his abandoned partners?) he should not have got involved. No doubt such adventures may be 'with acture', but the word 'acture' is a neologism, unscrupulously coined to mean 'what I happen to find an acceptable action'. 'They sought their shame that so their shame did find' is mere sophistry, since it is only at the most uselessly radical level that one can say that what is 'found' must have been 'sought', while the youth's assertion that the deserted girls take off his 'shame' when they reveal their own by admitting they have been seduced is a nasty piece of sexism which simply draws attention to the kind of heartlessness which allowed the maids to be betrayed in the first place. The reported rake goes on:

> ' "*Among the many that mine eyes have seen,*
> *Not one whose flame my heart so much as warmèd,*
> *Or my affection put to th'smallest teen,*
> *Or any of my leisures ever charmèd.*
> *Harm have I done to them, but ne'er was harmèd;*
> *Kept hearts in liveries, but mine own was free,*
> *And reigned commanding in his monarchy . . ."* '
>
> (lines 190–96)

Evidently the youth thinks it a recommendation that 'moving others' he was himself 'as stone'; he is glad to have wounded yet not be hurt; he relishes his 'power to hurt', and has done some (Sonnet 94.1 and 3).

In *Delia*, Daniel had shown chastity at two extremes: coldly unyielding in his mistress's case; all too weak in Rosamond's. The sonnets and the complaint illuminated each other by inversion. Something similar happens in Shakespeare's 1609 collection, because the poet of the complaint, detached from his tale by double rewording, stands by in appalled fascination as he hears how the unscrupulous young man seduced the 'fickle maid full pale', just as, in the later sonnets, he watches helplessly while the dark lady seduces his fickle young friend. There are two emotional triangles, and the poet is in both. But how comes it that the youth prevails in Shakespeare's complaint? Why is the maiden swayed by the youth's transparent Doublespeak? In one sense the answer is that of *All's Well That Ends Well*, a play which is (as I have already implied) involved in a triangular relationship with the two triangles of the 1609 collection. The 'crookèd curls' of the young man's 'browny locks', and all his physical charms, have the same devastating sexual allure as Bertram's 'curls' and 'hawking eye' (lines 85 and 80–133, I.1.93 and 81–97). The girl might be as sensible as Helena, and still succumb. But there is another force at work – something of the greatest significance for Shakespeare's Sonnets as a whole. Having boasted of his power to put girls' 'hearts in liveries', the youth gives the 'fickle maid' all the flattering tributes which those hearts have in the past paid him:

> ' "*Look here what tributes wounded fancies sent me,*
> *Of pallid pearls and rubies red as blood;*
> *Figuring that they their passions likewise lent me*

17

> *Of grief and blushes, aptly understood*
> *In bloodless white and the encrimsoned mood –*
> *Effects of terror and dear modesty*
> *Encamped in hearts but fighting outwardly . . .*"'
>
> (lines 197–203)

The gemstones signify by similitude (pearls for pallor, rubies for a blush), and 'deep-brained sonnets' apparently declare those likenesses. Locks of hair, a diamond 'beautiful and hard', an emerald, sapphire, and opal are added, and the whole collection is handed over:

> ' "*O, then, advance of yours that phraseless hand,*
> *Whose white weighs down the airy scale of praise;*
> *Take all these similes to your own command,*
> *Hallowed with sighs that burning lungs did raise;*
> *What me, your minister, for you obeys,*
> *Works under you, and to your audit comes*
> *Their distract parcels in combinèd sums . . .*"''
>
> (lines 224–31)

These are the tokens which the maiden sheds at the start of the poem, 'Tearing' the papers, 'breaking rings a-twain', and (as the poet tells us) throwing from her 'maund' or basket 'A thousand favours . . . | Of amber, crystal, and of beaded jet' (lines 6 and 36–8). 'Similes' betray her. A bundle of suasive metaphors – made up of gemstones and 'deep-brained sonnets' – is her undoing, for the similitudes never meant for her appear to validate the young man's panegyric of her. The 'fickle maid full pale' is a victim of praise and likeness, treacherous friends about which Shakespeare has much to say in his own 'deep-brained sonnets'.

*

For most renaissance writers, poetry was rooted in panegyric, praise of great and virtuous men being its moral end and historical beginning. Poets, thought Lorenzo de' Medici, are 'holy givers of praise'. They 'make others what they are themselves', wrote Scaliger: 'by the art which makes them immortal they confer immortality on those whom they celebrate.' E.K., that minor master of the literary commonplace, concurred. Glossing a phrase in Spenser's *Shepheardes*

Calender, he cites Plato's *Laws* to prove that 'the first invention of Poetry' lay in 'great solemn feasts called Panegyrica'. Poetry was conceived in praise and it could never escape its origins. Eulogistic in ancient Greece, it should be so again in renaissance Florence, Scaliger's France, and E.K.'s Elizabethan England.

In practice that entailed, of course, the promulgation of dismal hyperbole. The grounding of poetry in panegyric licensed flattery to a dangerous degree, and the Petrarchan tradition developed accordingly. The spiritual profundity of Michelangelo, and Wyatt's psychological vigour, central achievements of that tradition in the 1520s and 30s, became marginal to it as the century went on. With a few honourable exceptions, sonneteers devoted themselves to elaborating received conceits in praise of a type-cast mistress. Indeed, the first sonnet sequence to be published in English – Thomas Watson's *Hekatompathia* (1582) – directs its resources quite frankly, almost vauntingly, towards conventional encomium. Here, for instance, is its seventh poem, praising a mistress who, with the name Laura, sounds rather like the Laura that Petrarch had praised two hundred years before:

> *This passion of love is lively expressed by the Author, in that he lavishly praiseth the person and beautiful ornaments of his love, one after another as they lie in order. He partly imitateth herein Aeneas Silvius, who setteth down the like in describing Lucretia the love of Euryalus; and partly he followeth Ariosto cant. 7, where he describeth Alcina; and partly borroweth from some others where they describe the famous Helen of Greece; you may therefore, if you please, aptly call this sonnet, as a scholar of good judgement hath already christened it,* αἴνη παρασιτική.

> Hark you that list to hear what saint I serve:
> Her yellow locks exceed the beaten gold;
> Her sparkling eyes in heaven a place deserve;
> Her forehead high and fair of comely mould;
> Her words are music all of silver sound;
> Her wit so sharp as like can scarce be found:
> Each eyebrow hangs like Iris in the skies;
> [1]Her Eagle's nose is straight of stately frame;
> On either cheek a Rose and Lily lies;
> Her breath is sweet perfume, or holy flame;
> Her lips more red than any coral stone;
> Her neck more white than aged [2]swans that moan;

> *Her breast transparent is, like crystal rock;*
> *Her fingers long, fit for Apollo's lute;*
> *Her slipper such as [3]Momus dare not mock;*
> *Her virtues all so great as make me mute:*
>   *What other parts she hath I need not say,*
>   *Whose face alone is cause of my decay.*

[1] *Nasus Aquilinus ex Persarum opinione maiestatem personæ arguit.*

[2] *Quale suo recinit funere carmen Olor. Strozza. et vide Plin. de cantu Olorino lib. 10. nat. hist. cap. 23.*

[3] *Vide Chiliad I. cent. 5. adag. 74. vbi Erasm. ex Philostrati ad vxorem epistola mutuatur.*

This αἴνη παρασιτική, as Watson calls it, this 'derivative song of praise giving fame', is so secure in its praising purpose that it piles up comparisons far beyond the point of flattery and falsification. In doing so, it leaves itself vulnerable to the kind of sceptical intelligence which prompted Sidney to produce – without apparently knowing Watson's poem – its direct inversion, or 'antiblazon', in the second sonnet of his *Old Arcadia*. 'What length of verse can serve brave Mopsa's good to show' is, in effect, a cunningly gruesome parody of uncunningly gruesome pastiche. If Watson's mistress has crystal breasts and lips of coral stone, Sidney's Mopsa still more preciously has lips of 'sapphire' and 'skin like burnished gold'. While Watson praises the sparkling eyes and conventional high forehead of his Laura, Sidney hymns the pearly 'twinkling eyes' and 'jacinth' brow of his very rustic idol. Laura may have fingers fit for Apollo's lute and feet so quiet that Momus the churl would have to admire her poise; but Mopsa, not to be done down, has Saturn's beauty, Venus's chastity (the one was ugly, the other a flirt), and 'she borrows Momus' grace'. The satirist subverts, in short, the bejewelled figures of the eulogist, his commonplace comparisons in what Shakespeare calls 'distract parcels' and 'combinèd sums'. For there is a sense in which, as he accumulates his echoes of Aeneas Silvius, Ariosto, and the rest, Watson resembles in his writing the youth in *A Lover's Complaint*, praising the object of his admiration with second-hand 'similes' and 'deep-brained sonnets' snatched from others' pens. In this respect, if in no other, Watson is exemplary. Reading through *Zepheria, Fidessa, Chloris*, and the other sonnet sequences of the 1590s, it is easy to see why the 'deep-brained' sonnet became, during Shakespeare's lifetime, a byword for derivative mediocrity, far-fetched comparison, and flattering praise.

Of course, not all renaissance panegyric is heedless. Ben Jonson, for one, writes in the genre with vigilance and scruple. He seems never to have praised people he thought unworthy. And when disappointed by a lord he had once acclaimed (apparently Salisbury), he wrote a sharp epigram declaring that his panegyric had become a rebuke, a sort of satire on the object of his former adulation. Almost invariably, he avoided naming those who had offended him, but he thought it praise indeed to enshrine in verse the names of those who satisfied his high standards. Yet his naming and not-naming was not pursued with egotistical fervour. When, in the Cary-Morison Ode, he conforms to Scaliger's model, winning renown for two virtuous men as well as himself through loftily heroic but always defining images, the interjection of his own name across a stanza break – 'And there he lives with memory: And Ben || Jonson! Who sung this of him, ere he went | Himself to rest' (*Underwoods* LXX.84–6) – feels more like an act of friendship, and a considered endorsement of Morison's worth, than a vulgar bid for personal immortality.

Shakespeare's scruples went even deeper. If the bawdy quibbles on will are set aside as the fruits of an obsession, the poet's name never appears in his book. Indeed, it appears that, when he is most directly 'Will', he is nearest the spirit of riddling (see the note to 136.14). He says, several times, that his verse will 'wear this world out to the ending doom' (citing 55.12); but, modestly, he never claims that he, or his name, will be remembered, picked out for praise by posterity. He finds the dark lady so desirable that 'flesh . . . rising at thy name, doth point out thee | As his triumphant prize' (151.8–10); but just what this seductive 'name' might be, we are not told. Still more extraordinary is Shakespeare's treatment of the lovely youth. Time and again we are assured that the friend will live forever in the lines. 'Yet do thy worst, old Time,' the poet says; 'despite thy wrong, | My love shall in my verse ever live young' (19.13–14); 'And thou in this shalt find thy monument,' he writes, 'When tyrants' crests and tombs of brass are spent' (107.13–14); most striking of all, in Sonnet 81 he claims 'Your name from hence immortal life shall have' (line 5). Yet we never learn the young man's 'name'. Is it any wonder that post-Romantic readers should have clustered round the publisher's dedication to Mr W.H., in the hope that Thomas Thorpe might somehow redeem the poet's promise? Now it could be argued that

Shakespeare was not in complete control of his material when he allowed this discrepancy to emerge between what he so conventionally said and what he actually delivered. But it seems much more likely, in view of *A Lover's Complaint*, that the poet was prepared for this discrepancy to register because he wanted to communicate something important about praise and truth, similitude and seduction, poetry and morality. Indeed, he may have found it rewarding to write in sonnets precisely because the form conveyed to the reader panegyric and metaphoric assumptions of the kind he wished to work against.

Let us read, or reread, Sonnet 130:

> *My mistress' eyes are nothing like the sun;*
> *Coral is far more red than her lips' red;*
> *If snow be white, why then her breasts are dun;*
> *If hairs be wires, black wires grow on her head.*
> *I have seen roses damasked, red and white,*
> *But no such roses see I in her cheeks,*
> *And in some perfumes is there more delight*
> *Than in the breath that from my mistress reeks.*
> *I love to hear her speak, yet well I know*
> *That music hath a far more pleasing sound.*
> *I grant I never saw a goddess go;*
> *My mistress when she walks treads on the ground.*
> *   And yet, by heaven, I think my love as rare*
> *   As any she belied with false compare.*

This is not, as the critics seem to think, an anti-Petrarchan exercise. It refuses to submit the mistress to a convention, even by inversion. Although it also shadows *Hekatompathia* 7, it does not resemble Sidney's 'What length of verse can serve brave Mopsa's good to show', or any of the many loathly lady sonnets written in the renaissance, because it refuses to endorse praise by mispraising. (And 'reeks', it should be emphasized, would strike a realistic rather than insulting note for early readers; see the Commentary at 130.8.) When Sidney writes of Mopsa's 'jacinth' forehead and 'cheeks of opal hue', mistresses with 'velvet brows' and 'damasked cheeks' are exalted by contrast and the conventions of praise indirectly revived. Praise and its opposite prove mutually supportive. Hence a text like Donne's *The Comparison*, where the poet commits himself to eulogy and excoriation with an equal and interdependent gusto.

Shakespeare rejects both extremes, and in his plays and long poems shows the perils of invidious hyperbole. It is Valentine's extravagant eulogy on Sylvia which, in *The Two Gentlemen of Verona*, starts Proteus's drift towards sexual treachery. In *The Rape of Lucrece*, the poet who tells us in 'The Argument' that Tarquin was provoked to rape by Lucretia's beauty suggests, in his text, that her husband's vaunting praise prompted Tarquin – without ever seeing his victim – to a vicious 'envy of so rich a thing, | Braving compare' (39–40). And in *Love's Labour's Lost*, the King and his lords reveal their inadequacy as lovers – prepare us for the unhappy misunderstandings of Act V – when, in IV.3, they competitively compare their mistresses (first in 'deep-brained sonnets', then in dialogue) to the sun, the moon, a goddess, a rose, a raven, and an old boot. Here, in Sonnet 130, Shakespeare exposes the competitive roots of similitude by reminding us that 'as', that key-word in comparison ('pale as pearls, rubies red as blood'), carries a judgement of value and extent as well as of resemblance. Betraying the word's competitiveness, Shakespeare refuses to compete: 'by heaven, I think my love *as* rare | *As* any she belied with false compare.'

'False compare.' Comparisons are 'false' in Sonnet 130 not just because 'eyes' cannot really compete with the 'sun' for brightness but because to 'compare' is necessarily to belie. Similarity depends on difference; for without difference there is identity, not similitude. 'Identity', writes Wallace Stevens, 'is the vanishing point of resemblance.' Burns's 'love' was 'like a red, red rose' because in most respects she wasn't. Everywhere in the Sonnets, Shakespeare writes with a keen sense of the difference in similitude. In Sonnet 57, to take just one example, the poet's movement towards self-knowledge, towards a fond sense of his own folly, is marked by a shift from 'Being your slave, what should I do but tend | Upon the hours and times of your desire?' to '*like* a sad slave stay and think'; as the metaphorical basis of the poet's slavery is declared, his essential freedom is grasped. With Sonnet 130, 'My mistress' eyes', Shakespeare reacts more profoundly against the mendacity of metaphor. He derides similitude because it belies the nature of things. He finds comparisons odious because, when they conceal what a mistress's 'eyes' might actually be, or obscure what the 'sun' in itself is, they neglect particularity and being. It is the emotionally 'adulterate' Edward III, we remember, who would 'praise' his mistress by having her 'dazzle gazers like the sun'. Indeed, the Countess of Salisbury will, he says, 'brave the eye of heaven at noon', so radiantly comparable is she (II.1.110, 142–65). Eulogy in the drama, with its writing scene (see the note to 94.11), like encomium in the Sonnets, is seen to be competitive, and linked to the theme of betrayal.

Sonnet 21 has the same role in the first group of sonnets (1–126) as 130 in the second (127–52). 'So is it not with me as with that Muse,' it starts,

> *Stirred by a painted beauty to his verse,*
> *Who heaven itself for ornament doth use,*
> *And every fair with his fair doth rehearse,*
> *Making a couplement of proud compare*
> *With sun and moon, with earth and sea's rich gems,*
> *With April's first-born flowers, and all things rare*
> *That heaven's air in this huge rondure hems.*
> *O, let me, true in love, but truly write,*
> *And then, believe me, my love is as fair*
> *As any mother's child, though not so bright*
> *As those gold candles fixed in heaven's air.*
> > *Let them say more that like of hearsay well;*
> > *I will not praise that purpose not to sell.*

Again, Shakespeare exposes the invidious roots of similitude, refusing to put the youth into rivalry with the stars (since it belies both when 'my love' is compared with 'those gold candles'), and modestly asserting that his friend 'is *as* fair | *As* any mother's child'. The two kinds of competition – between tenor and vehicle, one love and another – are joined in the ambiguities of the opening lines, in 'every fair with his fair doth rehearse' (where 'every fair' is both 'every fair thing' and 'every fair beloved') and in the polyvalent 'couplement of proud compare'. The second quatrain, in that wonderfully complex list, enriches the rejection it advances. From the 'sun and moon', great rulers of the day and night, it moves through precious stones and pearls to the delightful but commonplace 'flowers' of 'April' and the thinly unadorned 'all things rare' (where 'rare' means 'scattered, sparse'); yet its diminution moves at the same time towards increase, the unique 'couplement' of 'sun and moon' giving way to handfuls of 'gems', to spring meadows spangled with 'flowers', and to innumerable numbers of 'things' which are, though common, 'rare' ('precious, valuable' emerging from 'distinct, individual'). The 'couplement of proud compare' dissolves into a Shakespearian multifariousness of things as they are, plentiful and vertiginously particular. Being is praised, not praise, for that is mercantile: 'Let them say more that like of hearsay well; | I will not praise that purpose not to sell.' Shakespeare tilts once more at the derivativeness of panegyric. He will not compare his mistress's hair to golden wire, nor couple the young man with the stars; it has all been said before; it is all poetic 'hearsay'. He will not, like Watson, write an αἴνη παρασιτική, nor, like the callous youth of *A Lover's Complaint*, try to steal the heart of his beloved by paying tributes already paid elsewhere, handing over a parcel of old, 'false', and vilely hyperbolic 'similes'.

'So is it not with me as with that Muse, | Stirred by a painted beauty to his verse' carries such weight because the opening lines of the previous sonnet (20) had declared the friend's beauty thoroughly ingrained: 'A woman's face, with Nature's own hand painted, | Hast thou, the master-mistress of my passion'. In the group of sonnets devoted to rival poets (78–86), Shakespeare pursues the distinction, staunchly protesting against the poetic praise which, daubing the youth with verbal cosmetics, conceals the natural painting of what he is, to leave him a merely 'painted beauty'. He insists that telling true – 'O, let me, true in love, but truly write', as he says in Sonnet 21 – is better far than such 'gross painting'. Even if the truths involved are disagreeable, he thinks, they should be told (hence Sonnet 35, where the poet rebukes himself for excusing the young man's faults with 'compare'). And when there is so much good to be found, why feign? 'When they have devised | What strainèd touches rhetoric can lend', he declares in the sestet of 82,

> Thou, truly fair, wert truly sympathized
> In true plain words by thy true-telling friend:
>   And their gross painting might be better used
>   Where cheeks need blood; in thee it is abused.

Sonnets 78–86 are perhaps the harshest in the volume. What rouses Shakespeare to unalloyed anger is not sexual infidelity but the exaggerated 'praise' and 'false compare' of rival poets. Consider, in this light, Sonnet 84:

> Who is it that says most which can say more
> Than this rich praise – that you alone are you,
> In whose confine immurèd is the store
> Which should example where your equal grew?

'Which hyperbolic poet,' Shakespeare asks, 'which most-sayer, can exceed this sublime truism, that "you alone are you". For you comprise the only things which, in honesty, you can be compared with; you already provide the semblance of You which these praisers pretend to offer.' The only honest course, he concludes, leads towards tautology:

> he that writes of you, if he can tell
> That you are you, so dignifies his story;
> Let him but copy what in you is writ,
> Not making worse what nature made so clear,
> And such a counterpart shall fame his wit,
> Making his style admirèd everywhere.

A poet like Watson could win himself 'fame' by reserving, not purveying, hyperbolic praise. But the rival poets have no scruples about 'false compare' and flattery. And they seduce the friend. 'You to your beauteous blessings add a curse,' the sonnet ends, 'Being fond on praise, which makes your praises worse.' To his horror, the poet of 84 discovers that the lovely youth – like the 'fickle maid' of *A Lover's Complaint* – has been corrupted by 'deep-brained sonnets', bundles of 'similes', 'praise'.

He, meanwhile, takes the path towards tautology, through 'you alone are you' to 'you are you'. Shakespeare has few mannerisms, but his habit of celebrating particularity and being through this kind of reflexive structure is surely one of them. 'I am that I am', in Sonnet 121, is merely the most extreme instance, the one which has given readers worried about blasphemy the most unnecessary trouble (just as 'I am not what I am' at *Othello* I.1.66 has left critics struggling for things to say about Iago's character when in a sense he says it all himself). 'I might as yet have been a spreading flower,' laments the maiden in *A Lover's Complaint*, 'Fresh to myself, if I had self-applied | Love to myself, and to no love beside' (lines 75–7). 'The summer's flower is to the summer sweet,' the poet writes in Sonnet 94, 'Though to itself it only live and die.' Such verbal reflexions are reflections, tautologies of selfhood, literal metaphors (as it were) of declared identity; and they are both commonplace in Shakespeare and central. 'In thyself thyself art made away', says Venus to Adonis; 'Narcissus so himself himself forsook' (lines 763 and 161). 'When he himself himself confounds', writes Shakespeare of Tarquin (*The Rape of Lucrece* 160); 'Myself myself confound', echoes King Richard III

(IV.4.399). Take 'I to myself am dearer than a friend' at *The Two Gentlemen of Verona* II.6.23, or 'I myself was to myself not mine' at *Much Ado About Nothing* IV.1.136. Consider those austerely noble lines on love in *The Phoenix and Turtle*, where 'the self' is 'not the same' but coupled in 'Single nature's double name | Neither two nor one'; and recall, climactically, that moment in *Pericles* where Shakespearian reflexivity expresses in the couplement of father and child the creative copiousness which lies at the heart of being:

> O Helicanus, strike me, honoured sir,
> Give me a gash, put me to present pain,
> Lest this great sea of joys rushing upon me
> O'erbear the shores of my mortality
> And drown me with their sweetness. O, come hither,
> Thou that beget'st him that did thee beget . . .

V.1.191–6

It should by now be clear why Shakespeare's Sonnets begin with the so-called 'breeding group', why poems on metaphor (like 21 and 78–86) follow a series of sonnets devoted to marriage, procreation, and what 1.1 calls 'increase'. In reproduction, Shakespeare found the most moral means to similitude. He found there a resemblance resembling tautology. 'O that you were yourself', he writes in Sonnet 13 (think of 'you alone are you' and 'you are you' in 84),

> but, love, you are
> No longer yours than you yourself here live.
> Against this coming end you should prepare,
> And your sweet semblance to some other give.

'Immurèd' in the youth's 'confine' (to persist in the language of 84) are perfect 'semblances' that can 'example' him in a fleshly 'issue':

> So should that beauty which you hold in lease
> Find no determination; then you were
> Yourself again after yourself's decease,
> When your sweet issue your sweet form should bear.

The trouble is, we have lost touch with the ideal of copiousness so dear to the Elizabethans. For us, the word 'copy', like 'reproduction' in art, implies debasement; but when Shakespeare says of Nature, elsewhere in the 'breeding group', 'She carved thee for her seal, and

meant thereby | Thou shouldst print more, not let that copy die'
(11.13–14), the 'seal' which prints is a 'copy' because, in sixteenth-
century English, a 'copy' was something from which copies were
produced. No original need be inferred, as it is with us, even when
describing the printer's copy from which copies of this book are
printed. A 'copy' was that which might produce 'semblances' which
could reproduce that 'copy'; so, in copying, 'identity' did, and yet did
not, push 'resemblance' to Stevens's 'vanishing point'. In other
words, couplets on breeding like 'This were to be new made when
thou art old, | And see thy blood warm when thou feel'st it cold'
(2.13–14) or 'Make thee another self for love of me, | That beauty
still may live in thine or thee' (10.13–14) advocate in life a plenitude,
a copiousness, resembling that *copia* which renaissance rhetoricians
thought texts should aspire to through a proliferation of eloquent
'figures'. Think of *De copia* itself, where Erasmus writes 'By your
letter was I mightily pleased' one hundred and forty-six times, yet
never quite repeats himself. Breeding promises an infinite extension
of such 'increase', a proliferation of 'figures' in a human sense, where
each is its other's 'copy'.

Yet how can Art match Nature's endless semblancing? When the
young man refuses to marry, what can the poet offer in breeding's
stead? One thing at least: a kind of protracted tautology. In Sonnet
84, it will be recalled, the poet advises rivals to (significant verb) 'copy
what in you is writ, | Not making worse what nature made so clear'.
This transcription will give them, he says, the young man's 'counter-
part' in verse. Now, such texts would be the subject's 'semblances' as
surely as his unbred children since, being copies, they could beget
others no less like him than themselves. 'O, know, sweet love,' the
poet declares in Sonnet 76 to the 'onlie begetter' of his sequence,

> *I always write of you,*
> *And you and love are still my argument;*
> *So all my best is dressing old words new,*
> *Spending again what is already spent:*
> *For as the sun is daily new and old,*
> *So is my love still telling what is told.*

That 'sun' which is love's writing, like the 'sun' used punningly in the
early sonnets to signify the young man's unbred offspring, his eldest
'son' (7.14), perfectly expresses the Shakespearian ideal of the
innocent similitude, where 'resemblance' does not so much 'vanish'

into 'identity' but is 'identified' with it. In recurrence, love's writing finds its end.

So repetition, that essential protracted tautology, became, for Shakespeare, perfect eloquence; and in poem after poem he celebrates the novelty of what he has already said, even while, in others, he purports to regret his staidness. Sonnet 108, which we glanced at in the context of 106–9, gives a particularly profound account of this paradox. The text's complexity is considerable, yet justified, since its poetic involution is seen to be the necessary product of an intricate intelligence pleading for simplicity without succumbing to self-regard. (In our own time, the work of Geoffrey Hill strikes the same troubled note.) However, if Sonnet 108 is a work of distinction, when the poet, instead of advocating repetition as tautology, indulges in it – genuinely practises what 76 preaches – the effect is, not unnaturally, a little flat. A poem like 105 is scrupulously and Shakespearianly dull, but it is dull nonetheless. The poet here offers no panegyric – and the praise he does offer might be considered, like Jonson's lines to Salisbury, a potential rebuke – beyond saying what it is that the youth might be. The text is stripped of metaphor; there are no false comparisons. And the poem transcribes the youth so thoroughly that it is impossible to say, in line 13, whether 'Fair, kind, and true' are what the youth comprises or the same in words (as in lines 9 and 10). Modern editors are hopelessly divided as to whether inverted commas should be used or not. The friend is co-extensive with the text; he really is 'all' its 'argument'; and the reader sees exactly what Shakespeare meant when, suppressing the young man's name, he said his friend would live forever 'in' his verse. Yet the result is a poem which, for all its charm (and integrity), lacks the compelling excitement of a metaphoric sonnet such as 60, 'Like as the waves make towards the pebbled shore'. In so far as Shakespeare exceeds the Erasmian *copia*, shunning 'variation' for the sake of tautologous recurrence, his verse palls.

For there is much truth in Constable Dogberry's assertion that, whatever else they may be, 'Comparisons are odorous'; and Shakespeare knew it. The point is not that he was an un-metaphoric writer. On the contrary, he was vividly metaphoric, and consistently alert to the latent images which constitute, in Carlyle's phrase, the 'muscle and living integuments' of common speech; but he was also a writer so alert to the ethical implications of his art that he led an inquiry into metaphor within that art. While the idea of Shakespeare as a nonchalant genius, put about by critics like John Bayley, includes a vital spark of truth, it is, once elaborated, very romantic and very misleading. In crucial respects, Shakespeare was the most, not the least, self-conscious of great artists, and his works are continuously shadowed by a sense that, though more or less likenesses of life, they cannot comprise life as in itself it is. If he was never laborious or crabbed in what he wrote, through the famous 'myriad-mindedness' which Coleridge described, what came forth in 'happy valiancy' was always scrutinized by a finely moral intelligence. That this anxiety led Shakespeare the sonneteer through tautology towards bare repetition is, by now, apparent. But the same scruples register in a correlative and equally important movement of feeling through the sequence, which – expressive, copious, and mythic – is ultimately compromised. For it seems highly significant, in the light of what has been said, that Shakespeare should think of his friend in violently reversed metaphors, subduing the nature of things for the sake of his beloved's particularity and being.

By 'violently reversed metaphors' is meant not 'My mistress' eyes are very like the sun' but 'the sun looks a little like my mistress' eyes', not Watson's 'Each eyebrow hangs like Iris in the skies' but 'The rainbow in the skies seeks to resemble my mistress' eyebrow'. The beloved becomes, in other words, not the world's tenor but its grand and elusive vehicle. In poetry, after all, the logically distant term frees language into suggestion; images lend resonance to their ground; Burns's 'rose' is symbolic, not his girl. And in the sonnets to the friend, Shakespeare lets his subject resound through 'all things rare' (21.7) until he writes a kind of pantheism. His 'rose', the youth, becomes his 'all'.

It is, indeed, a faith perceptible in the very first sonnet, where 'beauty's rose' is more freely associated with the youth than any other element in the 'world' he is charged to redeem. But it is not until the first metaphorically self-conscious sonnet in the 'breeding group', 18, that Shakespeare's reversing of metaphor makes its mark. 'Shall I compare thee to a summer's day?' as inevitably invites the response 'no' as 'Shall I compare my mistress's eyes to the sun?', yet the compliment which turns the sonnet – 'thy eternal summer shall not fade' – is of another order, since it makes the sense of the sestet run: 'the summer, whose lease is of too short a date, is an imperfect semblance of my friend'; the summer is as unlike him as his mistress's eyes are the sun, and in that order. In Sonnet 18 this reversal is merely incipient. It needs to be drawn out in analysis. But in sonnets like 31 – where the youth is said to include all the 'images' of the poet's lost loves – it is more explicit and mythic; and, by the time the reader reaches Sonnet 53, it has become unignorable. 'What is your substance, whereof are you made, | That millions of strange shadows on you tend?' writes Shakespeare, alluding in 'shadows' to all the world's particulars that, resembling the young man, 'tend' towards his being,

> *Since everyone hath, every one, one shade,*
> *And you, but one, can every shadow lend.*
> *Describe Adonis, and the counterfeit*
> *Is poorly imitated after you;*
> *On Helen's cheek all art of beauty set,*
> *And you in Grecian tires are painted new . . .*

The 'master-mistress' of Sonnet 20 becomes the cynosure of all loveliness, not only male and female but past as well as present, mythic as well as real. And, crucially, Adonis, Helen, and the rest resemble the youth rather than he them. Since he comprises everything, every thing you would expect to be a vehicle becomes a tenor, and the youth is made a kind of god:

> *Speak of the spring and foison of the year;*
> *The one doth shadow of your beauty show,*
> *The other as your bounty doth appear,*
> *And you in every blessèd shape we know.*
> *In all external grace you have some part,*
> *But you like none, none you, for constant heart.*

But if the young man is a god, an Adonis comprising the world's fertility as well as a Helen possessing its beauty, why does he tread 'on the ground'? And what of that last line: 'But you like none, none you, for constant heart?' Does not that denial of likeness and celebration of particularity approach hyperbole – false flattery even, since, in the immediately preceding sonnets, the poet has chastised the youth precisely for inconstancy?

One of the most fascinating things about this strand in the volume is its poet coming to recognize that, though violently reversed metaphor preserves the particularity and being of the beloved, it denies the tenor of the world, and lets flattery in by the back door. Here Sonnet 99 is crucial. In the text before, Shakespeare has described how, with the youth away, spring became meaningless to him. I did not 'wonder at the lily's white,' he says, 'Nor praise the deep vermilion in the rose'. With another poet, this remissness would be the result of love-melancholy; but not so in Shakespeare, or not simply so. 'They were but sweet,' he writes, 'but figures of delight, | Drawn after you, you pattern of all those.' According to the logic of this, the rainbow in the sky is somewhat like its 'pattern', the young man's brow, and his eyes are less like the sun than the sun resembles them (hence indeed 'that sun, thine eye' at 49.6). Yet Sonnet 98 is not wholly vain, since a tension at work in it, a sense of expectations overgone, of one idea turning into another, genuinely magnifies the friend. Not so Sonnet 99. There, finally, the poet so insistently expounds the notion that the world is the young man's likeness that we hear the unusual but unmistakable tones of Shakespeare writing without complete conviction:

> The forward violet thus did I chide:
> 'Sweet thief, whence didst thou steal thy sweet that smells,
> If not from my love's breath? The purple pride
> Which on thy soft cheek for complexion dwells
> In my love's vein thou hast too grossly dyed.'
> The lily I condemnèd for thy hand,
> And buds of marjoram had stol'n thy hair;
> The roses fearfully on thorns did stand,
> One blushing shame, another white despair;
> A third, nor red nor white, had stol'n of both,
> And to his robb'ry had annexed thy breath;
> But for his theft, in pride of all his growth
> A vengeful canker eat him up to death.
>> More flowers I noted, yet I none could see
>> But sweet or colour it had stol'n from thee.

It is surely most significant that here, where reversed semblancing has become unambiguously hyperbolic, and the world of things been reduced to a set of conventional types (the violet, the lily, the damasked roses) – it is surely striking that here, uniquely in the volume, Shakespeare has written directly through a source (an early sonnet in Constable's *Diana*), and even so produced something formally irregular: an odd fifteen lines. 'Unfinished', say the editors; 'unrevised'. But one wonders whether the author of *A Lover's Complaint*, the scourge of bloated praise and 'proud compare', could,

even in seeking to make his friend an Adonis, have wished to bring
such a poem as this quite round.

*

At the heart of *The Faerie Queene* Book III, 'The Legend of Brito-
martis. Or *Of Chastity*', lies the Garden of Adonis, the nursery of
Amoret and the fecund source of all the world's 'increase'. Here the
seeds of things take form and substance. Here Adonis can be enjoyed
by Venus, who visits the place to 'reape sweet pleasure of the wanton
boy'. And here 'There is continuall spring, and haruest there |
Continuall, both meeting at one time', for Time resolves itself in
process, 'eterne in mutabilitie'. Or does it? Some of Spenser's best
critics have thought so. 'Time', they say, 'is excluded from the
Garden'; Time assaults only that which leaves Adonis's care. So, no
doubt, it should be. So it would have been had Spenser here achieved
the synthesis he sought – the resolution he so nearly grasped in his
'Cantos of Mutabilitie'. But synthesis escaped Spenser in his third
book, and however sympathetic critics may be towards the poet's
project, they have no right to provide what his text cannot deliver. In
lines of desperate candour and extraordinary power – lines with
much to tell readers of Shakespeare's Sonnets – Spenser allowed
Time to destroy his vision of harmony. Writing of the 'flowre of
beauty', an equivalent of Shakespeare's 'beauty's rose' (1.2), he says:

> Great enemy to it, and to all the rest,
>   That in the Gardin of Adonis springs,
>   Is wicked Time, who with his scythe addrest,
>   Does mow the flowring herbes and goodly things,
>   And all their glory to the ground downe flings,
>   Where they do wither, and are fowly mard:
>   He flyes about, and with his flaggy wings
>   Beates downe both leaues and buds without regard,
> Ne euer pittie may relent his malice hard.

III.vi.39

Time indubitably *is* in the Garden. For Spenser, not only life but its
most secret springs are subject to Time's violence.

A medieval writer, faced with the same subject, would hardly have
thought so. Spenser's stanza draws on terrors peculiar to his age. For

the sixteenth century saw a dislocation in man's sense of himself and the world so massive that arguably nothing like it has been seen again until, in this century, man discovered that he had the power to destroy not only himself but 'the great globe itself, | Yea, all which it inherit'. The invention and dissemination of mechanical time in the renaissance brought about a complete reordering of sensibility. Spenser's monster with his 'flaggy wings' and swingeing 'scythe' was born and bred in a clock. Those who explain the Elizabethan obsession with Time by invoking the iconography of Saturn and Chronos (the god of chronology) confuse symptoms with cause. Time the Devourer, Time the Revealer, Time in rags with his scythe and hourglass: such figures were elaborated because they gave writers and artists emblems in which they could encapsulate their hopes and fears. The roots of Time's symbolism lie, not in classical literature and the iconographic tradition which it fostered, but in the springs, coils, and pendula of renaissance machinery.

In the middle ages, time almost was what Spenser tried to make it: an aspect of process. Candles burned to tell the time, sand seeped through tubes, water trickled from a pierced vessel, and the sun moved across the sky. Time was an abstraction from growth and decay, nothing without them. Being an aspect of process, time changed with it. Each day of the medieval year – summer and winter alike – was divided into twelve hours. So the hours were long in summer and short in winter. They dilated as harvest drew near, and contracted again as the days became cold. For most men, the music of time lay in the rhythm of the seasons and in seasonal labour, and, beyond that, in the sound of church bells. Bells rang out the hours of prayer; monasteries broadcast their own time to the fields; and people spoke of 'the hour of vespers' or 'before the first mass' when appointing times and dividing the day. The secular year began with spring, in late March, not, as now, on 1 January; but it was intimately bound up with ecclesiastical chronology – Lent, Advent, and the saints' days and holy days which recorded, in fasting and feasting, the life and death of Christ in every year, reminding men that the present world was to be damned and redeemed in timelessness.

At first, clockwork made little difference, because in the fifteenth century it found its way only into palaces, rich abbeys, and great cathedrals. As clocks and watches became cheap and compact, however, during the sixteenth century, the new music of time – cold, mechanical, inexorable – encroached on the lives of ordinary men and women. Clocks appeared in homes and workshops. Labour began to be regulated by machinery; domestic affairs were organized around the dial's hand. Moreover, time was increasingly subdivided. Seconds were not registered until the seventeenth century; the word is essentially post-Shakespearian in this sense, and when, in Sonnet 126, the poet wants to refer to puny units of time, he speaks of 'wretched minutes'. But during the reign of Elizabeth I, clocks with minute hands – machines capable of a much more exacting division of life than burning candles or a shadowy sundial – became widespread in England. Clock time invaded men's lives, and was, indeed, for city-dwellers like Shakespeare, the matrix of living. Yet every clock declared that an hour of life, considered another way, was an exact, irretrievable hour nearer death. As a sonnet by the Marinist poet Ciro di Pers (1599–1663) alarmingly declares, '*Mobile ordigno di dentate rote | lacera il giorno e lo divide in ore . . .* '. 'The moving engine, with its toothed cogs,' it might be rendered,

> *tears up the day and divides it into hours, and on its case in black letters it has written for whoever can read it:* WE ALL DIE *(and are dying always).*
> *While the concave metal ticks, a funereal voice resounds in my heart, nor can fate be better signified than by the cruel tenor of its brazen voice.*
> *Because I never hope for rest or peace, this, seeming at once a drum and trumpet, always dares me to confront voracious age. And with those beats from which the metal resounds, one's pace towards fugitive death quickens, and it* [the clock] *taps by the hour at the tomb to open* [ognor picchia a la tomba].

Italy saw the birth of clock-making, and, as this sonnet shows, the shocks of time were strongly felt there by the start of the seventeenth century. But Northern Europe has always, and rightly, been associated with the development of time-making and time-keeping. For the links between Protestantism and the clock, though complex and sometimes elusive, are undeniable. Clock-makers were notorious for religious dissent, and as the Counter-Reformation gathered momentum they were expelled from Catholic countries like Italy to congregate instead in such sympathetic cities as London and Geneva. In part, their views were born of literacy; being skilled workers, and able to read, they were much more susceptible than the illiterate peasantry of Catholic Europe to Protestantism – a religion of the Book circulated in books. But it is striking, too, that predestinarian Protestantism produced a picture of the world congruent with clock-making. When the God of Calvin created the universe, He determined its course by establishing natural laws and allotting men their doom, and even His 'special providences' (direct interventions in human life) were foreseen and purposeful – like the chimes of a clock confirming its function – rather than the result of man's prompting through prayer or ritual. Calvin's God constructed creation and retreated beyond it; he could not be moved by the intercession of the saints, or touched by tributes to the Blessed Virgin. It is ultimately no accident that Newtonian physics developed in Protestant England; and the path from Calvin to Newton lies through Kepler's 'The universe is not similar to a divine living being, but is similar to a clock' and Robert Boyle's assertion that the earth, the planets, and the stars constitute 'a great piece of clockwork'.

Moreover, time-keeping was allied with Protestantism in the conduct of daily life. 'A wise and well-skilled Christian', wrote the seventeenth-century divine Richard Baxter, 'should bring his matters into such order that every ordinary duty should know his place, and all should be . . . as the parts of a clock . . . which must be all conjunct and each right placed.' The good man's life conforms to God's order by resembling a clock, and the wise Christian is as careful of each passing hour as the vigilant hand on a timepiece. 'Let the time of your sleep be so much only as health requireth,' Baxter advises, 'for precious time is not to be wasted in unnecessary sluggishness . . . quickly dress you . . . and follow your labours with constant diligence.' By redeeming time, men witness the possibility of redemption. In wasting it, they reveal their godlessness. At which point, of course, spiritual striving allies itself to temporal prudence. The phrase 'Protestant work ethic' may not be exactly descriptive, but it does point to a recognizable, strenuous outlook post-dating the Reformation. In innumerable treatises, the 'spending' of time and money were equated, and the 'wasting' of both was opposed to a 'saving' which included the soul. Shakespearian drama, and especially its comedy, might represent in part a holiday from this prudential piety, but the works were formed within the context of that ethos and are significantly structured by it. Such a sense of time is found, for instance, in *The Comedy of Errors*, where clocks chime the hours for buying gold, paying debts, and discovering oneself. In Shakespeare's Pauline Ephesus (Acts 19, Ephesians), unlike the Epidamnus of the source play, Plautus's *Menaechmi*, time is mechanical and mercantile, but also, like debts and souls, capable – 'The hours come back', 'After so long grief, such nativity' (IV.2.54, V.1.407) – of redemption.

Whether Protestantism and technology were horse and cart or cart and horse is impossible to determine, but the spread of Luther's reformed faith and the dissemination of mechanical time went together because a clock or watch made time one man's property while reminding that man of his subjection to it. Protestant acquisitiveness, inwardness, and an acute sense of the individual's insignificance in the divine order conjoined in the mechanism. In Shakespearian England, watches frequently bore the owner's picture, and, as often, some reminder of that mortal's coming end – a moral tag, a skull among flowers. If, in the middle ages, time was natural and ecclesiastical, in the sixteenth century it became increasingly private yet impersonal, a source at once of piety and alienation. Jaques mocks the pieties of clockwork in his description of Touchstone, the motley fool of *As You Like It*, unleashed in Arden with a timepiece. 'And then', Jaques cries, in full descriptive flood,

> *he drew a dial from his poke,*
> *And looking on it, with lack-lustre eye,*
> *Says, very wisely, 'It is ten o'clock.'*
> *'Thus we may see', quoth he, 'how the world wags:*
> *'Tis but an hour ago since it was nine,*
> *And after one hour more 'twill be eleven,*
> *And so from hour to hour we ripe, and ripe,*
> *And then from hour to hour we rot, and rot,*
> *And thereby hangs a tale.' When I did hear*
> *The motley fool thus moral on the time,*
> *My lungs began to crow like Chanticleer*
> *That fools should be so deep-contemplative;*
> *And I did laugh, sans intermission,*
> *An hour by his dial.*

II.7.20–33

Yet how significant it is that Jaques should laugh 'like Chanticleer', that notable natural timekeeper, and then moreover time his laughter to a clockwork 'hour'. Despite his mockery, Jaques has been roused by Touchstone's pieties, and shortly after this launches into his own disquisition on mortality, 'All the world's a stage'. Like Touchstone, the melancholy Jaques is disturbed by the collocation of man's life with mechanical time. At the heart of the forest, in the seemingly regenerative 'green world', he is shaken into eloquence by the dial's assertion that man ripens into rottenness, declines ineluctably 'in his time' to 'second childishness, and mere oblivion' (lines 143, 166). And so, of course, is the poet of the Sonnets.

For Shakespeare conceded, more readily than Spenser or any of his great contemporaries, the mechanical origins of his anxiety. Here is Sonnet 12:

> When I do count the clock that tells the time,
> And see the brave day sunk in hideous night;
> When I behold the violet past prime,
> And sable curls all silvered o'er with white;
> When lofty trees I see barren of leaves,
> Which erst from heat did canopy the herd,
> And summer's green, all girded up in sheaves,
> Borne on the bier with white and bristly beard;
> Then of thy beauty do I question make,
> That thou among the wastes of time must go,
> Since sweets and beauties do themselves forsake,
> And die as fast as they see others grow;
> And nothing 'gainst Time's scythe can make defence
> Save breed to brave him when he takes thee hence.

The poet begins actively, counting the chimes of the clock. But as the mechanical rhythm of the first line – picked out by insistent alliteration – registers, we realize that the poet is passive, Time's subject, not its master. 'When *I* do *c*ount the *c*lock that *t*ells the *t*ime' so marks 'time' that 'tells' emerges from the sense 'conveys to me, informs me of' to mean 'counts out', as a bank-teller 'tells' coins. The poet does not count time; the clock does; and a recognition of that makes him look for a larger process to accommodate his new sense of mortality. He finds it in the old rhythm of the seasons and seasonal labour, in the 'green' which dies into grain, and 'Borne on the bier with white and bristly beard' is, with its bristling awn, a kind of fruitful corpse, an Adonis which dies to be 'reaped'. It is this sense of fertility in decay which makes the couplet of Sonnet 12 a consolation as well as a threat: if Time brings a scythe to life's harvest, life can at least bring a harvest to Time's scythe.

Shakespeare was fascinated by the idea that, appearing to possess time, man was possessed by it, and in a number of sonnets he explores that paradox with an insight the more devastating for his enacting the inquiry within its scope. Sonnet 115, for instance, records the power of time in an extraordinary syntactical disjunction:

> *Those lines that I before have writ do lie,*
> *Even those that said I could not love you dearer.*
> *Yet then my judgement knew no reason why*
> *My most full flame should afterwards burn clearer.*
> *But reckoning time . . .*

The poet begins to 'count the clock', reckoning up time's passing (and 'time' is the Quarto's lower-case reading); but a strong relative clause carries the argument out of his hands as Time, retrospectively requiring a capital letter, carries the poem away:

> *But reckoning Time, whose millioned accidents*
> *Creep in 'twixt vows and change decrees of kings,*
> *Tan sacred beauty, blunt the sharp'st intents,*
> *Divert strong minds to th'course of alt'ring things . . .*

Only with the accession of the sestet can the poet wrest the initiative back from Time. But now 'reckoning Time' has become a fearful thing:

> *Alas, why, fearing of Time's tyranny,*
> *Might I not then say 'Now I love you best,'*
> *When I was certain o'er incertainty,*
> *Crowning the present, doubting of the rest?*
> > *Love is a babe; then might I not say so,*
> > *To give full growth to that which still doth grow.*

The growth of Love, the argument (in effect) of Donne's *Love's Growth*, is something which, in Shakespeare, must be plucked from the very jaws of mortality. In the Sonnets, love does not grow as easily as Donne's 'blossoms on a bough' or his 'circles' in the 'water'. Its 'increase' requires an effort on the part of the poet – a 'war', as he says, 'with Time' (15.13).

That Time should 'Creep', 'Tan', 'blunt', and 'Divert strong minds' is hardly surprising. Shakespeare persistently withholds his personifications from abstraction, and Time is no exception. It registers in what it does, in how its violence feels. It builds up pyramids, razes towers, and makes hard 'brass' the 'slave to mortal rage'. It kills the rose and smears proud tombs with dust. On every side, its harsh calligraphy is seen. Violating the friend, it inscribes on his brow 'lines' which diminish that 'life' which the poet's 'lines' would give. Indeed, it appropriates the self, making the young man – as in Sonnet 104 – a kind of dial to register its passing:

> *To me, fair friend, you never can be old,*
> *For as you were when first your eye I eyed,*
> *Such seems your beauty still. Three winters cold*
> *Have from the forests shook three summers' pride,*
> *Three beauteous springs to yellow autumn turned*
> *In process of the seasons have I seen,*
> *Three April perfumes in three hot Junes burned,*
> *Since first I saw you fresh, which yet are green.*
> *Ah, yet doth beauty, like a dial hand,*
> *Steal from his figure, and no pace perceived . . .*

If the word 'Time' does not appear, that is only because it is comprised in the 'beauty' which steals from the friend's 'figure' – at once part of him, his very splendour, and something that pilfers from itself. The life of these lines depends, indeed, on Time being in command so obscurely. 'Beauty' wanes 'like a dial hand', or 'finger on a clock' leaving a digit; yet the 'hand' becomes alarmingly human, at the level of the imagery, when 'Steal from' and 'no pace perceived' conjure a thief with feet to 'pace'. 'Steal from' is thus made transitive for Time's explicit agent, the 'dial hand', though intransitive for its immediate subject (which is also the 'dial hand's' clearest object until the reader reaches 'figure'), 'beauty'. Finally, in 'his figure', three senses fuse. The 'figure' is the number on a clock face from which a 'dial hand' moves. It is a 'figure' or cynosure of 'beauty', a configuration of lovely perfection vulnerable to change. And, most concretely, it is the young man's 'figure', the 'shape' and 'body' from which 'beauty', and the 'dial hand', 'Steal'. Sonnet 104 is, in short, another poem of 'reckoning'. Shakespeare recounts the passing of time – reckons up the seasons – only to realize at the sonnet's volta that the clock 'tells' men what their span has been and is:

> *Ah, yet doth beauty, like a dial hand,*
> *Steal from his figure, and no pace perceived;*
> *So your sweet hue, which methinks still doth stand,*
> *Hath motion, and mine eye may be deceived;*
> *For fear of which, hear this, thou age unbred:*
> *Ere you were born was beauty's summer dead.*

That 104 should turn, like Sonnet 12 ('When I do count the clock'), to the circling seasons is significant. Shakespeare reacted against Time's onwardness by educing images of recurrence. Yet his victory in the Sonnets is never more than partial. In Barnabe Barnes's sequence *Parthenophil and Parthenophe* (1593), the twelve signs of the zodiac are deployed, each above a separate sonnet, so that the order implies recurrence. In Spenser's *Amoretti* (1595), while a central sequence of forty-seven sonnets corresponds to the days of Lent and Easter 1594, in which Spenser courted and won Elizabeth Boyle, the *Epithalamion* which ends the volume emblematically includes in its three hundred and sixty-five long lines an entire year, a complete cycle of the seasons, a circle of regeneration. The seasons in Shakespeare, by contrast, may modify the impact of Time but cannot recoup it. Nor, with any certainty, can the other large principles of recurrence to which the poet appeals. Prophecy, advanced in Sonnet 106 as a means of closing past and present, is shown to be an unhappy hallucination in Sonnet 107. Past 'praises' of the youth may have been 'prophecies | Of this our time, all you prefiguring' (106.9–10); but 'the prophetic soul | Of the wide world dreaming on things to come' is seen to be, when closely observed, wrong, and the 'sad augurs' are forced to 'mock their own presage' (107.1–2, 6). In the Sonnets, as in *King Lear*, prophecy is a delusion, and we learn there what the King's Fool tells us in the Folio, that the only reasonable prediction is that we cannot be sure what Time entails (III.2.79–96). In Sonnet 59, admittedly, the poet alludes to the fashionable Platonic view that the world repeats itself in six-hundred-year cycles, yet it seems important that Shakespeare cannot finally decide there 'Whether we are mended, or whe'er better they, | Or whether revolution be the same.' Recurrence remains no more than a possibility.

As though enforcing this, the overall movement of the poems to the friend is spiralling, uneven, discontinuous. Sonnet 104, for instance, the last text quoted in full – scanned eagerly by critics looking for biographical clues – is where it is less to smooth over a 'three summers'' gap in Shakespeare's verse autobiography than to empha-size the lacunae in a story sustained at bottom only by the onward movement of the Time whose progress it deplores. Arguably, it is precisely this unevenness – so different from the steady tenor of Spenser's Lent and Easter sonnets – which incites the reorderers to work so energetically: they seek to reduce a discontinuous sequence to a smoothly flowing story; but, in attempting to reconstruct such a pattern from the varied, troubled disposition of Shakespeare's material, they work against the poet's intentions, and against the grain of his collection. Certainly, those who, respecting the Quarto order, nevertheless seek a numerological structure in it can be seen striving to control the knotted, onward movement of events by appealing to some larger stasis. The various schemes proposed – such as Alastair Fowler's theory that the poems constitute a mystic pyramid of 153 (one sonnet is declared redundant) – may not fit the facts, but they witness strikingly to the success of Shakespeare's endeavour temporally to disconcert the reader. In practice, the only numerological argument that looks remotely plausible, far from offering stasis, points to a formal correlative of the anxiety about mechanical time registered in individual poems and turns of phrase. As has recently been noticed, the clock which chimes the twelve hours of the day is first invoked in Sonnet 12, and Sonnet 60 describes the 'minutes' which, in sixties, make up hours. How far this analysis may be pressed is still uncertain; but the nature of its irony is clear enough.

Only in the memory can two times definitively meet; and, for Shakespeare, recollection was always sadly flawed. Coriolanus cannot remember the name of the 'poor man' who, in Corioli, 'used [him] kindly' and deserved reward (I.9.81–90). Miranda cannot grapple, from the 'dark backward and abysm of time', those childhood affairs which most concern her on the magic island (*The Tempest* I.2.50). In *All's Well That Ends Well*, Helena finds she has 'forgot' the father who, through his skill, helps her cure the King (I.1.78–81). And, in *Hamlet*, the Prince promises that the ghost's instructions 'all alone shall live | Within the book and volume of [his] brain', only to find that this purpose, 'but the slave to memory', fades (I.5.102–3, III.2.198). With so many Shakespearian instances to choose from, any selection is invidious, yet Hamlet's interest in the memory as a 'book and volume' is striking, and underlined by what he says a few lines after his encounter with the ghost:

> *My tables – meet it is I set it down*
> *That one may smile, and smile, and be a villain.*
> *At least I am sure it may be so in Denmark.*
>   He writes
> *So, uncle, there you are.*

I.5.107–10

This, of course, is what stays with the Prince. The written declaration in his tables, that Claudius is a smiling villain, lingers while the tracings in 'the book and volume of [his] brain' become, as time passes, illegible. For someone whose works lived in speech, on stage – or perhaps *as* someone whose works lived thus – Shakespeare was peculiarly interested in the ancient image of remembrance as a written book, and its corollary, that writing is reified memory. Throughout the Sonnets this theme is strongly marked: we are told that 55 is 'The living record' of the young man's 'memory'; 74, contrariwise, shows us a poet remembered 'in' his textual 'memorial'; and, in 81, Shakespeare writes, 'From hence your memory death cannot take, | Although in me each part will be forgotten' – again, that setting of fallible remembrance against reliable reified recollection.

Just how keenly Shakespeare felt about this can be gauged from Sonnet 122, where the poet tries to excuse his losing or giving away a notebook which contained writings by the friend. This is one of those sonnets which suggest a life lived behind the text, so counter to Shakespeare's instincts is the direction of its argument. 'Thy gift, thy tables, are within my brain | Full charactered with lasting memory,' he writes, 'Which shall above that idle rank remain | Beyond all date, even to eternity –'. Yet, despite this bold attempt to scorn the book, that 'idle rank' of pages or lines on pages, the sonnet has hardly begun before Shakespeare feels compelled to subvert what he has said by admitting the frailty of memory:

> *Beyond all date, even to eternity –*
> *Or, at the least, so long as brain and heart*
> *Have faculty by nature to subsist;*
> *Till each to razed oblivion yield his part*
> *Of thee, thy record never can be missed.*

So the young man's gift will not live 'Beyond all date' but die when the heart and brain are 'razed' – wiped clean, like a *tabula rasa* – by 'oblivion'. The admission, once made, is so damaging that it reduces the sonnet which contains it to an awkward, almost sophistical exercise:

> *That poor retention could not so much hold,*
> *Nor need I tallies thy dear love to score;*
> *Therefore to give them from me was I bold*
> *To trust those tables [my memory] that receive thee more.*

43

> *To keep an adjunct to remember thee*
> *Were to import forgetfulness in me.*

Another poet – Wordsworth, for example, in *Tintern Abbey* and certain sonnets – would have meant that, finding a life in memory beyond the reach of art. But for Shakespeare recollection was weak and provisional, art fixed and 'of great constancy'. For him, past, present, and indeed future, most fruitfully conspired in inscription, where memory finds its lasting memorial.

Even in the most fluent, seemingly spontaneous of the sonnets to the friend there is a sense of formal achievement, a celebration of the text's capacity to survive the trials of time and give remembrance its memorial. Sonnet 71, for instance, assumes its insignificance, but with such verbal assurance that the text delivers through its execution a message at odds with its argument. 'No longer mourn for me when I am dead', it starts,

> *Than you shall hear the surly sullen bell*
> *Give warning to the world that I am fled*
> *From this vile world with vilest worms to dwell.*
> *Nay, if you read this line, remember not*
> *The hand that writ it, for I love you so*
> *That I in your sweet thoughts would be forgot*
> *If thinking on me then should make you woe . . .*

That 'hand' in line 5 is easily misread because so strangely un-Romantic. It is not Catherine Linton's, thrust through Mr Lockwood's casement on Wuthering Heights, nor John Keats's, once 'warm and capable | Of earnest grasping', but now 'in the icy silence of the tomb . . . see here it is – | I hold it towards you'; it is not Hallam's 'taken' as a 'pressure' by the mourning Tennyson at *In Memoriam* CXIX.12, nor even Christina Rossetti's, in that famous sonnet modelled on Shakespeare's 71st:

> *Remember me when I am gone away,*
> *Gone far away into the silent land;*
> *When you can no more hold me by the hand,*
> *Nor I half turn to go yet turning stay . . .*

For Shakespeare's 'hand' is inseparable from the writing which it was. 'Remember not | The hand that writ it' refers through the hand/writing which recorded the text and helped circulate it at a time when sonnets were passed about in manus/script, by virtue of that handwritten text being extant (and printed), to the 'warm scribe' which originally led the pen. That dead hand from the past will be remembered, in future, because of its inscription.

At which point we return to recurrence in love's writing. That a drift towards repetition was fostered by Shakespeare's mistrust of similitude is clear; but the same movement was seemingly encouraged by the poet's fear of Time. Through copying and tautology, and its attendant verbal ploys – echo, parallelism, rhyme – Shakespeare tries, that is, to recoup or cope with Time by recounting it. Even sonnets devoted to a description of Time's violence, like 12 ('When I do count the clock'), provisionally recover in their formal discipline something of what Time takes. Shakespeare seeks to 'control' time in the radical sense of that word explored in Sonnet 58: Anglo-Norman *contreroller*, 'to record in an account, enrol in a book, conclusively reckon'. His texts are to that extent essays in mastery (which do not always master), and lines like these, already scrutinized, describe the suspension of time as well as the tautology of pure praise:

> *O, know, sweet love, I always write of you,*
> *And you and love are still my argument;*
> *So all my best is dressing old words new,*
> *Spending again what is already spent:*
> *For as the sun is daily new and old,*
> *So is my love still telling what is told.*

76.9–14

Love's writing should take the initiative from Time, 'telling' before the clock can, and, in 'telling what is told', redeem time by recouping the past in the present, recovering what it can of what is lost. In such discourse, the ideal of recurrence sought in the circling seasons, in prophecy, and in the revolution of the Platonic year would be found; texts would recur like the sun which is 'old' yet 'new' each day. It is towards this condition that Shakespeare's Sonnets aspire, though they can no more finally achieve Time's suspension than they can match Nature's endless semblancing in a tautologous 'increase'. And it is, one might speculate, the poet's desire to recoup time by recounting it which explains the conduct of his sonnets, with their neglect of the dialectical resources of the fourteen-line form as usually practised – eight lines against six, divergent rhyme-schemes in octave and sestet (and from poem to poem) allowing a subtle orchestration of argument – in favour of a cumulative mode of writing which protracts poems for fourteen lines, or, more often and most characteristically, concedes in a couplet reversal that Time cannot be suspended for ever, that the hours cannot after all be entirely recouped by counting, nor the clock finally controlled.

*

When John Benson reprinted Shakespeare's Sonnets in 1640, he inflicted on them a series of unforgivable injuries. Responding to a shift in taste away from the fourteen-line form in the decades since 1609, he put numbers of the texts together to produce longer 'poems'; he began the long-running tiresome game of reordering; and omitted eight sonnets which somehow did not take his fancy. Most far-reaching of all, however, was a single recurring revision: he erratically emended the masculine pronouns used of the friend in 1–126 to 'she' and 'her', and replaced 'boy' (in 108) with love. The intervention was not without precedent. When, in 1623, Michelangelo's grand-nephew produced the first edited version of the sculptor's poems, he altered the pronouns of the love poetry to make it address a mistress. Those passionate if platonic sonnets addressed to the beauty of Tommaso de' Cavalieri, Michelangelo's 'armed Knight', were directed to some harmless imaginary female, who could not endanger the artist's reputation. Was Benson's revision similarly prudent? That the instincts of Michelangelo – who never married but was subject throughout his life to complicating attachments to younger men – were basically homosexual is not seriously in dispute. Can the same be said of Shakespeare 'the married man', a father, a burgher, and our National Poet?

What needs to be emphasized at once is the deep disapproval which homosexual activity attracted in Elizabethan England. The popular imagination associated sodomy with werewolves, basilisks, and papists. In church teaching, the vice lay outside the divine order: the devil himself would not practise it (though in copulation with witches he allegedly conceived sodomites), and God regarded it with such abhorrence that, as the Bible testified, he was prepared to destroy the Cities of the Plain to extirpate a few inverted miscreants. Burdened with the power of divine revenge, since their authority rested on Romans 13, magistrates felt obliged to act with similar rigour, and, when convictions were secured, 'beastly and obscene' offenders could expect to be put to death. If plagues, dearths, and other inexplicable scourges smote society, sodomites were blamed for bringing down God's wrath – along with such fleshly wrongdoers as adulterers, bawds, and drunkards. For, despite its supposed unnaturalness, homosexuality was not placed in a special spiritual category: it was thought to stem from the same carnal source as other sins of the fallen flesh; it was indeed, and alarmingly, a sin of which everyone (or, given the invisibility of lesbianism, every man) was capable. The situation was, to put it mildly, confused; and this creates some of the same problems for us, looking back on the period, as it did, much more painfully, for those who harboured homoerotic feelings in that society. Not only was homosexuality condemned: there was no language for coping with it, even as a misdemeanour. Indeed, the word 'homosexuality' did not exist, and the labels applied to the crime – 'buggery', 'sodomitical grossness', 'ingling' – muddled it hopelessly with bestiality and child abuse. However unconvincing the argot of modern psychology, with its proliferating terms used to discriminate the subtlest differences in observable sexual interest, it at least articulates and humanizes the range of psychosexual attitudes. Elizabethan England lacked that linguistic means: its legal codes and religious discourses could not accommodate the vice they abhorred. The age was, to that extent, neither sympathetic nor antagonistic towards inversion, but *pre*-homosexual.

As a consequence, one finds a curious lacuna in most contemporary accounts. The popular and biblical characterizations of the condition were so extreme that few people inclined to homoeroticism felt able to imagine that their own emotions and actions were of the kind condemned. We may look to writers for an honesty and insight greater than that to be found in other men and women, and expect them to forge a language linking orthodox codes to personal experience, where none exists; but the risks associated with homosexuality were such that very few authors dared deal with it directly, and where it was invoked, a cover of classical convention was typically deployed. Ironically, this strand in the tradition persuaded commentators like Oscar Wilde, J. A. Symonds, and Havelock Ellis that the homoerotic freedom of Plato's Athens and Virgil's Arcadia lay near the heart of renaissance England, when close reading suggests that Socrates, Alexis, and the rest were introduced evasively, to shield authors from rebuke. Spenser's *January Eclogue*, for instance, describes with considerable compassion and understanding the old shepherd Hobbinol's unrequited love for Colin Clout; but E.K. is quick to defend his friend from the imputation of pederasty by invoking in the notes, first 'Plato his dialogue called Alcibiades' and then, with equal approval, a Christian con mpt for the flesh – 'And so is paederastice much to be preferred before gynerastice, that is the love which enflameth men with lust toward womankind' – only to protest his ultimate dislike of the homoerotic, with a learned reference to prove it:

> But yet let no man think, that herein I stand with Lucian or his devilish disciple Unico Aretino, in defence of execrable and horrible sins of forbidden and unlawful fleshliness. Whose abominable error is fully confuted of Perionius, and others.

The protestations may seem as excessive as the nervous shifts in argument are comic, yet E.K. in his pedantic way reminds us how dangerous were the emotions with which Spenser was embroiled. What the annotator calls the 'savour' of the text might be homoerotic; but good reasons could be found – had to be found – for critically detaching the author from what so evidently engaged him.

With an author like Richard Barnfield, whose sequence *Cynthia* has already been mentioned, the situation is more complex, for he entices the reader with the irresistible but uncertain boldness of an inexperienced flirt:

> *Cherry-lipped Adonis in his snowy shape*
>   *Might not compare with his pure ivory white,*
>   *On whose fair front a poet's pen may write,*
> *Whose rosiate red excels the crimson grape;*
> *His love-enticing delicate soft limbs*
>   *Are rarely framed t'entrap poor gazing eyes;*
>   *His cheeks the lily and carnation dyes*
> *With lovely tincture which Apollo's dims.*
> *His lips ripe strawberries in nectar wet,*
>   *His mouth a hive, his tongue a honey-comb,*
>   *Where Muses (like bees) make their mansion.*
> *His teeth pure pearl in blushing coral set.*
>   *Oh, how can such a body sin-procuring,*
>   *Be slow to love, and quick to hate, enduring?*

What can be made of such a sonnet – so floridly reminiscent of Shakespeare's 99th, and its image of the friend as a kind of Adonis?

In *The Affectionate Shepherd* of 1594, Barnfield had risked similar sentiments ('If it be sin to love a lovely lad; | Oh, then sin I, for whom my soul is sad . . .'), but he had also, like Spenser in *January*, worked under the aegis of the famous Second Eclogue. As he says in the preface to the later sonnet sequence (1595), his pastorals were 'but an imitation of Vergil'. Why did the poet proceed to unfold the same material in a form unlicensed by classical precedent? Is this not flirtation of a peculiar kind? Ultimately one concludes that the sonnets written to the unknown friend – called I.U., and idolized as Ganymede – are exercises in a convention which fits the writer's needs so exactly that emotion in excess of the topos may be deduced.

Only in Marlowe, arguably, do we find an author prepared to explore the hiatus between homoerotic pleasure and the terrible image it bore in legal and religious literature. On occasion, it seems, he said things designed to spark provocatively across the gap between experience and orthodoxy. 'All they that love not tobacco and boys were fools' and 'St John the Evangelist was bedfellow to Christ and leaned always in his bosom, that he used him as the sinners of Sodoma' may be reported remarks, passed through the hands of a government informer with much to gain, but they ring convincingly when read alongside *Hero and Leander* – with its superbly erotic descriptions of male beauty – and parts of *Dr Faustus*. If Marlowe's views were exaggerated in the 'Baines note', there is little reason to doubt that he said stormy, sceptical things resembling those reported. Yet he was also capable of analysing the same terrain sensitively, and, in *Edward II*, he displays at once the wasteful vanity of homosexual dalliance and its glamour and tragic vulnerability. In the parasite Gaveston's lines especially, we hear the authentic voice of inverted seduction:

> *Sometime a lovely boy in Dian's shape,*
> *With hair that gilds the water as it glides,*
> *Crownets of pearl about his naked arms,*
> *And in his sportful hands an olive tree,*
> *To hide those parts which men delight to see,*
> *Shall bathe him in a spring . . .*

I.1.61–6

Against the allure of that, Marlowe pitches the sharp cruelty with which an uncomprehending nobility treats the homosexual, outcast by his proclivities. When Edward is murdered in squalor, with a red-hot poker up his anus, it must have been impossible for members of the original audience, though deeply imbued with the prejudices of the epoch, to feel that homosexuality deserved such 'apt' punishment: no one who had followed the King through the anguish of his fall, and observed the satanic malice of his murderers, could have withheld their sympathy. Yet the impact of the scene depends on that experience testing and contesting the audience's received image of the monstrous sodomite.

Shakespeare is less committed than Marlowe, decidedly more delicate than Barnfield, and less confined by convention than Spenser and E.K.; but he has something of them all. In his plays, he admits homoerotic feeling almost as freely as Marlowe did, if with greater subtlety. The inexplicable, or unexplained, passion which Antonio feels for Bassanio in *The Merchant of Venice* and the sudden anger of the sea captain in *Twelfth Night* when he thinks himself rejected by Sebastian are of this kind. Moreover, Shakespeare sometimes exploits the fact that, in his theatre, boy actors took women's parts to suggest a reorientation of sexual roles closer to those advocated by Gaveston than the orthodoxy of his age. When Rosalind, played by a boy actor, disguises herself as a boy (suggestively named Ganymede) in *As You Like It*, only to flirt with Orlando when pretending to be the Rosalind she is (except that she is a boy), a complex of role-playing so intricate results that the audience is drawn into homoerotic courtship merely by attending to its heterosexual surface. In Shakespeare's poetry, too, a delight in androgyny is evident. *Venus and Adonis* may be more equable in tone than Barnfield's 'Cherry-lipped Adonis', more coolly artful in its depiction of pubescent beauty, but the sexual alignment of the texts is not entirely different. When J. A. Symonds recalled, in his secret memoirs of 1889, the formative effect of the long poem on his adolescent sexuality – 'I dreamed of falling back like [Venus] upon the grass, and folding the quick-panting lad in my embrace' – his response may have been extreme, but it is indicative nonetheless. Most texts can bear a homoerotic reading, but few yield the homosexual reader such immediate rewards as Shakespeare's early epyllion. As for the Sonnets: there, perhaps, the likeness is with Spenser and E.K., except that the denial of fleshly interest is made within a first-person sonnet, rather than added in notes to a third-person eclogue, and the result is not, as might be expected, greater directness, but tantalizing ambiguity.

Certainly, Sonnet 20, addressed to the 'master-mistress' of the poet's 'passion', is as shiftily comic as E.K.'s note about Hobbinol and Clout, but self-consciously so, with an enigma in almost every line. Shakespeare uses feminine rhyme throughout, so that the claims of his argument, already disrupted by wordplay, are set against and upset by that odd combination of jovial patness and unconvinced falling away which such rhyming generates in the English pentameter. At a crucial stage in the argument, indeed, rhyming fails to clinch the point it is ostentatiously supposed to register, and the poet's claim to chastity is covertly endangered. In the bawdy lines,

> *Nature as she wrought thee fell a-doting,*
> *And by addition me of thee defeated,*
> *By adding one thing to my purpose nothing . . .*

that is, the concord with 'a-doting' is imperfect, and the decisive 'nothing' has a hollow ring. Though the text can hardly prove Shakespeare homosexual, it cannot be invoked, as it so often is, to demonstrate his unwavering heterosexuality.

In the last analysis, what one finds registered in the Sonnets is profound homosexual attachment of a scarcely sensual, almost unrealized kind. It is after all remarkable that the poems should tell us so little about the friend's appearance. He has damask cheeks and hair like marjoram; but nowhere in the sequence do we find the raptly detailed descriptions of erotic dotage. There is nothing, for instance, to compare with Marlowe's lingering catalogue of Leander's charms near the start of *Hero and Leander*. Faced with this mixture of sexual ambivalence and sensual restraint, one instinctively reaches for Coleridge's dictum 'a great mind must be androgynous', or Virginia Woolf's assertion that 'It is fatal for anyone who writes . . . to be a man or woman pure and simple; one must be woman-manly or man-womanly'; but Shakespeare might not approve or even understand this manoeuvre. If pressed, he would probably claim to have been working in the tradition of friendship literature – while conceding that his concealment of the young man's 'name' might seem protective. This literature, typically comparing the rival claims of heterosexual love and comradeship among young noblemen, was of central importance in European humanism, and, reaching England through writers like John Colet, Sir Thomas Elyot, and the translator Bryskett, it fed directly into Shakespeare's early comedies. Considered in this context, indeed, in the wake of plays like *The Two*

Gentlemen of Verona and *Love's Labour's Lost*, Antonio's 'passion' for his 'master-mistress' Bassanio, set against Bassanio's love for Portia, looks like the comradely side of love and friendship advancing into an erotically shady area. In claiming the same humanistic origin for his sonnets, Shakespeare might direct doubters towards a passage like this, from Ficino's influential commentary on Plato's *Symposium*, in which the deepest feelings of attachment are allowed between men without the imputation of unchastity:

> *Lovers exchange beauty for beauty. A man enjoys the physical beauty of a youth with his eyes; the youth enjoys the man's beauty with his mind. The youth, who is beautiful in body only, by this practice becomes beautiful also in soul; the man, who is beautiful in soul only, feasts his eyes upon bodily beauty. Truly this is a wonderful exchange, equally honourable, beneficial and pleasant to both . . .*

Shakespeare, of course, was not a neoplatonist. He was painfully aware of the way ideals like Ficino's are corrupted in practice, and of how imponderable true beauty is in the soul. The young man of 1–126 is conspicuously not improved by the attentions of the poet, who finds himself 'salving' and then castigating the friend's misdeeds. Moreover, Shakespeare was never sympathetic, as the neoplatonists were, to Love as an absolute, detached from the world and the erotic body. Brisk readers like Auden might find his sonnets to the youth directed towards the abstraction of Eros, but, though Shakespeare may have been drawn to the fecund loveliness of Adonis, he never adulated Love in quite that way. Some of his contemporaries did. Here, for instance, is Fulke Greville in the sequence *Caelica*:

> *Love is the peace, whereto all thoughts do strive,*
> *Done and begun with all our powers in one:*
> *The first and last in us that is alive,*
> *End of the good, and therewith pleased alone.*
> *Perfection's spirit, goddess of the mind,*
> *Passèd through hope, desire, grief, and fear,*
> *A simple goodness in the flesh refined,*
> *Which of the joys to come doth witness bear.*
> *Constant, because it sees no cause to vary,*
> *A quintessence of passions overthrown,*
> *Raised above all that change of objects carry,*

> *A nature by no other nature known:*
> *For glory's of eternity a frame,*
> *That by all bodies else obscures her name.*

(85)

As a description of absolute Love this is immensely accomplished, yet because it indicates only abstractly the difficulties inherent in striving towards 'Perfection's spirit', it reads coldly, almost inhumanly. Shakespeare's Sonnet 116, emerging from the love poems to the friend as an equally absolute statement, might almost be a rebuke to Lord Brooke:

> *Let me not to the marriage of true minds*
> *Admit impediments; love is not love*
> *Which alters when it alteration finds,*
> *Or bends with the remover to remove.*
> *O no, it is an ever-fixèd mark*
> *That looks on tempests and is never shaken;*
> *It is the star to every wandering bark,*
> *Whose worth's unknown, although his height be taken.*
> *Love's not Time's fool, though rosy lips and cheeks*
> *Within his bending sickle's compass come;*
> *Love alters not with his brief hours and weeks,*
> *But bears it out even to the edge of doom.*
>   *If this be error and upon me proved,*
>   *I never writ, nor no man ever loved.*

This sonnet has been misread so often and so mawkishly that it is necessary to say at once, if brutally, that Shakespeare is writing about what cannot be attained. The convoluted negatives of the last line have their point: they show the poet protesting too much, losing confidence in his protestations, or at least inviting disagreement with them (by anticipating rebuttal), at their climax. Indeed, the strenuousness subverts itself grammatically. With *Astrophil and Stella* 63, Sidney reminds us that 'Grammar says (to grammar who says nay) | That in one speech two negatives affirm', and Feste endorses this at *Twelfth Night* V.1.20–21, 'your four negatives make your two affirmatives'. The point was, in any case, widely understood, and the confusions it gave rise to were a comic commonplace. Has any man then ever loved? Lines 7 and 8 certainly suggest not, since the pole star guides the mariner by virtue of its being so far away that its 'height' does not alter. 'It is the star to every wandering bark, | Whose worth's unknown, although his height be taken': the lover can take Love's altitude, but not reach up and grasp the star, experience its 'worth'. In Greville, Love is 'Constant' and 'sees no cause to vary' because it is a small spark of 'Perfection' within man. In Shakespeare, its constancy depends on its being beyond man, and greater than Time – which man can never be. *Caelica* calls perfect Love 'A simple goodness in the flesh refined', a 'quintessence of passions over-thrown' by the individual will, which, 'Raised above all that change of objects carry', raises man. Shakespeare thinks all this too absolute for humankind. While Greville is buoyantly positive, Shakespeare de-fines true Love in the only way he can – through negation. His 'Love is not love | Which alters . . . Or bends'; 'O no!'; it 'alters not with his brief hours and weeks'. Since Love's 'worth's unknown' it can only be known by what it is not. Now it would be easy to read Sonnet 116 with an overplus of cynicism – asking, for instance, Why the poet begins so defensively ('Let me not . . . Admit'), Whether that love is humane which will not 'alter when it alteration finds', or What man can live long enough to love to the 'edge of doom'? – and that would be as mistaken as misreading the poem mawkishly. For those fourteen lines are committed to their 'unknown' absolute. The critical complication is simply that the poet's negative assertions work with the imagery to make a sceptical reading available. Othello could accept the poem, but so might Iago, and we must, like the poet, embrace both points of view. The sonnet celebrates Love as an absolute, but it is burdened with a sense that Love's 'Perfection' is divorced from the 'lips and cheeks' of the imperfect flesh.

The anxiety is intensely Shakespearian, and powerfully communi-cated in the Sonnets, where Love's Growth is as in Donne bound up with the body, its sexuality and decay, with the tangible being of the Other. The 'master-mistress' admired homosexually in Sonnet 20 becomes the androgynous 'Adonis' of 53 and the godlike source of fecundity in 98–9 by an access of potency, not by abstraction. However generalized by Shakespeare's inverted metaphors, the young man is never less than singular, himself alone, particular, and the poet's love is directed to him rather than beyond him at some absolute. As the object of love, he becomes love's end, the point where love declares itself as love. Indeed, love and the youth are so conjoined that there are many poems in which an interpretative effort is needed to determine whether the beloved or the poet's affection for him is comprised in the word 'love', and a number of places at which the two cannot be distinguished. When, for example, Shakespeare writes in Sonnet 80 'The worst was this: my love was my decay', you cannot tell whether tongue-tied passion or the youth himself has confounded the poet's verse. When, in 65, he hopes 'That in black ink my love may still shine bright', it is impossible to separate the friend from the loving thoughts which want to win him immortality. And when, in 107, the poet declares 'My love looks fresh', both the youth and the poet's affection are felt to flourish. The imaginative consequence of this conflation of love with love is that, through Love's Growth, the friend is magnified, finds 'increase'. He becomes 'A god in love' (110.12) without being abstracted from what he in himself is. And the sequence moves towards 126: 'O thou, my lovely boy, who in thy power | Dost hold Time's fickle glass, his sickle hour . . .'

*

If the sonnets to the youth grow out of comradely affection in the literature of friendship, those to the dark lady extend and degrade the rival attractions of heterosexual passion. While the comedies either accept the humanistic elevation of 'paederastice' over 'gynerastice' reluctantly, as in the last scene of *The Two Gentlemen of Verona*, or test and explicitly reject the claim of comradeship to dominance (as in *The Merchant of Venice*), the Sonnets as a collection come closer to the traditional view so vividly expressed by Montaigne in his essay 'Of Friendship':

> *To compare the affection towards women unto* [friendship], *although it proceed from our own free choice, a man cannot nor may it be placed in this rank: Her fire, I confess it to be more active, more fervent, and more sharp. But it is a rash and wavering fire, waving and diverse: the fire of an ague subject to fits and stints . . .*

(translated by Florio)

A stream of lines and images from Sonnets 127–54 pours into the reader's mind: 'My love is as a fever, longing still | For that which longer nurseth the disease' (147.1–2), 'Till my bad angel fire my good one out' (144.14), 'Cupid . . . his love-kindling fire', 'his heart-inflaming brand' (153.1 and 3, 154.2), 'Beshrew that heart that makes my heart to groan | For that deep wound' (133.1–2). But once

Sonnet 129, 'Th'expense of spirit', is remembered, it will not budge, as Montaigne's immovable analogue.

It is also, of course, the one poem in the dark lady group to stand entirely above the first person. As an absolute statement about 'the love which enflameth men with lust toward womankind', an account of lust's 'rash and wavering fire', it can be compared with 'Let me not to the marriage of true minds' in the primary sequence:

> Th'expense of spirit in a waste of shame
> Is lust in action, and, till action, lust
> Is perjured, murd'rous, bloody, full of blame,
> Savage, extreme, rude, cruel, not to trust,
> Enjoyed no sooner but despisèd straight,
> Past reason hunted, and no sooner had,
> Past reason hated as a swallowed bait
> On purpose laid to make the taker mad . . .

While 116 deals with Love complexly, however, questioning the absolute which it erects, 129 describes and enacts with single-minded, though cynically quibbling, forcefulness the distemperature of phallocentric lust. Fitful and fretting, such a passion squanders the moral powers along with the semen, committing both to a 'waste of shame' and 'shameful waist'. 'More active, more fervent, and more sharp' than comradeship, it goads men towards satisfaction, yet, once sated in the irrational frenzy of orgasm, it is queasy, woeful, and full of remorse:

> Mad in pursuit, and in possession so,
> Had, having, and in quest to have, extreme,
> A bliss in proof, and proved, a very woe,
> Before, a joy proposed, behind, a dream.
>   All this the world well knows, yet none knows well
>   To shun the heaven that leads men to this hell.

Lust is fixated by the moment: yearning towards emission, it lies sullied and futile in its wake, sourly foretasting hell, with nothing to hope for but further 'pursuit'. Its imaginative field is vorticose, centripetal, obsessive.

In this 129 provides an epitome of its group. While the sonnets to the youth are 'spiralling, uneven, discontinuous', they are neverthe-less caught up by the onward drift of time. They move inexorably onward, within, and from, poem to poem. The sub-sequence to the dark lady is, by contrast, disjunctive, wildly various, contained by a matrix of mood not pace, emotion not process. While poems 1–126 ultimately unfold sequentially, like one of those Elizabethan pictures recording an aristocrat's life – that of Sir Henry Unton, for instance – selecting and concentrating parts of the noble young man's life as he ages, the dark lady sonnets are fragmentary, juxtaposed, oddly modernist in effect. There are moments of terrible climactic insight which, outgone, are lost; the poet returns obsessively to anxieties already analysed into hopelessness. These poems do not operate under the aegis of Time – indeed, the word 'Time', so common in 1–126, does not appear in 127–54 – but are trapped in a chaos of inescapable passion. And here again, one might add, the reorderers respond wrongly to an urgently apprehended effect. It is precisely the fragmentariness of the dark lady sonnets which is their point, but also that which, making them detachable in ones and twos and threes, allows them, in the hands of reorderers, to ruin the coherence of the collection. To snatch such poems so promptly from emotional turmoil is merely to make innocuous Shakespeare's apposite unordering.

Which is not to say that the two groups are discrete. They are best regarded as foils of each other, like divergent areas of action in a Shakespeare play. As in the drama, links between the diverse threads of 'story' are ultimately complex yet incidentally explicit. There are, for example, the interlinked sonnets 21 and 130 on 'false' and 'proud compare'; there are paired poems on love and musical harmony (8 and 128); and there are several sonnets, verbally connected, on love-deluded eyes. This is 137:

> *Thou blind fool, Love, what dost thou to mine eyes*
> *That they behold and see not what they see?*
> *They know what beauty is, see where it lies,*
> *Yet what the best is take the worst to be.*
> *If eyes corrupt by over-partial looks*
> *Be anchored in the bay where all men ride,*
> *Why of eyes' falsehood hast thou forgèd hooks,*
> *Whereto the judgement of my heart is tied?*
> *Why should my heart think that a several plot,*
> *Which my heart knows the wide world's common place?*
> *Or mine eyes seeing this, say this is not,*

> *To put fair truth upon so foul a face?*
> *In things right true my heart and eyes have erred,*
> *And to this false plague are they now transferred.*

The sonnet is indicative as well as typical, when compared with such poems as 113–14, in that by virtue of its theme it is as much opposed to the sonnets written to the youth as it is in itself concerned with opposition: 'best' and 'worst', 'fair' and 'foul', feeling 'heart' against seeing 'eyes'. Indeed, it offers a hideous parody of those poems which seek to magnify the friend. The young man's sexuality includes a world of fruitful 'increase'; the dark lady, a 'bay where all men ride', is a kind of global whore, the 'wide world' of 107's 'common place'. If the sonnets to the lady parallel, they also refract and invert, those written to the youth: they behave like the sub-plot of a Shakespeare play.

Indeed, the two groups of sonnets, to the fair youth and dark lady, interact rather like the meshed 'stories' in *Othello*, where the fair Bianca ('white one') turns out to be a prostitute, though not finally evil, and the Moor can be judged, when heard with sympathy, 'far more fair than black' (I.3.287). In the period, colour prejudice, reinforced by the neoplatonic association between brightness and virtue, blackness and evil, ran so deep that it was impossible to extirpate, and to praise things dark inevitably sounded sophistical. Some writers welcomed this: Barnfield, in the second pastoral of *The Affectionate Shepherd*, for instance, argues at tedious length that 'white compared to black is much condemned'; and Shakespeare, possibly under Barnfield's influence, takes a similar line at *Love's Labour's Lost* IV.3.245–79, where Berowne defends the beauty of his dark lady Rosaline with bewildering ingenuity. The prevailing prejudice might be contested, then, but it remained in control. Hence, for example, Ben Jonson's difficulties when Queen Anne commanded him to present her and her ladies as Blackamoors in *The Masque of Blackness*. The resourceful poet had to argue that the women had grown dark by absorbing too much light – by basking too long, as it were, in virtue – but was careful to add that, if they saw more of King James, his sun-like presence would bleach them white again. In his Sonnets, as in *Othello*, Shakespeare welcomes and exploits the same prejudice to give his material – if not the stuff of life already – the unpredictability of life. The fair young man turns out to be, like Bianca, morally grey; and at first the lady seems to be his opposite. Helped, perhaps, by a shift of taste during the 1590s away from blond to dark hair (Daniel's Delia is fair in 1592, dark in the revised edition of 1601), and supported, certainly, by the convention that black could be sophistically defended, the poet says in 127 that, though ugly to some, the lady is to him 'far more fair than black'. Yet within four sonnets, in 131, he is claiming that, though 'fair', the woman is still 'black' – in her 'deeds'. So the fair friend is found to be less than fair, though forgivable, and the dark lady (like Othello, in the last extremity of anger) decidedly dark in the conduct of her love-life.

Elsewhere in the volume, the same uncertainties impinge. *A Lover's Complaint* may present its 'fickle maid' as the victim of 'false compare' and sexual charm, but the elaboration of her speech complicates our sense of her predicament. When she calls the young man 'maiden-tongued' though duplicitous, 'pure maid' in preaching but seductive in practice (lines 100 and 315), her own 'pure' and 'maiden' witness falls in doubt – not least because we learn that, seduced, she is no more a 'maid' than the youth. In the complaint as in the Sonnets, blame cannot be fixed on the corrupter alone, and what at first seemed morally fair turns out to have shades of grey. If anything, the complaint makes us more agnostic than the sequence, for it articulates an 'emotional triangle' from a single, turbulent point of view. Judgement is bound to be complex when the 'fickle maid', circumstantially unplaced, is also left unanswered by the poet (see page 425). The conventions of the genre encourage us to credit the speaker, yet a vehemence so self-undoing (notably at lines 316–29) prompts us to deduce, and then trace back to the underlying plot, deception. As in the dark lady sonnets – and the more surely since the complaint is read and reread after those texts – we sense duplicity doubling. Indeed, the youth's voice blends with the maiden's to the point at which his false words are hers. Especially in the quarto, where Jacobean typography eschews quotation marks round reported speech, their two tongues seem to fuse and his vaunting becomes her 'boast' (line 246). What registers in 1–126 as godlike androgyny here becomes the mastery of a mistress, and 127–52's flattery by lies (see 'fickle', line 5, note) urges ethical alertness on the reader.

If opposition and symmetry, with intermittent suggestions of moral equivalence, characterize relations between the fair friend poems and those to the dark lady, when these structures converge and become explicit, in 144, the result is one of the strongest sonnets in the volume:

> *Two loves I have, of comfort and despair,*
> *Which like two spirits do suggest me still;*
> *The better angel is a man right fair,*
> *The worser spirit a woman coloured ill.*
> *To win me soon to hell, my female evil*
> *Tempteth my better angel from my side,*
> *And would corrupt my saint to be a devil,*
> *Wooing his purity with her foul pride.*
> *And whether that my angel be turned fiend*
> *Suspect I may, yet not directly tell;*
> *But being both from me, both to each friend,*
> *I guess one angel in another's hell.*
> > *Yet this shall I ne'er know, but live in doubt*
> > *Till my bad angel fire my good one out.*

The poet suspects that his friend has become a fiend, seduced by the dark lady, thrall to E.K.'s 'love which enflameth men with lust' and Montaigne's 'rash and wavering fire', and he breaks out in a frenzy of sordid quibbling. Thus, 'I guess one angel in another's hell', while ostensibly extending the idea of suffering found in line 5 ('To win me soon to hell') to mean 'I presume that one angel is making the other miserable', uses a slang sense of 'hell' to clinch its rhyme in a bawdy joke ('I guess the good angel is in the bad one's cunt') while alluding at the same time to the game of barley-break, in which couples tried to run through a home base called 'hell' without being caught. And that last line, apparently meaning 'Until my mistress stops seeing my friend', is darkly fraught with the suggestion that the good angel has become an animal to be smoked out of its burrow, the lady's vagina ('He that parts us shall bring a brand from heaven', Lear cries at V.3.22–3, 'And fire us hence like foxes'), while hectically glancing at the proverb 'One fire drives out another', and touching – via the standard Elizabethan quibble on 'angel' (both 'spirit' and 'gold coin stamped with the figure of Michael') – on a financial apophthegm commonly known as Gresham's Law, 'Bad money drives out good', only to be tortured still further by the sexual implication of 'fire . . . out': 'Till my bad angel gives my good one a dose of the pox (confirming that he has been in her hell)'.

What seems most striking in the polysemy of 144, however, is the ambivalence of 'love' in line 1. Those 'two loves' must register as different modes of feeling – comforting and hopeless – until the second line makes them 'spirits'. Two kinds of loving are summed in two individuals, and the ambiguity we found in such poems to the youth as 65, 80, and 107 recurs, with 'love' at once emotion and the loved object. But the 'bad angel' represents only the 'dark' side of love; she is 'the love which enflameth men with lust toward woman-kind'. Once again, 129 clamours for quotation:

> *Mad in pursuit, and in possession so,*
> *Had, having, and in quest to have, extreme,*
> *A bliss in proof, and proved, a very woe,*
> *Before, a joy proposed, behind, a dream.*
> > *All this the world well knows, yet none knows well*
> > *To shun the heaven that leads men to this hell.*

Beyond time, indeed Time, and the process of Love's Growth, the dark lady's 'love' is not imaginatively 'redeemable'; its infertile delusions have no purchase on 'increase'; morally she inhabits, as she sexually enshrines, a 'hell'. Is it any wonder that 127–52 should include, as 1–126 could not, a religious sonnet, the poet's palinode, a Donne-like cry from the heart of corruption, 'Poor soul, the centre of my sinful earth' (146)?

Nowhere is the woman more clearly identified with debased 'love' than in 151, 'Love is too young to know what conscience is'. At the end of a complicated and extravagantly obscene argument, which copes with guilt, deception, and the fall of man *en route*, the poet declares: 'No want of conscience hold it that I call | Her "love" for whose dear love I rise and fall.' So the sonnet equates the lady with 'love'. Yet, oddly, the love involved is Cupid, not his mother, the 'young' god, not the Venus who (according to renaissance mythographers) gave birth to Cupid in the Garden of Adonis. At first sight this seems unaccountable; but other poems in the secondary sequence associate the lady with Cupid (137 and 145, for instance), and all these lead to 153–4. In some respects a buffer group, with the function of the anacreontics and epigrams in *Delia*, the *Amoretti*, *Phillis*, and the rest, these sonnets about Cupid and his brand are also the logical outcome of the dark lady sonnets, since they make visible the erotic principle at work in them. Not 'obviously linked' with what precedes them, they are nevertheless inseparable from 127–52, and essential to those poems' effect. Shakespeare has taken the Daniel-esque convention of a three-part structure and, with characteristic revivifying economy, made its central term work twice, separating the sonnets from *A Lover's Complaint* but concluding the dark lady group. Indeed, he has, like Richard Linche, used the fourteen-line form as his textual link to signal his intentions. Nor can there be thought a contradiction between the structure of these texts and their epigrammatic content; nine of Sir John Davies's forty-eight *Epigrams* are in sonnet form, and Shakespeare's 153–4 would have been effortlessly read by early readers as simultaneously sonnet–epigrams.

These poems record, of course, how Cupid's 'heart-inflaming brand' was stolen by a nymph of Dian's train and quenched in 'a cold valley-fountain' or 'cool well by'. In the first, the torch is reignited; in the second, with perhaps greater claims to resolution, it simply makes the water seethe. Yet such a description makes the poems sound naive when they are very knowing. As a number of critics have pointed out, the sonnets contain innuendoes which are not the less blatant for being baroque. The burning 'brand' reignited at 'my mistress' eyes' (the 'eyes' which are 'nothing like the sun' in 130) is patently phallic; it is the 'flesh' which 'rises' and 'falls' for 'love' in Sonnet 151. And the 'cool well' made a healthful bath 'For men diseased' by the 'brand' of 'love' is distinctly reminiscent of the sweating tubs used to cure the pox in Jacobethan London. The sonnets may be deft, but they are sordid too. This 'little Love-god', unlike the 'god in love' of Sonnet 110, inhabits a sterile landscape. Like his bizarre human correlative, the dark lady, the 'boy' Cupid brings sensation, where the poet's 'lovely boy' is a god of 'increase'.

For we are back, finally, with the question of a sub-plot. Just as, in Sonnet 137, the lady offers a ghastly parody of the young man's amplitude, a 'wide world's common place' to his 'spring and foison of the year', so, in the conflation of her 'love' with Cupid, there is an echo of Shakespeare's exaltation of the youth into a 'god in love'. The two final sonnets on Cupid find their lofty equivalent in the last poem to the young man, Sonnet 126:

> *O thou, my lovely boy, who in thy power*
> *Dost hold Time's fickle glass, his sickle hour,*
> *Who hast by waning grown, and therein show'st*
> *Thy lovers withering, as thy sweet self grow'st;*
> *If Nature, sovereign mistress over wrack,*
> *As thou goest onwards, still will pluck thee back,*
> *She keeps thee to this purpose, that her skill*
> *May Time disgrace and wretched minutes kill.*

> *Yet fear her, O thou minion of her pleasure;*
> *She may detain, but not still keep her treasure.*
> *Her audit, though delayed, answered must be,*
> *And her quietus is to render thee.*

The poem resonates with material from the early sonnets: treasure and the treasury, the audit, skill, the 'sweet self', and, of course, Time's wrack. But here, the powers of Adonis reach their full height, and the young man grows by waning, increasing in decay. Like Spenser's 'wanton boy' in the Garden of Adonis, Shakespeare's 'lovely boy' dwindles into foison, producing, in the words of his Venus, seeds from seeds, beauty from beauty (*Venus and Adonis* 167). In 107, a 'mortal moon' had been 'eclipsed'; but in 126 Time's 'sickle' is borrowed by 'waning' in line 3, to make the youth a moon that grows when it is shaded. He is 'eterne in mutabilitie', favoured by Nature as Spenser's 'boy' was favoured by Aphrodite Pandemos, the Venus of the natural world. And like that youth, he is apparently above Time: 'O thou, my lovely boy, who in thy power | Dost hold Time's fickle glass, his sickle hour'. Many critics have quoted that, as though it were the end of the matter. But this last poem to the friend includes a reversal quite as violent as Spenser's at *The Faerie Queene* III.vi.39. Nature is in debt to Time, and, despite her dotage, she 'must' render the 'lovely boy' to mortality. The youth cannot escape from Time. Beauty cannot save him, nor all the poet's labours, which strive to make the friend a 'god', and try to recoup, by recounting, the clock. In Shakespeare's Sonnets, at the last, Time circumscribes the natural world and the very springs of life, while verse can only make memorials, inscribing what, without art, would always already be gone.

FURTHER READING

THE bibliography of relevant works is enormous – Herbert S. Donow's *The Sonnet in England and America: A Bibliography of Criticism* (Westport, Conn., 1982) lists 1,898 items on the Sonnets alone – but much of the literature tends to lunacy and is dispensable. What follows is highly selective. Many works of merit have been excluded because duplicated or replaced by later studies, though certain other well-publicized books have been left ou deliberately, on scholarly grounds.

Editions, Textual and Related Studies

The original texts are best read in *Shakespeare's Poems: A Facsimile of the Earliest Editions*, published for the Yale Elizabethan Club (New Haven, Conn., 1964), which includes *The Passionate Pilgrim*. Among older editions, those by Edmond Malone (1780, 1790), Edward Dowden (1881), and George Wyndham (1898) are still of enormous interest. Most readers, however, will find all they want of the older scholarship in Hyder Edward Rollins's New Variorum Editions of *The Sonnets* (Philadelphia, Pa., 1944, 2 vols.) and, for *A Lover's Complaint*, *The Poems* (Philadelphia, Pa., 1938). What Rollins lacks in critical sophistication he makes up in stout astuteness. The New Cambridge *Sonnets*, edited by J. Dover Wilson (Cambridge, 1966, 1967) is late undistinguished work by an important scholar, while J. C. Maxwell's *Poems* in the same series (Cambridge, 1966) is disappointingly perfunctory in its treatment of *A Lover's Complaint*. Martin Seymour-Smith's edition of the Sonnets for Heinemann Educational (London, 1963) is admirable in its own, necessarily restricted, terms. William Burto's Signet *Sonnets* (New York, 1964) is chiefly noteworthy for its introduction by W. H. Auden (reprinted in Edward Mendelson's selection from Auden's prose, *Forewords and Afterwords*, New York, 1973, 88–108). Altogether more ponderable is *Shakespeare's Sonnets*, edited by W. G. Ingram and Theodore Redpath (London, 1964, 1978); it often seems impossible to improve on the annotation of these editors. Stephen Booth's edition of the Sonnets (New Haven, Conn., 1977, 1978), which interleaves the 1609 text in facsimile with modernized but conservative, lightly punctuated versions, is by contrast both inspiring and infuriating. Elaborately annotated, on the ultra-Empsonian principle that any extractable meaning is significant, it too often lapses into perverse intricacy, and, in the discovery of impossible innuendoes, sinks into puerility. Though much can be said against this edition, it is nevertheless compulsory reading for all close students of Shakespeare, and for those who think literary value inheres in wordplay it is indispensable.

The insufficiently sung hero of Sonnets scholarship is Macd. P. Jackson, whose 'Punctuation and the Compositors of Shakespeare's *Sonnets*, 1609', *The Library*, 5th series, 30 (1975), 1–24, finally set the textual criticism of these poems on a sensible footing. His pamphlet *Shakespeare's 'A Lover's Complaint': Its Date and Authenticity*, University of Auckland Bulletin 72, English Series 13 (Auckland, 1965), is equally important, since, with the help of Kenneth Muir's '"A Lover's Complaint": A Reconsideration' (conveniently reprinted in Muir's *Shakespeare the Professional and Related Studies*, London, 1973, 204–19), it establishes Shakespeare's authorship of a poem for long denied him. The older, anti-Shakespearian view can be consulted in J. W. Mackail's 'A Lover's Complaint', *Essays and Studies* 3 (1912), 51–70, and in *Shakespeare and Chapman* by J. M. Robertson (London, 1917). Recently, confirmation of Muir and Jackson's work has been offered by Eliot Slater, 'Shakespeare: Word Links Between Poems and Plays', *Notes and Queries* 220 (1975), 157–63, and by A. C. Partridge, whose *Substantive Grammar of Shakespeare's Nondramatic Texts* (Charlottesville, Va., 1976), is continuously illuminating about linguistic usage in the collection.

Neither Muir and Jackson nor Slater and Partridge argues for Shakespearian authority on the basis of the Delian tradition. Here the credit must go to Malone, who declared that 'Daniel's Sonnets . . . appear to me to have been the model that Shakespeare followed', and to few others. In her generally unrewarding 'The Structure of English Renaissance Sonnet Sequences', *English Literary History* 45 (1978), 359–89, Carol Thomas Neely notices the tendency of sequences to be attached to complaints. Thomas P. Roche fruitfully remarks, in 'Shakespeare and the Sonnet Sequence' (*English Poetry and Prose, 1540–1674*, edited by Christopher Ricks, London, 1970, 101–18), the tripartite form of Q. And Alastair Fowler's numerological analysis of the Sonnets, in *Triumphal Forms: Structural Patterns in Elizabethan Poetry* (Cambridge, 1970), at least pays *A Lover's Complaint* the compliment of arithmetical inclusion. Most important, however, is Katherine Duncan-Jones's 'Was the 1609 *Shakespeares Sonnets* Really Unauthorized?', *Review of English Studies*, new series, 34 (1983), 151–71, which, after building on Leona Rostenberg's characterization of 'Thomas Thorpe, Publisher of "Shake-Speares Sonnets"', *Papers of the Bibliographical Society of America* 54 (1960), 16–3′, and arguing, attractively but unconvincingly, for an echo of the structure of Sidney's *Astrophil and Stella* in the poems to the friend, sets about reconstructing the tradition which leads towards Q. It is the claim of this edition, of course, that Malone's insight, the corollary of which he never grasped, has far-reaching critical as well as structural and editorial implications.

Manuscript versions of Sonnets 1 (conflated with 2 and 54), 2, 8, 32, 33, 68, 71, 106, 107, 116 (as a lyric), 128, and 138 are listed by Peter Beal in Volume I, part ii, of the *Index of English Literary Manuscripts* (London, 1980). Mary Hobbs's 'Shakespeare's Sonnet II – "A Sugred Sonnet"?', *Notes and Queries* 224 (1979), 112–13, raises important issues, pursued by Gary Taylor in 'Shakespeare's Sonnets: a Rediscovery', *Times Literary Supplement*, 19 April 1985, 450, and 'Some Manuscripts of Shakespeare's Sonnets', *Bulletin of the John Rylands Library* 68 (1985–6), 210–46. On the manuscript text of Sonnet 128, see Robin Robbins, 'A Seventeenth-Century Manuscript of Shakespeare's Sonnet 128', *Notes and Queries* 212 (1967), 137–8. Willa McClung Evans's 'Lawes' Version of Shakespeare's Sonnet CXVI', *PMLA* 51 (1936), 120–22, is of considerable interest, though the editorial value of Lawes's text is minimal. For an absorbing account of the poems in Elizabethan manuscript culture see Arthur F. Marotti, 'Shakespeare's Sonnets as Literary Property', in Elizabeth D. Harvey and Katharine Eisaman Maus, eds., *Soliciting Interpretation: Literary Theory and Seventeenth-Century English Poetry* (Chicago, 1990). Margreta de Grazia does equally valuable work on the later reception of the poems, especially as edited by John Benson (1640), in her *Shakespeare Verbatim: The Reproduction of Authenticity and the 1790 Apparatus* (Oxford, 1991). Research into *The Passionate Pilgrim* has hardly advanced since the 1960s. For alternative views on authority and authorship see F. T. Prince's new Arden edition of *The Poems* (London, 1960) and J. C. Maxwell's volume, noted above.

Leslie Hotson's dating of certain sonnets, such as 107, to the 1580s (*Shakespeare's Sonnets Dated, and Other Essays*, London, 1949) has been convincingly refuted by, among others, F. W. Bateson ('Elementary My Dear Hotson', *Essays in Criticism* 1 (1951), 81–8), J. M. Nosworthy ('All too Short a Date: Internal Evidence in Shakespeare's Sonnets', *Essays in Criticism* 2 (1952), 311–24), and Walter B. Stone ('Shakespeare and the Sad Augurs', *Journal of English and Germanic Philology* 52 (1953), 457–79). Claes Schaar's elaborate attempt to date large numbers of the poems before 1594, and some before 1592 (*Elizabethan Sonnet Themes and the Dating of Shakespeare's Sonnets*, Lund Studies in English 32, Lund, 1962), already subjected to damaging scrutiny by Winifred Nowottny in the *Review of English Studies*, new series, 15 (1964), 423–9, is tellingly challenged over a representative detail by MacD. P. Jackson in 'Shakespeare's "Sonnets", "Parthenophil and Parthenophe", and "A Lover's Complaint"', *Notes and Queries* 217 (1972), 125–6. The issue of dating is, however, inordinately complex and contentious. Students concerned to date the crucial 107, for instance, would have to add the following to Slater and the studies already mentioned, for even a basic reading list: F. S. Boas, 'Dr Hotson's Arguments', *Times Literary Supplement*, 7 July 1950, 421; Samuel Butler, 'Shakespeare's Sonnets', *Athenaeum*, 30 July 1898, 161; E. K. Chambers, 'The "Mortal Moon" Sonnet', *Times Literary Supplement*, 25 January 1934, 60 (compare his

Shakespearean Gleanings, Oxford, 1944); Leo Daugherty, 'Sir John Davies and the Question of Topical Reference in Shakespeare's Sonnet 107', *Shakespeare Quarterly* 30 (1979), 93–5; J. A. Fort, 'The Date of Shakespeare's 107th Sonnet', *The Library*, 4th series, 9 (1929), 381–4; G. B. Harrison, 'The Mortal Moon', *Times Literary Supplement*, 29 November 1928, 938; Garrett Mattingly, 'The Date of Shakespeare's Sonnet CVII', *PMLA* 48 (1933), 705–21; Laurence Michel, 'Shakespeare's Sonnet 107', *Journal of English and Germanic Philology* 54 (1955), 301–5; John Middleton Murry, 'The Mortal Moon' in *John Clare and Other Studies*, London, 1950, 246–52; I. A. Shapiro, 'Dr Hotson's Arguments', *Times Literary Supplement*, 21 April 1950, 245. The best overview of the dating question (which produces results broadly in line with those arrived at, independently, for this edition), is by A. Kent Heiatt, Charles W. Heiatt and Anne Lake Prescott, 'When Did Shakespeare Write *Sonnets* 1609?', *Studies in Philology* 88 (1991), 69–109. Despite the objections of Hilda Hulme ('Sonnet 145: "I Hate, From Hathaway She Threw"', *Essays in Criticism* 21 (1971), 427–9), Andrew Gurr's hypothesis that Sonnet 145 is early, and punningly directed at Anne Hathaway, remains persuasive: 'Shakespeare's First Poem: Sonnet 145', *Essays in Criticism* 21 (1971), 221–6. The same critic has also written the most convincing in a succession of articles on 'You and Thou in Shakespeare's Sonnets', *Essays in Criticism* 32 (1982), 9–25.

Reorderings of the sequence up to 1940 are summarized by Rollins (II, 74–116). Since then, only Brents Stirling's *The Shakespeare Sonnet Order* (Berkeley, Calif., 1968), S. C. Campbell's *Only Begotten Sonnets: A Reconstruction of Shakespeare's Sonnet Sequence* (London, 1978), and John Padel's *New Poems by Shakespeare: Order and Meaning Restored to the Sonnets* (London, 1981) deserve attention, and none remotely persuades. The controversy surrounding the identity of Mr W.H. and/or the addressee of Sonnets 1–126, the dark lady, and the rival poet(s), is outlined with admirable restraint by Kenneth Muir in appendixes to his study, *Shakespeare's Sonnets* (London, 1979). His notes and allusions provide a sufficient chart to this unrewarding territory.

Criticism

Peter Jones's *Casebook* (London, 1977) provides an intelligent selection of comments up to 1938, important extracts from the work of Sir Sidney Lee, Robert Graves and Laura Riding ('A Study in Original Punctuation and Spelling', which can be read in context in *The Common Asphodel*, London, 1949, 84–95), and William Empson (*Seven Types of Ambiguity*, London, 1947, 1953), and the following indispensable discussions: L. C. Knights, 'Shakespeare's Sonnets' (*Scrutiny* 3 (1934), 133–60, first reprinted in

Knights's *Explorations*, London, 1946); John Crowe Ransom, 'Shakespeare at Sonnets' (*Southern Review* 3 (1937–8), 531–3, first reprinted in Ransom's *The World's Body*, New York, 1938, which should be read in the light of Ransom's apologetic 'Postscript on Shakespeare's Sonnets', *Kenyon Review* 30 (1968), 523–31); Winifred Nowottny, 'Formal Elements in Shakespeare's Sonnets: Sonnets I–VI' (*Essays in Criticism* 2 (1952), 76–84); G. K. Hunter, 'The Dramatic Technique of Shakespeare's Sonnets' (*Essays in Criticism* 3 (1953), 152–64); G. Wilson Knight, 'Symbolism' (from his uneven *The Mutual Flame*, London, 1955); M. M. Mahood, on quibbling (from *Shakespeare's Wordplay*, London, 1957) and 'Love's Confined Doom' (*Shakespeare Survey 15*, Cambridge, 1962, 50–61); Yvor Winters, from *Four Poets on Poetry* (edited by Don Cameron Allen, Baltimore, Md, 1959, 44–75); F. T. Prince, 'The Sonnet from Wyatt to Shakespeare' (*Elizabethan Poetry*, edited by John Russell Brown and Bernard Harris, Stratford-upon-Avon Studies 2, London, 1960, 10–29); Joan Grundy, 'Shakespeare's Sonnets and the Elizabethan Sonneteers' (*Shakespeare Survey 15*, Cambridge, 1962, 41–9); Jan Kott, from *Shakespeare our Contemporary* (London, 1965, 1967); Inga-Stina Ewbank, from 'Shakespeare's Poetry' in *A New Companion to Shakespeare Studies* (edited by Kenneth Muir and S. Schoenbaum, Cambridge, 1971); C. F. Williamson, 'Themes and Patterns in Shakespeare's Sonnets' (*Essays in Criticism* 26 (1976), 191–207).

This collection is usefully complemented by Hilton Landry's gathering of specially commissioned pieces, *New Essays on Shakespeare's Sonnets* (New York, 1976). Among the nine essays – by Rodney Poisson, Martin Seymour-Smith, W. G. Ingram, Winifred Nowottny, Anton M. Pirkhofer, Landry himself (already the author of the useful *Interpretations in Shakespeare's Sonnets*, Berkeley, Calif., 1963), Marshall Lindsay, Paul Ramsey, and Theodore Redpath – those by Nowottny ('Some Features of Form and Style in Sonnets 97–126') and, in its different way, Redpath ('The Punctuation of Shakespeare's Sonnets') stand out. Slightly older, but at least as valuable, are the essays in *The Riddle of Shakespeare's Sonnets*, edited by Edward Hubler (New York, 1962). In addition to Hubler's synthesizing 'Shakespeare's Sonnets and the Commentators' and Oscar Wilde's 'The Portrait of Mr W.H.' (reprinted from the enlarged version of 1895), this includes distinguished work by Northrop Frye, Leslie Fiedler, Stephen Spender, and R. P. Blackmur.

Some other essay-length discussions worth serious attention are: Michael J. B. Allen, 'Shakespeare's Man Descending a Staircase: Sonnets 127 to 154', *Shakespeare Survey 31* (Cambridge, 1978), 127–38; C. L. Barber, Introduction to *The Sonnets by William Shakespeare*, edited by C. J. Sisson (New York, 1960), reprinted in *Elizabethan Poetry: Modern Essays in Criticism*, edited by Paul Alpers (New York, 1967), 299–320; John Barrell, 'Editing Out: The Discourse of Patronage in Shakespeare's Twenty-Ninth Sonnet', and the opening pages of 'Masters of Suspense: Syntax and Gender in

Milton's Sonnets', both in his *Poetry, Language and Politics* (Manchester, 1988), pp. 18–43, 44ff.; John Bayley, 'Who Was the "Man Right Fair" of the Sonnets?', *Times Literary Supplement*, 4 January 1974, 108; John D. Bernard, '"To Constancie Confin'de": The Poetics of Shakespeare's Sonnets', *PMLA* 94 (1979), 77–90; Rosalie Colie, Chapters 1 (on the Sonnets and *Love's Labour's Lost*) and 2 (on couplets, epigrams, and Shakespeare's sequence) of *Shakespeare's Living Art* (Princeton, N.J., 1974); Patrick Cruttwell, 'Shakespeare's Sonnets and the 1590's' in *The Shakespearean Moment and its Place in the Poetry of the Seventeenth Century* (London, 1954); Janette Dillon, '"Walls of glass"; The Sonnets' in *Shakespeare and the Solitary Man* (London, 1981); Ch. 3 of Heather Dubrow, *Captive Victors: Shakespeare's Narrative Poems and Sonnets* (Ithaca, NY, 1987); Philip Edwards, 'The Sonnets to the Dark Woman' in *Shakespeare and the Confines of Art* (London, 1968); Anne Ferry, *All in War with Time: Love Poetry of Shakespeare, Donne, Jonson, Marvell* (Cambridge, Mass., 1975), 3–63, and *The 'Inward' Language: Sonnets of Wyatt, Sidney, Shakespeare, Donne* (Chicago, 1983), 1–70 (the English renaissance sonnet), 170–214 and 251–5 (on Shakespeare and Sidney); Thomas M. Greene, 'Pitiful Thrivers: Failed Husbandry in the Sonnets', in Patricia Parker and Geoffrey Hartman, eds., *Shakespeare and the Question of Theory* (London, 1985), pp. 230–44; L. C. Knights, 'Time's Subjects: The Sonnets and *King Henry IV, Part II*', *Some Shakespearean Themes* (London, 1959), 45–64; Pauline Kogan, 'A Materialist Analysis of Shakespeare's Sonnets', *Literature and Ideology* 1 (1969), 8–21; Murray Krieger, 'The Innocent Insinuations of Wit: The Strategy of Language in Shakespeare's Sonnets' in *The Play and Place of Criticism* (Baltimore, Md., 1967), 19–36; Richard Lanham, 'Superposed Poetics: The Sonnets' in *The Motives of Eloquence* (New Haven, Conn., 1976); C. S. Lewis, *English Literature in the Sixteenth Century, Excluding Drama, Oxford History of English Literature*, Volume 3 (Oxford, 1954), 502–8; A. C. Partridge, *The Language of Renaissance Poetry: Spenser, Shakespeare, Donne, Milton* (London, 1971), 119–40; Christopher Ricks, glancingly, in his *Critical Inquiry* essay 'Lies' (conveniently reprinted in *The Force of Poetry*, Oxford, 1984, 369–91); Jane Roessner (Ritchie), 'Double Exposure: Shakespeare's Sonnets 100–114', *English Literary History* 46 (1979), 357–78; George Rylands, 'Shakespeare the Poet' in *A Companion to Shakespeare Studies*, edited by Harley Granville-Barker and G. B. Harrison (Cambridge, 1934), 89–115, perceptively praising *A Lover's Complaint*; B. F. Skinner, 'The Alliteration in Shakespeare's Sonnets: A Study in Literary Behaviour', *Psychological Record* 3 (1939), 186–92; Hallett Smith, 'Bare Ruined Choirs: Shakespearean Variations on the Theme of Old Age', *Huntington Library Quarterly* 39 (1976), 233–49; Caroline Spurgeon, *Keats's Shakespeare* (Oxford, 1928), especially pages 38–41; Roger Warren, 'Why Does It End Well? Helena, Bertram, and the Sonnets', *Shakespeare Survey 22* (Cambridge,

1969), 79–82, and '"A Lover's Complaint", "All's Well", and the Sonnets', *Notes and Queries* 215 (1970), 130–32.

Equally valuable, though more narrowly focused, are: on Sonnet 15, Raymond B. Waddington, 'Shakespeare's Sonnet 15 and the Art of Memory' in *The Rhetoric of Renaissance Poetry from Wyatt to Milton*, edited by Thomas O. Sloan and Waddington (Berkeley, Calif., 1974), 96–122; on 73, Roger Fowler, 'Language and the Reader: Shakespeare's Sonnet 73' in *Style and Structure in Literature: Essays in the New Stylistics*, edited by Fowler (Oxford, 1975), 79–122, Winifred Nowottny, *The Language Poets Use* (New York, 1962), 76–86, and, on line 4 of the sonnet, Bateson versus Empson and Charles B. Wheeler, *Essays in Criticism* 3 (1953), 7–9, 357–63, and 4 (1954), 224–6; on Paul Celan's translation of 79, and Stefan George and Karl Kraus's translations of 87, George Steiner, *After Babel* (Oxford, 1975), 382–93; on 94, conspicuously, Empson, 'They That Have Power', *Versions of Pastoral* (London, 1935), rebuked by, among others, Veronica Forrest-Thomson, in *Poetic Artifice: A Theory of Twentieth-Century Poetry* (Manchester, 1978), 1–17; on 111, and 'infected' especially, Geoffrey Hill, 'Our Word Is Our Bond', reprinted in *The Lords of Limit* (London, 1984), page 153; on 116 and related texts, Sigurd Burckhardt, 'The Poet as Fool and Priest', *English Literary History* 23 (1956), 279–98, reprinted in *Shakespearean Meanings* (Princeton, N.J., 1968), 22–46, Hilton Landry, 'The Marriage of True Minds: Truth and Error in Sonnet 116', *Shakespeare Studies* 3 (1967), 98–110, and Carol Thomas Neely, 'Detachment and Engagement in Shakespeare's Sonnets: 94, 116 and 129', *PMLA* 92 (1977), 83–95; on 124, Arthur Mizener, 'The Structure of Figurative Language in Shakespeare's Sonnets', *Southern Review* 5 (1940), 730–47, reprinted most accessibly in *Essays in Shakespearean Criticism*, edited by James L. Calderwood and Harold E. Toliver (Englewood Cliffs, N.J., 1970), 85–100; on 126, and especially line 2, Jon R. Russ, 'Time's Attributes in Shakespeare's Sonnet 126', *English Studies* 52 (1971), 318–23; on 129, inauguratively, Roman Jakobson and Lawrence G. Jones, *Shakespeare's Verbal Art in th'Expence of Spirit*, De Proprietatibus Litterarum, Series Practica, 35 (The Hague, 1970), surveyed and approved by I. A. Richards in 'Jakobson's Shakespeare: The Subliminal Structures of a Sonnet', *Times Literary Supplement*, 28 May 1970, 589–90, and pursued by Helen Vendler in 'Jakobson, Richards, and Shakespeare's Sonnet CXXIX' (*I. A. Richards: Essays in His Honour*, edited by Reuben Brower, Helen Vendler, and John Hollander, New York, 1973, 179–98) and, less directly, by B. F. Skinner in the same volume ('Reflections on Meaning and Structure', pages 199–209); on 146, Donald A. Stauffer, 'Critical Principles and a Sonnet', *The American Scholar* 12 (1942–3), 52–62, B. C. Southam, 'Shakespeare's Christian Sonnet? No. 146', *Shakespeare Quarterly* 11 (1960), 67–71, Charles A. Huttar, 'The Christian Basis of Shakespeare's Sonnet 146', *Shakespeare Quarterly* 19 (1968), 355–65, and Michael West, 'The Internal Dialogue of Shakespeare's Sonnet 146', also in *Shakespeare Quarterly* 25 (1974), 109–22; on 153–4, James Hutton, 'Analogues of Shakespeare's Sonnets 153–4: Contributions to the History of a Theme', *Modern Philology* 38 (1941), 385–403, reprinted in Hutton's *Essays on Renaissance Poetry*, edited by Rita Guerlac (Ithaca, New York, 1980), 149–68. The numerological analysis praised on page 42 is by René Graziani, 'The Numbering of Shakespeare's Sonnets: 12, 60, and 126', *Shakespeare Quarterly* 35 (1984), 79–82.

Much of the liveliest recent criticism of the Sonnets has been influenced by gender studies. See, for instance, Joseph Pequigney, *Such is My Love: A Study of Shakespeare's Sonnets* (Chicago, 1985), Bruce R. Smith, *Homosexual Desire in Shakespeare's England: A Cultural Poetics* (Chicago, 1991), pp. 228–70, Gregory W. Bredbeck, *Sodomy and Interpretation: Marlowe to Milton* (Ithaca, NY, 1991), pp. 167–80, and Raymond B. Waddington, 'The Poetics of Eroticism: Shakespeare's "Master-Mistress"', in Claude J. Summers and Ted-Larry Pebworth, eds., *Renaissance Discourses of Desire* (Columbia, Miss., 1993), pp. 13–28. For work which moves intelligently between textual and interpretative questions on the one hand and the history of sexuality on the other, see Peter Stallybrass, 'Editing as Cultural Formation: The Sexing of Shakespeare's Sonnets', *Modern Language Quarterly* 54 (1993), 91–103 and Margreta de Grazia, 'The Scandal of Shakespeare's Sonnets', *Shakespeare Survey* 46 (1993), 35–49. The three best extended studies of the Sonnets are probably: J. B. Leishman's *Themes and Variations in Shakespeare's Sonnets* (London, 1961), Stephen Booth's *Essay on Shakespeare's Sonnets* (New Haven, Conn., 1969) – a subtle and searching book, quite free from the excesses of Booth's later edition – and Giorgio Melchiori's *Shakespeare's Dramatic Meditations: An Experiment in Criticism* (Oxford, 1976). These individually distinguished works are also complementary in that, while Leishman places the poems in a broad tradition of love poetry reaching back to Catullus, Ovid, and Horace, Booth is sensitive to rhythm, structure, and sequence, and Melchiori makes his larger points by attending with microscopic – some would say myopic – care to the details of five sonnets (20, 94, 121, 129, 146). For an attempt to read the Sonnets *Beyond Deconstruction*, see Chapter 5 of Howard Felperin's book (Oxford, 1985). The most sustainedly intricate post-structuralist analysis is Joel Fineman's *Shakespeare's Perjured Eye: The Invention of Poetic Subjectivity in the Sonnets* (Berkeley, 1986).

'A Lover's Complaint' remains neglected, though critical interest has begun to stir. Sources and analogues are established, socio-historical contexts provided, and close reading advanced in John Kerrigan, ed. *Motives of Woe: Shakespeare and 'Female Complaint'. A Critical Anthology* (Oxford, 1991). Theoretical arguments which illuminate 'A Lover' Complaint' – though it is not itself an object of scrutiny – can be found in Elizabeth D. Harvey, *Ventriloquized Voices: Feminist Theory and English Renaissance Texts* (London, 1992). Various texts generically related to the poem are discussed by Götz Schmitz in *The Fall of Women in Early English Narrative Verse* (Cambridge, 1990).

Background

T. W. Baldwin's *On the Literary Genetics of Shakespeare's Poems and Sonnets* (Urbana, Ill., 1950), though not exhaustive, is formidably thorough. A. Kent Hieatt plugs one gap with 'The Genesis of Shakespeare's *Sonnets*: Spenser's *Ruines of Rome: by Bellay*', *PMLA* 98 (1983), 800–814, but the debt is not as important as Hieatt implies. J. W. Lever's *The Elizabethan Love Sonnet* (London, 1956) helpfully supplements the work of Prince, Grundy, and Ferry discussed above, and is usually more perceptive than C. S. Lewis's volume for the *Oxford History of English Literature*. M. C. Bradbrook has some suggestive things to say about dramatic and non-dramatic verse in *Shakespeare and Elizabethan Poetry* (London, 1951). On the social context of sonneteering (in an essay which properly stresses the importance of wooing patrons), see Arthur F. Marotti, '"Love is Not Love": Elizabethan Sonnet Sequences and the Social Order', *ELH* 49 (1982), 356–428. An equally important background, however, is provided by the literary tradition of poetic 'imitation'. For an attempt to relate the breeding motif in Shakespeare's poems to classical and Renaissance ideas of *imitatio*, see John Kerrigan, 'Between Michelangelo and Petrarch: Shakepeare's Sonnets of Art', in Yasunari Takada, 'Surprised by Scenes: Essays in Honour of Professor Yasunari Takahashi' (Tokyo, 1994), pp. 142–63.

O. B. Hardison's *The Ei uring Monument: A Study of the Idea of Praise in Renaissance Literary Theory and Practice* (Chapel Hill, N.C., 1962) remains the standard introduction, though *Praise in 'The Faerie Queene'* by Thomas H. Cain (Lincoln, Nebr., 1978) includes much interesting material, and has up-to-date references. On medieval time, Jacques Le Goff's essays in *Time, Work, and Culture in the Middle Ages* (Chicago, Ill., 1980) and Jean Leclerq's 'Experience and Interpretation of Ti e in the Early Middle Ages' in *Studies in Medieval Culture* 5, edited by John R. Sommerfeldt *et al.* (Kalamazoo, Mich., 1975) are outstanding. E. P. Thompson's 'Time, Work-Discipline, and Industrial Capitalism', *Past and Present* 38 (1967), 56–97, deals with England in the seventeenth, eighteenth, and nineteenth centuries. David S. Lande's *Revolution in Time: Clocks and the Making of the Modern World* (Cambridge, Mass., 1983) does not entirely displace Carlo M. Cipolla's elegant *Clocks and Culture: 1300–1700* (London, 1967). Exellent in itself, Alan Bray's *Homosexuality in Renaissance England* (London, 1982) includes a useful list of books and articles for those wishing to pursue this elusive theme further. For work which builds on Bray's study, and establishes new theoretical and historical perspectives, see Jonathan Goldberg, *Sodometries: Renaissance Texts, Modern Sexualities* (Stanford, 1992). The annotation in A. C. Hamilton's edition of *The Faerie Queene* (London, 1977) offers immediate help with Spenser's Adonis, and the works of Ellrodt, Roche, Ramsay, and Tonkin (1973b) listed in Hamilton's bibliography provide further enlightenment. For Shakespeare's Adonis see, especially, Geoffrey Bullough, *Narra ive and Dramatic Sources of Shakespeare*, Volume I (London, 1957). On the variety of renaissance Cupids see Jean Seznec, *The Survival of the Pagan Gods* (Princeton, N.J., 1953), Erwin Panofsky, *Studies in Iconology* (Oxford, 1939), Chapter iv, Edgar Wind, *Pagan Mysteries in the Renaissance* (London, 1958, 1967), especially Chapters iv, ix, and x. Panofsky also writes well about 'Father Time' (Chapter iii), and Wind, illuminatingly, on androgyny and the 'blest Hermaphrodite' (Chapter xiii). Sears Jayne's 'Ficino and the Platonism of the English Renaissance', *Comparative Literature* 4 (1952), 214–38, provides a lucid if provisional survey.

In 'The Development of Rhyme-Scheme and of Syntactic Pattern in the English Renaissance Sonnet', *Philologica* (Acta Universitatis Palackianae Olumucensis) 4 (1961), 167–85, and his earlier 'On the Relations of Language and Stanza Pattern in the English Sonnet' (*Worte und Werke: Bruno Marckwardt zum 60. Geburtstag*, Berlin, 1960, 214–31), Jiří Levý establishes with dry rigour that the Shakespearian rhyme scheme emerges naturally, almost inevitably, from the economy of our language. With similar analytical steadiness, G. P. Jones compares the disposition of pronouns in Shakespeare's Sonnets with their use in contemporary collections: 'You, Thou, He or She? The Master-Mistress in Shakespearian and Elizabethan Sonnet Sequences', *Cahiers Élisabéthains* 19 (April 1981), 73–84.

At the margin which should be central, two authors make a stron; case for Shakespearian involvement in *Edward III* (see the note to 94.14): Kenneth Muir, in *Shakespeare as Collaborator* (London, 1960), and G. R. Proudfoot, '"The Reign of King Edward the Third" (1596) and Shakespeare', British Academy Shakespeare Lecture 1985 (forthcoming in *Proceedings of the British Academy* 72 [London (Oxford), 1986]). At the centre which might be marginal, Samuel Schoenbaum's *William Shakespeare: A Compact Documentary Life* (Oxford, 1977) is standard, while, for those with leisure and a sense of humour, the same author's *Shakespeare's Lives* (Oxford, 1970) can be recommended as a wittily-turned account of the innumerable crackpot theories about the poet's life and love life – fantasies in which the Sonnets have played a large part.

THE SONNETS

From fairest creatures we desire increase,
That thereby beauty's rose might never die,
But as the riper should by time decease,
His tender heir might bear his memory;   4
But thou, contracted to thine own bright eyes,
Feed'st thy light's flame with self-substantial fuel,
Making a famine where abundance lies,
Thyself thy foe, to thy sweet self too cruel.   8
Thou that art now the world's fresh ornament
And only herald to the gaudy spring
Within thine own bud buriest thy content,
And, tender churl, mak'st waste in niggarding. 12
   Pity the world, or else this glutton be,
   To eat the world's due, by the grave and thee.

When forty winters shall besiege thy brow,
And dig deep trenches in thy beauty's field,
Thy youth's proud livery, so gazed on now,
Will be a tattered weed of small worth held.   4
Then being asked where all thy beauty lies,
Where all the treasure of thy lusty days,
To say within thine own deep-sunken eyes
Were an all-eating shame and thriftless praise. 8
How much more praise deserved thy beauty's use
If thou couldst answer 'This fair child of mine
Shall sum my count and make my old excuse,'
Proving his beauty by succession thine.   12
   This were to be new made when thou art old,
   And see thy blood warm when thou feel'st it cold.

Look in thy glass and tell the face thou viewest
Now is the time that face should form another,
Whose fresh repair if now thou not renewest
Thou dost beguile the world, unbless some mother.   4
For where is she so fair whose uneared womb
Disdains the tillage of thy husbandry?
Or who is he so fond will be the tomb
Of his self-love to stop posterity?   8
Thou art thy mother's glass, and she in thee
Calls back the lovely April of her prime;
So thou through windows of thine age shalt see,
Despite of wrinkles, this thy golden time.   12
    But if thou live remembered not to be,
    Die single, and thine image dies with thee.

Unthrifty loveliness, why dost thou spend
Upon thyself thy beauty's legacy?
Nature's bequest gives nothing, but doth lend,
And being frank she lends to those are free.   4
Then, beauteous niggard, why dost thou abuse
The bounteous largess given thee to give?
Profitless usurer, why dost thou use
So great a sum of sums yet canst not live?   8
For having traffic with thyself alone
Thou of thyself thy sweet self dost deceive;
Then how when Nature calls thee to be gone,
What acceptable audit canst thou leave?   12
    Thy unused beauty must be tombed with thee,
    Which, usèd, lives th'executor to be.

5

Those hours that with gentle work did frame
The lovely gaze where every eye doth dwell
Will play the tyrants to the very same
And that unfair which fairly doth excel;   4
For never-resting Time leads summer on
To hideous winter and confounds him there,
Sap checked with frost and lusty leaves quite gone,
Beauty o'ersnowed and bareness everywhere.   8
Then, were not summer's distillation left
A liquid prisoner pent in walls of glass,
Beauty's effect with beauty were bereft,
Nor it nor no remembrance what it was.   12
    But flowers distilled, though they with winter meet,
    Leese but their show; their substance still lives sweet.

6

Then let not winter's ragged hand deface
In thee thy summer ere thou be distilled.
Make sweet some vial; treasure thou some place
With beauty's treasure ere it be self-killed.   4
That use is not forbidden usury
Which happies those that pay the willing loan –
That's for thyself to breed another thee,
Or ten times happier be it ten for one.   8
Ten times thyself were happier than thou art,
If ten of thine ten times refigured thee;
Then what could death do if thou shouldst depart,
Leaving thee living in posterity?   12
    Be not self-willed, for thou art much too fair
    To be death's conquest and make worms thine heir.

7

Lo, in the orient when the gracious light
Lifts up his burning head, each under eye
Doth homage to his new-appearing sight,
Serving with looks his sacred majesty;   4
And having climbed the steep-up heavenly hill,
Resembling strong youth in his middle age,
Yet mortal looks adore his beauty still,
Attending on his golden pilgrimage;   8
But when from highmost pitch, with weary car,
Like feeble age he reeleth from the day,
The eyes, 'fore duteous, now converted are
From his low tract and look another way: 12
   So thou, thyself outgoing in thy noon,
   Unlooked on diest unless thou get a son.

8

Music to hear, why hear'st thou music sadly?
Sweets with sweets war not, joy delights in joy;
Why lov'st thou that which thou receiv'st not gladly,
Or else receiv'st with pleasure thine annoy?   4
If the true concord of well-tunèd sounds,
By unions married, do offend thine ear,
They do but sweetly chide thee, who confounds
In singleness the parts that thou shouldst bear.   8
Mark how one string, sweet husband to another,
Strikes each in each by mutual ordering;
Resembling sire, and child, and happy mother,
Who, all in one, one pleasing note do sing;   12
   Whose speechless song, being many, seeming one,
   Sings this to thee: 'Thou single wilt prove none.'

9

Is it for fear to wet a widow's eye
That thou consum'st thyself in single life?
Ah, if thou issueless shalt hap to die,
The world will wail thee like a makeless wife; 4
The world will be thy widow and still weep
That thou no form of thee hast left behind,
When every private widow well may keep
By children's eyes her husband's shape in mind. 8
Look what an unthrift in the world doth spend,
Shifts but his place, for still the world enjoys it;
But beauty's waste hath in the world an end,
And kept unused, the user so destroys it. 12
   No love toward others in that bosom sits
   That on himself such murd'rous shame commits.

10

For shame, deny that thou bear'st love to any,
Who for thyself art so unprovident!
Grant if thou wilt, thou art beloved of many,
But that thou none lov'st is most evident; 4
For thou art so possessed with murd'rous hate,
That 'gainst thyself thou stick'st not to conspire,
Seeking that beauteous roof to ruinate,
Which to repair should be thy chief desire. 8
O, change thy thought, that I may change my mind!
Shall hate be fairer lodged than gentle love?
Be as thy presence is, gracious and kind,
Or to thyself at least kind-hearted prove. 12
   Make thee another self for love of me,
   That beauty still may live in thine or thee.

11

As fast as thou shalt wane, so fast thou grow'st
In one of thine from that which thou departest;
And that fresh blood which youngly thou bestow'st
Thou mayst call thine, when thou from youth convertest.   4
Herein lives wisdom, beauty, and increase;
Without this, folly, age, and cold decay.
If all were minded so, the times should cease,
And threescore year would make the world away.   8
Let those whom Nature hath not made for store –
Harsh, featureless, and rude – barrenly perish.
Look whom she best endowed she gave the more;
Which bounteous gift thou shouldst in bounty cherish.   12
   She carved thee for her seal, and meant thereby
   Thou shouldst print more, not let that copy die.

12

When I do count the clock that tells the time,
And see the brave day sunk in hideous night;
When I behold the violet past prime,
And sable curls all silvered o'er with white;   4
When lofty trees I see barren of leaves,
Which erst from heat did canopy the herd,
And summer's green, all girded up in sheaves,
Borne on the bier with white and bristly beard;   8
Then of thy beauty do I question make,
That thou among the wastes of time must go,
Since sweets and beauties do themselves forsake,
And die as fast as they see others grow;   12
   And nothing 'gainst Time's scythe can make defence
   Save breed to brave him when he takes thee hence.

O that you were yourself; but, love, you are
No longer yours than you yourself here live.
Against this coming end you should prepare,
And your sweet semblance to some other give. 4
So should that beauty which you hold in lease
Find no determination; then you were
Yourself again after yourself's decease,
When your sweet issue your sweet form should bear. 8
Who lets so fair a house fall to decay,
Which husbandry in honour might uphold
Against the stormy gusts of winter's day
And barren rage of death's eternal cold? 12
   O, none but unthrifts! Dear my love, you know
   You had a father; let your son say so.

Not from the stars do I my judgement pluck,
And yet methinks I have astronomy;
But not to tell of good or evil luck,
Of plagues, of dearths, or seasons' quality; 4
Nor can I fortune to brief minutes tell,
Pointing to each his thunder, rain, and wind,
Or say with princes if it shall go well
By oft predict that I in heaven find. 8
But from thine eyes my knowledge I derive,
And, constant stars, in them I read such art
As truth and beauty shall together thrive
If from thyself to store thou wouldst convert; 12
   Or else of thee this I prognosticate,
   Thy end is truth's and beauty's doom and date.

When I consider everything that grows
Holds in perfection but a little moment,
That this huge stage presenteth naught but shows
Whereon the stars in secret influence comment;   4
When I perceive that men as plants increase,
Cheerèd and checked even by the selfsame sky,
Vaunt in their youthful sap, at height decrease,
And wear their brave state out of memory;   8
Then the conceit of this inconstant stay
Sets you most rich in youth before my sight,
Where wasteful Time debateth with Decay,
To change your day of youth to sullied night;   12
   And all in war with Time for love of you,
   As he takes from you I engraft you new.

16

But wherefore do not you a mightier way
Make war upon this bloody tyrant Time,
And fortify yourself in your decay
With means more blessèd than my barren rhyme?   4
Now stand you on the top of happy hours,
And many maiden gardens, yet unset,
With virtuous wish would bear your living flowers,
Much liker than your painted counterfeit.   8
So should the lines of life that life repair
Which this time's pencil or my pupil pen
Neither in inward worth nor outward fair
Can make you live yourself in eyes of men.   12
   To give away yourself keeps yourself still,
   And you must live drawn by your own sweet skill.

Who will believe my verse in time to come
If it were filled with your most high deserts?
Though yet, heaven knows, it is but as a tomb
Which hides your life and shows not half your parts.   4
If I could write the beauty of your eyes,
And in fresh numbers number all your graces,
The age to come would say 'This poet lies;
Such heavenly touches ne'er touched earthly faces.'   8
So should my papers, yellowed with their age,
Be scorned, like old men of less truth than tongue,
And your true rights be termed a poet's rage
And stretchèd metre of an antique song.   12
   But were some child of yours alive that time,
   You should live twice, in it and in my rhyme.

18

Shall I compare thee to a summer's day?
Thou art more lovely and more temperate.
Rough winds do shake the darling buds of May,
And summer's lease hath all too short a date.   4
Sometime too hot the eye of heaven shines,
And often is his gold complexion dimmed;
And every fair from fair sometime declines,
By chance or nature's changing course untrimmed.   8
But thy eternal summer shall not fade,
Nor lose possession of that fair thou ow'st,
Nor shall Death brag thou wand'rest in his shade,
When in eternal lines to time thou grow'st.   12
   So long as men can breathe or eyes can see,
   So long lives this, and this gives life to thee.

Devouring Time, blunt thou the lion's paws,
And make the earth devour her own sweet brood;
Pluck the keen teeth from the fierce tiger's jaws,
And burn the long-lived phoenix in her blood; 4
Make glad and sorry seasons as thou fleet'st,
And do whate'er thou wilt, swift-footed Time,
To the wide world and all her fading sweets.
But I forbid thee one most heinous crime: 8
O, carve not with thy hours my love's fair brow,
Nor draw no lines there with thine antique pen;
Him in thy course untainted do allow
For beauty's pattern to succeeding men. 12
 Yet do thy worst, old Time; despite thy wrong,
 My love shall in my verse ever live young.

A woman's face, with Nature's own hand painted,
Hast thou, the master-mistress of my passion;
A woman's gentle heart, but not acquainted
With shifting change, as is false women's fashion; 4
An eye more bright than theirs, less false in rolling,
Gilding the object whereupon it gazeth;
A man in hue all hues in his controlling,
Which steals men's eyes and women's souls amazeth. 8
And for a woman wert thou first created,
Till Nature as she wrought thee fell a-doting,
And by addition me of thee defeated,
By adding one thing to my purpose nothing. 12
 But since she pricked thee out for women's pleasure,
 Mine be thy love, and thy love's use their treasure.

So is it not with me as with that Muse,
Stirred by a painted beauty to his verse,
Who heaven itself for ornament doth use,
And every fair with his fair doth rehearse, 4
Making a couplement of proud compare
With sun and moon, with earth and sea's rich gems,
With April's first-born flowers, and all things rare
That heaven's air in this huge rondure hems. 8
O, let me, true in love, but truly write,
And then, believe me, my love is as fair
As any mother's child, though not so bright
As those gold candles fixed in heaven's air. 12
   Let them say more that like of hearsay well;
   I will not praise that purpose not to sell.

My glass shall not persuade me I am old
So long as youth and thou are of one date;
But when in thee Time's furrows I behold,
Then look I death my days should expiate. 4
For all that beauty that doth cover thee
Is but the seemly raiment of my heart,
Which in thy breast doth live, as thine in me.
How can I then be elder than thou art? 8
O, therefore, love, be of thyself so wary
As I, not for myself, but for thee will,
Bearing thy heart, which I will keep so chary
As tender nurse her babe from faring ill. 12
   Presume not on thy heart when mine is slain;
   Thou gav'st me thine, not to give back again.

As an unperfect actor on the stage,
Who with his fear is put besides his part,
Or some fierce thing replete with too much rage,
Whose strength's abundance weakens his own heart;   4
So I, for fear of trust, forget to say
The perfect ceremony of love's rite,
And in mine own love's strength seem to decay,
O'ercharged with burden of mine own love's might.   8
O, let my books be then the eloquence
And dumb presagers of my speaking breast,
Who plead for love and look for recompense
More than that tongue that more hath more expressed.   12
    O, learn to read what silent love hath writ;
    To hear with eyes belongs to love's fine wit.

Mine eye hath played the painter and hath stelled
Thy beauty's form in table of my heart;
My body is the frame wherein 'tis held,
And perspective it is best painter's art,   4
For through the painter must you see his skill
To find where your true image pictured lies,
Which in my bosom's shop is hanging still,
That hath his windows glazèd with thine eyes.   8
Now see what good turns eyes for eyes have done:
Mine eyes have drawn thy shape, and thine for me
Are windows to my breast, wherethrough the sun
Delights to peep, to gaze therein on thee.   12
    Yet eyes this cunning want to grace their art;
    They draw but what they see, know not the heart.

Let those who are in favour with their stars
Of public honour and proud titles boast,
Whilst I, whom fortune of such triumph bars,
Unlooked for joy in that I honour most.   4
Great princes' favourites their fair leaves spread
But as the marigold at the sun's eye,
And in themselves their pride lies burièd,
For at a frown they in their glory die.   8
The painful warrior famousèd for fight,
After a thousand victories once foiled,
Is from the book of honour razèd quite,
And all the rest forgot for which he toiled.   12
 Then happy I that love and am beloved
 Where I may not remove nor be removed.

Lord of my love, to whom in vassalage
Thy merit hath my duty strongly knit,
To thee I send this written ambassage,
To witness duty, not to show my wit –   4
Duty so great, which wit so poor as mine
May make seem bare, in wanting words to show it,
But that I hope some good conceit of thine
In thy soul's thought, all naked, will bestow it;   8
Till whatsoever star that guides my moving
Points on me graciously with fair aspect,
And puts apparel on my tattered loving
To show me worthy of thy sweet respect.   12
 Then may I dare to boast how I do love thee,
 Till then, not show my head where thou mayst prove me.

Weary with toil, I haste me to my bed,
The dear repose for limbs with travel tired;
But then begins a journey in my head
To work my mind when body's work's expired;4
For then my thoughts, from far where I abide,
Intend a zealous pilgrimage to thee,
And keep my drooping eyelids open wide,
Looking on darkness which the blind do see;8
Save that my soul's imaginary sight
Presents thy shadow to my sightless view,
Which like a jewel hung in ghastly night
Makes black night beauteous and her old face new.12
Lo, thus by day my limbs, by night my mind,
For thee, and for myself, no quiet find.

How can I then return in happy plight
That am debarred the benefit of rest,
When day's oppression is not eased by night,
But day by night and night by day oppressed,4
And each, though enemies to either's reign,
Do in consent shake hands to torture me,
The one by toil, the other to complain
How far I toil, still farther off from thee?8
I tell the day, to please him, thou art bright
And dost him grace when clouds do blot the heaven;
So flatter I the swart-complexioned night,
When sparkling stars twire not, thou gild'st the even.12
But day doth daily draw my sorrows longer,
And night doth nightly make grief's length seem stronger.

When, in disgrace with Fortune and men's eyes,
I all alone beweep my outcast state,
And trouble deaf heaven with my bootless cries,
And look upon myself and curse my fate,   4
Wishing me like to one more rich in hope,
Featured like him, like him with friends possessed,
Desiring this man's art, and that man's scope,
With what I most enjoy contented least;   8
Yet, in these thoughts myself almost despising,
Haply I think on thee, and then my state,
Like to the lark at break of day arising
From sullen earth, sings hymns at heaven's gate;   12
    For thy sweet love remembered such wealth brings
    That then I scorn to change my state with kings.

When to the sessions of sweet silent thought
I summon up remembrance of things past,
I sigh the lack of many a thing I sought,
And with old woes new wail my dear time's waste;   4
Then can I drown an eye, unused to flow,
For precious friends hid in death's dateless night,
And weep afresh love's long since cancelled woe,
And moan th'expense of many a vanished sight;   8
Then can I grieve at grievances foregone,
And heavily from woe to woe tell o'er
The sad account of fore-bemoanèd moan,
Which I new pay as if not paid before.   12
    But if the while I think on thee, dear friend,
    All losses are restored and sorrows end.

Thy bosom is endearèd with all hearts
Which I by lacking have supposèd dead;
And there reigns love and all love's loving parts,
And all those friends which I thought burièd.   4
How many a holy and obsequious tear
Hath dear religious love stol'n from mine eye,
As interest of the dead, which now appear
But things removed that hidden in thee lie.   8
Thou art the grave where buried love doth live,
Hung with the trophies of my lovers gone,
Who all their parts of me to thee did give;
That due of many now is thine alone.   12
   Their images I loved I view in thee,
   And thou, all they, hast all the all of me.

32

If thou survive my well-contented day,
When that churl Death my bones with dust shall cover,
And shalt by fortune once more resurvey
These poor rude lines of thy deceasèd lover,   4
Compare them with the bettering of the time,
And though they be outstripped by every pen,
Reserve them for my love, not for their rhyme,
Exceeded by the height of happier men.   8
O, then vouchsafe me but this loving thought:
'Had my friend's Muse grown with this growing age,
A dearer birth than this his love had brought
To march in ranks of better equipage;   12
   But since he died, and poets better prove,
   Theirs for their style I'll read, his for his love.'

Full many a glorious morning have I seen
Flatter the mountain tops with sovereign eye,
Kissing with golden face the meadows green,
Gilding pale streams with heavenly alchemy, 4
Anon permit the basest clouds to ride
With ugly rack on his celestial face,
And from the forlorn world his visage hide,
Stealing unseen to west with this disgrace. 8
Even so my sun one early morn did shine
With all triumphant splendour on my brow;
But out, alack, he was but one hour mine,
The region cloud hath masked him from me now. 12
    Yet him for this my love no whit disdaineth;
    Suns of the world may stain when heaven's sun staineth.

Why didst thou promise such a beauteous day
And make me travel forth without my cloak,
To let base clouds o'ertake me in my way,
Hiding thy brav'ry in their rotten smoke? 4
'Tis not enough that through the cloud thou break
To dry the rain on my storm-beaten face,
For no man well of such a salve can speak
That heals the wound and cures not the disgrace. 8
Nor can thy shame give physic to my grief;
Though thou repent, yet I have still the loss.
Th'offender's sorrow lends but weak relief
To him that bears the strong offence's cross. 12
    Ah, but those tears are pearl which thy love sheeds,
    And they are rich and ransom all ill deeds.

No more be grieved at that which thou hast done:
Roses have thorns, and silver fountains mud,
Clouds and eclipses stain both moon and sun,
And loathsome canker lives in sweetest bud;   4
All men make faults, and even I in this,
Authorizing thy trespass with compare,
Myself corrupting, salving thy amiss,
Excusing thy sins more than thy sins are;   8
For to thy sensual fault I bring in sense –
Thy adverse party is thy advocate –
And 'gainst myself a lawful plea commence.
Such civil war is in my love and hate   12
   That I an accessory needs must be
   To that sweet thief which sourly robs from me.

Let me confess that we two must be twain,
Although our undivided loves are one.
So shall those blots that do with me remain
Without thy help by me be borne alone.   4
In our two loves there is but one respect,
Though in our lives a separable spite,
Which, though it alter not love's sole effect,
Yet doth it steal sweet hours from love's delight.   8
I may not evermore acknowledge thee,
Lest my bewailèd guilt should do thee shame;
Nor thou with public kindness honour me,
Unless thou take that honour from thy name.   12
   But do not so; I love thee in such sort
   As, thou being mine, mine is thy good report.

37

As a decrepit father takes delight
To see his active child do deeds of youth,
So I, made lame by Fortune's dearest spite,
Take all my comfort of thy worth and truth   4
For whether beauty, birth, or wealth, or wit,
Or any of these all, or all, or more,
Entitled in thy parts do crownèd sit,
I make my love engrafted to this store.   8
So then I am not lame, poor, nor despised
Whilst that this shadow doth such substance give
That I in thy abundance am sufficed
And by a part of all thy glory live.   12
    Look what is best, that best I wish in thee.
    This wish I have, then ten times happy me!

38

How can my Muse want subject to invent,
While thou dost breathe, that pour'st into my verse
Thine own sweet argument, too excellent
For every vulgar paper to rehearse?   4
O, give thyself the thanks, if aught in me
Worthy perusal stand against thy sight;
For who's so dumb that cannot write to thee
When thou thyself dost give invention light?   8
Be thou the tenth Muse, ten times more in worth
Than those old nine which rhymers invocate;
And he that calls on thee, let him bring forth
Eternal numbers to outlive long date.   12
    If my slight Muse do please these curious days,
    The pain be mine, but thine shall be the praise.

O, how thy worth with manners may I sing
When thou art all the better part of me?
What can mine own praise to mine own self bring,
And what is't but mine own when I praise thee?   4
Even for this let us divided live,
And our dear love lose name of single one,
That by this separation I may give
That due to thee which thou deserv'st alone.   8
O absence, what a torment wouldst thou prove,
Were it not thy sour leisure gave sweet leave
To entertain the time with thoughts of love,
Which time and thoughts so sweetly dost deceive,   12
   And that thou teachest how to make one twain
   By praising him here who doth hence remain.

Take all my loves, my love, yea, take them all;
What hast thou then more than thou hadst before?
No love, my love, that thou mayst true love call;
All mine was thine, before thou hadst this more.   4
Then if for my love thou my love receivest,
I cannot blame thee for my love thou usest;
But yet be blamed, if thou thyself deceivest
By wilful taste of what thyself refusest.   8
I do forgive thy robb'ry, gentle thief,
Although thou steal thee all my poverty;
And yet love knows it is a greater grief
To bear love's wrong than hate's known injury.   12
   Lascivious grace, in whom all ill well shows,
   Kill me with spites; yet we must not be foes.

Those pretty wrongs that liberty commits,
When I am sometime absent from thy heart,
Thy beauty and thy years full well befits,
For still temptation follows where thou art. 4
Gentle thou art, and therefore to be won;
Beauteous thou art, therefore to be assailed;
And when a woman woos, what woman's son
Will sourly leave her till she have prevailed? 8
Ay me, but yet thou might'st my seat forbear,
And chide thy beauty and thy straying youth,
Who lead thee in their riot even there
Where thou art forced to break a twofold truth: 12
    Hers, by thy beauty tempting her to thee,
    Thine, by thy beauty being false to me.

That thou hast her, it is not all my grief,
And yet it may be said I loved her dearly;
That she hath thee is of my wailing chief,
A loss in love that touches me more nearly. 4
Loving offenders, thus I will excuse ye:
Thou dost love her because thou know'st I love her,
And for my sake even so doth she abuse me,
Suff'ring my friend for my sake to approve her. 8
If I lose thee, my loss is my love's gain,
And, losing her, my friend hath found that loss;
Both find each other, and I lose both twain,
And both for my sake lay on me this cross. 12
    But here's the joy: my friend and I are one.
    Sweet flatt'ry! Then she loves but me alone!

43

When most I wink, then do mine eyes best see,
For all the day they view things unrespected;
But when I sleep, in dreams they look on thee,
And, darkly bright, are bright in dark directed.   4
Then thou, whose shadow shadows doth make bright,
How would thy shadow's form form happy show
To the clear day with thy much clearer light,
When to unseeing eyes thy shade shines so!   8
How would, I say, mine eyes be blessèd made,
By looking on thee in the living day,
When in dead night thy fair imperfect shade
Through heavy sleep on sightless eyes doth stay!   12
    All days are nights to see till I see thee,
    All nights bright days when dreams do show thee me.

44

If the dull substance of my flesh were thought,
Injurious distance should not stop my way;
For then despite of space I would be brought,
From limits far remote, where thou dost stay.   4
No matter then although my foot did stand
Upon the farthest earth removed from thee;
For nimble thought can jump both sea and land
As soon as think the place where he would be.   8
But ah, thought kills me that I am not thought,
To leap large lengths of miles when thou art gone,
But that, so much of earth and water wrought,
I must attend time's leisure with my moan;   12
    Receiving naught by elements so slow
    But heavy tears, badges of either's woe.

The other two, slight air and purging fire,
Are both with thee, wherever I abide;
The first my thought, the other my desire,
These present-absent with swift motion slide. 4
For when these quicker elements are gone
In tender embassy of love to thee,
My life, being made of four, with two alone
Sinks down to death, oppressed with melancholy; 8
Until life's composition be recured
By those swift messengers returned from thee,
Who even but now come back again, assured
Of thy fair health, recounting it to me. 12
   This told, I joy, but then no longer glad,
   I send them back again, and straight grow sad.

Mine eye and heart are at a mortal war
How to divide the conquest of thy sight;
Mine eye my heart thy picture's sight would bar,
My heart mine eye the freedom of that right. 4
My heart doth plead that thou in him dost lie,
A closet never pierced with crystal eyes;
But the defendant doth that plea deny,
And says in him thy fair appearance lies. 8
To 'cide this title is impanellèd
A quest of thoughts, all tenants to the heart;
And by their verdict is determinèd
The clear eye's moiety and the dear heart's part: 12
   As thus – mine eye's due is thy outward part,
   And my heart's right thy inward love of heart.

Betwixt mine eye and heart a league is took,
And each doth good turns now unto the other.
When that mine eye is famished for a look,
Or heart in love with sighs himself doth smother,   4
With my love's picture then my eye doth feast,
And to the painted banquet bids my heart.
Another time mine eye is my heart's guest
And in his thoughts of love doth share a part.   8
So, either by thy picture or my love,
Thyself, away, are present still with me;
For thou not farther than my thoughts canst move,
And I am still with them, and they with thee;   12
  Or, if they sleep, thy picture in my sight
  Awakes my heart to heart's and eye's delight.

How careful was I when I took my way
Each trifle under truest bars to thrust,
That to my use it might unusèd stay
From hands of falsehood, in sure wards of trust!   4
But thou, to whom my jewels trifles are,
Most worthy comfort, now my greatest grief,
Thou best of dearest and mine only care,
Art left the prey of every vulgar thief.   8
Thee have I not locked up in any chest,
Save where thou art not, though I feel thou art,
Within the gentle closure of my breast,
From whence at pleasure thou mayst come and part;   12
  And even thence thou wilt be stol'n, I fear,
  For truth proves thievish for a prize so dear.

Against that time – if ever that time come –
When I shall see thee frown on my defects,
Whenas thy love hath cast his utmost sum,
Called to that audit by advised respects; 4
Against that time when thou shalt strangely pass,
And scarcely greet me with that sun, thine eye,
When love, converted from the thing it was,
Shall reasons find of settled gravity; 8
Against that time do I ensconce me here
Within the knowledge of mine own desert,
And this my hand against myself uprear
To guard the lawful reasons on thy part. 12
    To leave poor me thou hast the strength of laws,
    Since why to love I can allege no cause.

How heavy do I journey on the way
When what I seek, my weary travel's end,
Doth teach that ease and that repose to say
'Thus far the miles are measured from thy friend.' 4
The beast that bears me, tired with my woe,
Plods dully on, to bear that weight in me,
As if by some instinct the wretch did know
His rider loved not speed being made from thee. 8
The bloody spur cannot provoke him on
That sometimes anger thrusts into his hide,
Which heavily he answers with a groan
More sharp to me than spurring to his side; 12
    For that same groan doth put this in my mind:
    My grief lies onward and my joy behind.

Thus can my love excuse the slow offence
Of my dull bearer, when from thee I speed:
From where thou art why should I haste me thence?
Till I return, of posting is no need. 4
O, what excuse will my poor beast then find
When swift extremity can seem but slow?
Then should I spur, though mounted on the wind;
In wingèd speed no motion shall I know. 8
Then can no horse with my desire keep pace;
Therefore desire, of perfect'st love being made,
Shall neigh, no dull flesh in his fiery race;
But love, for love, thus shall excuse my jade: 12
    Since from thee going he went wilful slow,
    Towards thee I'll run and give him leave to go.

So am I as the rich whose blessèd key
Can bring him to his sweet up-lockèd treasure,
The which he will not every hour survey,
For blunting the fine point of seldom pleasure. 4
Therefore are feasts so solemn and so rare,
Since, seldom coming, in the long year set,
Like stones of worth they thinly placèd are,
Or captain jewels in the carcanet. 8
So is the time that keeps you as my chest,
Or as the wardrobe which the robe doth hide,
To make some special instant special blest,
By new unfolding his imprisoned pride. 12
    Blessèd are you whose worthiness gives scope,
    Being had, to triumph, being lacked, to hope.

What is your substance, whereof are you made,
That millions of strange shadows on you tend?
Since everyone hath, every one, one shade,
And you, but one, can every shadow lend.   4
Describe Adonis, and the counterfeit
Is poorly imitated after you;
On Helen's cheek all art of beauty set,
And you in Grecian tires are painted new.   8
Speak of the spring and foison of the year;
The one doth shadow of your beauty show,
The other as your bounty doth appear,
And you in every blessèd shape we know.   12
   In all external grace you have some part,
    But you like none, none you, for constant heart.

O, how much more doth beauty beauteous seem
By that sweet ornament which truth doth give!
The rose looks fair, but fairer we it deem
For that sweet odour which doth in it live.   4
The canker blooms have full as deep a dye
As the perfumèd tincture of the roses,
Hang on such thorns and play as wantonly
When summer's breath their maskèd buds discloses;   8
But for their virtue only is their show
They live unwooed and unrespected fade –
Die to themselves. Sweet roses do not so;
Of their sweet deaths are sweetest odours made.   12
   And so of you, beauteous and lovely youth,
    When that shall vade, by verse distils your truth.

Not marble nor the gilded monuments
Of princes shall outlive this powerful rhyme,
But you shall shine more bright in these contents
Than unswept stone, besmeared with sluttish time.　　4
When wasteful war shall statues overturn,
And broils root out the work of masonry,
Nor Mars his sword nor war's quick fire shall burn
The living record of your memory.　　8
'Gainst death and all oblivious enmity
Shall you pace forth; your praise shall still find room
Even in the eyes of all posterity
That wear this world out to the ending doom.　　12
　　So, till the judgement that yourself arise,
　　You live in this, and dwell in lovers' eyes.

Sweet love, renew thy force; be it not said
Thy edge should blunter be than appetite,
Which but today by feeding is allayed,
Tomorrow sharpened in his former might.　　4
So, love, be thou; although today thou fill
Thy hungry eyes even till they wink with fullness,
Tomorrow see again, and do not kill
The spirit of love with a perpetual dullness.　　8
Let this sad interim like the ocean be
Which parts the shore where two contracted new
Come daily to the banks, that, when they see
Return of love, more blest may be the view;　　12
　　As call it winter, which being full of care
　　Makes summer's welcome thrice more wished, more rare.

Being your slave, what should I do but tend
Upon the hours and times of your desire?
I have no precious time at all to spend,
Nor services to do, till you require. 4
Nor dare I chide the world-without-end hour
Whilst I, my sovereign, watch the clock for you,
Nor think the bitterness of absence sour
When you have bid your servant once adieu. 8
Nor dare I question with my jealous thought
Where you may be, or your affairs suppose,
But like a sad slave stay and think of naught
Save where you are how happy you make those. 12
    So true a fool is love that, in your will
    Though you do anything, he thinks no ill.

That god forbid that made me first your slave
I should in thought control your times of pleasure,
Or at your hand th'account of hours to crave,
Being your vassal bound to stay your leisure. 4
O, let me suffer, being at your beck,
Th'imprisoned absence of your liberty,
And, patience-tame to sufferance, bide each check
Without accusing you of injury. 8
Be where you list, your charter is so strong
That you yourself may privilege your time
To what you will; to you it doth belong
Yourself to pardon of self-doing crime. 12
    I am to wait, though waiting so be hell,
    Not blame your pleasure, be it ill or well.

59

If there be nothing new, but that which is
Hath been before, how are our brains beguiled,
Which, labouring for invention, bear amiss
The second burden of a former child! 4
O that record could with a backward look
Even of five hundred courses of the sun
Show me your image in some antique book,
Since mind at first in character was done, 8
That I might see what the old world could say
To this composèd wonder of your frame;
Whether we are mended, or whe'er better they,
Or whether revolution be the same. 12
   O, sure I am the wits of former days
   To subjects worse have given admiring praise.

60

Like as the waves make towards the pebbled shore,
So do our minutes hasten to their end;
Each changing place with that which goes before,
In sequent toil all forwards do contend. 4
Nativity, once in the main of light,
Crawls to maturity, wherewith being crowned,
Crookèd eclipses 'gainst his glory fight,
And Time that gave doth now his gift confound. 8
Time doth transfix the flourish set on youth,
And delves the parallels in beauty's brow,
Feeds on the rarities of nature's truth,
And nothing stands but for his scythe to mow. 12
   And yet to times in hope my verse shall stand,
   Praising thy worth, despite his cruel hand.

Is it thy will thy image should keep open
My heavy eyelids to the weary night?
Dost thou desire my slumbers should be broken
While shadows like to thee do mock my sight?   4
Is it thy spirit that thou send'st from thee
So far from home into my deeds to pry,
To find out shames and idle hours in me,
The scope and tenor of thy jealousy?   8
O no, thy love, though much, is not so great;
It is my love that keeps mine eye awake,
Mine own true love that doth my rest defeat,
To play the watchman ever for thy sake.   12
  For thee watch I, whilst thou dost wake elsewhere,
  From me far off, with others all too near.

Sin of self-love possesseth all mine eye,
And all my soul, and all my every part;
And for this sin there is no remedy,
It is so grounded inward in my heart.   4
Methinks no face so gracious is as mine,
No shape so true, no truth of such account,
And for myself mine own worth do define,
As I all other in all worths surmount.   8
But when my glass shows me myself indeed,
Beated and chopped with tanned antiquity,
Mine own self-love quite contrary I read –
Self so self-loving were iniquity: 12
  'Tis thee, myself, that for myself I praise,
  Painting my age with beauty of thy days.

Against my love shall be as I am now,
With Time's injurious hand crushed and o'erworn;
When hours have drained his blood and filled his brow
With lines and wrinkles, when his youthful morn   4
Hath travelled on to age's steepy night,
And all those beauties whereof now he's king
Are vanishing or vanished out of sight,
Stealing away the treasure of his spring;   8
For such a time do I now fortify
Against confounding Age's cruel knife,
That he shall never cut from memory
My sweet love's beauty, though my lover's life.   12
    His beauty shall in these black lines be seen,
    And they shall live, and he in them still green.

When I have seen by Time's fell hand defaced
The rich proud cost of outworn buried age,
When sometime lofty towers I see down-razed,
And brass eternal slave to mortal rage;   4
When I have seen the hungry ocean gain
Advantage on the kingdom of the shore,
And the firm soil win of the wat'ry main,
Increasing store with loss and loss with store;   8
When I have seen such interchange of state,
Or state itself confounded to decay,
Ruin hath taught me thus to ruminate –
That Time will come and take my love away.   12
    This thought is as a death, which cannot choose
    But weep to have that which it fears to lose.

65

Since brass, nor stone, nor earth, nor boundless sea,
But sad mortality o'ersways their power,
How with this rage shall beauty hold a plea,
Whose action is no stronger than a flower? 4
O, how shall summer's honey breath hold out
Against the wrackful siege of battering days,
When rocks impregnable are not so stout,
Nor gates of steel so strong, but Time decays? 8
O, fearful meditation! Where, alack,
Shall Time's best jewel from Time's chest lie hid?
Or what strong hand can hold his swift foot back?
Or who his spoil of beauty can forbid? 12
  O, none, unless this miracle have might,
  That in black ink my love may still shine bright.

66

Tired with all these, for restful death I cry:
As to behold desert a beggar born,
And needy nothing trimmed in jollity,
And purest faith unhappily forsworn,
And gilded honour shamefully misplaced, 4
And maiden virtue rudely strumpeted,
And right perfection wrongfully disgraced,
And strength by limping sway disablèd, 8
And art made tongue-tied by authority,
And folly, doctor-like, controlling skill,
And simple truth miscalled simplicity,
And captive good attending captain ill. 12
  Tired with all these, from these would I be gone,
  Save that, to die, I leave my love alone.

Ah, wherefore with infection should he live
And with his presence grace impiety,
That sin by him advantage should achieve
And lace itself with his society? 4
Why should false painting imitate his cheek
And steal dead seeming of his living hue?
Why should poor beauty indirectly seek
Roses of shadow, since his rose is true? 8
Why should he live, now Nature bankrupt is,
Beggared of blood to blush through lively veins,
For she hath no exchequer now but his,
And, 'prived of many, lives upon his gains? 12
  O, him she stores, to show what wealth she had
  In days long since, before these last so bad.

Thus is his cheek the map of days outworn,
When beauty lived and died as flowers do now,
Before these bastard signs of fair were borne,
Or durst inhabit on a living brow; 4
Before the golden tresses of the dead,
The right of sepulchres, were shorn away
To live a second life on second head –
Ere beauty's dead fleece made another gay. 8
In him those holy antique hours are seen
Without all ornament, itself and true,
Making no summer of another's green,
Robbing no old to dress his beauty new; 12
  And him as for a map doth Nature store,
  To show false Art what beauty was of yore.

Those parts of thee that the world's eye doth view
Want nothing that the thought of hearts can mend;
All tongues, the voice of souls, give thee that due,
Uttering bare truth, even so as foes commend.   4
Thy outward thus with outward praise is crowned,
But those same tongues that give thee so thine own
In other accents do this praise confound
By seeing farther than the eye hath shown.   8
They look into the beauty of thy mind,
And that in guess they measure by thy deeds;
Then, churls, their thoughts (although their eyes were kind)
To thy fair flower add the rank smell of weeds;   12
  But why thy odour matcheth not thy show,
  The soil is this – that thou dost common grow.

That thou are blamed shall not be thy defect,
For slander's mark was ever yet the fair;
The ornament of beauty is suspect,
A crow that flies in heaven's sweetest air.   4
So thou be good, slander doth but approve
Thy worth the greater, being wooed of time;
For canker vice the sweetest buds doth love,
And thou present'st a pure unstainèd prime.   8
Thou hast passed by the ambush of young days,
Either not assailed, or victor being charged;
Yet this thy praise cannot be so thy praise
To tie up envy, evermore enlarged.   12
  If some suspect of ill masked not thy show,
  Then thou alone kingdoms of hearts shouldst owe.

No longer mourn for me when I am dead
Than you shall hear the surly sullen bell
Give warning to the world that I am fled
From this vile world with vilest worms to dwell. 4
Nay, if you read this line, remember not
The hand that writ it, for I love you so
That I in your sweet thoughts would be forgot
If thinking on me then should make you woe. 8
O, if, I say, you look upon this verse,
When I, perhaps, compounded am with clay,
Do not so much as my poor name rehearse,
But let your love even with my life decay; 12
   Lest the wise world should look into your moan,
   And mock you with me after I am gone.

O, lest the world should task you to recite
What merit lived in me that you should love
After my death, dear love, forget me quite;
For you in me can nothing worthy prove, 4
Unless you would devise some virtuous lie
To do more for me than mine own desert,
And hang more praise upon deceasèd I
Than niggard truth would willingly impart. 8
O, lest your true love may seem false in this,
That you for love speak well of me untrue,
My name be buried where my body is
And live no more to shame nor me nor you; 12
   For I am shamed by that which I bring forth,
   And so should you, to love things nothing worth.

That time of year thou mayst in me behold
When yellow leaves, or none, or few, do hang
Upon those boughs which shake against the cold,
Bare ruined choirs where late the sweet birds sang. 4
In me thou seest the twilight of such day
As after sunset fadeth in the west,
Which by and by black night doth take away,
Death's second self, that seals up all in rest. 8
In me thou seest the glowing of such fire
That on the ashes of his youth doth lie,
As the deathbed whereon it must expire,
Consumed with that which it was nourished by. 12
   This thou perceiv'st, which makes thy love more strong,
   To love that well which thou must leave ere long.

But be contented when that fell arrest
Without all bail shall carry me away;
My life hath in this line some interest
Which for memorial still with thee shall stay. 4
When thou reviewest this, thou dost review
The very part was consecrate to thee.
The earth can have but earth, which is his due;
My spirit is thine, the better part of me. 8
So then thou hast but lost the dregs of life,
The prey of worms, my body being dead,
The coward conquest of a wretch's knife,
Too base of thee to be rememberèd. 12
   The worth of that is that which it contains,
   And that is this, and this with thee remains.

So are you to my thoughts as food to life,
Or as sweet seasoned showers are to the ground;
And for the peace of you I hold such strife
As 'twixt a miser and his wealth is found;   4
Now proud as an enjoyer, and anon
Doubting the filching age will steal his treasure;
Now counting best to be with you alone,
Then bettered that the world may see my pleasure;   8
Sometime all full with feasting on your sight,
And by and by clean starvèd for a look;
Possessing or pursuing no delight
Save what is had or must from you be took.   12
  Thus do I pine and surfeit day by day,
  Or gluttoning on all, or all away.

Why is my verse so barren of new pride,
So far from variation or quick change?
Why with the time do I not glance aside
To new-found methods and to compounds strange?   4
Why write I still all one, ever the same,
And keep invention in a noted weed,
That every word doth almost tell my name,
Showing their birth and where they did proceed?   8
O, know, sweet love, I always write of you,
And you and love are still my argument;
So all my best is dressing old words new,
Spending again what is already spent: 12
  For as the sun is daily new and old,
  So is my love still telling what is told.

Thy glass will show thee how thy beauties wear,
Thy dial how thy precious minutes waste;
The vacant leaves thy mind's imprint will bear,
And of this book this learning mayst thou taste: 4
The wrinkles which thy glass will truly show
Of mouthèd graves will give thee memory;
Thou by thy dial's shady stealth mayst know
Time's thievish progress to eternity; 8
Look what thy memory cannot contain
Commit to these waste blanks, and thou shalt find
Those children nursed, delivered from thy brain,
To take a new acquaintance of thy mind. 12
 These offices, so oft as thou wilt look,
 Shall profit thee, and much enrich thy book.

So oft have I invoked thee for my Muse
And found such fair assistance in my verse
As every alien pen hath got my use
And under thee their poesy disperse. 4
Thine eyes, that taught the dumb on high to sing
And heavy ignorance aloft to fly,
Have added feathers to the learnèd's wing,
And given grace a double majesty. 8
Yet be most proud of that which I compile,
Whose influence is thine, and born of thee:
In others' works thou dost but mend the style,
And arts with thy sweet graces gracèd be; 12
 But thou art all my art, and dost advance
 As high as learning my rude ignorance.

Whilst I alone did call upon thy aid,
My verse alone had all thy gentle grace;
But now my gracious numbers are decayed,
And my sick Muse doth give another place. 4
I grant, sweet love, thy lovely argument
Deserves the travail of a worthier pen,
Yet what of thee thy poet doth invent
He robs thee of, and pays it thee again. 8
He lends thee virtue, and he stole that word
From thy behaviour; beauty doth he give,
And found it in thy cheek; he can afford
No praise to thee but what in thee doth live. 12
   Then thank him not for that which he doth say,
   Since what he owes thee thou thyself dost pay.

O, how I faint when I of you do write,
Knowing a better spirit doth use your name,
And in the praise thereof spends all his might
To make me tongue-tied speaking of your fame. 4
But since your worth, wide as the ocean is,
The humble as the proudest sail doth bear,
My saucy bark, inferior far to his,
On your broad main doth wilfully appear. 8
Your shallowest help will hold me up afloat
Whilst he upon your soundless deep doth ride;
Or, being wrecked, I am a worthless boat,
He of tall building and of goodly pride. 12
   Then if he thrive and I be cast away,
   The worst was this: my love was my decay.

Or I shall live your epitaph to make,
Or you survive when I in earth am rotten,
From hence your memory death cannot take,
Although in me each part will be forgotten.   4
Your name from hence immortal life shall have,
Though I, once gone, to all the world must die.
The earth can yield me but a common grave
When you entombèd in men's eyes shall lie.   8
Your monument shall be my gentle verse,
Which eyes not yet created shall o'er-read,
And tongues to be your being shall rehearse
When all the breathers of this world are dead.   12
    You still shall live – such virtue hath my pen –
    Where breath most breathes, even in the mouths of men.

82

I grant thou wert not married to my Muse,
And therefore mayst without attaint o'erlook
The dedicated words which writers use
Of their fair subject, blessing every book.   4
Thou art as fair in knowledge as in hue,
Finding thy worth a limit past my praise;
And therefore art enforced to seek anew
Some fresher stamp of the time-bettering days.   8
And do so, love; yet when they have devised
What strainèd touches rhetoric can lend,
Thou, truly fair, wert truly sympathized
In true plain words by thy true-telling friend: 12
    And their gross painting might be better used
    Where cheeks need blood; in thee it is abused.

I never saw that you did painting need,
And therefore to your fair no painting set;
I found, or thought I found, you did exceed
The barren tender of a poet's debt;   4
And therefore have I slept in your report,
That you yourself, being extant, well might show
How far a modern quill doth come too short,
Speaking of worth, what worth in you doth grow.   8
This silence for my sin you did impute,
Which shall be most my glory, being dumb;
For I impair not beauty, being mute,
When others would give life and bring a tomb.   12
     There lives more life in one of your fair eyes
     Than both your poets can in praise devise.

Who is it that says most which can say more
Than this rich praise – that you alone are you,
In whose confine immurèd is the store
Which should example where your equal grew?   4
Lean penury within that pen doth dwell
That to his subject lends not some small glory,
But he that writes of you, if he can tell
That you are you, so dignifies his story;   8
Let him but copy what in you is writ,
Not making worse what nature made so clear,
And such a counterpart shall fame his wit,
Making his style admirèd everywhere.   12
     You to your beauteous blessings add a curse,
     Being fond on praise, which makes your praises worse.

My tongue-tied Muse in manners holds her still,
While comments of your praise, richly compiled,
Reserve thy character with golden quill
And precious phrase by all the Muses filed.   4
I think good thoughts whilst other write good words,
And, like unlettered clerk, still cry 'Amen'
To every hymn that able spirit affords
In polished form of well-refinèd pen.   8
Hearing you praised, I say ''Tis so, 'tis true,'
And to the most of praise add something more;
But that is in my thought, whose love to you
(Though words come hindmost) holds his rank before.   12
    Then others for the breath of words respect,
    Me for my dumb thoughts, speaking in effect.

Was it the proud full sail of his great verse,
Bound for the prize of all-too-precious you,
That did my ripe thoughts in my brain inhearse,
Making their tomb the womb wherein they grew?   4
Was it his spirit, by spirits taught to write
Above a mortal pitch, that struck me dead?
No, neither he, nor his compeers by night
Giving him aid, my verse astonishèd.   8
He, nor that affable familiar ghost
Which nightly gulls him with intelligence,
As victors, of my silence cannot boast;
I was not sick of any fear from thence.   12
    But when your countenance filled up his line,
    Then lacked I matter; that enfeebled mine.

87

Farewell, thou art too dear for my possessing,
And like enough thou know'st thy estimate.
The charter of thy worth gives thee releasing;
My bonds in thee are all determinate.
For how do I hold thee but by thy granting,
And for that riches where is my deserving?
The cause of this fair gift in me is wanting,
And so my patent back again is swerving.
Thyself thou gav'st, thy own worth then not knowing,
Or me, to whom thou gav'st it, else mistaking;
So thy great gift, upon misprision growing,
Comes home again, on better judgement making.
  Thus have I had thee as a dream doth flatter,
  In sleep a king, but waking no such matter.

88

When thou shalt be disposed to set me light
And place my merit in the eye of scorn,
Upon thy side against myself I'll fight
And prove thee virtuous, though thou art forsworn.
With mine own weakness being best acquainted,
Upon thy part I can set down a story
Of faults concealed wherein I am attainted,
That thou in losing me shall win much glory.
And I by this will be a gainer too,
For, bending all my loving thoughts on thee,
The injuries that to myself I do,
Doing thee vantage, double-vantage me.
  Such is my love, to thee I so belong,
  That for thy right myself will bear all wrong.

Say that thou didst forsake me for some fault,
And I will comment upon that offence.
Speak of my lameness, and I straight will halt,
Against thy reasons making no defence.   4
Thou canst not, love, disgrace me half so ill,
To set a form upon desirèd change,
As I'll myself disgrace, knowing thy will.
I will acquaintance strangle and look strange,   8
Be absent from thy walks, and in my tongue
Thy sweet belovèd name no more shall dwell,
Lest I, too much profane, should do it wrong
And haply of our old acquaintance tell.   12
   For thee, against myself I'll vow debate,
   For I must ne'er love him whom thou dost hate.

Then hate me when thou wilt, if ever, now,
Now, while the world is bent my deeds to cross,
Join with the spite of Fortune, make me bow,
And do not drop in for an after-loss.   4
Ah, do not, when my heart hath 'scaped this sorrow,
Come in the rearward of a conquered woe;
Give not a windy night a rainy morrow,
To linger out a purposed overthrow.   8
If thou wilt leave me, do not leave me last,
When other petty griefs have done their spite,
But in the onset come; so shall I taste
At first the very worst of Fortune's might,   12
   And other strains of woe, which now seem woe,
   Compared with loss of thee will not seem so.

Some glory in their birth, some in their skill,
Some in their wealth, some in their body's force,
Some in their garments, though new-fangled ill,
Some in their hawks and hounds, some in their horse; 4
And every humour hath his adjunct pleasure,
Wherein it finds a joy above the rest.
But these particulars are not my measure;
All these I better in one general best. 8
Thy love is better than high birth to me,
Richer than wealth, prouder than garments' cost,
Of more delight than hawks or horses be;
And, having thee, of all men's pride I boast – 12
   Wretched in this alone, that thou mayst take
   All this away, and me most wretched make.

But do thy worst to steal thyself away,
For term of life thou art assurèd mine;
And life no longer than thy love will stay,
For it depends upon that love of thine. 4
Then need I not to fear the worst of wrongs,
When in the least of them my life hath end.
I see a better state to me belongs
Than that which on thy humour doth depend. 8
Thou canst not vex me with inconstant mind,
Since that my life on thy revolt doth lie.
O, what a happy title do I find,
Happy to have thy love, happy to die! 12
   But what's so blessèd-fair that fears no blot?
   Thou mayst be false, and yet I know it not.

93

So shall I live, supposing thou art true,
Like a deceivèd husband; so love's face
May still seem love to me, though altered new,
Thy looks with me, thy heart in other place. 4
For there can live no hatred in thine eye;
Therefore in that I cannot know thy change.
In many's looks, the false heart's history
Is writ in moods and frowns and wrinkles strange, 8
But heaven in thy creation did decree
That in thy face sweet love should ever dwell;
Whate'er thy thoughts or thy heart's workings be,
Thy looks should nothing thence but sweetness tell. 12
  How like Eve's apple doth thy beauty grow,
  If thy sweet virtue answer not thy show!

94

They that have power to hurt and will do none,
That do not do the thing they most do show,
Who, moving others, are themselves as stone,
Unmovèd, cold, and to temptation slow; 4
They rightly do inherit heaven's graces
And husband nature's riches from expense;
They are the lords and owners of their faces,
Others but stewards of their excellence. 8
The summer's flower is to the summer sweet,
Though to itself it only live and die;
But if that flower with base infection meet,
The basest weed outbraves his dignity: 12
  For sweetest things turn sourest by their deeds;
  Lilies that fester smell far worse than weeds.

How sweet and lovely dost thou make the shame
Which, like a canker in the fragrant rose,
Doth spot the beauty of thy budding name!
O, in what sweets dost thou thy sins enclose!   4
That tongue that tells the story of thy days,
Making lascivious comments on thy sport,
Cannot dispraise but in a kind of praise;
Naming thy name blesses an ill report.   8
O, what a mansion have those vices got
Which for their habitation chose out thee,
Where beauty's veil doth cover every blot,
And all things turns to fair that eyes can see!   12
   Take heed, dear heart, of this large privilege;
   The hardest knife ill-used doth lose his edge.

Some say thy fault is youth, some wantonness,
Some say thy grace is youth and gentle sport;
Both grace and faults are loved of more and less;
Thou mak'st faults graces that to thee resort.   4
As on the finger of a thronèd queen
The basest jewel will be well esteemed,
So are those errors that in thee are seen
To truths translated and for true things deemed.   8
How many lambs might the stern wolf betray,
If like a lamb he could his looks translate;
How many gazers might'st thou lead away,
If thou wouldst use the strength of all thy state!   12
   But do not so; I love thee in such sort
   As, thou being mine, mine is thy good report.

How like a winter hath my absence been
From thee, the pleasure of the fleeting year!
What freezings have I felt, what dark days seen –
What old December's bareness everywhere! 4
And yet this time removed was summer's time,
The teeming autumn, big with rich increase,
Bearing the wanton burden of the prime,
Like widowed wombs after their lords' decease. 8
Yet this abundant issue seemed to me
But hope of orphans and unfathered fruit;
For summer and his pleasures wait on thee,
And, thou away, the very birds are mute; 12
  Or if they sing, 'tis with so dull a cheer
  That leaves look pale, dreading the winter's near.

From you have I been absent in the spring,
When proud-pied April, dressed in all his trim,
Hath put a spirit of youth in everything,
That heavy Saturn laughed and leaped with him. 4
Yet nor the lays of birds, nor the sweet smell
Of different flowers in odour and in hue,
Could make me any summer's story tell,
Or from their proud lap pluck them where they grew. 8
Nor did I wonder at the lily's white,
Nor praise the deep vermilion in the rose;
They were but sweet, but figures of delight,
Drawn after you, you pattern of all those. 12
  Yet seemed it winter still, and, you away,
  As with your shadow I with these did play.

The forward violet thus did I chide:
'Sweet thief, whence didst thou steal thy sweet that smells,
If not from my love's breath? The purple pride
Which on thy soft cheek for complexion dwells   4
In my love's veins thou hast too grossly dyed.'
The lily I condemnèd for thy hand,
And buds of marjoram had stol'n thy hair;
The roses fearfully on thorns did stand,   8
One blushing shame, another white despair;
A third, nor red nor white, had stol'n of both,
And to his robb'ry had annexed thy breath;
But for his theft, in pride of all his growth   12
A vengeful canker eat him up to death.
   More flowers I noted, yet I none could see
   But sweet or colour it had stol'n from thee.

Where art thou, Muse, that thou forget'st so long
To speak of that which gives thee all thy might?
Spend'st thou thy fury on some worthless song,
Darkening thy power to lend base subjects light?   4
Return, forgetful Muse, and straight redeem
In gentle numbers time so idly spent;
Sing to the ear that doth thy lays esteem,
And gives thy pen both skill and argument.   8
Rise, resty Muse, my love's sweet face survey,
If Time have any wrinkle graven there,
If any, be a satire to decay,
And make Time's spoils despisèd everywhere.   12
   Give my love fame faster than Time wastes life;
   So thou prevene'st his scythe and crookèd knife.

O truant Muse, what shall be thy amends
For thy neglect of truth in beauty dyed?
Both truth and beauty on my love depends;
So dost thou too, and therein dignified.   4
Make answer, Muse! Wilt thou not haply say
'Truth needs no colour with his colour fixed,
Beauty no pencil, beauty's truth to lay;
But best is best if never intermixed?'   8
Because he needs no praise, wilt thou be dumb?
Excuse not silence so, for't lies in thee
To make him much outlive a gilded tomb,
And to be praised of ages yet to be.   12
 Then do thy office, Muse; I teach thee how
 To make him seem, long hence, as he shows now.

My love is strengthened, though more weak in seeming;
I love not less, though less the show appear.
That love is merchandised whose rich esteeming
The owner's tongue doth publish everywhere.   4
Our love was new, and then but in the spring,
When I was wont to greet it with my lays;
As Philomel in summer's front doth sing,
And stops his pipe in growth of riper days.   8
Not that the summer is less pleasant now
Than when her mournful hymns did hush the night,
But that wild music burdens every bough,
And sweets grown common lose their dear delight.   12
 Therefore, like her, I sometime hold my tongue,
 Because I would not dull you with my song.

Alack, what poverty my Muse brings forth,
That, having such a scope to show her pride,
The argument all bare is of more worth
Than when it hath my added praise beside.   4
O, blame me not if I no more can write!
Look in your glass, and there appears a face
That overgoes my blunt invention quite,
Dulling my lines and doing me disgrace.   8
Were it not sinful then, striving to mend,
To mar the subject that before was well?
For to no other pass my verses tend
Than of your graces and your gifts to tell;   12
    And more, much more, than in my verse can sit
    Your own glass shows you when you look in it.

To me, fair friend, you never can be old,
For as you were when first your eye I eyed,
Such seems your beauty still. Three winters cold
Have from the forests shook three summers' pride,   4
Three beauteous springs to yellow autumn turned
In process of the seasons have I seen,
Three April perfumes in three hot Junes burned,
Since first I saw you fresh, which yet are green.   8
Ah, yet doth beauty, like a dial hand,
Steal from his figure, and no pace perceived;
So your sweet hue, which methinks still doth stand,
Hath motion, and mine eye may be deceived;   12
    For fear of which, hear this, thou age unbred:
    Ere you were born was beauty's summer dead.

Let not my love be called idolatry,
Nor my belovèd as an idol show,
Since all alike my songs and praises be
To one, of one, still such, and ever so.   4
Kind is my love today, tomorrow kind,
Still constant in a wondrous excellence;
Therefore my verse, to constancy confined,
One thing expressing, leaves out difference.   8
'Fair, kind, and true' is all my argument,
'Fair, kind, and true', varying to other words;
And in this change is my invention spent,
Three themes in one, which wondrous scope affords.   12
    Fair, kind, and true have often lived alone,
    Which three till now never kept seat in one.

106

When in the chronicle of wasted time
I see descriptions of the fairest wights,
And beauty making beautiful old rhyme
In praise of ladies dead and lovely knights;   4
Then, in the blazon of sweet beauty's best,
Of hand, of foot, of lip, of eye, of brow,
I see their antique pen would have expressed
Even such a beauty as you master now.   8
So all their praises are but prophecies
Of this our time, all you prefiguring,
And, for they looked but with divining eyes,
They had not skill enough your worth to sing: 12
    For we, which now behold these present days,
    Have eyes to wonder, but lack tongues to praise.

Not mine own fears nor the prophetic soul
Of the wide world dreaming on things to come
Can yet the lease of my true love control,
Supposed as forfeit to a confined doom. 4
The mortal moon hath her eclipse endured,
And the sad augurs mock their own presage,
Incertainties now crown themselves assured,
And peace proclaims olives of endless age. 8
Now with the drops of this most balmy time
My love looks fresh, and Death to me subscribes,
Since, spite of him, I'll live in this poor rhyme,
While he insults o'er dull and speechless tribes. 12
    And thou in this shalt find thy monument,
      When tyrants' crests and tombs of brass are spent.

What's in the brain that ink may character
Which hath not figured to thee my true spirit?
What's new to speak, what now to register,
That may express my love or thy dear merit? 4
Nothing, sweet boy; but yet, like prayers divine,
I must each day say o'er the very same,
Counting no old thing old – thou mine, I thine –
Even as when first I hallowed thy fair name. 8
So that eternal love in love's fresh case
Weighs not the dust and injury of age,
Nor gives to necessary wrinkles place,
But makes antiquity for aye his page, 12
    Finding the first conceit of love there bred
      Where time and outward form would show it dead.

O, never say that I was false of heart,
Though absence seemed my flame to qualify.
As easy might I from myself depart
As from my soul, which in thy breast doth lie. 4
That is my home of love; if I have ranged,
Like him that travels I return again,
Just to the time, not with the time exchanged,
So that myself bring water for my stain. 8
Never believe, though in my nature reigned
All frailties that besiege all kinds of blood,
That it could so preposterously be stained
To leave for nothing all thy sum of good; 12
　For nothing this wide universe I call
　Save thou, my rose; in it thou art my all.

Alas, 'tis true, I have gone here and there,
And made myself a motley to the view,
Gored mine own thoughts, sold cheap what is most dear,
Made old offences of affections new. 4
Most true it is that I have looked on truth
Askance and strangely; but, by all above,
These blenches gave my heart another youth,
And worse essays proved thee my best of love. 8
Now all is done, have what shall have no end;
Mine appetite I never more will grind
On newer proof, to try an older friend,
A god in love, to whom I am confined. 12
　Then give me welcome, next my heaven the best,
　Even to thy pure and most most loving breast.

O, for my sake do you with Fortune chide,
The guilty goddess of my harmful deeds,
That did not better for my life provide
Than public means which public manners breeds.   4
Thence comes it that my name receives a brand,
And almost thence my nature is subdued
To what it works in, like the dyer's hand.
Pity me then, and wish I were renewed,   8
Whilst, like a willing patient, I will drink
Potions of eisel 'gainst my strong infection;
No bitterness that I will bitter think,
Nor double penance to correct correction.   12
    Pity me then, dear friend, and I assure ye
    Even that your pity is enough to cure me.

112

Your love and pity doth th'impression fill
Which vulgar scandal stamped upon my brow;
For what care I who calls me well or ill,
So you o'er-green my bad, my good allow?   4
You are my all the world, and I must strive
To know my shames and praises from your tongue;
None else to me, nor I to none alive,
That my steeled sense or changes right or wrong.   8
In so profound abysm I throw all care
Of others' voices, that my adder's sense
To critic and to flatterer stoppèd are.
Mark how with my neglect I do dispense: 12
    You are so strongly in my purpose bred
    That all the world besides methinks they're dead.

Since I left you, mine eye is in my mind,
And that which governs me to go about
Doth part his function and is partly blind,
Seems seeing, but effectually is out; 4
For it no form delivers to the heart
Of bird, of flower, or shape, which it doth latch.
Of his quick objects hath the mind no part,
Nor his own vision holds what it doth catch; 8
For if it see the rud'st or gentlest sight,
The most sweet-favour or deformèd'st creature,
The mountain, or the sea, the day, or night,
The crow, or dove, it shapes them to your feature. 12
 Incapable of more, replete with you,
 My most true mind thus mak'th mine eye untrue.

Or whether doth my mind, being crowned with you,
Drink up the monarch's plague, this flattery?
Or whether shall I say mine eye saith true,
And that your love taught it this alchemy, 4
To make of monsters and things indigest
Such cherubins as your sweet self resemble,
Creating every bad a perfect best
As fast as objects to his beams assemble? 8
O, 'tis the first, 'tis flattery in my seeing,
And my great mind most kingly drinks it up.
Mine eye well knows what with his gust is greeing,
And to his palate doth prepare the cup. 12
 If it be poisoned, 'tis the lesser sin
 That mine eye loves it and doth first begin.

Those lines that I before have writ do lie,
Even those that said I could not love you dearer.
Yet then my judgement knew no reason why
My most full flame should afterwards burn clearer.   4
But reckoning Time, whose millioned accidents
Creep in 'twixt vows and change decrees of kings,
Tan sacred beauty, blunt the sharp'st intents,
Divert strong minds to th'course of alt'ring things –   8
Alas, why, fearing of Time's tyranny,
Might I not then say 'Now I love you best,'
When I was certain o'er incertainty,
Crowning the present, doubting of the rest?   12
   Love is a babe; then might I not say so,
   To give full growth to that which still doth grow.

Let me not to the marriage of true minds
Admit impediments; love is not love
Which alters when it alteration finds,
Or bends with the remover to remove.   4
O no, it is an ever-fixèd mark
That looks on tempests and is never shaken;
It is the star to every wandering bark,
Whose worth's unknown, although his height be taken.   8
Love's not Time's fool, though rosy lips and cheeks
Within his bending sickle's compass come;
Love alters not with his brief hours and weeks,
But bears it out even to the edge of doom.   12
   If this be error and upon me proved,
   I never writ, nor no man ever loved.

Accuse me thus: that I have scanted all
Wherein I should your great deserts repay,
Forgot upon your dearest love to call,
Whereto all bonds do tie me day by day; 4
That I have frequent been with unknown minds,
And given to time your own dear-purchased right;
That I have hoisted sail to all the winds
Which should transport me farthest from your sight. 8
Book both my wilfulness and errors down,
And on just proof surmise accumulate;
Bring me within the level of your frown,
But shoot not at me in your wakened hate; 12
    Since my appeal says I did strive to prove
    The constancy and virtue of your love.

Like as to make our appetites more keen
With eager compounds we our palate urge;
As to prevent our maladies unseen
We sicken to shun sickness when we purge: 4
Even so, being full of your ne'er-cloying sweetness,
To bitter sauces did I frame my feeding;
And, sick of welfare, found a kind of meetness
To be diseased ere that there was true needing. 8
Thus policy in love, t'anticipate
The ills that were not, grew to faults assured,
And brought to medicine a healthful state,
Which, rank of goodness, would by ill be cured. 12
    But thence I learn, and find the lesson true,
    Drugs poison him that so fell sick of you.

What potions have I drunk of siren tears
Distilled from limbecks foul as hell within,
Applying fears to hopes and hopes to fears,
Still losing when I saw myself to win!   4
What wretched errors hath my heart committed,
Whilst it hath thought itself so blessèd never!
How have mine eyes out of their spheres been fitted
In the distraction of this madding fever!   8
O, benefit of ill! Now I find true
That better is by evil still made better;
And ruined love, when it is built anew,
Grows fairer than at first, more strong, far greater.   12
   So I return rebuked to my content,
   And gain by ills thrice more than I have spent.

That you were once unkind befriends me now,
And for that sorrow which I then did feel
Needs must I under my transgression bow,
Unless my nerves were brass or hammered steel.   4
For if you were by my unkindness shaken,
As I by yours, y'have passed a hell of time,
And I, a tyrant, have no leisure taken
To weigh how once I suffered in your crime.   8
O that our night of woe might have remembered
My deepest sense how hard true sorrow hits,
And soon to you, as you to me then, tendered
The humble salve which wounded bosoms fits!   12
   But that your trespass now becomes a fee;
   Mine ransoms yours, and yours must ransom me.

'Tis better to be vile than vile esteemed
When not to be receives reproach of being,
And the just pleasure lost which is so deemed
Not by our feeling but by others' seeing.   4
For why should others' false adulterate eyes
Give salutation to my sportive blood?
Or on my frailties why are frailer spies,
Which in their wills count bad what I think good?   8
No, I am that I am, and they that level
At my abuses reckon up their own;
I may be straight though they themselves be bevel.
By their rank thoughts my deeds must not be shown,   12
    Unless this general evil they maintain:
    All men are bad and in their badness reign.

Thy gift, thy tables, are within my brain
Full charactered with lasting memory,
Which shall above that idle rank remain
Beyond all date, even to eternity –   4
Or, at the least, so long as brain and heart
Have faculty by nature to subsist;
Till each to razed oblivion yield his part
Of thee, thy record never can be missed.   8
That poor retention could not so much hold,
Nor need I tallies thy dear love to score;
Therefore to give them from me was I bold
To trust those tables that receive thee more.   12
    To keep an adjunct to remember thee
    Were to import forgetfulness in me.

No, Time, thou shalt not boast that I do change.
Thy pyramids built up with newer might
To me are nothing novel, nothing strange;
They are but dressings of a former sight.   4
Our dates are brief, and therefore we admire
What thou dost foist upon us that is old,
And rather make them born to our desire
Than think that we before have heard them told.   8
Thy registers and thee I both defy,
Not wondering at the present nor the past;
For thy records and what we see doth lie,
Made more or less by thy continual haste.   12
   This I do vow, and this shall ever be:
   I will be true despite thy scythe and thee.

If my dear love were but the child of state,
It might for Fortune's bastard be unfathered,
As subject to Time's love, or to Time's hate,
Weeds among weeds, or flowers with flowers gathered.   4
No, it was builded far from accident;
It suffers not in smiling pomp, nor falls
Under the blow of thrallèd discontent,
Whereto th'inviting time our fashion calls.   8
It fears not Policy, that heretic
Which works on leases of short-numbered hours,
But all alone stands hugely politic,
That it nor grows with heat, nor drowns with showers.   12
   To this I witness call the fools of Time,
   Which die for goodness, who have lived for crime.

Were't aught to me I bore the canopy,
With my extern the outward honouring,
Or laid great bases for eternity,
Which proves more short than waste or ruining? 4
Have I not seen dwellers on form and favour
Lose all and more by paying too much rent,
For compound sweet forgoing simple savour,
Pitiful thrivers, in their gazing spent? 8
No, let me be obsequious in thy heart,
And take thou my oblation, poor but free,
Which is not mixed with seconds, knows no art
But mutual render, only me for thee. 12
   Hence, thou suborned informer! A true soul
   When most impeached stands least in thy control.

O thou, my lovely boy, who in thy power
Dost hold Time's fickle glass, his sickle hour,
Who hast by waning grown, and therein show'st
Thy lovers withering, as thy sweet self grow'st; 4
If Nature, sovereign mistress over wrack,
As thou goest onwards, still will pluck thee back,
She keeps thee to this purpose, that her skill
May Time disgrace and wretched minutes kill. 8
Yet fear her, O thou minion of her pleasure;
She may detain, but not still keep her treasure.
Her audit, though delayed, answered must be,
And her quietus is to render thee. 12

In the old age black was not counted fair,
Or, if it were, it bore not beauty's name;
But now is black beauty's successive heir,
And beauty slandered with a bastard shame: 4
For since each hand hath put on nature's power,
Fairing the foul with art's false borrowed face,
Sweet beauty hath no name, no holy bower,
But is profaned, if not lives in disgrace.   8
Therefore my mistress' eyes are raven black,
Her brows so suited, and they mourners seem
At such who, not born fair, no beauty lack,
Sland'ring creation with a false esteem.   12
   Yet so they mourn, becoming of their woe,
   That every tongue says beauty should look so.

How oft, when thou, my music, music play'st
Upon that blessèd wood whose motion sounds
With thy sweet fingers when thou gently sway'st
The wiry concord that mine ear confounds,   4
Do I envy those jacks that nimble leap
To kiss the tender inward of thy hand,
Whilst my poor lips, which should that harvest reap,
At the wood's boldness by thee blushing stand.   8
To be so tickled, they would change their state
And situation with those dancing chips
O'er whom thy fingers walk with gentle gait,
Making dead wood more blest than living lips.   12
   Since saucy jacks so happy are in this,
   Give them thy fingers, me thy lips to kiss.

Th'expense of spirit in a waste of shame
Is lust in action, and, till action, lust
Is perjured, murd'rous, bloody, full of blame,
Savage, extreme, rude, cruel, not to trust, 4
Enjoyed no sooner but despisèd straight,
Past reason hunted, and no sooner had,
Past reason hated as a swallowed bait
On purpose laid to make the taker mad; 8
Mad in pursuit, and in possession so,
Had, having, and in quest to have, extreme,
A bliss in proof, and proved, a very woe,
Before, a joy proposed, behind, a dream. 12
 All this the world well knows, yet none knows well
 To shun the heaven that leads men to this hell.

My mistress' eyes are nothing like the sun;
Coral is far more red than her lips' red;
If snow be white, why then her breasts are dun;
If hairs be wires, black wires grow on her head. 4
I have seen roses damasked, red and white,
But no such roses see I in her cheeks,
And in some perfumes is there more delight
Than in the breath that from my mistress reeks. 8
I love to hear her speak, yet well I know
That music hath a far more pleasing sound.
I grant I never saw a goddess go;
My mistress when she walks treads on the ground. 12
 And yet, by heaven, I think my love as rare
 As any she belied with false compare.

Thou art as tyrannous, so as thou art,
As those whose beauties proudly make them cruel;
For well thou know'st to my dear doting heart
Thou art the fairest and most precious jewel.   4
Yet in good faith some say that thee behold
Thy face hath not the power to make love groan;
To say they err I dare not be so bold,
Although I swear it to myself alone.   8
And to be sure that is not false I swear,
A thousand groans, but thinking on thy face,
One on another's neck, do witness bear
Thy black is fairest in my judgement's place.   12
   In nothing art thou black save in thy deeds,
   And thence this slander, as I think, proceeds.

Thine eyes I love, and they, as pitying me,
Knowing thy heart torment me with disdain,
Have put on black, and loving mourners be,
Looking with pretty ruth upon my pain.   4
And truly not the morning sun of heaven
Better becomes the grey cheeks of the east,
Nor that full star that ushers in the even
Doth half that glory to the sober west,   8
As those two mourning eyes become thy face.
O, let it then as well beseem thy heart
To mourn for me, since mourning doth thee grace,
And suit thy pity like in every part.   12
   Then will I swear beauty herself is black,
   And all they foul that thy complexion lack.

Beshrew that heart that makes my heart to groan
For that deep wound it gives my friend and me.
Is't not enough to torture me alone,
But slave to slavery my sweet'st friend must be?   4
Me from myself thy cruel eye hath taken,
And my next self thou harder hast engrossed.
Of him, myself, and thee, I am forsaken;
A torment thrice threefold thus to be crossed.   8
Prison my heart in thy steel bosom's ward,
But then my friend's heart let my poor heart bail;
Whoe'er keeps me, let my heart be his guard;
Thou canst not then use rigour in my jail.   12
    And yet thou wilt, for I, being pent in thee,
    Perforce am thine, and all that is in me.

So, now I have confessed that he is thine,
And I myself am mortgaged to thy will,
Myself I'll forfeit, so that other mine
Thou wilt restore to be my comfort still.   4
But thou wilt not, nor he will not be free,
For thou art covetous, and he is kind;
He learned but surety-like to write for me
Under that bond that him as fast doth bind.   8
The statute of thy beauty thou wilt take,
Thou usurer that put'st forth all to use,
And sue a friend came debtor for my sake;
So him I lose through my unkind abuse.   12
    Him have I lost, thou hast both him and me;
    He pays the whole, and yet am I not free.

Whoever hath her wish, thou hast thy Will,
And Will to boot, and Will in overplus;
More than enough am I that vex thee still,
To thy sweet will making addition thus.   4
Wilt thou, whose will is large and spacious,
Not once vouchsafe to hide my will in thine?
Shall will in others seem right gracious,
And in my will no fair acceptance shine?   8
The sea, all water, yet receives rain still
And in abundance addeth to his store;
So thou being rich in Will add to thy Will
One will of mine, to make thy large Will more.   12
    Let 'no' unkind no fair beseechers kill;
    Think all but one, and me in that one Will.

If thy soul check thee that I come so near,
Swear to thy blind soul that I was thy Will,
And will, thy soul knows, is admitted there;
Thus far for love my love-suit, sweet, fulfil.   4
Will will fulfil the treasure of thy love,
Ay, fill it full with wills, and my will one.
In things of great receipt with ease we prove
Among a number one is reckoned none.   8
Then in the number let me pass untold,
Though in thy store's account I one must be;
For nothing hold me, so it please thee hold
That nothing me, a something, sweet, to thee.   12
    Make but my name thy love, and love that still,
    And then thou lov'st me for my name is Will.

Thou blind fool, Love, what dost thou to mine eyes
That they behold and see not what they see?
They know what beauty is, see where it lies,
Yet what the best is take the worst to be.   4
If eyes corrupt by over-partial looks
Be anchored in the bay where all men ride,
Why of eyes' falsehood hast thou forgèd hooks,
Whereto the judgement of my heart is tied?   8
Why should my heart think that a several plot,
Which my heart knows the wide world's common place?
Or mine eyes seeing this, say this is not,
To put fair truth upon so foul a face?   12
  In things right true my heart and eyes have erred,
  And to this false plague are they now transferred.

When my love swears that she is made of truth
I do believe her, though I know she lies,
That she might think me some untutored youth,
Unlearnèd in the world's false subtleties.   4
Thus vainly thinking that she thinks me young,
Although she knows my days are past the best,
Simply I credit her false-speaking tongue;
On both sides thus is simple truth suppressed.   8
But wherefore says she not she is unjust?
And wherefore say not I that I am old?
O, love's best habit is in seeming trust,
And age in love loves not to have years told.   12
  Therefore I lie with her, and she with me,
  And in our faults by lies we flattered be.

O, call not me to justify the wrong
That thy unkindness lays upon my heart;
Wound me not with thine eye but with thy tongue;
Use power with power and slay me not by art.   4
Tell me thou lov'st elsewhere; but in my sight,
Dear heart, forbear to glance thine eye aside;
What need'st thou wound with cunning when thy might
Is more than my o'erpressed defence can bide?   8
Let me excuse thee: 'Ah, my love well knows
Her pretty looks have been mine enemies,
And therefore from my face she turns my foes,
That they elsewhere might dart their injuries.'   12
   Yet do not so; but since I am near slain,
   Kill me outright with looks and rid my pain.

Be wise as thou art cruel; do not press
My tongue-tied patience with too much disdain,
Lest sorrow lend me words, and words express
The manner of my pity-wanting pain.   4
If I might teach thee wit, better it were,
Though not to love, yet, love, to tell me so;
As testy sick men, when their deaths be near,
No news but health from their physicians know.   8
For if I should despair, I should grow mad,
And in my madness might speak ill of thee.
Now this ill-wresting world is grown so bad
Mad sland'rers by mad ears believèd be.   12
   That I may not be so, nor thou belied,
   Bear thine eyes straight, though thy proud heart go wide.

In faith, I do not love thee with mine eyes,
For they in thee a thousand errors note;
But 'tis my heart that loves what they despise,
Who in despite of view is pleased to dote. 4
Nor are mine ears with thy tongue's tune delighted,
Nor tender feeling to base touches prone,
Nor taste, nor smell, desire to be invited
To any sensual feast with thee alone. 8
But my five wits nor my five senses can
Dissuade one foolish heart from serving thee,
Who leaves unswayed the likeness of a man,
Thy proud heart's slave and vassal wretch to be. 12
    Only my plague thus far I count my gain,
     That she that makes me sin awards me pain.

Love is my sin, and thy dear virtue hate,
Hate of my sin, grounded on sinful loving.
O, but with mine compare thou thine own state,
And thou shalt find it merits not reproving; 4
Or if it do, not from those lips of thine,
That have profaned their scarlet ornaments
And sealed false bonds of love as oft as mine,
Robbed others' beds' revenues of their rents. 8
Be it lawful I love thee as thou lov'st those
Whom thine eyes woo as mine importune thee.
Root pity in thy heart, that, when it grows,
Thy pity may deserve to pitied be. 12
    If thou dost seek to have what thou dost hide,
     By self-example mayst thou be denied.

Lo, as a careful housewife runs to catch
One of her feathered creatures broke away,
Sets down her babe, and makes all swift dispatch
In pursuit of the thing she would have stay;   4
Whilst her neglected child holds her in chase,
Cries to catch her whose busy care is bent
To follow that which flies before her face,
Not prizing her poor infant's discontent: 8
So run'st thou after that which flies from thee,
Whilst I, thy babe, chase thee afar behind;
But if thou catch thy hope, turn back to me
And play the mother's part – kiss me, be kind.   12
   So will I pray that thou mayst have thy Will,
   If thou turn back and my loud crying still.

Two loves I have, of comfort and despair,
Which like two spirits do suggest me still;
The better angel is a man right fair,
The worser spirit a woman coloured ill.   4
To win me soon to hell, my female evil
Tempteth my better angel from my side,
And would corrupt my saint to be a devil,
Wooing his purity with her foul pride.   8
And whether that my angel be turned fiend
Suspect I may, yet not directly tell;
But being both from me, both to each friend,
I guess one angel in another's hell.   12
   Yet this shall I ne'er know, but live in doubt
   Till my bad angel fire my good one out.

Those lips that Love's own hand did make
Breathed forth the sound that said 'I hate'
To me that languished for her sake.
But when she saw my woeful state, 4
Straight in her heart did mercy come,
Chiding that tongue that ever sweet
Was used in giving gentle doom,
And taught it thus anew to greet: 8
'I hate' she altered with an end
That followed it as gentle day
Doth follow night, who, like a fiend,
From heaven to hell is flown away. 12
 'I hate' from hate away she threw,
 And saved my life, saying 'not you.'

Poor soul, the centre of my sinful earth,
[ ] these rebel powers that thee array,
Why dost thou pine within and suffer dearth,
Painting thy outward walls so costly gay? 4
Why so large cost, having so short a lease,
Dost thou upon thy fading mansion spend?
Shall worms, inheritors of this excess,
Eat up thy charge? Is this thy body's end? 8
Then, soul, live thou upon thy servant's loss,
And let that pine to aggravate thy store;
Buy terms divine in selling hours of dross;
Within be fed, without be rich no more: 12
 So shalt thou feed on Death, that feeds on men,
 And Death once dead there's no more dying then.

My love is as a fever, longing still
For that which longer nurseth the disease,
Feeding on that which doth preserve the ill,
Th'uncertain sickly appetite to please.   4
My reason, the physician to my love,
Angry that his prescriptions are not kept,
Hath left me, and I desperate now approve
Desire is death, which physic did except.   8
Past cure I am, now reason is past care,
And frantic-mad with evermore unrest;
My thoughts and my discourse as madmen's are,
At random from the truth, vainly expressed: 12
   For I have sworn thee fair, and thought thee bright,
   Who art as black as hell, as dark as night.

148

O me, what eyes hath love put in my head,
Which have no correspondence with true sight!
Or, if they have, where is my judgement fled,
That censures falsely what they see aright?   4
If that be fair whereon my false eyes dote,
What means the world to say it is not so?
If it be not, then love doth well denote
Love's eye is not so true as all men's 'no'.   8
How can it, O, how can love's eye be true,
That is so vexed with watching and with tears?
No marvel then though I mistake my view;
The sun itself sees not till heaven clears.   12
   O cunning love, with tears thou keep'st me blind,
   Lest eyes well-seeing thy foul faults should find.

Canst thou, O cruel, say I love thee not,
When I against myself with thee partake?
Do I not think on thee when I forgot
Am of myself, all tyrant for thy sake?   4
Who hateth thee that I do call my friend?
On whom frown'st thou that I do fawn upon?
Nay, if thou lour'st on me, do I not spend
Revenge upon myself with present moan?   8
What merit do I in myself respect
That is so proud thy service to despise,
When all my best doth worship thy defect,
Commanded by the motion of thine eyes?   12
  But, love, hate on; for now I know thy mind:
  Those that can see thou lov'st, and I am blind.

150

O, from what power hast thou this powerful might
With insufficiency my heart to sway?
To make me give the lie to my true sight
And swear that brightness doth not grace the day?   4
Whence hast thou this becoming of things ill
That in the very refuse of thy deeds
There is such strength and warrantise of skill
That in my mind thy worst all best exceeds?   8
Who taught thee how to make me love thee more,
The more I hear and see just cause of hate?
O, though I love what others do abhor,
With others thou shouldst not abhor my state.   12
  If thy unworthiness raised love in me,
  More worthy I to be beloved of thee.

Love is too young to know what conscience is;
Yet who knows not conscience is born of love?
Then, gentle cheater, urge not my amiss,
Lest guilty of my faults thy sweet self prove.   4
For, thou betraying me, I do betray
My nobler part to my gross body's treason:
My soul doth tell my body that he may
Triumph in love; flesh stays no farther reason,   8
But, rising at thy name, doth point out thee
As his triumphant prize. Proud of this pride,
He is contented thy poor drudge to be,
To stand in thy affairs, fall by thy side.   12
   No want of conscience hold it that I call
   Her 'love' for whose dear love I rise and fall.

In loving thee thou know'st I am forsworn,
But thou art twice forsworn, to me love swearing;
In act thy bed-vow broke, and new faith torn
In vowing new hate after new love bearing.   4
But why of two oaths' breach do I accuse thee,
When I break twenty? I am perjured most,
For all my vows are oaths but to misuse thee,
And all my honest faith in thee is lost;   8
For I have sworn deep oaths of thy deep kindness,
Oaths of thy love, thy truth, thy constancy,
And to enlighten thee gave eyes to blindness,
Or made them swear against the thing they see;   12
   For I have sworn thee fair – more perjured eye,
   To swear against the truth so foul a lie.

Cupid laid by his brand and fell asleep.
A maid of Dian's this advantage found,
And his love-kindling fire did quickly steep
In a cold valley-fountain of that ground;   4
Which borrowed from this holy fire of Love
A dateless lively heat, still to endure,
And grew a seething bath, which yet men prove
Against strange maladies a sovereign cure.   8
But at my mistress' eye Love's brand new-fired,
The boy for trial needs would touch my breast;
I, sick withal, the help of bath desired,
And thither hied, a sad distempered guest,   12
   But found no cure; the bath for my help lies
   Where Cupid got new fire – my mistress' eyes.

The little Love-god lying once asleep
Laid by his side his heart-inflaming brand,
Whilst many nymphs that vowed chaste life to keep
Came tripping by; but in her maiden hand   4
The fairest votary took up that fire,
Which many legions of true hearts had warmed;
And so the general of hot desire
Was, sleeping, by a virgin hand disarmed.   8
This brand she quenchèd in a cool well by,
Which from Love's fire took heat perpetual,
Growing a bath and healthful remedy
For men diseased; but I, my mistress' thrall,   12
   Came there for cure, and this by that I prove:
   Love's fire heats water, water cools not love.

A LOVER'S COMPLAINT

From off a hill whose concave womb reworded
A plaintful story from a sist'ring vale,
My spirits t'attend this double voice accorded,
And down I laid to list the sad-tuned tale;
Ere long espied a fickle maid full pale,   5
Tearing of papers, breaking rings a-twain,
Storming her world with sorrow's wind and rain.

Upon her head a platted hive of straw,
Which fortified her visage from the sun,
Whereon the thought might think sometime it saw   10
The carcass of a beauty spent and done.
Time had not scythèd all that youth begun,
Nor youth all quit, but spite of heaven's fell rage
Some beauty peeped through lattice of seared age.

Oft did she heave her napkin to her eyne,   15
Which on it had conceited characters,
Laund'ring the silken figures in the brine
That seasoned woe had pelleted in tears,
And often reading what contents it bears;
As often shrieking undistinguished woe,   20
In clamours of all size, both high and low.

Sometimes her levelled eyes their carriage ride,
As they did batt'ry to the spheres intend;
Sometime diverted their poor balls are tied
To th'orbèd earth; sometimes they do extend   25
Their view right on; anon their gazes lend
To every place at once, and nowhere fixed,
The mind and sight distractedly commixed.

Her hair, nor loose nor tied in formal plat,
Proclaimed in her a careless hand of pride;   30
For some, untucked, descended her sheaved hat,
Hanging her pale and pinèd cheek beside;
Some in her threaden fillet still did bide,
And, true to bondage, would not break from thence,
Though slackly braided in loose negligence.   35

A thousand favours from a maund she drew,
Of amber, crystal, and of beaded jet,
Which one by one she in a river threw,
Upon whose weeping margin she was set;
Like usury applying wet to wet,   40
Or monarch's hands that lets not bounty fall
Where want cries some, but where excess begs all.

Of folded schedules had she many a one,
Which she perused, sighed, tore, and gave the flood;
Cracked many a ring of posied gold and bone,   45
Bidding them find their sepulchres in mud;
Found yet more letters sadly penned in blood,
With sleided silk feat and affectedly
Enswathed and sealed to curious secrecy.

These often bathed she in her fluxive eyes,   50
And often kissed, and often 'gan to tear;
Cried 'O false blood, thou register of lies,
What unapprovèd witness dost thou bear!
Ink would have seemed more black and damnèd here!'
This said, in top of rage the lines she rents,   55
Big discontent so breaking their contents.

A reverend man that grazed his cattle nigh,
Sometime a blusterer that the ruffle knew
Of court, of city, and had let go by
The swiftest hours observèd as they flew,   60
Towards this afflicted fancy fastly drew,
And, privileged by age, desires to know
In brief the grounds and motives of her woe.

So slides he down upon his grainèd bat,
And comely distant sits he by her side,   65
When he again desires her, being sat,
Her grievance with his hearing to divide.
If that from him there may be aught applied
Which may her suffering ecstasy assuage,
'Tis promised in the charity of age.   70

'Father,' she says, 'though in me you behold
The injury of many a blasting hour,
Let it not tell your judgement I am old:
Not age, but sorrow, over me hath power.
I might as yet have been a spreading flower,   75
Fresh to myself, if I had self-applied
Love to myself, and to no love beside.

'But woe is me! too early I attended
A youthful suit — it was to gain my grace —
O, one by nature's outwards so commended   80
That maidens' eyes stuck over all his face.
Love lacked a dwelling and made him her place;
And when in his fair parts she did abide,
She was new lodged and newly deified.

'His browny locks did hang in crookèd curls,   85
And every light occasion of the wind
Upon his lips their silken parcels hurls.
What's sweet to do, to do will aptly find:
Each eye that saw him did enchant the mind;
For on his visage was in little drawn   90
What largeness thinks in paradise was sawn.

'Small show of man was yet upon his chin;
His phoenix down began but to appear,
Like unshorn velvet, on that termless skin,
Whose bare out-bragged the web it seemed to wear; 95
Yet showed his visage by that cost more dear,
And nice affections wavering stood in doubt
If best were as it was, or best without.

'His qualities were beauteous as his form,
For maiden-tongued he was, and thereof free;   100
Yet, if men moved him, was he such a storm
As oft 'twixt May and April is to see,
When winds breathe sweet, unruly though they be.
His rudeness so with his authorized youth
Did livery falseness in a pride of truth.   105

'Well could he ride, and often men would say
"That horse his mettle from his rider takes;
Proud of subjection, noble by the sway,
What rounds, what bounds, what course,
        what stop he makes!"
And controversy hence a question takes,   110
Whether the horse by him became his deed,
Or he his manage by th'well-doing steed.

'But quickly on this side the verdict went:
His real habitude gave life and grace
To appertainings and to ornament,   115
Accomplished in himself, not in his case;
All aids, themselves made fairer by their place,
Came for additions; yet their purposed trim
Pieced not his grace, but were all graced by him.

'So on the tip of his subduing tongue   120
All kind of arguments and question deep,
All replication prompt and reason strong,
For his advantage still did wake and sleep.
To make the weeper laugh, the laugher weep,
He had the dialect and different skill,   125
Catching all passions in his craft of will,

'That he did in the general bosom reign
Of young, of old, and sexes both enchanted,
To dwell with him in thoughts, or to remain
In personal duty, following where he haunted.   130
Consents bewitched, ere he desire, have granted,
And dialogued for him what he would say,
Asked their own wills, and made their wills obey.

'Many there were that did his picture get
To serve their eyes, and in it put their mind,   135
Like fools that in th'imagination set
The goodly objects which abroad they find
Of lands and mansions, theirs in thought assigned,
And labouring in more pleasures to bestow them
Than the true gouty landlord which doth owe them.   140

'So many have, that never touched his hand,
Sweetly supposed them mistress of his heart.
My woeful self, that did in freedom stand,
And was my own fee-simple, not in part –
What with his art in youth, and youth in art –   145
Threw my affections in his charmèd power,
Reserved the stalk and gave him all my flower.

'Yet did I not, as some my equals did,
Demand of him, nor being desirèd yielded;
Finding myself in honour so forbid,   150
With safest distance I mine honour shielded.
Experience for me many bulwarks builded
Of proofs new-bleeding, which remained the foil
Of this false jewel, and his amorous spoil.

'But ah, who ever shunned by precedent   155
The destined ill she must herself assay?
Or forced examples, 'gainst her own content,
To put the by-past perils in her way?
Counsel may stop awhile what will not stay;
For when we rage, advice is often seen   160
By blunting us to make our wits more keen.

'Nor gives it satisfaction to our blood
That we must curb it upon others' proof,
To be forbod the sweets that seems so good,
For fear of harms that preach in our behoof.   165
O appetite, from judgement stand aloof!
The one a palate hath that needs will taste,
Though Reason weep, and cry "It is thy last!"

'For further I could say this man's untrue,
And knew the patterns of his foul beguiling,   170
Heard where his plants in others' orchards grew,
Saw how deceits were gilded in his smiling,
Knew vows were ever brokers to defiling,
Thought characters and words merely but art,
And bastards of his foul adulterate heart.   175

'And long upon these terms I held my city,
Till thus he 'gan besiege me: "Gentle maid,
Have of my suffering youth some feeling pity,
And be not of my holy vows afraid.
That's to ye sworn to none was ever said;   180
For feasts of love I have been called unto,
Till now did ne'er invite nor never woo.

'"All my offences that abroad you see
Are errors of the blood, none of the mind;
Love made them not; with acture they may be,   185
Where neither party is nor true nor kind.
They sought their shame that so their shame did find;
And so much less of shame in me remains
By how much of me their reproach contains.

'"Among the many that mine eyes have seen,   190
Not one whose flame my heart so much as warmèd,
Or my affection put to th'smallest teen,
Or any of my leisures ever charmèd.
Harm have I done to them, but ne'er was harmèd;
Kept hearts in liveries, but mine own was free,   195
And reigned commanding in his monarchy.

'"Look here what tributes wounded fancies sent me,
Of pallid pearls and rubies red as blood;
Figuring that they their passions likewise lent me
Of grief and blushes, aptly understood   200
In bloodless white and the encrimsoned mood –
Effects of terror and dear modesty
Encamped in hearts but fighting outwardly.

'"And, lo, behold these talents of their hair,
With twisted metal amorously empleached,   205
I have received from many a several fair,
Their kind acceptance weepingly beseeched,
With the annexions of fair gems enriched,
And deep-brained sonnets that did amplify
Each stone's dear nature, worth, and quality.   210

'"The diamond? why, 'twas beautiful and hard,
Whereto his invised properties did tend;
The deep-green em'rald, in whose fresh regard
Weak sights their sickly radiance do amend;
The heaven-hued sapphire and the opal blend   215
With objects manifold; each several stone,
With wit well blazoned, smiled, or made some moan.

'"Lo, all these trophies of affections hot,
Of pensived and subdued desires the tender,
Nature hath charged me that I hoard them not,   220
But yield them up where I myself must render –
That is, to you, my origin and ender;
For these, of force, must your oblations be,
Since, I their altar, you enpatron me.

'"O, then, advance of yours that phraseless hand,   225
Whose white weighs down the airy scale of praise;
Take all these similes to your own command,
Hallowed with sighs that burning lungs did raise;
What me, your minister, for you obeys,
Works under you, and to your audit comes   230
Their distract parcels in combinèd sums.

'"Lo, this device was sent me from a nun,
Or sister sanctified, of holiest note,
Which late her noble suit in court did shun,
Whose rarest havings made the blossoms dote;   235
For she was sought by spirits of richest coat,
But kept cold distance, and did thence remove
To spend her living in eternal love.

'"But, O my sweet, what labour is't to leave
The thing we have not, mast'ring what not strives,   240
Paling the place which did no form receive,
Playing patient sports in unconstrainèd gyves!
She that her fame so to herself contrives,
The scars of battle 'scapeth by the flight,
And makes her absence valiant, not her might.   245

'"O, pardon me, in that my boast is true!
The accident which brought me to her eye
Upon the moment did her force subdue;
And now she would the cagèd cloister fly.
Religious love put out religion's eye.   250
Not to be tempted, would she be immured,
And now to tempt all liberty procured.

'"How mighty then you are, O, hear me tell!
The broken bosoms that to me belong
Have emptied all their fountains in my well,   255
And mine I pour your ocean all among.
I strong o'er them, and you o'er me being strong,
Must for your victory us all congest,
As compound love to physic your cold breast.

'"My parts had power to charm a sacred nun,   260
Who disciplined, ay, dieted in grace,
Believed her eyes when they t'assail begun,
All vows and consecrations giving place.
O most potential love! vow, bond, nor space,
In thee hath neither sting, knot, nor confine,   265
For thou art all, and all things else are thine.

'"When thou impressest, what are precepts worth
Of stale example? When thou wilt inflame,
How coldly those impediments stand forth,
Of wealth, of filial fear, law, kindred, fame!   270
Love's arms are peace, 'gainst rule, 'gainst sense,
          'gainst shame,
And sweetens, in the suff'ring pangs it bears,
The aloes of all forces, shocks, and fears.

'"Now all these hearts that do on mine depend,
Feeling it break, with bleeding groans they pine,   275
And supplicant their sighs to you extend
To leave the batt'ry that you make 'gainst mine,
Lending soft audience to my sweet design,
And credent soul to that strong-bonded oath
That shall prefer and undertake my troth."   280

'This said, his wat'ry eyes he did dismount,
Whose sights till then were levelled on my face;
Each cheek a river running from a fount
With brinish current downward flowed apace.
O, how the channel to the stream gave grace!   285
Who glazed with crystal gate the glowing roses
That flame through water which their hue encloses.

'O father, what a hell of witchcraft lies
In the small orb of one particular tear!
But with the inundation of the eyes   290
What rocky heart to water will not wear?
What breast so cold that is not warmèd here?
O cleft effect! cold modesty, hot wrath,
Both fire from hence and chill extincture hath.

'For lo, his passion, but an art of craft,   295
Even there resolved my reason into tears;
There my white stole of chastity I daffed,
Shook off my sober guards and civil fears,
Appear to him as he to me appears –
All melting; though our drops this diff'rence bore: 300
His poisoned me, and mine did him restore.

'In him a plenitude of subtle matter,
Applied to cautels, all strange forms receives,
Of burning blushes, or of weeping water,
Or swooning paleness; and he takes and leaves,   305
In either's aptness, as it best deceives,
To blush at speeches rank, to weep at woes,
Or to turn white and swoon at tragic shows;

'That not a heart which in his level came
Could 'scape the hail of his all-hurting aim,   310
Showing fair nature is both kind and tame;
And, veiled in them, did win whom he would maim.
Against the thing he sought he would exclaim;
When he most burned in heart-wished luxury,
He preached pure maid and praised cold chastity.   315

'Thus merely with the garment of a grace
The naked and concealèd fiend he covered,
That th'unexperient gave the tempter place,
Which, like a cherubin, above them hovered.
Who, young and simple, would not be so lovered?   320
Ay me! I fell; and yet do question make
What I should do again for such a sake.

'O, that infected moisture of his eye,
O, that false fire which in his cheek so glowed,
O, that forced thunder from his heart did fly,   325
O, that sad breath his spongy lungs bestowed,
O, all that borrowed motion, seeming owed,
Would yet again betray the fore-betrayed,
And new pervert a reconcilèd maid.'

COMMENTARY

WHAT Shakespeare would make of these notes one scarcely dares think, but it is arguable that the sonnet as a form – with its densities and ellipses enforced by close patterning, and its structural modifications of ostensible meaning – most aptly finds resolution in a critical apparatus. Certainly, the first surviving sonnet sequence, Dante's *Vita Nuova*, includes an elaborate authorial commentary; and, on a lower level, the first extended sequence in English, Thomas Watson's *Hekatompathia* (1582), was published with framing glosses, source notes, and generally appreciative comments (for an example see the Introduction, pages 19–20).

The annotation in this edition broadly follows New Penguin practice, but it is slow to enumerate meanings – since it is felt that, especially in mature sonnets and *A Lover's Complaint*, the verse opens fields of significance rather than sharply distinguishing primary, secondary, and tertiary senses – and it glosses in longer spans than is usual, on the Coleridgean principle that 'Shakespeare goes on creating, and evolving B. out of A., and C. out of B., and so on, just as a serpent moves, which makes a fulcrum of its own body, and seems forever twisting and untwisting its own strength'. The commentary also includes more illustrative material than its companion volumes on the plays, because it is believed that the peculiar interpretative difficulties of the non-dramatic poetry are best eased by quotation. In preparing these notes, the editions by Rollins (1944), Ingram and Redpath (1964, 1978), and Stephen Booth (1977, 1978) have been closely consulted and sometimes echoed. In two respects this editor has been more fortunate than his precursors: he has been able to consult R. W. Dent's *Shakespeare's Proverbial Language: An Index* (Berkeley, Calif., 1981) and has been assisted in the assessment of rhymes and puns by Fausto Cercignani's *Shakespeare's Works and Elizabethan Pronunciation* (Oxford, 1981) – an altogether more reliable guide than the much-cited *Shakespeare's Pronunciation* by Helge Kökeritz (New Haven, Conn., 1953). With rhyming the policy has been to assure readers that almost all of the rhymes which look or sound false today were acceptable in 1609, and to provide rough indications of how they worked. Inevitably, this policy is compromised, since one should, to be consistent, gloss all the other rhymes in the collection, to remind readers that what looks and sounds perfect now was not invariably full then. Similarly with sources: obvious echoes are noted, but lesser reverberations and motifs shared from common stock are not. A glancing indication of the dense intertextuality within which the poems are inscribed is given in, e.g., the note to *A Lover's*

Complaint 59, but this commentary would ideally quote in full the sequences of Sidney, Spenser, Daniel, Constable, Drayton, and others.

In what follows, 'Q' refers to Thorpe's quarto (1609); quotations from that and other early editions of Shakespeare preserve old spelling but modernize 'long s' (ſ). Biblical quotations are modernized from the Bishops' Bible (1568 etc.), the version that was probably best known to Shakespeare; quotations from the prayer book are modernized from the Elizabethan Book of Common Prayer.

THE SONNETS

The Dedication

When the Sonnets and *A Lover's Complaint* were first published in 1609, they were prefaced by the following lapidary dedication, centred, capitalized, and impressive: 'TO.THE.ONLIE.BEGETTER.OF. | THESE.INSVING.SONNETS. | Mʳ.W.H. ALL.HAPPINESSE. | AND.THAT.ETERNITIE. | PROMISED. | BY. | OVR.EVER-LIVING.POET. | WISHETH. | THE.WELL-WISHING. | ADVENT-VRER.IN. | SETTING. | FORTH. || T.T.'. Most editors print this before the Sonnets, as though T.T.'s words deserved the same kind and degree of attention as Shakespeare's poems; but they do not. Indeed, with the exception of 'ONLIE.BEGETTER' (negotiated at length in the Introduction, pages 25–9), they are of minimal literary interest.

'T.T.' is evidently Thomas Thorpe, the publisher of the Sonnets, who, as the publisher of *Volpone* two years before, had demonstrated his interest in lapidary acknowledgement by laying out the dedication page of Jonson's quarto in the same way as Shakespeare's (though without full stops). 'BEGETTER' is more contentious, but, as Ingram and Redpath conclude in their edition, it is virtually certain that the actual or inspirational origin of the 'INSVING.SONNETS' is invoked, not the procurer of the manuscript. Jacobean usage is uniform on this point; Thorpe could scarcely have employed 'begetter' in the sense 'getter' and still expect to be understood. An examination of the other Thorpe prefaces reveals a man with rhetorical pretensions, but not someone so floridly inept as to stumble into misconstruction. (Which does not rule out the possibility that Thorpe sought to be misconstrued when dedicating the Sonnets; many have thought his words a blind.) 'ONLIE' modifies 'BEGETTER', meaning 'sole' and 'incomparable'. As for 'Mʳ.W.H.', that has usually been read as a clue to the identity of the young man and friend in the poems. Some candidates are mentioned above (page 10). Of the two favourites, Henry Wriothesley, Earl of Southampton (1573–1624), and William Herbert, Earl of Pembroke (1580–1630), this editor finds the former a more plausible addressee than the latter.

Shakespeare's association with Southampton in the early 1590s – when, on stylistic grounds, the first sonnets seem to have been written – is indisputable. The poet dedicated *Venus and Adonis* to Wriothesley in 1593–4, and, more warmly (using Thorpe's 'all happiness' in the process), *The Rape of Lucrece* in 1594. The Earl's patronage of the arts and interest in the theatre during the 1590s and 1600s is well-attested. Certain parallels can be drawn between his life and events described by the Sonnets, and the one highly datable poem, 107, arguably alludes to his situation in 1603 (see page 319). Herbert, by contrast, was associated with Shakespeare less and later, and he seems too young to have been the subject of urgent exhortations to procreate in the early 1590s. It is, however, a premiss of this edition that, in reading Shakespeare's Sonnets, biography need not impinge. This is not to deny that lived experience lies behind the text. Yet there may have been two, three, or more young men involved in Shakespeare's idea of the friend; in one sense, indeed, there must have been many men involved in the production of that single image. And an 'idea' or 'image' the friend will certainly have become once transmuted into poetry, with a created identity distinct from Southampton's or Herbert's, and from what Shakespeare may have known of them. To interpret the Sonnets through the medium of biography is in principle no different from analysing the motives of Shakespeare's Richard III through a study of fifteenth-century history.

Returning to Thorpe's dedication: neither Henry Wriothesley nor William Herbert squares readily with 'Mʳ.W.H.', since earls are not called 'Mr'; on the other hand, if Thorpe is assumed to be revealing his knowledge of the friend's identity tactfully, Herbert's initials are right (though, once tact is admitted, 'W.H.' might be Southampton's H.W. in reverse). It is also possible that our 'WELL-WISHING. | ADVENTVRER', Thorpe, was mistaken in his identification of the friend. 'OVR.EVER-LIVING.POET' refers, of course, to Shakespeare, and the 'ETERNITIE. | PROMISED' by him is presumably the immortality assured the youth in sonnets like 81 and 107. 'THE.WELL-WISHING | ADVENTVRER.IN. | SETTING. | FORTH.', finally, makes play with printing as voyaging. Explorers and traders 'set forth' in ships as printers 'set' text; Thorpe sends his quarto into the world as a brave venture. Though a few scholars have sought to read these words as Thorpe's 'signing off', with 'WISHETH' governed by 'Mʳ.W.H.' (so that he becomes the author of the dedication, Thorpe only his agent), the natural way to read the enigma is with the subject of the main verb last: 'T. T.'.

Sonnet 1

1   *creatures* living things (not just, as in modern English, 'animals')
      increase procreation (as when Lear curses Gonerill, 'Dry up in her
      the organs of increase', I.4.276), offspring ('her womb's increase',

> *Coriolanus* III.3.114), fruitful produce (as in Prospero's masque for
> the lovers Ferdinand and Miranda, 'Earth's increase, foison plenty, |
> Barns and garners never empty', *The Tempest* IV.1.110–11)

2   *That* so that

> *thereby* through *increase* (though also 'by means of *fairest creatures*')
> *rose.* The first of three dozen words picked out with italics and a
> capital letter in Q Sonnets, *rose* has sometimes been read as a clue to
> the identity of Shakespeare's young man. Yet it is far from certain
> that Southampton's family name, Wriothesley, could be pronounced
> 'Rose-ly' in the sixteenth century. What is apparent is that this *rose* –
> with its powerful development towards 109.14 – puts the Sonnets, at
> the outset, in a tradition of courtly, learned love poetry stretching
> from the *Roman de la Rose* of Guillaume de Lorris and Jean de
> Meung to the rose lyrics of early Yeats and Rilke.

2, 4   *die . . . memory.* A full rhyme, sounding closer to the diphthong 'i-ee'
> than modern 'eye', with a secondary stress on the 'y' of *memory*.

3   *as.* The primary sense is 'while', but the suggestion of propriety (if
> not obligation) in *should* allows *as* to link lines 3–4 by a tacit elliptical
> 'just *as . . .* so'.

4   *His . . . his* its . . . its. A standard possessive in Elizabethan English,
> often used in the Sonnets subtly to personify (and here suggesting
> that the *heir* of the *riper* might be the young man's child).

> *tender* young, sensitive, loving. Modern English has lost the full
> range of meaning illustratively exploited by Lear when he asks his
> *heir*, Cordelia, why she does not love him: 'So young, and so
> untender?' (I.1.106).

> *tender heir might bear his memory.* The dominant idea is of the *riper*'s
> offspring, or *heir*, *bear*ing his memory into the future by *bear*ing his
> features and reminding others of him; but there may be a quibbling
> glance, via *mollis aer* as a false etymology for Latin *mulier* ('woman'),
> at the *tender* mother who *might bear* in her womb the *riper*'s memorial.
> The same pun on *heir* and learned invocation of *mollis aer* for *mulier*
> recurs at *Cymbeline* V.5.444–50, where the Soothsayer interprets
> the prophecy to Posthumus and the King:

> > (*To Cymbeline*)
> > The piece of tender air, thy virtuous daughter,
> > Which we call 'mollis aer', and 'mollis aer'
> > We term it 'mulier'; (*to Posthumus*) which 'mulier' I divine
> > Is this most constant wife, who even now
> > Answering the letter of the oracle,
> > Unknown to you, unsought, were clipped about
> > With this most tender air.

5   *contracted.* Though the dominant sense is 'betrothed', the word
       tacitly alludes to its consequences: by staying single the youth has
       lost the chance to *increase* and has *contracted* or 'shrunk' into himself.
6   *Feed'st thy light's . . . fuel.* The image is of a pyre, torch, or candle,
       nourishing its *flame* by giving itself up. The line apparently echoes
       Metamorphoses III.463–4, where Ovid's Narcissus recognizes him-
       self reflected in a forest pool: '*iste ego sum: sensi, nec me mea fallit
       imago; | uror amore mei: flammas moveoque feroque*'. In Arthur
       Golding's translation of 1567 – a work which Shakespeare knew,
       and which lies behind many of the sonnets to the youth, directly or
       obliquely – this is diffusely rendered:

> It is myself I well perceive, it is mine image sure,
> That in this sort deluding me, this fury doth procure.
> I am enamoured of myself, I do both set on fire,
> And am the same that swelteth too, through impotent desire.

9   *fresh* youthful, vigorous, hale
10   *only* outstanding, unique. 'These are the only men', says Polonius of
       the actors (*Hamlet* II.2.400–401), meaning that they are excellent at
       what they do.
       herald to messenger of. The young man is sent by *spring* to announce
       that season's approach.
       gaudy showy (though not necessarily, as in modern usage, 'garish'),
       festive (as at *Antony and Cleopatra* III.13.182, 'Let's have one other
       gaudy night'), joyful (compare the Latin *gaudium*, 'joy'). Conceivably
       gaudy was chosen to give the *spring* a dash of colour by association
       with the compound 'gaudy-green' (the tint of rustic cloth when dyed
       with the juices of a hedgerow plant called weld).
11   *buriest* (two syllables)
       content (1) happiness (which lies in marriage); (2) children (the
       offspring which a future father 'contains')
12   *tender churl.* An echo of line 4 (*tender heir*) and bundle of paradoxes –
       'sensitive boor', 'loving begrudger', 'young old skinflint' – preparing
       the image of *niggarding* used at the end of the line and in Sonnet 2.
       churl . . . niggarding. An echo of Isaiah 32.5: 'Then shall the foolish
       niggard be no more called gentle, nor the churl liberal.' Wycliff
       introduced 'niggard' as a noun, but its extension here into the verb
       and gerund is probably new. Of the three examples cited in the
       Oxford English Dictionary, two are from Shakespeare and one from
       Robert Armin, a member of his theatre company.
       mak'st waste in niggarding. Another paradox: the young man is a
       wastrel because he hoards himself up. Compare Rosaline in *Romeo
       and Juliet* who, having sworn to live unmarried, 'in that sparing

makes huge waste. | For beauty, starved with her severity, | Cuts beauty off from all posterity' (I.1.218–20).

13   *glutton.* The poem's paradoxes converge on a word: wastefully starving, the youth greedily denies his appetite.

14   *the world's due.* The young man's children, his *increase*, here regarded as a 'duty' or a 'debt'.

     by the grave and thee. The *due* is twice devoured: by the young man (who consumes his *self-substantial fuel*), and by the *grave* (which consumes him, *thee*). An overlap with *Venus and Adonis* 757–60 is unmissable:

> 'What is thy body but a swallowing grave,
> Seeming to bury that posterity
> Which by the rights of time thou needs must have,
> If thou destroy them not in dark obscurity? . . .'

On a larger congruence between the early sonnets and this narrative poem, see the Introduction, pages 33, 38 and 62–3.

Sonnet 2

An early version of this sonnet is discussed and reprinted below, pages 442–3 and 444. The underlying influence on 1–19 of an Erasmian letter urging a young man to breed, not visible in 1609 until 3.5–6 (see the note), is particularly clear in the manuscript text; note the quotation on page 442.

1   *forty.* Here, as often, an indefinite large number: 'many'.
     winters (the passing years at their most chillingly destructive)
     brow forehead

2   *deep trenches* (wrinkles, dug by the years as they besiege the young man's *beauty*)
     field. The word has scope enough to contain its transformation by violence. The pleasant 'meadow' of the youth's *beauty* becomes a 'battle*field*' (as at *Henry V* III.5.39, for instance: 'More sharper than your swords, hie to the field!') scored with *trenches*. *Field* also suggests 'face, feature' (compare *The Rape of Lucrece* 72, 'her fair face's field'), an image evoked by *brow*. And the word has heraldic connotations, particularly appropriate to the well-born youth: a field is the background of an escutcheon on which devices are displayed. (Compare Sidney's claim that on Stella's face 'roses gules are borne on silver field', *Astrophil and Stella* 13.11.)

2, 4   *field . . . held.* The rhyme apparently sounded more like 'e' than 'ee', though something closer to 'fild . . . hild' is also possible.

3   *proud* magnificent (with perhaps a hint of vanity)
     livery. A stock description of the face and its expression ('her face

wore sorrow's livery', *The Rape of Lucrece* 1222, and so on), enlivened
by the surrounding metaphors. The *livery* is a 'soldier's uniform' –
gallant *now*, but after *forty winters* in the *field*, sadly *tattered*. The *livery*
is arguably also 'servant's attire' – the usual sense of the word,
though secondary here – in that the young man's *beauty* is not
properly his but lent him for a period of employment.

4   *weed* (1) garment; (2) wild plant. The latter, drawn out by *beauty's
field* (with its echo of *beauty's rose* in Sonnet 1, as though that flower
became, after *forty winters*, an aged and torn hedgerow pest), is
enriched by the Q spelling of *tattered*, 'totter'd', which implies not
just ragged disorder but the slumped unsteadiness of a plant past its
prime.

5–8   *Then being asked . . . praise.* A clear allusion to the parable of the
talents (Matthew 25.14–30), in which God is a lord who gives his
servants money for *use* (see line 9 and the note) and who chastises as
a thrifty unthrift the servant who hoards up the loan for safety's sake.

6   *lusty* vigorous, spirited (with evident sexual overtones)

7   *thine own deep-sunken eyes.* The *eyes* which were *bright* at 1.5, sunk
into a spare aged face. Conceivably the *eye* for 'I' pun, prominent in
such later sonnets as 148 and 152, acts here to identify as selves the
children buried in the self.

8   *all-eating shame* (1) matter for such shame that you would be
consumed by self-recrimination; (2) shameful piece of gluttony (see
1.13–14) to have to admit to
thriftless praise (1) praise for your wasteful unprofitableness; (2)
praise which will not profit you

9   *deserved thy beauty's use* the prudent investment (or 'profitable em-
ployment') of your beauty would deserve. At this point, 'usury' is
merely latent in *use*, and its bawdy implication, explicit at 6.5–6, is
only hinted.

11   *sum my count* add up the balance sheet of my doings (and) make up
the odds in the audit of my life
make my old excuse justify me when I am old

12   *Proving.* The logical and mathematical sense elicited by line 11,
complicated by hints of a legal hearing, is modified by the idea of
'verifying through experience'.
succession right of inheritance

13   *were* would be
new made when thou art old. What had seemed an inversion in line 12
becomes a paradox: the youth, grown old, will somehow inherit the
beauty of his *child*.

14   *And see thy blood . . . cold.* The line turns on two notions not now
credited: that the *blood* of a young man, being full of fiery passion, is
distinctly hotter than that of an old; that the *blood* which flows in

a son's veins is essentially the same as that which flows through his father's. Hence Henry V to his soldiers at Harfleur, 'On, on, you noblest English, | Whose blood is fet from fathers of war-proof!' (III.1.18–19), or, in lines which bear directly on the early sonnets (and especially the vial images of 5 and 6), the Duchess of Gloucester at *Richard II* I.2.11–22, comparing Edward III's sons to 'seven vials of his sacred blood'.

Sonnet 3

1   *glass* mirror

2   *another. Face* should be understood, though the Q spacing, 'an other', helpfully points towards its extension, 'an Other, another person'.

3   *repair* condition (maintained by restoration, upkeep, care)

4   *beguile* seductively deceive, cheat

    unbless some mother deprive some woman of maternity (using *mother* before she exists to make the youth's denial theft. This use of 'blessing' was standard; hence Hamlet's riddle (II.2.184–6): 'Conception is a blessing. But as your daughter may conceive, friend, look to't'.)

5–6   *For where is . . . husbandry.* Echoes a model letter in Erasmus's *De Conscribendis Epistolis* in which a young nobleman is urged to marry. Shakespeare apparently knew the epistle from Thomas Wilson's translation included in his *Art of Rhetoric* (1553): 'If that man be punished who little heedeth the maintenance of his tillage . . . what punishment is he worthy to suffer that refuseth to plough that land which, being tilled, yieldeth children.'

5   *uneared* unploughed (so not reduced to *tillage*). For the sexual implication of 'to ear' (from Old English *erian*, 'to plough'), see *Antony and Cleopatra* II.2.233, 'He ploughed her, and she cropped.' Cropping points, however, to the further suggestion that the *womb*, being unploughed and uncultivated, is not yet fruitful, lacks the 'ears' of grain with which children might be compared.

6   *husbandry* (1) agricultural duties; (2) sexual responsibilities as a husband

7–8   *Or who is . . . posterity.* Reverting to the theme of *Venus and Adonis* 757–60; see the second note to 1.14.

7   *fond* (1) loving (here, self-loving); (2) foolish

    tomb. Frequently in Shakespeare the resting place of several generations of a noble family (compare the tombs of the Andronici, *Titus Andronicus* I.1, or the Capulets, *Romeo and Juliet* V.3). The youth entombs the future of his house.

8   *Of.* Elliptically 'because of' as well as simply possessive.

9   *glass* mirror. In Elizabethan usage, *glass* – and indeed 'mirror' –
      suggests an exemplary, rather than merely faithful, image. Hence
      Ophelia's praise of Hamlet as 'The glass of fashion and the mould of
      form' (III.1.154). Shakespeare begins to hint at the main theme of
      his sestet: that paradoxical inversion which makes a child's features
      the model for its parent's. In line 11, the vitreous mirror wittily
      transmutes into a casement.

10   *April.* 'In the April of one's age' was proverbial. On the season see
      the note to 18.3.
      prime. 'Point of greatest excellence', as in modern English, but with
      stronger overtones of 'early' (as in 'primal' or 'primary'). *Prime* was
      also used to mean 'spring' (see 97.7), and this is drawn out here by
      April.

11   *windows of thine age* eyes bleared by old age. Elizabethan windows
      were much less transparent than our own.

12   *Despite of wrinkles* in spite of your wrinkles. This phrase abandons
      neither the *windows* of line 11 nor the *glass* (line 9) which prompted
      them, for it suggests the gazer peering *through* translucent *windows* at
      a child, only to *see*, in the *glass* before him, the outline of his *face* and
      the lines upon his *brow*.

13   *remembered not to be* only to be forgotten. There is an undercurrent of
      intention ('in order that you'll not be remembered') which makes the
      young man's singleness seem particularly wilful.

14   *image.* A word which, starting from the notion of a mirror-image
      (lines 1 and 9), suggests reproduction on several levels, from
      mechanical copying (as at 11.14) to an imagined impression or
      mental *image* or *remembered* idea (and *The Tempest* I.2.43–4, 'Of any
      thing the image tell me, that | Hath kept with thy remembrance', is
      relevant). The notion that nature forged itself like art, and that art
      fleshed out its works like nature, stayed with Shakespeare to the end:
      'Your mother . . . did print your royal father off, | Conceiving you',
      says Leontes to Florizel; 'Were I but twenty-one, | Your father's
      image is so hit in you, | His very air, that I should call you brother'
      (*The Winter's Tale* V.1.123–7).

Sonnet 4

In the next ten sonnets, and residually thereafter, the influence of Marlowe's
Hero and Leander (published in 1598, but available in manuscript during the
early 1590s) is important. Particularly relevant are these lines from the First
Sestiad, in which the lover, Leander, woos his mistress:

> Then treasure is abused
> When misers keep it; being put to loan,
> In time it will return us two for one . . .
> Who builds a palace and rams up the gate,
> Shall see it ruinous and desolate.
> Ah simple Hero, learn thyself to cherish;
> Lone women like to empty houses perish.
> Less sins the poor rich man that starves himself
> In heaping up a mass of drossy pelf,
> Than such as you: his golden earth remains,
> Which, after his decease, some other gains;
> But this fair gem, sweet in the loss alone,
> When you fleet hence, can be bequeathed to none.
> Or if it could, down from th'enamelled sky
> All heaven would come to claim this legacy,
> And with intestine broils the world destroy,
> And quite confound nature's sweet harmony . . .
> One is no number; maids are nothing then,
> Without the sweet society of men.
> Wilt thou live single still? one shalt thou be,
> Though never-singling Hymen couple thee . . .
> Base bullion for the stamp's sake we allow,
> Even so for men's impression do we you.
> By which alone, our reverend fathers say,
> Women receive perfection every way.

(lines 234–68)

1   *Unthrifty* (1) wasteful; (2) unprofitable. Compare *thriftless* at 2.8.
     spend. As the sonnet unfolds, 'use, expend' gives way to 'dispose of
     cash'.

2   *thy beauty's legacy* your inheritance of *loveliness*

4   *frank . . . free*. Both words mean 'generous', but the latter also implies
     sexual liberality. Shakespeare playfully glances at the stock phrase
     'frank and free', meaning 'not a serf', 'nobly open in temperament',
     and 'without let or hindrance'.
     those those who

5   *beauteous* (two syllables)

6   *bounteous* (two syllables)

7–8 *Profitless usurer . . . live* usurer making no profit (with a hint of 'usurer
     no good to anybody'), why is it that although you loan out for interest
     (but actually 'use up, exhaust') so many sizeable sums of money you
     still can't get enough to live on? The last phrase, *yet canst not live*, also
     has suggestions of 'don't really lead a full life' (being childless) and
     'are not able to survive after death' (picking up the imagery of

3.13-14). Compare the play on *live* at *The Merchant of Venice* IV.1.373-4, where the *usurer*, Shylock, says to the Duke: 'You take my life | When you do take the means whereby I live.'

8   *sum of sums* quantity of quantities-of-money. A stock phrase, derived from the Latin tag *summa summarum* and meaning 'the grand total, the ultimate result', here wittily redeployed.

9   *having traffic with* (1) trading with; (2) being sexually fascinated by. Some readers find in *traffic with thyself* a hint of masturbation; but the innuendo can be nothing more.

9, 11   *alone . . . gone.* The first of several such rhymes, based on long 'o' (sounding like the vowel in 'wart' or 'ward' in Scottish English now).

12-13   *What acceptable audit . . . thee.* Adopting the imagery of 2.11 and 3.7-8. *Acceptable* is accented on the first syllable, with a lesser stress on the third. An *audit* – important image in the Sonnets and developed towards 126.11 – is, of course, a 'final account, summary reckoning'.

13   *unused* not invested for profit

14   *executor* person appointed by a testator to see that his assets are disposed of according to the terms of his will

Sonnet 5

1   *hours* (two syllables). Probably referring to the Seasons (the *Horae* of Latin poetry) as well as to units of time; hence *summer* and *winter* in lines 5-6, 9, and 13.
gentle work (1) tenderly careful industry; (2) refined workmanship. And compare the note to *frame*.
frame make. But *work* suggests a substantive behind the verb, and an image of the *hours* as *gentle*women weaving the young man's beauty in a tapestry-*frame* results.

2   *gaze* object raptly looked upon (but it is impossible to exclude a sense that what is viewed so eagerly is itself a *gaze*, eyes meeting eyes)
dwell linger

3   *play the tyrants to* cruelly oppress (in harsh opposition to *gentle* in line 1. The phrase 'play the tyrant' remains idiomatic.)

4   *unfair* make ugly (something *unfair*, indeed, in the sense 'unjust')
fairly (1) in loveliness; (2) completely; (3) without cheating in any way. (An inaugurative ambiguity, expressing a knot of concerns explored later, in poems on false and dishonest beauty.)

5   *leads . . . on* (1) acts as guide to; (2) goes before like a herald (which makes *summer* merely *winter's* servant); (3) lures, beguiles into disadvantage. The enjambed movement from line 5 to 6 makes (3), initially latent, suddenly and shockingly primary.

6   *confounds* destroys. Informed, as often in Shakespeare, by the im-
      plications of Latin *confundere*: 'to pour together, topple in confusion,
      bewilder, disastrously mingle'.

7   *checked.* Because it is generally applied to moving things 'curbed' or
      'halted', *checked* here implies the circulation of the *Sap* which it stops.
      lusty full of vigour, bursting with the joy of growth

8   *bareness everywhere.* The phrase is moved towards paradox ('nothing
      all over the place') by its own *bareness*, striking after the strongly
      personified *hideous winter* and *Beauty* (supported by 1.2, 2.2, and 4.2
      and 13) and the vividly concrete line 7.

9–14   *Then, were not . . . sweet.* In Sidney's *Arcadia* (published in 1590),
      Cecropia recommends marriage thus: 'Have you ever seen a pure
      rose-water kept in a crystal glass, how fine it looks, how sweet it
      smells while that beautiful glass imprisons it? Break the prison, and
      let the water take its own course; doth it not embrace dust and lose all
      his former sweetness and fairness? Truly so are we, if we have not
      the stay, rather than the restraint, of crystalline marriage' (III.5).
      Shakespeare adopts Sidney's image, but he makes the vial an
      emblem not of married chastity but of what Sonnet 1 calls *increase*: it
      is the child who will preserve his father's beauty (5.9–14), or the
      procreative womb of that child's mother (6.3–4). See the note to
      2.14.

9   *summer's distillation* the essence of summer (understood as the
      perfume of its flowers)

9–10   *left | A liquid prisoner.* The formal break and rhyme on *left* delicately
      suspend line 10, without insisting that it be read as a parenthesis.

10   *A liquid prisoner pent in walls of glass.* The suggestion of con-
      straint seems significant. Is the poet's approval of breeding already
      qualified?

10, 12   *glass . . . was.* A perfect rhyme, both words using the short 'a' still
      current in northern pronunciations of *glass*, and with the 's' of *was*
      like 'ss' not 'z'.

11   *effect* (1) property; (2) consequence, impact. Most immediately,
      Beauty's effect is the *summer's distillation* of line 9.
      were bereft would be taken away

12   *Nor it nor no remembrance what it was.* Elliptical and ambiguous: 'and
      we would be left both without beauty and without a reminder (or the
      memory) of what beauty had been'.

14   *Leese* lose. An unusual form – found nowhere else in Shakespeare
      and unrecorded after the seventeenth century – doubtless employed
      for a pun on 'lease'; compare 13.5, *that beauty which you hold in lease.*
      show . . . substance. The phrase 'More show than substance' was
      proverbial.
      still (1) nevertheless; (2) always

Sonnet 6

1   *Then let not.* The argument continues from Sonnet 5.
       ragged rough in appearance (and conduct), shaggy, clad in beggarly
       rags (compare 'churlish winter' at *2 Henry IV* I.3.62)
       deface. The loving attention paid to the young man's *face* in Sonnets
       1, 2, 3, and 5 lends this verb an aggressive physicality: 'unface,
       ravage the features'.

3   *treasure* (1) cherish; (2) fill with treasure

5–6 *That use . . . loan* usurers are not forbidden to lend money for interest
       when their debtors are willing to be in debt on usurious terms and
       pleased to repay what they owe. *That use* distinguishes 'that kind of
       use' from the other kind ('profitable investment') discussed in earlier
       sonnets. *Not forbidden* consequently negotiates a moral problem:
       Elizabeth legalized usury in 1571, but it was frowned on long
       after. The lines apply to the youth, of course, because the *vial* of
       line 3 is a 'mother's womb' (see the note to 5.9–14) and be-
       cause *use* could carry a sexual sense: 'that *use* which is inter-
       course is entirely acceptable when it makes some woman (who, by
       returning the young man's seed as progeny, *pays the willing loan*)
       happy'.

6, 8 *loan . . . one.* Another full rhyme using the long 'o' discussed in the
       note to 4.9, 11.

7   *That's for thyself to breed another thee* that is, when you beget a child in
       your likeness

8   *ten times happier be it ten for one* you (or 'she', the happied mother of
       line 6, or simply 'the situation') would be *ten times happier* if instead of
       one child you had *ten*. *Ten for one* alludes to and wittily inverts the top
       legal rate of interest, 10 per cent, 'one for ten'.

9   *Ten times thyself were happier than thou art* (1) you would be happier if
       you lived in ten likenesses rather than just as you do; (2) it would
       indeed be a fortunate state of affairs (happier than now) if you lived
       in ten likenesses of yourself

10   *If ten of thine ten times refigured thee* if you had ten children all
       duplicating you (with a play on 'figure' as 'numeral', and an allusion,
       through the same word, to one of the young man's physical excel-
       lences). On a secondary level, the line runs away with itself, *ten of
       thine ten times* suggesting one hundred grandchildren, a joyous
       proliferation of the *posterity* described by line 12.

12   *Leaving thee living in posterity.* Subtly paradoxical, since *Leaving*
       includes both the *depart*ure of line 11 and the 'staying behind' of
       living in posterity; while a third sense registers because *in posterity*
       means 'in perpetuity' as well as 'in your children', so that *Leaving thee*
       can be 'bequeathing yourself'.

13   *self-willed* (1) obstinate; (2) bequeathed to yourself (instead of to your children, 'in perpetuity')

14   *death's conquest* (1) someone overcome by Death; (2) property acquired (in this context, at or by *death*) without inheritance (the standard sense of *conquest* in feudal law, still employed in Scotland) *and make worms thine heir.* As the body conquered by Death decays and feeds worms, *conquest* (in its legal sense) becomes inheritance.

Sonnet 7

A number of the sonnets – 7 being the first, 19 and 60 the most distinguished – are indebted to Ovid's *Metamorphoses* XV.214–36:

> Our bodies also aye
> Do alter still from time to time, and never stand at stay.
> We shall not be the same we were today or yesterday.
> The day hath been, we were but seed and only hope of men,
> And in our mother's womb we had our dwelling place as then,
> Dame Nature put to cunning hand and suffered not that we
> Within our mother's strainèd womb should aye distressed be,
> But brought us out to air, and from our prison set us free.
> The child newborn lies void of strength. Within a season though
> He waxing fourfooted learns like savage beasts to go.
> Then somewhat faltering, and as yet not firm of foot, he stands
> By getting somewhat for to help his sinews in his hands.
> From that time growing strong and swift, he passeth forth the space
> Of youth, and also wearing out his middle age apace,
> Through drooping age's steepy path he runneth out his race.
> This age doth undermine the strength of former years, and throws
> It down: which thing old Milo by example plainly shows.
> For when he saw those arms of his (which heretofore had been
> As strong as ever Hercules in working deadly teen
> Of biggest beasts) hang flapping down, and nought but empty skin,
> He wept. And Helen when she saw her aged wrinkles in
> A glass, wept also: musing in herself what men had seen,
> That by two noble princes' sons she twice had ravished been.
> Thou time, the eater up of things, and age of spiteful teen,
> Destroy all things. And when that long continuance hath them bit,
> You leisurely by lingering death consume them every whit.
>
> (Golding's translation)

1   *Lo* behold (but doubtless with a play on 'low', since the sun at sunrise only just peeps over the horizon)
            orient. Both 'east' and 'East'. For the latter sense, and perhaps the

imagined background of this sonnet's sun-worship, see *Love's Labour's Lost* IV.3.219–23:

> Who sees the heavenly Rosaline
> That, like a rude and savage man of Inde
>   At the first opening of the gorgeous east,
> Bows not his vassal head and, strucken blind,
>   Kisses the base ground with obedient breast?

    gracious (exploiting a cluster of connotations, 'noble, indulgent to inferiors, graceful in bearing and aura, holy, admired')
    light (the sun, defined by its most striking quality)

2   *under* (1) below (on the ground); (2) socially inferior (as at *The Winter's Tale* IV.2.35, 'I have eyes under my service'). The implicit 'over eye' is glossed by 18.5.

2, 4   *eye . . . majesty.* A full rhyme, resembling *die* and *memory* at 1.2 and 4.

4   *Serving* (1) worshipping (like those at a church service); (2) attending (servant-like)
    sacred majesty. His makes this a title, like 'his Holiness, the Pope', while claiming for the sun the quality of *sacred majesty*.

5   *steep-up* precipitous
    heavenly (1) of the sky; (2) sacred

6   *Resembling strong youth in his middle age.* At its zenith, the sun is like a strong youth grown middle-aged (though there is a suggestion that the sun retains the vigour of his youth at noon).

7   *Yet mortal looks adore his beauty still* nevertheless (although the first flush of youth is off him) mortals continue to reverently admire his beauty

8   *Attending on* watching. But the idea that *looks* are services paid to a king by inferiors (see line 4) persists, so that the sun is pictured as a monarch on a progress surrounded by attendants.

9–12   *But when . . . another way.* It was proverbial that 'The rising, not the setting, sun is worshipped by most men.' Hence the references in *Richard II* to the King in decline as a setting sun (II.4.21–2, III.3.178–83), and hence Apemantus's pithy 'Men shut their doors against a setting sun' at *Timon of Athens* I.2.142.

9   *highmost pitch* (1) very highest point; (2) loftiest and steepest slope. The sun's fall is anticipated: a *pitch* is the height to which a falcon flies before it stoops, and 'to *pitch*' is 'to throw down'.
    car chariot (traditional vehicle of Phoebus, the sun god)

11   *'fore* before
    converted turned aside

12   *tract* track, course

13   *thyself outgoing.* Like the concentrated poetry of selfhood in Shakespeare's *The Phoenix and Turtle*, this is hardly glossable.

'Outliving yourself (by outlasting maturity)', enlivened by the idea of extinguishing, of a *light* 'going out', in *outgoing* (hyphenated in Q).

13, 14   *noon . . . son*. Rhyming on a vowel rather like the 'u' in 'educated' southern 'put', lengthened.

14   *get* (1) acquire; (2) beget

son. If the young man is a 'sun', his *son* will be the same. The pun triumphs over a logical objection – would people not turn their eyes from a setting to a rising sun at least as promptly as from a setting sun with no successor? – by invoking the notion established in the sestet of Sonnet 6, that offspring recapitulate a parent.

Sonnet 8

For a variant text, conceivably incorporating authoritative early readings, see pages 442–3 and 444–5 below.

1   *Music to hear*. Anticipating the second half of line 1, 'Hearing music . . .', this also acts as a vocative, 'O you, whose voice is like music to my ears' – a sense which prevails by the end of line 2.

sadly gravely. But the sense 'regretfully, unwillingly' lies ready for line 3.

3–4   *Why lov'st thou . . . thine annoy*. The jest, 'why do you like music if it doesn't please you (and it can hardly please you if it makes you sad)', rests on the common experience described by Jessica at *The Merchant of Venice* V.1.69: 'I am never merry when I hear sweet music.'

4   *annoy* that which annoys (with the accent on *ennui*, the annoyance of melancholy and boredom)

5–8   *If the true . . . bear*. As at 5.9–14 and 6.3–4, Shakespeare reworks Cecropia's speech on marriage in *Arcadia* III.5: 'And is a solitary life as good as this? Then can one string make as good music as a consort.'

5   *true concord* finely toned harmony

6   *By unions married*. Alluding to the harmonies and unisons of polyphony (see the second note to line 8), but using terms with a general rather than specifically musical reference, to prepare the moral application of the metaphor in lines 7–14.

6, 8   *ear . . . bear*. The rhyme was nearer modern *bear* than *ear*, and apparently full.

7   *They* (the sounds which make up the *concord*. This use of a plural pronoun for singular subject helps draw attention to the paradoxical unity-in-variety of harmony.)

Sweetly chide thee gently chastise you. Until the object is reached, 'ring out loud and clear' also registers; compare *A Midsummer*

Night's Dream IV.1.111–17, where Hippolyta describes the 'music' of hounds in the field; 'Such gallant chiding ... So musical a discord, such sweet thunder.')

confounds destroys by mixing together, ruins by blending (see 5.6 and the note)

8   *singleness* (1) bachelorhood; (2) one thread of tune (as against pleasing polyphony)

   parts that thou shouldst bear (1) lines of melody which you should sing (as in a 'part-song') or, more likely, play; (2) talents which you should maintain (by breeding them into others); (3) other people, so close to you that they are *parts* of you, that you should support (compare *The Comedy of Errors* III.2.61, where Antipholus of Syracuse woos Luciana by calling her 'thyself, mine own self's better part'); (4) roles which you should perform (for you could be a husband and father instead of just a bachelor – indeed, you could also be a child, your own *image*, three parts in place of one; see lines 9 and 11)

9–12   *Mark how ... do sing.* Obscure. If the poet still has *concord* in mind, *mutual ordering* would refer to clever fingering on a lute or viol, designed to bring disparate strings into harmonious order (compare *The Taming of the Shrew* III.1.63, where, in a lute lesson, Hortensio promises to teach Bianca 'the order of my fingering'), while *Strikes each in each* would allude to the mutually ordered strings' bracingly percussive agreement (*Strikes* as both 'hits' and 'strikes a deal'), and *one pleasing note* would loosely cover the unity of diverse strings in *concord*. But it may be that the poet is thinking of sympathetic resonance on a double-strung lute, in which case the *mutual ordering* might refer to tuning (each string being brought to the same tension as its comrade), and *each in each* to the double resonance which creates the multiple unison of *one pleasing note.*

11   *sire* father

13   *speechless* wordless

14   *Thou single wilt prove none.* The *speechless song* wittily alludes to the proverb 'One is no number' (see the quotation from *Hero and Leander* in the headnote to Sonnet 4, and compare 136.8), while assuring the young man that if he remains unmarried and has no children he will be the last of his line.

Sonnet 9

3   *issueless* without children
   hap chance

4   *makeless wife* wife without a mate (*make*). The mild oxymoron is resolved in line 5.

5   *still* (1) constantly; (2) forever. With perhaps a hint of 'nevertheless'

(that is, 'despite the care you took not to leave a tearful *widow* behind').

6   *form* likeness. In the sense 'type' rather than modern 'copy', or as 'copy' is used in Shakespeare (see the note to 11.14 and the Introduction, pages 27–8). Arguably enriched by 'physical appearance, *shape*' (line 8), the *form* the *form* would take.

7   *private* (1) particular, individual (as against the *world* as *widow*); (2) living quietly out of the public eye (as widows should, taking *world* in the common Shakespearian sense 'sphere of public affairs'); (3) deprived, suffering (through a pun on 'private')

8   *By* by means of, by looking at
     eyes. As at 2.7, a pun on 'I's' is possible; certainly, the clever redeployment of the stock coupling of *eyes* with *mind* (see Sonnets 113–14 and *A Lover's Complaint* 89 and 135) prompts the reader to look for wordplay.

9   *Look what* whatever (though, as often, 'look here, consider that what . . .' registers)
     unthrift wastrel
     spend (1) expend, waste beyond recall; (2) outlay as cash

10   *his* its (though *his* can be applied, on another level, to the *unthrift* who falls in the social order because of his extravagance)
     still (1) even after it is spent; (2) nevertheless; (3) forever (since coins continue to circulate after what they buy has been consumed)
     enjoys has the use of, takes pleasure in

11   *beauty's waste* beauty prodigally spent. But there are hints of 'waste by a beautiful person' and 'beauty's decay'.

12   *And kept unused, the user so destroys it.* The line turns on the ambiguity of *use*: 'utilize, invest, turn to usury' and 'spend, consume, waste'. *So* means 'thus'.

13   *sits*. In Elizabethan literature, abstractions and minor gods like *love* are often presented as dignitaries enthroned. Compare, for example, *Richard III* V.3.352, 'Victory sits on our helms', or *The Two Noble Kinsmen* IV.2.12–14, 'What an eye, | Of what a fiery sparkle and quick sweetness, | Has this young prince! Here love himself sits smiling.'

14   *himself* (the *bosom* becomes the youth it represented by synecdoche)
     murd'rous shame shameful murder. (But a suggestion that *shame* will kill the young man if chastity doesn't is no doubt intended.)

Sonnet 10

1   *For shame*. Initially, this means 'Shame on you!' Reading on, and in the light of *murd'rous shame* at 9.14 (compare the *murd'rous hate* of

10.5), the editorial comma after *shame* falls away and 'Out of a sense of your own shame' results. The tonal duplicity is typical of this poem. On the surface politely critical, banteringly censorious (as befits a sonnet rebuking a social superior), it conveys a concern commensurate with the growing devotion registered in line 13's *for love of me* (with its first use of a first-person pronoun in the sequence, even if oblique). Words like *possessed*, *ruinate*, and *hate* (in lines 5, 7, and 10) seem slightly – yet revealingly – too strong for the argument they carry. And the recurring imperatives (*deny*, *Grant*, *change*, *Be*, *Make*), ostensibly softening from command (in line 1) to request (in the sestet), accumulate strenuously.

3   *Grant if thou wilt.* The parallel with *For shame, deny* adds assertion to a phrase which usually means, in all modesty, 'I admit . . .'.

5   *possessed with* (as though invaded by devils)

6   *thou stick'st not* you do not hesitate even

7   *Seeking that beauteous roof to ruinate.* The young man seeks to destroy his lovely body (conventionally the house of the soul) by refusing to *increase*; he therefore threatens destruction to his family, the house to which he belongs, and possibly (by implication) puts a real *roof* in jeopardy by leaving his property to chance and decay by neglecting to provide an heir. The image was probably suggested by *Hero and Leander* I.239–42 (see the headnote to Sonnet 4), Sonnet 7 in Spenser's *Ruines of Rome* (a translation of Du Bellay's *Antiquitez de Rome*, published in 1591), 'time in time shall ruinate | Your works and names' (referring to buildings), and the Erasmian letter discussed in the note to 3.5–6. Wilson's translation includes:

> Seeing also you are a man of great lands and revenues by your ancestors, the house whereof you came being both right honourable and right ancient, so that you could not suffer it to perish, without your great offence and great harm to the common weal. You notwithstanding cannot want great rebuke, seeing it lieth in your hands to keep that house from decay, whereof [you are] lineally descended, and to continue still the name of your ancestors.

The influence of Spenser's sequence on Shakespeare's is not as far-reaching as has recently been claimed (see Further Reading, page 72), but its thirty-three poems on the decline and decay of Rome seem to have left clear traces in Shakespeare's memory (see, for instance, 15.13, 63.2 and the notes). Moreover, in the light of *A Lover's Complaint*'s debt to *The Ruines of Time* (see pages 390–92) it seems likely that the *Ruines of Rome* – reinforced by Marlowe and Wilson – formatively linked in the poet's mind, as Hieatt claims, the potential ruin of the young man's beauty and the ruin of a city.

8	*repair* keep in good order
9	*change thy thought, that I may change my mind* think differently, so that I can alter my opinion of you
10	*be fairer lodged* have a better, more attractive, lodging (under the *roof* which is you)
11	*presence.* A word with a wide range of senses, from 'demeanour' to 'personality' and 'person'. The latter transmutes the first half of line 11 into a persuasive tautology: 'be as you are . . .'.
	kind. For Elizabethan readers, *kind*ness was that generosity which should be shown towards other members of human*kind* and particularly towards *kind*red. So the word incites the youth to create kin to be *kind* to.
13	*Make thee another self* breed a child in your likeness. With perhaps a hint of 'change your ways', as at *2 Henry IV* V.5.61, where Hal, become a stiffly unexceptionable Henry V, says to Falstaff 'I have turned away my former self'.
14	*still may* may continue to, may always
	live in (1) survive in; (2) lodge in (see line 10 and the note)
	thine or thee. Shakespeare employs a phrase often used to place someone in the context of her or his kin (see, for instance, *Titus Andronicus* I.1.49–50, 'so I love and honour thee and thine, | Thy noble brother Titus and his sons'), but reversed, to rehearse the paradox raised in line 13. Thus 'your children or your-children-who-are-you' might be the gloss.

Sonnet 11

1	*fast* quickly and steadily
2	*one of thine* a child of thine (see 10.4)
	that which thou departest (your youth)
2, 4	*departest . . . convertest.* A feminine rhyme sounding '-artest' not '-ertest', and the first of several in the Sonnets using the 'ar' for 'er' which persisted in certain words from medieval into Elizabethan spoken English.
3	*blood* lifeblood, life (passed through the family; see 2.14 and the note. Perhaps *departest* is marginally transitive, making *blood* 'semen'; certainly sperm was thought a distillation of the *blood*.)
	youngly (1) in youth; (2) with youthful vigour; (3) upon a youngling (a child)
	bestow'st (1) confer; (2) invest, give for keeping
4	*convertest* turn aside (as at 7.11, but with financial overtones here; currency can be 'converted')
5–6	*Herein lives . . . cold decay* within the scope of this policy, *wisdom,*

beauty, and increase reside, and if the plan is not effected, *folly, age, and cold decay* will accrue. *Herein* more obliquely refers to the child who would contain and convey the young man's virtue and virility.

7   *times* generations (extending a standard Shakespearian use of *time* for the span of someone's life)

8   *year* (not, as now, a markedly archaic plural)
     make . . . away dispose of
     the world (of men. But, for the first time in the poems, extending easily into the hyperbole 'everything on earth' and, in Elizabethan though not modern English, 'the cosmos'.)

9   *for store* (1) as breeding stock (farmers still speak of *store*-cattle); (2) for hoarding up (children inheriting parental qualities)

10   *featureless* without marks of distinction, shapeless, ugly
     rude crude, rough, bare

11   *Look whom* whomever
     Look whom she best endowed she gave the more. Like God in the parable of the talents, Nature gave more – including, perhaps, greater powers of generation – to those who already had most. The wit and authority of Shakespeare's tautology depends on its shadowing Matthew's paradox so closely: 'For unto everyone that hath shall be given, and he shall have abundance: But he that hath not, from him shall be taken away, even that which he hath' (25.29).

12   *bounteous . . . in bounty* generous . . . generously (shading into 'fecund . . . by increase')
     cherish. A word associated, in Elizabethan English, with nurturing and rearing.

13   *seal.* Not the wax but the stamp which marks it. A *seal* authenticates and displays authority; the young man shows the world what nature is and can do.

14   *copy.* Like *form* at 9.6, a 'pattern, type, something capable of producing copies' (rather than, as in modern usage, 'debased reproduction'). See the Introduction, pages 27–8.

Sonnet 12

Like the octave of Sonnet 73 – where the debt is, however, less apparent – heavily influenced by Ovid's *Metamorphoses* XV.199–216.

> What? seest thou not how that the year as representing plain
> The age of man, departs itself in quarters four? first bain [supple]
> And tender in the spring it is, even like a sucking babe.
> Then green, and void of strength, and lush, and foggy is the blade,
> And cheers the husbandman with hope. Then all things flourish gay.
> The earth with flowers of sundry hue then seemeth for to play,

And virtue small or none to herbs there doth as yet belong.
The year from springtide passing forth to summer, waxeth strong,
Becometh like a lusty youth. For in our life throughout
There is no time more plentiful, more lusty, hot, and stout.
Then followeth harvest when the heat of youth grows somewhat cold,
Ripe, mild, disposed mean betwixt a youngman and an old,
And somewhat sprent with greyish hair. Then ugly winter last
Like age steals on with trembling steps, all bald, or overcast
With shirl [rough] thin hair as white as snow. Our bodies also aye
Do alter still from time to time, and never stand at stay.
We shall not be the same we were today or yesterday.

(Golding's translation)

1   *count* add up (what the *clock* strikes)
     tells (1) utters; (2) counts out. The latter is evoked so strongly by *count*
     that the *clock* takes on a shrewdly calculating life of its own. (On
     which, and the poem in general, see the Introduction, page 38.)
2   *brave* splendid, gallantly clad
     hideous (two syllables, or three refusing to quite be two)
3   *violet* (three syllables)
     past prime (1) after its first excellence; (2) when the spring is over (a
     standard Elizabethan sense of *prime*)
4   *sable* black
     all silvered o'er. Q's 'or siluer'd ore' has been variously emended, but
     only the present reading and 'o'er-silvered all' seem plausible.
     'O'er-silvered all' is effective but static, emblematic rather than
     revelatory. If a head is 'o'er-silvered', then it must be 'all' covered
     with white; 'all' is pleonastic. But *all silvered o'er* simultaneously
     re-creates the shock of seeing a head which is *all* – ah yes – *silvered
     o'er*, and frees *all* and *o'er* from tautology by releasing *all*'s sense of
     intensity: 'absolutely grey all over' as well as 'all somehow grey all
     over'. (Observe, too, the subtle variation in line 7, *all girded up . . .*).
     'O'er silver'd all' is, in short, good Spenser, *all silvered o'er* good
     Shakespeare.
5   *lofty* high (but with the implication 'proud, arrogantly noble')
     barren (not just 'bare'; echoing the fear and threat of infertility raised
     at 11.10 by *barrenly perish*)
6   *erst* formerly
6, 8 *herd . . . beard.* Rhymed on a vowel nearer modern 'er' than 'ar'.
7   *girded* tied, bundled
8   *bier* (1) barrow for carrying harvested hay and grain; (2) stand upon
     which a corpse rests or is carried. One word catches up the lives of
     men and *plants* (see 15.5–8) as they reach a common conclusion.
     Perhaps Shakespeare meant to conflate a festive 'harvest home' (in

which the last load of grain is brought in with flowers and images)
with a solemn funeral.

white and bristly beard. The awn which grows on grains like oats and
barley; but consider, too, a man lying on his *bier*, bearded (as most
Elizabethan men were), or bearing on his face the stubble which
grows after death.

9   *of thy beauty do I question make* I speculate about your beauty
(wondering how long it will last)

10   *thou among the wastes of time must go* you must take a place among the
things destroyed by Time. But a mysterious 'you must wander in
Time's waste-lands' – gesturing, perhaps, towards an after-life –
also registers.

11   *sweets and beauties* sweet and lovely things
themselves forsake (1) change from what they were (through decay);
(2) depart from themselves, or their selves (towards and into death.
Compare *thyself outgoing* at 7.13.)

12   *others.* Primarily 'other *sweets and beauties*'; but the suggestion that
'*others* of perhaps less note' will sprout where excellence has been is
distinctly felt.

13   *scythe.* Time's traditional weapon, sharpened here by association
with the reaping of lines 7–8.

14   *brave* defy

Sonnet 13

The poet takes a further step towards intimacy (for the first, see 10.13 and
the note to 10.1) by shifting from 'thou' to 'you'. Usage was complex in the
late sixteenth century, and in some contexts 'thou' remained more familiar
than 'you' (as with modern French *tu* and *vous*). This older pattern of address
was modified, however, by the increasingly archaic, formal ring of 'thou' in
literary circumstances, so that, in seeking a less conventional idiom,
Shakespeare – like Samuel Daniel when writing poems to patrons in the
same period – substituted 'you' for 'thou'. 'Thou' recurs in Sonnet 14 – as
though the liberty so convolutedly taken in 13 were too great – and in many
sonnets thereafter (especially in invocatory contexts, where the formal timbre
of 'thou' is consciously exploited). Significantly, it is invariable in poems to
the dark lady, though the generally anomalous 145 admits a 'you' used of the
poet to clinch a rhyme.

1   *O that you were yourself.* Initially supported by a play on 'you are not
yourself', meaning 'you are out of sorts', the paradox becomes more
weighty with *you yourself* in line 2. The first *yourself* is an imagined
absolute, beyond chance and Time, the latter quotidian, subject to
the decay described by Sonnet 12.

1, 3   *are . . . prepare.* Rhymed on a long 'a' in *are* not standard at the time.
        In sound, the final effect would be closer to modern 'ar' than 'er'.

2   *here* (in the world)

3   *Against* in expectation of
        this (making concrete and tangible what might, with 'the', seem
        merely abstract)

4   *semblance* likeness

6   *determination* conclusion, termination. In legal language, an ended
        lease has 'determined'.

6–7   *you were . . . decease* you would be *yourself* (sense of line 2 supported by
        that of line 1) once more after the death of *yourself* (sense of line 2).
        Q's 'You selfe again' might just be right, meaning 'you, the very
        same, over again'; but the real temptation is to follow Q's spacing for
        'your selfes decease', underlining the ambiguity on which the line
        depends.

8   *your sweet issue . . . bear* (1) your children (stamped with your
        likeness) would look like you; (2) your children would give birth to
        children resembling you; (3) your children would carry *your sweet
        form* on *the bier* (echoing the corresponding line of the previous
        sonnet to promise the young man that he can be alive even as he is
        carried to the grave)

9   *lets* allows (with a quibbling echo of *lease*)
        house. As with *roof* at 10.7, the body and kin predominate over images
        of bricks and mortar.

10   *husbandry* management of a *house*hold (with an obvious play on
        'being a husband'). In Shakespeare, generally applied to good
        economy (as against the waste of line 13's *unthrifts*).

12   *barren rage* anger which robs the world of fertility. In Elizabethan
        English, *rage* lies somewhere between 'furious passion' and the
        'savagery' produced by fury. But the shock of the phrase lies less in
        its concretion of *rage* than in its inversion of violence and violence's
        consequence (the *barren*ness being put before the rage), a reversal
        which make's *death's* anger seem as *barren* of purpose as in effect.

13–14   *O, none but . . . say so.* Q's punctuation is ambiguous, and an
        alternative (though less dramatic) punctuation would endstop line
        13: 'O, none but unthrifts, dear my love. You know | you had a father
        – let your son say so.' The intimacy of *Dear my love* (a clear advance
        from 10.13's *for love of me*) confirms the gesture made in using *you*,
        not 'thou' (see the headnote).

14   *let your son say so.* Generous duress: the words deliver the *son* which is
        being urged, so that to deny him would seem more like murder than
        indifference.

Sonnet 14

1   *judgement pluck.* Though *judgement* could mean 'wisdom' (and some-
     thing of that registers here), the predominant sense is *knowledge* (as
     in line 9). *Pluck* is carefully nonchalant: 'pick like fruit off a tree'.

2   *have astronomy* understand astrology

4   *seasons' quality* the nature of the seasons (whether spring will be wet
     this year, etc.)

5   *to brief minutes.* See the second note to 126.8 and the Introduction,
     page 35.

6   *Pointing to each his* assigning to each minute its. The satirical edge
     apparent in *pluck* (line 1) is sustained in *Pointing*, with its suggestion
     that the astrologer commands the elements by deciphering the stars.

6, 8 *wind . . . find.* Apparently rhymed on a diphthong resembling 'u-ee'
     or 'i-ee'.

7   *with princes if it shall go well* whether certain rulers will be fortunate

8   *By oft predict that I in heaven find* by means of frequent predictions
     which I find signified in the sky. *Oft* can be applied either to the
     predictor or to the message which he decodes.

9–10 *thine eyes . . . constant stars.* A commonplace comparison, but evi-
     dently inspired here by the twenty-sixth sonnet ('Though dainty wits
     dare scorn astrology') of Sidney's *Astrophil and Stella* (published in
     1591). Central to that poem, and functioning like Shakespeare's
     constant stars, are the 'two stars in Stella's face'.

10–11 *in them I read such art | As* in those eyes I discover such learning as, in
     effect, that. On a secondary level, the idiomatic association *such . . .
     As* allows *art* to be the object of thrive, so that *truth and beauty* seem to
     conspire to make a higher *art* than astrology succeed.

10, 12 *art . . . convert.* Rhyming on 'ar', not 'er', like 11.2 and 4 (see the
     note).

12   *If from . . . convert* if you would turn from yourself (eschewing
     narcissism) and breed children. See 11.4 and 9 and the notes.

14   *end* death (but with a censorious suggestion of intent: 'you purpose
     the destruction of *truth and beauty*')
     date limit in time (probably 'fixed by decree'. In the *constant stars* of
     line 10, the poet sees that, if the young man does not breed, those
     eyes decree destruction to themselves and to the *truth and beauty*
     which in one sense they are.)

Sonnet 15

1–2   *When I consider . . . moment.* The shock which registers when *Holds*
     jolts line 1 out of the pattern established by 2.1 and 12.1 into an
     ellipsis ('*When I consider* that *everything that grows*') is functional: the

great sweep of the first line records the grandeur of a world suddenly shown to be vulnerable at the turn into line 2.

2   *Holds in perfection* (1) stays at the point of perfection; (2) preserves perfection within itself

3   *this huge stage presenteth naught but shows.* A renaissance commonplace; compare *As You Like It* II.7.138–40, 'This wide and universal theatre | Presents more woeful pageants than the scene | Wherein we play in', and Jaques' reply, 'All the world's a stage . . .'.

4   *Whereon the stars in secret influence comment.* The *stars*, watching the world like the audience in a theatre (or like the 'gods' who 'laugh' at the 'unnatural scene' in *Coriolanus* V.3.184–6), make unheard criticisms which change the course of the action. Renaissance astrologers believed that the *stars* affected men by pouring down an ethereal fluid; this they called *influence*. (The line is not Alexandrine; *influence* has two syllables; and *comment* is accented on the first syllable, producing a feminine ending.)

6   *Cheerèd* encouraged
      checked restrained, rebuked
      even (one syllable)
      the selfsame sky the very same heavens (the *sky* which the *stars* of line 4 inhabit. More broadly, perhaps, 'the heavens, which, despite their fluctuating appearance, temper, and effect on men, remain essentially the same'.)

6, 8 *sky . . . memory.* A full rhyme, resembling 1.2 and 4.

7   *Vaunt in their youthful sap* exult in the possession of youthful vitality. But *in* also registers temporally (young men exult while they are young) and, looking back from a sonnet like 108, almost sartorially (youths swagger about, adorned with the flush of their vigour).
      at height decrease reaching the height of their powers, men (like plants which reach full growth and then decay) immediately start to decline

8   *And wear their brave state out of memory.* The line unfolds ambiguities as it proceeds. The *brave state* ('boldly vigorous condition'; 'splendid attire'; 'gallant air') that the *men* of line 5 *wear* ('enjoy'; *wear* quite literally; 'display') at their *height* (line 7) gradually *wears out* ('becomes exhausted, is lost with use'; 'gets reduced to rags') and so *wears out of memory* ('is eroded from the world's, and perhaps *their* own, recollection of what they once were').

9   *conceit* (1) apprehension; (2) idea of an intricate or far-fetched sort. The latter suggests the poet's bewilderment that life should be so strangely directed towards decline.
      this inconstant stay. Recalling the first quatrain, *this* evokes 'point of rest held fleetingly' from *inconstant stay*; recalling the second, 'residence in the mutable, sojourn in the uncertain'. For the latter, see Ovid's *Metamorphoses* XV.177–80 in Golding's translation: 'In all

the world there is not that that standeth at a stay. | Things ebb and flow, and every shape is made to pass away. | The time itself continually is fleeting like a brook.'

10   *rich in* (1) full of; (2) enriched by. If Shakespeare's young man was an aristocrat, the scion of some great house, there would be a third, complimentary, and literal sense, 'wealthy at the time of your'.

11   *Where* (in the poet's *sight*)
      wasteful destructive, squandering

11–12   *Time debateth with Decay,* | *To.* 'Time and Decay discuss how best they may', or 'Time and Decay compete to be the promptest to', or 'Time, through the agency of Decay, contends (against you) to'. That last can hardly be primary, but it does anticipate line 13, where *Time* is offered as the youth's sole foe.

12   *sullied night.* The contrast with *day of youth* suggests 'old age, with all its disfigurements' rather than 'death'.

13   *all in war* battling with all my might. The poet replaces *Decay* as *Time*'s antagonist.
      war with Time. Like 10.7, echoing Sonnet 7 of Spenser's *Ruines of Rome*: 'And though your frames do for a time make war | 'Gainst Time'.

14   *As he takes from you I engraft you new* as Time wastes you I give you new life. An engrafter introduces a cutting from one plant into the stock of another to produce flowers and fruit from new growth; similarly, the poet makes the young man flourish as he ages by grafting him into his verse. Though a pun on *graphein* (Greek for 'to write') can probably be ruled out – *engraft* seems fully motivated by the vegetable imagery of lines 5–8 – the idea of writing does clinch the poem, and this marks an important point in Shakespeare's argued meditation on breeding and verse as means to immortality (Sonnets 1–19).

Sonnet 16

1   *But wherefore.* The argument continues from Sonnet 15.
     a mightier way by a more potent method (than my engrafting)
     mightier (two syllables)

3   *fortify* strengthen. A suggestion of siege-works and fortification, following from *war* (line 2).
     in your decay in your decaying condition. *Fortify* elicits 'within' from *in*, creating an image which anticipates 146.1–4.

4   *With means more blessèd* (1) through something more effectual (interpreting *blessèd* as 'favoured with success'); (2) by breeding

(allowing *barren* to evoke the sexual connotations of *blessèd*: see 3.4 and the note on *unbless*)

my barren rhyme. Beyond the obvious ('unlike wombs, my poems bear no children') lies an elegant apology ('my verses are so inadequate'), anticipating such sonnets as 76.

5   *top* zenith (from which *you* must decline. The *highmost pitch* of 7.9 and *height* of 15.7.)

6   *unset* unplanted

6, 8   *unset . . . counterfeit*. Though the pronunciation 'counterfit' was common in the period, '-et' is the basis of this rhyme.

7   *With virtuous wish would bear your living flowers* would willingly but chastely bear your children

virtuous (two syllables)

8   *liker* more like (to you)

counterfeit portrait

9   *lines of life* (1) lineage (with a suggestion of the *lines* used on genealogical charts to show descent); (2) offspring (vital, not merely *painted*, portraits of the young man's living outline, the *form* of the youth reborn in his children); (3) lines on the hand (examined by palmists to judge life expectancy, extrapolated here by lineage and offspring)

10   *this time's pencil or my pupil pen* the brushes wielded by today's painters or the quill which I, a mere beginner in poetry, employ. Q's accidentals – 'this (Times pensel or my pupill pen)' – are unacceptable, though sometimes accepted; for if 'this' (as 'this sonnet') can be equated with 'my pupill pen' by metonymy, it can scarcely stand in apposition to 'Times pensel'.

11   *inward worth* excellence of character

outward fair beauty of appearance

12   *live* survive as

in eyes of men before men's eyes. The phrase is enriched by a suggestion of 'in the world's opinion', and by the possibility that *men* refers to the youth's offspring (compare 9.8).

13   *give away yourself* ('in marriage' or 'to your children')

keeps maintains, preserves (quibblingly opposed to *give away*)

still (1) despite the giving; (2) even after the giving; (3) forever

14   *you must live drawn by your own sweet skill*. Various emphases are possible: 'if you want to survive, you must do so through your sexual artistry, not through my verse or other men's painting'; 'you have a positive obligation to live by breeding yourself'; 'if you produce children you will definitely live after your death'. The penis, mightier than the word, replaces the *pencil* and *pen* of lines 10–12; see Gratiano's explicit 'I'll mar the young clerk's pen' at *The Merchant of Venice* V.1.237.

Sonnet 17

1–8   *Who will believe . . . faces.* Some editors put a question mark after line
      1, making 2–8 a single sentence with a two-line parenthesis (3–4);
      but the present arrangement (based on Q) seems more Shake-
      spearian.

1, 3 *come . . . tomb.* A common rhyme in the Sonnets, with a silent 'b' and
      vowel probably resembling the short 'u' of 'educated' southern 'put'
      (though perhaps long, sounding like the 'oo' of 'mood').

2   *were filled with your most high deserts* fully expressed (and so rewarded)
      your merits. Exploiting an ambiguity in *deserts*: both 'deservings' and
      what they earn.

2, 4 *deserts . . . parts.* This rhyme, characterized at 11.2 and 4 (see the
      note), is spelled out by Q's 'desart' at 49.10.

3   *yet* as yet. Having a *pupil pen* (16.10), the poet writes badly, but hopes
      to improve.

3, 8 *heaven . . . heavenly* (one and two syllables)

3–4   *a tomb | Which hides your life.* Initially paradoxical (*a tomb* usually
      covers a corpse), the words settle into sense as the memorial
      inscriptions on sepulchres come ironically to mind. The poet is
      preparing a metaphorical monument which is so badly composed
      that it fails to communicate the quality of the young man's *life* (the
      brilliance of his 'career', his exquisite 'vitality').

4   *parts* good qualities

5   *write the beauty of your eyes.* A direct object declares the poet's radical
      ambition: not to write about but inscribe beauty on the page. In later
      sonnets the implications of this desire are involutedly pursued.

6   *fresh numbers* novel and stimulating verses

8   *heavenly touches.* In the imagined sonnet these 'ravishing strokes of
      art' derive from the youth, in the youth himself from God (which
      makes them, indeed, *heavenly*).

10   *old men of less truth than tongue* (alluding to the proverb 'Old men and
      far travellers may lie by authority'. *Less truth than tongue* means 'more
      talkative than honest'.)

10, 12 *tongue . . . song.* There was some freedom in the pronunciation of
      these words. The rhyme probably rests on a vowel like 'educated'
      southern 'u' ('sung' for *song*), though 'o' ('tong' for *tongue*) is
      possible.

11   *your true rights.* A pun on 'rites' allows 'the ritual of praise appropriate
      to you' as well as, primarily, 'the praise which is your due'.
      a poet's rage the frenzied outpourings of an inspired (rather than
      dispassionate) writer (alluding to the classical *furor poeticus*)

12   *stretchèd metre of an antique song* far-fetched piece of verse (with a
      modestly unnecessary apology for writing not-quite-metrical,

stretchèd, numbers) in an old-fashioned (with a quibble on 'antic', meaning 'bizarre') poem

antique (accented on the first syllable)

14   *rhyme* verse

Sonnet 18

1   *Shall I compare thee to a summer's day.* Glancing perhaps at the proverb 'As good as one shall see in a summer's day' (summer days being long, with lots of time for looking). *Day* could mean 'period, term' ('I saw not better sport these seven years' day', *2 Henry VI* II.1.2), and though this sense is initially only latent it registers retrospectively when *summer* becomes a season (lines 4 and 9). On the questioned comparison see the Introduction, pages 30–31.

2   *temperate* equable

2, 4 *temperate . . . date.* Rhymed on long 'a', resembling the 'a' in southern English 'bat', 'bad', lengthened.

3   *May.* In the 1590s our calendar lagged several days behind the European system – something not corrected till the late eighteenth century. Shakespeare's *May* thus reached into our June and was a *summer*, not spring, month.

4   *lease hath all too short a date* allotted time (of tenancy) expires all too soon

5, 7 *Sometime . . . sometime.* Making play with two senses: 'sometimes (from time to time) . . . eventually (at some time)'.

5, 6 *eye of heaven . . . gold complexion* (developing the sun imagery of 7.1–2)

7   *fair from fair* beautiful thing from its state of beauty

8   *changing course* (through altering seasons, in unpredictable weather)
     untrimmed stripped of ornament, robbed of trimming

10   *Nor lose possession.* Despite the tremor of doubt in *ow'st*, this *summer* contrasts with the *lease*-holder of line 4 by enjoying *possession* (the word carries a strong legal implication) of its property, beauty.
     fair thou ow'st beauty you own (with a trace of 'beauty you're supposed to repay')

11   *Nor shall . . . shade.* Echoing Psalms 23.3: 'Yea though I walk through the valley of the shadow of death, I will fear no evil: for thou art with me, thy rod and thy staff be the things that do comfort me.'

12   *eternal lines* (1) immortal verses (see lines 13–14); (2) links of lineage (see the *lines of life* at 16.9)
     to time thou grow'st. The young man will flourish as long as *time*

stands, waxing *to*wards its unknown limit, since his growth through *eternal limits* is also grafted *in* (bound by *eternal lines*) *to* the root stock of *time*.

14   *this* (the sonnet, written in *eternal lines*)

Sonnet 19

Though some experienced readers have found Sonnets 1–17 a coherent group, others (with better reason) regard 19 as the conclusion of an opening sequence. Here the displacement of breeding by verse, begun in 15, is completed, and the poet feels able to defy Time on his own terms. Sonnet 20 marks a fresh start by abandoning the theme of Time, and by shifting decisively in timbre through its use of feminine rhymes.

1   *Devouring Time.* A stock translation of Ovid's '*tempus edax rerum*' (*Metamorphoses* XV.234; see Golding's loose rendering, page 180), based on the proverb, widely current in the sixteenth century, 'Time devours all things'.

2   *make the earth devour her own sweet brood* (all life returning to *the earth*, after Time has wasted it)

2, 4   *brood ... blood.* An ambiguous rhyme, apparently attainable with either long 'u' (pronounced 'oo' as in 'mood') or short (as in 'educated' southern 'put').

4   *burn the long-lived phoenix in her blood.* The chastity, longevity, and uniqueness of the *phoenix* were familiar lore in the period – partly because the bird was often used as an emblem of Queen Elizabeth. If Shakespeare needed to consult classical authority, he would have turned to Pliny's *Natural History* X.2 or to Ovid's *Metamorphoses* XV. 392–402:

> One bird there is that doth renew itself and as it were
> Beget itself continually. The Syrians name it there
> A phoenix. Neither corn nor herbs this phoenix liveth by,
> But by the juice of frankincense and gum of amomye [amomum].
> And when that of his life well full five hundred years are past,
> Upon a holmtree or upon a date tree at the last
> He makes him with his talents [talons] and his hardened bill a
>   nest:
> Which when that he with cassia sweet and nardus [nard] soft
>   hath dressed,
> And strowed it with cinnamon and myrrha [myrrh] of the best,
> He rucketh [crouches] down upon the same, and in the spices
>   dies.

> Soon after, of the father's corpse men say there doth arise
> Another little phoenix which as many years must live
> As did his father.

(Golding's translation)

Pliny and Ovid both emphasize the dignity of the phoenix's death; for them it is prepared, almost chosen. Shakespeare, by contrast, puts the bird completely at the mercy of Time. Indeed, *burn . . . in her blood* does more than describe a painful death: it quibbles on the idiom 'to be in blood', meaning 'to be in one's prime', to imply that Time can kill the phoenix whenever it wants. Despite the bestiaries and their lore, Time need not wait for the bird's old age. Pliny and Ovid marvel at the bird's regenerative powers. These Shakespeare ignores, as though suggesting what he declares in *The Phoenix and Turtle*, that his phoenix dies without 'posterity' ('heirs' and 'future').

5   *fleet'st.* Editors often emend this, the Q reading, to 'fleets', for the sake of a rhyme with *sweets.* But Shakespearian rhymes can be imperfect; *-t'st* is musically superior to '-ts' (because of the patterning of 't' and 's' throughout lines 5–8 and because of *And* at the start of line 6); and the slight pause imposed by the clustering of consonants in *fleet'st* helps articulate the syntax.

6   *swift-footed.* A familiar attribute of *Time*; compare 65.11, *As You Like It* III.2.297, and the proverb 'Time flees away without delay'.

7   *sweets* lovely things

10   *Nor.* Not indicating an alternative but emphasizing with negative force the poet's twice-stated resistance to a wrinkled forehead.

     antique (accented on the first syllable) old, aged. The sense is partly transferred from the pen to the thing inscribed; thus 'ageing, old-making'. And the play on 'antic' hinted at 17.12 here registers strongly: Time's *pen* is 'bizarre', and it makes brows 'grotesque' with wrinkles.

11   *course* rapid passage. *Swift-footed* running gives way, with *untainted*, to horse-riding. *In thy* adds a frightening logic to Time's depredations, 'in course' being a stock phrase meaning 'in the regular order . . .'.

     untainted (1) unsullied; (2) untouched by Time's lance (the language of jousting), unmarked

12   *pattern* ideal, model

13   *do thy worst.* The poet's stock cry of defiance is on one level touching and naive because it construes a few wrinkles on the young man's brow as more terrible than the burning of a *phoenix* (it is Time's *worst*), but on another (as the assumption of parallelism gives way to the idea of a future, with *ever*), it gestures realistically towards the fate (a new *worst*) which awaits the youth beyond old age.

wrong. The culpable and injurious *worst* (however interpreted) inflicted by *Time*; and perhaps, by extension, the quality of *wrong*, of evil, essential to *Time*.

13, 14   *wrong . . . young*. The rhyme probably resembled *tongue . . . song* at 17.10 and 12 (see the note).

14   *My love shall in my verse ever live young* my beloved will always be a young man in my verse (though *love*, as often in the Sonnets, is 'affection' as well as the 'person loved')

Sonnet 20

The only poem in the volume to use feminine rhymes throughout.

1   *with Nature's own hand painted* (1) beautified by Nature herself; (2) coloured naturally, not (as *A woman's face* so often is) by cosmetics

2   *thou, the master-mistress of my passion.* The hint of eroticism flusters interpreters and drives them into extremes. Some save Shakespeare's reputation by reading the line as a literary joke ('you, praised in this love poem (one sense of the word *passion*) like the conventional sonnet mistress, are nevertheless male'), while others, of coarser fibre, prefer 'you, the seductively androgynous object of my homosexual lust'. Though both extremes can be dismissed, where one stands between them will depend less on the content of this calculatedly paradoxical line than on the quality of the love unfolded before, and indeed after, Sonnet 20. On this, and renaissance androgyny, see the Introduction, pages 46–52, and Further Reading, page 73.

4   *as is false women's fashion* as is the way with morally (or 'emotionally' or, with a glance back to the cosmetics of line 1, 'visually') deceitful women. The comparison is with 'all women, all false', not 'such women as happen to be false'.

5   *rolling* roving

6   *Gilding the object whereupon it gazeth* adding lustre to whatever it looks on. Though metaphors of *Gilding*, or 'filming with gold', can be problematic in Shakespeare, and even expressive of evil (see 55.1, 101.11, and *A Lover's Complaint* 172), and though the line might therefore describe the gazing of *false women* (despite the disjunction between *theirs* in line 5 and *it*), it seems more likely that the poet is praising the youth by comparing his *eye* with the sun, thought capable of transmuting into gold base metals on or near the surface of the earth. (According to the prevailing theory of sight, the *eye* produced light to see by; hence the commonplace assumed here and mocked at 130.1.) See 33.4, where Shakespeare elaborates this theme, and the note.

7   *A man in hue all hues in his controlling.* A *hue* is a 'form', an 'appearance' (with strong implications of comeliness), or 'colour' (by extension 'complexion', with the probable implication 'in the pink, hale' when combined with *in*). *In his controlling* means 'under his aegis, in his power, subject to his challenge' and, by extension, 'contained by him'. This haunting, complex line therefore includes, or makes available, senses such as these: 'a fine-looking man, he enthrals everyone', 'though his complexion is manly, touched by *all hues* it is womanly too' (see lines 1–2), 'he is so comely that all complexions (blushing or turning pale) lie in his power'. Moreover, though the youth is not yet the godlike figure described in such sonnets as 53, the following senses remain in readiness, to be discerned with hindsight: 'a mere man in appearance, he controls all living forms', 'though he looks like a man, he has the power to adopt any form he chooses'. Finally, early readers would have been struck by the comparative strangeness of *hue*. Though revived later, and now common, the word had fallen into disuse by the 1590s, except in some verse.

8   *Which.* The antecedent is probably *hue* but possibly 'his act of *controlling'.*
     amazeth overwhelms, stuns

9   *for a woman* to be female, a woman in form

9, 11 *created... defeated.* This rhyme may be inexact or it may depend on a complicated merger of 'ai' ('defeature' is sometimes spelled 'defaiture' in the period) with 'ah' ('cre-ahted, defahted').

10   *fell a-doting* became besotted (with you). But *doting* implies mad folly as well as affection: the poet suggests that *Nature* 'went mildly dotty' over the youth; certainly (he implies) she must have been crazy to deprive the poet of the perfect girl by making him a boy. On the rhyme with *nothing* see below.

11   *by addition* (1) by honouring you ('I came to kill thee, cousin, and bear hence | A great addition earnèd in thy death', *Troilus and Cressida* IV.5.140–41); (2) by adding something (your penis)
     me of thee defeated deprived me of you

12   *thing* (with a bawdy quibble)
     to my purpose nothing. 'Of no interest to me' shading into 'irrelevant to my concerns' shading into 'irrelevant here, in this context, this poem'. Rhyming, already doubtful with *created... defeated*, becomes distinctly shaky here (though 'th' was harder, closer to 'd' and 't', than now), and this underlines at the level of form the elegant evasiveness of the disclaimer ('irrelevant in this poem' being so clearly overlaid, though itself ambiguous). The line is enlivened residually, in its opposition of *one thing* and *nothing*, by the *nothing* being effectively, the poet claims, in the bawdy sense, 'no thing' – 'no

sexual organ to speak of' – to him. Critics who argue that this disposes of homoeroticism misconstrue teasing inconsequence as unambiguous statement, though the weight of the verb *defeated* in line 11 cannot be overlooked.

13   *pricked thee out* (1) selected you from a list (on this method of marking paper irreversibly see *Julius Caesar* IV.i.1); (2) gave you a prick *for women's pleasure* to please women (especially sexually)

14   *Mine be thy love, and thy love's use their treasure.* Primarily a clever appeal for lots of affection – 'give me your love and let the profits of your love go to women as treasure' (so that the poet enjoys the capital while women divide the interest) – the line rests on a double, almost coital, bawdy jest: first, 'give me your love and let your sexual activity (see 6.5–6 and the note) be precious to women'; second, 'give me your love and let women's cunts (see 136.5 and compare 'There serve your lust . . . And revel in Lavinia's treasury', *Titus Andronicus* II.i.130–31) be sexually enjoyed by you'. Both bawdy senses, paradoxically, work to free the poet from the imputation of sexual interest in the young man, and implicitly exalt the *love* which he wants from the youth over the *love* (inseparable from *use*) which the women deserve.

Sonnet 21

On the sonnet in general, and its relationship with 130, see the Introduction, pages 24–5.

1   *So is it not with me as with that Muse* my state is not the same as that of the poet

2   *Stirred* inspired (though the verb carries a scornful suggestion of some base appetite provoked)
      painted beauty (1) beautiful person daubed with cosmetics; (2) beauty merely painted. It is characteristic of Shakespeare, with his intense dislike of cosmetics, that (1) should slip so easily into (2).

3   *heaven itself for ornament doth use* beautifies his beloved by comparing her or him with the heavens (with an imputation of blasphemy, since *heaven* could mean 'God')

4   *every fair with his fair doth rehearse* speaks of every fair thing and his painted beauty in the same breath (which implies, of course, 'compares every fair beloved with his *painted beauty*'. *Rehearse* is here pejorative: the other *Muse* goes through the motions, repeating – someone else's? – words mechanically, like an actor in rehearsal.)

5–6   *Making a couplement of proud compare | With* (1) presenting his beloved as equal in grandeur to; (2) producing a vaunting metaphorical comparison between his beloved and. In both cases, implicitly contrasting *his fair* with others.

6–7   *sun and moon . . . things rare*. See the Introduction, page 24.

8   *in this huge rondure hems* confines in this great round of the universe. The life of that phrase comes from the paradoxical relation of *huge* to *hems* (the confined enclosure is enormous), and from *rondure* – a word which only affects affectation, being fashionably neologistic (unrecorded before Shakespeare) but also expressive. The poet beats *that Muse* at its own game.

9   *true in love* since I am faithful to you. If 'you who are true in love to me' is implied, it only anticipates disappointment.

   truly honestly, straightforwardly (without ornament)

10   *then* (1) when that happens; (2) on account of that

11   *any mother's child*. Employing a stock phrase still visible in 'mother's boy', and probably, like that, implying a degree of cossetting. 'Anyone' shading into 'any flattered and pampered brat'.

12   *those gold candles fixed in heaven's air* the stars. Another jibe at literary affectation, though Shakespeare uses the image himself in his plays (for instance, at *The Merchant of Venice* V.1.220).

13   *that like of hearsay well* who thoroughly enjoy empty talk

14   *I will not praise that purpose not to sell*. Like 102.3–4, and the parallel sequence at *Love's Labour's Lost* IV.3.237–9, where Berowne lauds Rosaline – 'Fie, painted rhetoric! O, she needs it not! | To things of sale a seller's praise belongs: | She passes praise; then praise too short doth blot' – alluding to the proverb 'He praises who wishes to sell'.

Sonnet 22

The opening contrast with Sonnet 3 (*Look in thy glass*) alerts readers to an increased emphasis on the poet as against the youth, while the conspicuous use of *nurse* and *babe* in line 12, as similes for the youth and the young man's heart, marks the ousting of the breeding theme by the complementariness of selves (something developed towards the extreme of 62.13).

1   *glass* mirror

2   *of one date* coextensive, as long-lasting as each other

3   *in thee* (made suddenly physical, 'inscribed in your flesh', by *furrows*)
   Time's furrows wrinkles (like the *deep trenches* of 2.2)

4   *look I death my days should expiate* I hope (and expect) that death will end my days peacefully. Perhaps the commoner sense of *expiate* is felt, suggesting a purging of guilt by death.

5–7   *For all . . . art*. Shakespeare takes a conventional motif of love poetry (the one explored by Sidney in 'My true love hath my heart, and I have his'), makes it wittily literal, and adapts it to the grand concern of the early sonnets – mortality. In the process, arguably, he uses *live* to glance at the proverb 'The lover is not where he lives but where he loves'. Compare 109.3–4.

6   *seemly* becoming, decorous

9   *be of thyself so wary* look after yourself (involutedly expressed, *so* passing through a flicker of 'thus')

10   *will* (be *wary*)

11   *chary* carefully

12   *tender* loving (with a trace, perhaps, of 'she who tends')

13   *Presume not on* do not count on recovering

Sonnet 23

1   *unperfect actor* player who has not properly learned his lines, not-word-perfect actor. Perhaps also 'actor with an imperfect technique'.

2   *with his fear* by stagefright
      put besides made to forget (as in 'put out')

3   *fierce thing replete with too much rage* wild creature full to bursting with excessive fury (*too much* for it, and *too much* anyway)

4   *Whose.* Although the antecedent is strictly *thing, rage* participates.
      heart. 'Courage' or 'taste for action' as well as the literal sense.

5–8   *So I ... love's might.* Lines 5–6 parallel 1–2, making the poet an unnerved actor; lines 7–8 compare him with the *fierce thing* of 3–4.

5   *for fear of trust.* Although 'afraid to trust myself, lacking self-confidence' is primary, 'afraid that I will not find trust, unnerved by anticipated disapproval' registers. The phrase is enlivened by the paradoxical reliance posited by *of* between *fear* and *trust*.

6   *perfect* memorized exactly and executed flawlessly (recalling *unperfect* from line 1), exquisitely pleasing (because so flawless)
      love's rite. The Q spelling 'right' alerts us to a secondary sense: 'due' as well as 'ritual'. Compare 17.11 and 117.6.

7   *decay* weaken

8   *O'ercharged* overloaded

9   *books.* Not, as now, 'writings, printed and bound', but text on paper at any length (thus *Cymbeline* V.4.133, 'A book? O rare one!', of a single handwritten sheet). *Books* probably refers to the Sonnets themselves, forwarded to the youth, but those who favour the identification of the young man with Henry Wriothesley may be right in thinking them *Venus and Adonis* and *The Rape of Lucrece*, published in 1593 and 1594 and dedicated to Southampton.

9–10   *the eloquence | And dumb presagers of my speaking breast.* This strand of playful sophistry depends on *eloquence* meaning 'inventive and accomplished utterance', so that the *dumb* pages are voluble and the *speaking breast* (where *breast* is a common Shakespearian synecdoche for 'heart') is in practice *dumb*.

10   *presagers* heralds ('those who go before to inform', not 'those who indulge in prophecy')

11   *Who.* Though the ultimate antecedent is *books*, that *Who* not 'which' is used suggests that Shakespeare thought *dumb presagers* most immediately commanding.

11-12   *look for recompense . . . expressed* seek greater rewards than *that tongue* which has spoken more grandly and more copiously (or often). The implication is that, whereas the *tongue* looks for material *recompense*, the poet's *books* seek that worthier prize, the young man's love. Though this text anticipates the later sonnets concerned with the rival poet(s), *that tongue* probably refers by synecdoche to the kind of imagined author identified in Sonnet 21 as *that Muse.*

13   *O, learn to read what silent love hath writ.* Possibly based on the proverb 'Whom we love best to them we can say least'.

14   *fine wit* acute intelligence

Sonnet 24

The poet looks, or imagines himself looking, into the eyes of the young man.

1   *played the* acted like a, behaved like a

     stelled fixed. Q's 'steeld' is a possible reading if taken to mean 'engraved with a steel tool' or 'inscribed with a stylus' (the imperfect rhyme with *held* is not an insuperable difficulty); but *painter* tells strongly against it.

2-3   *Thy beauty's . . . held.* A conventional image, though bizarre. Compare, for example, Sonnets 45 and 47 of Thomas Watson's *Tears of Fancy* (1593): 'With steadfast eye she gazèd on my heart, | Wherein she saw the picture of her beauty'; 'My mistress seeing her fair counterfeit | So sweetly framèd in my bleeding breast . . .'.

2   *table* board on which a picture is painted (commonly used to image the heart, as at *All's Well That Ends Well* I.1.94, 'our heart's table')

3   *frame* picture-frame (with a quibble on 'physical frame, body')

4   *perspective it is best painter's art.* Interpretation depends on whether Q 'Painters' is taken as a singular or plural, whether *perspective* (accented on the first syllable) is read as a noun, adverb, or both, and whether *art* refers to a skill or the product of that skill: (1) 'the *art* of making a *perspective* (a distorted painting which looks right from only one point of view) is the best a *painter* could have' (see *Twelfth Night* V.1.214, 'A natural perspective, that is and is not', and *Richard II*

II.2.18–20, 'perspectives which, rightly gazed upon, | Show nothing but confusion; eyed awry, | Distinguish form'); (2) 'skill in *perspective* (the science of proportion and the relation of size to distance) is the best bit of artistic equipment a painter could have (thus, is a skill held by the best painters)'; (3) 'seen from the right angle (obliquely, through my eyes), the picture of you in my heart is splendid painterly work' (compare *Henry V* V.2.315, 'you see them perspectively . . .'); (4) 'seen through a *perspective* (optical device designed to produce pleasingly distorted images – represented here by the poet's eyes), it looks like the best portrait a painter could paint' (see *All's Well That Ends Well* V.3.48–9, 'Contempt his scornful perspective did lend me, | Which warped the line of every other favour'). Sense (2) must remain speculative because without parallel in the canon.

5–8   *For through . . . eyes.* Another bizarre notion which is essentially conventional. Compare, for instance, these lines modernized from 'Sonnetto nono' in Constable's *Diana* (1592, reprinted in 1594 as Sonnet 5 in the first decad):

> Thine eye, the glass where I behold my heart;
> Mine eye, the window through the which thine eye
> May see my heart, and there thyself espy
> In bloody colours how thou painted art!

5–6   *through the painter . . . find* you must look through *Mine eye* to the painting of you in *my heart* if you want to judge that eye's *art* (a conceit supported by an etymological quibble on *perspective*, which derives from Latin *perspicere*, 'to look through', and by the more obvious but indubitably secondary sense, 'the painter's skill can only be judged when he exercises it in works of art') and, by doing this looking in order to judge, to discover. (There may be a suggestion that the *eye* is skilful because it can see backwards into the self, finding the young man on the *heart*.)
you . . . yours. This brief excursion from *Thy*, *thine*, and *thee* (lines 2, 8, 10, 12) was probably motivated by a desire for euphony, though some have found the shift tonally significant. It is, intriguingly, the only point in the collection where 'you' is mixed with 'thou' (see the headnote to Sonnet 13).

6   *true* faithfully drawn

7   *bosom's shop* (the heart. The poet's body, in line 3 a picture-frame, here includes an artist's studio and retail outlet.)
still (1) constantly; (2) forever

8   *That hath his windows glazèd with thine eyes.* The *windows* of the poet's *bosom* (his eyes) are glassed over by the young man's, because as the poet looks into his friend's *eyes* those *eyes* can be seen reflected across the surface of his own; which must mean that the young man's *eyes*

are as well-depicted in the *windows* of the *bosom* as behind them (in the *true image* displayed in the *shop*).

9   *good turns* favours (with a suggestion of 'loving glances'). Lines 10–11 make clear that there is a reference here, as at 47.2, to the proverb 'One good turn deserves another'.

13   *cunning* skill

      grace give grace to, ornament

      their art (both 'their artistic execution' and 'the art-object possessed by them')

14   *They draw but what they see, know not the heart.* Meaning that the poet cannot judge whether the youth loves him as he does the youth. But the possibility of duplicity, of the youth deceiving the poet (confirmed later), may also register.

Sonnet 25

1   *who are in favour with their stars* whose stars are favourable. The astrological allusion scornfully severs advancement from merit, attributing success to chance.

3   *of* from

      triumph. The *honour* and *titles* of line 2; but perhaps, also, the 'triumphing', the *boast*ing, which accompanies public success.

4   *Unlooked for* (1) unregarded, out of the public eye; (2) unexpectedly. 'Beyond all expectation' may also be relevant.

      joy in that I honour most delight in the person (the loving beloved of line 13) whom I most honour. Delight and devotion are linked the more firmly by a secondary 'joy in the fact that I honour the object of my honour more than anyone else honours (him)'. There may also be an astrological quibble: a planet 'joys' when it inhabits a heavenly house which enhances its qualities by agreement, and the poet's *joy* apparently stems from the congruence of his and his beloved's love (see lines 13–14).

5   *favourites* (three syllables)

6   *But* only, merely

      marigold. The plant's sensitivity to light is often remarked in Elizabethan literature; compare 'the marigold which opens and shuts with the sun' in Nashe's *The Unfortunate Traveller*, or lines 5–6 of the Constable sonnet quoted in the headnote to Sonnet 99.

7   *in themselves their pride lies buried.* Approached from line 6, 'left alone (without the *sun* of *favour*), their glorious display folds up'; read in the light of line 8, 'their handsome show dies with them, leaving nothing lasting'. Either way, *pride* is pejorative (the favourites are 'vain' about their transitory 'splendour').

8   *frown*. Displeasure darkens the patron's face; a cloud passes over the
     sun.

9   *painful*. Being 'painstaking', the assiduous warrior is 'full of pain'
     (both 'pain-dealing, wounding' and doubtless 'pained, often hurt').
     warrior (two syllables)
     famousèd renowned
     fight. Q's 'worth' can hardly be correct. (Some editors preserve it,
     emending *quite* in line 11 to 'forth' for the sake of the rhyme; but this
     sacrifices unnecessarily *quite*'s forcefulness.) *Fight* rhymes with *quite*,
     is phonetically appropriate (the poem is full of emphatic *f*s), and,
     through alliteration with *famousèd*, nicely pompous (the *warrior*
     evidently deserves some of the scorn-and-pity directed at the
     favourites).

11   *razèd quite* completely erased

12   *the rest* (the *thousand victories* of line 10)

13, 14   *beloved . . . removed*. The first of many points at which 'love' and its
     compounds rhyme with '-ove' words now dissimilar in sound (*mov-
     ing, prove, move, approve, remove, reproving*). The rhyme, apparently,
     was full in Shakespearian English, with a vowel between 'educated'
     southern short 'u' and long 'o' (sounding 'orh').

14   *remove* be unfaithful (compare 116.4)
     be removed (from favour)

Sonnet 26

Frequently compared with the dedication to *The Rape of Lucrece* ('Were my
worth greater, my duty would show greater; meantime, as it is, it is bound to
your lordship'), and used to identify the youth of the Sonnets with the object
of that dedication, Henry Wriothesley, this poem seems rather to take its
bearings from the commonplace literary language of courtly love. Lines 1–2
would no doubt seem more interesting if they could be shown to describe the
poet's relationship with an identifiable patron, but the idiomatic overlap with
the prose address is too slight to be in itself significant.

1   *vassalage* allegiance. A feudal bond, sustained in verse by its promi-
     nence in courtly love poetry, or an image of the lover's loyalty to his
     mistress.

2   *duty* devotion, willingness to serve

3   *ambassage* message (usually oral, so *written* is an important quali-
     fication. Arguably, this pursues the paradox advanced at 23.9–10;
     which raises the possibility that, like the eloquent *books* of the earlier
     sonnet, the *ambassage* involves more than the immediate poem.)

4   *witness* bear witness to

4–5 *wit . . . wit* literary ingenuity . . . intelligence

6   *bare* meagre, unadorned
    wanting lacking, needing

7   *But* except
    good conceit (1) kind opinion; (2) excellent literary figure, splendid far-fetched fancy

8   *thy soul's thought.* Simultaneously the place where the good conceit will be produced and the place where the youth will *bestow* ('securely place') the poet's *all naked* ('completely *bare*') *ambassage*.

9   *moving* actions. On the rhyme with *loving*, see the note to 25.13, 14.

10   *Points on* directs its rays on to, pours its influence upon
    fair favourable
    aspect (accented on the second syllable) astrological influence

11   *puts apparel on* clothes, dresses up
    loving. 'Statement of praise, formal wooing' and 'being in love'. An ambiguity which helps the reader from the *ambassage* which dominates the octave to its writer, the *I* of the couplet.

12   *thy sweet respect.* Some editors follow Q's 'their', arguing that the poet wants to be *worthy* of the *Duty* and *wit* (or the *Duty, star,* and *loving*) which pay the young man *sweet respect*; but *sweet* surely claims too much for things called *bare, naked,* and *tattered.* 'Their'/'thy' errors are so common in Q (see the Collations, pages 437–8) that it seems better to emend, *sweet respect* becoming the 'kindly regard' shown to the poet by the man who lodged and clothed his lines.

13–14   *dare . . . not show my head.* Alluding to the proverb 'He dares not show his head (for debt)'.

13, 14   *love thee, prove me.* Double rhyme; see the note to 25.13, 14.

14   *prove* test

Sonnet 27

2   *travel.* Modernization of Q's 'trauaill' sacrifices an ambiguity which leads wittily from *toil* (line 1) to *journey* (line 3). That the dominant sense here is *travel* can be deduced less from Sonnet 27 itself than from 27's relation to 28.

3   *begins a journey in my head.* The verb is displaced ('a journey in my head begins'), partly for the sake of a strong substantive rhyme, partly to emphasize *work* in line 4 (heightening, in turn, the clash with *work's*).

4   *To work my mind.* Idiomatic, not forced for *work's* sake; compare *Henry V* III Chorus 25: 'Work, work your thoughts . . .'.
    when body's work's expired (1) when the physical *toil* of the day is finished; (2) when bodily activity stops in sleep

5   *from far.* Understand 'away from you'.

6 *Intend* set out on (from Latin *iter intendere*. But the usual sense is felt strongly enough to give *thoughts* their own volition and thus that independence from the thinker characteristic of hopeless and distressing fancies.)

9 *Save* except

10 *thy shadow* the image of you. Some editors preserve Q's 'their', but this forces the reader into pointless contortions: 'the image which my *thoughts* (line 5) sketch of you'. There is a suggestion that the *journey* of line 3 has reversed, the young man haunting the poet as a 'shade'; note *ghastly* ('having to do with ghosts' as well as 'horrible') in the next line. Compare 61.5–8.

 sightless view unseeing sight. Paradox (line 8) reduced to oxymoron.

11–12 *like a jewel . . . beauteous.* The young man glimmers like Juliet, who, according to Romeo, 'hangs upon the cheek of night | As a rich jewel in an Ethiop's ear' (I.5.45–6). The Elizabethans believed that some jewels could be seen in *darkness* because they produced their own glowing light (see, for instance, *Titus Andronicus* II.3.226–30, where a *jewel* lights a gloomy pit, and compare *A Lover's Complaint* 213–14).

12 *black . . . beauteous.* The first appearance of that conventional opposition which plays such an important part in the sonnets to the dark lady. See the Introduction, pages 58–9.

 old hag-like (having been *night* every day for centuries)

14 *For thee, and for myself, no quiet find.* The correspondence with line 13 is inexact, unless the poet labours with his *limbs* for the young man or is undertaking a journey for his sake. *For* is twice used in a double sense: the poet lies awake 'because of' the friend and 'for his sake'; so, 'because of' his devotion, he finds *no quiet* 'for the sake of' himself.

Sonnet 28

1 *in happy plight* in a good state

2 *debarred* forbidden

3 *day's oppression is not eased by night.* After the oppressive *toil* and *travel* (27.1–2) of his *day*, the poet finds no refreshment *at night*; personified 'Night' will not help him resist the tyranny of 'Day'. There may be a hint behind the former of 'oppressive' weather: the kind that makes *travel* exhausting and sleep hard to come by. The latter prepares the opposition and league of line 4.

4 *day by night and night by day oppressed.* As 'Day' and 'Night' struggle, each a foe *to either's reign* (line 5), the *day* ('day-time') quashes *night* ('night-time') and *night* the *day* alternately; meanwhile (reading the line another way), the poet is sleepless (which befits *day*) at *night* and

weary (which befits *night*) during the *day*, the virtue of each time
transferred to and oppressing the other. The line alludes to a stock
formula for expressing monotony (used straightforwardly at *Titus
Andronicus* V.2.58), 'day by day'.

6   *in consent shake hands* having come to an understanding make a pact

7   *the other to complain* the other party (*night*) giving me the opportunity
       (through sleeplessness) to lament

8   *still* (1) always; (2) even

9   *I tell the day, to please him, thou.* Some editors leave this unpunctuated
       (producing the sense 'I tell the day to be glad that you'); but *flatter I* in
       line 11 counts strongly in favour of the commas.

10, 12 *heaven . . . even.* Rhymed with a long first vowel not unlike the 'ar' in
        modern 'scarce', 'scares'. Q points to this, and underlines the
        concord (both here and at 132.5 and 7), by spelling 'eauen' for *even*.

11   *flatter* please (a little deceitfully)
        swart-complexioned dark-skinned. A consciously poetic compound:
        though *swart* (Old English 'sweart') survived in verse until the
        nineteenth century, it was superseded in prose by 'black' before the
        renaissance.

12   *When sparkling . . . even* (the gist of what the poet tells the *night*)
        twire peep, peer. A verb of uncertain origin, unrecorded before the
        Sonnets, but probably (like *swart*) archaic by the 1590s.
        gild'st. This is the usual emendation of 'guil'st', supported by *A
        Midsummer Night's Dream* III.2.187–8, where it is said that Helena
        'more engilds the night | Than all yon fiery oes and eyes of light [the
        stars]'; though, if the *even* could be said to be 'beguiled' by light, Q
        might stand.

13–14   *longer . . . length . . . stronger.* Night intensifies the sorrow already
        lengthened out by day. Suppressing wordplay, the common
        emendation 'longer . . . strength . . . stronger' makes the couplet
        excessively predictable.

Sonnet 29

1   *disgrace* disfavour

2   *outcast state* (1) position as social pariah (*state* as 'status'); (2) feelings
       of unwantedness (*state* as 'state of mind')

3   *bootless* useless

4   *And look upon myself.* The poet is not navel-gazing but has be-
       come the spectator of his own predicament (compare *3 Henry VI*
       II.3.25–8, 'Why stand we like soft-hearted women here . . . And
       look upon, as if the tragedy | Were played in jest . . . ?').

5   *one more rich in hope* a man with better prospects (of worldly success.

The poet's despondency ensures that 'having more hope than I' also registers.)

6   *Featured like him, like him with friends possessed* having that other man's looks, and being equipped, like that second, with a set of friends

6, 8   *possessed . . . least.* The rhyme depends on 'ea' shortening to 'e' before the consonant group 'st'. Q indicates the basis of the rhyme by reading 'possest' in line 6.

7   *art . . . scope.* Impossible to gloss precisely, but *art* involves 'skill, craft, learning, literary achievement' while *scope* includes 'range of accomplishment, plentiful opportunities, mental stamina'.

8   *most enjoy* (1) possess most securely; (2) take most pleasure in (relating paradoxically to *contented least*)

9   *Yet.* 'Still, even then', transformed by 'even so' when the recollection of the youth is related. The expected *then* (compare *When . . . Then* at 2.1, 5, 12.1, 3, 5, 9, and 15.1, 5, 9) is delayed, seemingly displaced, until the second half of line 10.

10   *state.* The emphasis is on 'state of mind', not 'status'.

11–12 *Like to the lark . . . earth.* Compare *Cymbeline* II.3.19–20: 'Hark, hark! the lark at heaven's gate sings, | And Phoebus 'gins arise'. In the sonnet, the lark almost is the sun, rising above the rim of earth at dawn.

12   *sullen.* 'Sluggish, heavy, dull in colour', but also 'sulky', because the poet's *sullen* melancholy is replaced in the sestet by *lark*-like joy.

13   *wealth.* The image, although startling, has been carefully prepared; consider *one more rich in hope* (line 5) and *Fortune* (line 1) as latently a financial 'fortune'.

14   *scorn to change* wouldn't consider changing
       state. To the social and psychological senses of the word used in line 2, *wealth* adds a third appropriate to the *kings*: 'lavish worldly pomp'.
       kings. The ear may assume an apostrophe: 'kings''.

Sonnet 30

1   *sessions* court sittings

2   *summon up.* As though *remembrance* were a defendant, served with a 'summons' by the court.
       remembrance of things past. Echoing Wisdom 11.12, 'For their grief was double [compare *Love's Labour's Lost* V.2.747], and mourning for the remembrance of things past'.

2, 4   *past . . . waste.* The first of several rhymes in which Shakespeare calls on the short 'a' available as a variant pronunciation in the period for normally long 'a' words like *waste*.

3-4 *I sigh the lack . . . waste.* In line 3 *old* disappointments cause *new* grief; in line 4 the *time* lying between the *old* and *new* becomes an additional source of sorrow. *My dear time's waste* can be read either impersonally – 'the decay/ruin' of 'my precious time, the best years of my life' or 'each thing and person dear to me' – or as a self-rebuke: 'my frittering away of valuable time, my waste of the best years of my life'. 'Each person dear to me', a sense which barely registers here (since the 'persons' are but an inference from the generalized *thing*s of line 3), becomes dominant as the poem proceeds and as it gives way to Sonnet 31. In the sestet of Sonnet 30, as in its successor, the *friends* of 30.6 are the poet's main *remembrance*. Because of this development, it is hard to reread 30.3–4 without assuming, against the pull of the text, that 'Each person dear to me' is primary.

3, 8 *many a* (two syllables)

5 *unused to flow* not prone to tears

6 *dateless* endless

7 *long since cancelled woe.* The *woe* is like a bond or legally recorded debt, *cancelled* ('paid off, annulled') long ago. Part of the thread of legal and financial imagery which starts with *sessions* and *summon up*, continues with *dateless* (for bonds and leases reach fruition and expire at their 'date'), and concludes in lines 11–14 with *sad account*, *pay*, *paid*, and *losses*.

8 *moan* bewail
   expense of many a vanished sight (1) loss of many things once seen; (2) expenditure of many fruitless sighs; (3) cost to myself of frequent and fruitless sighs. Senses (2) and (3) both depend on *sight* as a variant form of 'sigh' in sixteenth-century English. Sense (3) should be read in the light of the 'blood-consuming sighs' and 'blood-drinking sighs' of *2 Henry VI* III.2.61 and 63; the Elizabethans believed that sighing consumed the blood.

9 *grievances foregone* (1) sorrows past (griefs gone before the present grief); (2) sorrows left off (for griefs, like pleasures, are difficult to put aside)

9, 11 *foregone . . . moan.* The first of several rhymes involving *gone* and *moan*. Though a long 'o' ('foregorhn, morhn') seems likelier than a short ('forgon, mon'), either is possible.

10 *heavily* sadly, wearily

10-11 *tell o'er . . . moan* count up the sorry total of laments already uttered. *Fore-bemoanèd moan* is vocal enough to make *tell o'er | The sad account* suggest 'recount the sad story, relate the sorry tale'.

14 *losses.* The things, time, and, above all (see the note to lines 3–4), friends lost in the past. Emotion is inseparable from loss, and the word *losses* inevitably conjures 'recurring feelings of loss'; but *sorrows*, later in the line, seems meant to cover the *woe* long past as

well as those wept *afresh*: *losses* are thus concrete, *sorrows* emotional.
restored. See the headnote to Sonnet 31.

Sonnet 31

This poem explains how the *losses* of 30.14 (see the note) are not so much
'made up for' as *restored*. The sonnet is intimately linked with its predecessor,
in vocabulary (*lack/lacking* at 30.3 and 31.2, for example), imagery (*interest*
and *due*, 31.7 and 12, pick up the financial metaphors of 30), and the
deployment of material (31.5–6 matches 30.5–6), as well as in its concern
with the past. But the poem also has affinities with Sonnets 53, 98, and 99
and *A Lover's Complaint* 253–80, for it presents the beloved as the focus, the
inclusive centre, of love and beauty. The difficult first quatrain announces
this theme, and the sestet clarifies and extends it: since the youth contains all
the human beauty that the poet has ever loved (line 13), the poet must give
him all the love he has ever felt (lines 11–12). As the seat of such love (almost
of Love itself), the young man seems to comprise *all they* (line 14) – all those
friends previously lost to *death's dateless night* (30.6).

1   *endearèd with all hearts*. Initially 'loved by the hearts of all men' and so
'richly adorned with the hearts of all men' (exploiting, like Sonnet
22, the convention that lovers' *hearts* reside in their beloved's *bosom*);
then, with the turn into line 2, 'made precious by including all those
loved people (assuming, as often in Shakespeare, the synecdochic
equivalence of *hearts* and their owners), enriched with all those
friends (compare 30.6 and 31.4)'. The former exalts the youth as the
most beautiful object imaginable, someone loved by *all* men, even
those ignorant of him (because they love the beauties he includes):
the latter explains why he so consoles the grieving poet of Sonnet 30.
This second sense becomes primary as the poem unfolds.

2   *lacking* not having (because *hid* in what 30.6 calls *death's dateless night*.
Taken with *hearts* in line 1, a clever adaptation of the idiom 'to lack
heart', meaning 'to be cowardly and demoralized'.)

3   *there reigns love and all love's loving parts*. Initially 'there Eros reigns
among his loveful aspects/attributes'; then, as the poem proceeds
(and particularly in the sestet), a secondary 'there (the emotion of)
love and all the loving pieces of (my) love hold sway' dominates. The
latter prepares for – at least by not excluding – the identification of
the poet and his *love* advanced strongly in line 11.

5   *many a* (two syllables)
    obsequious (three syllables) funereal, having to do with obsequies

6   *dear* tender, precious, heartfelt, grievous
    religious assiduous, full of faith, reverent, pure

6   *stol'n. Love* is a thief (though *religious*) because it provokes unnecess-
     ary fears; the poet need not weep for dead *friends* if they are alive in
     the young man's *bosom*. But *stol'n* is not included just for paradox'
     sake; it suggests *tear*s wept despite the weeper, sincere *tear*s secretly
     shed.

7   *interest* (1) legal right; (2) return due to investors (here the dead. The
     latter sense is picked up in line 12.)
     which who

7–8 *now appear* | *But* are now seen to be only

8   *removed* absent. Ellipsis allows the lovers' removal to be either active
     or passive.
     thee. The Q reading, 'there', is weak, but – as a reference to *Thy
     bosom* – not impossible.
     lie are (but with a suggestion of 'lodge'. The young man is a dwelling
     about to become a *grave*.)

9   *buried love* (the fractions of emotion discussed in line 3)
     doth live (1) resides; (2) has life, survives
     buried love doth live (transforming line 4, with life after burial)

10   *Hung with the trophies of my lovers gone.* It was classical and classicizing
     renaissance practice to hang emblems and wreaths commemorat-
     ing a dead man's successes in life over his grave (compare *Titus
     Andronicus* I.1.388–9, 'There lie thy bones, sweet Mutius, with thy
     friends, | Till we with trophies do adorn thy tomb', and *All's Well
     That Ends Well* II.3.137–8, 'on every grave | A lying trophy'). Here
     the poet says that the *trophies* of his dead *friends* (recording,
     presumably, their emotional triumphs over him) adorn the young
     man's *bosom*.

10, 12 *gone . . . alone.* Like *foregone . . . moan* at 30.9 and 11, rhymed on
     either long or short 'o': perhaps, in this case, the latter.

11   *their parts of me.* See line 3 and the note; the friends inherited not just
     the poet's love but, hyperbolically, him.

12   *due of many* that *love*, and self, which is owed to many (the *interest* of
     line 7)

13   *Their images I loved I view in thee.* Syntactical distortion allows the line
     to balance paradoxically between *Their* and *thee*, and thus to set up
     the bold equation *thou, all they* in line 14.

14   *thou, all they, hast all the all of me.* Holding in his breast *all those friends
     which* the poet *thought buried* in earth, the youth comprises – indeed
     'is' (see line 13 and the note) – *all they*; and he consequently inherits
     (according to the logic of lines 3 and 11) both *all love's loving parts*
     (see the note, sense 2) and *all their parts of me.* In other words,
     because he 'is' the lost *friends*, the young man possesses *all the all* of
     the poet – *all* his 'everything', where 'everything' is not only 'all the
     friends I ever loved' and 'all the love I ever gave' but 'all that I am'.

This climactic conceit, which catches up *all the all*s of the poem (see lines 1, 3, 4, 11, and 14), is clinched in wordplay: 'the all of all' is a stock tag (used, for example, at *Love's Labour's Lost* V.1.103) meaning 'summary conclusion', and *all the all* sums and concludes the sonnet.

Sonnet 32

1   *my well-contented day* the day which I welcome (when I shall pay my debt to nature. 'To content' could mean 'to pay in full'.)

2   *churl. Death* is seen as rough, base, begrudging.
    Death my bones with dust shall cover. The flesh will turn – or, as Genesis 2.7 and the burial service in the Elizabethan Book of Common Prayer remind us, will return – to *dust* on the *bones*, and the *bones*, being buried, will be covered with the *dust* of the earth.

3   *by fortune* by chance, perchance, fortune permitting
    resurvey look over again (with the implication 'reassess')

4   *rude* unrefined, not polished

5   *Compare them with* consider them in the context of, read them in the light of
    the bettering of the time the age's cultural progress. On this, and style, see Sonnet 106.
    bettering (two syllables)

7   *Reserve* keep, preserve
    for my love (1) for the sake of my love of you (which they display); (2) out of love towards me
    rhyme literary quality

8   *height* pitch of achievement
    happier more fortunate. The *men* may be more talented, or they may just live in a better age for writing.

9   *vouchsafe me but* deign to grant me just

10 *growing* (towards cultural maturity)

11 *dearer birth* more precious child of fancy, better poem. That composition resembled parturition was a commonplace; the image recurs in several sonnets.
    than. Modernization of Q's 'then' destroys a secondary sense of the line: 'then his love (which can be inferred from this, written long ago) would have produced something more stylish'.

12 *To march in ranks of better equipage* to take its place as an equal among better-turned-out lines of verse. Based on a military image, often used in the period to express the idea of equality. The sense flows naturally from the syntax of line 11, and has contemporary parallels (such as Marston's claim in *Pygmalion's Image* (1598) that his

'stanzas . . . like soldadoes of our warlike age, | March rich bedight in warlike equipage'). On a secondary level, however, *To march* is an ellipsis ('so that he could justifiably march'), and 'to take his place as an equal alongside better-equipped poets' registers.

13   *better prove* are improved, turn out to be better

13, 14 *prove . . . love*. See the note to 25.13, 14.

14   *Theirs* their *lines*

for their style . . . for his love. The double implication of *their style* (both the *poets' style* and the *style* of their *lines*) shrinks into the single modesty of *love* – since, though *lines* can show *love*, *his* cannot mean *their* – and the parallel with line 7 (*for my love*) underlines this in the reduction of two senses (see the second note to line 7) to a devoted 'because of his love towards me'.

Sonnet 33

It was proverbial that 'The morning sun never lasts the day'.

1   *Full* very

2   *Flatter.* 'Stroke, caress' ('They flattered me like a dog', says Lear, IV.6.96–7) as well as 'gratifyingly delude'.

sovereign eye. The sun (compare 18.5); like a king, the *morning* flatters everything he deigns to look upon.

2, 4   *eye . . . alchemy.* A full rhyme; compare *eye . . . majesty* at 7.2 and 4 and, hence, 1.2 and 4.

4   *Gilding pale streams with heavenly alchemy.* See 20.6 and the note; compare *Venus and Adonis* 856–8 ('The sun ariseth in his majesty; | Who doth the world so gloriously behold | That cedar-tops and hills seem burnished gold') or *King John* III.1.77–80:

> To solemnize this day the glorious sun
> Stays in his course and plays the alchemist,
> Turning with splendour of his precious eye
> The meagre cloddy earth to glittering gold.

5–8   *Anon permit . . . disgrace.* Frequently and suggestively compared with *1 Henry IV* I.2.193–201, where the future *sovereign*, Hal, likens himself to 'the sun, | Who doth permit the base contagious clouds | To smother up his beauty from the world'.

5   *Anon* soon

basest (1) lowest in rank (the sun is a king); (2) lowest in altitude (thinking of dull cumulus *clouds*); (3) darkest in hue (compare the 'base Indian' of *Othello* V.2.343); (4) most mean of substance (as in 'base metal', *alchemy* enforcing this distinction between the sun's *golden face* and the *basest clouds*)

6   *rack* scudding clouds (with perhaps a hint of 'wrack' as 'damage, ruin')

7   *forlorn* (accented on the first syllable)

8   *Stealing.* The morning (become the *sun* which lightens it) moves slowly and furtively.
    to west (1) to the west; (2) in order to west. The verb has become obsolete (though Hardy's Drummer Hodge was buried where 'foreign constellations west | Each night above his mound'), but it was current in the sixteenth century.
    disgrace (1) dishonour; (2) disfigurement ('dis-grace')

9   *Even* (one syllable)

10 *triumphant* glorious (rather than 'victorious')
    splendour. Enriched by *shine*, which draws attention to the etymology; Latin *splendere* means 'to be bright and shining'.
    brow forehead

11 *out, alack* alas. The expression of grief reflects its cause, *out* suggesting both the *cloud*'s extinction of the *sun*'s light and the *sun*'s departure to the *west*.

12 *region* of the upper air, high

13 *this* (the sun's departure after *but one hour*)
    no whit not a jot, not at all

14 *Suns of the world* (1) great men (who are like *Suns* among lesser human planets); (2) mere mortals (punning on 'sons')
    stain (1) lose brightness and allure; (2) be dishonoured (by a blotted reputation)
    heaven's (one syllable)
    staineth. The sun 'stains' when clouds cover it; but even when it shines freely it 'stains' in the now obsolete sense 'drains light away', for it takes lustre from other bright things. (As the Countess of Pembroke, Sidney's sister, puts it in her translation of Psalm 72, 'The sun . . . all lights shall stain'.) Thus line 14 on one level attains the pithy generality of proverb, and *when* in *when heaven's sun staineth* tilts still further from 'when it happens that' to 'given that, since'.

Sonnet 34

Continuing the argument of Sonnet 33.

1–2 *Why didst thou . . . cloak.* The poet has shunned the proverbial advice, 'Although the sun shines, leave not your cloak at home'.

1   *beauteous* (two syllables)

3   *To* only to
    base. See 33.5 and the second note.

4   *brav'ry* splendid finery

4 *rotten smoke* unwholesome vapours

5, 7 *break . . . speak*. Rhyming on a vowel close to 'ar' in modern 'scarce'.

6 *To* in order to

7 *well* favourably

8 *That heals the wound and cures not the disgrace*. Like 33.8, this depends
  on the ambiguity of *disgrace*: both 'disfigurement' (here the scar left
  by the healed *wound*) and 'dishonour' (suffered by the poet when
  rejected by the youth). The line advances a commonplace; compare,
  for example, Wyatt's 'Sure I am, Brian, this wound shall heal again, |
  But yet, alas, the scar shall still remain' (*Sighs are my Food*), or *The
  Rape of Lucrece* 731–2: 'Bearing away the wound that nothing
  healeth, | The scar that will, despite of cure, remain'.

9 *shame* regret at having done (me) wrong
  physic medical help, medicine

10 *still* (1) nevertheless; (2) even afterwards

12 *bears the . . . cross* endures the . . . affliction. As in the phrase 'that is
  the cross I must bear' (based on Matthew 10:38, 'And he that taketh
  not his cross, and followeth me, is not worthy of me').

13 *those tears are pearl* (therefore precious. And probably curative; the
  Elizabethans thought the dust of ground pearl medicinal.)
  sheeds. An obsolete variant of 'sheds', retained from Q for the sake of
  rhyme. That the rhyme is 'sought' in this way, requiring a variant
  form, may or may not show the *I* of the poem working hard to wrest
  his text towards last-minute restitution.

14 *ransom all ill deeds*. The biblical resonance of line 12 (see the note)
  supports a hint of Christian imagery. As Christ died on the *cross* to
  ransom – the verb was commonly used – mankind from the effects of
  the fall and *all ill deeds*, so the young man's *tears* atone for his *ill deeds*
  against the poet.

Sonnet 35

1 *No more* no longer (but with a secondary suggestion of quantity)

2 *Roses have thorns* (proverbial: 'No rose without a thorn', or, as Lyly
  puts it in *Euphues*, 'The sweetest rose hath his prickle' – compare
  sweetest bud in line 4)
  silver (the colour of water as it wells and splashes in *fountains*)

3 *stain* dim (but suggesting 'corrupt', which connects the *moon and sun*
  directly to the youth. Compare, of course, Sonnets 33 and 34.)

4 *loathsome canker lives in sweetest bud*. By alluding to the proverb 'The
  canker soonest eats the fairest rose', Shakespeare suggests not only
  that 'excellent things are liable to flaw' but that 'flaws come quickest
  to the most excellent things'.

canker worm (caterpillar or larva) which destroys flowers

5 *All men make faults* (another proverbial truism: 'Every man has his faults')

even I I myself

in this (1) by doing this, namely; (2) in this poem (or, if the Q comma after *this* is read through, 'in this poem, which sets about')

6 *Authorizing* (accented on the second and fourth syllables)

Authorizing thy trespass with compare justifying your wrongdoing by comparison. See the Introduction, page 25.

6, 8 *compare . . . are.* Rhymed in the same way as 13.1 and 3 (see the note).

7 *salving.* As at 34.8, the sense of palliation exceeds that of cure.

amiss offence (though the young man is himself *amiss*, like a cankered bud or muddy fountain)

8 *Excusing thy sins more than thy sins are.* Once Q's 'their . . . their' is emended and the line's transitional position recognized, the difficulties dissolve. As he provides the young man with comparisons potent enough to excuse him from sins worse than those he has actually committed, the poet *makes faults* not only by tolerating misconduct but by displaying the doting weakness which makes him over-indulgent to his beloved, and by bringing sophistry (the *sense* of line 9) to the defence of *sensual*ity, using a faculty which should know better than to absolve an instinctive *amiss*.

9 *For to thy sensual fault I bring in sense* because in order to excuse your *sensual fault* I introduce sophistical reasoning. Malone drew attention to one quibble when he proposed the emendation 'incense' (something sweet and obfuscatory used in adoration); a second depends on the rejected sense of *sense* ('that which is receptive to *sensual* stimuli').

10 *Thy adverse party is thy advocate.* The client of the prosecution speaks for the defence.

10, 12 *advocate . . . hate.* Rhymed on a long 'a', resembling the 'a' in southern English 'bat', 'bad' lengthened.

11 *lawful* (1) in proper legal form; (2) just

commence. The correct legal term for 'begin an action'.

12 *in.* A lesser poet would have written ''tween': Shakespeare refuses to simplify the emotions by abstraction, and throws them into a turmoil (*civil war*) *in* which the alliances can only be assumed.

13 *accessory* accomplice

14 *sourly* churlishly (in action), bitterly (in effect)

Sonnet 36

1   *Let me confess* I must admit (so, permit me)
    twain parted (invoking 'coupled, pair' only to reject it. Pandarus
    makes the same joke at *Troilus and Cressida* III.1.96, where he says of
    Cressida and Paris, 'they two are twain'.)

2, 4   *one . . . alone.* The first of several rhymes between these words,
    resting on a long 'o' sounding like the 'ar' of 'ward' in Scottish
    English.

3   *blots* (of dishonour. Perhaps the *disgrace* of Sonnet 29; perhaps the
    stain inherited from the young man in 33–5.)

4   *borne* carried (like the *cross* of 34.12), endured
    alone (1) only; (2) in solitude (because the *two* will be *twain*)

5   *but* only
    respect. In this context, difficult to pin down: 'centre of attention',
    'thing honoured', 'act of esteeming', 'appearance' (with a suggestion
    of bodily identity between the *two*), 'degree' (relevant to the diverse
    social positions of the poet and the young man).

6   *separable spite* vexing separation

7   *love's sole effect* the single (and unique) action of our love. *Effect*
    suggests 'property' as well as 'working'; the *two* are a single thing in
    love's possession.

8   *steal sweet hours from love's delight* (by keeping the *two* apart, though
    one, and thus unable to enjoy each other's company)

9   *not evermore* nevermore (though Shakespeare also employs the
    circumlocution to imply a thwarted constancy: 'not, as I did and
    expected in future, continually to . . .')

10   *my bewailèd guilt* (note the *blots* of line 3)

11   *public kindness* kindness to me in public

12   *Unless thou take that honour from thy name* without accordingly
    dishonouring yourself, unless you are prepared to lower your
    standing

13–14 *But do not . . . report.* The same couplet, intriguingly, concludes
    Sonnet 96. See the note to 96.13–14.

13   *in such sort* in such a way

14   *As* that
    being (one syllable)
    report reputation

Sonnet 37

3   *made lame.* Though metaphorical – compare, for instance, the
    Quarto *King Lear* IV.6.221, 'A most poore man made lame by

Fortunes blowes' – used by biographical critics to cripple the poet.
dearest direst, most grievous (and 'heartfelt' on *Fortune's* part)
spite ill-will, malicious injury

4 *comfort* cheer, consolation
 of from
 truth honesty, fidelity, soundness (the young man not being *lame*)

5 *wit* intelligence

7 *Entitled in thy parts do crownèd sit* having the right and title, sit throned
 like a king among your good qualities

8 *make my love engrafted to this store* add my love to this stock (or
 'copious plenitude') of virtues so that it draws strength thence and,
 fused with you, flourishes

9 *then* (1) therefore; (2) at that time

9, 11 *despised . . . sufficed.* If the rhyme is not indeed imperfect, it relies on
 the second 's' in *despised* sounding, as it could, as such, rather than as
 'z'.

10 *this shadow doth such substance give.* A *shadow* is usually the product of
 a *substance*, and the former's inferiority to the latter was proverbial;
 but the young man's *shadow* (his image, made up of *worth and truth*
 and all the *store* of good *parts*) here gives 'tissue' and 'strength' (two
 Elizabethan senses of *substance*) to the *decrepit* poet.

11 *abundance* (in *store*, but also in giving)
 sufficed adequately supplied, satisfied

12 *part* portion (a quibbling deflection of sense from *parts*, line 7)

13 *Look what* whatever

14 *then ten times happy me.* Wishing the youth the *best*, the poet grants, or
 rediscovers, the *best* (of *beauty, birth, or wealth, or wit*) in him; as a
 result, he is infused with happiness at the *store* transfused to him.

Sonnet 38

1, 9, *Muse.* Used in the restricted sense 'creative faculty' in lines 1 and 13,
13 but in 9 evoking the nine sister-goddesses supposed to inspire
 learning and the arts.

1 *want subject to invent* lack subject-matter for literary creation (allud-
 ing to the rhetorical process *inventio*, 'the finding out of a topic')

2 *that* who

3 *Thine own sweet argument* you, as an attractive literary theme

4 *vulgar paper* commonplace composition (by metonymy)
 rehearse repeat (for the pejorative implications, see the note to 21.4)

5 *in me* (by metonymy, 'in my verse'. Compare the doubly personal and
 literary *sweet argument* of line 3.)

6   *stand against thy sight* meet your eye. *Stand* modestly suggests 'bear looking at'.

7   *dumb.* Although the modern American sense, 'stupid', was not current in Elizabethan English, 'unresponsive', 'dull', and 'insensible' would be understood here in addition to 'lacking in eloquence'.

8   *When thou thyself dost give invention light.* By being himself (that is, a *sweet argument* incarnate), the youth illuminates (like the sun) or lights the way (like a torchbearer) for, or else finds out or digs up (and thus brings to *light*), rhetorical *invention*. His mere being ensures that the poet has matter.

9, 11   *worth . . . forth.* The rhyme depends, it seems, on a vowel resembling 'u' in 'educated' modern 'put' – a pronunciation available at the time, though not standard.

10   *invocate* invoke. Used mostly in theological contexts from the sixteenth to the nineteenth century; now obsolete.

11   *bring forth* (suggesting parturition. Compare 32.11 or 76.8.)

12   *Eternal numbers* verses that will live forever
      outlive long date. A hyperbole (the work will live not to but beyond a far distant *date*), intensified by *date*'s secondary sense 'end, point of expiring' (the work will survive even its far distant extinction, it will never die).

13   *slight* inconsiderable
      curious fastidious in fancy, hypercritical

14   *pain* effort, trouble (as in 'take pains')
      thine shall be the praise (because you are the *sweet argument* of the verse)

Sonnet 39

Close in its concerns to Sonnet 36.

1   *with manners* decently (here 'without self-praise')

2   *the better part of me.* Shakespeare apparently took this phrase (repeated at 74.8) from Golding's Ovid, where it translates '*parte . . . meliore mei*' (*Metamorphoses* XV.875). Ovid simply means 'my soul'; but Shakespeare has in mind the proverbial saw 'A friend is one's second self' – recurring at 42.13, 62.13, and 133.6 – and, beyond that, the Platonic and Pauline notion that lovers are part-selves capable of mutual completion (compare Aristophanes' fable in the *Symposium* and Ephesians 5.28–31, 'He that loveth his wife, loveth himself . . . For this cause shall a man leave father and mother, and shall be joined unto his wife, and two shall be made one flesh'). The idea recurs in the plays: at *The Comedy of Errors* III.2.61, for example,

or *Julius Caesar* II.1.274, where Portia, addressing Brutus, calls herself 'your self, your half'.

3–4   *What can . . . thee* where's the profit in praising myself, and what kind of praise is it if not self-praise when I praise you?

5   *Even for* precisely because of

6   *dear* (1) heartfelt; (2) precious
    name of single one the reputation of being unique and undivided, the title of unity. *Divided* in line 5 – which implies separation between *parts* of some natural whole – makes this loss particularly bitter.

6, 8   *one . . . alone.* See the note to 36.2, 4.

8   *That due* that owed payment, that which is owed. *Due* works twice and, in the latter elliptical sense, underwrites the second half of line 8 by tautology.

9   *O absence.* When the poet reveals that the separation of line 7 is only physical, the argument of the second quatrain (which had implied a spiritual and emotional severance) retrospectively weakens. Yet that supports, in turn, the ambivalently climactic last lines of the sonnet.

9, 11   *prove . . . love.* See the note to 25.13, 14.

11   *entertain the time* pass the time pleasantly

12   *so sweetly dost deceive* with utter sweetness *thou* (from line 9) *dost* beguile. *So* perhaps suggests 'thus'. Despite *thy* in line 10, and *thou* (again) in line 13, some editors feel *thou* too distant an antecedent; they read 'doth' (governed by *love* and/or *Which time and thoughts*) or, less plausibly, 'do' (taking *Which* as a relative pronoun and *time and thoughts* as plural).

13   *And that thou teachest how.* Elliptical; to be read in the light of lines 9–10: 'And *were it not* that thou, *O absence*, teachest how'.

13–14   *to make . . . remain.* The straightforward conceit – that by writing laudatory verses about the young man the poet makes him present though absent and thus *one twain* – is accompanied by a return to the theme of lines 1–4; the poet and the young man are on an emotional level *one twain*, and the youth can be praised *here* though *hence* because, despite their physical separation, the young man is still the poet's *better part*, a piece of himself bound to be wherever he is. ('Our separation so abides and flies', as Antony says to Cleopatra when leaving her at 1.3.102–3, 'That thou residing here goes yet with me, | And I hence fleeting here remain with thee.')

Sonnet 40

Whatever *ill deeds* lie behind, or are imagined in, Sonnets 34–6, the treachery described here and in the next two poems resembles so closely the poet's betrayal by the dark lady and his youthful friend – discussed in several sonnets between 133 and 152 – that it is usually assumed that the two situations are one.

1 *all my loves* all those I love and all the love I give them

2 *then* (1) at that time; (2) in that case, therefore

3–4 *No love . . . more.* Since the young man already enjoyed the poet's *love*, any extra *love* which he now takes can only be false. *My love* means 'my affection', but the ambiguity of line 1 persists strongly enough to allow the bitter wordplay of lines 5–6.

5 *for my love* (1) out of affection for me (liking what I love because you love me); (2) to win *more* of my affection (by taking the love the mistress apparently enjoys); (3) as a substitute for my affection (lending a dark undercurrent to the line)
  thou my love receivest you entertain my mistress. More than a tactful euphemism, *receivest* largely absolves the youth by making him a passive agent.

6 *I cannot . . . usest.* The coolly reasonable 'I can't blame you for your conduct because you do it for love of me' (compare 42.6) is undercut by a sardonic 'I can't blame you for sexually enjoying my mistress'.

7 *thyself deceivest.* Some editors retain Q's 'this selfe' for *thyself*; but the poet is clearly not deceived (though he may be meant to be), whereas the youth does (according to line 8) delude himself.

8 *wilful* stubborn, perverse, lustful. For the last, sexual sense, see Sonnets 134–6.
  taste of sampling of, testing of (and, perhaps, 'relish for')
  what thyself refusest what you really (deep in the *self*) balk at. As often, something is lost in modernizing Q's 'thy selfe'.

9 *gentle.* Contrast with *my poverty* supports the suggestion of good birth.

10 *steal thee* take for yourself
  all my poverty what little I have. Echoing *all* from line 1, pointedly, and (if *my poverty* is taken as a title for the mistress) subtly insulting a treacherous woman.

11 *love knows* my love (all I am) can tell that. With a hint of 'Love knows' by analogy with 'God knows'.

12 *love's wrong* wrong committed by a loved one. But 'wrong suffered by a loving person' and 'wrong done to love (or Love)' also contributes.

13 *Lascivious.* Modified in any case by *grace*, the word is milder than it might appear – is in keeping with the tact of the poem – in that, in Elizabethan English, it could mean 'wanton, sportive' as well as 'lustful'.
  grace charm, loveliness (with spiritual implications which link the word paradoxically with *Lascivious*, and thus anticipate the oxymoron *ill well* later in the line)

14 *spites* malicious vexations, injuries

Sonnet 41

1   *pretty* (1) attractive (used ironically, as at *Dr Faustus* I.1.130 in the 1606 text, 'A pretty case of paltry legacies!'); (2) slight, small (a sense played on in the proverb 'Little things are pretty'); (3) sportive, wanton
    liberty licence (the *liberty* of libertines)

2   *sometime* sometimes
    absent from thy heart (by being forgotten)

3   *befits.* The subject is *wrongs*; such disagreements between verb and noun are not uncommon in Elizabethan English.

4   *still* constantly, always

5   *Gentle thou art, and therefore to be won.* Echoing and wittily inverting the commonplace 'She is a woman and therefore to be won' (used by Shakespeare at, for instance, *1 Henry VI* V.3.79 and *Titus Andronicus* II.1.83–4). Perhaps the woman, it is implied, was to some extent wooed and won. As at 40.9, *gentle* involves both tenderness (which makes the young man winnable) and good birth (which makes him a prize worth winning).

6   *to be assailed* worth seducing (a conventional love/war image)

8   *she.* Some editors retain Q's 'he', ignoring the irony of the second quatrain. Just as line 5 reverses in the reader's mind, returning to its proverbial base, so *she* implies 'he'.

9   *my seat* place which belongs to me. In Shakespeare, frequently, an image of power, possession, and sexual rights (hence Iago's 'I do suspect the lusty Moor | Hath leaped into my seat', *Othello* II.1.286–7).
    forbear deny yourself, refuse to take

10–11   *thy beauty and thy straying youth | Who lead thee.* Aspects of the young man, given an independent life (hence *Who* not 'Which'), and seen as raffish bad company.

11   *riot* chaotic dissipation, debauchery

12   *truth* troth

Sonnet 42

In Sonnet 40 the poet accuses the youth of treachery yet absolves him from the offence (see, especially, lines 5–6 and the notes). In 41 the critical note is more pronounced (see lines 5 and 8 and the notes), but the poet still contrives to excuse the friend by blaming the *beauty* and *youth* which led him on (lines 9–12). Here, in Sonnet 42, the anxieties are resolved as the poet manages to admit the youth's duplicity while demonstrating to himself that the offence has effectively not been committed (and, interestingly, that he and his friend are closer than the friend and the mistress).

2   *loved* (significantly placed in the past tense)

3   *of my wailing chief* the main cause of my sorrow

4   *loss in love* (involving not just emotion, as in line 2, but a beloved, the youth, to the mistress)

        touches concerns, affects

        nearly intimately

5   *Loving offenders.* A paradox, and quibble (the *offenders'* offence is *Loving*, as is their relationship with each other and the poet), resting on a common form of salutation (compare 'most loving liege', for instance, at *Richard II* I.1.21).

        excuse provide excuses for (though the poet's object in providing the apologia is to persuade himself to *excuse* the pair emotionally)

6, 8 *love her . . . approve her.* On this feminine rhyme see the note to 25.13, 14.

7   *even* (one syllable)

        abuse wrong, deceive (by being unfaithful)

8   *Suff'ring* tolerating, allowing

        approve put to proof, try out sexually. Conceivably the suggestion of 'insult' in *abuse* elicits 'commend', by contrast.

9   *my loss* (the double *loss in love* described in line 4 and the note)

        my love's (the mistress's)

10   *losing her* in my *losing her* to him

        found that loss recovered the lost love (both 'affection' and 'beloved', as in lines 8 and 4)

11   *and.* Following Q, where 'and' might, however, be the old form of 'an', meaning 'if'. *And I lose both twain* would thus parallel *If I lose thee* (line 9), comparing the effects of a double with a single loss.

12   *for my sake* out of love for me (lines 5–8)

        lay on me this cross lay this cruel burden upon me (see 34.12 and the note)

13   *my friend and I are one* (as the poet established in Sonnet 39)

13, 14 *one . . . alone.* See the note to 36.2, 4.

14   *flatt'ry* pleasing delusion

        but me alone only me

Sonnet 43

1   *When most I wink, then do mine eyes best see.* Playfully developing the proverb 'Although I wink, I am not blind'. The implication of this saw is moral, with *wink* meaning, in our idiom, 'turn a blind eye'. Hence Macbeth's 'Let not light see my black and deep desires. | The eye wink at the hand' (I.4.52–3). The sonnet thus develops its interest in night, sight, and sleep (already explored in Sonnets 27

and 28) from a line suggestive of the theme of the three preceding poems: the poet's ignoring faults in the friend. Setting aside its moral sense, *wink* means 'close the eyes', as in modern English, but also 'nod off' (we still 'take forty winks'), 'sleep'. *Best see* is most immediately 'see most clearly'; but 'see the best there is to see (the youth)' can be discerned on rereading the sonnet.

2   *unrespected* regardlessly, without discrimination (and, perhaps, 'not worthy respect', not being the youth)

4   *darkly bright* blindly seeing, radiant though not releasing light (brilliant behind the eyelids' shutters. Informed by the renaissance notion that eyes create the light by which they see.)

bright in dark directed. Interpretation depends on *bright*: it can be adjectival (the *bright* eyes are *directed* by night though wandering by day), adverbial (the eyes look 'cunningly' in *darkness*), or part of an adverbial compound, 'bright-in-dark' (which usefully anticipates line 5).

5   *Then.* Following *When . . . then* in line 1, temporal; but this gives way to 'therefore' as the quatrain develops.

whose shadow shadows doth make bright whose image brightens darkness

6   *thy shadow's form* the substance which lies behind your dream-shadow, the *form* or model of that *shadow* which is your body's *form*. Using the terms inverted at 37.10 directly, though with a paradoxical twist.

form happy show create a pleasing spectacle

7   *clear* (1) bright (compare 'my clear sun' at *Henry VIII* I.1.226); (2) absolute (the *day* when free from all traces of *night*); (3) illustrious, glorious ('O that estates, degrees, and offices | Were not derived corruptly, and that clear honour | Were purchased by the merit of the wearer!' laments Arragon at *The Merchant of Venice* II.9.41–3).

clearer (1) brighter; (2) more visible; (3) more illustrious (see above, and compare 'the clearest gods' at *King Lear* IV.6.73. *Clear* and *clearer* relate paradoxically through their primary senses; for why would a bright object seem more striking in daylight than darkness?)

9   *How would, I say.* Ostensibly repetitious, the sestet moves beyond the idea of seeing a *shadow* in *clear day* to seeing the youth there himself.

10 *the living day.* The real day may be 'full of life', unlike *dead night* (line 11), but *living* also acts as a partly transferred epithet, since the poet means to see the *living* youth, not his *shadow*.

11 *dead* (1) lifeless (as opposed to *living*); (2) absolute (as in 'dead centre')

imperfect (because insubstantial, and because seen by *night* instead of *day*)

11   *shade*. As in the sestet of Sonnet 27, there is a suggestion of ghostly haunting (elicited here by *dead*); compare 61.5–8.

12   *heavy*. A word so often associated with 'ponderous, leaden' *sleep* that, in Shakespeare, 'to be heavy' often means 'to be fatigued'. Here, though, a second sense, 'sorrowful' ('a heavy tale', 'my heart is exceedingly heavy', commonplace in Shakespeare), arguably contributes.

       stay linger, reside

14   *show thee me*. The primary sense is clearly 'show thee to me'; but Shakespeare's inversion allows 'show me to thee', so that the poet's visions (*me* seeing *thee*) become touchingly like encounters (each seeing the other).

Sonnet 44

Though clearly linked with Sonnet 43, this poem is paired explicitly with 45, and both are twinned with 50 and 51. At *Henry V* III.7.11–78, in the Dauphin's eulogy on his horse, ideas rehearsed in these four sonnets (space, time, travel, the four elements) recur most interestingly, but at too great length for quotation here.

1   *dull* sluggish, heavy

2   *Injurious* (three syllables) malicious, wounding
      stop block
      way course, path

3   *despite* in spite

4   *limits* districts. In the context of *far remote*, 'extremities' registers; the poet *would be brought* from the ends of the earth.
      where to where
      stay linger, reside (the former carrying a hint of blame not felt, of course, at 43.12)

5   *No matter then although my foot did stand* it would not then matter if I sojourned

6   *farthest earth removed from* corner of the world most distant from

8   *he* (personifying *thought*)

10   *large lengths of miles* many long miles, long miles by the mile

10, 12 *gone . . . moan*. See the note to 30.9, 11.

11   *so much of earth and water wrought* being so thoroughly compounded of *earth and water*. Here and in Sonnet 45 Shakespeare relies on the old division of matter into four elements: *earth and water*, heavy, slow, and base; *air* and *fire*, light, quick, and noble. Ovid relates the four thus:

> This endless world contains therein I say
> Four substances of which all things are gendered. Of these four,

> The earth and water for their mass and weight are sunken lower.
> The other couple, air and fire, the purer of the twain,
> Mount up, and naught can keep them down.
>
> *Metamorphoses* XV.239–43 (Golding's translation)

It is probably significant that the poet is separated from the young man by the very elements of which he is *wrought* (the *sea and land*, line 7).

12   *attend time's leisure* (1) wait for time to pass; (2) wait until Time is ready to work in my favour (the poet is a humble petitioner waiting on the whims of a great man)

13   *by* from, by courtesy of

14   *heavy* (1) sorrowful; (2) weighty

badges indications, signs. Knights were identified by *badges* (devices) and tradesmen bore them (as brooches and emblems) to denote their skills.

either's woe the woe of each (element. The *tears* represent *earth* by being *heavy* and *water* by being wet.)

Sonnet 45

1   *other two* (elements. The argument continues from the previous sonnet.)

slight insubstantial

purging purifying

4   *present-absent*. Both 'simultaneously' and 'alternately' *present* and *absent*. The former concentrates the hyperbole of line 2 into a paradox; the latter, enforced by *swift motion*, introduces the idea of travel from self to beloved.

5   *For*. The emendation 'So' (assuming a compositorial misreading of 'soe' in secretary hand) is attractive.

quicker speedier, more vital, sharper, and clearer (of *air*), burning more strongly (of *fire*)

5, 7 *gone . . . alone*. See 31.10, 12 and the note.

6   *embassy of love to thee* mission bearing my love for you to you. Enriched by the ambiguity of *to thee*.

7   *being* (one syllable)

two alone only two

8   *Sinks down*. On the ponderous weight of *earth and water*, see the note to 44.11.

oppressed with melancholy weighed down with brooding despondency. Context incites the reader to take *melancholy* in its physiological sense, for 'black bile' (translating melancholy from the Greek) is a body fluid associated with *earth* and credited with the power to create despondency when present in excess. *Melancholy* makes the line hypermetrical, unless 'a' is elided. Opinion divides over stress: elsewhere Shakespeare accents the first and third syllables, *mElanchOly*, but contemporary instances of *melAncholY* are easily found. If the usual Shakespearian stress applies, the unstressed 'y' of *melancholy* rhymes awkwardly – in deliberate sluggish clumsiness? – with the stressed *thee* of line 6.

9   *life's composition be recured* the balance and blend of elements necessary for life be restored

10   *those swift messengers* (*air* and *fire*)

11   *even but now* just this moment. *Even* is here monosyllabic.

13-14   *This told . . . sad.* Hearing that the young man is well, the poet rejoices; but he then becomes anxious and, needing reassurance, sends his *swift messengers* away, only to become (devoid of *fire* and *air*) sad.

Sonnet 46

Sonnets 46 and 47 rehearse and resolve a conflict, conventional in renaissance poetry, between the *eye* and the *heart* – apparently in the light of a portrait of the friend. As at *A Lover's Complaint* 134-40, where the picture of a lovely youth attracts similar devotion, the problem of outward show and inward life arises: should the grounds of love be beauty (pleasing to the *eye*) or moral character (satisfying mind and *heart*)?

1, 3   *war . . . bar.* Rhymed on a flat 'a', like the vowel in northern English 'bat', 'bad'.

2   *conquest* (1) spoils of war; (2) legal acquisition without inheritance (see 6.14 and the note). The former continues the imagery of *mortal war*; the latter carries the poem into the courtroom.

      of thy sight which is the sight of you

3   *bar* prohibit (by order)

4   *freedom of that right* liberty to excuse the right (of seeing). As with *bar*, there are legal overtones.

5   *thou in him dost lie.* A poetic commonplace – that the beloved resides (one sense of *lie*) in the lover's *heart* – extended to 'you are in his possession, you are at his disposal, it lies in him to say who or what should see you'.

6   *closet.* In Elizabethan usage both 'small private room' and 'box or cabinet (used for storing valuables)'. Either might be meant here.

      crystal eyes. The suggestion of cliché (compare Pistol's bombastic use of the image at *Henry V* II.3.51) is deliberate; the *heart* is deriding the *eye*.

9   *'cide* settle, decide. It is possible that Q's 'side' should not be

modernized in this way but interpreted as a verb meaning 'assign to one or other side in a dispute'.

title legal right of possession

impanellèd enrolled on a jury (the correct legal term)

10   *quest* jury, inquest

thoughts, all tenants to the heart. The jury has been 'packed' to the advantage of the *heart*. The *heart* is often presented as a rational, or at least thinking, organ in Shakespeare; compare 69.2.

12   *moiety* (two syllables) portion (not necessarily a half)

13–14   *mine eye's . . . heart.* The jury finds in favour of the *heart*, despite its granting the disputed *sight* to the eye; for it grants the *eye* enjoyment of the young man's *appearance*, the *heart* enjoyment of his *love*.

Sonnet 47

The argument continues from the previous sonnet.

1   *a league is took* an alliance is struck

2   *each doth good turns now unto the other.* Invoking directly the proverb glanced at in 24.9, 'One good turn deserves another'.

now (after the disagreements recorded in Sonnet 46)

4   *Or heart* or when my heart

himself itself

5   *With* on (the usual Elizabethan locution in such a context)

6   *painted banquet.* Glancing, perhaps, with the help of *banquet* ('formal dessert of sweetmeats and fruit'), at Zeuxis' *painted* grapes – a commonplace image, in the period, of art rivalling nature: 'Zeuxis, for proof of his cunning, brought upon the scaffold a table wherein were clusters of grapes so lively painted that the very birds of the air flew flocking thither for to be pecking at the grapes' (Holland's translation of Pliny). Compare the note to 75.13.

8   *share a part.* The echo of 46.12 reminds readers of the dispute now so amicably resolved.

9, 11   *love . . . move.* See the note to 25.13, 14.

10   *are.* Some editors emend to 'art'; but Shakespeare elsewhere uses this form before consonants, for the sake of euphony.

12   *still* constantly

13–14   *thy picture . . . delight.* So intimate have the foes of Sonnet 46 become that the previously contentious *sight* is now a source of shared pleasure; indeed, line 14 is ordered in such a way as to suggest that, although the *eye* can see the young man without the *heart*'s help, it can only *delight* in seeing after its friend the *heart* has joined the fun.

Sonnet 48

1   *took my way* set out on my journey. Whether the sonnet was written on the occasion of some particular Shakespearian journey is, of course, a matter for speculation.

2   *trifle* thing of little worth
    truest firmest (probably with a metaphorical 'most honest')
    bars that which prevents entry (though, beyond this bland abstraction, *wards* in line 4 suggests another sense – the *bars* which cover prison windows)

3   *to my use* (1) ready for me to use; (2) to my profit

3–4 *stay | From* remain out of

4   *hands of falsehood* untrustworthy hands (of thieves)
    in sure wards of trust behind sure and trustworthy guards. *Wards*, immediately abstract here, often means – and here suggests – 'cell walls' and 'metal ridges round a lock (designed to ensure that the right key is used)'.

5   *to whom my jewels trifles are* compared with whom my jewels are trifles. Line 2 does not after all ascribe to the poet an absurdly tight-fisted caution (what he there diminishes as *trifles* are *jewels*).

5, 7 *are . . . care.* Rhymed in the same way as 13.1 and 3.

6   *worthy* esteemed, valuable
    grief cause of anxious distress

7   *care* sorrow, anxiety (though it is no doubt significant that the line's antithesis cannot quite suppress the positive sense 'loving concern')

14 *truth proves thievish for a prize so dear* honesty itself becomes thievish for the sake of such a precious prize. The passive 'you will be taken from my breast by some thief' is primary, but line 12 allows 'you will steal away from my breast'. The youth will be *stol'n* so easily, perhaps, that the volition will be partly his. It was proverbial that 'Rich preys do make true men thieves'.

Sonnet 49

1, 5, 9 *Against* in preparation for

2   *defects* (accented on the second syllable)

3   *Whenas thy love hath cast his utmost sum* when your love for me has made its final reckoning (thus closing the account. The image is, with cold irony, derived from commerce, but a phrase taken from dicing, 'at last cast', meaning 'in extremity, near ruin', informs *cast his utmost*.)

4   *advised respects* pondered considerations, well-informed reflection, careful heed

5   *strangely* like a stranger

5, 7   *pass . . . was.* Rhymed on a short 'a', like the vowel in northern English 'bat', 'bad', with the 's' of *was* like that in *pass*, not 'z'.

6   *scarcely* hardly
        that sun, thine eye. An image prepared by 18.5, 20.6, 33, 34.4–6, 35.3, and interestingly at odds with 130.1.

6, 8   *eye . . . gravity.* A full rhyme; compare 7.2, 4 and, hence, 1.2, 4.

7   *converted* changed
        the thing it was its former quality

8   *Shall reasons find of settled gravity* (1) will find reasons for behaving with dignified reserve (towards me); (2) will find ponderously plausible excuses (for changing its nature)

9–12   *Against that time . . . thy part.* The quatrain has caused difficulties, presumably because the poet's double desire to defend himself (lines 9–10) and excuse the young man for rejecting him (lines 11–12) turns a logical 'But' in line 11 into *And*. Arguably, it is necessary for the poet to establish his *desert* in lines 9–10 if he is to qualify as a witness responsible enough to excuse the friend in lines 11–12.

9   *ensconce* shelter, fortify

10, 12 *desert . . . part.* Q's 'desart' points up the basis of the rhyme.

11   *this my hand against myself uprear.* The poet is like a witness who swears (with raised *hand*) to testify against himself, and (especially in the light of *guard*, line 12) like a soldier who threatens himself with his own *hand*.
        against. This time the sense is 'in opposition to'.
        uprear raise

12   *lawful* (picking up the legal imagery of line 11)
        reasons arguments, excuses

14   *to love* (in general, or 'me')
        allege (another legal term) offer, propose
        no cause no reason, no grounds. But one has only to think of Cordelia's 'No cause, no cause' (*King Lear* IV.7.75) to grasp how sharply Shakespeare condemns the youth in the poet's so painfully excusing him. Having asked, with Cordelia, Is love to be calculated? (lines 3–4), the poet now implies, But who can *allege* a *cause* why I or anyone should be loved?

Sonnet 50

See the headnote to Sonnet 44, though it should be added that *Astrophil and Stella* 49 – a sonnet which wittily correlates the moods of a horse and rider – offers a non-Shakespearian analogue. More distantly, both Sidney and

Shakespeare draw on a convention of indivisibility in good horsemanship also invoked at *A Lover's Complaint* 107 (see the note).

1   *heavy* (1) sadly; (2) slowly

2–4 *When what ... friend* when what I'm looking for, the goal and conclusion of my exhausting journey (the alternative sense of Q's 'trauel', that is 'toil', contributes here), only instructs the comfort and rest that I win at my *travel's end* to tell me that I am so many miles away from my *friend*. (Here, and throughout the sonnet, abstractions are subtly personified.) It is possible that the *travel's end* comes each day at dusk, and that the poet laments nightly that he has journeyed further from the young man.

5   *tired with my woe* (1) wearied by my sorrow; (2) clad in ('attired with') my grief. The phrase modifies either *me* or the *beast* – indeed, both – a human-animal confusion continued through the poem. Compare *Love's Labour's Lost* IV.2.125–6: 'Imitari is nothing. So doth the hound his master, the ape his keeper, the tired horse his rider.'

6   *dully*. Though 51.2 enforces this emendation – which may, in any case, merely be a modernization – of Q's 'duly', the original reading is not impossible. 'Duly' would mean 'methodically' and, perhaps, 'following a straight course' (as in 'due west'). Indeed, a pun may be intended (it is just workable in Elizabethan English), invoking both dullness and dutiful plodding.
     to bear in bearing
     that weight (the *woe* of line 5)

7   *some* (conceivably quibbling on the word 'sum', still current in the period in the sense 'quantity which one horse can carry, horse-load')
     instinct (stressed on the second syllable)

7–8 *did know ... thee* knew that his rider disliked the making of hasting-away from you. *Being made from* can also yield 'when he is being carried away from' and 'because he is being carried away from'.

8   *being* (one syllable)

9, 11 *on ... groan*. Rhyming on a long 'o' (pronounced like 'ar' in Scottish English 'wart', 'ward').

11   *heavily* sadly, grievously. The dwindling of two senses to one (contrast *heavy*, line 1) marks an important stage in the sonnet's modulation from partly physical to essentially emotional terms.

12   *sharp* painful (though, in the latter part of line 12, also *sharp* as spurs are)

14   *onward ... behind*. While the primary sense is spatial, 'future' and 'past' contribute.
     my joy. Perhaps the young man as well as the emotion he arouses; Cordelia is Lear's 'joy' (I.1.82), and Constance calls Arthur 'My life, my joy, my food, my all the world!' (*King John* III.4.104).

Sonnet 51

Obviously linked to Sonnet 50.

1   *love.* Here 'affection' rather than 'beloved'.

    slow offence offence of slowness

2   *my dull bearer.* The horse which *Plods dully* in Sonnet 50.

    speed. Though the poet's departure is *slow*, it is still too fast; hence the *haste* of line 3.

4   *of posting is no need* there is no need to ride post-haste

5, 7 *find . . . wind.* See the note to 14.6, 8.

6   *swift extremity* the most extreme speed

7   *though* even if I was

8   *In wingèd speed no motion shall I know* travelling with the speed of a winged thing, I still won't feel as though I'm moving

9   *Then can no horse* at that time no horse will be able to

10   *perfect'st* (standardizing Q's metaplasmic 'perfects'. The reading has troubled editors, who object that 'perfect' can have no superlative form; but Shakespeare embraces that impossibility to express the super-distilled quality of *desire*. Compare 'the perfectest report' at *Macbeth* I.5.2.)

    being (one syllable)

11   *neigh.* Frequently emended; but the poet's *desire* is here imagined making a horse-like noise to match the human sound made by the horse in the corresponding line of the previous sonnet. (Compare the stallion in *Venus and Adonis*, which 'neighs' with sexual desire at lines 265 and 307.)

    fiery race (1) proud lineage, spirited breeding (contrasted with the *dull flesh* of the poet's *jade*); (2) fierce career, passionate gallop (suggesting competitive contrast as *desire* outstrips the poet's *slow* horse)

12   *But love.* The 'affection' of line 1, incorporating the *desire* of lines 9 and 10 and suggesting 'Love' in the form of Cupid.

    for love (1) for its own sake; (2) out of charity; (3) on account of *love* (the poet's for *thee* and, conceivably, the kindness shown the poet by his horse at 50.6–8)

    jade nag

13   *wilful* (adjective as adverb)

14   *Towards thee . . . go.* In his eager *desire* the poet will dash home even faster than the horse carrying him (and horses that go *wilful slow* are likely to be leaving their stables and inclined to retrace their tracks with corresponding speed). *Give him leave* suggests a distinctly dismissive 'give him permission' as well as an unreined freedom to gallop; *to go*, playfully contrasted with *from thee going* in line 13, means 'to walk' as well as 'to move'

(*desire* is so swift that it makes the horse's homeward gallop seem a plod).

Sonnet 52

1   *So am I as the rich* I am just like the rich man
         blessèd (because 'happying')

1, 4   *key . . . survey.* For some speakers, apparently, inexact, the rhyme
         tended towards 'kay, survey'.

3–4   *The which . . . pleasure* (prudently heeding the proverb 'A seldom use
         of pleasures maketh the same the more pleasant')

4   *For* for fear of
         fine (1) slender, delicate; (2) splendid
         seldom infrequent

5   *Therefore are feasts* that is why feast-days are
         solemn. 'Ceremonious because special', and thus 'festive' rather than
         'glumly formal'. Context draws attention to the word's Latin root,
         sollemnis, 'annual, customary, wonted, orderly'.
         rare excellent, uncommon, widely separated, dispersed, distinct

5, 7   *rare . . . are.* Resembling the rhyme at 13.1 and 3.

6–7   *set,* | *Like stones of worth.* Despite Q's logically correct comma, an
         enjambed 'set like stones of worth' also registers.

7   *thinly placèd* distributed sparsely

8   *captain* chief
         jewels (two syllables)
         carcanet jewelled necklace or collar

9   *So is the time that keeps you as my chest.* After an initial parallel with *the
         rich* of line 1, *the time* becomes *as a chest* (that is, 'like a chest'),
         containing the youth. It is the poet who resembles *the rich*, having
         access to a *chest* which holds the friend as *treasure*. The primary
         impact of *the time* lingers, however, into lines 11 and 12, where it
         contributes markedly.

11   *some special instant special blest.* The echo of *blessèd* in line 1, and the
         obvious association of *instant* and *time*, revives the initial impact of
         line 9, put into abeyance by the syntax of 9 and 10.

12   *unfolding* (when opened, though the active verb harks back to *the time*
         as agent)
         his its (that is, *the time*'s)
         pride (1) splendour; (2) that of which *the time* is proud

13   *Blessèd.* The blessing, refracted in line 11, here passes from the
         opener of the casket to the *treasure* within.

13–14   *gives scope . . . hope* allows the owner (the poet and, perhaps, *the time*),

when you are his, to rejoice, and when you are not, to hope for your
return

Sonnet 53

The poem enlivens, and deepens towards philosophical profundity (see the
Introduction, pages 30–31), a sonneteering commonplace: that the beloved
comprises all worldly beauty. Shakespeare satirized the same topic in a poem
of Orlando's, at *As You Like It* III.2.121–50. Explaining how Rosalind
became 'The quintessence of every sprite | Heaven would in little show' (that
is, the type of all lesser beauties), the lover writes, in lines intriguingly close to
Sonnet 53:

> Therefore Heaven Nature charged
>   That one body should be filled
> With all graces wide-enlarged.
>   Nature presently distilled
> Helen's cheek, but not her heart,
>   Cleopatra's majesty,
> Atalanta's better part,
>   Sad Lucretia's modesty.
> Thus Rosalind of many parts
>   By heavenly synod was devised,
> Of many faces, eyes, and hearts,
>   To have the touches dearest prizèd.
> Heaven would that she these gifts should have,
> And I to live and die her slave.

1–2 *substance . . . shadows.* The opposition so deftly invoked at 37.10 here
  becomes the basis of a poem. As a result, its Platonic potential is
  realized. *Substance* is popularly the 'stuff of an object', but context
  requires 'essential nature', and the mild paradox posed by the
  conflicting senses answers the Platonic requirement that the 'form'
  or 'idea' (the 'quintessence' of Orlando's panegyric) be both ab-
  stracted from and more essentially real than its replicas or *shadows*.

1 *whereof* of what

2 *strange* (1) exotic; (2) not your own. The following lines make (2)
  paradoxical, for, although the *shadows* do not belong to the young
  man, they are pieces of him, fragments and flawed reflections.

  tend. The primary sense is 'follow like servants, attend on you': the
  shadows serve the young man, much as *summer and his pleasures wait
  on* him at 97.11. This retrospectively elicits 'wealth' from *substance*
  (as we still understand 'a man of substance'), and the question posed
  by line 1 looks new (for a young man with *millions* of lackeys would
  have to be of extraordinary *substance*). *On you tend* might be meant to

237

suggest 'incline towards you' and thus 'strive to reach your state of perfection'; *shadows* do *tend* to match a form, and invariably, through distortion, fail. It is difficult to agree with those who find 'ghosts' in *shadows* – as though the youth's beauty resembled black magic in its power to draw spirits into his service – unless it be that the shadows of Adonis, Helen, and other dead beauties haunt his features.

3   *everyone hath, every one, one shade* every single person has his own unique shadow. Some editors retain Q's spacing of 'euery one, hath' in three words, to produce the all-embracing assertion: 'every single person, thing, or phenomenon has its own unique shadow'. While the sweep of this is consistent with the tone of the poem, it robs line 3 of a characteristic piece of wordplay. Nor does it seem Shakespearian to anticipate quite so obviously the shift from human *beauty* to elemental *beauty* and *bounty* effected at the turn of the sonnet. (For early readers 'euery one' would have been, of course, admirably ambiguous; on the problem of modernizing such words, see the Account of the Text, pages 431–2.)

5–7   *Adonis ... Helen.* The beautiful boy wooed by Venus in Ovid's *Metamorphoses* (X.298–559, 708–39) and in Shakespeare's *Venus and Adonis*; and Helen of Troy, presented – satirically – by Shakespeare in *Troilus and Cressida.* The poet's *master-mistress* (20.2) combines so supremely the best of man and woman that he outdoes in beauty the loveliest representatives of each sex.

5   *counterfeit.* The 'picture' evoked by the description which *Describe* prompts; but also *Adonis* himself, an inauthentic copy of the friend.

5, 7   *counterfeit ... set.* Rhymed in the same way as 16.6 and 8.

6   *after.* Referring less to style (as in 'after Rembrandt') than to the *counterfeit*'s subject-matter: *you.*

7–8   *On Helen's cheek ... new* (1) concentrate all the arts which deal with beauty on reproducing the beauty of Helen's cheek and what results is a picture of you in Grecian head-dress; (2) paint Helen's cheek with artful cosmetics and the result will be a copy of you in Grecian head-dress. Sense (1), which stresses the difficulty art has in reproducing Helen's beauty, makes Helen worth comparing with the young man; but (2) reminds us how far short of him she nevertheless falls. *New* means 'afresh, once again', but its commoner sense 'recent, novel' registers through paradox in the context of that old work of beauty, *Helen's cheek.* The young man contains the best of what has been, as well as the best that the present world's *shadows* can contribute.

9   *foison* abundant harvest. By identifying 'autumn' through its action and property, and introducing *of the year*, Shakespeare contrives to return to the word *spring* some of its primal vigour: 'source and rising of the seasons'.

11   *The other as your bounty doth appear*. The young man resembles the
       Antony described by Cleopatra: 'For his bounty, | There was no
       winter in't; an [autumn] 'twas | That grew the more by reaping'
       (V.2.86–8).

12   *And you in every blessèd shape we know* and we recognize you in every
       happily-favoured shape. If the line is read as an ellipsis, 'and you
       appear in every happily-favoured shape known to us' can also be
       extracted.

13   *In all external grace you have some part*. Like *strange* (sense 2) this
       exploits the paradoxical relationship between what Orlando calls the
       'quintessence' and 'every sprite': 'you contribute (*lend*) something to
       every graceful worldly appearance (or manner)'; 'you have some-
       thing of the grace of every appearance (or manner) in the world'.

14   *you like none, none you, for constant heart* when it comes to constancy,
       you resemble nobody and nobody resembles you. The double
       likeness of line 13 (the youth is like the world since the world
       resembles him) here becomes a double disparity, and resemblance
       takes on strong connotations of value. Although the line could be
       read ironically (in the light of Sonnets 35 and 40–42), the immediate
       context seems to require 'in constancy you exceed everybody,
       nobody can compare with you in that'. The line resolves the sonnet
       in the rhythms of lines 3–4.

Sonnet 54

In Sonnets 15–19 the poet had raised, rejected, and then happily embraced
the idea that his verse could make the young man live after death, providing
child-like substitutes for children. Here he returns to the theme. Alluding to
the rose and perfume imagery of Sonnets 5 and 6, he suggests that verse, not
children or women's wombs, will best contain the youth's distilled self.

1, 13   *beauteous* (two syllables)
2   *By* through the agency of
         truth integrity, truth to self. But 'honesty' and 'fidelity, constancy' are
         also implied.
3–4   *rose . . . sweet*. The association was proverbial; see line 12 and the
         note, and 98.10–11.
4   *For* because of
5   *canker blooms* flowers of the dog-rose (which have no perfume)
         have full as deep a dye are as strong in colour. Elizabethan cultivated
         roses were less vividly coloured than are modern hybrids.
5, 7   *dye . . . wantonly*. The rhyme is full, resembling *die . . . memory* at 1.2
         and 4.
6   *tincture* colour, pigment (but with a suggestion of 'essence', elab-
         orated in lines 12–14)

239

7   *such* the same kind of
        play flutter, frolic
        wantonly sportively, roguishly

8   *maskèd* concealed. The buds are *maskèd* by calyxes, which open out
        in the summer breeze, revealing rose petals. There is probably a pun
        on 'damasked' (in the sense 'mingled white and red'), a word often
        used of roses. For the implied comparison with the youth's com-
        plexion, effected by the pun, see 99.10, 130.5–6, and the 'cheeks of
        damask roses' described by the Wooer of the Gaoler's Daughter at
        The Two Noble Kinsmen IV.1.74.
        discloses opens out, reveals

9   *for their virtue only is their show* (1) because their only excellence is the
        pretty display they make; (2) because they only make a pretence of
        virtue. The latter is decidedly secondary, but the moralistic opening
        lines of the sonnet enforce it.

10   *unrespected* unregarded (but with traces of the modern sense,
        'winning no respect, thought ill of')

11   *Die to themselves* die alone, without affecting or being affected by
        another (94.9–10 clarifies this. There is a suggestion that the
        unwooed and unrespected roses *fade* because, thus neglected, they
        'become completely indifferent *to themselves*'.)

12   *Of their sweet . . . made.* The *roses* are crushed and made into scent.
        Given the bawdy overtones of *deaths* ('to die' could mean 'achieve
        orgasm'), it is probable that the sexual imagery of Sonnets 5 and 6 is
        invoked here, with the roses' *deaths* in aromatic pain recalling the
        fertilization of a woman's womb (*Make sweet some vial*, 6.3) – only for
        the poet to wrest the emblem another way, and make his text a *vial*.

13   *of you* from you (being *rose*-like), with regard to you
        lovely. 'Worthy to be loved' as well as 'attractive'.

14   *vade.* Both 'depart' (compare Latin *vadere*) and 'fade away, wither'
        (indeed, *vade* was and sometimes is regarded as a variant form of
        'fade').
        by verse distils your truth your *truth* will distil (into a lasting essence)
        through the medium of verse. The *ornament* of line 2 becomes
        essential – indeed, an essence. Some editors emend *by* to 'my',
        turning *distils* into a transitive verb.

Sonnet 55

Evidently indebted to Horace, *Odes* III.30.1–9, and the closing lines of
Ovid's *Metamorphoses*, two passages frequently echoed in renaissance poetry:

> More durable than bronze, higher than Pharaoh's
> Pyramids is the monument I have made,

A shape that angry wind or hungry rain
Cannot demolish, nor the innumerable
Ranks of the years that march in centuries.
I shall not wholly die: some part of me
Will cheat the goddess of death, for while High Priest
And Vestal climb our Capitol in a hush,
My reputation shall keep green and growing.

(Horace, translated by James Michie, Penguin Classics)

Now have I brought a work to end which neither Jove's fierce wrath,
Nor sword, nor fire, nor fretting age with all the force it hath
Are able to abolish quite. Let come that fatal hour
Which (saving of this brittle flesh) hath over me no power,
And at his pleasure make an end of mine uncertain time.
Yet shall the better part of me assured be to climb
Aloft above the starry sky. And all the world shall never
Be able for to quench my name. For look how far so ever
The Roman Empire by the right of conquest shall extend,
So far shall all folk read this work. And time without all end
(If poets as by prophecy about the truth may aim)
My life shall everlastingly be lengthened still by fame.

(Ovid, translated by Golding)

Strikingly, though, Shakespeare promises to preserve the young man in verse, not himself. This has led to the citation of a third possible 'source', the conclusion to the second elegy in Propertius, Book III:

Happy you who have been celebrated in my book! My songs shall be so many monuments of your beauty. For neither the starward-raised costliness of the Pyramids, nor the heaven-imitating house of Jove at Elis, nor the rich abundance of Mausolus's tomb are exempt from Death's ultimate condition. Fire or rain will steal away their glories or, stricken by the years, they will collapse under their own weight. But the name acquired by genius shall not fall from memory through lapse of time: for genius there abides undying [in] renown.

(translated by J. B. Leishman)

Propertius, however, was not much read. Traces of his influence may be found – in, for example, Jonson's *Poetaster* – but he remained marginal until the twentieth century. Thus, while a Propertian debt cannot be ruled out, it seems more likely that Shakespeare adapted Ovid and Horace in Sonnet 55, and virtually certain that early readers would have understood the lines that way. On the modesty of Shakespeare's aims and claims see 107.11–12 and the note, and the Introduction, pages 21–2.

2   *this powerful rhyme.* Either 'this poem' or 'the verse I've written about

you'. *Powerful*, three syllables asked to do the work of two, tests its strength within the line, like a flexed muscle.

3   *these contents* what is contained in *this powerful rhyme* (either sense. If a plurality of poems is assumed, the reference might be to a collection of sonnets 'contained' in a book.)

contents (accented on the second syllable)

4   *Than unswept stone.* The phrase makes good sense as the completion of *you shall shine more bright: you* makes *stone* a memorial statue over a tomb; *unswept*, and the notion of writing *contents*, suggests a *stone* set in a dirty church floor, its inscription obliterated by rushes and muddy feet. Yet the proximity of *in these contents* simultaneously turns the phrase into an ellipsis lacking 'in': 'than in the grubby stone of a tomb (the dirt of which will sully your reputation)'.

besmeared with sluttish time. The extraordinary power of this stems partly from its lofty dismissal of a force elsewhere considered potent – *sluttish* meaning 'slovenly', but with a strong suggestion of 'lewd' and 'whorish' – and partly from the ambiguous density of *besmeared with . . . time*: 'smeared in the course of time', 'smeared with time' (as though *time* were muck), 'smeared by Time' (*sluttish* provoking the personification; *with*, as often in Shakespeare, meaning 'by')

5   *wasteful* destructive, full of *waste* (which, with the word *war*, forms a distinctively Shakespearian triangle with *time*)

6   *broils* tumults, skirmishes

work of masonry (1) structures built of stone; (2) products of the stonemason's art. The phrase is enriched by the military sense of *work*, 'fortification'.

7   *Nor Mars his sword nor war's quick fire shall burn* neither Mars's sword nor the swiftly vigorous fire of war shall burn. A zeugma; strictly, a *sword* cannot *burn. Quick* is enlivened, given the sense 'full of life', by the *living record* of line 8.

8   *record of your memory.* For the written bias of this *record* see 59.5, 63.11 and notes.

9   *all oblivious enmity.* The strongest implications are: 'utterly regardless enmity'; 'every bit of unheeding enmity'; 'enmity which forgets (or causes to be forgotten) everything'. *Oblivious* has three syllables.

pace forth stride confidently forwards (into the future and the fray suggested by '*Gainst*)

10   *praise shall . . . find room* (it will not need to jostle for admittance)

still (1) always; (2) nevertheless (despite *death* and *enmity*)

11   *Even in the eyes of* in the very opinion of. But also, as line 14 demonstrates, literal, readerly. *Even* is here monosyllabic.

12   *That wear this world out to the ending doom* that will last until the world arrives at the doomsday which will end it. The antecedent of *That* is *eyes*.

13   *judgement that yourself arise* Day of Judgement when you will rise from
     the dead. Although the use of *that* for 'when' was acceptable in
     Elizabethan English, early readers probably also detected 'verdict
     that you should rise from the dead'.

14   *live in* (1) survive in, survive by virtue of; (2) inhabit (drawn out by
     dwell in)
     this (the *powerful rhyme* and *contents* of lines 2 and 3)
     lovers' eyes the eyes of your admirers (people forced to love you even
     as they read *this*. But the poet may simply have in mind the
     renaissance convention that love poetry is usually read by lovers
     trying to comprehend their affliction in the light of another's
     experience.)

Sonnet 56

1   *love* (the emotion, not the beloved)
1, 3 *said ... allayed*. Although the pronunciation 'sed' is sometimes
     required in Shakespeare, the standard Elizabethan 'sayd' obtains
     here, making the rhyme with *allayed*.
2   *should ... be* is
     appetite hunger (elicited by line 3), craving (supporting line 6)
3   *but* only for. A hint of 'this very' adds immediacy.
4   *his* its
6   *even* (one syllable)
     wink with fullness close dozily, being sated
7   *see* (by opening the *eyes* closed by gluttony *today*)
8   *spirit* (one syllable)
     perpetual (three syllables)
     dullness (1) lethargy; (2) bluntness (playfully echoing the knife
     imagery of lines 2 and 4)
9–12 *Let this ... view*. The quatrain has caused critical difficulties, partly
     because its metaphorical basis has been misunderstood – when *this
     sad interim* ('this unfortunate and miserable intermission in loving')
     is compared to *the ocean*, a temporal gap becomes spatial – and partly
     because the implications of *Let* have been overlooked. The poet is
     not saying that an *interim* compares easily with an *ocean*. He is
     saying: 'let us interpret our estrangement as though it were an *ocean* parting
     recently betrothed lovers (*two contracted new*), and then we might
     start to anticipate love's renewal (*Return of love* suggesting both the
     reciprocation of affection and the recovery of love lost) as such lovers
     do when they come to the shore each day to look for a known sail'.
13   *As call it* as appropriate, it is, to compare *the sad interim* to. A second

interpretative metaphor is added to, and through *As* loosely compared with, the one unfolded in lines 9–12.

care anxiety, sorrow

14 *summer's welcome.* Both the 'greeting that summer (which is like *love*) extends (to us)' and '(our) greeting of summer (which is like *love*)'.

thrice more wished, more rare. Desire and excellence are presented in parallel (*summer's welcome* is both *more wished* and *more rare*) but they also act as cause and effect (being *more wished*, *summer's welcome* is *more rare*). The suggestion that wishing can create the excellence it wants comes aptly at the close of a sonnet concerned to persuade love that if it puts itself into the position of one wanting love it might begin to be rewarded. (Notice, here, the optimistic deployment of the seasons: as *summer* follows *winter*, lines 13–14, so love will be renewed.)

Sonnet 57

1–2 *tend | Upon* wait on, attend

2 *times of your desire* occasions when you want this or that (from me. The poet might have said 'your every whim', but he anticipates *time*, *world-without-end* and *clock* by concentrating on the way desire changes with the *times* – the theme of Sonnet 56.)

3 *precious time at all to spend.* The poet's *time* is not *precious* till spent for the young man (line 4); yet the adjective is there in any case, suggesting that the poet knows the value of the *time* which he claims he cannot value till his beloved employs it. The sonnet's first glint of irony.

4 *services* acts of use to others

require (1) need, desire; (2) order. The latter is in a sense primary, but Shakespeare founds the line on the notion that the friend has only to want something for its fulfilment to become binding on the poet. To that extent (2) follows from (1).

5 *chide the world-without-end hour* castigate the seemingly endless hour. An idea so odd that the reader is prompted to take the words as an ellipsis for what the poet can't bring himself to say: 'chastise you, my friend, for the apparently endless hour (which you make, or have made, me wait)'.

6 *watch the clock.* As now, a proverbial instance of impatience making time pass slowly.

7 *Nor think the bitterness of absence sour.* Ironic self-awareness here becomes more pronounced. The line effectively declares: 'and persuade myself that the *bitterness* (of your absence from me) is not sour'.

8   *When you have bid your servant once adieu.* Although the poet relishes
     the young man's company, he is so anxious not to displease him that,
     being *once* bad farewell, he obediently departs. *Adieu* (which is not *au
     revoir*) augurs a longer separation than the *hour* of line 5. *Bid* is a
     regular, though now obsolete, past tense.

9   *question with* (1) ask by means of; (2) debate with. The fruitlessness
     of asking produces the futility of a debate (between the self, or *I*, and
     its *thought*).
     jealous mistrustful, watchful, envious (of some rival, real or imagin-
     ary. The adjective modifies the negation *Nor dare* (compare the
     effect of *precious*, line 3): the poet's *thought* doubts, even though it
     does not.

10   *your affairs suppose* imagine what you are doing. In Elizabethan
     English, *affairs* does not immediately suggest 'illicit love affairs'.

11   *like a sad slave.* On the distance measured from line 1 by the insertion
     of *like*, see the Introduction, page 23.

12   *Save where . . . those* except how happy you make those who are where
     you are

13   *true* (1) faithful; (2) absolute
     fool. Love attends its master simple-mindedly but with doting faith,
     like the Fool in Quarto *King Lear*. Compare the *fools of Time* at
     124.13.
     will desire (with connotations of sexuality and wilfulness. Q prints a
     capital W, but an allusion to Will[iam Shakespeare] seems unlikely.)

14   *he* (that is, *love*. The implication is that, although the poet is not in
     control of his besotted passion, he is not identified with it either; by
     the end of the sonnet, at least, he distinguishes the *I* from its *love*.)

Sonnet 58

Echoing Sonnet 57 in theme and diction.

1–2 *That god . . . should* may the god (presumably Love) who first made
     me your slave forbid that I should. An appeal which implies, of
     course, that the poet may not be able to stop himself wanting the
     youth controlled.

2   *in thought* (1) in my mind; (2) even speculatively
     control (1) regulate, curb; (2) call to account. Shakespeare uses the
     word with an eye to etymology: Anglo-Norman *contreroller* means 'to
     record in an account, enrol in a book, conclusively reckon'; hence
     th'account of line 3.
     your times of pleasure. Like *will* (57.13), *pleasure* has sexual overtones
     As a whole, the phrase constitutes a more explicit version of *times of
     your desire* (57.2).

3   *at* from

4   *Being your vassal* since I am your feudal dependant (compare *Being your slave*, 57.1)

      bound obliged, duty-bound

      stay await. But just as lines 1–3 register the poet's desire to *control* the young man's *times of pleasure* by saying that those *times* should not be controlled, so in line 4 *stay* suggests a desired 'stop' as well as the dutiful 'await'.

5   *suffer* (1) allow; (2) endure the pain of

      beck (and call)

6   *imprisoned* imprisoning (by prolepsis. There is no doubt a suggestion that the poet can do nothing useful – is effectively in chains – when the friend is away.)

      absence of your liberty separation which is the product of your being free (and of your libertinism. Perhaps, also, 'lack of being free to enjoy you'.)

7   *And, patience-tame to sufferance, bide each check* and, tame as patience itself (or 'made tame by patience') in the face of suffering (or 'to the point of abject submission'), I put up with every rebuke (and 'setback'). Q's possible but hardly likely 'And patience tame, to sufferance bide each check' has been variously repunctuated. 'And patience, tame to sufferance, bide each check' is often adopted. Compare *Troilus and Cressida* I.i.27–8, 'Patience herself, what goddess e'er she be, | Doth lesser blench at sufferance than I do.' As in that quotation, *sufferance* is contracted to two syllables.

8   *injury* hurtful injustice

9   *where you list* wherever you wish

      your charter is so strong your acknowledged right is so powerful. In the sestet the young man is likened to a feudal lord possessed of a *charter* which allows him to grant rights and judge in legal disputes.

10–11 *privilege your time* | *To what you will* give your time official permission to be employed in whatever way you like

12   *Yourself to pardon of self-doing crime* to pardon yourself the offences which you commit. With a suggestion of 'against yourself' (the young man's *liberty* being as bad for him as for the poet).

13   *I am to* it is expected of me that I should

      wait . . . waiting. The repetition suggests a residual pun on *wait* as 'attend, serve' (see 57.1–2).

14   *blame* condemn, complain about, bewail

      your pleasure, be it ill or well. In line 2, *pleasure* refers exclusively to worldly diversions enjoyed by the young man. Here the friend's attitude to the poet falls within the word's compass – as though the youth were a king, at whose *pleasure* things might or might not happen. The implications of *ill or well* are thus different from those of *ill* at 57.14, involving cruelty and kindness as well as conduct.

Sonnet 59

1–2   *If there be . . . before.* The idea of recurrence is a very old one; the Pythagoreans maintained it, as did the older Stoics. For Elizabethan readers, the obvious analogue would be Ecclesiastes 1.9–10: 'The thing that hath been, cometh to pass again, and the thing that hath been done, shall be done again: There is no new thing under the sun. Is there anything whereof it may be ṣaid, lo, this is new? for it was long ago in the times that have been before us.' Indeed, 'There is nothing new under the sun' was already proverbial. Q's comma after *is* points up and relishes the infolded tautology of line 1 before it enjambs.

1, 3   *is . . . amiss.* The rhyme depends on 's' instead of 'z' in *is*.

3   *invention* (in the rhetorical sense used at 38.1)

3–4   *bear . . . The . . . burden of.* A pleasing image of pregnancy and birth (*bear* suggests both), darkened by *amiss* and diverted by *labouring* into 'toil painfully under the oppressive weight of'.
   amiss mistakenly (because the born or borne *child* is already born. Even, perhaps, 'abortively, imperfectly'.)

5   *record* (accented on the second syllable) memory (imagined as a written account, as at *Hamlet* I.5.92–105 or *Twelfth Night* V.1.243), historical recollection (which tends to involve writing)

6   *Even* (one syllable)
   five hundred courses of the sun. Alluding to the ancient belief that the heavens move in 540, 600, 12,960, 36,000, or 49,000 annual cycles. The poet here speculates that 600 years ago, when the heavens last held their present astrological configuration, someone resembling the young man lived and was written about. (The word *hundrað* in Old Norse originally meant 120. In English it has usually been applied to the decimal hundred, but traces of the older usage have lingered, and Shakespeare here invokes the 'great' or 'long' hundred of six score.)

7   *antique* (accented on the first syllable)

8   *Since mind at first in character was done* written at any time since thought was first expressed in writing

9   *see what the old world could say.* As at 23.13–14, reading is treated as a paradoxical process of hearing through sight.

10   *To* in response to. But in so far as the idea of recurrence is treated lightly, 'to compare with'.

10   *composèd wonder of your frame* well proportioned and assembled
      miracle which is your form

11   *Whether we are mended, or whe'er better they.* The poet's speculation
      here ranges beyond recurrence to the old ideas (often associated
      with Lucretius and Ovid respectively) of continual human progress
      and constant decline. Some editors reverse Q's elision, reading
      'Whe'er . . . whether'.

12   *revolution be the same* cycles revolve to produce the same phenomena
      regularly

13   *wits* intelligences, men of intellect

14   *subjects worse* (1) inferior topics; (2) people of worse character. It is
      difficult to determine the degree of irony which should be attached
      to (2). As so often, it depends on whether the sonnet is taken
      individually (in which case the line is complimentary) or in the
      context of the sequence, involving more critical poems (in which
      case the ironies are pronounced).
      given (one syllable)

Sonnet 60

1–4   *Like as . . . contend.* Inspired by Ovid's *Metamorphoses* XV.178–85:

> Things ebb and flow, and every shape is made to pass away.
> The time itself continually is fleeting like a brook.
> For neither brook nor lightsome time can tarry still. But look
> As every wave divers other forth, and that that comes behind
> Both thrusteth and is thrust itself: Even so the times by kind
> Do fly and follow both at once, and evermore renew.
> For that that was before is left, and straight there doth ensue
> Another that was never erst.
>
> (Golding's translation)

1   *Like as* just as
      make towards the pebbled shore move up the shingle beach. Presumably
      pebbled is preferred because shingle makes the tide's progress more
      clearly discernible than sand. *Towards* is monosyllabic.

4   *In sequent toil* successively and laboriously, through successive
      efforts
      contend strive. The *waves* compete, each endeavouring to outstrip its
      precursor; as a result, *contend* suggests conflict (see *fight*, line 7, and
      the note).

5   *Nativity* the new-born child ('birth' made concrete. In astrology, the
      configuration of heavenly bodies at the moment of birth constitutes a

Nativity. This sense becomes relevant in line 7, with *Crookèd eclipses*).

once (1) no sooner (requiring 'than it' at the end of the line); (2) once, formerly (reflecting the speed with which 'no sooner' takes effect)

the main of light. For Shakespeare, a *main* was any 'broad expanse' but, particularly, as in modern English, the open sea. In lines 1–4 the movement of *the waves* suggested the passing of life; here *the main* becomes 'the sea of life, all full of light'. Indeed, *the main* is, because of its *light*, the sky beneath which the living live; so *Nativity* leaves the darkness of not-being and the womb's shadow to discover *light* in an ocean of air. (Whereupon, arguably, the logic of Sonnet 7 takes over, at least secondarily, with life reaching its zenith in line 6 only to be eclipsed in line 7.)

6   *Crawls* moves slowly (like the tide) on all fours (like a growing baby) *wherewith* (1) with which; (2) whereupon

7   *Crookèd* malignant (taking *eclipses* astrologically. There is, however, a strong suggestion of the tormenting distortions which age inflicts on the body, 'eclipsing' its youthful vigour.)

      his (*Nativity*'s, grown mature)

      fight. The hint of battle in *contend* (line 4) anticipates a combat now grown fierce.

8   *confound* ruin, destroy. See 5.6 and the note.

9   *transfix.* Almost certainly 'pierce through', anticipating *delves*, but perhaps 'unfix, tear off'. The word is rare, definition difficult and contested.

      flourish lovely embellishment. Importantly, it was used in the period to mean 'blossom, bloom of health', the *flourish* of beauty on fine skin.

      set on youth. Beauty adorns *youth* as an artist's *flourish* does a painting, or a musician's ornamentation a theme: it is essential to the effect. Yet, this being Shakespeare, *set on* suggests a degree of superficiality – hypocrisy even – almost sufficient to explain the vulnerability of beauty to attack.

10   *delves the parallels* digs wrinkles that look like military trenches. The image grows out of *contend*, *confound*, and *fight*. Compare 2.1–2. Conceivably, Shakespeare meant *parallels* to suggest 'lines of latitude'; at *Twelfth Night* III.2.74–6, Malvolio is said to 'smile his face into more lines than is in the new map with the augmentation of the Indies.' At all events, the *parallels* recall the *waves* of lines 1–4, moving up the beach in insidious ranks, and, like wrinkles, auguring death.

10, 12   *brow . . . mow.* Rhymed, apparently, on a diphthong including 'i' as in 'bit', or 'a' unstressed as in 'ago', plus 'u' as in 'educated' southern 'put'.

11   *Feeds on the rarities of nature's truth* devours the delicacies which

nature in her integrity produces, consumes the most excellent things comprised in nature's perfection

12   *but* except
      scythe. See 12.13 and the note.

13   *to times in hope* until futures only dreamed of. The imagery of line 12, taken with the echo of *stands* in *stand* (lines 12–13), gives *to* a suggestion of 'against': 'against the destructive powers of the future'. *in hope . . . stand.* Shakespeare redeploys the standard idiom 'stand in hope' (meaning 'wait hopefully for'); attaching *hope* to the future (making the *times* merely hypothetical), he allows a defiant weight to the end-positioned, strongly stressed *stand*.

14   *Praising thy worth.* For an extended gloss on this avoidance of personal praise, see the Introduction, pages 21 and 29.
      cruel (two syllables)

Sonnet 61

Compare Sonnets 27 and 43.

1, 3   *open . . . broken.* One of the few cases of imperfect rhyme in the Sonnets.

2   *heavy* dull, oppressed
      weary night (1) night in which men are weary; (2) night run far along its course

4   *shadows* images (but preparing for the supernaturalism of the second quatrain)

5   *spirit* immaterial being, ghostly essence

6, 8   *pry . . . jealousy.* The rhyme is full, resembling 1.2 and 4.

7   *shames* shameful deeds
      idle hours wasted time (though one has a right to be *idle* in the *hours* of night)

8   *scope and tenor* aim and purport, target and chief concern. Probably defining the *shames and idle hours* of line 7, not *me*.

9, 11   *great . . . defeat.* The rhyme resembles *break . . . speak* at 34.5 and 7.

10–11 *my love . . . Mine own true love.* Primarily, of course, the poet's affection (enforced, in part, by *thy love* in line 9); but 'you, my beloved' indubitably contributes.

12   *To play the watchman ever for thy sake.* Alluding to the proverb which quibblingly underlies the poem: 'One good friend watches for (looks out for, looks after) another'. A *watchman* is a constable who patrols the streets by night; *ever* means 'always, for ever'.

13   *For thee watch I* (1) I keep vigil for you (in the hope of seeing you); (2) I stay awake (in the 'watches' of the night) because of you (kept waking by the pangs of love)

wake. A quibble, 'lie awake, vigilantly' – paralleling *watch* – gives way to the cynical 'revel' (compare 'The King doth wake tonight and takes his rouse', *Hamlet* I.4.8).

13, 14   *Elsewhere . . . near*. Rhymed on long 'e', and closer in sound to '-ere' than '-ear'.

14   *with others all too near*. A jealous reference to the poet's rival(s) and/or, in the light of 40–42, his mistress (*near* him emotionally when physically *near* the friend).

Sonnet 62

A rigorous expression of the Other-as-Self topos – emergent in Sonnets 36 and 39 – complicated here by false immodesty and *age* against *thy days*. (Having urged the breeding of copies, and projected verse as creatively equivalent, the *I* now relates, covertly, to its *love*, the youth, as progenitor.)

1   *possesseth* holds, owns, grips (like madness or an evil spirit. The word reverberates with dark suggestions.)

1, 3   *eye . . . remedy*. A full rhyme, resembling 7.2, 4 and, hence, 1.2, 4.

4   *grounded inward in my heart*. Echoing, perhaps, the Prayer Book: 'grafted inwardly in our hearts'.

5   *Methinks* it seems to me
         gracious lovely, charming (but with an implication of moral worth, elicited by *Sin*, lines 1 and 3)

6   *true* well-formed
         truth integrity, constancy (resisting Time. The line moves from physical to moral perfection.)
         of such account so valuable

7   *for myself* (1) by myself (such assessments are usually made by others); (2) for my own satisfaction, to gratify myself
         define determine, judge

8   *As* (1) since that, in as much as; (2) namely that; (3) as though. The first sense follows confidently from line 7 (the poet must take his own measure since no one else is worthy to), the second is more neutral, and the third indicates creeping uncertainty in advance of the sestet.
         all other in all worths surmount overtop everyone else in every kind of merit

9   *indeed* as I really am

10   *Beated* weather-beaten
         chopped cracked and lined, chapped: 'Her cheeks with chaps and wrinkles were disguised' (*The Rape of Lucrece* 1452).
         with tanned antiquity. A typically Shakespearian convolute: 'by leathery tanned Old Age which tans skin to leather'. Pale soft skin

was, of course, the ideal; sun-tans became fashionable only in this century.

11 *quite contrary I read* I interpret in quite another way

12 *Self so self-loving were iniquity* it would be wicked for the self to be so conceited

13 *for myself* (echoing *for myself* in line 7, with the same range of senses)

14 *Painting my age with beauty of thy days* describing my aged state as though it was your youthful beauty

Sonnet 63

1   *Against my love* in preparation for the time when my beloved

2   *injurious* (three syllables) unjustly harmful
    crushed and o'erworn (like a garment creased and worn from years of use. In the light of *injurious*, another glancing echo of Spenser's *Ruines of Rome*, where 'The which injurious time hath quite outworn' appears in Sonnet 27.)

3   *hours have drained his blood.* Shakespeare turns the traditionally beneficent *Horae* into something resembling vampires.
    filled. Balanced against *drained*, *filled* suggests liquid repletion; but *lines and wrinkles* conjure a smooth surface cross-hatched with care. The Q spelling 'fild' is fruitfully ambiguous, for it prompts 'filed' as well as *filled*; but we cannot be sure that it is Shakespearian.

4   *lines and wrinkles.* The pleonasm is functional, because it draws attention to a word used in the couplet to carry the burden of the poem's argument. The effectiveness of Shakespeare's handling of *lines* can be judged from the parallel passage in Drayton's 1599 *Idea* (Sonnet 43): 'Whilst thus my pen strives to eternize thee, | Age rules my lines with wrinkles in my face'. Forced to the point of punning, the ambiguity becomes merely grotesque.

4–5 *when his youthful morn | Hath travelled on to age's steepy night.* Eleven words seem to contain the entire substance of Sonnet 7. Modernization of Q's 'trauaild' inevitably obscures the effort made by the *morn* as it moves towards its ruin in *night*. *Steepy* suggests both the irreversible rapidity of the day's decline (compare 7.5, 9–10) and the 'soaking' or 'steeping' of the *morn* in the darkness which is death.

6   *those beauties whereof now he's king* the charms and physical graces which are his. But there is a supporting suggestion of 'the beautiful people who pay him allegiance and love'.

7   *Are vanishing or vanished out of sight.* The *beauties* fade as we read, *vanishing*, then *vanished*. But the repetition, and use of *or*, also give *vanished* the air of being transitive, as though some vanisher made

the *beauties* fade (and the sestet introduces a plausible agent in the figure of *Age*).

8   *Stealing away the treasure of his spring.* The young man's fading *beauties* quietly and dishonestly carry off the *treasure* which belongs to (and which is) his youth (the *spring* of his life) as they vanish *out of sight*. But the *beauties* actually are the *treasure* of his *spring*, and *Stealing*, placed in parallel with *vanishing*, turns from theft to 'creeping away'; so the young man's *treasure* – as surely as his beauties – makes itself away, and does not.

9   *fortify* build defences

9, 11   *fortify . . . memory.* For the rhyme see 1.2 and 4.

10   *confounding* wrecking, destroying

       Age's. The personification creeps upon the reader, from *age's steepy night* (where *age* is a future property of the young man, though more powerful than he), through *vanished* in line 7 (see the note).

       cruel (two syllables)

11   *That* so that

       memory. Rather the *living record* of Sonnet 55 than the poet's private recollection.

12   *My sweet love's.* The *love* of line 1; not the poet's affection.

       though my lover's life (1) though he will cut off *My sweet love's* life; (2) though he will cut the details of *My sweet love's* life from the public *memory*; (3) though he will cut off my life as a lover. Without suggesting that the young man's *life* will not bear scrutiny, sense (2) scrupulously points to the discrimination exercised by the poet in recording his *sweet love's* life: the young man's *beauty*, not the untidy details of his daily living, fill the *black lines* of the poem.

13   *beauty . . . black.* Opposing principles; see 27.12 and the note, and the Introduction, pages 58–9.

14   *still* (1) even (after death); (2) constantly, for ever

       green. A fresh, youthful, lover's colour ('Green indeed is the colour of lovers', says Armado at *Love's Labour's Lost* I.2.83), associated with the spring, and with living, growing things.

Sonnet 64

1   *fell* cruel, deadly

1, 3   *defaced . . . down-razed.* Apparently a rhyme, based on a long 'a' sounding like the 'a' of southern English 'bat', 'bad', lengthened.

2   *rich* lavish, intricate, ostentatiously splendid

       proud gorgeous, showy, vain

       cost object(s) procured with cost, extravagantly precious thing(s)

       outworn (1) worn out, exhausted; (2) outmoded

2   *buried*. The lost *cost* is *buried* in the past, 'forgotten', like a treasure trove covered with earth.

      age (1) antiquity; (2) aged things

3   *When sometime lofty towers I see down-razed* (1) when I see once-high towers razed to the ground; (2) when, from time to time, I see *lofty towers* lying in ruin

4   *eternal*. An adjective modifying *brass*, placed with Latinate tardiness (and recalling the Horatian '*aere perennius*' behind 55.1), but also an adverb: '*And brass* (which is) eternally the *slave to*'.

      mortal rage fury of mortality, death's destructiveness

5–7   *When I have . . . main*. Some argue that the movement of the tides up and down the shore is evoked here (compare 60.1); but the *hungry ocean* and *firm soil* seem too decisive for such a gentle to-and-fro. The sea brings down cliffs and devours fields, while the land asserts itself in the main, putting out spurs, laying down salt-marsh, and so forth. Shakespeare's source – Ovid's *Metamorphoses* XV.261–4 – confirms this:

> Even so have places oftentimes exchanged their estate.
> For I have seen it sea which was substantial ground alate
>   [formerly],
> Again where sea was, I have seen the same become dry land,
> And shells and scales of seafish far have lain from any strand,
> And in the tops of mountains high old anchors have been found.
>   (Golding's translation)

8   *Increasing store with loss and loss with store*. Shakespeare conflates the victories described in lines 6–7 in such a way that he seems to prove that by losing one has more, and vice versa.

9–10   *state . . . state*. In line 10, the sense 'worldly pomp' is added to the 'condition' (with a quibble on *kingdom*) which prevails in line 9.

10   *confounded to decay* ruined to the point of dilapidation. Some editors preserve Q's comma after *confounded*, but that enlivens *state itself* at the cost of making the *interchange of state* of line 9 *decay*, when it is the poet's point that that alone never will.

12   *love* beloved

13   *which*. The antecedent is *thought*. Shakespeare allows it, in line 14, the tears and terror which it creates.

14   *to have* because it has

Sonnet 65

1   *Since* since there is neither

2   *sad*. Though 'grievous and grief-inflicting' is ultimately dominant, 'grave, solemnly determined' registers strongly.

     o'ersways overrules. *Sad mortality* is a monarch stronger than *brass*, *stone*, and the rest; he *o'ersways* because he curbs *their ~~power~~* by oscillation, mutability, what 64.9 calls *interchange of state*.

2, 4 *power ... flower*. Between one and two syllables; neither a regular pentameter nor quite a feminine ending.

3   *this rage*. The *mortal rage* of 64.4.

     hold a plea uphold a suit, prevail in (legal) argument

4   *action*. The primary sense is 'law-suit', prompted by *plea*; but *flower* elicits 'activity of growing' or 'being (declared in activity)', and the military imagery of lines 5–6 makes beauty's *action* the conduct of a 'battle'.

     than a flower. Elliptical: 'than a flower's àction is'. But also a direct equivalence, the abstract *action* compared to the material *flower*.

6   *wrackful* destructive, vindictive

     of (maintained by)

     battering days. The *days* pound like a *battering*-ram against *summer's honey breath*. (Q's 'battring' indicates scansion, but also the force of three syllables compressed to two.) There is nothing indulgent about the metaphor, extravagantly mixed though it is, since it expresses the pathetic – indeed, the absurd – fragility of *beauty* when it stands against *Time*. For early readers this fragility would have been communicated in part by the hint of cliché in *honey breath* (compare *Venus and Adonis* 16, 452, and 538, *Titus Andronicus* II.4.25, *Hamlet* II.1.157, or, more comically, Marlowe's *Hero and Leander* I.21–4, where Hero is encumbered by honey bees attracted to her sweet breath).

7   *impregnable* unconquerable, invincible. Line 6 grounds the word in war (compare *Richard II* III.2.167–70, where the King denies that the 'flesh which walls about our life' is 'brass impregnable' or a strong 'castle wall'); but *rocks* generalizes beyond the idea of besieged walls to boulders strewn about the landscape, toughly resisting erosion.

     stout sturdy, strong

8   *gates of steel*. Presumably fortified doors set in city walls.

     but Time decays (them, the *gates*)

9   *fearful*. Like 'frightful', *fearful* conveys little terror in modern English; but for Elizabethan and Jacobean speakers the word was evidently potent ('full of fear'). Death seems a 'fearful thing' to Claudio (*Measure for Measure* III.1.119), and the ghost of Hamlet's

father returns to Purgatory on hearing the 'fearful summons' of a crowing cock (I.1.150).

9–10   *Where, alack . . . hid.* The young man is a beautiful gem lent to the world by Time; and Time will be sure to reclaim him, locking him up in his jewel-case (suggesting a coffin), wherever he hides. The words compare interestingly with 52.9.

11   *his swift foot.* See 19.6 and the note.

12   *spoil* ruin, despoliation

13   *might* force (both strength and efficacy)

14   *love* beloved (as at 63.1. Compare lines 13–14 of the same sonnet.)

Sonnet 66

Compare Hamlet's famous soliloquy 'To be, or not to be' (III.1.56–90), where the Prince describes 'Th'oppressor's wrong, the proud man's contumely' and analogous evils, and Lucrece's eloquent complaint against Opportunity (*The Rape of Lucrece* 848–924).

1   *Tired with* wearied by

1, 3   *cry . . . jollity.* The rhyme is full, resembling 1.2 and 4.

2   *As* for instance

2–12   *desert . . . captain ill.* Q grants initial capitals to 'Doctor' and 'Captain', and to 'Nothing', 'Folly', 'Truth', 'Simplicity'. Some editors use initial capitals for all the poem's abstractions, turning them into characters from personification allegory or Morality drama; but *desert, nothing,* and the rest seem more suggestive in lower case, implying personification without excluding that sense of metonymy which allows 'a worthy person' or 'a worthless spendthrift'.

2   *desert* Merit (and 'a worthy individual') born into beggary

3   *And needy nothing trimmed in jollity.* Editors keen to attribute a modern social conscience to Shakespeare interpret *needy nothing* as 'he who goes in need of nothing'; but 'beggarly worthlessness' seems more relevant. The poet (and no doubt the Stratford burgher who stands behind him) laments that the *needy* should compound their need by squandering the little they have on *jollity* ('revelry', but also, because of *trimmed,* which suggests attire, 'tawdry gewgaws and fancy gear').

4   *purest faith unhappily forsworn* most absolute (and morally spotless) Fidelity (or 'oath' or even 'religion') regrettably (or 'wretchedly' or 'maliciously') abandoned (or, if *faith* is read as 'oath', 'broken')

5   *gilded honour.* Although *gilded* can be pejorative (as the note to 20.6 explains), when applied to 'titles' and 'rank' *shamefully misplaced* ('distributed with a shameful disregard for merit'), the sense 'having

the mere appearance of gold' is excluded by 'eye-catchingly attract-
ive' and 'golden' (compare 28.12).

6   *strumpeted.* Either 'prostituted' or 'given the false reputation of
        sexual laxity'. The latter provides a better parallel for line 7.

7   *right* genuine (but *wrongfully* evokes 'correct', 'just', and 'morally
        true')
        disgraced disparaged (robbed of a good name's *grace*)

8   *limping sway* slow and erratic Authority, a weak and uncertain ruler
        disablèd (four syllables, 'disable-ed')

9   *art.* 'Learning' in both the arts and sciences (and so 'a learned
        person') as well as 'artistry, creativity'.
        made tongue-tied by authority (1) stifled by tradition and precedent; (2)
        forced into inactivity (or frankly censored) by the powers that be. It is
        not clear whether one or both senses are intended.

10   *doctor-like* putting on an air of learning, like a learned scholar with
        authority over students
        controlling (1) directing; (2) curbing; (3) apparently refuting in a
        formal disputation

11   *simple truth.* Both 'straightforward honesty' and 'plain fact'.
        miscalled slandered as
        simplicity. 'Stupidity' and 'a naive misinterpretation of something',
        matching the two senses of *simple truth*.

12   *captive.* Like *captain*, both an adjective ('trapped, oppressed by
        servitude') and a noun ('prisoner-of-war').
        attending (1) serving; (2) hearkening to
        captain. 'Chief, dominating' as well as a military rank; see the note on
        captive.

13, 14 *gone . . . alone.* See the note to 31.10, 12.
14   *to die* if I die, in dying
        alone solitary. But with a hint of wordplay: the beloved is 'all one'
        ('just one, only a single thing'), but he nevertheless outweighs *all
        these*.

Sonnet 67

In its reference to the friend as *he*, this poem – especially in the wake of 66,
with its self-pitying lament – marks a crucial stage in the poet's account of the
youth. It uniquely anticipates (if 5, resolved by 6, is excepted) the issues of 94,
as 69 – within a group which arguably extends from this sonnet to 70 –
anticipates, particularly in lines 9–12, that poem, with its third-person (but,
further, impersonal) account.

1–4   *Ah, wherefore . . . society.* The young man is ostensibly the innocent
        victim of *sin*, which uses him as a front to conceal its ugliness; but the

youth's moral shortcomings are emphasized so strongly in earlier
sonnets that it is difficult to ignore an ironic undertow: 'Oh, why
should he be allowed to live, corrupted as he is, only to make impiety
look gracious through his charm, so that sin profits from his loose
loveliness, becoming his bosom friend?'

1   *wherefore* why
    with infection in a sickly corrupted world (presumably that described
    in the previous sonnet)

1, 3   *live . . . achieve.* The rhyme was closer to modern '-ive' than '-ieve',
    as Q's spelling 'atchiue' indicates.

2   *grace* adorn, make attractive (the spiritual implication of the word
    being notable by its absence)

3   *That* with the result that
    advantage should achieve should profit

4   *lace itself with his society* (1) wind itself into his company (as a *lace* runs
    through a shoe); (2) embellish itself with his company (as though
    trimmed with fine *lace*)

5–6   *Why should . . . hue.* why should cosmetics be applied to other
    cheeks to make them look like his, taking a lifeless appearance
    from (or 'copying the mere appearance of') his living *hue* ('com-
    plexion, colour, form, air, being', that cluster of senses exploited
    at 20.7)? The old theory that *painting* refers to portraiture is hardly
    plausible; more persuasive is the suggestion that poetic 'depiction'
    is touched on (compare the cosmetic imagery of Sonnets 82 and
    83).

7   *poor beauty.* The 'lesser loveliness', if not positive 'plainness', of
    those cheeks which cosmetically copy the *cheek* of the lovely youth.
    Alternatively, *poor* suggests 'worthy of pity' and *beauty* is firmly
    personified: poor old Beauty, though *beauty* itself, is less lovely than
    the young man.
    indirectly seek try to obtain through the devious obliquity of *false
    painting*

8   *Roses of shadow* unreal roses (the rosiness of rouged cheeks rather
    than the 'cheek-roses' which Lucio finds on Isabella's face at
    Measure for Measure I.4.16)
    since. 'Just because' gives way to 'because after all'; the temptation to
    copy and emulate should submit to a readiness to pay the young man
    homage.
    his rose is true the rosiness of his cheeks comes from native *beauty*.
    Recalling the first sonnet of the sequence, with its celebration of
    beauty's rose.

9   *now Nature bankrupt is* (by giving all her treasures to the friend,
    making him beautiful. The idea is too commonplace to need much
    elaboration on the poet's part; compare, for example, *Love's Labour's*

Lost II.1.9–12. *Bankrupt* is both an adjective and, supplying 'a', a noun.)

10   *Beggared* destitute

to blush. In context, transitive: 'to send in a red flush'.

lively. Like *living* in line 6, redolent of spontaneity, hope, vigour.

11   *exchequer* treasury (of beauty)

12   *'prived.* Q has 'proud', which is workable. The idea would be that *Nature* is 'conceited' about her *many*, inferior to and derivative from the young man though they are when it comes to *beauty*. But *'prived* fits the financial imagery of bankruptcy and beggary much more satisfactorily than 'proud', and it provides a neat paradox when set against *gains*. It is easy to imagine one of the Q compositors misreading a manuscript 'priu'd' as 'proud'; the words look alike in secretary hand.

many (treasuries of *beauty*. The lovely living things which *Nature* owned before all the world's true *beauty* was lavished on the friend.)

13   *stores* reserves, keeps in store. Conspicuously not associated here, as earlier, with breeding; see the note to 11.9.

14   *In days long since.* In lines 9–12, the blame had almost been the young man's for bankrupting *Nature*; but now it seems that Time, that familiar Shakespearian enemy, has deprived *Nature* and her progeny of *beauty*, leaving only the young man as a relic of the better past (perhaps, as 68.1 and 9–10 suggest, as good and long gone as the golden age).

these last these most recent days

Sonnet 68

1   *Thus.* The argument continues from Sonnet 67.

map epitome, record

days outworn times past

2   *as flowers do now* (that is, naturally, with no help from crafty art)

3   *bastard signs of fair.* Those marks and features which seem to signify beauty in modern faces and forms are illegitimate (base as well as ill-founded and false) because they derive from other faces and forms than the ones they garnish.

borne. This, the Q spelling, would function as both 'borne' and 'born' for Elizabethan readers, the former connecting with *signs* (though suggesting 'tolerated' as well as 'carried') and the latter with *bastard* (as well as *living* and *dead* in lines 4 and 5).

4   *brow* forehead

5–8   *Before the golden . . . gay.* Wigs were often made with hair cut from corpses. Compare *The Merchant of Venice* III.2.73–107, where

Bassanio mentions this practice – 'those crispèd snaky golden locks ... the dowry of a second head, | The skull that bred them in the sepulchre' – in his indictment of what he and the poet of the Sonnets call *ornament* (line 10).

5, 8   *golden tresses ... fleece.* Blond hair (fashionable in Elizabethan England, and therefore valuable), resembling the golden *fleece* for which Jason and the Argonauts ventured.

6   *The right of sepulchres* the rightful possession of the grave

8   *Ere ... gay* before the hair of one dead beauty was used to make *another* (not necessarily in his or herself beautiful) lovely. But the generalized *beauty* of line 2 also makes itself felt, and the *dead fleece* thus partly belongs to 'Beauty'. Shakespeare often uses *gay* to suggest gaudy allure – at *The Comedy of Errors* II.1.94, for instance, 'gay vestments' are those of whores; compare 146.4, where *gay* is again associated with dubious display.

9   *holy antique hours* blessed ancient times (of the golden age)
     antique (accented on the first syllable)

10   *all* any
     itself and true. As a *map of days outworn*, the young man presents an image of the golden age in all its honest integrity. *Itself* refers immediately to *hours*; in Elizabethan English, plural expressions of time were sometimes treated as singular.

11   *Making no summer of another's green.* Attention here shifts from the *cheek* as a *map* to the *cheek* itself, unadorned by cosmetics, set under the young man's own hair, not another's.

12   *old.* An adjective ('*Robbing no old* thing') tending to become substantive.

13   *as for a* to act as a

14   *what beauty was* (1) what beauty consisted of; (2) how much beauty there was

Sonnet 69

1   *parts* (1) portions; (2) attributes

2   *Want* lack
     thought of hearts heartfelt thoughts (thought up by *hearts* in the sense 'people')
     mend improve upon

3   *due* what is owed

4   *Uttering bare truth, even so as foes commend* telling the simple truth about your *outward*, in the way enemies (not inclined to flatter or over-praise their foes) commend. The claim is not (or not yet) that *All tongues* are the young man's *foes*; but the simile does suggest a

degree of antagonism, and, in doing so, it anticipates the second quatrain.

even (one syllable)

5   *Thy outward* (the *parts of thee that the world's eye* can *view*)

outward praise commendation appropriate to *Thy outward* (but with at least a hint of 'merely apparent, not substantial, *praise*': see the following note)

6   *those same tongues that give thee so thine own* the very *tongues* (and their owners, those who wag them) which give you in this way what is properly owing to you. The idea that commendation is a kind of return is underwritten by line 5, where the young man's *outward* is said to receive *outward praise*.

7   *In other accents* (1) using quite another language; (2) laying altogether different emphases

confound (1) confute; (2) destroy (see 5.6 and the note)

8   *the eye* (of line 1)

shown revealed to scrutiny

9   *look into* investigate (following easily from *the eye*)

10   *in guess they measure* they guessingly estimate

11   *Then, churls, their thoughts.* Q is unpunctuated, and some editors prefer no comma after *Then*, making the *thoughts*, not their thinkers, *churls*.

12   *To thy fair flower add the rank smell of weeds.* Here, as often in Shakespeare, *flower* means 'finest part' (compare 'the flower of chivalry') as well as 'blossom, bloom' (used, as in line 2 of the previous sonnet, to image beauty). The friend's *outward* is said to be his *flower* (both implications), his *mind* and moral character are found *rank* as *weeds* (quibblingly, only the natural, organic sense of *flower* is answered).

13   *odour* reputation. Probably, at the time, as dead a metaphor as now ('to be in bad odour'), enlivened here by *smell*.

14   *soil.* Complex, misprinted in Q ('solye'), and consequently much emended. But no editorial suggestion ('solve, toil, sully') matches *soil* in its capacity to contain the sonnet. A metaphoric 'ground, logical foundation, basis' co-exists with the literal 'earth (in which a *flower* and *weeds* grow)' – the latter leading to one sense of *common* in this line. *Soil* is also the aphetic form of 'assoil', meaning 'solution, explanation', but the poet's 'conclusion' here involves a 'blemish' – a further sense of *soil* – on the young man's reputation.

common vulgar, commonplace, cheap. With a quibble on 'public pasture, unenclosed field', the kind of *soil* in which *weeds* proliferate.

Sonnet 70

Answering the *churls* of 69.11 – to the point, indeed, of excusing the *soil* admitted at 69.14.

1   *are.* Another example of 'art' evaded for the sake of euphony.

     thy defect your flaw. 'Considered a fault on your part' is a rough expansion of the ellipsis.

1, 3   *defect . . . suspect.* A masculine rhyme, both words stressed on their second syllable (the usual accent for them in the period).

2   *mark* target (alluding to the proverb 'Envy shoots at the fairest mark')

3   *The ornament of beauty is suspect* suspicion is that which adorns beauty

4   *A crow* (comparing *suspect* to a bird familiarly associated with malice, ugliness, and the powers of evil)

5   *So* provided that, as long as

     doth but approve only proves. But *slander* evokes 'approval', a sense reinforced by line 6, with its paradoxically posed assertion (relying on *approve* as proof) that *worth* lies in opinion.

5, 7   *approve . . . love.* See the note to 25.13, 14.

6   *being wooed of time* since you are seductively tempted by the (corrupt) present day (but do not succumb, remaining *good*). A secondary strand explains why the young man is so subject to seduction: 'since you are favoured by Time (which handles your *beauty* tenderly)'.

7   *canker vice* vice like a cankerworm

     canker . . . the sweetest buds doth love. Another proverbial allusion; see 35.4 and the note.

8   *unstainèd* (1) unblotted; (2) unfaded

     prime youth, freshness (enlivened by the images of line 7, so that 'spring', 'spring of life, blossoming time' emerge)

9   *the ambush of young days* (thinking of the dangers and undesirable company which lie in wait for unwary youth)

10   *charged* attacked (and perhaps, since *slander* is the theme, 'accused, blamed' in the legal sense)

11–12   *so . . . To* so much . . . as to

12   *evermore enlarged* which is constantly being set free (and 'growing greater' or 'spreading further afield'). *Envy* seems a rampaging monster, like the Blatant Beast in Book V of *The Faerie Queene*.

13–14   *If some . . . owe* if a hint or suspicion of badness did not disguise your true appearance, entire nations would be in thrall to you. As in line 3, *suspect* is stressed on its second syllable; *owe* means 'own'. The image of masking arguably harks back to the sun metaphors of Sonnets 33–4; note especially 33.12.

Sonnet 71

2   *Than*. Something is lost by modernizing Q – where the old am-
     biguous 'Then' is used, preceded by a comma – since against, or
     suspended in, the main syntax, a familiar temporal progression can
     be felt: 'when I am dead, | Then you shall heare the surly sullen bell'
     (Q).
     the surly sullen bell (a passing bell)

3   *warning* notice (but also, insidiously, *warning* of others' deaths.
     'Never send to know for whom the bell tolls', Donne writes, 'It tolls
     for thee.')

3, 4 *world* (of mankind, as against 'earth', which line 4 makes the poet's
      dwelling)

4   *vile . . . vilest*. Q heightens this climax by employing a now obsolete
     form (with great phonic bite), 'vildest'.

5–6 *remember not | The hand that writ it*. See the Introduction, pages 44–5.

6, 7 *so* (1) so much; (2) in such a way. The approach to 'in order' is
      welcome, given the illogicality of love.

7   *sweet thoughts*. There is, perhaps, a trace of arm-twisting here, since
     'affectionate *thoughts*' are – the poet implies – inevitably expected
     from so *sweet*-natured and *sweet*-favoured a thinker.

8   *on* about
     make you woe cause you sorrow. But *woe* also operates, by transfer, as
     a verb: 'cause you to sorrow'.

9   *this verse*. Immediately, the *line* of line 5, but broadening to include
     the sonnet or some unknown gathering from the collection.

11   *rehearse* say over

12   *even with* at the same time as. *Even* is monosyllabic.
     decay (to the point of extinction)

13   *look into* inquire into, investigate
     moan complaint, lamentation

13, 14 *moan, gone*. See the note to 30.9, 11.

14   *with me* (1) on my account; (2) together with *me* (so clearly not worth
     your remembering; see Sonnet 72)

Sonnet 72

The poet explains why the *wise world* might *mock* the friend (71.13–14) for
remembering him after his death.

1   *task* (1) challenge; (2) command
     recite tell, describe

2   *lived* was, was included, was alive (before *my death*. The antithesis
     seems implicit.)

that (1) to account for the fact that; (2) which. The latter is secondary, but it usefully prepares for the discussion of *desert*, *praise*, and *shame* later in the sonnet by connecting the young man's *love* to the poet's disputed *merit*.

2–3   *you should love | After my death.* Though Q is unpunctuated, some editors insert a comma after *love*. This limits *After my death* unnecessarily. As the text stands, the phrase truthfully and ruefully marks a time in which the friend should *love* and (simultaneously) a time in which he should *forget*.

2, 4   *love . . . prove.* For the rhyme see the note to 25.13, 14.

4   *worthy.* There may be a passing quibble on 'worth thee'.

prove (1) find; (2) demonstrate. The latter is dominant, but it depends on the former.

5   *would* (more 'should want to' than 'should happen to')

virtuous (two syllables) (1) morally creditable (paradoxically related to *lie*); (2) potent, efficacious

6   *than mine own desert* (1) than I deserve; (2) than my own merit does

6, 8   *desert . . . impart.* On this rhyme, sounding 'ar', see the notes to 14.10, 12 and 17.2, 4.

7   *hang more praise upon deceasèd I.* The image is of a tomb hung with trophies (see the note to 31.10), though the parallel which comes first to mind is *Much Ado About Nothing* V.3, where Claudio reads Hero's *praise* from an epitaph hung *upon* her tomb (see V.1.271–2).

8   *niggard* miser (also acting as an adjective here, 'miserly')

impart hand out, utter

9   *lest your true love may seem false.* The primary sense, 'in case your constant affection should seem inconstant', turns on a quibble, *false* meaning 'dishonest' as well as 'inconstant', and the playful paradox is that the dishonesty which would make the friend *false* and therefore 'inconstant' would only be perpetrated because of the constancy which would make him loyal to the poet, *true* not *false*. On a secondary level, the words suggest 'in case your faithful beloved (me, the poet) should appear to be misrepresented (falsified, however favourably)'.

9, 11   *this . . . is.* Rhymed with the sound 's' not 'z' in *is*.

10   *for love* (1) out of charity; (2) for *your true love* (line 9, both senses, 'affection' and 'beloved')

speak well of me untrue (1) praise flawed me; (2) praise me dishonestly (*untrue* as adverb). *Well* also suggests 'eloquently' while *untrue* serves to oppose securely what *false* had balanced ambiguously.

11   *My name be* let my name be. Conceivably, the ellipsis should be supplied by *may* (line 9).

12   *nor . . . nor* neither . . . nor

13   *that which I bring forth* (my sonnets, my verse. Or, if Shakespeare's

life is felt to be the proper context for construing the poems, 'my
literary and theatrical works, and what I say or do'.)

13, 14   *forth ... worth.* See the note to 38.9, 11.

14   *should you* you ought to be ashamed
things (those works *which I bring forth*)
nothing worth without value, worth nothing (with a ripple of wordplay
when set beside *things*)

Sonnet 73

On the octave's debt to Ovid, see the headnote to Sonnet 12.

2   *or none, or few.* Although the comma is in Q, some editors remove it,
creating alternatives ('either none or few') which can be reconciled
('only a few, if any'). Sometimes explicitly, they prefer the gradation
'or few, or none'. But, setting aside euphony, Shakespeare's point is
that, where *leaves* are concerned, *few* is worse than *none* (just as
twilight exceeds *night* in pathos, and glowing *fire, ashes*), because a
fading thing sadly shows what it was.

3, 4   *those boughs ... Bare ruined choirs.* Though the essential metaphoric
connexion is invariably granted – it is earned by the *sweet birds* which
sang in the tree as choristers sing in *choirs* – considerable controversy
surrounds the degree of correspondence imagined, or imaginable,
here (see Further Reading, page 70). At an extreme of concretion it
may be observed that the stonework or woodwork in medieval *choirs*
– referring to that part of a church, east of the crossing, in which
divine services are sung – was frequently foliate. Less immediately,
choirs is enriched by a self-referential image of books and writing
(note the burden of 72.13–14). In Q it is spelt 'quiers', which usually
alerts the reader, already (with hindsight) sensitized by *yellow leaves*,
to a pun on 'quires'. The poet, one might infer from these traces (as
from elsewhere), finds his writings, once tuneful, old and barren.
For *yellow leaves* as written sheets see 17.9, and, for an equally
subordinate but more fully developed strand of book imagery, the
sestet of 108 (and its notes).

3   *shake against the cold.* The ambiguity of *against* serves to place the
boughs on the chilling edge of winter: they 'tremble in a cold autumn
wind' and 'shiver in anticipation of winter's ice and snow'.

4   *where late the sweet birds sang.* The *sweet birds* which *sang* in summer,
and are now silent, are like choirboys (see above), because they sing
in piping treble voices in chorus and because choirboys look rather
like birds when dressed in fluttering, ruffed plumage. Whether a
further parallel can be drawn is doubtful, but if, as has often been
suggested, the *choirs* of line 4 are monastic churches, sacked and

ruined at the dissolution, the absent birds would be like pre-Reformation choristers, who sang formerly but not now. (The difficulty with such a reading is that, while *late* can mean 'formerly', it is usually applied to some recent event – which the dissolution by no means was when the Sonnets were written.)

8   *Death's second self.* A standard description of sleep, here applied to *night* (but note *rest* at the end of the line, signifying sleep but suggesting death).

seals up all in rest. There are three threads of imagery entangled here: *night* is like a coffin in which the day's life is sealed; *night* resembles a letter writer, bringing the day to completion by folding it up and sealing it, or a testator, sealing a will on his *deathbed*; *night* closes all eyes, like the falconer who 'seels' or 'stitches up' the eyes of his hawk (compare *Macbeth* III.2.46–7, 'Come, seeling night, | Scarf up the tender eye of pitiful day').

10   *his* its

12   *with.* Both 'by' and 'along with', as the *ashes* choke their own *fire*. Line 12, with its lovely absorbed image, is curiously reminiscent of 1.5–7.

14   *that* (the poet. But also, inevitably, 'your life'.)

leave forgo. But 'depart from' (echoing the journeying image of line 7) registers to support the secondary implications of *that*: the young man must *leave* life as the *leaves* of line 2 the tree.

Sonnet 74

As the argument proceeds through Sonnets 73 and 74 it becomes increasingly Christian in tenor. The Ovidian association between man and the seasons which informs 73.1–4 (see the headnote to Sonnet 12) gives way, after the *Bare ruined choirs* are introduced, to echoes of Job 17.11–13:

My days are past, and my counsels and thoughts of my heart are vanished away, changing the night into day, and the light approaching into darkness. Though I tarry never so much, yet the grave is my house, and I have made my bed in the dark.

But it is not until the second quatrain of Sonnet 74 that the stark despair of Job 17.14–15 is invoked:

I said to corruption, thou art my father, and to the worms, you are my mother and my sister. Where is then now my hope? Or who hath considered the thing that I look for? These shall go down with me into the pit, and lie with me in the dust.

Compare with line 7 the following words in the Elizabethan burial service (in

the Book of Common Prayer), 'earth to earth, ashes to ashes, dust to dust',
and its scriptural analogue: 'Then shall the dust be turned again unto earth
from when it came, and the spirit shall return unto God who gave it'
(Ecclesiastes 12.8). This suggests, in turn, 1 Corinthians 15.53–5 (also
included in the burial service), with its message of hope:

> For this corruptible, must put on incorruption, and this mortal [must] put
> on immortality. When this corruptible hath put on incorruption, and this
> mortal hath put on immortality, then shall be brought to pass the saying
> that is written, Death is swallowed up into victory. O Death, where is thy
> sting?

And yet the sonnet, by no means orthodox in its treatment of the flesh, the
spirit, and immortality, harnesses Christian *contemptus mundi*, it might be
said, for its own secular ends.

1   *But . . . arrest.* Some editors insert a colon after *contented*; but it seems
unreasonable to expunge an expressive, if quiet, paradox for the sake
of logical clarity.
contented tranquil, free of distress
fell cruel, deadly
arrest (1) stop; (2) taking into custody (as by an officer. Compare
Hamlet V.2.330–31, 'this fell sergeant, Death, | Is strict in his
arrest'.)

2   *Without all bail* without any chance of release. No one can pay Death
in surety to win a respite for the poet, or be the poet's substitute in
custody.

3   *in this line some interest* some title to this verse, some degree of
involvement in and right of possession over this line of poetry

4   *for memorial* (1) as a reminder; (2) as a monument. *Memorial* has
three syllables.
still (1) always; (2) despite (Death's *fell arrest*)

5   *reviewest . . . review.* Mildly quibbling; 'read critically' becomes the
same plus 'see again', *re-view*.

6   *part* (of me, identified in line 8)
consecrate to solemnly devoted to, reserved for. The religious con-
notations prepare for the allusion to the burial service in line 7.

7   *his* its

8   *spirit.* The Christian context suggests 'soul', the poetic 'creative
powers' (compare 80.2, 85.7, and 86.5), and the elemental 'volatile
properties' (in contrast with the *earth* and *dregs* of the body).
the better part of me (the *spirit*, the *part* of line 6. See 39.2 and the
note.)

9   *So then* (when I die. But the ingenuity of the argument elicits 'so,
therefore'.)
but only

11   *The coward conquest of a wretch's knife.* Perhaps the body is a *coward*
      because it timorously gives up its life to something as slight as a *knife*;
      more likely the *wretch* with the *knife* makes a *coward* (acting as
      adjective) *conquest* when it stealthily assassinates the body. The
      former explains the nature of the body (so that the line runs in
      parallel with *the dregs of life*), the latter how it came to be the corpse it
      (in the future) is. If the *wretch* is the poet, the subject is suicide;
      if some hypothetical ruffian, the line expresses the same contempt
      for Death as Donne's 'Thou art slave to Fate, Chance, kings,
      and desperate men'; but the most plausible identification is with
      Mortality – as at 63.10, *confounding Age's cruel knife.*

12   *of* by

13-14 *The worth . . . is this* the value of the body resides in the *spirit* which it
      contains, and that can be identified with this poetry

14   *with thee remains* (1) endures, along with you; (2) stays with you. The
      former grows into the latter.

Sonnet 75

1   *So are . . . life* you are to my thoughts what food is to life

2   *sweet seasoned* (1) gentle and temperate; (2) spring (traditionally 'the
     sweet season'); (3) imbued with sweetness (a culinary image con-
     nected with *food* in line 1)

3   *And for . . . strife.* Clarity is sacrificed to chiasmus, to the balance of
     peace against *strife* and *you* against *I. For* can mean 'in order to (win)',
     'for the sake of', 'because of', and 'instead of'; *the peace of you* might
     be 'the tranquillity which you bring me' or 'the quietly secure
     enjoyment of your love'.

4   *As 'twixt . . . found* as is exemplified by a miser's relationship with his
     wealth, namely (though the proximity of *strife* makes *'twixt* suggest
     conflict between the poet and friend in ways consistent with the
     sequence at large and, arguably, with the love-hate involved in *a
     miser*'s possessiveness)

5   *proud as an enjoyer* exulting as a possessor
     anon immediately, at the next moment

5, 7 *anon . . . alone.* Probably rhymed on a long 'o' sounding like the vowel
     in Scottish English 'wart', 'ward', lengthened.

6   *Doubting* suspecting that
     filching thieving

7   *counting* accounting it, thinking it (an appropriately calculating verb
     for a *miser*, sitting, no doubt, in his *counting*-house)

8   *Then bettered . . . pleasure* then thinking it even better (*counting* the *best*
     to have been *bettered*) that people can see (with a hint of 'when people

see') me enjoying your company (or just 'you, who give me, indeed are, *my pleasure*')

9   *Sometime* at one time (paralleling *Now* in lines 5 and 7)

10   *clean* wholly

a look. Although *your sight* in line 9 means straightforwardly 'my seeing you', it is difficult not to read *a look* without thinking of a desired glance from the friend, or *a look* exchanged.

12   *Save what . . . took* except for what is received from you or must be taken from you (because no one else can give it)

13   *pine* (1) starve; (2) languish with desire. Compare *Venus and Adonis* 601–2, where Shakespeare again sets *pine* against *surfeit* to illustrate the workings of desire; the goddess of love, touching Adonis but not rousing him, resembles 'poor birds, deceived with painted grapes' that 'surfeit by the eye and pine the maw'. On the birds' pining see the note to 47.6 and, in the light of *feasting, starvèd, pine*, and *surfeit* in the sonnet's sestet, the images of sightful eating throughout 47.

14   *Or . . . or* either . . . or

all away possessing nothing

Sonnet 76

See the Introduction, pages 28–9 and 45.

1   *barren* bare

new pride new-fangled adornment, novel ornamentation

2   *variation or quick change*. In classical rhetoric, *variation* includes nimbleness of expression and variety in argument, so *or* means 'or what might be called' rather than 'or, alternatively'. As a deft Englishing, *quick change* resembles some of Puttenham's glosses in *The Art of English Poesy* (1589): '*hyperbole* or the over-reacher, otherwise called the loud liar', '*ironia* or the dry mock'.

3   *with the time* as is fashionable these days. But the poet claims such staunch constancy in the sestet that 'with each change of taste that the passing of time produces' would also be a plausible interpretation.

glance turn sharply

4   *methods* creative procedures. In this context, the word has a faintly technical ring: 'Poesy', Puttenham says, was not an art 'until by studious persons fashioned and reduced into a method of rules and precepts'. Medical associations may also be involved (compare *compounds strange*): it has been pointed out that a 'method' was a course of treatment, and that the three schools of classical medicine were called Dogmatic, Methodic, and Empiric.

compounds strange exotic compound words (of the kind used by modish poets like Marston and Joseph Hall). Because composite drugs and poisons were called *compounds* – as against 'simples', the refined extract from single sources – Shakespeare can suggest that fashionable diction resembles odd and probably dangerous substances. Moreover, since the word *compound* was novel as a noun (the *Oxford English Dictionary*, somewhat tardily, first records it in the chemical sense in *Cymbeline, c.* 1611), the *compounds strange* are themselves (as Shakespeare's own *compound* says) *new-found*. For a similar instance of the poet enacting the abuses he adverts to, see 21.8 and the note.

5   *still* always, ever (as in lines 10 and 14)
      all one only one way, the same

6   *keep invention in a noted weed.* According to the prevailing aesthetic, writing involved the 'inventing' or 'finding out' of a topic (see 38.1 and the note), and then the dressing of that *invention* – the clothing image was commonplace – in language. Here the poet laments that he should *keep* or 'maintain' his subject-matter in a 'familiar, well-known' discursive 'garb' or 'dress' (*noted weed*).

7   *That* so that

8   *their . . . they.* The antecedent is *every word* (treated as a plural).
      where they did proceed (1) where they issued from, whence they came; (2) where they graduated from. The idea of (2) is that, having been born in the poet, *every word* is educated there and issues into poetry rather like a young man who, having taken a degree, begins to make his way in the world. Compare the quibble on 'proceeding' at *Love's Labour's Lost* I.1.95.

9   *sweet love.* A fleeting uncertainty, resolved by *you and love* in line 10; the poet is here addressing his 'gentle beloved'.

10 *argument* theme

11 *all my best* the best I can manage
      dressing (1) arranging; (2) clothing. Compare the sartorial imagery of line 6.
      new anew, over again. But 'in a new way' is prompted by *old*, modifying the modesty of the octet.

12 *spent* (1) paid out; (2) exhausted, worn out. The financial metaphor, *Spending . . . spent*, translates: 'used so often in the past that it lacks literary interest'.

13 *For as the sun is daily new and old.* If *old words new* registers as an apology for mediocrity, *new and old* are here linked by the sun's blaze of glory. The poet's love is as predictable – yet as dazzlingly beautiful – as the *sun*. If he lacks originality, that is only a consequence of his being inviolably true.

14 *telling what is told.* The financial-for-literary imagery of line 12 turns into wordplay: saying things *already* said, the poet 'once more counts

over the coinage of love'. (Compare the *counting* of the *miser* in Sonnet 75.)

Sonnet 77

1   *glass* mirror

wear. 'Endure, last out' registers only to heighten the impact of 'diminish, fade away'. Q's spelling, 'were', reveals a possible ambiguity; the young man's *glass* will lead him to reflect that his 'worn' *beauties* are not what they 'were'.

2   *dial* (two syllables). The *shady stealth* of line 7 defines the *dial* as the face of a 'sundial' rather than some other kind of timepiece. Why *dial* instead of 'sundial'? Presumably Shakespeare used the part for the whole to parallel line 1 more precisely: both the *glass*, showing the young man's face, and the *dial* (the 'face' of the timepiece) register the progress of time.

waste decay, wear away

3, 4,   *vacant leaves ... this book ... these waste blanks ... thy book.* The
10, 14   sonnet was almost certainly meant to accompany the gift of a blank notebook. Compare Sonnet 122.

4   *taste* sample, experience. The bizarre link with the *mouthèd graves* of line 6 (which gape, *taste*, and devour men) is probably deliberate.

6   *give thee memory* remind you. Presumably the young man's *wrinkles* prompt him to think of *mouthèd graves*; they mark his mortality, his drift towards death. Despite 2.2 and 60.10, it is difficult to equate the *wrinkles* directly with *graves*.

7   *shady stealth* slowly moving shadow. The hint of theft in *stealth* sets up the imagery of line 8.

8   *thievish progress to* thief-like (and thieving) advance towards. Two ideas meet: *Time* moves with all the stealth of a thief on the job; his movement towards *eternity* constitutes theft because it robs the world of its *beauties*. Compare the 'thievish minutes' of *All's Well That Ends Well* II.1.166. Lines 7 and 8 seem to vary the proverb 'We perceive the shadows of a dial passed, but perceive it not passing'.

9   *Look what* whatever

10   *Commit* consign. An aptly chosen verb, mediating between *memory* and the *waste blanks*; Elizabethans 'committed' things to *memory*, as we do; but they also 'committed' matters to writing.

waste blanks blank pages

10–12   *shalt find ... thy mind* will find those ideas of yours matured (like children past nursing) and ready to be newly acquainted (as though new acquaintances) with your mind

13   *offices* duties (of looking at the *glass* and *dial*, and producing thoughts

for the *book*. The young man's meditations would resemble the thoughts of a clergyman saying his *offices*.)

so oft as often

14   *much enrich thy book* (the assumption being that, when the *offices* are done, the young man will feel compelled to *commit* them to paper)

Sonnet 78

The first of several sonnets concerned with poetic rivalry. In Sonnet 21 a similar theme was entertained, but as this group unfolds, a distinct and characterized opponent – the so-called 'rival poet' – seems to emerge. Whether he was Marlowe, Chapman, Jonson, Turberville, or a conflation of more than one figure cannot be the concern of this edition. Despite the contingent details offered in Sonnet 86, it is impossible to identify the rival with confidence. Moreover, while it seems unlikely that the antagonist was merely invented (wrought from the concerns of the sequence), he is, in the development of its anxieties, a 'wondrous necessary man', and, as a being projected by the verse, subordinate in interest, at every point, to the poetic issues raised by his existence.

1   *for* as, to be

2   *fair* helpful, favourable. Such assistance as a *fair* ('lovely, attractive') youth would grant.

3   *As* that

      alien other, strange, stranger. An adjective tending towards a noun.

3, 7,   *pen . . . feathers . . . style.* The links have been obscured by biros and
11   typewriters. Shakespeare wrote with a quill; *feathers* provided his *pen*. Indeed, the word *pen* (based on Latin *penna*, 'feathers') was used of *feathers* well into the nineteenth century. The same word anticipates *style* because *style* lies close to its Latin origin (*stilus*, 'writing implement') in Elizabethan English. And *mend the style* seems obliquely related to line 7, with its imping of *pen*s.

4   *under thee* under your protection, in your service, with you as patron

5–6   *Thine eyes . . . fly.* Modest disclaimers by the poet: until inspired by the young man's eyes, he was dully ignorant and altogether without eloquence; now he sings with full-throated ease (*on high* means 'aloud, loudly', while quibblingly anticipating *aloft*) and, no longer *heavy*, soars into the sky.

6, 8   *fly . . . majesty.* A full rhyme, resembling 1.2 and 4.

7   *added feathers to the learnèd's wing.* A metaphor from falconry. The poet's *learnèd* rivals have been imped (given extra wing feathers) by their master, and now they fly even higher than they did.

8   *given grace a double majesty* doubled the glorious superiority of already excellent wits

9   *compile* compose, write. The word inherits from its Latin root (*compilare*, 'to rob, plunder') a strong implication of derivativeness, here from the friend.

10   *Whose influence is thine* whose nature is determined by you. The *influence* is astrological. Presumably the image was prompted by the educative *eyes* of line 5; here, as at 14.10, the *eyes* become stars.
      born of thee is your child. The poet's verses are the intellectual offspring of the young man; on the centrality of this and other images of creation as parturition, see the Introduction, pages 27-9.

11   *mend* correct, improve
      style (as opposed to content. But see the note to *pen . . . feathers*.)

12   *arts* learning and literary skills

12-14   *graces gracèd . . . high . . . learning . . . ignorance*. Echoing key-words from the octet.

13   *thou art all my art*. Reducing to wordplay the bold claim that the young man is a *Muse*, a goddess giving *art* by being *art*'s epitome.
      advance. A word which suggests movement upwards as well as forwards ('Advance thy halberd higher than my breast' at *Richard III* I.2.40 is typical); hence *high* in line 14.

Sonnet 79

2   *had all thy gentle grace* received all your kind favour, contained and expressed all your elegantly graceful graciousness, was every bit as gently graceful as you

3   *gracious numbers* verses possessed of *gentle grace*
      decayed declined in quality

4   *sick Muse* ailing inspiration, failing literary gifts
      doth give another place makes way for another (*Muse*, and so poet)

5   *thy lovely argument* the lovely theme of lovely you. Compare Sonnet 38, particularly line 3.

6   *worthier* (two syllables)

7   *of thee* concerning you. Shakespeare wittily reverses the words in the same foot in the next line.
      invent find out as a literary subject. (Compare 76.6 and 38.1.)

9   *lends* ascribes to (but with a quibble on loaning and borrowing which leads, via *afford* in line 11, to the starkly financial *owes* and *pay*)

9, 11   *word . . . afford*. Uncertain, since the rhyme might depend on a short 'u' like the one in 'educated' southern 'put', but probably relies on the old 'o'-based pronunciation of *word* ('ward . . . afford' rather than 'wurd . . . affurd').

10   *behaviour*. 'Bearing' and 'manner' as well as 'conduct'. The word has

become neutral, but for early readers it would imply comeliness and elegance in deportment.

11   *can afford* is able to offer (with financial associations, like *lends*)

14   *owes* is obliged to pay. Whether in return for patronage or out of some obscure prompting which makes poets praise beauty is not quite clear. See 83.4 and the note.

thyself (with a flicker of wordplay, signalled in Q by the admittedly standard 'thy selfe'. The friend repays his self himself.)

Sonnet 80

1   *faint* lose heart, languish

2   *a better spirit* (some more accomplished poet. *Spirit* is monosyllabic.)
     use your name (as subject-matter, the basis of his eulogy)

3–4 *spends all his might* | *To make me tongue-tied.* As we read into line 4 the sincerity of the rival falls in doubt. It is intimated that he partly praises the friend for the pleasure of making the poet *tongue-tied*.

4–12 The extended image of seas and shipwreck recalls Nestor's speech on valour at *Troilus and Cressida* I.3.33–45, where the large 'strong-ribbed bark' again comes out well and the 'saucy boat' badly – fleeing to harbour 'Or made a toast for Neptune' when the sea gets rough.

5   *wide as the ocean is* which is as wide as the ocean

6   *humble.* Shakespeare, it might be thought, avoids the imputation of pride which would follow from calling himself the 'humblest *sail*' by implying the superlative through the equivalence suggested in *as*.
     as as well as, just as well as
     proudest grandest, most gallant. But a suggestion of sinful pride is evident.

6, 8 *bear . . . appear.* Rhymed on a vowel nearer the 'ea' in modern *bear* than in *appear* (for confirmation see *A Lover's Complaint* 93, 95–6).

7   *saucy* impertinent (for braving the *wide ocean* and tacitly claiming equality with the rival's grand craft)
     inferior (three syllables)

8   *main* open sea
     wilfully out of choice, stubbornly, perversely

9–10 *Your shallowest help . . . ride.* The poet is so devoted that a few favours from the young man suffice to keep his *bark* buoyant; the rival is implicitly rebuked.

9   *shallowest* most meagre, scantiest

10   *soundless* unfathomable, not to be sounded

12   *tall building* sturdy and imposing construction
     pride. Compare *proudest* (line 6) and the note.

13   *cast away* (1) spurned; (2) shipwrecked

14 *my love* (which prompted me to put to sea in an *inferior* craft. It is possible that *love* should also be interpreted 'beloved'; at *worst*, the poet reflects, he would suffer at the hands of someone he loved.)
    decay ruin, cause of my ruin

Sonnet 81

1-2 *Or ... Or* whether ... or
1   *make* compose. Poets were sometimes called 'makers'.
3   *From hence* from the world. But readers familiar with this or earlier sonnets concerned with poetry as immortality might anticipate the sestet and add 'from these lines'.
4   *in me each part* all the qualities in me, all of me
5   *from hence.* The phrase used in line 3 is redeployed with a different emphasis: 'from these lines' remains available, but 'from the world' is ousted by 'henceforth'.
5, 7 *have ... grave.* Probably rhymed on long 'a', resembling the vowel in southern English 'bat', 'bad', lengthened.
6   *to all the world must die.* 'I must be dead to (unresponsive towards) all the world' accompanies 'I must be downright dead (my reputation defunct as well as my body) as far as the world is concerned'; the confusion enriches the couplet, suggesting that the young man will not only *live* in the world's memory but somehow himself *live*.
7   *yield* (a perverse harvest)
     but only, just
     common undistinguished
8   *entombèd in men's eyes.* Evoking one of those fine renaissance tombs on which the dead lie, at eye level, in effigy, bust, or family group. If the friend of this sonnet is the well-born youth addressed in Sonnets 1-19, such a tomb would be his due, and the turn into line 9 would imply 'Despite this, *Your* real *monument ...*', drawing on the priorities established in such sonnets as 55.
9-12 *Your monument ... dead.* Q punctuates loosely, with commas after each line. This allows line 11 a double life, simultaneously ending the quatrain and introducing the couplet. Logical modern pointing requires that the ambiguity be suppressed.
9   *monument* (1) sepulchre, stone memorial; (2) written record. In the wake of the octave, the former seems dominant; as the sestet unfolds, it is ousted by (2), a usage now obsolete but current into the nineteenth century.
10, 12 *o'er-read ... dead.* The rhyme depends on a long-vowelled pronunciation of *dead* apparently already archaic in Elizabethan English.
11   *rehearse* recount, repeat (by saying over the poet's *verse*)

275

12 *this world* the world as it now is, this generation
13 *You still shall live* (1) you'll continue to live; (2) you'll live nevertheless
14 *even in the* in the very. *Even* is monosyllabic.

Sonnet 82

2 *attaint* dishonour. Perhaps quibbling on 'a taint'.
   o'erlook peruse
3 *dedicated* (1) devoted; (2) committed to you by virtue of an Author's
   Dedication (the kind of text which prefaces *Venus and Adonis* and *The
   Rape of Lucrece*)
4 *blessing every book.* Perhaps the *fair subject* ('lovely you') does the
   blessing; perhaps the *dedicated words which writers use*; probably both,
   with a glance, *via* the sexual sense of *blessing* (see the second note to
   3.4), at the youth as verbal 'begetter'.
5 *Thou art as fair in knowledge as in hue* you are as *fair* ('just, honest') in
   comprehension as you are *fair* ('lovely, attractive') in *hue* (with most
   of the senses evoked by 20.7).
6 *Finding thy worth a limit past my praise* in deciding that your merit
   forms a region beyond the reach of my praise, when you discover that
   your merit extends to a boundary beyond the range of my praise
7 *therefore* (because you are so *fair*, but most immediately on account of
   your *Finding*)
   enforced obliged
8 *stamp* impression (or instrument for stamping one. Often used in the
   context of printing; compare the concerns of lines 3–4.)
   time-bettering days days which have brought such improvements (in
   the arts. Compare *the bettering of the time* at 32.5.)
10 *strainèd.* Nicely ambiguous: 'straining' to the *limit* of line 6, the poets'
   'strains' become attenuated, far-fetched, and, frankly, *strainèd.*
   touches artful strokes (of painted *rhetoric*. Also 'pluckings and strum-
   mings' on the lyre of language.)
11 *truly fair.* Presumably *fair* in a way which joins *fair* loveliness to *fair*
   justice (see lines 4 and 5).
   truly sympathized accurately and feelingly depicted
12 *true . . . true-telling* honest . . . truthful
   plain frank, unadorned (by *rhetoric*), clear
13 *gross* thick, heavily laid on
   painting. Praise construed as cosmetic: compare *Love's Labour's Lost*
   IV.1.17–18, 'Nay, never paint me now! | Where fair is not, praise
   cannot mend the brow', or, in the light of line 6, IV.3.237–9, quoted
   in the note to 21.14; and see the Introduction, page 25.

14   *in thee* (1) in your case; (2) on your features
      abused misused

Sonnet 83

The continuity with Sonnet 82 is obvious.

2   *fair* beauty
      set applied

3   *or thought I found.* At first, the poet seems to waver in the confidence
      earned at 82.9–14, but it emerges, as the sonnet proceeds, that this
      parenthesis stems, not from some renewed sense of other men's
      powers, but from a disappointed recognition that the friend approves
      painting (something which leads to a frank rebuke in the couplet of
      84).

4   *barren tender of a poet's debt* sterile and worthless tribute which a poet
      is obliged to *tender* you (in return for patronage or just because your
      beauty requires praise. Compare the obligation at 79.14). *Barren*
      only confirms the insufficiency of *tender*, a word which implied in the
      period 'mere promise, only an offer'; at *Hamlet* I.3.105–7, Polonius
      tells Ophelia: 'Think yourself a baby | That you have ta'en these
      tenders for true pay | Which are not sterling.'

5   *slept in your report* (1) kept quiet about you; (2) stayed quiet in the
      midst of your reputation, said nothing though I heard your praises
      vaunted on all sides

6   *That* so that
      being (one syllable)
      extant (1) still existing, alive now; (2) conspicuous, evident. The
      latter registers when the reader reaches *well might show*.

7   *modern* (1) ordinary, trite; (2) up-to-date, of the present. As usual in
      Shakespeare, the former is dominant, but it rests here on the latter.
      In the context of *quill* there may also be a reference to *modern* as
      against 'ancient' (that is, classical) writing – the latter carrying more
      prestige (though that was contested with increasing vigour and
      complexity throughout the seventeenth century). The implication of
      such an allusion would be that, if Ovid or some other ancient writer
      were the poet's rival, the *quill* might not fall so *short*.

8   *of worth, what worth.* The uncharacteristic awkwardness marks a
      moment of hesitation, or stalling, at the idea of the friend's *worth*.
      The poet betrays an anxiety already visible in the parenthesis of line
      3 and explicit in the sestet.
      what worth how much value, such value as. Both nuances are felt in
      any reading, but knowledge of the sestet makes the latter, more
      sceptical implication especially strong.

9   *for* as
10   *being dumb*. An ellipsis, requiring 'I'. This seemingly banal and
       tautologous explanation of the poet's *silence* yields a fuller signifi-
       cance in lines 11–12 and, more strikingly, in the conclusion of
       Sonnet 85.
10, 12 *dumb . . . tomb*. Employing a short 'u' to rhyme fully, like *come . . .*
       tomb at 17.1 and 3.
12   *When others . . . tomb*. The poet directs at his rivals the criticism he
       made of himself at 17.3–4.
14   *both*. Despite the plurality of *others* (which might be, in any case, a
       darkly general reference to a single other), probably the poet plus
       rival rather than two rivals.

Sonnet 84

For a more discursive paraphrase of the first quatrain, and an account of the
whole sonnet, see the Introduction, pages 25–6.

1–2   *Who is it . . . this* where is that most extravagant of eulogists who can
       say more than this. Some editors prefer to punctuate lines 1–2 as a
       pair of challenges directed at the rival(s): 'Who is it that says most?
       Which can say more | Than this . . . ?'
2   *you alone are you* you are the only you there is, you are absolutely
       unique, no one can compare with you
3–4   *In whose . . . grew* within whom is confined that abundance of
       qualities which should identify the place where your exemplar and
       equal grows (but doesn't because it just identifies you). As his own
       model the peerless young man defies the imaging extravagance of
       poets. *Immurèd*, 'walled', and *grew* subtly conjure the image of a
       walled garden.
5   *penury* (reversing *rich* and playfully anticipating *pen*)
       pen (as a metonymy for 'poet', with perhaps a quibbling glance back
       to *confine*)
6   *his* its (though *pen* is so clearly metonymic that the modern sense,
       referring back to 'poet', passes muster)
8   *so* thereby, thus. But 'to such an extent' also registers, carrying the
       argument across the turn into the sestet (allowing a silent 'that').
9   *but* only, just
       copy. See the note to 11.14 and the Introduction, pages 27–9.
10   *clear* (1) bright; (2) pure (both 'absolute' and 'innocent'); (3) illus-
       trious, distinguished; (4) lucid, free from crabbed obscurity. For a
       similar but not identical range of senses, see 43.7 and the note.
10, 12 *clear . . . everywhere*. The rhyme was apparently full, and nearer
       modern '-ere' than '-ear'.

11   *counterpart* likeness, reproduction
      fame his wit make his intelligence famous

12   *style* manner of writing, idiom (but with a quibbling reference back to
      pen. See the note to 78.3, 7, 11.)

13   *beauteous* (two syllables)
      blessings (1) gifts from God, excellences; (2) praises, words spoken by
      those who bless you (see 82.4 and the note)

14   *Being fond . . . worse.* If the Q comma is read through, the following
      results: '*Being fond* of the kind of panegyric which, praising the wrong
      things in you, debases itself (and so degrades you)'.
      Being (one syllable) that of being, in that you are
      fond on. 'Too fond of' carried as far as 'besotted by' (*fond* in the sense
      'dotingly idiotic').
      makes your praises worse debases the praise bestowed on you (because
      however eloquent it is, your eagerly undiscriminating reception of it
      turns it to flattery)

Sonnet 85

1   *in manners holds her still* keeps quiet (and doesn't jostle for attention)
      out of politeness. There may be a secondary 'continues to act in a
      well-mannered fashion'.

2   *comments of your praise* treatises detailing your merits, tracts in praise
      of you
      richly compiled elaborately written

3   *Reserve* store, lay up
      thy character (1) your nature and manner; (2) the writing which you
      are. The two senses are doubly linked: (1) implies (2) because the
      comments which record the young man's *character* belong to that
      genre of prose personality sketch so popular in the early seventeenth
      century, the Theophrastan Character (and it is relevant that Q gives
      character, like *hymn* in line 7, a capital letter); (2) implies (1) because
      of the sestet of the previous sonnet, where it is said that the young
      man is inscribed with a self which poets should set out to *copy*. Those
      recent editors who retain Q's 'their' sacrifice half the sense of the
      phrase, and, with it, Shakespeare's suggestion that the young man's
      being is beyond comparing.
      golden precious, aureate (describing the product of the quill rather
      than the pen itself)

4   *phrase* style, phraseology, language (rather than the restricted
      modern sense)

5   *other* others (a standard form of the plural)

5, 7 *words . . . affords.* For the rhyme, see the note to 79.9, 11.

6   *unlettered* illiterate

     clerk. Character and *quill* suggest 'scribe', but this dissolves to be replaced by 'minor cleric' and 'parish clerk, lay assistant to the priest' as we read *Amen* and *hymn*.

     still constantly

6–7   *still cry 'Amen'* | *To every hymn that able spirit affords.* An echo of 1 Corinthians 14.16: 'Else when thou blessest with the spirit, how shall he that occupieth the room of the unlearned say Amen at thy giving of thanks, seeing he understandeth not what thou sayest.' *Spirit* is monosyllabic.

7   *hymn* song of praise (directed at something of more than human worth)

     that. Since the poem deals with a plurality of rivals, 'which (any)' rather than '(which) *that*'.

     able spirit gifted poet. One possessed with a *Muse* which is not *tongue-tied.*

     affords offers, provides

8   *In polished form of well-refinèd pen* in the smooth and shapely style which flows from a thoroughly cultivated writer. Or *pen* may be, like *quill*, a metonymy for writing rather than a writer: 'in the smooth and shapely style (and perhaps "the elegantly shaped lettering", for calligraphy was taken very seriously) of thoroughly civilized writing'.

10   *most of praise* utmost praise. Compare the first line of Sonnet 84.

11   *that* (the poet's addition to *the most of praise*)

11–12 *whose love to you ... holds his rank before.* Conjuring a procession: although the poet's *words* are so undistinguished that they come at the rear, his loving *thoughts* are so puissant that they have a place in the front rank of marchers.

13   *breath of* (suggesting insubstantiality, if not insincerity)

14   *in effect* in what I do, in practice

Sonnet 86

In its imagery the poem recalls Sonnet 80 (compare, for example, 86.1 with 80.6 and 12), but its argument connects with Sonnet 85. Here the poet explains why the *good thoughts* of 85.5 had to go unspoken. The details of this sonnet have been scrutinized with microscopic attention by scholars attempting to establish the identity of the rival poet (see the headnote to Sonnet 78). Their labours have met with little success, though it should be conceded that, if an identification had to be made on the basis of Sonnet 86 alone, Chapman would seem a strong candidate. In their admirable annotation, Ingram and Redpath summarize the case, to which they are also uncommitted, thus: 'Line 1 would fit the fourteeners of his *Iliad* [seven books of which appeared in 1598]. Lines 5–8 would readily apply to his labours in translating the classics and his heavy reliance on past writers. "Above a mortal pitch" would describe well the high epic style and theme of his great translation. And lines 9–10 might refer to his rhetorical claim in his *Tears of Peace* to have been constantly prompted by the spirit of Homer. The double reference to night, moreover, might well, in this case, allude to the motto of his poem *The Shadow of Night* (1594), *Versus mei habebunt aliquantum noctis*.'

Perhaps the chief problem in interpreting the poem, and pondering the nature of its reference, is the degree of credence to be attached to the paranormal implications of *spirits* and *familiar ghost* and the degree of literalness allowed *compeers*. Are these loftily ironic ways of describing literary derivativeness, or the depiction of a particular author's erudite and self-regarding superstition?

1   *proud full sail.* A complex phrase: *proud* implies splendour, the swelling of the *sail* with a good following wind, and (through a 'proudful' conflation with *full*) high arrogance; *full* supports the idea of billowing (the canvas is *full* of air), while suggesting (when taken with *sail*) a *full*-rigged ship moving *full* ahead; and this last impression, of movement, makes *sail* evoke not just a roped and straining canvas but the action which the *sail* effects, that of 'sailing' (Hamlet exploits the same ambiguity when he praises Laertes' 'quick sail' at V.2.115).

2   *Bound for . . . you.* The rival is a galleon setting out to win treasure in the rich New World, or a formidable privateer looking for booty on the high seas.

3   *ripe* matured and ready (for birth)
       inhearse entomb, bury. The word was apparently coined by Shakespeare in writing this poem, in the form given here, with *in-*. Later authors preferred 'enhearse', and ruthless modernization might call for that spelling here. Since, however, the word has not been used enough for the orthodoxy to be tyrannous, and since *inhearse* is semantically richer (representing the results as well as the process of putting something *in* a *hearse*), Q's 'inhearce' is substantially followed.

5   *spirit . . . spirits.* The wordplay depends on *spirit* meaning 'vigorous mind, sprightly temperament, aspiring powers' while *spirits* refers to literary associates of the rival, whether living (compare 85.7) or ghostly and/or devilish (compare, in the light of lines 9–10, the 'familiar spirits' which tend on Joan of Arc in *1 Henry VI* V.3). But Shakespeare was capable of construing the *spirit* as a kind of daemon and, beneath the wordplay, this may also register (compare *Antony and Cleopatra* II.3.18–31, where the Soothsayer discusses the rivalry between Antony and Caesar in precisely those terms).

5–6   *write | Above a mortal pitch.* Falconry informs this, a *pitch* being the

281

'height to which a bird of prey soars before stooping' as well as a 'level of attainment'.

6 *struck me dead.* This heightening of 'struck me dumb' is supported by the death-silence imagery of lines 3–4.

7 *compeers* associates, fellows (implying equality and, as sometimes in the English of the period, contempt)

 compeers by night. The phrase looks back to *spirits*, and the rival is imagined in nocturnal converse with his literary friends, with the mighty dead (as he supposes), or with evil wraiths. The idea of communication with dead writers is immediately attractive, since it fades into scornful literalness if the phrase is read as a high-sounding account of the inspiration drawn from reading books *by night*. The suggestion of equality and trace of contempt in *compeers* – which would fit the rival's literary friends directly – would then resonate ironically in that the poet would equate the rival with great *spirits* (Chapman, as it were, would be Homer's peer) while conde-scending incredulously – a mixture of flattery and dismissal central to the tone of the poem. But Shakespeare does not give us enough to be sure.

8 *astonishèd* stunned (into silence)

9 *He, nor* neither he nor

 affable courteously complaisant, conversable, friendly

 familiar ghost attendant spirit. The phrase *affable familiar ghost*, though singular, is evidently linked to *spirits*, and so to *compeers*. Here, as in line 5, the eccentric is mixed up with the sinister (if *affable* sounds amiable enough, *familiar* is usually used of devils), and, as in line 7, there is a sense of pretensions scorned. What distinguishes this phrase, obviously, is its emphasis on the supernatural (which need not retrospectively disambiguate *spirits* and *compeers*) and its peculiar contingency (see the headnotes to this sonnet and to 78).

10 *gulls* (1) dupes; (2) crams, gorges. The latter (from French *engouler*, 'to send down the throat') was not common in the period, but it probably contributes here.

 intelligence information

12 *of* with, from

13 *countenance* (1) face and feature ('Clear up, fair Queen, that cloudy countenance', *Titus Andronicus* I.1.263), manner and bearing ('Lift up your countenance', says Florizel to the downcast Perdita at *The Winter's Tale* IV.4.49), pleasing appearance ('the evil which is here wrapped up | In countenance', *Measure for Measure* V.1.117–18); (2) regard and approval ('[a sponge] that soaks up the King's counten-ance, his rewards, his authorities', *Hamlet* IV.2.15–16), patronage, favour, and protection (thus, at *2 Henry IV* V.1.33–4 and 38–9, Davy asks Justice Shallow 'to countenance William Visor of Woncot

against Clement Perkes o'th' Hill', insisting that 'a knave should have some countenance at his friend's request')

filled up. The young man's *countenance* provided subject-matter for, and (like plaster filling cracks in a badly made wall) repaired deficiencies in, the rival's verse.

14   *lacked I matter* I had nothing left to write about

    that (lack of *matter*)

Sonnet 87

All the rhymes are feminine except *estimate . . . determinate.* Compare Sonnet 20, which has feminine rhymes throughout.

1   *thou art too dear for my possessing.* The primary 'you are too costly for my purchase' implies either 'too emotionally exhausting for me to continue loving' (*dear* bearing something of the sense 'grievous') or 'too expensive for the likes of humble me because too ready to sell yourself to the highest bidder (to offer yourself for the purchase of praise: see especially 84.13–14)'. 'You are too deeply loved by me to be won by me (for you take my love for granted, my doting bores you)' also registers; as does 'you are too high in rank to be won by me' (resting on a common connotation of *dear*, as at *1 Henry IV* IV.4.31–2, 'many more corrivals and dear men | Of estimation and command in arms').

1, 3   *possessing . . . releasing.* Rhymed on short 'e', not the 'ea' of modern *releasing.*

2   *like enough* very probably

    estimate value (in the world's eyes. Here almost 'market price'.)

3   *The charter of thy worth.* From 'the initial document conferring rank and privilege upon you' – which incidentally implies that the friend, like the youth of Sonnets 1–19, is well-born – come 'the (metaphorical) *charter* created by (which is) your worth' and 'the privileged scope for action which your *worth* allows you'. *Worth* hovers uneasily between 'true value (inherent *worth*)' and the *estimate* (judged *worth*) assigned by the market-place.

    releasing ('legal exemption' as a wider 'liberation, freedom')

4   *bonds in thee* (1) legal agreement with you; (2) emotional claim over you

    determinate ended, terminated

5   *hold* keep. A physical 'embrace' can be felt beneath the legalistic 'hold title to'.

    by thy granting with your permission, by virtue of a legal *grant* from you

5, 7   *granting . . . wanting*. Rhymed on a short 'a' like the one in modern *granting*, not as 'gronting, wonting'.

6   *for that riches where is my deserving* in what way do I deserve that wealth (which is the *granting* of *dear* you by you)

7   *The cause of this fair gift in me is wanting* I lack those qualities which should prompt you to grant me *this fair gift* (which is lovely you)

8   *patent* right of ownership (apparently clinched by the *bonds* of line 4)
        back again is swerving reverts to you

10   *Or me . . . else mistaking* or else you misunderstood my character (took me, almost, for someone else)

11   *upon misprision growing*. The young man's *gift* was grounded in and rose from *misprision*. Perhaps Shakespeare means to suggest that the *gift* grew, became more precious, while it lodged mistakenly with the poet.
        misprision. One word for 'error' covers both the *not knowing* of line 9 and the *mistaking* of 10.

12   *on better judgement making* on (your) having second (and *better*) thoughts

13   *had* possessed

14   *In sleep a king, but waking no such matter* (a dream of wealth and power which, on waking, proves insubstantial, nothing of the kind, a fraud)

Sonnet 88

In many ways a recapitulation of Sonnet 49.

1   *set me light* value me little, hold me cheap

2   *place my merit in the eye of scorn* hold my good qualities up to ridicule. The poet modestly alludes to a proverbial illustration of insignificance: 'One might put *x* in one's eye and never see the worse'. The exhibited *merit* will be virtually indiscernible.

4   *virtuous* (two syllables)

6   *Upon thy part* on your side, in support of your case. It may be significant that the phrase can be read with *faults concealed*, subverting lines 6–7: 'I can set down a story of faults concealed by you and blamed on me'.

7   *attainted* dishonoured

8   *That* so that
        losing me. The Q spelling, 'loosing me', draws attention to an obvious quibble: 'setting me free' accompanies 'ceasing to possess me'. The irony of this imagined liberation is pointed by the implicit 'make me lost' ('ruin me, bring me to destruction', common in Elizabethan English and still current in 'lost at sea'); by freeing the poet, the youth would destroy him. Moreover, by balancing *losing* and *win*, the

poet equates loss with defeat. This puts pressure on the young man not to 'loose' his lover; for no sane man seeks defeat.

10   *bending . . . on* turning . . . towards

12   *vantage* advantage, benefit

       double-vantage me do me a double benefit. The poet is so much a part of the young man (*to thee I so belong*, line 13) that a service done to the youth profits him; but he is, of course, distinct (as *belong* assumes), so that when both profit there is a *double-vantage*, despite that *double-vantage*'s being initially injurious to the poet.

13   *so* so absolutely

14   *for thy right.* Suggestively ambiguous: *for* means both 'for the sake of (establishing)' and 'because of'; and *thy right* is both 'your virtue, your righteousness' (which links with lines 5–8) and, alluding to the concerns of the previous few sonnets, 'your privilege (which allows you to make massive emotional demands on other people)'.

Sonnet 89

1   *Say.* 'Assert' rather than 'suppose'; in parallel with *Speak* in line 3.

       fault. The *offence* of line 2, not a 'defect'. Lines 1–2 deal with transgressions; 3–4 with flaws.

2   *comment* discourse at large upon

3   *lameness* inadequacy. See 37.3 and the note.

       I straight will halt. Dense with quibbles; beyond 'I will stop (arguing) immediately' come 'I, erect and sound of limb, will become crippled', 'I, moving *straight*, will meander forthwith', and 'I will immediately start to limp'.

4   *reasons* arguments

5   *disgrace* (1) dishonour; (2) dismiss from favour. Perhaps also 'deprive of beauty' (actually, by making *me* upset and ugly, or in repute, by talking about *my lameness*).

5   *ill* to my discredit (but a sorrowing 'wrongfully' also registers)

6   *To set* (1) in order to set; (2) in setting

       set a form upon give shape and order (and so make attractive. But the hint of hypocrisy, of cosmetic covering, in *upon* is reinforced by *form*, which suggests the 'appearance' and 'show' of order rather than its true substance.)

       desirèd (by you)

7   *knowing thy will* being aware of what you want. Some editors begin a new sentence here.

8   *acquaintance* my acquaintance with you, our familiarity

       strangle violently stifle

       look strange behave like a stranger, eye you coldly. Compare 49.5–6.

9   *Be absent from thy walks* avoid the places where you go for walks. Perhaps the formal *walks* (the paths and avenues) of a garden owned by the young man.

        in my tongue on my lips, in my uttering ('the news I bring | Is heavy in my tongue' says Marcade at *Love's Labour's Lost* V.2.714–15). Presumably also 'in my peculiar poetic language, in my idiom'.

9, 11   *tongue . . . wrong.* Rhyming like *tongue . . . song* at 17.10 and 12.

11   *profane* (1) unworthy; (2) blasphemous. What the poet is, and what he might be when using the young man's name. If the *walks* of line 9 are formal ways in the friend's garden, Latin *profanus* (in the sense 'not entitled to enter a sacred place') might also contribute.

12   *haply* (1) by chance; (2) perhaps

13, 14 *For . . . For* on behalf of . . . because

13   *myself.* One of those points at which Q's unmodernized 'my selfe' seems helpfully to posit an instructable self.

        debate argument, conflict, struggle (not always, as now, verbal)

Sonnet 90

1   *Then* Therefore. The argument flows on from Sonnet 89. *When* and the double *now,* | *Now* point to a quibble on the temporal sense of *Then*.

1, 9   *wilt.* Desire is dominant, not futurity.

2   *Now . . . cross.* Carrying line 1 to a conclusion, 2 simultaneously initiates 3–4.

        bent resolved

        cross thwart

3   *spite of Fortune.* See 37.3, and compare it with 89.3.

4   *drop in for an after-loss* fall upon me, crushingly, as a belated loss. For *drop in* as 'fall upon' see *Antony and Cleopatra* II.13.158–62:

> Ah, dear, if I be so,
> From my cold heart let heaven engender hail,
> And poison it in the source, and the first stone
> Drop in my neck: as it determines, so
> Dissolve my life!

        The received interpretation of *drop in*, 'call in casually', relies on a usage not currrent until a century later, and is bathetic.

5   *this sorrow* (the world's present enmity)

6   *in the rearward* behind, in the rearguard (of that metaphorical army, *woe*)

7   *Give not a windy night a rainy morrow.* Because, as the proverb says, 'A blustering night [presages] a fair day.'

8   *linger out* prolong (by postponing the final *overthrow*)
        purposed (by the friend, Fortune, or both)
9, 11   *last . . . taste*. On the short 'a' in *taste* see the note to 30.2, 4.
10   *petty griefs*. The 'sorrows' (or 'grievous acts' which cause them) seem
        slight compared with the friend's leaving the poet. (There is, of
        course, no suggestion that *griefs* are inherently *petty*.)
11   *in the onset* at the outset, in the first wave of an attack (by the army of
        woe)
13   *strains* (1) kinds, varieties; (2) stresses

Sonnet 91

1   *glory in*. The suggestion of boastful pride is deliberate (compare the
        play in *all men's pride I boast*, line 12).
        skill cleverness, craft, art
2   *body's*. A good case could be made for a plural possessive on the basis
        of Q's 'bodies'.
3   *new-fangled ill* nastily fashionable, badly executed bits of trendiness.
        The ambiguity, essentially uninteresting, derives from *new-fangled*'s
        double work as adjective and participle.
4   *horse*. Probably plural, as sometimes in Shakespeare (compare the
        'team of horse' at *The Two Gentlemen of Verona* III.1.264), and thus
        answering *hawks and hounds*.
5   *humour* temperament, kind of character (alluding, ultimately, to the
        four Hippocratic humours, phlegm, blood, choler, and the *melan-
        choly* of 45.8: see the note)
        his its
        adjunct corresponding, associated
6   *finds* (1) discovers; (2) concludes that there is. Though distinctly
        secondary, the latter gives the poet's *But* in line 7 considerable bite.
        above the rest. Probably 'greater than in any other *pleasure*', perhaps
        'more than other men do (in that *pleasure*)', conceivably 'more than
        other men do (in any other *pleasure*)' – or all three senses mixed.
7   *particulars* (1) things listed (in lines 1–4); (2) single things, distinct
        sources of *pleasure*
        my measure (1) the things to judge me by; (2) enough for me,
        sufficient to satisfy me; (3) the things I use to judge happiness. This
        last persists most strongly in line 8.
8   *better* outdo, encompass, and exceed
        one general best. The idea of inclusion, expressed strongly in Sonnet
        53 and restated vehemently in Sonnets 98–9, here lends *of* in line 12
        a particular possessive weight, essential to the resolution of the
        poem.

10   *prouder* more splendid
        cost showy extravagance

10, 12 *cost . . . boast*. The rhyme depends on a variant pronunciation of *boast*,
        using short 'o', resembling the vowel in modern 'wart', 'ward'. (The
        final effect would thus approximate 'corst . . . borst'.)

12   *all men's pride* all the splendid things men possess. But *pride* is
        ambiguous here – like *glory* in line 1, and playfully unlike *prouder* in
        line 10 – so that 'all that men take pride in' easily slips into the
        suggestion in *boast* that the poet brags with 'the arrogance of all
        mankind lumped together'. This rash pride, or the self-conscious
        trace of it, sets the poet up for undercutting in the couplet.

13, 14 *Wretched . . . wretched* in an unhappy position (and unhappy about it)
        . . . unhappy

Sonnet 92

1   *But*. The argument flows on from Sonnet 91.
        do thy worst to steal. Inverting the idiom 'do your best (plus infinitive)'
        to recall a stock cry of defiance (employed at 19.13): *do thy worst!*
        steal thyself away rob me of you. But *steal* also registers as 'creep,
        move stealthily', a quibble already deployed to effect at 63.8 and
        77.7–8.

2   *For term of life* (a legal formula) for the duration of life. Lines 3–4
        suggest that the *life* is the poet's, and 6 confirms it.
        assurèd mine (1) pledged to me; (2) certainly mine. 'Assured' was
        often used to mean 'betrothed'; compare *King John* II.1.533–5,
        where Lewis and Blanche are contracted:

KING PHILIP
    It likes us well. Young princes, close your hands.

AUSTRIA
    And your lips too – for I am well assured
    That I did so when I was first assured.

3   *stay* remain
4   *depends upon* relies on and is sustained by
5   *the worst of wrongs* (your loss, the *worst* mentioned in line 1)
6   *the least of them* (the slightest sign of coolness or infidelity)
7   *state* (of affair. But *belongs* allows and probably solicits the more
        psychological interpretation, 'manner of being'.)
8   *humour*. 'Mood' and 'whim' as well as the 'temperament' and
        'character' (see 91.5 and the note) which underlie them.
9–10   *Thou canst . . . lie* you can't distress me with your inconstancy just
        because (indeed, precisely because) my life hangs on your change of

allegiance. The ambiguity of *Since that* is crucial, for it shows strength growing from submission.

11   *happy.* 'Fortunate' as well as 'joyful'.
title legal right of ownership
find discover

12   *Happy . . . happy.* As much opposed as equivalent; absolute joy, and an escape from despair.

13   *But what's . . . blot.* This seems to refer to the *title*, the poet's situation in life and love, until, in line 14, the *blot* sticks to the young man.

14   *Thou mayst . . . not.* Though the line's primary reference involves fear for the future ('you may one day be false, and I nevertheless not know it'), *mayst* allows a darker and more immediate threat, which *yet* supports ('you may be being false and I as yet not know of it'). As these anxieties bite, a quibble on the second clause (picked out in Q by the comma after *false*) shows the poet, perhaps, rallying with brave reassurance: 'you may be false in the future, and may even be being false, and yet, oh, I don't know, I don't suppose you really would be.'

Sonnet 93

1   *So* (1) therefore (having weighed up the implications of 92.13–14); (2) in the following fashion
supposing. Not 'if we can assume for the moment that' but 'imagining that' touched (by virtue of 92.13–14) with 'persuading myself that'.

2   *so* with the result that
love's face. The 'appearance of love' is identified with the young man's *face*; in lines 3–4 the *face* becomes less *love's* and more the beloved's.

3   *May* (1) can; (2) might perhaps
seem love to me appear to me to be love towards me. *To me* acts twice.
though altered (referring to *love's face*)
new (1) recently; (2) into a new appearance

4   *looks* (1) features, countenance (referring back to the *face* of line 2); (2) glances (preparing *thine eye* in line 5)
heart affection

5   *For* because, since

5, 7   *eye . . . history.* A full rhyme, resembling 7.2 and 4 and, hence, 1.2 and 4.

7   *many's looks* the features of many people

8   *moods* visible marks of feeling (with a strong negative implication: 'signs of treachery, petulance, angry melancholy')
wrinkles strange. Not the lines etched by Time but 'bizarre markings' drawn by habitual scowls, sneers, faked smiles; or, if these *wrinkles*

are the immediate effect of such grimaces, 'unfamiliar' and 'coldly
distant, estranged expressions' (see 49.5–6, and the situation envis-
aged there).

9   *heaven* (one syllable)

11   *heart's workings* movements of feeling, desires. Compare the 'work-
       ing of the heart' at *Love's Labour's Lost* IV.1.33.

13–14 *How like . . . show.* Compare Genesis 3.6 (on the beauty of the fatal
       tree) and, more immediately, the proverb, also used at *The Merchant
       of Venice* I.3.98–9, 'An apple may be fair without and bad within'.

13   *grow* become. And if *beauty* can *grow*, it has indeed 'become' like an
       apple.

14   *virtue.* Both 'nature and quality' and 'moral goodness'.
       answer not thy show doesn't correspond to your appearance

Sonnet 94

This elusive poem is perhaps the most discussed in the collection. Its ironies
are almost inordinate, an ebb and flow between approval and disapproval
ambiguating the text, whose iterative patterns – *moving* and *Unmovèd, base*
and *basest, sweet* and *sweetest, flower* and *flower, weed* and *weeds* – offer a
security which, in reading, dissolves. Yet the lines are not opaquely indeter-
minate. Though it can hardly be the function of commentary to dictate
interpretation, it should be said that the general reluctance to read the poem
in context stems from an unreasonable mistrust of Q. Shakespearian
involvement in the ordering of Thorpe's quarto is argued for and assumed in
this edition, and whatever anxiety one may harbour elsewhere, the section of
the book within which 94 falls is peculiarly connective: 92 follows 91 with
But, and 93 picks up with *So;* 95 is essentially a development from the couplet
of 94, and 96 continues to worry at the *faults* discussed in all these poems. If it
is read in this light, 94 looks like an intense meditation on the issues raised in
92 and confronted in 93. For the first and almost the last time in the
sequence, Shakespeare writes impersonally, neither addressing the friend
nor describing him explicitly as *he,* and scrupulously avoiding *I* and *me* and
my. 'What can be said in favour of such inscrutability?' the poet seems to ask,
recalling the conclusion of 93, 'taking it at its best, yet not flinching from the
unpalatable implications which may follow.' But the poet's feelings about the
friend, obliquely registered in the octave, are more keenly felt in the sestet,
where the poem turns towards motifs strongly associated with *thou* and *you* in
earlier poems (husbandry, the ownership of great estates, the *flower*). Finally,
as in 92 and 93, the couplet is pithily critical of the kind of corruption which is
concealed – only here, the issue having been brought into the open by the
sonnet itself, there is an image of visible and stinking vileness.

It follows that a larger sequential context contributes to our experience of the sonnet. The *flower* of lines 9 and 11, for example, is the image of frail beauty offered in Sonnets 1–19 as an instance of loveliness made vulnerable by barrenness (hence the transition from the *stone* in lines 3–4, a development which would otherwise seem incomprehensible); but this *flower* has been modified by texts like 54 (where the friend of 94 and 95.1–4 is a *flower* essentially preservable and worth preserving), and it will be so again in poems like 124 (where the collocation with *weeds* recurs). Hence a secondary complication. The sonnet resonates with issues still unsettled in the sequence at large, and is fraught with ironies and uncertainties not strictly part of itself, though inseparable from it.

1 *They that have power to hurt and will do none.* Alluding to the commonplace '*posse et nolle, nobile*'. Compare Sidney's *Arcadia* II.15, 'the more power he hath to hurt, the more admirable is his praise, that he will not hurt', or Jonson's *The Case is Altered* I.7.71–3 (where the source is pseudo-Ausonius), 'The property of the wretch is, he would hurt and cannot, of the man, he can hurt and will not'. The sonnet starts coolly with a common saw, and ends in the savage chill of another.

 will (expressing desire as well as futurity)

2 *That do not do the thing they most do show* who do not do what their appearance suggests they will do. Line 1 makes this seem laudatory – 'who look dangerous but (because of their self-control) behave well' – without quite suppressing the suggestion of unreliability – 'who do not act in the way one is led to expect they will' – or, indeed, the imputation of hypocrisy: 'who do one thing while seeming to do another'.

3–4 *Who, moving . . . cold.* Such people, *moving others* emotionally while remaining detached, are as *cold* as the proverbial *stone* – a frequent image, in Shakespeare, of unrelenting indifference. There may also be a glance at *stone* as 'lodestone', since the *Unmovèd* attract *others* through what we now call 'magnetism'.

4 *and to temptation slow.* If line 2 subverts the praise tendered by *They that have power to hurt and will do none*, this points to an irrefutable if negative virtue enshrined in the *cold* natures of line 3.

5 *They rightly do inherit.* Taking *inherit* in the now familiar sense 'receive through inheritance', *rightly* means 'by right'; allowing it the Elizabethan or Jacobean implication 'enjoy, have the use of', *rightly* can also mean 'in the proper way, wisely'.

 heaven's graces (1) charms which are absolutely heavenly, divine attractiveness; (2) favour from heaven, God's gifts

6 *husband nature's riches from expense* protect the riches of nature (here, primarily, beauty and charm) from wasteful expenditure by means of prudent management

7 *They are the lords and owners of their faces.* Lines 1–4 encourage the

interpretation 'they have complete control over their features (because *Unmovèd* and *cold*)'; but lines 5–6, and more especially 8, describe a thoroughgoing self-possession which makes the *faces* seem a synecdoche for the *lords and owners* who bear them.

8   *but stewards* only custodians, just managers

their excellence. Suggestively ambiguous: the *lords and owners* of line 7 possess the *excellence*, and 8 describes the way hordes of *Others* tend the *cold* and fortunate few (compare 53.1–2); at the same time, *Others* is the antecedent of *their*, and the poet is contrasting the *lords and owners'* secure possession of *heaven's graces* and *nature's riches* (that mode of ownership which is as intimate as self-possession) with the tenuous tenancy of *excellence* which the *Others*, mere *stewards*, hold. The former may be enriched and underwritten by *excellence* as an honorary title (the *stewards* tend upon their master, his Excellence).

9–10 *The summer's . . . die* a flower that blooms in summer gives out its sweetness to that season (and those who inhabit it, which and who accordingly enjoy its sweetness) even though it blooms and fades alone (and therefore merely *lives and dies* (*only* works twice), unfertilized by another or itself, unseeding, futureless). As in the third quatrain of Sonnet 54, the poet suggests the sterility of glamour, yet concedes here through *Though* that the *flower* is justified even if it just *lives and dies*; the bloom is under no pressing obligation either to breed, as in the first nineteen sonnets, or to be distilled, as in 54. See the headnote. For modern readers the *flower* is a sudden vivid emblem; early readers – accustomed to *flower* in the sense 'very best of, refined extraction' – would feel it grow, during line 9, from the 'excellence of the summer' which it represents. On its probable connexion with *stone*, see the headnote.

9, 13 *sweet . . . sweetest.* Like *base* and *basest* (and, to a certain extent, the sonnet's other ostensibly fixed terms), in recurring, these change. Line 9 uses *sweet* of smell and appearance; line 13 introduces taste (compare *sourest*) and temperament, and no doubt morals.

10, 12 *die . . . dignity.* A full rhyme, resembling that at 1.2 and 4.

11, 12 *base . . . basest* vile . . . humblest

11   *infection* (suggesting a stain, or what 92.13 and 95.11 call a *blot*, as well as disease. See 111.10 and the note.)

12   *outbraves his dignity* surpasses his rank. The *weed*'s social superiority is marked sartorially, for *dignity* can mean 'outward state' and *outbraves* makes good sense as 'goes more bravely than, is clad more gallantly than'. Such an interpretation is prompted by the ambiguity of *weed*, which can mean 'costume' as well as 'wild plant' (petals and foliage both clothe plants); compare 2.3–4.

13   *sweetest things turn sourest by their deeds.* That persons such as the

poem describes are *Unmovèd, cold, and to temptation slow* does not
mean that, once tempted, they are fastidious. Angelo in *Measure for
Measure* is sufficient warning of the depths to which such natures
sink once tempted (when there are *deeds* to judge them by). See the
next note.

14   *Lilies that fester smell far worse than weeds.* Supporting line 13 with an
apophthegm which, proverbial in origin – 'The fairest flowers
putrefied, stink worse than weeds', 'The lily is fair in show but foul in
smell' – also occurs in *Edward III* (published in 1596), an anonymous
history play often attributed in part to Shakespeare. The Countess of
Salisbury's father, Edward's reluctant pandar, tells his daughter that
the King's wicked advances are the worse because of his status and
authority:

> The freshest summer's day doth soonest taint
> The loathèd carrion that it seems to kiss;
> Deep are the blows made with a mighty axe;
> That sin doth ten times aggravate itself
> That is committed in a holy place;
> An evil deed done by authority
> Is sin and subornation; deck an ape
> In tissue, and the beauty of the robe
> Adds but the greater scorn unto the beast.
> A spacious field of reasons could I urge
> Between his glory, daughter, and thy shame:
> That poison shows worst in a golden cup;
> Dark night seems darker by the lightning flash;
> Lilies that fester smell far worse than weeds . . .

II.1.438–51

Within the economy of the poems, compare 69.12–14, and see the
headnote to Sonnet 67. Without, observe the congruity of Warwick's
words and Isabella's to Angelo (compare the note to line 13):

> man, proud man,
> Dressed in a little brief authority,
> Most ignorant of what he's most assured,
> His glassy essence, like an angry ape
> Plays such fantastic tricks before high heaven
> As makes the angels weep . . .

Measure for Measure II.2.117–22

But then, the Countess of Salisbury scenes connect with a great deal
in Elizabethan Shakespeare. In their entirety, they bear close read-
ing beside the middle-span sonnets. Indeed, II.1.25–193, in which
verses are composed by the King and Lodowick *praising* the Coun-

tess's qualities, elaborates doubts about *flattery* and *compare* continuous with those found central to the sequence (see the Introduction, pages 18–33). Such links strengthen the case for Shakespearian authorship advanced by Muir and, more sweepingly, Proudfoot (see the Further Reading, page 73), elaborated by Eliot Slater in a forthcoming, partly statistical, study.

'Better than beautiful thou must begin', the King tells his confidant:

> Devise for fair a fairer word than fair,
> And every ornament that thou wouldst praise,
> Fly it a pitch above the soar of praise.
> For flattery fear thou not to be convicted;
> For, were thy admiration ten times more,
> Ten times ten thousand more the worth exceeds
> Of that thou art to praise, thy praise's worth.

With these echoes or pre-echoes of, for instance, 6.8–10, 78.5–8, 83.7–8, 86.5–6, Edward commands Lodowick to 'Begin', and write. Soon, however, he finds himself perplexed by the fickleness of images:

> Write on, while I peruse her in my thoughts.
> 'Her voice to music or the nightingale' –
> To music every summer-leaping swain
> Compares his sunburnt lover when she speaks;
> And why should I speak of the nightingale?
> The nightingale sings of adulterate wrong,
> And that, compared, is too satirical;
> For sin, though sin, would not be so esteemed,
> But, rather, virtue sin, sin virtue deemed.
> 'Her hair, far softer than the silkworm's twist,
> Like to a flattering glass, doth make more fair
> The yellow amber' – *like a flattering glass*
> Comes in too soon; for, writing of her eyes,
> I'll say that like a glass they catch the sun,
> And thence the hot reflection doth rebound
> Against my breast, and burns my heart within.

In fact, when the mirroring of 'eyes' and 'sun' recurs, an edge in brilliance is granted to the mistress. Lodowick reads his poetic effort to the King, ' "More fair and chaste than is the queen of shades"–', only to be interrupted:

> That line hath two faults, gross and palpable:
> Comparest thou her to the pale queen of night,

Who, being set in dark, seems therefore light?
What is she, when the sun lifts up his head,
But like a fading taper, dim and dead?
My love shall brave the eye of heaven at noon,
And, being unmasked, outshine the golden sun . . .
Say she hath thrice more splendour than the sun,
That her perfections emulates the sun,
That she breeds sweets as plenteous as the sun,
That she doth thaw cold winter like the sun,
That she doth cheer fresh summer like the sun,
That she doth dazzle gazers like the sun;
And in this application to the sun,
Bid her be free and general as the sun,
Who smiles upon the basest weed that grows
As lovingly as on the fragrant rose.

After these echoes of, especially, 18.5–6, 130.1, line 12 of this sonnet, and 95.2 after 94.14, Edward's perplexity remains. For, once read truly, instead of being thought mere painting, likenesses prove volatile, fraught, critical – and, again, Shakespeare shows himself alert to the moral burden of comparison. '"More fair and chaste than is the queen of shades"', Lodowick repeats, '"More bold in constancy"–', and the King interrupts another time: '"In constancy"! Than who?' '"Than Judith was."' Judith, of course, decapitated Holofernes, for pressing his tyrannical suit. She was Isabella without the passivity. 'O monstrous line!', the King declares. 'Put in the next a sword, | And I shall woo her to cut off my head. | Blot, blot, good Lod' wick!'

Sonnet 95

1, 4   *sweet . . . sweets*. Appealing, like 94.9 and 13, to a range of senses which includes the moral, but consciously excluding virtue from the sweetness the youth can claim.

2   *canker* cankerworm. Compare 54.5–11, in the light of Sonnet 94, and 35.4, 70.7, and 99.13.

3   *budding name* reputation just coming into flower. The cupped petals of the *rose*, its scattered perfume, its air of grace, used metaphorically of the friend. This assumes that *fragrant* describes the *rose* as it is, making *spot* refer to blotches becoming visible but offset by the sweetness. Alternatively, *fragrant* is proleptic, or describes the kind of *rose* being dealt with; the bloom is *budding* in the sense 'closed up

tight in a bud just beginning'; and *spot* refers to the single small hole bored by the *canker* invading the bud.

6   *lascivious comments on* salacious remarks about. *Lascivious* has three syllables here.

      sport play, recreation (especially sexual)

7–8   *Cannot . . . report.* The punctuation is editorial. Q has 'Cannot dispraise, but in a kinde of praise, | Naming thy name, blesses an ill report', which obscures the antithesis of line 7 for the sake of a secondary sense. An ideal reading would encompass both syntaxes.

12   *all things . . . that eyes can see.* Shakespeare employs a phrase which usually implies 'absolutely everything' to mean 'what is visible to the eyes', so that we are made aware of what the *eyes* miss.

      turns to fair. If the subject is *beauty's veil*, this means 'makes lovely'; but if, as seems less likely, *turns* is an '-s' plural with *all things* as its subject, it means 'become beautiful'.

13   *large privilege* extensive freedom

13, 14   *privilege . . . edge.* Rhyming on *edge* as 'idge', with a secondary stress on the last syllable of *privilege*.

14   *The hardest knife ill-used doth lose his edge.* Unrecorded as a proverb, but clearly commonplace, like the final lines of 93 and 94.

      his its

Sonnet 96

1   *wantonness* (1) playfulness, exuberance; (2) lechery

2   *gentle* fit for a gentleman, honourable though spirited

      sport. See 95.6 and the note. *Gentle sport* is a generous interpretation of what line 1 calls *wantonness*.

3   *of more and less* by all social classes, by high and low people alike

4   *mak'st faults graces that to thee resort* turn the faults which repair to you into graces. See 95.9–10 and 12.

6   *basest.* Certainly 'least valuable' and 'most undistinguished'; perhaps also 'most counterfeit' and 'made of material of the very lowest grade'.

      jewel (two syllables)

      well esteemed. Both 'judged to be good' and 'thoroughly admired'.

7   *errors.* Both 'moral flaws' and the 'faulty deeds' which declare them. The latter extends *in thee* to 'in your deeds, in your being you'.

8   *truths.* 'Virtues' and 'good deeds'.

      translated transformed. The usual word for metamorphosis, as, famously, at *A Midsummer Night's Dream* III.1.112–13, 'Bless thee, Bottom! Bless thee! Thou art translated!' Line 4 notes the young man's ability to make his *faults graces*, and this capacity is remarked again (with an echoic *translate*) at lines 9–10; but line 6 firmly ascribes to the friend's admiring viewers the responsibility for line 8's distorting *truths translated*.

for true things deemed judged to be virtues and good deeds

9–10   *the stern wolf . . . like a lamb*. Invoking the proverbial 'wolf in a lamb's skin'. *Stern* in this context means 'grim, cruel'.

9   *betray* treacherously deceive

10   *his looks translate*. In lines 7–8, seen things are *translated*; here, by contrast, seeing things change.

11   *lead away* lead astray (morally as well as in perception)

12   *wouldst* wanted to

strength of all thy state force of all that glamour, rich array, and eminence (with its corollary, power – since the youth has some of the allure and status of a *thronèd queen*) which are at your command. The exclamation point after *state* rests on Q's '?', often the mark in the period for both exclamations and questions. Some such ambiguous sign would, of course, be ideal here.

13–14   *But do not . . . report*. The same couplet ends Sonnet 36, arguably with better decorum. Corruption of some kind cannot be ruled out – though if the printer was short of a couplet he showed considerable ingenuity in returning to a poem so close to 96 in its concerns, so far back (and one might rather expect him, as after 126, to signal the 'missing' text with brackets). Equally, Shakespearian indolence or uncertainty is not impossible; quartos based directly on authorial manuscript often show loose ends and patches of incompleteness which are not dissimilar. If, however, one takes the couplet as consciously deployed, it is immediately striking that 36 and 96 end the first and last groups of sonnets critical of the youth (35–6, 92–6). The common couplet makes the two groups rhyme, as it were, pointing up their relationship with a duplication entirely consistent with the intricate, echoing, repetitive mode of these late sonnets, reconsidering early concerns.

Sonnet 97

1   *absence*. Probably physical separation, though some editors prefer to read the word in the light of Sonnets 92–6, emphasizing emotional estrangement. Certainly, *freezings* and *dark days* in line 3 suggest chilling, depressed days without love.

2   *thee, the pleasure of the fleeting year*. Probably 'you, the sum of what is delightful in the swiftly-passing year'; but perhaps 'you, who delight the year as it swiftly passes'. The two interpretations are not quite incompatible.

2, 4   *year ... everywhere.* Probably rhymed nearer modern '-ere' than
'-ear' (with a vowel like 'ar' in standard 'scare', 'scarce'), but possibly
'yeer ... everywheer'.

2, 3, 4   In Q each line ends with an exclamatory '?' (see the notes to 96.12).
Most editors follow Q's plethora of pointing, but within our own
conventions this makes the quatrain read too effusively; given the
modernized spelling and the principle of modernized punctuation,
the marks should be tempered.

4   *old December's bareness. December* comes late, when the year is *old*, and
it is cold, dispirited, and full of things nearly dead. *Old* also suggests
familiarity; as an *old* acquaintance *December's* ways are only too
well-known.

everywhere. 'Plentiful' (a sense now restricted to Midlands dialect) as
well as 'all over the place'.

5   *time removed* period of separation (compare 25.14, 44.6, and 116.4.
Perhaps also 'time now past (when we were apart)'.)

summer's time. Not, quibblingly, 'summer-time' but the 'time when
summer laboured to bear offspring' (that is, early autumn); compare
The Winter's Tale II.2.25, where Emilia says that Hermione is
'something before her time delivered'.

6   *teeming.* 'Pouring out (as from a cornucopia)', informed by 'full of
life, fecund'.

increase. See 1.1 and the note.

7   *Bearing.* Like *teeming*, a word which suggests delivery as well as store.
wanton (1) sportive (as young animals are in early autumn); (2)
luxuriating in an overplus of growth and gathering fruition; (3)
amorously indulgent (looking forward to *prime* and thus back to the
season which first bred autumn's *rich increase*)

prime spring

8   *Like widowed wombs after their lords' decease.* The *autumn* is spring's
widow, the *rich increase* of the fall spring's posthumous child.

9–10   *Yet this ... fruit.* Complicated by the sonnet's time scheme, and its
incipient worship of the friend as nature's epitome (see the Intro-
duction, pages 30–33, and, more immediately, Sonnets 98 and 99).
Looking back to the period of separation, which was *summer's time*,
the poet says that in its emotional winter he had anticipated a harvest
orphaned (the word *orphans* is used loosely, unless *autumn* is meant
to die in childbirth) by the young man's absence. His being away, the
rich increase or *abundant issue*, alike unborn (*issue* is implicitly prolep-
tic), offered no more *hope* than that, being born, they would be
fatherless (since the friend is, by implication, lord of the year).

11   *his* its

wait on thee. 'Serve you, look after you', but also 'rely on you' and so
'are at your disposal'. Compare 53.2.

12   *thou away* when you are absent
13   *with so dull a cheer* so gloomily, with so downcast a mien and manner
14   *leaves look pale* (losing their summer green)

Sonnet 98

The poet recalls another period of separation which was also wintry, though not coinciding with winter.

2   *proud-pied* gorgeously variegated. The hyphen is editorial, and Q's 'proud pide' could be said to impute jaunty arrogance to *April*.
      his. Not, as often, 'its', because *April* is personified (compare *him*, line 4).
      trim elaborate clothing, finery (flowers like jewels, leafy branches like ribboned sleeves, and so on)
3   *spirit* (one syllable)
4   *That* so that
      heavy Saturn. Like the planet bearing his name, this god was associated with a dignified but ponderous melancholy. *Heavy* suggests the sombre gravity of the saturnine temper, but playfully preserves its physical sense 'weighty'. Hence *laughed and leaped*, the former adverting to *heavy* as a mood, the latter concerned with something 'weighty' become nimble.
5   *Yet nor . . . nor* even so, neither . . . nor
      lays songs
6   *different flowers in* flowers differing in. The metre requires 'diff'rent flow'rs'.
7   *summer's story tell*. Usually interpreted as 'speak (or write) cheerfully', in opposition to the stock 'winter's tale'. 'A sad tale's best for winter', says Mamillius at *The Winter's Tale* II.1.25. *Cymbeline* III.4.11–14 also seems relevant:

> Why tender'st thou that paper to me with
> A look untender? If't be summer news,
> Smile to't before; if winterly, thou need'st
> But keep that count'nance still.

8   *proud* showy
      lap (of earth. Compare *Richard II* V.2.47: 'the green lap of the new-come spring'.)
9   *the lily's white*. Q's 'Lillies' could be plural (yielding 'the white lilies'), a plural possessive, or the singular (but general) possessive adopted here in parallel with *the rose* of line 10. 'White as a lily' was proverbial.
10–11   *rose . . . but sweet*. Like 54.3–4, alluding to the proverbial comparison 'As sweet as a rose'.

11–14   *They were ... play*. As in Sonnet 53, the poet praises the friend by making him a natural epitome, a *pattern* of excellences scattered in little throughout creation. See the Introduction, pages 31–2.

11   *They ... delight* they (the *lily* and the *rose*) were only *sweet* (attractively pretty and nicely perfumed), only pleasing configurations (of the complete *delight* which is *you*). The poet is not dismissing *sweet* things or *figures of delight*, only remarking his friend's superiority. What Shakespeare meant by *figures* can still be felt in our word 'prefigures', except that an absolute (rather than a temporal) priority is assumed.

12   *after* in the likeness of. See 53.6 and the note.

13   *you away*. See 97.12 and the note.

14   *shadow* image. See 53.2 and the note to lines 11–14 above.

    these (the flowers of lines 9–12, unless those editors who end the poem with a colon are correct in thinking that the *violet*, *lily*, *marjoram*, and *roses* of Sonnet 99 are directly invoked.)

    play. This most Shakespearian of words aptly mediates between joyful fun and the futility of pretence. The poet could not join *April* and *Saturn* in their full-blooded jollity, but played by finding pleasure in the mockery of entertaining *shadows*.

Sonnet 99

Among the 154 sonnets in Q, only two are genuinely aberrant in form (since 126 is designedly different, acting as a coda). One is 145, with its fourteen octosyllabic lines, probably early work. The other is 99, with its stray iambic pentameter. It is true that contemporary sequences include fifteen-line sonnets – Barnabe Barnes's *Parthenophil and Parthenophe* (1593), for instance, or Bartholomew Griffin's *Fidessa* (1596) – but, in a collection as formally consistent as Shakespeare's, the irregularity of 99 is startling. The poem is often judged to be a draft, and, while that suggests a stage of composition which it has clearly passed beyond, it is easy to accept that the text has not been finally brought to resolution. In what way, however, might Shakespeare find Sonnet 99 troublesome, not quite in his grasp, not completely assimilable to the sequence? There is a further, related issue: the poem is in a second, equally important sense not quite 'his'. Though numerous sonnets in Q glancingly echo works by Shakespeare's contemporaries, none relies directly on a source – except 99, which works up 'Sonetto decisette' of Constable's *Diana* (1592, reprinted in 1594 as Sonnet 9 in the first decad):

My lady's presence makes the roses red,
Because to see her lips they blush for shame.
The lily's leaves, for envy, pale became,
And her white hands in them this envy bred.

The marigold the leaves abroad doth spread,
Because the sun's and her power is the same.
The violet of purple colour came,
Dyed in the blood she made my heart to shed.
In brief, all flowers from her their virtue take;
From her sweet breath their sweet smells do proceed;
The living heat which her eyebeams doth make
Warmeth the ground and quickeneth the seed.
   The rain, wherewith she watereth the flowers,
   Falls from mine eyes, which she dissolves in showers.

For an attempt to solve the problems raised by this sonnet, see the Introduction, pages 32–3.

1   *forward* (1) precocious, early-flowering; (2) presumptuous
        violet (three syllables)

2–5   *Sweet thief... dyed.* Compare the closing stanzas of *Venus and Adonis*, particularly lines 1165–70:

> By this, the boy that by her side lay killed
> Was melted like a vapour from her sight,
> And in his blood that on the ground lay spilled
> A purple flow'r sprung up, check'red with white,
>   Resembling well his pale cheeks, and the blood
>   Which in round drops upon their whiteness stood.

Here, as in the sonnet, Shakespeare is assisted by the vagueness of *purple*, a word which, in Elizabethan and Jacobean English, covers everything from the crimson of fresh blood to the violet of the *violet*.

2, 15   *sweet* sweetness of odour (in an *ad hoc* absolute formulation, prompted by the chiasmic contrast *Sweet thief... steal thy sweet*, and echoed from line 2 in 15)

3   *pride* splendour

4   *for complexion* (1) as colouring (with a hint of cosmetic deceit); (2) as a complexion (of flesh and blood. Something not usually associated with flowers, and therefore liable to invite, as possessing stolen goods invites, an accusation of theft.)

5   *my love's veins* (the friend's *veins*, and not, as in lines 7–8 of Constable's sonnet, the poet's)
        grossly (1) heavily, thickly; (2) flagrantly. But the latter becomes dominant and less restrained ('shamelessly, brutally') as *dyed* obliquely suggests 'dying' by violence – a confusion easily exploited in Q, with its fluid spelling conventions. On the idea of a young man's death feeding flowers with lifeblood, see the passage from *Venus and Adonis* quoted in the note to lines 2–5 above.

6 *for* for stealing the whiteness and smooth texture of

7 *And buds of marjoram had stol'n thy hair* and *I condemnèd* the herb sweet marjoram for stealing your hair. The accusation is designed to praise the young man's *hair* for its fairness, thickness of growth, and odour. As John Gerard notes in his *Herbal* (1597):

> Sweet Marjoram is a low and shrubby plant, of a whitish colour and marvellous sweet smell, a foot or somewhat more high. The stalks are slender, and parted into divers branches, about which grow forth little leaves soft and hoary; the flowers grow at the top in scaly or chaffy spiked ears, of a white colour like unto those of candy organy. The root is compact of many small threads. The whole plant and every part thereof is of a most pleasant taste, and aromatical smell, and perisheth at the first approach of winter.

8 *on thorns did stand.* Both 'grew on thorny stems' and 'were in a state of anxiety'. The latter was proverbial; compare 'O, the thorns we stand upon' at *The Winter's Tale* IV.4.582.

9 *One blushing shame, another white despair.* With a flicker of not particularly interesting wordplay (or clumsiness) based on syntax. At first *One blushing shame* seems a participial modifier of *stand* (the red rose flushes with *shame*), but *another white despair* modifies this (since one cannot strictly blush *white*) and the line is resolved into a pair of emblems, the red rose Shame personified and the white Despair.

10 *A third, nor red nor white, had stol'n of both.* The *third* rose is evidently damasked; see 54.8 and the note, and 130.5-6.

 nor . . . nor neither . . . nor

11 *to his robb'ry had annexed thy breath* had added (appropriated, included) your breath in his theft

12 *But for* however, on account of (and in punishment for)

 in pride of in the glory of

13 *canker* cankerworm

 eat ate. The usual form of the past tense, arguably a candidate for decisive modernization; but neither *eat* nor 'ate' makes much difference to Q's slack line.

14 *But* except

Sonnet 100

In the next four sonnets the poet elegantly blames, and excuses, himself for neglecting the friend in verse.

3 *Spend'st thou* do you expend, are you using up

 fury. A creative *furor poeticus* rather than destructive anger. The *Muse* is inspiring texts, not raging at their mediocrity.

4   *Darkening* (two syllables) (1) sullying; (2) burning up (like a candle which loses itself to give *light*: compare 1.6)
to lend in order to give
base (1) lowly; (2) dark (see the notes to 33.5)

5   *straight* immediately

5–6   *redeem ... time.* Compare *1 Henry IV* I.2.215 (Hal's 'Redeeming time when men think least I will') and the common source, Ephesians 5.15–16: 'Take heed therefore how ye walk circumspectly: not as unwise, but as wise, Redeeming the time, because the days are evil.'

6   *gentle numbers* noble (not *base*) verse
idly foolishly, profligately (not necessarily 'lazily')

8   *argument* subject-matter, material

9   *resty.* A *resty* animal is out of handling, stubborn and unresponsive, perhaps lazy, perhaps nervously energetic.
survey regard, look at. But if the third quatrain is felt to divide after line 10 rather than 9, *survey*, | *If* is read through and 'scrutinize to see whether' results.

10   *If Time have any wrinkle graven there.* It is impossible to couple the line firmly to either 9 or 11–12; its syntactical status remains ambiguous.
have (subjunctive)

11   *satire to* satirist of. Drawing on the renaissance association between satire as a genre and the classical satyr (half man, half goat) which allegedly indulged in poetic savagery in the satiric vein. Q alerts readers to this by giving *satire* italics and a capital *S*; indeed, if these marks are taken to indicate a borrowing from Latin or Greek, the modernized text should prefer 'satyr' to *satire*. At *Hamlet* I.2.140, significantly, the second Quarto (printed from authorial manuscript and therefore likely to reflect Shakespearian spelling) reads 'Hyperion to a satire', invariably modernized to 'satyr'.

12   *spoils* deeds of destruction, acts of spoliation. Despite certain editors, the booty itself is clearly not to be *despisèd*.

14   *So thou prevene'st* thus you forestall, in that way you thwart. Though editors have, since 1711, preferred 'prevent'st', Q's 'preuenst' represents (as Stanley Wells has shown) a distinct verb common in the sixteenth and seventeenth centuries.
scythe and crookèd knife. Perhaps a conscious tautology – a hendiadys or 'saying the same thing in other words'. More likely an elaboration of the image designed to avoid the potential flatness, or bluntness, of *scythe* as an attribute for *Time*. The repetition is supported by earlier poems: by the *Crookèd eclipses* of 60.7, for instance, which bring old age; and by *confounding Age's cruel knife* at 63.10.

Sonnet 101

1   *what shall be thy amends* what reparation will you make, what excuse will you offer

2   *truth in beauty dyed* moral integrity (both honesty and faith) imbued with beauty. See line 6.

3   *Both truth and beauty on my love depends.* Compare 14.11 and 14.

    depends. A third-person plural; the '-s' ending was not particularly unusual.

4   *therein dignified* through that dependence you, *Muse*, are given dignity (indeed, 'given that office which you hold')

5   *haply* perhaps

6   *Truth needs no colour.* Proverbial; *colour* includes 'excusing' and 'disguise' ('Why hunt I then for colour or excuses', 'Under what colour he commits this ill', *The Rape of Lucrece* 267 and 476) and 'deceiving rhetoric' (the metaphor was commonplace). Quibblingly, Shakespeare exploits a secondary, literal notion: *colour* as pigment, used for make up and portraiture.

    with his colour fixed (1) in addition to his ingrained (and therefore natural) colouring; (2) since his colour is secure. *Twelfth Night* I.5.227 – where Olivia assures Viola that her face's beauty is 'in grain' – is often compared, but the whole comic sequence (211–43) clarifies the poem. In unveiling herself to Viola, to 'draw the curtain and show you the picture' (portraits often were so covered), Olivia echoes the sonnet's play between the face and painting (*fixed* suggests a 'fixative agent' used to stiffen *colour*); and, in stressing her neglect of cosmetics ('*'Tis in grain*'), she follows the poet in his declared dislike of making up. Moreover, Olivia's prosaic cataloguing of her beauties, with its scornful question 'Were you sent hither to praise me?', alerts us to the sonnet's links with earlier texts on the rival poet(s), and its involvement with the problem of praise (see the Introduction, pages 18–26).

7   *Beauty no pencil, beauty's truth to lay* Beauty needs no fine-tipped brush (the kind used by artists and by women touching up their features with paint) to apply (or 'sketch out') true beauty (or 'that truth which is the proper adjunct of beauty'). The assumption is that *beauty's truth* already lies in the young man's complexion.

8   *best is best.* Despite much recent work in proverbs, this has not been recorded as a saw, though 'Better is better' and 'The best may amend' have been. Presumably Shakespeare is playing on those, and bettering 'Better is better', while echoing – in the light of *Truth* and *truth* in lines 6–7 (with their slight and implicitly quibbling semantic shift) – the apophthegm 'Truth is truth'.

    intermixed alloyed, adulterated

9, 11   *dumb . . . tomb.* For the rhyme see the note to 83.10, 12.

10   *lies in thee* is in your power

11   *gilded tomb.* Compare 55.1 and see the note to 20.6.

13   *thy office* your duty

      I teach thee how. Some editors, encouraged by the commas which enclose this in Q, treat it as a parenthesis; line 14 then becomes a definition of the Muse's *office* rather than a lesson to the Muse contained in a claim of the poet's. Either way, the distinction between *I* and the *Muse* puts the self in the right (as against its gifts), preparing for the defence offered in Sonnet 102.

14   *seem . . . shows.* Having stressed throughout the sonnet the young man's *truth and beauty*, the poet feels able to venture verbs which suggest deceit and *colour*. They echo in the opening two lines of the next sonnet.

Sonnet 102

1   *love* affection

      in seeming in appearance, apparently

2   *less the show appear* (1) *the show* may seem to be less; (2) *the show* is less in evidence. 'Outward manifestation, appearance' is the primary sense of *show*; but there is a hint of 'ostentatious display, mere *seeming*' which helps excuse the poet's reticence.

2, 4   *appear . . . everywhere.* A full rhyme, like 84.10 and 12.

3–4   *That love . . . everywhere.* See 21.14 and the note.

3   *merchandised* treated like merchandise (because offered for sale)

      whose rich esteeming the rich estimate of whose worth

4   *publish* make public knowledge, broadcast

5   *in the spring* (of its growth. The seasonal reference is, as yet, secondary.)

6   *greet* salute, welcome

      it (the *love* of line 5)

      lays songs. The echo of 101.7 is probably deliberate; visual artistry becomes verbal.

7   *As Philomel in summer's front doth sing* just as the nightingale sings at the start of the summer. For *front* as 'onset, beginning' see *The Winter's Tale* IV.4.2–3, where Perdita is called 'Flora | Peering [appearing] in April's front'. But a quibble on *front* as 'forehead' ('Grim-visaged war hath smoothed his wrinkled front', complains Richard III at I.1.9) seems certain; it makes *summer* a personification, and its sets *Philomel* singing on the season's brow like a jewel glittering on the forehead of a beautiful woman.

8   *stops his pipe* ceases singing. In so far as the metaphor is alive,

Philomel resembles a shepherd(ess) playing pan-pipes in a pastoral landscape. Many editors emend Q's 'his' to 'her', noting *her* in lines 10 and 13, and respecting the sex of *Philomel* in legend. Their intervention may be justified. Clearly, those editors who defend Q's 'his' on the grounds that only cock nightingales sing can be mocked, and those who argue that *his* impersonally means 'its' are – on the basis of *her* elsewhere – on hardly safer ground. Nor is *his* likely to be, in the handwriting of the period, a compositorial (or scribal) misreading of a manuscript 'her'. The chances are that this is a lapse from 'her' to *his*, and authorial: that the shift to *his* shows Shakespeare briefly thinking of the bird as the poet that the bird is like. Should Shakespearian errors be corrected? In some cases, clearly; but when, as here, the apparent slip is not serious enough to trouble readers (and would probably not trouble the poet if it were pointed out to him), and where, again, the lapse supports a subcurrent in the text which Shakespeare evidently cared about (the poet being identified with the nightingale), then the Q reading must be respected.

in growth of riper days as summer wears on. *Riper* suggests both the maturity of the season and its quiet progress towards autumn's fruition.

9   *the summer* (of *Our love*. But the seasonal metaphors have become so vital and the nightingale so alluring that *the summer* is taken as much for its own sake as for *love*'s.)

10   *mournful hymns*. Perhaps an allusion to Philomela's tragic story; raped and mutilated by Tereus of Thrace, she turned into a lamenting nightingale (see Ovid's *Metamorphoses* VI.412–674).

hush the night. When *Philomel* sings, the *night* quietens, as though the owls, foxes, insects had stopped their work to listen to her *hymns*. And it is true that the song of a bird – distracting us from slighter sounds that carry on regardless – can seem to *hush the night* by filling it with music. (On a metaphoric level this suggests the nightingale hushing the night with a lullaby, like a mother or nurse.)

11   *But that*. In parallel with *Not that*; *that* is not a demonstrative adjective.

wild music hectic melody, tumultuous singing (uttered, significantly, by *wild* birds)

burdens weighs down. The verb suggests (*music* being so light) inordinate quantities of song, and (*music* being, after all, weightless) *bough*s bent by the tiny bodies of singing birds. It also anticipates line 12 by suggesting that, in late summer, bird-song has become so *common* that it encumbers and proves burdensome to trees which had, a few months before, gladly cradled the nightingale. And perhaps *burdens* registers, fleetingly, as a plural form of the noun meaning 'chorus, refrain'. This last would support the idea that, if the poet is *Philomel*, the birds that sing *wild music* after *Philomel* has shown the way and then grown silent are the rivals discussed in Sonnets 78–86.

12   *sweets ... delight.* Complementing, if not rehearsing, the proverb 'Familiarity breeds contempt.'
    sweets pleasant things
    common (implying vulgarity as well as plenitude)
    dear precious, loved

13   *sometime* from time to time

13, 14   *tongue ... song.* For the rhyme see the note to 17.10, 12.

14   *dull you* bore you. But there may be a suggestion of 'take the edge and lustre off you (by publishing your excellence so widely that the world takes you for granted)'; unlike his rivals (see the note on *burdens* in line 11), the poet will not merchandise the young man.

Sonnet 103

1   *what poverty* what poorness, what poor stuff, how poor is that which *my Muse brings forth* my inspiration delivers. The virginal *Muse* becomes a mother giving birth to bad verse.

1, 3   *forth ... worth.* For the rhyme see the note to 38.9, 11.

2   *That, having.* The ellipsis expands to 'in that, her having', or, unpacking still further, 'if you consider that, when she has (in writing about you)'.
    scope. 'Free range of subject-matter', and the 'opportunity' which this allows. A compliment to the young man; there is so much that can be said about him.
    show her pride. A wry 'display her dazzling creative powers (such as they are)' and 'display the gorgeous verses (such as they are) which she inspires'. Perhaps also 'show the world how proud she is of you' and 'show the world her pride and joy (namely, you)'.

3   *The argument all bare is of more worth* the unadorned theme is more precious. Possibly alluding to the proverb 'Truth shows best being naked.'

4   *beside* as well

5   *no more can write.* 'Can write nothing better than I do' or 'can write nothing better than the mere *argument* which is you'. In the light of Sonnets 100–102, 'can write no longer' registers, and lines 1–4 become an apology complementing 101.6–8.

7   *overgoes* (1) surpasses; (2) overwhelms
    blunt dull (not finely-honed enough to sketch your fine features),

stupid (not clever enough to describe you accurately), forthright but coarse (not verbally adroit enough to cope with your beauty)

invention (here 'creative powers')

8   *Dulling my lines* making my verse seem dull (by comparison with your lustre)

doing me disgrace putting me to shame

9–10   *striving to mend,* | *To mar* trying to improve, to spoil. Conventional wisdom; compare *King Lear* I.4.343, 'Striving to better, oft we mar what's well.'

10   *subject.* The 'subject-matter' which is you, an 'object, person, I', and your qualities.

11   *pass* end, effect

13   *sit* take its place, be enthroned

14   *shows you* (1) shows to you; (2) shows you to be. The echo of *show her pride* is doubtless deliberate; it supports the poet's suggestion that poetry, which adds to the youth's beauty by subtraction, is vain. Yet, in other ways, the poem is extraordinarily cool towards the youth, and what might have been clear praise in earlier sonnets feels – in the wake of 92–6 – tainted. By celebrating the friend's *face* and what *appears* in the *glass* (lines 6–8), and then humbly insisting that his verse deals with mere *graces* and *gifts* (clearly, more important), Shakespeare makes the contemplation of the *glass* in line 14 seem self-regarding, and what it *shows* superficial: the *glass* only *shows* what *shows*.

Sonnet 104

For an account of this sonnet, and especially its sestet, see the Introduction, pages 39–40.

2   *your eye I eyed* I saw you (reading *your eye* as either metonymy or a pun, 'your I', or as both)

3, 4,   *Three winters cold . . . three summers' pride,* | *Three beauteous springs . . .*

5, 7   *Three April perfumes . . . three hot Junes.* There are sonnets by Ronsard, Desportes, and Daniel celebrating the same period of loving devotion. Horace, *Epodes* XI.5–6, also bears comparison: '*hic tertius December, ex quo destiti* | *Inachia furere, silvis honorem decutit*' ('The third December, since I ceased to lust after Inachia, now is shaking the glory from the forests'). Such analogues must cast doubt on, or at least complicate, the arguments of those who use 104 to date the Sonnets and link them directly with Shakespeare's lived experience. See the Introduction, pages 10–12, and the headnote to Sonnet 107.

3   *winters.* Some editors add an apostrophe, paralleling *summers'* in line

4; but this makes *cold* (singular) the subject of *Have* (plural), and 'Three winters' cold . . . three summers' pride' squarely symmetrical in ways which seem un-Shakespearian.

4   *shook* shaken (a standard form of the participle; 'I have shook my head and wept', *Timon of Athens* II.2.142)

    pride splendour, glorious show

5   *beauteous* (two syllables)

6   *process* the progress, the course

7   *Three April perfumes* the perfumes of three Aprils. But, inevitably, 'three Aprils as sweet as perfume'.

    burned (parched and scorched by the *three hot Junes*. Perhaps Shakespeare means to suggest incense, that sweet concoction of *perfumes . . . burned* in a censer; the *three hot Junes* are hazy with the odours they destroy.)

8   *fresh . . . green.* Roughly synonymous; 'youthful, vigorous, full of hope'.

    which yet are who is still

9   *yet.* The temporal 'still, now as before' of line 8 is gradually eclipsed, as the sestet unfolds, by 'even so, nevertheless'.

9–10   *beauty, like a dial hand . . . no pace perceived.* See the Introduction, page 40, and, for an underlying proverb, the note to 77.8.

11   *So your sweet hue.* The correspondence with *his figure* is direct, though dominant here are the *beauty* that slips away and the 'shape' and 'body' of the friend. For *hue*'s full range of meaning, see the note to 20.7.

    methinks. In line 3, *seems* had seemed impersonal, almost objective; now its risky subjectivity is exposed.

    still doth stand (1) doesn't move, shows no alteration; (2) survives intact, remains what it was. The former makes play with the idea of moving by foot in *no pace perceived*.

13   *For fear of which* to provide against which possibility (namely, that *mine eye* is being *deceived*)

13, 14   *thou . . . you.* The pronouns mark a shift in attention from the single *age* to the plural individuals who inhabit it.

13   *unbred* unborn

Sonnet 105

The poet's persona is strongly registered here, since the sonnet draws its strength from the weakness of its argument. The 'I' projected by *my verse* is read or heard defending – with such obvious sophistry that one assumes some excess is being concealed – his devotion to the youth. He tries to refute the charge of *idolatry* by demonstrating that his *love* is monotheistic – indeed, trinitarian, like orthodox Christianity – and directed at someone whose unique blend of beauty, generosity, and truth is almost miraculous; but although polytheism was, for most Elizabethan readers, ineluctably idolatrous, *idolatry* is not necessarily polytheistic, and the tone of the sestet – the manner of the poet's defence of *love* – supports a suggestion that he thinks his friend a worldly god, an *idol*. At the same time, the sonnet is not particularly complex. Almost bare of metaphor, with a chaste rhetorical 'colour' scheme, it exemplifies in verbal terms the flatness of *constancy*. On this, and the decorum of love poetry, see the Introduction, pages 18–33, and especially page 29.

2   *show* appear, be displayed

3–4   *Since all . . . so*. For some critics, these are grounds for the charge of *idolatry*, reported, or broodingly thought up; for others, they constitute the beginnings of a defence against the accusation. Both interpretations are right because the poet outlines the charge against himself so negatively (*Let not . . .* meaning 'on no account') that his determination to resist it registers very strongly. The ambiguity of line 4 adds another complication: if *still such, and ever so* refers to the poet's *songs and praises*, lines 3–4 incline more towards the prosecution than the defence; but if it refers to the *constant* young man – the *one* of line 4 who is loved – then the contrary holds. (The sestet explains, without resolving, this confusion, by insisting that the poet just inscribes what the young man is.) Line 4 echoes the *Gloria Patri* – 'Glory be to the Father, and to the Son, and to the Holy Ghost. As it was in the beginning, is now, and ever shall be: world without end' – and it may be significant that, as Stephen Booth has noted, a similar echo occurs in a text read regularly in Elizabethan churches, the 'Homily against Idolatry': '. . . images in temples and churches be indeed none other but idols, as unto the which idolatry hath been, is, and ever will be committed'.

5   *Kind*. See the notes to line 9.
6   *constant* (1) the same; (2) faithful
7   *to constancy confined* restricted in subject-matter to the theme of sameness-and-fidelity (for the *verse* is *confined* by the poet's mood, and the poet *confined* by his enthralled admiration for the *constant* young man. Since *constancy* is changeless, and *confined* completely binding, 'absolutely and eternally restricted to the theme of *constancy*' would not be over-emphatic.)
8   *leaves out difference*. The poet means 'ignores other literary subjects' and 'needs not record diversity (because you are so *constant*)'; but 'fails to mention disagreements (between us)' and 'excludes changes of mood (in you)' must also register. The poet's idolatrous self-deception is subtly exposed; you cannot *leave out* what isn't there.
9   *'Fair, kind, and true' is all my argument*. Though used to restrict, *all*

suggests much (indeed, 'everything'), and the three adjectives seem to expand in denotation until they include not only each other (see *Three themes in one* in line 12 and the note) but all virtue. *Fair* suggests beauty, justice, and kindness; *kind*, generosity, gentleness, affection, naturalness; *true*, natural integrity, spontaneous honesty, constancy, true rather than feigned beauty. Q has no inverted commas. Most editors employ them each time the trinity of virtues turn up. This text adds them only in lines 9 and 10, without complete conviction, on the grounds that, in line 13, the poet refers to the qualities themselves and not to the names by which he knows them.

10   *varying to other words* expressed in different terms (though still alluding to the same qualities. Compare 76.5 and 9–14.)

10, 12 *words . . . affords.* For the rhyme see the note to 79.9, 11.

11   *change* (of *words*)

      invention (here 'inventiveness, creative ingenuity')

      spent (1) employed; (2) used up, exhausted, squandered

12   *in one* (1) united in one theme, encompassed in a single virtue (see the note to line 9); (2) contained in a single person (the *one* of line 4). For the religious implications of (2) taken with *Three*, see the headnote.

      wondrous scope affords provides an amazing range of literary opportunities (because so vast an area of subject-matter. The *scope* of 103.2.)

13   *lived alone* lodged separately (in different people). Line 13 probably glances at the proverb 'Beauty and chastity (or honesty) seldom meet'.

13, 14 *alone . . . one.* For the rhyme see the note to 36.2, 4. There is perhaps a trace of wordplay here, *in one* providing the unity which 'all-one' (*alone*) seems to offer but actually does not.

14   *kept seat* (1) resided, *lived* (as in 'the Earl spent the weekend at his country seat'); (2) sat enthroned

Sonnet 106

On the links between the next four poems – a group often divided by those who reorder the Sonnets – see the Introduction, pages 8–9. For a variant text, which may incorporate authoritative early readings, see pages 443 and 445 below.

1   *wasted* past, used up, gone to ruin, laid waste. The drift towards violent *waste* is encouraged by *time*, which here, ostensibly ruined, is felt – on the basis of lines like 15.11 and 100.13 (and see the note to 55.5) – to be ruinous.

2   *wights* persons. Despite some editors, archaic in the 1590s and early 1600s: hence its relevance to *old rhyme*.

3–4   *And beauty . . . knights*. As in Sonnet 105, a deliberate confusion
between excellence written and written about. The poet finds *beauty*
(of style, which is the trace of Beauty) *making beautiful* some *old rhyme*
composed *in praise of* long-dead *wights*; and he finds *ladies dead and
lovely knights* themselves *making beautiful* the *old rhyme* which pre-
serves their *beauty*.

4   *In praise of* (referring to a kind of discourse as well as the motive for it)
lovely. The word could mean 'attracting love' as well as 'handsome',
and both operate here.

5   *blazon* commendatory catalogue of qualities. Derived from heraldry,
where the word means 'coat of arms' (which a *lovely knight* would
carry on his shield to declare his character and breeding). The noun
has historical links with the verb 'to blaze' ('to trumpet forth, bruit,
loudly proclaim'), and these contribute to the ring of the line.
      beauty's. The usual modernization of Q's 'beauties', but other
versions are possible, tracing interpretations available to Q's first
readers: 'Beauty's', pursuing the primary sense of lines 3–4;
'beauties'', echoing those lines' secondary implication.

6   *brow* forehead

7   *I see*. Not the 'I behold' of *I see* in line 2 but a shrewder 'I discern,
perceive'.
      their. Although the pronoun comes from nowhere, it causes no
problem. Behind the 'old writing' or 'ancient penning' of the *antique
pen* lie the poets who once wielded the quills which wrote *old rhyme*.
      antique (accented on the first syllable)
      would have sought to, wished to

8   *Even* (one syllable)
      master control, possess

9–10 *So all . . . prefiguring*. Almost certainly influenced by the first quatrain
of a Constable sonnet recorded in the Todd MS (exact date
unknown; here modernized):

> Miracle of the world! I never will deny
>   That former poets praise the beauty of their days;
>   But all those beauties were but figures of thy praise,
> And all those poets did of thee but prophesy.

Significantly, in the light of 105, this sonnet ends 'thou that goddess
art, | Which only we without idolatry adore.'
      all their praises . . . all you prefiguring. The old texts anticipate the
friend figurally, rather as the Old Testament prefigures (in its
typology) the coming of Christ. *All*, repeated, changes its signifi-
cance, since *all you prefiguring* can be read 'prefiguring all that is you
(which is a great deal)'.

9, 11   *prophecies . . . eyes.* All full rhyme, resembling 7.2 and 4 and, hence, 1.2 and 4.
11, 13   *for they . . . For we* because they . . . for even we
11   *but* only
         divining peering into the future (as though by divination)
12   *They had not skill enough.* If Q's 'still' is retained (in the sense 'as yet' or 'quite'), a word like *skill* ('ability' or just plain 'understanding') must nevertheless be understood. 'Still' can be read as an obsolete form of 'style', current in the sixteenth century (though archaic), but 'style' consorts so much less easily with *divining* than *skill* that modernization along those lines seems unattractive (which is not to say that early readers would not have sometimes resolved the crux by taking 'still' as 'style'). For two early texts reading *skill*, see pages 443 and 445 below.
14   *wonder* look with astonishment (at you)

Sonnet 107

As in Sonnet 106, the survival of poetry through time and the character of prophecies about the present preoccupy the poet. Here, however, the present events are realized so vividly that they can be read as topical allusions. As a result, the poem has played a crucial role in attempts to date the Sonnets – and rightly (see Further Reading, pages 67–8).

Shakespeare invokes public events to express and magnify the poet's situation. Some general movement of prophetic anxiety, a period of national foreboding, is followed by the proclamation of peace and the settling of doubts, and that revives the state. At the same time, in parallel, the poet's *fears* about his *love* (apparently waning, as 102 reports) turn out to be unfulfilled: his *love*, as though revived by the general relief, appears to him *fresh*, as at first. (In a secondary strand of significance – emerging, as so often, from the ambiguity of *love* – the friend, admitted in 104 to be ageing, if not in the poet's eyes, is found *fresh*, youthful, full of sap.) The immediacy of all this is emphasized by the turn into the sestet, *Now*. It follows that any dating of the poet's change of heart can be linked to the public events described in lines 5–9, as either written at the time or (less likely) retrospectively set in that context. And this means that, if the allusions are unlocked, they probably date the poem, and certainly set a *terminus a quo* for its composition.

To start with the first allusive verse, line 5: *The mortal moon hath her eclipse endured.* Setting aside the really wild guesses, five interpretations remain. (1) The *mortal moon* is the Spanish Armada, which fought the English in a crescent formation in 1588 and was defeated (taking *mortal* to mean 'deadly' and *endured* 'undergone' or 'suffered'). (2) The *moon* (which is *mortal* to the extent that it waxes, wanes, and apparently dies when eclipsed) has survived (a common sense of *endured*) its astrologically portentous *eclipse* (one such occurred without consequence in 1595). (3) Queen Elizabeth (frequently compared to Diana, the chaste *moon* goddess, though herself *mortal*) has survived her Grand Climacteric (her sixty-third year, thought to be a crucial and dangerous phase of life because numerically the product of the mystical numbers 7 and 9); this fell in 1595–6. (4) Queen Elizabeth has survived a serious illness (and it was rumoured that she was gravely ill in 1599–1600, though in fact she was not). (5) Queen Elizabeth has *endured* or 'suffered' an *eclipse* from which she, being *mortal*, cannot recover; she died in 1603.

In their edition of the Sonnets (1964, 1978), Ingram and Redpath question the validity of (1) and (5) on the basis of *endured*. 'Shakespeare never uses the word "endure" in the sense "succumb to",' they write, 'but only in one or other of the senses "undergo", "suffer", "survive", "last", and (though not relevant here) "put up with".' The difficulty is illusory. That Shakespeare does not use a word in a particular sense is irrelevant if the way in which he usually uses it allows for (1) and (5). Clearly, the Armada and Queen Elizabeth could be said to have 'undergone' or 'suffered' an *eclipse* in 1588 and 1603. It is striking, moreover, that when (5) is set against (4) or (3), which Ingram and Redpath prefer, its poetic quality is seen to be greater, its language more expressive. For, if *endured* alludes to the survival of a climacteric or illness, *mortal* acts as a flat denotative adjective, distinguishing the Diana-like Queen from the heavenly *moon*, while, if *endured* means the undergoing and suffering of a deadly *eclipse*, *mortal* works twice, to distinguish the Queen from a planet and to explain why this *moon* cannot survive the *eclipse* it suffers. As Robert Giroux notes in *The Book Known as Q* (London, 1982), Edgar's lines in *King Lear*, 'Men must endure | Their going hence even as their coming hither; | Ripeness is all' (V.2.9–11), sufficiently answer E. K. Chambers's assertion, 'it is not easy to think that to "endure" an eclipse can mean to die'.

Initially, then, all five readings seem plausible. Line 6, however, begins to favour (5), while drastically weakening (1). A paraphrase of the line would read: 'and the grave and pessimistic augurers (presumably those who judged that disaster would follow the *mortal moon*'s *eclipse*) now deride their past predictions' (though they may still be, despite the tone of what follows, *sad*, saddened, mourning perhaps, in some way). What seems to be in question is formal augury, as against the kind of foreboding discussed in line 7: almanacs and prophetic broadsheets, plentiful in the period and avidly read, are invoked. And here, as Walter B. Stone has demonstrated, 1588 can be ruled out as a likely date on even circumstantial grounds. There was no substantial literature of dread anticipating its advent; the 'prediction of Regiomontanus', which has been adduced, was discredited in 1583 and was revived and applied to the Armada only years later, when hindsight made it relevant. (Compare Bernard Capp, *Astrology and the Popular Press* (London, 1979), page 166.) What of the other dates? Although the eclipse of 1595 and the Queen's Grand Climacteric tempted *sad augurs* to prophesy, a considerable outburst of anxious astrology and prediction also preceded the Queen's death. As her health worsened and the political picture remained obscure, foreboding grew. Much was at stake. Elizabeth had announced no successor, and both Catholics and Puritans feared the accession of a ruler less sympathetic to their religious liberty than the moderate Protestant Queen had been. More than a dozen claimants maintained their right to the throne, some within the kingdom, some without (including the Infanta of Spain), and the people anticipated either invasion from abroad or civil strife of the kind which laid the country waste during the Wars of the Roses, before the Tudor settlement.

These *Incertainties* – since we are now talking about the general forebodings of line 7 – were only resolved at the coronation of James VI of Scotland, the successor that Elizabeth named on her deathbed. He came to power with an ease which was as widely welcomed as it was found surprising – the general fear of unrest simultaneously rallying people behind this 'heir' and astonishing them that the transition should be so smooth. Bacon's letters attest to this mood with particular immediacy, and Donne, looking back on the *Incertainties* in a sermon of 1617, declared – with joy and weeping, *prophetic* writing and 'that Queen' in mind:

Consider the tears of Richmond this night, and the joys of London, at this place, at this time, in the morning; and we shall find prophecy even in that saying of the poet, *Nocte pluit tota*, showers of rain all night, of weeping for our sovereign. And we would not be comforted, because she was not. And yet, *redeunt spectacula mane*, the same hearts, the same eyes, the same hands were all directed upon recognitions, and acclamations of her successor in the morning. And when every one of you in the city were running up and down like ants with their eggs bigger than themselves, every man with his bags, to seek where to hide them safely, Almighty God shed down his spirit of unity, and recollecting, and reposedness, and acquiescence upon you all. In the death of that Queen, unmatchable, inimitable in her sex; that Queen, worthy, I will not say of Nestor's years, I will not say of Methusalem's, but worthy of Adam's years, if Adam had never fallen; in her death we were all under one common flood, and depth of tears. 'But the Spirit of God moved upon the face of that depth'; and God said, 'Let there be light, and there was light, and God saw that that light was good.' God took pleasure, and found a savour of rest, in our peaceful cheerfulness, and in our joyful and confident apprehension of blessed days in his government, whom he had prepared at first, and preserved so often for us . . . It would have troubled any king but him, to have come in succession, and in comparison with such a Queen. And in them both we may observe the unsearchableness of the ways of God; of them both, we may say, *Dominus fecit*, 'It is the Lord that hath done it, and it is wonderful in our eyes'. First, that a woman and a maid should have all the wars of Christendom in her

315

contemplation, and govern and balance them all. And then, that a King, born and bred in a warlike nation, and so accustomed to the sword, as that it had been directed upon his own person, in the strength of his age, and in his infancy, in his cradle, in his mother's belly, should yet have the blessed spirit of peace so abundantly in him, as that by his counsels, and his authority, he should sheathe all the swords of Christendom again.

Certainly, in line 7 of the sonnet, *crown* and *assured* carry especial weight. *Assured* expresses a degree of contentment associated with a long-term solution, which the passing of an eclipse or Elizabeth's recovery from a climacteric or illness would surely not invite. And *crown* suggests not only the decisiveness of this conclusion – 'The end crowns all' is a proverb used four times by Shakespeare in his plays – but the crowning of a king.

The entire context is clarified by Joseph Hall's *The King's Prophecy*, a poem published in 1603 (with the subtitle 'Weeping Joy') and celebrating the smooth transfer of power to James. As F. S. Boas notes, in a letter published in *The Times Literary Supplement* (7 July 1950, page 421), Hall

describes vividly the fears of evils to come that had so beset him that

Oft did I wish the closure of my light,
Before the dawning of that fearfull day
Which should succeed *Elizaes* latest night.

But now, with the new King on the throne, all the gloomy omens are belied, and Hall cries ecstatically:

O turned times beyond all mortall feare,
Beyond all mortall hopes! Not till this day
Began the fulnesse of our bliss appeare;
Which dangers dimmed erst with fresh dismay;
Still ever checking ioy with seruile care,
Still charging vs for Tragick times prepare.
False starres and falser wizards that foresaine
By their aspects the state of earthly things:
How bene your bold predictions proved vaine,
That here brake off the race of British Kings,
Which now alone began; when first we see
Fair *Britaine* formed to a Monarchie.

Then Hall proceeds to further raptures about the blessings brought by King James to 'Earth's Second Paradise,' including peace with a promise of 'eternall comfort' in times to come.

This certainly looks like an analogue – and Shakespeare's mention of *peace* makes the *Prophecy* unignorable. When James came to the throne in 1603, England had been at war with Spain continuously since 1585, and for much of that time (including 1599–1600, when the Queen's supposed *eclipse* in sickness coincided with Essex's unhappy campaign) she was embroiled in Ireland too. James resolved to end that. Peace with Spain quickly followed his accession, conflict was suspended in Ireland, and in his public statements James laid claim, as a king, to the *olives* of *peace*. As his first address to Parliament emphasized – and it was published, circulated, and echoed in lesser pronouncements throughout the realm – 'outward peace', or peace abroad, was 'The first' of the several 'blessings' he brought the realm:

> I have ever, I praise God, yet kept peace and amity with all, which hath been so far tied to my person, as at my coming here you are witnesses I found the state embarked in a great and tedious war, and only my arrival here, and by the peace my person, is now amity kept, where war was before, which is no small blessing to a Christian commonwealth . . .

Nor is this his only claim to peace-making. Glancing at the nation's fear of civil strife, James says:

> But although outward peace be a great blessing; yet is it as far inferior to peace within, as civil wars are more cruel and unnatural than wars abroad. And therefore the second great blessing that God hath with my person sent unto you, is peace within, and that in a double form.

'Double', he explains, because he unites England and Wales with Scotland – ending that centuries-long rivalry which made the North subject to destructive Scottish incursions – and because, drawing his own blood from the union of the white and red roses, he continues the Tudor settlement. The King came, 'not with an olive branch in his hand, but with a whole forest of olives round him', Gervase Markham recalled in *Honour in Her Perfection* (1624), and his peaceful unification of three kingdoms in one – the opposite of Lear's disjection – arguably incited Octavius's prophetic and 'imperial theme', 'the three-nooked world | Shall bear the olive freely' (*Antony and Cleopatra* IV.6.6–7). Here, at all events, is the spirit of unity and *peace* recalled by Donne.

Yet, if this illuminates *peace proclaims olives* – and incidentally underlines the inappropriateness of such an allusion being made in the eighteen years up to 1603 – what of *endless age* (or what Hall calls 'eternall comfort' in times to come)? James's speech, already substantially absorbed with the theme of lasting *peace*, goes on:

> Now although these blessings before rehearsed of inward and outward peace, be great: yet seeing that in all good things, a great part of their goodness and estimation is lost, if they have not appearance of perpetuity or long continuance; so hath it pleased Almighty God to accompany my person also with that favour, having healthful and hopeful issue of my body . . . for continuance and propagation of that undoubted right which is in

my person; under whom I doubt not but it will please God to prosper and continue for many years this union, and all other blessings of inward and outward peace which I have brought with me.

Line 9 finally clinches the case for 1603. It is true that *the drops of this most balmy time* have caused confusion, and some desperation – Garrett Mattingly, for instance, in an otherwise distinguished essay dating Sonnet 107 to 1603 (*PMLA* 48 (1933), 705–21), weakly concludes that the *drops* are of rain, in the mild spring of that year – but the words are not as opaque as has sometimes been assumed. Balm is a fragrant unguent made from aromatic resins (especially those exuded by the balsam) and volatile oils. It was highly prized for its perfume, texture, and healing properties. So the *time* soothes the *world* back to health, by using *drops* of drugs (see *A Lover's Complaint* 300 and the note). The image is darkly but richly supported by line 8; somehow, *peace* oozes from its *olives* (the 'olive-branches' associated with *peace*), like sap becoming resin, as the *drops* of the *balmy time*. Inevitably, this recalls Othello's 'subduèd eyes' which, in 1603–4, 'Drop tears as fast as the Arabian trees | Their med'cinable gum' (V.2.344–7), and tear*drops* shed for Elizabeth add an undertow of salt bitterness to the cure proposed by *balmy*. Compare the corrosive property of 'drugs', cited by Brabantio against the Moor (I.2.73–5, I.3.60–61), and the paradox of Hall's 'Weeping Joy'. And hence, indeed, what would be strongest of all for Shakespeare's early readers: a connexion between *balmy time* and the *crown* of line 7. Balm was used in the coronation ceremony, and it was a familiar symbol of regal authority. Listing the adjuncts of his office, Henry V orders them thus: 'the balm, the sceptre, and the ball, | The sword, the mace, the crown imperial, | The intertissued robe of gold and pearl . . .' (IV.1.253–5). Compare Richard II's claim, 'Not all the water in the rough rude sea | Can wash the balm off from an anointed king' (III.2.54–5). Or, in words which closely shadow those of the sonnet, the dying Henry IV's rebuke of his ambitious son, after he has taken the crown from his father's sick-bed:

What, canst thou not forbear me half an hour?
Then get thee gone, and dig my grave thyself,
And bid the merry bells ring to thine ear
That thou art crownèd, not that I am dead.
Let all the tears that should bedew my hearse
Be drops of balm to sanctify thy head;
Only compound me with forgotten dust.   *2 Henry IV* IV.5.110–16

It would be natural for Shakespeare to draw on this cluster of images from the late 1590s if he were celebrating, in 1603 or a little later, the death of Elizabeth and hopeful accession of James. Correspondingly, he would be unlikely to use such images in a poem devoted to the Queen's recovery from illness or her survival of a climacteric. And 1588 has already been displaced.

One might go further, and become mildly speculative. In the light of the secondary sense of *My love looks fresh* it is remarkable that one of the first acts of the newly-crowned King was to release the Earl of Southampton – often thought the addressee of Sonnets 1–126 – from the prison in which he had languished ever since his participation in the ill-fated Essex rebellion of 1601. If Wriothesley was indeed, to some emotional extent, the *you* and *thou* and *love* of 1–126, both he and the poet's affection for him would have been refreshed and renewed by the events of 1603. And Shakespeare's sonnet would take its place alongside the verse congratulations on Southampton's release offered by Samuel Daniel and John Davies of Hereford.

On the basis of allusions, in short, 1603 seems the obvious date – with all which that implies for the dating of the sequence. Stylistic evidence supports this. As J. M. Nosworthy has demonstrated, 107 is more immediately congruent with *Antony and Cleopatra* (1606–7) than anything in the Elizabethan Shakespeare. At this point, however, the case for late dating becomes indistinguishable from arguments affecting other sonnets; see the Account of the Text, pages 429 and 430.

1–2 *prophetic soul | Of the wide world.* Imagining the soul, as often in Shakespeare, a seat of intuition and premonition ('O my prophetic soul' cries Hamlet at I.5.40). Here *soul* represents the collective consciousness of the world at large (the *world* of men and women, not of earth and its objects), fearful for the future.

2 *dreaming on* musing about, predicting (regarded scornfully. Caesar dismisses the Soothsayer as a 'dreamer' at *Julius Caesar* I.2.24, and Hotspur mocks 'the dreamer Merlin and his prophecies' at *1 Henry IV* III.1.144.)

2, 4 *come . . . doom.* Probably rhymed on a long 'o' (pronounced like the vowel in Scottish 'wart', 'ward'), but conceivably using the short 'u' (as in 'put') likely with *come . . . tomb* (see the note to 17.1, 3).

3 *yet.* Variously interpreted; probably 'now' ('as yet' is still used in a temporal sense), but possibly an intensifier like 'even' attached retrospectively to *Not . . . nor.*

lease period of tenure

true love faithful affection

control (1) challenge; (2) curb; (3) overpower. The significances merge since, in each case, the assumption is 'set a temporal limit to'.

4 *Supposed as forfeit to a confined doom* thought destined to expire after a limited period. The poet has in mind the apparent waning remarked in 102, and anticipates with *Supposed* both the sestet of this sonnet and the delight in love's growth expressed in 115. *Forfeit* means both 'subject to' and 'legally owed to'; *confined* (accented on the first syllable) expressively confounds cause with effect, for it must be interpreted 'confining'; and *doom* means 'judgement' as well as 'fate' (so that the word meshes with *forfeit* in its legal sense).

5–9 *The mortal moon . . . time.* On the topical allusions here, and their role in dating the sonnet, see the headnote.

7 *Incertainties* uncertainties

8 *And peace proclaims olives of endless age.* The association of *olives* – here 'olive branches' – with peace, reconciliation and hope is ancient; see, for instance, Genesis 8.11. At *2 Henry IV* IV.4.87, Shakespeare had already enlivened the familiar iconography by writing 'Peace puts forth her olive everywhere'. Here he goes further, making the abstraction which the symbol stands for seem to stand for the symbol.

9 *the drops of this most balmy time.* On this image and its topical significance, see the headnote.

10 *My love looks fresh* my affection looks green and vigorous (like the sprouting *olives*. With a subsidiary tribute to the *thou* of line 13, the poet's *love*, on whom see the headnote.)
 to me subscribes submits to me, acknowledges that I am his superior

11 *spite of* despite, in spite of

11–12 *I'll live . . . tribes.* The grand claim of Horace and Ovid, resisted in Sonnet 55 (see its headnote). Yet, even while he makes his boast, the poet tempers it; if *poor* adds insult to *Death*'s injury (the verse which mortality submits to is not even distinguished), it registers most immediately as a modest disclaimer. If I live after death, the poet implies, the praise must be Poetry's, not mine. Lines 13–14 also recall Sonnet 55 and its sources.

12 *insults* triumphs, exults, gloats
 dull and speechless tribes. The hordes of those who, making no *rhyme* when alive, are forgotten when dead. Being *dull* and inarticulate, they are, by hyperbole, *speechless* in life as in death.

14 *crests.* Perhaps the 'battle helms' of warrior *tyrants*; more likely the 'coats of arms' which traditionally adorned the *tombs* of noblemen and kings.
 spent consumed, wasted away

Sonnet 108

1 *character* write

2 *figured* sketchily shown, represented, displayed
 true constant, honest

2, 4 *spirit . . . merit.* Though the rhyme perhaps remained imperfect, it will have tended towards a short 'e' sound in *spirit* (compare Old French *esperit . . . merite*); thus, giving both words the two syllables they here enjoy, 'sperit . . . merit'.

3 *what now to register* what remains unrecorded. Some editors emend

Q's 'now' to 'new', balancing *new to speak* (and anticipating *old thing old* in line 7).

4   *dear* precious, loved

5   *yet* (1) nevertheless; (2) still, now as before

7   *Counting no old thing old* accounting no phrase much used by me (and perhaps 'no stale lovers' cliché') outworn. *Old thing* has all the vague dismissiveness of affectionate familiarity.

thou mine, I thine. Probably what the poet's daily sayings boil down to rather than a direct quotation from his office (though at least one editor has enclosed the words in inverted commas). There may be an echo of the Song of Solomon 2.16: 'My love is mine, and I am his, which feedeth among the lilies until the day break.'

8   *Even* (one syllable)

hallowed thy fair name. An echo of the Lord's Prayer ('hallowed be thy name') brings home to the reader the resemblance of the poet's office to *prayers divine*.

9   *So that.* 'And it is in a similar way that' as well as 'and so it is that', for the sestet broadens the scope of the octet to consider the ageing of lovers in the light of the *old* loving *prayers*.

eternal forever constant

in love's fresh case (1) in the (constantly) fresh circumstances of (truly true) love; (2) contained in affection's sprightly (though *old*) argument (meaning 'my love poetry'); (3) covered by affection's youthful vigour (*case* suggesting 'skin', and thus the *wrinkles* of line 11); (4) clad in affection's sprightly garb (common meaning of *case* in the period)

10–11   *Weighs not . . . place.* The writing theme is sustained by the suggestion that a lover's *case* (his 'poetic argument') 'finds no reason to mention *the dust and injury of age*, and has no room for talk of wrinkles'; but the main concern of these lines is to establish that *eternal love*, forever *fresh*, 'is not put off by the decay and harm which ageing inflicts on a loved person (or the *dust and injury* which characterize old age) and does not weaken when confronted by the inevitable *wrinkles*'. This strand of sense intertwines with the two visual images evoked in line 9 by *case*: skin, dry and wrinkled with age; clothing, rubbed and creased with long use – these resemble (and if they do not it is because they are) the loved one in *age*.

12   *But makes antiquity for aye his page.* 'But finds good service in *age*' gives the gist, but none of the life, of the line. *Antiquity* adheres to both the beloved and the poetry written about him: just as *age* can attract *love* (see *case*, sense 1), so an *old thing* can be *love's fresh case* (sense 2). The emotional argument is extended by *for aye*, which looks back to the constancy, the renewing *fresh*ness, of *eternal love*; while the writing theme leads beyond the servant-boy who is

antiquity itself (sprucely clad, no doubt, in an old but *fresh case*) to the page inscribed with *antiquity* – the 'leaf of paper' bearing some old thing of the poet's written in praise of the young man. And, reading the lines in the light of the sequence at large, it is difficult to exclude a sense that *age* and *antiquity* are figures of Time, overwhelmed here by love and poetry, put in servitude by the pen.

13   *the first conceit of love* (1) love as it was first (at the start of the affair) understood; (2) the first literary conceit used of the beloved

13–14   *there . . . Where.* By now both 'in the beloved' and 'in the verse written to the beloved'.

13   *bred.* Suggestively ambiguous in tense. The *first conceit of love* is still being *bred* where it once was *bred. Antiquity* remains *fresh*.

14   *would show it.* 'Make it seem' gives way to 'try to make it appear' and a still weaker 'want to make it seem'.

Sonnet 109

2   *flame* passion
      qualify moderate

3   *easy* (1) easily; (2) easy in my mind, contentedly

3–4   *from myself . . . lie.* For this play on a double commonplace see 22.5–7 and the note.

5   *ranged* wandered away, strayed

6   *him* one, that person
      travels. Used in rough antithesis to *ranged*: a traveller does not stray but journeys purposefully, eventually returning home.

7   *Just to the time, not with the time exchanged* exactly punctual, not altered by the period (of *absence*). Doubly quibbling, for *Just* means 'righteous, honest' as well as 'prompt' (so that it stands opposed to *exchanged* in the sense 'changed, inconstant, *false of heart*'), and *time* serves first as 'hour of the day' and then as 'period of separation'.

8   *water for my stain.* Presumably tears, which wash away the *stain* of his offence.

9   *reigned* prevailed

10   *All frailties that besiege all kinds of blood* all the moral weaknesses incident to every kind of temperament. Building metaphorically on the renaissance notion that the quality of a man's blood (its distinctive balance of humours) influenced not only his character but his susceptibility to certain kinds of disease.

10, 12   *blood . . . good.* Ambiguous; the rhyme may rest on the long 'u' noted at 19.2 and 4 (sounding like 'oo' in modern 'mood') or on a long 'o' (sounding in the period like 'ar' in Scottish 'ward', 'wart').

11   *preposterously* unnaturally, absurdly. Shakespeare found the word
      newly coined and free of its modern implication of risibility.
      stained made dishonourable. *Blood* extends this, evoking a standard
      sense of *stained* in the period: 'shown to be of base descent'.

12   *for nothing* (1) for the sake of something utterly worthless (another
      lover); (2) as though . . . worthless (inserting '*all thy sum of good* was');
      (3) for no reason

13   *For nothing this wide universe I call* because I account this wide
      universe worthless

14   *Save* except for
      my rose. On this echo of the early sonnets, see the Introduction, page
      9, and the notes to 1.2.
      in it thou art my all. Although the *universe* is called *nothing*, the *rose*
      which is less than it (because placed *in it*) is, for the poet at least, *all*
      that there is.

Sonnet 110

Though the poet confesses in earlier sonnets to verbal deficiencies, and to
the fault of excusing the friend's faults, and though he hints at some
estrangement in Sonnets 100-103 and 109, this is the first sonnet in which
he roundly accuses himself of emotional betrayal.

1   *Alas, 'tis true, I have gone here and there.* Some editors omit the Q
      comma after *true*, changing the tone of the sonnet in consequence.
      As the text stands, the poet concedes even as we read that he has
      ranged (109.5) to his dishonour; the sestet then announces his
      determination to reform. Emended, the text suggests – since the
      sestet is held in reserve rather than reached towards – an apology
      bolstered by self-righteousness.

1, 3 *there . . . dear.* Rhymed like *clear . . . everywhere* at 84.10 and 12.

2   *a motley to the view* a fool in the eyes of the world. Professional jesters
      wore *motley* – coarse mixed cloth or, as here (see *Gored*, sense 2),
      parti-coloured clothing. The metonymy is Shakespearian; compare
      As You Like It III.3.71, 'Will you be married, motley?' Some scholars
      read this in the light of 111.6-7, arguing that Shakespeare here
      alludes to his life as an actor.

3   *Gored* (1) wounded, made gory; (2) furnished with gores (triangular
      pieces of cloth), dressed in *motley*; (3) dishonoured (because in
      heraldry a 'gore' is a mark interposed between two charges to define
      an abatement of honour)
      dear (1) precious; (2) beloved

4   *Made old offences of affections new* made new attachments further
      instances of the same old infidelity

5   *truth* honesty, constancy, true love

6   *Askance and strangely* with disdainful surprise and reserve. *Askance* can also mean 'sideways, obliquely'; compare sense (2) of *blenches* in line 7.

        by all above by heaven

7   *blenches* (1) swervings (from the straight and narrow, and from *thee*); (2) sideways glances (catching new lovers' eyes); (3) blemishes, stains (to my honour and good name). In sense (2) rare, and possibly obsolete, with this exception, since the fourteenth century.

        gave my heart another youth rejuvenated my affections

8   *worse essays proved thee my best of love* less satisfactory experiments in loving showed you to be my best lover, and experiences of less honourable love proved your love the best that could be

9   *Now all is done* now that all the motley infidelity is done with

        have what shall have no end receive (from me) something that will last forever. *What* could be translated 'my love', or 'the fidelity which I describe in lines 10–12'.

10–11 *Mine appetite . . . friend.* The poet revives a dead metaphor ('to whet one's appetite'), making the grindstone's *proof* ('trial by experience') *try* ('test out, provoke, afflict' and so 'sharpen, whet') the friend as well as his own *appetite*.

11   *newer . . . older.* Compare line 4, with its balanced *old . . . new.*

12   *A god in love.* Probably 'who is a god as far as my love is concerned' rather than 'who loves like a god'.

        I am confined. Loving is spatial restriction, as infidelity is movement *here and there.* The echo of 107.4 seems significant.

13   *next my heaven the best.* Probably 'you, who are to me the next best thing to my life in heaven'; but the requested *welcome* might be the almost heavenly thing.

13, 14 *heaven . . . Even* (both monosyllabic)

14   *most most loving.* This hyperbole – prompted, perhaps, by the poet's guilt – aptly ends a poem which inclines throughout towards comparatives and superlatives: *most dear, Most true, worse essays, best of love, newer proof, older friend, the best.*

Sonnet 111

1   *O, for my sake do you with Fortune chide.* As the text stands, a straightforward but passionate imperative: 'O, chide Fortune for my sake'. Retaining Q's 'wish': 'O, wish for my sake that Fortune chide' (making the *guilty goddess* an independent deity), 'O, you wish Fortune to chide me for my own good', or 'O, surely you don't for my sake wish Fortune to chide me (don't you know what she has done to

me already) . . . ?' None of the senses that can be squeezed from Q seems quite satisfactory. It is true that 'wish' can hardly be a misprint for *with*; as Randall McLeod has ingeniously observed, 'wish' is printed with a 'sh' ligature which comes from a section of the Jacobean compositor's printing case quite distinct from 't' and 'h' ('Unemending Shakespeare's Sonnet 111', *Studies in English Literature* 21 (1981), 75–96). But 'wish' might stem from a misreading of *with* in the author's manuscript or scribal transcript, and could certainly arise from misremembering by a compositor moving from copy to setting stick.

2   *The guilty goddess of my harmful deeds* the goddess who is guilty of my misdeeds (because she caused them. No doubt the faults recorded in Sonnets 109 and 110.)

3   *better* (1) more adequately; (2) something better (more honest and honourable)
        life survival, living, livelihood

4–7   *Than public . . . hand.* Most critics agree with Shelley's gloss: 'The author seems here to lament his being reduced to the necessity of appearing on the stage, or writing for the theatre.' Yet if Shakespeare is expressing through the script of the poet distaste for the theatrical life which supported him, his reservations must be read in the light of the tributes paid to acting in his plays (most notably *Hamlet*) and in the context of a society which only slowly and reluctantly granted actors the status they felt they deserved. For many, acting was associated with vagabondage, vanity, and subversion. (Which is not to say that all those with voices to be heard reacted so: there are, indeed, verses in John Davies of Hereford's *Microcosmos* (1603) and *Scourge of Folly* (1611?) which look like replies to this sonnet, or at the least the sentiments expressed therein – the former with marginal initials W.S., and the latter addressed to the poet as named in 135–6, Will.)

4   *public means* a livelihood won in public (by means of acting and presenting composed plays. *Means* operates twice, as a 'way' and an 'income'. By extension, 'a career dependent on public approval if not indeed sheer vulgar acclaim'.)
        which public manners breeds (1) which makes one familiar with all and sundry (and thus prone to wander *here and there* (110.1) in love); (2) which encourages vulgar display and unfeelingly superficial charm

5–6   *Thence . . . thence.* Referring to the *guilty* deeds of *Fortune*, but most immediately to the *public means* which those deeds delivered.

5   *my name receives a brand.* Criminals were sometimes branded (Ben Jonson, for example, received a brand on his thumb in 1598 for killing the actor Gabriel Spencer in a duel). So the poet's 'reputation is dishonoured'. It is possible that Shakespeare means to allude to

the Roman practice of marking with *notae* the names of citizens guilty of immorality where they appeared on census lists. And see the note to 112.1–2.

6–7   *subdued | To* overpowered by, made subject to

7   *like the dyer's hand* (which is coloured by the dye into which it dips cloth. Distantly, the image suggests the poet's *hand*, writing, steeping language in rhetorical 'colours'.)

8   *renewed* restored. In the light of lines 9–10, 'cured'.

9   *Potions of eisel* concoctions of vinegar. Often used *'gainst* ('as a cure for') the plague; but employed, too, for removing stubborn stains (for cleaning *the dyer's hand*).

   strong infection powerful disease, firmly-rooted sickness. However, as Geoffrey Hill has noted (see Further Reading, page 70), *infection* meets, at its Latin root, *the dyer's hand*, since *inficere* means 'to dip in, stain'. Compare the uses of *eisel*, above.

11   *No bitterness that I will bitter think.* Elliptical; supply 'there is *No bitterness* . . .'. Mildly quibbling: *bitterness* describes the tase of *eisel*, but *bitter* moves towards line 12 by introducing, in addition, the sourness of becoming embittered.

12   *Nor double penance to correct correction* nor will I think a twofold penance, designed to correct what has already (with the first penance) been corrected, bitter. The poet promises to be mercilessly persistent in his pursuit of a complete cure.

13   *then* (1) therefore; (2) at that time. The latter is prompted by the *will* . . . *will* which *willing* foregrounds in lines 9–11.

14   *Even that your pity is enough* that that pity of yours is (and *will* be, *then*, when I take my richly deserved medicine) in itself enough. *Even* is monosyllabic.

Sonnet 112

1–2   *Your love . . . brow.* The *brand* of 111.6 turns up on the poet's forehead (where Roman slaves and criminals might be marked), but the *pity* of 111.13–14, apparently granted, erases the scar.

1   *doth* do. A common form of the plural; compare 123.11.

2   *vulgar scandal.* Both 'base detraction' and 'public disgrace'.

3   *calls me well or ill* speaks good or ill of me, gives me a good or bad name. Compare 111.5.

4   *So* as long as

   o'er-green my bad. The friend covers the poet's *bad* (mostly his 'disgrace', but partly the 'evil doing' which earned it) with fresh *love and pity*, rather as green ivy grows over dead trees and ugly ruins, or, if *o'er-green* (which seems to be Shakespeare's coinage) is read in

326

strict accordance with *fill*, by inlaying greenery to conceal an unsightly blemish (as, for instance, when a damaged lawn is patched with fresh turf).

my good allow. The friend recognizes what is *good* in the disgraced poet. Arguably, the phrase cannot be entirely detached from *o'er-green my bad* so that, once *allow* registers in the sense 'concede that I have, approve', *o'er-green* starts to mean 'gloss over, regard as attractive (in your own mind, whatever the *world* says)'.

5   *my all the world* everything to me (but see the note to line 14)

6, 8   *tongue . . . wrong.* Rhyming like *tongue . . . song* at 17.10 and 12; compare 89.9 and 11.

7–8   *None else . . . wrong* for there is no one else who exists for me, or for whom I exist, in such a way that they can change my hardened sensibility (my by now obdurate will) towards either virtue or evil. *Strive* in line 5 and *steeled* support this strenuous interpretation of *changes*, but the idea of *changes* in appearance wrought by the friend's point of view (quatrain one) persists, perhaps, to a degree.

9   *in so profound* into such a deep
        abysm (two syllables)

9, 11   *care . . . are.* Resembling the rhyme at 13.1 and 3.

10   *Of* about

10–11   *my adder's . . . are.* 'As deaf as an adder' was proverbial, though Shakespeare here calls on the context provided by Psalm 58, 'the deaf adder that stoppeth her ears, and will not hear the voice of charmers, though he be never so skilful in charming' (verse 4). As this passage suggests, the adder was not thought naturally deaf but quick to close its ears (by fixing one orifice to the ground and stopping the other with its tail, some argued). *Critic* here means 'unfavourable commentator'; still a relatively new word (not recorded as a noun, in anglicized form, before *Love's Labour's Lost, c.* 1595), it was not associated with literary analysis until the later seventeenth century; it thus refers to carping about the poet's life, not to adverse 'reviewing' or 'literary criticism'.

11   *flatterer* (two syllables: 'flatt'rer')

12   *Mark . . . dispense* note how I excuse my neglect (of *others' voices.* Though some scholars understand 'of you', recalling the poet's apologies in Sonnets 100–103 and, more immediately, 109–11.)

13   *in my purpose bred* nurtured (like a child in the womb) in my purposeful (my conscious and committed) thoughts. *Purpose* properly expresses the subject-matter of thought, and thus formulated conscious thinking; the friend is not tucked away 'at the back of' the poet's 'mind'.

14   *all the world besides methinks they're dead* I think only you, in the whole world, alive. The echo of *my all the world* is obvious, though here an

emphasis on 'people, world of men and women' in *world* is clearer. Q's 'all the world besides me thinkes y'are dead' has been variously emended (see the Collations, page 435), but the sonnet's argument seems to require 'they are' or the *they're* offered. Presumably 'y' is used in Q as an archaic form of the still more archaic 'þ', sounded 'th' (as in 'Ye Olde Tea Shoppe', which Shakespeare's contemporaries would have read, correctly, as 'The Olde . . .'), producing 'th'are', a common contraction of 'they are' in the period. To adopt *they're* is thus, strictly, to modernize, not emend; though in modernizing, as sometimes happens, the original is distorted, with the loss of Q's two stark monosyllables 'th'are dead' for the sake of the more modulated modern forms.

Sonnet 113

1   *mine eye is in my mind.* The poet regards the world through what Hamlet calls the 'mind's eye' (I.2.185), through visioning fancy, because he is in love. As Helena observes at *A Midsummer Night's Dream* I.1.234, 'Love looks not with the eyes, but with the mind'.

2   *that* the eyesight. Such a gloss rationalizes, however, the bizarre suggestion – made by *eye* in line 1 and the singulars *that, his, is,* and *is* in lines 2–4 – that one *eye* is turned within and the other out, making the poet a combination of stylized seer and Cyclops. (The conceit merely carries to an extreme Claudius's 'one Auspicious, and one Dropping eye' at Folio *Hamlet* I.2.11.)
    governs guides

3   *Doth part* (1) divides; (2) departs from, abandons; (3) does part of, partly does. Sense (3) only really registers when we reach *partly blind.*

3, 7, 8   *his* its

4   *Seems seeing* apparently sees, pretends to see
    effectually is is effectively, is in effect
    out. Certainly 'inaccurate and ineffectual because out of condition and off the mark' (compare *Love's Labour's Lost* IV.1.134, 'Wide o'the bow hand! I'faith, your hand is out'), and probably 'snuffed out, lustreless' (recalling the renaissance notion that the *eye* creates the beams by which it sees); perhaps, too, 'plucked out' (like Gloucester's eyes in *King Lear* III.7).

5   *the heart.* As often in Shakespeare, a sentient, conscious organ; compare 69.2.

6   *latch* apprehend, catch sight of. Compare *Macbeth* IV.3.193–5, 'But I have words | That would be howled out in the desert air, | Where hearing should not latch them', and the still-current idiom 'latch on to'. This emendation of Q's 'lack' is almost universal.

7   *Of his quick objects hath the mind no part* the mind (with its inward *eye*)
       has no share of the *quick* things seen by the outward eye of sight.
       Quick means both 'lively, vivid' and 'fleeting'; the former sense
       touches perhaps on 'lifelike, real (rather than fancied)'. Notice how
       part, already complex in line 3, yields a further sense as a substantive.

8   *Nor his own vision holds what it doth catch* nor does the sight retain an
       impression of what it glimpses

9   *rud'st* most uncouth
       gentlest cultivated, well-bred, and courteous

10   *sweet-favour.* Almost invariably emended, either to 'sweet favour'
       ('agreeable countenance, pleasant appearance') or 'sweet-favoured'
       ('sweetly featured'). However, as Stanley Wells points out to me, Q's
       hyphen implies an adjectival form with the '-ed' assumed from
       deformèd'st. The sense, then, is 'sweet-favoured', but interference
       with Q would be on this showing unnecessary (unless, as a radical
       modernizer, one felt compelled to insert '-ed' to update a form that
       must always have been rare and is now obsolete). Those defending
       'sweet favour' compare that other substantive *creature*; but if context
       is to count, *creature* actually weakens the case. Lines 7–12 show an
       increasing concentration, as paired units lead to the list of single
       things in 11–12. Thus *mind* and *vision* enjoy a line each, then *the*
       rud'st or gentlest sight are opposed within line 9; in line 10 *sweet-favour*
       and *deformèd'st* are compacted as qualifiers of *creature*, and *The*
       mountain, sea, day then follow.

12   *feature.* Like *favour*, a word which can be used of a complete 'figure'
       and 'form' but tends to refer to the 'countenance'.

13   *Incapable of* unable to cope with

14   *true* faithful, devoted, constant. But not (and here is the irony)
       'honest'.
       mak'th mine eye untrue. Q's 'maketh mine vntrue' can hardly be right
       (though some editors retain it). Among the better emendations,
       'maketh m'eyne untrue' fails to satisfy because it makes plural an *eye*
       singular throughout the sonnet, while 'maketh mind untrue' (though
       paleographically acceptable) divorces the conclusion of the poem
       from the divorce described in the sestet. *My most true mind mak'th*
       mine eye untrue has the advantage of ending the sonnet aptly by
       echoing, but inverting, its first line. And it simply assumes the
       omission of one word by the compositor ('maketh' for *mak'th* is an
       unremarkable irregularity – compare Q's 'flatterer' and 'flatry' at
       112.11 and 114.9, both two syllables).
       untrue unreliable, deceitful, false

329

Sonnet 114

Elaborating the argument of Sonnet 113.

1, 3   *Or whether . . . or whether* (indicating alternatives advanced as ques-
tions. 'Is it the case that my mind . . . drinks up' and 'or shall I say that
my eye . . .')

1   *being* (one syllable)
crowned with you made a king by having you as my friend, triumphant
in loving you

2, 9   *flattery* pleasing delusion. Three syllables in line 2, two in line 9.

4   *your love* my love for you. No doubt *your* (which initially suggests *love*
coming from the friend) was prompted by *mine* in line 3.
alchemy. Employed here because alchemists purport to transmute
base matter into stuff of value and beauty.

5–6   *To make . . . resemble* to make monstrous forms (probably animate)
and shapeless things (presumably inanimate) resemble such angels
as resemble lovely you. The suggestion is that *cherubins* are as
inferior to the young man in grace and beauty as are *monsters and
things indigest* to *cherubins*.

8   *As fast as objects to his beams assemble* as quickly as things seen take
shape in its (the *eye*'s) gaze. Alluding, again, to the idea that the *eye*
creates the *beams* by which it sees.

9   *'tis the first.* The theory advanced in lines 1–2 is correct, not the
notion floated in 3–4.
'tis flattery in my seeing. 'I . . . fear to find | Mine eye too great a
flatterer for my mind', says Olivia, after falling in love with Cesario
(*Twelfth Night* I.5.298–9).

10   *great.* Used ironically; 'pompously grand, overweeningly conceited'.
most kingly in a kingly fashion. Inevitably, the words exert an
adjectival influence over *mind* while adhering immediately to the
verb *drinks*.
drinks it up. Compare line 2; but this time the dead metaphor is
brought back to life. In lines 11–12, the eye is a butler and taster to
the *mind*, apparently betraying his *kingly* master (see the previous
note) with a poisoned *cup*.

11, 12   *his* its (the *mind*'s)

11   *gust* taste
is greeing agrees. Most editors read ''greeing', unnecessarily: the
verb 'to gree', aphetized from 'agree' or deriving from Old French
greer, is recorded regularly between the fourteenth and nineteenth
centuries.

12   *to* to suit

13   *If.* 'Even though' is as prominent here as 'if perhaps'.

13–14   *'tis the . . . begin* it makes the eye's sin less black that, liking the brew, it drinks first. For the *eye* sees the world as the friend before the *mind* receives that message from the *eye*, and it *loves* what it sees.

Sonnet 115

Frequently compared with Donne's *Love's Growth*.

2   *Even those* the very ones. *Even* is here monosyllabic.

3   *Yet* (1) however (introducing an apology for the *lie*); (2) as yet (placing the *lie* in *Time* and preparing *then*)

4   *most full* (1) as intense as could be; (2) very intense. The poet finds (2) where he had once understood (1).
     flame (of love)

5   *reckoning* (three syllables treated here as two)
     reckoning Time. Initially 'counting up time, when I reckon up time', but the relative clause beginning *whose* makes *reckoning* an adjectival modifier of *Time*, until the original construction is resumed in line 9 – but with a decisively personified *Time*. Merely to mention time is fearfully to remember *Time*. On the impact of this ambiguity see the Introduction, pages 38–9. Modernization sadly obscures the effect since Q's 'time' here and in line 9, where 'time' is clearly personified, allows the reader to be lulled into the first construction before she or he is wrested into the second by the relative clause. (It is true that compositorial practice probably dictated the lower-case 't', but that indicates a degree of indifference to capitals in 1609, impossible under modern conventions, which would have allowed Shakespeare's ambiguity to bite had another compositor, readier to capitalize, set the poem. A capital is adopted in this edition to conform to the pattern throughout; ideally the text should have *reckoning time*, turning to *Time* once read.)
     millioned numbered by the million. Although the noun 'million' is a fourteenth-century borrowing (from French), this is the first recorded use of the word plus 'd'. Conceivably Q's 'milliond' is a variant form of 'million' (influenced by 'hundre*d*', 'thousan*d*'). That 'millions' occurs in Q Sonnet 53 need not matter, since the poems were probably set by different compositors (one of whom might respect a manuscript form with 'd', while the other standardized).
     accidents events ('These bloody accidents', *Othello* V.1.94), chance occurrences ('accidents unpurposed', *Antony and Cleopatra* IV.14.84), misfortunes ('by some unlooked accident cut off', *Richard III* I.3.213). Only as lines 6–8 unfold do the sombre implications – strongest in modern English – take command.

6   *'twixt vows*. 'Between the oaths of people who swear to something'

(one thinks of lovers' *vows*, betrayed by *Time*), and so, prompted by *'twixt*, 'between *vows* and their keeping'.

change decrees of kings. As time passes, the fixed *decrees of kings* are amended and rescinded.

7   *Tan* darken, turn leathery. Compare 62.10, where *Time*'s ally, *antiquity*, is the villain.

sacred adorable, worthy of fervent devotion

sharp'st intents keenest intentions, most urgently intended purposes

8   *course* tending, way. There is a suggestion of 'current', as though the *alt'ring things* flowed in torrents towards decay.

9–10   *why . . . Might I not then say* why . . . was I not entitled *then* ('when I wrote *Those lines*', with a hint of 'therefore') to say

11   *certain o'er incertainty* steadfastly sure (that my love for you, being complete, was at its zenith)

12   *Crowning the present* (1) thinking the present the best that could be (believing it to be a king among times); (2) glorifying the present in my thoughts. The former flows into the latter. The echo of 114.1 may be deliberate; by association with *incertainty*, *Crowning* also recalls 107.7.

doubting of the rest. 'Dubious about the value of the future' as well as 'apprehensive about what the future would bring'.

13   *Love is a babe* (because Cupid is so depicted)

then might I not say so. Shakespeare recapitulates line 10 (*so* standing for '*Now I love you best*') with a significant change of emphasis. In the earlier line, *then* primarily means 'at that time', and 'therefore' is only hinted; in line 13, by contrast, *then* is mostly 'therefore', and the temporal sense of the word is hardly felt. The poet's defence becomes his apology: 'why should I not at that time say "Now I love you best"?' modulates to 'that is why I was wrong to say "Now I love you best"'.

14   *To give full growth to that which still doth grow* attributing maturity to something (*Love* as 'my love for you') which is *still* (both 'even now' and 'forever') growing. Perhaps *still* draws on its sense 'nevertheless', making *still doth grow* suggest 'grows, regardless of what is said about it'.

Sonnet 116

On this much misread sonnet, see the Introduction, pages 53–4. For an adaptation of the text, see pages 441 and 445–6 below.

1, 2,   *marriage . . . impediments . . . the edge of doom*. Quietly invoking the
12   Elizabethan Book of Common Prayer: 'I require and charge you (as you will answer at the dreadful day of judgement, when the secrets of

all hearts shall be disclosed) that if either of you do know any impediment, why ye may not be lawfully joined together in matrimony, that ye confess it. For be ye well assured, that so many as be coupled together otherwise than God's word doth allow, are not joined together by God, neither is their matrimony lawful.'

2   *Admit* concede (that there are, that there might be), permit the consideration of

2–12   *Love is not love . . . the edge of doom.* In some ways a secular variation on St Paul's account of love in 1 Corinthians 13.

2–4   *love . . . remover to remove.* The overall, confident assertion is clear: true love does not change when it finds some change (of appearance, circumstance, affection) in the loved one; nor does it incline, if the beloved is inconstant, to stray. Whether one detects an undertow of irony – should love not accommodate itself to change, be flexible, make allowances? and should it not, in some sense (see, for example, Sonnets 45–6), *bend with the remover?* – depends on the extent to which one finds the *love* of the poem inhuman in its absoluteness. Certainly, the unwavering fixity of *love* here conflicts suggestively with the growing emotion described in 115.

2, 4,   *love . . . remove . . . proved . . . loved.* For the rhyme see 25.13 and 14
13, 14   and the note.

5–8   *it is . . . be taken.* Shakespeare alludes to a tradition of love poems (deriving from Petrarch's '*Passa la nave mia colma d'oblio*') in which the lover is a mariner adrift on a raging sea.

5   *ever-fixèd mark.* Presumably the kind of lighthouse or beacon referred to at *Coriolanus* V.3.74–5: 'a great sea-mark, standing every flaw | And saving those that eye thee!'

7   *star* guiding star. It is natural to think of the pole star, and (because of *ever-fixèd* in line 5) of Caesar's boast at *Julius Caesar* III.1.60–62: 'But I am constant as the northern star, | Of whose true-fixed and resting quality | There is no fellow in the firmament.'
    bark boat

8   *worth's unknown.* 'Value' and 'quality' can both be felt in *worth*, while *unknown* suggests 'not tried in experience' as much as 'not understood, beyond understanding'.
    height be taken altitude be measured. Mariners estimate latitude by measuring in degrees the *height* of the pole star above the horizon.

9   *Love's not Time's fool* true love is not the laughingstock of Time. Compare *the fools of Time* at 124.13, and Hotspur's sententious allusion to 'life, time's fool' at *1 Henry IV* V.4.80.

10   *bending.* Time's *sickle* is doubly *bending* because, curved in shape, it cuts through its harvest in sharp curved sweeps. It is malicious and highly active, for 'to bend' could mean 'to level at, aim for' ('I told him the revenging gods | 'Gainst parricides did all the thunder

333

bend', says Edmund at *King Lear* II.1.44–5) and 'to proceed, head towards' (as at *1 Henry IV* V.5.35–6, 'You, son John, and my cousin Westmorland, | Towards York shall bend you with your dearest speed'). The *sickle* seems to encompass the sonnet's *rosy lips and cheeks*, with cruel conviction, as we read. *Love*'s antagonism to *Time* is marked here, too; for *love* never *bends* (line 4), though Time's *sickle* does.

compass range, scope. But the final effect is much more complex, since *compass* links with the navigational images of the second quatrain (magnetic compasses point north, towards the pole star), and since the combination of the *fixèd mark* and *wandering* suggests, in a submerged way, a geometrical *compass* in which one foot is *fixed* while the other wanders (and by remaining *fixed* dignifies itself by remaining the centre of the erring limb's wanderings).

10, 12   *come . . . doom*. For the rhyme see the note to 107.2, 4.

11   *his brief hours and weeks*. Though the earlier instances of *his* are unambiguous (lines 8 and 10), here the immediate reference of the *brief hours and weeks* to *Time* is complicated by a secondary suggestion that *Love*, refusing to be subordinate to *Time*, sets *his* own time scheme, in which devotion (and pleasure) make *hours and weeks* seem *brief* when compared with *Time*'s objective reckoning.

12   *bears it out* endures
to the edge of doom until the day of judgement

13   *If this be error and upon me proved*. More than witty pleading is involved: the poet does not withdraw in his couplet from the gravity of his three quatrains. *Error* and *proved* carry legal associations, *error* meaning 'fault in procedure or judgement' and *upon me proved* 'demonstrated in evidence against me'. Indeed, as M. C. Bradbrook reminds me, *error* would have suggested, in the light of the spiritual issues and biblical echoes contained in the poem, theological *error*, heresy – the kind of *error* encountered, for instance, in 'Error's Den' near the start of *The Faerie Queene* Book I. In this context, *proved* might mean 'tested', with hints of interrogation and torture. (The poet claims an orthodoxy or true faith which would bear proof.) It is no accident, presumably, that a text closely related to 116 in both its verbal palette and its interest in constancy – Sonnet 124 – calls *Policy* in love, specifically, *that heretic*. Conceivably, early readers found the theological implication dominant in line 13: judgement would then weaken in two stages, from the final *doom* of line 12 to the inquisition and torment of line 13, with its secondary legal suggestion, to the legalistic in Sonnet 117. As 117.7–8 and 9 make plain, Shakespeare is alert to the etymology of *error*, which, derived from Latin *errare* ('to wander'), associates the couplet with the *wandering bark* of lines 7–8.

14   *I never writ, nor no man ever loved*. On the Shakespearian vulnerability

of this clamorously negative assertion, see the Introduction, page 53. Within the generalizing sweep of *nor no man ever loved*, 'nor did I ever love the young *man* of these sonnets (which I clearly did)' can be felt.

Sonnet 117

Although Sonnet 117 is quite different in tone from 116, it discusses some of the same subjects (constancy, removing, proof, measure, worth), it shares at least two metaphors (of navigation and the legal proof of love), and it echoes some of its predecessor's diction (*minds* and *unknown* at 116.1 and 8 become the *unknown minds* of 117.5, and *error* at 116.13 becomes *errors* at 117.9, while the rhyme words of both final couplets are close).

1   *Accuse me thus*. As *bonds* and *Book* suggest, and *appeal* confirms, the poet is outlining, like a lawyer, a case for the prosecution. See the note to 116.13.

       scanted stinted on, neglected

1–2   *all | Wherein* everything by which

2   *your great deserts repay* reward your excellent qualities (repaying you for the pleasure I have taken in them)

3–4   *Forgot . . . day.* An impression of neglect is vividly conveyed, though the details are left obscure. Perhaps the poet *Forgot* his daily offices of *love* (see Sonnet 108), failing to *call upon* the friend's *love* in the sense 'invoke'. Perhaps he *Forgot* to 'visit' (another sense of *call upon*) the friend's *love*, either in the place where the friend lived or in his own heart (which would make *Forgot upon your dearest love to call* straightforward forgetting). The *bonds* of line 4 are ties of love and duty, and perhaps oaths sworn before God, regarded as legal obligations. They *tie* the poet *day by day*, each *day* another loop fastening him to the responsibility which he chooses to ignore (though this last is barely hinted).

5   *frequent been with* often been with, frequented the company of, been familiar (a lost sense of *frequent*) with

       unknown minds strangers, I don't know who, nonentities

5, 7 *minds . . . winds.* The rhyme resembles *wind . . . find* at 14.6 and 8, with a diphthong sounding like 'u-ee' or 'i-ee'.

6   *given* (one syllable)

       given to time your own dear-purchased right given up to idle hours (in wasteful frittering) that love rite (not necessarily sexual) which, purchased by the precious authority of your love, is yours by right. Compare the right/rite ambiguity at 17.11 and 23.6. *Given to time* also suggests procrastination: 'left until the time served'.

7   *all the winds.* An extraordinary access of reckless freedom; from *all bonds* to *all* this.

9   *Book . . . down* write down, record
         wilfulness headstrong liberty, determined perversity
         errors. On the contribution made by etymology, see the note to
         116.13.

10   *on just proof surmise accumulate* pile on top of what you can prove
         everything you suspect

11   *level* range and aim (as when Leontes complains that Polixenes is
         'quite beyond mine arm, out of the blank | And level of my brain,
         plot-proof', *The Winter's Tale* II.3.5–6)

12   *your wakened hate* your state of roused hatred, the heat of your new
         hate

13   *appeal* plea (against sentence)
         prove test

13, 14   *prove . . . love.* For the rhyme see the note to 25.13, 14.

14   *virtue.* Already a ponderable word in the sequence, it resonates here
         with its full semantic range: strength, quality, value, moral integrity.
         your love (for me)

Sonnet 118

1, 5   *Like as . . . Even so* just as . . . in the same way

1   *appetites.* As at 56.2 there are sexual implications.

2   *eager compounds* pungent concoctions (sharp sauces, spicy appetizers
         and suchlike). For the latent medical sense of *compounds* – stirred by
         lines 3–4, 8, 11, and 14, and by Sonnet 119 – see the second note to
         76.4.
         urge prompt, stimulate

3   *prevent* forestall, ward off by anticipating
         unseen not yet evident, hypothetical (for the potions of line 4 are
         prophylactic)

4   *We sicken to shun sickness when we purge.* Laxatives of sickening
         strength were frequently prescribed by doctors to guard against
         disease.

5   *Even . . . being* (both monosyllabic)
         ne'er-cloying. The old emendation 'neare cloying' (dating back to
         Benson's edition of 1640) points to a possible pun. Compare *Richard
         II* V.1.88, 'Better far off than, near, be ne'er the nea'er', and the
         proverb which arguably activates the quibble here, 'Too much honey
         cloys the stomach'.

6   *bitter sauces.* The *eager compounds* of line 2, with a quibbling glance at
         the people they represent (since the poet has been seeking love
         elsewhere): a *sauce* is an 'impudent and undesirable person' (see
         128.13 and the notes). 'Sweet meat must have sour sauce' was

proverbial, as was 'Sweet sauce begins to wax sour' (bearing in mind the possible wordplay in *ne'er-cloying*).

frame direct, order

7   *sick of* (1) surfeited with, wearied by; (2) made ill by. This fleeting quibble sets up the jest which ends the poem.

welfare (1) good fare, healthy eating; (2) good health

found a kind of meetness somehow found it fitting, thought it in some way admirable

8   *true needing* real need to be

9   *policy*. As at 124.9, 'short-sighted cunning' rather than 'prudence'.

anticipate provide against, *prevent* (line 3)

10   *ills* (1) diseases; (2) evils. The latter is elicited by the primary sense of *faults*.

grew to faults assured (1) became real errors (in my conduct); (2) developed into indubitable (not just anticipated) diseases

11   *brought to medicine* brought to the point of needing medicine

a healthful state (what had previously been) a condition of complete health

12   *Which* (referring to the patient's condition when *healthful*)

rank of gorged with, sickened by

goodness. The friend's 'excellence' and 'virtue', which left the poet 'feeling well'.

would by ill be cured wanted to be cured by *ill*. If the *ills* of line 10 refer primarily to 'diseases', here *rank of goodness* makes 'evil' dominate 'sickness'.

13   *thence* (from these nasty experiences)

14   *Drugs poison him that so fell sick of you*. The black joke seems to be not just that the poet *fell sick of* being *healthful* and took *Drugs* to make himself *ill* (see *sick of* in line 7 and the note), but that the poet has proven by his experience that being in love with the young man is an incurable though benign disease (take *Drugs* to expel the *sickness* and they *poison* you). There is a secondary play in *that so fell sick*: 'who fell so sick' and 'who fell sick in this way'. The *Drugs poison* and *benefit of ill* (119.9) motif links this phase of 1–126 with Sonnets 147 and 148 in the dark lady group. For a larger Shakespearian context, see the note to *A Lover's Complaint* 300.

Sonnet 119

1–2   *What potions ... within*. The imagery is traditional (at *Troylus and Criseyde* IV.519–20, for example, Chaucer writes, 'Troylus in teris gan distille, | As licour out of a lambic ful faste'), but *siren*, *Distilled*, *limbecks*, and the quibble on *evil still* in line 10 (see the note) together suggest a debt to Sonnet 49 of Barnabe Barnes's *Parthenophil and Parthenophe* (1593). After calling his mistress a 'siren', the poet says: 'From my love's 'lembic [have I] still 'stilled tears.'

1   *What potions have I drunk of siren tears* what drug draughts of alluring tears I have drunk. Compare the imagery of 114.1–2 and 9–14. Sirens are mythological chimeras (part bird, part woman), known to lure mariners to destruction with their sweet singing. Ulysses heard them, bound to the mast, while his sailors (their ears stuffed with wax) worked his ship.

2   *limbecks* alembics, stills

     foul as hell within. Echoed at 147.14, where the poet complains that the dark lady, though outwardly *fair*, is inwardly *as black as hell, as dark as night.* The parallel is made the more striking by the common subject-matter of the sonnets: disease, false medicine, frantic madness. Perhaps nothing should be made of the overlap between 119 and 147; but it is tempting to infer (and the reader is encouraged to make the inference by the feminine connotations of *siren*) that 119 considers the affair analysed in 147 in the context of the poet's love for the young man.

3   *Applying fears to hopes and hopes to fears.* In so far as line 3 explicates 1–2, it suggests that, in taking *tears* as *potions* to delude himself, the poet has administered draughts of fear to his *hopes* and draughts of hope to his *fears.* Yet the line feels detached from what it follows: it evokes through abstraction the turbulence of love, *hopes* and *fears* together clamouring to possess the lover.

4   *Still* always

     losing when I saw myself to win. Inheriting from line 3 both rhetorical antithesis (*losing . . . win*) and the theme of self-deception, line 4 is nevertheless independent. It alludes to a series of mistakes: tricked by *siren tears*, the poet made gains which were losses.

5   *errors* (the mistakes of line 4; lapses in both judgement and conduct. For the latter, see *errors* as 'regrettable wanderings' at 117.9.)

6   *so blessèd never* never before so fortunate

6, 8   *never . . . fever.* Ambiguous; rhymed with a short first 'e' in *fever*, or with a long first 'e' (resembling the 'ar' in modern 'scarce', 'scares') in *never.*

7–8   *How have . . . fever.* Difficult lines which quibblingly entangle cause and effect. During his malaise, his metaphoric malady (lines 1–6), the poet apparently suffered bouts of *madding fever* which made his eyeballs roll about their sockets, *fitted* ('convulsed by fits') out of their proper orbits like wandering stars thrust from the crystal *spheres* in which they should be fixed. (The astronomical analogy was commonplace; compare, for example, *Hamlet* I.5.17, 'Make thy two eyes like stars start from their spheres', and *The Two Noble Kinsmen*

338

V. 1.113–14, 'Torturing convulsions from his globy eyes | Had almost drawn their spheres'.) What caused (yet also was, and resulted from) the poet's *distraction* is declared by *spheres* in the sense 'social orbits': neglecting the friend, the poet *looked . . . Askance and strangely* (see 110.5–8 and the notes), finding (at least one) lover in a different social milieu (perhaps a difference of class can be inferred – the 'huge sphere' of great men at *Antony and Cleopatra* II.7.14 seems relevant, as does Polonius's reported advice to Ophelia, 'Lord Hamlet is a prince, out of thy star . . .', II.2.141).

9   *ill* (1) wrongdoing; (2) evil; (3) disease, sickness
    find true discover that it is true

10   *better is by evil still made better.* Initially the line suggests balance and recovery: just as superior things always look better when contrasted with bad, so we *still* (that is, 'constantly') witness recovery when a person of excellence is cured (*made better*) by vile medicines – when, indeed, he is cured by the distilment of an *evil still* (for this quibble see lines 1–2 and the note). As lines 11–12 demonstrate, however, there is a secondary, or tertiary, significance here, dependent on *made better* as improvement, and *still* modifying *better*: superior things are made even more so by being touched with *evil*, and rallying.

10, 12   *better . . . greater.* The rhyme apparently rests on the use of the old comparative 'gretter'; in everyday Jacobean speech the consonance would have been imperfect.

11–12   *ruined love . . . greater.* The lines, which emerge from line 10 (see the note), are rooted in common experience, and in such saws as 'The falling out of lovers is a renewing of love'; but the architectural metaphor is characteristically Shakespearian: 'Shall love in building grow so ruinous?' (*The Comedy of Errors* III.2.4); 'O thou that dost inhabit in my breast, | Leave not the mansion so long tenantless, | Lest, growing ruinous, the building fall | And leave no memory of what it was!' (Valentine to the absent Silvia, turning his breast into the dwelling of love, *The Two Gentlemen of Verona* V.4.7–10). The constructive power claimed for poetry in sonnets like 55 and 107 begins to become an attribute of *love* (see the headnote to Sonnet 124).

12   *Grows* (like a flower. But also, as part of the architectural image, 'becomes'.)
    fairer. A comparative adjective modifying *love*, *fairer* links adverbially with *Grows*. As a result, *love* becomes *greater*, *more strong*, while we read.

13   *my content* the relationship which contents me, you who are my contentment

14   *ills.* The same range of sense as *ill* in line 9. Indeed, encouraged by

the parallel (and by the singular *evil* of line 10), some editors emend this to *ill*. But the poet is looking beyond the generalized sooths of lines 9–10 to the *potions* and *errors* of lines 1–6.

Sonnet 120

1   *That you were once unkind.* Inevitably recalling Sonnets 35–6, 40–42, and, most recently, 92–6 – clusters in which the poet claims that the friend has betrayed him emotionally.

2   *for* because of

3   *my transgression.* Perhaps that described by Sonnet 119, taking all the *errors* together.

4   *nerves.* The imagery of line 3 elicits 'sinews, tendons' (compare Coriolanus's 'nervy arm', II.1.153) while *sorrow* in line 2 prompts 'feelings, sensibility' (resting on a sense of *nerves* still current).

6   *a hell of time* a hellish time, a time (metaphorically) in hell. Circumlocution harnesses the energy of phrases like 'a hell of ugly devils' and 'a hell of pain' (*Richard III* I.3.226, *Troilus and Cressida* IV.1.59) while directing blame not so much towards *hell* as, typically, *time*. Meanwhile, *time* extends itself by eliciting from *hell* the notion of eternal punishment: the hellish time, by implication, seemed endless.

7–8   *no leisure taken | To weigh* set aside no time to consider. The suggestion that suffering can be tested by weight is obscurely supported by the imagery of line 3.

9   *our night of woe* distressing period of dark estrangement which we endured

    remembered reminded, brought to the memory of. Standard usage in the period; compare 'Let me remember thee what thou hast promised' (*The Tempest* I.2.243), or 'Thou but rememberest me of mine own conception' (*King Lear* I.4.66–7).

9, 11   *remembered ... tendered.* As in modern English, an imperfect feminine rhyme.

10   *deepest sense* most profound level of apprehension (where, through the ambiguity of *sense*, thoughts and emotion are indistinguishable)

11   *And soon to you, as you to me then, tendered* and that *our night of woe* (or, rather, *My deepest sense* through which the *night* should have worked, or, most immediately, the 'I' which *My* posits) *might have* offered to you, as you *then* (when making up after being *unkind*) offered to me. Q has a comma after *to you*, but no other punctuation. Some editors prefer to place a second comma before *then*, leaving the reader to provide a *then* (from line 2, as it were) in *as you to me.* The advantage of this arrangement is that it points up the balance (the reciprocal

340

'weighing') of *And soon to you* and *as you to me*. Perhaps the line should be left unpunctuated; certainly, when read aloud, Q's *then* tends towards a (not particularly interesting) ambiguity which makes it refer either to the period when the poet was abandoned and offered *salve*, or simply to the period when, after abandonment, the poet was offered *salve*.

12   *humble salve* salving humility, healing balm of a humble apology
      which wounded bosoms fits which is just the thing for wounded bosoms
      (and for the injured hearts which lie in them)

13   *that your trespass* that offence of yours
      fee payment

14   *ransoms . . . ransom.* As the balance of *Mine . . . yours* shifts to *yours*
      . . . me, the verb modulates from 'provides recompense for' to 'pays
      for the release of, redeems'.

Sonnet 121

1–2   *'Tis better . . . being.* It was proverbial that 'There is small difference
      to the eye of the world in being naught (that is, morally and/or
      sexually at fault) and being thought so'.

1   *vile esteemed* thought contemptible, said to be wicked

2   *not to be* not being *vile*

3–4   *And the . . . seeing.* After an initial ironic 'and you don't even get the
      pleasure appropriate to being *vile*', the lines clarify in the wake of *not
      to be* into a complaint about the way love can be marred by the
      insinuations of ignorant onlookers: 'and the legitimate *pleasure* of an
      honourable affection is *lost* because judged *vile* not by those who
      experience it but by those who look on'.

5   *adulterate.* The primary sense is undoubtedly 'corrupt, impure' (a
      substance becomes *adulterate* when mixed with base matter); but
      'adulterous' may also be implied (compare the ghost's description
      of Claudius at *Hamlet* I.5.42, 'that incestuous, that adulterate beast',
      and, more obliquely, *A Lover's Complaint* 175). On both levels the
      idea is that *adulterate eyes* misconstrue innocent love as jaundiced
      eyes see yellow.

6   *Give salutation to my sportive blood* greet my lusty gusto (with famili-
      arity. Presumably the *eyes* wink and exchange 'knowing' looks with
      the discomfited, outraged poet. *Blood*, the physiological basis of
      character, as at 109.10, was particularly associated with sexual
      passion; hence *A Lover's Complaint* 162 and 184. For *sportive*ness
      close to vice, see 95.6 and 96.2.)

6, 8   *blood . . . good.* For the rhyme see the note to 109.10, 12.

7   *Or on my frailties why are frailer spies* and why do people more flawed
     than I spy on my peccadilloes, and how comes it that people less
     moral than myself are spies looking for my weaknesses

8   *Which* who
     in their wills in the faculties which contain and direct their (cor-
     rupted) desires. Perhaps 'wilfully, out of sheer perversity' also
     registers.
     think. So the poet consults reason, a higher faculty than the will
     which directs the *frailer* folk of line 7.

9   *I am that I am.* God's words to Moses at Exodus 3.14, used ruefully,
     as though 'I'm not God, but I'm less flawed than some think'.
     Asserting his integrity, the poet puts himself as far from Iago (that
     arch-misconstruer of others' affairs) as possible: 'I am not what I am'
     (*Othello* I.1.66). Compare *you alone are you* at 84.2. Here is the other
     tautologous extreme; between these verbal poles, equally respectful
     of human opacity (and for a riddling *I am*, see the notes to 136.14),
     the complex poetry of interchange and identity unfolds.

9–10 *level | At* (1) guess at ('according to my description level at my
     affection', says Portia to her maid, describing the character of her
     wooers, *The Merchant of Venice* I.2.35–6); (2) aim (critical remarks) at
     (compare 'the deadly level of a gun' at *Romeo and Juliet* III.3.103, and
     117.11)

10   *abuses* misdeeds
     reckon up enumerate, list (recalling *count* in line 8)
     their own the *abuses* which they commit themselves. Contracted to
     'what is theirs' because *abuses* are so essentially of the nature of the
     poet's critics.

11   *straight* (as a die. Both 'steady in character, honest' and 'free from
     curvature and irregularity'.)
     bevel. The opposite of *straight* in the geometrical sense (in heraldry, a
     bevel line is broken to form a Z) and, by implication, in the ethical;
     opposing, too, its rhyme word, *level*, from which it elicits the sense
     'flat' (in building and carpentry, *bevel* angles slant from the hori-
     zontal)

12   *By* (1) through the agency of; (2) by analogy with
     rank lustful, luxuriating, diseased, fetid
     must not (1) should not; (2) cannot

13   *this general evil.* Describing both the tone of the proposition (glibly
     generalizing and cynically corrupt) and its content (its assertion that
     evil is *general*, universal).

14   *All men are bad and in their badness reign.* The ambiguity of *in their
     badness* is crucial. That *All men are bad* is easily conceded (see 35.5);
     that they sometimes *reign* ('prosper, prevail') in life (*in their badness*)
     is evident: but only corrupt cynics could *maintain* that *badness*

necessarily explains success, that it is *in their badness* ('when being bad') that men *reign*. Seeing the poet's success in love (lines 1-8), *bevel* individuals conclude that he is *bad*, when he is only – well, *bad* in the way good men are.

Sonnet 122

The poet apologizes for giving away – or excuses himself for losing (thus *missed*, line 8) – a notebook apparently inscribed with the friend's writings. In Sonnet 77 the poet urges the young man to record his thoughts in a blank notebook sent, it seems, with the poem; some critics believe that this book, filled in and returned to the poet, is the one discussed in 122. Both sonnets have been urged to show that Shakespeare's sequence grew directly out of lived experience: for why else would such trivial objects as notebooks turn up there? But, as one particularly close analogue of Sonnet 122 reminds us, Shakespeare was not the first poet to write about *tables*:

Il ne falloit, Maitresse, autres tablettes
Pour vous graver, que celles de mon cœur,
Où de sa main Amour nostre veinqueur
Vous a gravée, et vos graces parfaites . . .
Ronsard, Les Amours diverses (1578), Sonnet 4

Any argument in favour of a biographical reference in Sonnet 122 must start a stage further back, asking why Shakespeare should have chosen to write on a theme which, however conventional, challenged, indeed contradicted, his deepest instincts about memory and mortality. See the note to lines 4-5 and the Introduction, pages 43-4.

The sonnet presents a further difficulty: so accustomed is the reader at this stage in the sequence to associate writing and anxiety about writing with the poet that the script discussed keeps shifting, in reading, from the friend to the apologetic *I*. Particularly striking is *that idle rank* (line 3): how could the poet, one feels inclined to ask, call the friend's writings *idle*, when attempting to excuse himself and regain favour? Must he not mean that his own verse is so? It is not finally possible, however, to read the text as an apology for losing *tables* inscribed by the poet – *tables* given him, blank, by the friend. And one concludes, again, that Shakespeare found himself tackling a theme which he could not handle with assurance (because the idea of writing carried such weight); biography impinges, once more, through inelegance of argument.

1   *tables* notebooks
2   *Full charactered* written in full, packed with script
     with by. Perhaps also 'in (the medium of)'.
3   *Which . . . remain* which *lasting memory* will survive longer than that trifling list (of jottings) and remain superior in status to it. A

quibblingly compact line turning on the ambiguity of *idle rank*: 'worthless status' as well as 'futile list of commonplaces ranked in your notebook' (some commentators would add 'ineffectual series of pages set out like ranks of soldiers').

4   *all date* every conceivable time-limit, every possible date of expiry
     even (one syllable)

4–5   *to eternity – | Or, at the least.* As the poet's apology carries him towards a contradiction of his own most firmly held views, he balks. See the Introduction, pages 43–4.

6   *Have faculty by nature to subsist* have the power to survive naturally, are granted by Nature the power to survive. The word *faculty* contributes a glancing quibble, dissolving the *brain and heart* of line 5 into mental and emotional capacities.

7   *each* (referring to the *brain and heart*, as themselves and as capacities)
     razed oblivion blank obscurity. Implying 'Oblivion which erases and ruins (see 25.11 and 64.3) everything'.
     oblivion (three syllables)
     his its

7–8   *part | Of thee.* Here *part* includes the friend's physical charms and accomplishments, possessed, each in *part* (a bizarre touch, softened by the general currency of the word), by the *brain and heart* of the poet. Until the line enjambs, however, *part* refers back to the 'role' played in *memory* by the *brain* and the *heart*.

8   *missed* found missing, lacked, lost

9   *poor retention* (referring to the notebook. *Retention* is here 'the capacity for retaining things, memory' made concrete; so *Poor* simultaneously characterizes the *retention*, calling it 'beggarly, ignoble' (for who needs a notebook to recall his true love?), and its quality of *retention*, 'frankly inadequate, positively amnesiac'.)

10   *Nor . . . score.* The notebook is scornfully compared to *tallies*, sticks notched (*scored*) with records of debt. Judging from *2 Henry VI* IV.7.31–3, where the rebel Jack Cade speaks strongly in their favour, the 'score and tally' were regarded as basely rustic devices.

11   *Therefore . . . bold* so (that's why) I took the liberty of giving them away

12   *To* so that I might instead
     those tables (of memory. The echo of *thy tables* in line 1 clinches the apology.)
     that receive thee more (1) which contain more of you (see lines 1–2 and 9); (2) which hold you for longer (see lines 3–8). An excellent example of constructive vagueness; the arguments unfolded in lines 1–12 echo in a phrase which itself eludes paraphrase.

13   *adjunct* aid, assistant

14   *Were to import* would imply, would be a sign of. There may be a quibble on 'would introduce', for keeping a notebook might *import*

forgetfulness by encouraging one to write things down instead of remembering them.

forgetfulness poor memory, absent-minded neglect, incivility. As the connotations gather, the sonnet reverts to the question of good conduct. The poet claims that he was right to give away the young man's gift: it would have been discourteous to keep it; it would have shown a lack of respect for the young man.

Sonnet 123

2   *pyramids.* It has been suggested that Shakespeare had particular structures in mind – the Egyptian obelisks set up in Rome during the late 1580s by Pope Sixtus V, certain triumphal monuments erected in 1603 for the coronation of James I – but it seems more likely that the word was used because it suggested, in Jacobean English, a whole range of inspiring contemporary buildings (lofty spires and steeples, pinnacles, conical roofs) without losing its roots in Egyptian antiquity, and thus the past (lines 3–4). (The point is worth emphasizing. When Cleopatra, who ought to know about Egyptian *pyramids*, declares, 'make | My country's high pyramides my gibbet' (V.2.60–61), she is clearly thinking of something steeper than the *pyramids* by the Nile. Dowden's gloss is apt in its grand indefinition: 'all that Time piles up . . . all his new stupendous erections'.)

built up with newer might constructed with new power. The *might* lies in the *pyramids*, with their massy construction; but also in the labour and art which built them.

3   *nothing . . . nothing.* Either substantives or adverbs (meaning 'not at all').

nothing novel, nothing strange. See 59.1–2 and the note.

4   *dressings* reworkings (though, this being Shakespeare, the clothing metaphor, often expressive in his work of deceit and show, is strongly felt)

5   *Our dates* our allotted periods of time, the span of our lives
     admire wonder at, venerate

6   *What thou dost foist upon us that is old* whatever old thing you palm off on us (as *novel* and *strange*)

7   *make them born to our desire* (1) construe them as the product of our own conceptions, imagine them to be invented by us; (2) make them new in wanting them (assuming that because we want them they are as new to the world as new-*born* babies)

8   *think* (1) believe; (2) call to mind, remember
     told (1) talked about; (2) reckoned up

9   *registers* records, chronicles

345

9   *defy* scorn (with a suggestion of challenge, of duelling 'defiance', overweening in the circumstances)

10   *wondering* marvelling (two syllables)

10, 12 *past . . . haste.* For the rhyme see the note to 30.2, 4; the short 'a' in *haste* is underlined in Q by the spelling 'hast'.

11   *For thy records and what we see doth lie* since your chronicles of the past and our experience of the present are both deceptive. *Records*, the *registers* of line 9, is accented on the second syllable. *Doth*, as at 112.1, is used in the plural.

12   *Made more or less by thy continual haste.* Time's hasty and unresting passage prompts us to misjudge everything. The *present* and its works seem more significant than they should, while the *past* and its achievements, diminished by distance, are undervalued; meanwhile, the *present* becomes the past. (The passage is illuminated by *The Winter's Tale* IV.1, where Time celebrates his power to 'make stale | The glistering of this present'.)
        continual (three syllables)

13   *this shall ever be* (as far as I am concerned. Also, residually, 'as long as this line stands'.)

14   *true* honest, faithful to love

Sonnet 124

A sonnet of beautiful complexity, drawing many of its images and concerns from 116. *Love* is here, however, lived and inward, its monumental status resting on groundedness. In this last group of poems to the youth – beginning perhaps with the sestet of 119 (see the note to 119.11–12) – writing yields in strength to emotion, verbs of making are given over (so that *render*, for instance, is, after *no art* in 125.11–12, *Nature*'s at 126.12), and sonneteering becomes less sufficient (its form indeed breaking down with 126).

1   *dear love* deeply felt affection (though 'dear beloved' is kept in play until *It* in line 2)
        but the child of state only the produce of circumstance. There may be a glance at the state of the young man, his 'high rank' and 'wealthy grandeur' (the connexion between this sonnet and the next; see the headnote to 125): the poet says his love is not the mere product of deference and social climbing. In so far as *state* registers in that way, *dear love* retains its secondary implication (the friend is not 'just an aristocrat's son', but someone special to the poet).

2   *for* as
        be unfathered be disowned by its apparent father (the friend)

2, 4   *unfathered . . . gathered.* The feminine rhyme was almost certainly

346

exact, and probably relied on long 'a' (sounding like the vowel in southern English 'bat', 'bad', lengthened).

3   *As* since, because
subject to Time's love, or to Time's hate. If the poet's *love* was *the child of state* it would be governed by *Fortune* and her fellow, *Time*, shifty controllers of the *state* of things

4   *Weeds . . . gathered.* The mature style at its best, in verse as resistant to paraphrase as it is near perfection. If the poet's *love were . . . the child of state*, it would lack fine singularity; it would be dispersed, plural, transient, like *weeds* and *flowers* in the fields. And as the scattered feelings grew, they would adapt to their situation, becoming *Weeds among weeds* if *Time's hate* thrust *love* among the ugly and idle, or *flowers with flowers* if *Time's love* agreed. Such feelings could – indeed would – be *gathered* as easily as *weeds* and *flowers*, e.g., taken down in swathes by a labourer, because in losing its constancy the poet's *love* would become mortal, as *subject* to Time's scythe as any commonplace affection. *Flowers* is monosyllabic after *or*, disyllabic after *with*.

5   *accident* the working of chance, chance's influence. *Accident* derives from the Latin intransitive verb *accidere*, 'to befall, happen'; but in the context of lines 4, 7, and 8, the transitive sense of *accidere*, 'to cut short, ruin' also makes itself felt.

6   *suffers not* does not deteriorate
in smiling pomp (1) when surrounded by the favours of the great; (2) when clad in cheerful finery

6–7   *nor falls . . . discontent.* If this is read in parallel with *suffers not in smiling pomp* (if *the blow* is struck), 'nor does it succumb when assaulted in some way by the discontented lowly' and 'nor does it succumb when thrust injuriously into the kind of servitude which usually prompts discontent' register. But if *falls | Under* is interpreted as 'comes beneath', the sense moves on, through the notion that the poet's *love* is too considerable to be attacked by base malcontents or subjected to weary servitude, to something which runs easily into line 8: 'nor is it ever afflicted with obsessive melancholy (*discontent* held in thrall)'.

8   *Whereto th'inviting time our fashion calls* towards which the seductive present day beckons *our fashion* ('our behaviours, our *mores*' or 'men of our ilk, men like us'). Melancholy *discontent* was in vogue during the late 1590s and early 1600s; Shakespeare anatomizes it in his characterization of Jaques in *As You Like It*.

9   *Policy, that heretic* Policy (expediency and canny scheming personified), that unprincipled and faithless fellow. In line 11, the prudence of *Policy* is invoked; here (as at 118.9) its pragmatism.

10   *works on leases of short-numbered hours* only enters into and operates according to short-term commitments

11   *all alone stands hugely politic* stands, massively provident (also 'gigan-
      tic in prudence'), in solitary (unique and self-sufficient) splendour.
      There is at least a suggestion in *all alone* that the poet's *love* is, rightly
      considered, the only prudent thing there is.

12   *That* (1) in that; (2) so that
      nor... nor neither... nor
      nor grows with heat, nor drowns with showers. A fleeting hint of *weeds*
      and *flowers*, subjected to *Time's* changing favour.

13   *To this I witness call* I call as witness to support my claim. The poet
      argues his case in a metaphorical court of law; compare the couplet
      of the next sonnet.
      the fools of Time those who follow *Time* as professional *fools* their
      masters (prostituted to every whimsical beck and call), those who do
      as the times require, the timeservers. Hence 'Time's laughing-
      stocks, those who are gulled by Time (whose power they could
      escape in true *love*)'; and hence the echo of 116.9.

14   *Which die for goodness, who have lived for crime.* The *fools of Time* only
      espouse *goodness* when circumstances make it politic; after living
      lives of immoral pragmatism they repent on their deathbeds in the
      hope of getting to heaven; or they die as martyrs after committing
      criminal, perhaps terrorist, acts; or they denounce their own crimes
      before dying, possibly on the scaffold. Various attempts have been
      made to identify *the fools of Time* on the basis of this last line. The
      Marian martyrs and Elizabethan Jesuits (suggestions apparently
      prompted by the appearance of *heretic* in line 9), Essex and his rebels,
      Guy Fawkes and his fellow conspirators, Christopher Marlowe,
      George Peele, and Thomas Nashe – they have all been invoked. But,
      while some of these suggestions can be dismissed, and while the
      Gunpowder Conspirators have the advantage of a likely date (1605,
      executed 1606), no certainty is possible since the grandeur of the
      phrase depends on scornful generality. (Indeed the more delimited
      the reference, the less functional it becomes in a poem about
      uncalculating *love*.)

Sonnet 125

The poet responds to the criticism of an onlooker (perhaps one of those
described in Sonnet 121), who has apparently suggested that his *love* is just
the child of state (124.1), by insisting that he recognizes the vanity of pomp and
circumstance and has been impressed in the past by the folly of those
seduced by appearances.

1   *Were't aught to me* would it matter to me, would there be any
      advantage to me

I bore the canopy. It is not quite clear whether the *canopy* is literal (a 'lavishly embroidered awning borne over the head of a processing dignitary'), metonymical ('pomp, supported by servitude and acclaim'), or metaphorical ('praising poetry', for example). Nor is *bore* unambiguous in tense and mood. Perhaps the poet is saying that, although he once carried the *canopy*, the privilege means nothing to him (supplying the ellipsis before *I bore* with 'that'); but it seems more likely that he is insisting that he is so wary of display that even the privilege of carrying the *canopy* would mean nothing to him if it came his way (reading 'if' before *I bore*).

2 *With my extern the outward honouring* doing honour to the public aspect of someone through my appearance and actions

3 *Or laid great bases for eternity*. The *great bases* seem to be 'massy foundations' *laid* for some monumental structure designed to last 'forever' (or, as *for eternity* insinuates, 'for eternity to rest on, to support eternity'). But literal building work (though hypothetical, and so imagined) need not be implied, as it is at 123.1–4; the poet may have in mind some act of valour winning public renown, or some literary triumph such as the Sonnets themselves (see the headnote to 124). Line 3 is unsettled, like line 1, by its verb, ambiguous in both tense and mood.

4 *Which . . . ruining* which *bases* prove shorter-lived than the forces of decay or destruction. (Although '-s' forms of the plural are common in Jacobean English, some editors prefer to interpret *proves* as a singular, making eternity the antecedent of *Which*.) The implications of *waste* are picked up in the second quatrain.

5 *dwellers on* people who linger over. The dwellers become 'tenants, inhabitants' when line 6 introduces *rent*.

   form and favour (1) courtly formality and status; (2) figure and face

6 *Lose all and more* run through their wealth and into debt. The *waste* is, of course, metaphorical; see the next note. *All and more* is based on idioms like 'all and whole', 'all and some' (both meaning 'absolutely all').

   paying too much rent (in obsequious fascination)

6–7 *Lose all . . . savour*. Q has no punctuation at the end of line 6 and a semi-colon after *sweet*. The present text restores the antithesis to line 7, but by punctuating logically it suppresses the fleeting but fruitful impression that the *rent* was paid *For compound sweet* (which in a sense it was).

7 *compound sweet . . . simple savour* saccharine sophistication . . . wholesome plainness. Extraordinarily complex since all four terms can be read as adjectival or substantive (forcing *savour* into a new area of expression), since *sweet* and *savour* suggest both taste and smell, and since the whole line is modified by the pharmaceutical suggestions of

> *compound* and *sweet* (see the second note to 76.4 and compare 118.2 and *A Lover's Complaint* 259).

8   *Pitiful* wretched, pathetic, contemptible
    thrivers people of enterprise, prosperous folk
    in their gazing spent used up by looking on. With a glance at financial profligacy; the *thrivers*, obsessed with advancement, squander themselves by dwelling in *form and favour*.

9   *obsequious* (three syllables)
    in thy heart (rather than at court)

10 *oblation* offering (especially to God. Indeed, the context of *compound sweet ... simple savour* suggests an echo of Leviticus 1.13: 'an oblation made by fire for a sweet savour unto the Lord.')
    poor but free humble but freely given

11 *not mixed with seconds* free of inferior matter, unadulterated. We still call damaged or inferior goods *seconds*. Conceivably the poet is also implying that the friend has no rival, that love is going to no 'other' or 'others' (*seconds* in an extended sense).

11–12 *knows no art | But mutual render*. Untouched by the low craft of those who adulterate wares in order to rook the public, and innocent of the high artifice of those who use a courtly manner to thrive, the poet's unsophisticated *oblation* comprehends only honest straightforward exchanging. Some editors preserve Q's comma after *art*, interpreting *But* as 'but is rather'.

13 *suborned informer*. See the headnote. The *informer* has been 'procured to bear false witness' – the poet angrily suggests – and very probably 'bribed'.

14 *impeached* accused
    control power. For the suggestion of financial accounting (relevant to lines 5–8) see 58.2 and the note.

Sonnet 126

The formal peculiarities of this poem (twelve pentameters rhymed in couplets), added to its concentration on the sequence's dominant themes up to 125 (love, mortal beauty, treasure, finance and its growth, Time), tend to support its placing in Q – as an envoy to the series of sonnets addressed to the friend. The failure of the poem to be a sonnet (see the headnote to Sonnet 124) is emphasized in Thorpe's text by two sets of brackets, indented after line 12, where a final couplet might have been. Conceivably authorial, but more likely added by a scribe or someone connected with the script's publishing or printing, these brackets are excluded from the present edition, not without regret, as accidentals. What they usefully point up in Q is a sense of poetic shortfall, as though the recoiling, inconclusive quality of earlier sonnet couplets (see the Introduction, page 46) had been concentrated in a single poem, consisting entirely of such rhymed endings, which 'rounded off' the sub-sequence (was a couplet conclusion to the meta-poem) without solving by aesthetic means the problems it addressed. On this insufficiency, and for signs of congruence with Sonnets 153–4, see the Introduction, pages 61–3; for a distant source, or intriguing cluster of verbal analogues, see *A Lover's Complaint* 59–60 and the note.

1   *lovely* beautiful, inviting love

1–2   *in thy . . . hour.* The *lovely boy* controls the flow of time through Time's treacherously-sifting hourglass (compare *The Winter's Tale* IV.1.16, where Time, speaking as Chorus, turns his *glass*), and he determines the *hour* when Time will reap life into death (alluding to the traditional iconography of Time, that gaunt figure holding an hourglass in one hand and a scythe in the other). Some editors preserve Q's comma after *sickle*, granting Time three adjuncts (though not, apparently, three hands): an uncanonical looking-*glass* (which shows how *fickle* beauty is, like the *glass* in Sonnet 77), the *sickle* which should be a scythe, and an hourglass rudely truncated (apparently without precedent in Elizabethan and Jacobean English) to *hour*.

3   *Who hast by waning grown.* Extraordinarily suggestive. *Thy lovers withering* in line 4 makes 'who has grown more beautiful in ageing' primary, but much more seems implied. The life of the phrase stems partly from wordplay (*grown* means 'grown older, aged' as well as 'somehow increased, grown more impressive'), and partly from the suggestion (made by *sickle* and *waning*) that the friend renews like the moon. See *grow'st*, line 4, and the note.

       show'st. The friend 'reveals' that the *lovers* are *withering* by 'showing them up'.

4   *thy lovers withering.* Some editors add a possessive apostrophe, reading 'lovers''', but *withering* (both 'shrivelling up' and, in an anticipation of line 7, 'departing') seems too strong to be a property of the *lovers*: it happens to them and they do it; they have no control. (A crude gloss would be 'thy lovers who are withering'.) The argument for 'lover's' is weakened by *my* in line 1 (making a third-person self-account less likely), by the fruitfully double opposition between self and other, single and plural in the text as printed, and by the plurality, elsewhere in the sequence, of the friend's *lovers*.

       self. At once the mundane *self* – taking *thy sweet self* to be 'thyself' (or, as Q would space it, 'thy selfe') with *sweet* inserting itself (as a tribute which, as it were, cries out to be made) – and the essential stuff of selfhood, postulated.

       grow'st. Though the full range of significance registered in *grown* operates here, growing old seems dominant, and a flicker of word-play is consequently felt between lines 3 and 4. This underlines the paradox that the friend grows in growing old, grows somehow more impressive as his lovers wither.

5   *wrack* ruin, decay

6   *As thou goest onwards* (on a journey through life towards death)
     still always (which the sonnet gradually subdues to 'continually')

7   *keeps* holds on to, maintains (as her *minion*), guards, detains
     to for

8   *disgrace* discredit, rob of honour
     wretched minutes kill. Nature's victory is so complete that she obliter-ates even the smallest, most beggarly units of time ('seconds' were not in general use in a temporal sense, *pace* Booth, until the mid-seventeenth century).

9   *Yet* (1) nevertheless; (2) still, even now
     minion (1) darling; (2) lowly servant, slave

10   *She may detain, but not still keep her treasure* (preserving Q's expressive single comma, though strict logic would require a second mark after *keep* or no punctuation at all)

11   *audit* final account, reckoning. It was commonplace, proverbial that 'To pay one's debt to nature' was to die.
     answered made good by payment. The books must be balanced by sacrifice of the friend to death.

12   *her quietus is to render thee* she is discharged from her responsibilities when she relinquishes you. A *quietus* is a quittance given when accounts are cleared by due payment ('*quietus est*' used to be written on receipts). *Render* also has mercantile associations (touched on at 125.12), for accounts were settled by 'rendering' (settling by an exchange); hence *Much Ado About Nothing* IV.1.328, 'Claudio shall render me a dear account.' On a hinted, distant 'fix as by depiction', art deferring at the last to *Nature*, see the headnote to Sonnet 124.

General Note to Sonnets 127–54

With Sonnet 127 our attention switches from the *lovely boy* to a dark-favoured mistress, generally assumed to be the woman whose betrayal of the poet with the friend is first discussed in Sonnets 40–42. Much has been made of the lady's darkness, and rightly; but it is not without precedent. Indeed, Shakespeare seems to be developing traits visible in Sidney's Stella when he gives the mistress black hair and eyes. 127.10 and 132.3 clearly echo the seventh sonnet of Sidney's sequence:

When Nature made her chief work, Stella's eyes,
In colour black, why wrapped she beams so bright?
Would she in beamy black, like painter wise,
Frame daintiest lustre, mixed of shades and light?
Or did she else that sober hue devise,
In object best to knit and strength our sight,
Lest if no veil those brave gleams did disguise,
They sun-like should more dazzle than delight?
Or would she her miraculous power show.
That whereas black seems Beauty's contrary,
She even in black doth make all beauties flow?
Both so and thus, she minding Love should be
    Placed ever there, gave him this mourning weed,
    To honour all their deaths who for her bleed.

If literary convention played its part in the characterization of the poet's mistress, that does not mean that there never was a dark lady, or someone like her, in Shakespeare's life. Who might have acted as model for the mistress of the sequence is, however, impossible to say on present information. For a sane and amusing survey of the many candidates, or nigrates, offered, see Samuel Schoenbaum's 'Shakespeare's Dark Lady: a question of identity' in *Shakespeare's Styles: Essays in honour of Kenneth Muir*, edited by Philip Edwards, Inga-Stina Ewbank, and G. K. Hunter (Cambridge, 1980), pages 220–39.

Sonnet 127

1–2   *In the old age ... name* in the olden days darkness was not considered beautiful (with a play on 'light in colour'), or, if it were, it was not called so. On a possible significance of the contrast between *the old age* and *now* (line 3), see the Introduction, pages 58–9.

3–4   *now is ... shame* nowadays darkness, considered the legitimate heir of Beauty, is granted *beauty's name* (and the respect which goes along with that), while *beauty* (whatever is *fair*), regarded as Beauty's illegitimate offspring, loses (as bastards might in Elizabethan England) the name of its parent

5   *since* (1) ever since; (2) in as much as
      each hand hath put on nature's power everybody has usurped powers rightly nature's. And every *hand* has *put* cosmetics *on* its complexion, changing what only nature should change.
      power (one syllable)

6   *Fairing ... face* making ugliness fair with a deceiving mask of cosmetics

7   *Sweet beauty hath no name* (and thus no repute or pride of lineage).

353

Compare the plight of Coriolanus after leaving Rome: he 'forbade all names; | He was a kind of nothing, titleless, | Till he had forged himself a name i'th'fire | Of burning Rome' (V.1.12–15). *But is profaned* adds, however, another possibility: that *beauty* is *slandered* by the blasphemous misuse of her titles, all sorts of painted faces being called *fair*.

no holy bower no sacred abode. As the preserve of a principle, Beauty, the *bower* is not localized, unless, that is, the Q comma is read across and *But is profaned* involved. Then the abstract *bower* is violated (roughly by the vile use of cosmetics), and in the process an idea resembling *Love's Labour's Lost* IV.3.256–63 (and consider the Introduction, page 25) emerges: *Sweet beauty* can dwell in no *fair* face without being blasphemously maligned, because every *beauty* is suspected of painting.

8   *But is profaned.* To the interpretations offered above (in the last two notes) another must be added: Sweet beauty, wherever it lives, is *profaned* by those who, wishing to be modish, paint. Even the beautiful use cosmetics, violating beauty's *bower* with greasy pigments.

if not (1) or even; (2) or else

lives in disgrace lives in disrepute, suffers dishonour. *Bower* makes *disgrace* seem a kind of allegorical dwelling by invoking 'resides at, inhabits' from *lives in*. And if the *bower* is a 'naturally lovely face' sometimes abused with painting (see the previous note), *disgrace* would be the kind of cosmetic disfigurement behind which such a face would shelter out of obedience to the fashion of the times (a *fair* face behind a *fair* but *false borrowed face*).

9   *Therefore* and that's the reason why. The poet persuades himself (or claims to) that his mistress had some choice in the matter.

raven black. 'As black as a raven' was proverbial.

10   *Her brows so suited* and for the same reason her forehead is clad in *black* (referring to dark eyebrows). *Suited* suggests 'matched (with the eyes)' as well as 'clothed'. See the General Note above.

11   *At such ... lack* on account of those who, naturally plain, look beautiful (because they use cosmetics)

12   *Sland'ring ... esteem* (1) slandering *creation* by making real *beauty* indistinguishable from *false* (causing the truly *fair* to be abused); (2) slandering *creation* by seeming to do what only nature does (so that people think *nature* no more impressive than a box of cosmetics); (3) slandering *creation* by giving people the wrong idea of what *beauty* is (making them prefer *art* to *nature*). Other levels of sense can be dimly discerned. *Creation* seems to divide between 'nature's working' and 'all Nature's Works' (it may be significant that Thorpe's Quarto gives the word a capital letter).

13–14   *Yet so . . . That* but they mourn in such a way, their woe gracing them, that. Some editors drop Q's comma after *mourn* to heighten the influence of *so* over *becoming*.

14   *look so* have such colouring (and so 'look like my mistress'. With perhaps a hint of 'have that expression, seem to be in mourning for its betrayal'.)

Sonnet 128

Apparently the ingenious elaboration of a conceit so well-worn by the end of the 1590s that Jonson mocked it in *Every Man Out of His Humour* (1599), making the 'Neat, spruce, affecting Courtier' Fastidious Brisk say of his mistress Saviolina, as she plays the viola da gamba: 'You see the subject of her sweet fingers, there? . . . Oh, she tickles it so, that . . . she makes it laugh most divinely . . . I'll tell you a good jest now, and yourself shall say it's a good one: I have wished myself to be that instrument, I think, a thousand times, and not so few, by heaven' (III.9.101–6). Shakespeare approaches lines 3–6 in a more serious context at *Titus Andronicus* II.4.44–7: 'O, had the monster seen those lily hands | Tremble like aspen leaves upon a lute | And made the silken strings delight to kiss them, | He would not have touched them for his life!' For a variant text, probably recording authoritative early readings, see pages 442 and 446 below.

1   *my music.* Compare 8.1, where the young man is *Music to hear.*

2   *that blessèd wood.* The wooden keys of the virginals, graced by her touch.
      whose motion the movement of which, which by being moved
      sounds. Both transitive (with *The wiry concord* as object) and intransitive.

3   *With* (1) through the action of; (2) in concord with
      sway'st. Like *sounds*, both transitive (the object, again, *The wiry concord*, which is 'ruled' and 'set in undulating motion' by the lady) and intransitive (the poet, pretending to listen to the music, is enthralled by the movements of the player's body).

4   *wiry concord* harmony of strings (aptly suggesting the sinewy twanging which characterizes the virginals)
      mine ear confounds amazes my ear (with delight)

5   *envy* (accented on the second syllable)

5–6   *those jacks . . . hand.* Though it is sometimes suggested that Shakespeare here depicts the dark lady cupping her hand over the striking mechanism of her instrument as she tunes it, the probability is that he uses *jacks* in Q – strictly, the vertical extensions of keys designed to carry plucking quills to the strings when the keys are pressed by a player – to refer to the whole key mechanism, so that he can make the keys 'common fellows' (compare *Richard III* I.3.71–2, 'Since every Jack became a gentleman | There's many a gentle person made a Jack') allowed to kiss the lady's *hand* to the poet's chagrin. For early readers, *nimble* presumably clinched this quibbling personification; certainly, the expression 'nimble jack', meaning 'sprightly rascal', was current in the second half of the seventeenth century. The poet's envy of what the manuscript calls 'kies' is perfectly understandable: Elizabethans and Jacobeans regarded the *tender inward* of the *hand* (whether the palm or the soft underside of the fingers) as highly erogenous. Hence Leontes' objections when Polixenes takes his wife's hand: 'But to be paddling palms and pinching fingers, | As now they are ... Still virginalling [significant verb] | Upon his palm?' (*The Winter's Tale* I.2.115–16, 125–6).

8   *by* beside

blushing. The poet's *lips* (like the rest of him, though all he can think of when he sees the keys' good fortune is *lips*) flush with *envy* and desire.

stand. The lips do not quite have feet; but as the poet *stand*s by the lady, they represent what he is to him.

9–10   *state | And situation* nature and position

10   *dancing chips* (of wood. The keys that leap in time *With thy sweet fingers.*)

11   *gentle* soft, delicate, well-bred. (It was, after all, a *gentle* accomplishment to play the virginals.)

13   *saucy jacks* impertinent *chips*, shameless rascals. *Jacks* were at least as proverbially *saucy* as they were *nimble*; see *Henry V* IV.7.136–9, 'If he be perjured, see you now, his reputation is as arrant a villain and a Jack-sauce as ever his black shoe trod upon God's ground and His earth, in my conscience, la!'

happy blessed, fortunate, and contented

Sonnet 129

Of the 154 sonnets in Q, only 94 compares with this in impersonal profundity, in its illumination of the sequence by means of indirect because general statement. While 94 moves steadily, however, undercutting itself by the recoil of one clause or line upon another, 129 is rapid, almost frenetic, in its pursuit of lust, satiety, and despair. Q sustains this pace by punctuating lightly: apart from a full stop after octave and sestet, it uses commas throughout, and sparingly. Though Q's punctuation cannot always be trusted, and though it should never be judged conclusively authorial (see the Account of the Text, pages 429–31), it has seemed appropriate here to preserve the spirit of Q's light pointing. For a series of intelligent accounts –

some directly concerned with Q's punctuation, and its merits – see Further Reading, pages 68 (Graves and Riding), 69 (Redpath), and 71.

1–2   *Th'expense... action* lust is satisfied by a lavishing of vital energy in an orgy of shameful extravagance, lust is satisfied by the dissipation of the spirit in a gross wasteland of guilt. *Shame* enriches this by suggesting not just *shame*ful *waste* and the 'guilt' attendant on *lust* but the 'chaste modesty' lost and violated by its *action* (compare *A Midsummer Night's Dream* III.2.285, 'Have you no modesty, no maiden shame', *Measure for Measure* II.4.101–4, 'Th'impression of keen whips I'd wear as rubies, ... ere I'd yield | My body up to shame', and the complex of senses released by the repetition of *shame* at *A Lover's Complaint* 187). Moreover, the language is so sexually suggestive that a further level of sense is exposed as the abstracts concrete: 'lust achieving intercourse is the emission of semen (or "the ejaculation of the penis") into a shameful waist'. *Till action* later in line 2 does much to effect this ambiguity, since the repetition of *action* shifts the word (with hindsight) into the bawdy sense used at *Pericles* IV.2.8–9: '[the whores] with continual action are even as good as rotten'. *Spirit* as 'generative spirit' and so 'sperm' was commonplace, and the phallic connotations of the word can be gauged from Mercutio's lines at *Romeo and Juliet* II.1.23–7:

> This cannot anger him. 'Twould anger him
> To raise a spirit in his mistress' circle
> Of some strange nature, letting it there stand
> Till she had laid it and conjured it down.
> That were some spite.

As for *waste* as 'waist', the pun is apparent if *Hamlet* I.2.198, 'In the dead waste and middle of the night', is set alongside the sonnet.

3   *perjured, murd'rous, bloody* (lying, killing and maiming its way to satisfaction)
       full of blame utterly culpable (yet 'quick to recriminate')

4   *Savage* wild (both 'unrestrained' and 'uncivil, half bestial')
       extreme (and therefore violent, but see the note to line 10)
       rude brutal
       cruel (two syllables)
       not to trust not to be trusted

5   *Enjoyed no sooner but despisèd straight* despised as soon as *enjoyed* (a word which ironically declines from 'pleasurably indulged' to flatly 'exercised' as *despisèd* registers. *But* wrenches the line towards regret more violently than the expected *than* could.)

6   *Past reason hunted* unreasonably (illogically and intemperately) sought. From here to line 8, and in lines 10–12, the enjoyment of *lust*

357

is central, not *lust* itself; or, allowing Shakespeare a characteristically composite subject, *lust in action* starts to display its active, instead of its craving, aspect.

had (carrying, as in modern English, in such a context, sexual implications)

7   *Past reason hated.* Suggesting insanity (compare *mad*, line 8) rather than, as in line 6, merely unreasonable conduct.

7–8   *a swallowed ... mad.* Two passages in the plays are illuminating: *Macbeth* I.3.83–4, where Banquo asks the protagonist 'have we eaten on the insane root | That takes the reason prisoner?', and *Measure for Measure* I.2.127–9, where Claudio explains to Lucio his lapse into mild sexual irregularity: 'Our natures do pursue, | Like rats that ravin down their proper bane, | A thirsty evil, and when we drink we die.' In the sonnet *On purpose* suggests both intent (in which case, whose?) and 'on top of *purpose*, as a burden on volition', and Claudio's 'proper' (meaning 'own, self-created') indicates the source of that intent upon intent.

10   *in quest to have, extreme.* Q's 'in quest, to haue extreame' has been famously defended by Robert Graves and Laura Riding (see Further Reading, page 68), but, while it points up a secondary identification of *lust in action* with the desire to possess (an) *extreme*, to capture an extremity of passion (the *bliss* of line 11, but also the *woe*), it involves an ellipsis so pronounced that, in a modernized edition, it must give way to the text as printed.

11   *in proof* when tested, being experienced, *in action*
        proved once tested
        a very woe a veritable sorrow, a complete calamity

12   *Before ... behind* in prospect ... in retrospect
        proposed promised, anticipated
        a dream (and therefore insubstantial, transient, and deceptive. Compare *The Rape of Lucrece* 211–12, where Tarquin anticipates the fruits of *lust in action*: 'What win I if I gain the thing I seek? | A dream, a breath, a froth of fleeting joy.')

13–14   *All this ... To* everybody knows this perfectly well, but nobody is wise enough to

14   *heaven* (of *bliss*. By extension, however, *heaven* refers to 'woman' in general, as a sex, and so, contextually (rather as 94 refers to the friend), to the particular woman discussed in Sonnets 127–8 and 133–44. One syllable.)
        hell (of guilt and misery. The slang sense 'pudendum', evidently working at 144.12, does not seem relevant here, despite the erotic implication of *heaven*.)

358

Sonnet 130

The poet mocks the stock comparisons of Elizabethan love poetry, and flouts the reader's expectation that the blazon of a mistress will involve hyperbolic praise. Compare Sonnet 21 and see the Introduction, pages 22–5. Ironically, some of the metaphors satirized in Sonnet 130 are used of the young man in earlier poems.

1   *My mistress' eyes are nothing like the sun.* Compare Daniel's *Delia* 31.7 (1601 edition), 'thine eye's bright sun', and, of course, Shakespeare's Sonnet 49, *And scarcely greet me with that sun, thine eye* (line 6). It may be significant that 132.5–6 gives every appearance of comparing the dark lady's *eyes* to the *sun*.
     nothing not at all

2   *Coral . . . lips' red.* Compare Linche's *Diella* 31.2, 'sweet lips of coral hue but silken softness'; Watson's long sonnet, quoted on pages 19–20, at line 11, 'Her lips more red than any coral stone'; and the 'sweet coral mouth' and 'coral lips' of *Venus and Adonis* 542 and *The Rape of Lucrece* 420.

3   *If snow . . . dun.* 'As white as snow' was proverbial, the snowiness of skin a commonplace.

4   *If hairs . . . head.* The conventional *mistress* of Elizabethan love poetry had blond tresses (see the General Note, pages 352–3), frequently compared to *wires* or drawn gold, the kind of precious thread used in fine embroidered cloth. (See, for example, Spenser's *Amoretti* 15.11, 'her locks are finest gold on ground', and *The Ruines of Time* 10, 'yeolow locks, like wyrie gold', page 390 below, or Watson, page 19 above, line 2.) Line 4 is more subtly witty than 1–3 in that, instead of rejecting a cliché outright, it accepts it only to expose its absurdity by invoking the *mistress*'s dark beauty.

5–6 *I have . . . cheeks.* Though the young man's cheeks resembled the damask rose, mingling *red* with *white* (see 99.10). It has been plausibly suggested that Shakespeare here exploits a confusion in the history of the word 'damask' which makes it refer not only to *roses* (and swords) but soft silken cloth – an apt comparison for a woman's cheeks. For the convention used more slackly see, as Ingram and Redpath note, Barnes's *Parthenophil and Parthenophe* Ode 16, 'Her cheeks to damask roses sweet | In scent and colour were so like, | That honey bees in swarms would meet | To suck!'

7–8 *And in some . . . reeks.* Compare Linche's *Diella* 31.4, 'Sweet breath that breaths incomparable sweetness!', and 48.6 with 29.8 of the 1594 and 1619 editions of Drayton's *Idea*: 'The sweet of Eden [is like] to her breath's perfume', 'My smelling won with her breath's spicery'. If lines 5–6 echo 99.10, 7–8 seem close to 99.11.

8   *reeks.* The modern connotations are distracting; *reeks* was more
        neutral than offensive for early readers, close to 'emanates' or
        'exhales'. (Compare, for instance, *Love's Labour's Lost* IV.3.137–8, 'I
        heard your guilty rhymes, observed your fashion, | Saw sighs reek
        from you, noted well your passion.') The recent *O-Scz Supplement* of
        the *Oxford English Dictionary* confirms that, in the sense 'To emit an
        unwholesome or disagreeable vapour', the verb is unrecorded be-
        fore Swift.

9–10   *I love ... sound.* Compare Sidney's *Astrophil and Stella* 100.11,
        'While sobbed out words a perfect music give', Watson, page 19
        above, line 5, or, indeed, 8.1 in Shakespeare's sequence.

11   *I grant I never saw a goddess go.* Compare Daniel's *Delia* 5.3 (1592
        edition), 'a Goddess chaste', or Spenser's *Amoretti* 22.13, '[my heart]
        vouchsafe O goddesse to accept'. Sonnet 105 and 110.12 are also
        relevant.

12   *treads on the ground* (like other mortals)

13   *heaven* (one syllable)
        rare. Though the dominant sense is clearly 'extraordinary, precious',
        that depends – see the Introduction, pages 24–5 – on the particu-
        larity and individuality denoted by *rare* in the period (compare 21.7
        and 52.5).

14   *false* erroneous, deceitful, artificial, artful

Sonnet 131

1   *tyrannous* domineeringly pitiless
        so as thou art just as you are (in 130 and earlier poems, dark, *black*, not
        even *fair*)

2   *proudly make them cruel.* The prose order would be 'make them
        proudly cruel', but the poet reorders the line to personify *beauties* (so
        that *those* cannot claim entire possession of a loveliness which,
        dishonourably provoking them to scorn, is incidental, not finally of
        them).

2, 4   *cruel ... jewel* (two syllables, or tending to that, with a feminine
        rhyme)

3   *dear.* Adjective, adverb, or both; 'tender(ly)', 'earnest(ly)', or both;
        and, in its adverbial aspect, 'costly' (the *doting* taking its toll on the
        heart); see, moreover, *precious*, line 4 and the note.
        doting adoring, loving to distraction. As at 20.10, the word carries a
        suggestion of besotted idiocy and raving.

4   *fairest* (though *black*. Quibbling, as often, on fairness of colour and
        fairness as beauty.)
        precious (retrospectively igniting 'valuable' in *dear*, offered so mod-

estly that the only suggestion of cost lay in what was offered the mistress in *doting*)

5 *in good faith* (1) verily (as an interjection); (2) speaking in good faith, believing what one says to be true (modifying *say*)

6 *love* (in the form of a lover)

7 *say*. Repetition creates, as almost invariably, a quibbling modification of meaning: *say* as in line 5, but *say* also as 'speak out, declare in public'.

8 *alone* in private (and, perhaps damagingly, 'not to anyone else')

9 *And to be sure that is not false I swear* (1) and in order to be sure that what I swear is true; (2) and, certainly, that which I swear is true. Although the latter sharply disrupts the movement of the sestet, it is undoubtedly felt through the parallel with *in good faith* (sense 2); indeed, some editors (including Benson in 1640) make it primary by punctuating strongly after *swear*.

10 *but thinking on* just thinking about. It seems inconceivable that the *groans* might be *thinking*, until each sigh is given a *neck* in line 11.

11 *One on another's neck.* Not piled up but in quick succession, jostling. That 'One misfortune comes on the neck of another' was proverbial.

12 *Thy black is fairest* (making explicit the paradox assumed at line 4, but with the extra twist that *Thy black* means both 'your blackness' and 'the particular kind of excellent blackness which is yours')
    in my judgement's place in my consideration, to my mind. Thinking of the mind as a courtroom, a place in which one might *swear*, *witness*, and make a *judgement*. Perhaps also 'in the ranking which my *judgement* reaches'.

13 *nothing* no particular, no way
    black (in the sense 'ugly, foul, immoral')

14 *this slander* (the one reported in line 6)
    as I think I presume

Sonnet 132

Despite the idiom 'to say black is *x*'s eye', meaning 'to find fault with', the poet praises his mistress's dark *eyes*, which are *nothing like the sun*. In so doing, he follows the example of Sidney, an author echoed in line 3 (see the note).

1 *as* as if
   pitying (two syllables)

2 *Knowing thy heart torment me with disdain.* An elliptical parenthesis ('knowing that your heart torments me with disdain'), modifying *Thine eyes*.

3 *Have put on black, and loving mourners be.* Compare 127.10, where the

361

eyebrows are mourners clad in black, and the likely source of both images, quoted in the General Note, pages 352-3.

4   *ruth* pity

5   *morning sun* (with a quibble on 'mourning', aided by *sun* recalling the *eyes* of 130 which are, here, in line 3, *mourners*)

5, 7   *heaven . . . even.* On the rhyme, and Q's 'Eauen', see the note to 28.10, 12.

6   *Better becomes* is more becoming to, looks better in
     the grey cheeks of the east (clouds lit by the dawn sun. Compare *Romeo and Juliet* III.5.19-20: 'I'll say yon grey is not the morning's eye; | 'Tis but the pale reflex of Cynthia's brow'.)

6, 8   *east . . . west.* That *east* could sound 'est' in the period presumably explains the rhyme.

7   *that full star . . . even* Hesperus, the evening star
     full intense, bright

8   *sober* sombre, calm

10   *as well* (1) also; (2) as appropriately
     beseem become, look well in. Once common, the word was rare by the 1590s, and obsolete in the seventeenth century. (Its use elsewhere in Shakespeare is restricted to a few instances in the early plays.) Even if the sonnet was circulated in manuscript before 1609, its first readers will have found the word archaic, 'poetic' in resonance.

11   *To mourn . . . grace.* Persuasion stems from a quibble in *mourn for*, both 'sorrow for' and 'wear mourning for', the seemliness of the latter encouraging the former. Compare 127.13 on the grace of *mourning*.

12   *suit . . . like* (1) clothe in the same way; (2) make alike, make consistent
     in every part (in the *heart* as well as the *eyes*)

14   *And all they foul* and that all those are foul who
     complexion. 'Disposition' as well as 'skin colouring' and 'complexion' in the modern sense; an important quibble.

Sonnet 133

On the triangular situation described here, and in some later sonnets, see the Introduction, pages 7, 10, 17, 55, and 59-60.

1   *Beshrew* fie upon

2   *For* because of
     deep wound grave injury

3   *alone* only

4   *slave to slavery* utterly enslaved, enslaved by a slavish devotion (drawing on the love-as-slavery topos raised in Sonnets 57-8,

though more conventionally in that the enslaver is here the mistress. It has been suggested that *slavery* might mean 'one who is a slave, someone base', in the way 'antiquity' can mean 'old man'; this would add the sense 'enslaved by a worthless creature', consonant with what the poet says about the dark lady elsewhere, though the reading seems forced in this context.)

5   *cruel* (two syllables)

6   *my next self* (the friend. On the basis of the image, and its currency elsewhere in Q, see 39.2 and the note.)
     harder with greater firmness, more cruelly
     engrossed. In its two dominant senses, the word cuts opposite ways: while the friend is *engrossed* in being 'fascinated, absorbed, obsessed', he is 'bought up in gross, taken into possession' by the lady; his passion is outward-going, hers is mercantile and selfish. At the same time, *engrossed* suggests 'made gross, degraded', not a common usage in the period, but strongly felt here in the debasement of the friend by his passion.

6, 8 *engrossed . . . crossed.* Possibly rhymed on long 'o' (sounding like the vowel in Scottish English 'wart', 'ward'), but, equally, a rhyme on short 'o' (roughly as in standard modern English) is possible.

7   *myself* (the *Me* of line 5)
     forsaken. Both 'deprived' and 'abandoned'.

8   *A torment.* Elliptical; supply 'it is'.
     crossed thwarted

9   *Prison* (imperative verb)
     ward. The abstract sense is 'care', but *Prison* enforces 'jail cell, dungeon' (implications now obsolete, though lingering in 'prison warder').

9, 11 *ward . . . guard.* Probably rhymed on a short 'a' resembling the vowel in northern English 'bat', 'bad'.

10   *then* (1) in that case; (2) at that time
     poor unworthy, pathetic, unfortunate
     bail. 'Redeem, release' registers until line 11 draws out the rarer, quite opposite sense, 'confine, enclose'.

11   *keeps* retains possession of, preserves, guards, holds captive
     his (the friend's)
     guard. Probably 'guard-house, place of imprisonment' rather than 'warder'.

12   *Thou . . . jail.* There could be no more *torture* of the *friend* because he would fall within the jurisdiction of the poet.

13   *pent* imprisoned

14   *and all* and so is everything

Sonnet 134

The argument flows on from Sonnet 133.

1   *So* well, so there we are
     now now that

2   *mortgaged to* pledged to comply with (and liable to forfeiture)
     wi¹¹ (1) wishes, purpose; (2) carnal appetite. The wilful quibbles of
     Sonnet 135 cannot be detected here.

3   *so* (1) provided that; (2) in order that
     that other mine (the *next self* of 133.6)

4   *still* always

5   *nor he will not be free* (1) nor will he be released; (2) nor does he want
     to be set free (because *kind* and, in the words of 133.4, *slave to slavery*)

6   *covetous* possessive, grasping, selfish
     kind benevolent, kindly, sympathetic, well-bred, naturally generous

7–8 *He learned . . . bind.* The young man was persuaded to underwrite the
     bond which committed the poet to the lady, but it turned out that the
     bond to which he set his pen committed him as well as the poet. The
     suggestion (supported by line 11) is that the young man, sent to
     recommend the poet's love to the lady, fell in love with the lady on his
     own account.

8   *fast* firmly, securely

9   *The statute . . . take* you will exact the full forfeiture stipulated by the
     bond, to which seizure, indeed, your beauty entitles you. The poet
     and the friend both stand in the lady's power.
     put'st forth all to use. The lady is like a *usurer* who 'lends out every-
     thing on interest'; she 'prostitutes beauty for gain' and perhaps
     even (given the bawdy implications of *use*) 'makes every kind of
     sexual favour available'.

11   *sue* (1) bring a legal suit against (to recover the full forfeiture); (2)
     follow, pursue; (3) woo. The decisive ambiguity here is (1) against
     (3); compare *Love's Labour's Lost* V.2.426–7, where, hearing
     Berowne call his state 'forfeit', Rosaline replies, 'It is not so; for how
     can this be true, | That you stand forfeit, being those that sue?'
     came debtor who became a debtor

12   *lose* am bereft of. In the light of *be free* and *fast doth bind*, Q's
     ambiguous spelling 'loose' may draw attention to another sense; the
     friend is loosed to loss.
     through my unkind abuse. Probably referring to the heartless (the
     unkind) wrongs done the poet by the lady (*abuse* which entailed the
     downfall of the friend under the terms of the *bond*); conceivably
     alluding to the poet's unnatural (one sense of *unkind*) employment of
     the friend to woo the lady (an *abuse* which led to the friend's loss).

13   *hast* (with a bawdy innuendo)

14   *He pays . . . free* he (as *surety*) pays the entire debt, but I am still not
released (from my *bond*). But the *double entendres* of *use* and *hast* elicit
'hole' from *whole*, and, from the full line, 'he gives you what should
be complete sexual satisfaction, but, insatiable as you are, you want
some more from me'. *Yet* implies both a logical ('nevertheless') and
temporal ('even now') impatience.

Sonnet 135

Here and in the following poem Shakespeare quibbles compulsively on six
senses of *will* (examples appended): (1) what is wanted (*thou hast thy Will*
135.1); (2) lust, carnal desire (*thou being rich in Will* 135.11); (3) shall (*Will*
will fulfil the treasure of thy love 136.5); (4) penis (*hide my will* 135.6); (5) vagina
(*thy sweet will* 135.4); (6) *William* (*my name is Will* 136.14). The distribution
of (6) is controversial. Some scholars maintain that every time Q italicizes
and gives a capital letter to *will* the name William is invoked. (This editor
reduces the italics to roman and, somewhat reluctantly, retains all the capital
Ws; see the third note to 1.2.) If every '*Will*' in Q invokes a name, 135.1–2
apparently proves that the friend and the dark lady's husband were, like the
poet, named William. On the biographical issues raised here – particularly by
the sonnet's obscurities – see the Introduction, pages 10–12, and the
discussion of Thorpe's dedication of Q to 'Mʳ.w.ʜ.', pages 168–9 above.

1   *Whoever hath . . . Will.* Echoing the proverb 'A woman will have her
will'. As the *will*s proliferate in line 2, the proverb 'Will will have will
though will win woe' is felt. If the dark lady is imagined as married to
a spouse called *Will*, the idiom 'to be wedded to one's will' registers
playfully. Each proverbial echo enforces the headnote's glossing of
Will as 'what is wanted'; but the suggestion is not that only one sense
is invoked here. In second and subsequent readings, *Will* is felt to be
pregnant with ambiguities.

2   *to boot* in addition
in overplus in excess

3   *vex* (1) annoy (presumably by stubborn wooing); (2) agitate, stir (with
a sexual innuendo)
still constantly, now as before

4   *making addition thus* (by being *in overplus*, or simply by fucking)

5, 12   *large* (1) great in size, capacious; (2) unrestrained, licentious
('th'adulterous Antony' is 'most large | In his abominations' with
Cleopatra, III.6.93–4); (3) bountiful (compare Lear's 'largest
bounty' at I.1.52, a sense related to 'largess'). The last, complimen-
tary significance comes in a poor third.

5, 7   *spacious . . . gracious* (trisyllabic)

365

7   *will in others* others' wills
    right thoroughly
8   *in my will* in the case of my (that is *Will*'s) will
    fair acceptance kindly reception, courteous admittance (with a bawdy insinuation)
    shine (1) appear, be visible; (2) smile, grace favourably
9   *The sea . . . still.* Compare the proverbs 'The sea refuses no river', 'The sea is never full' and Shakespeare's less seamy application of the same wisdom at *Twelfth Night* I.1.9–11: 'O spirit of love, how quick and fresh art thou, | That, notwithstanding thy capacity, | Receiveth as the sea'. (Arguably, indeed, the image unfolded in this sestet, and at 137.5–8 and *A Lover's Complaint* 253–9, displays the dark side of the synthesizing power discussed by sonnets like 53 and 98–9. See the Introduction, pages 30–33 and 62.)
10 *in abundance* (1) already abundantly provided (modifying *sea*); (2) abundantly (modifying *addeth*)
    his its
    store (1) stock; (2) plenty (another *abundance*)
11 *So* in the same way
    being (one syllable)
13 *Let 'no' unkind no fair beseechers kill. Unkind* (see the note on *kind* at 134.6) describes the sexual refusal *'no'*, though it can also function as a description of the lady (whose generosity is selfish, her kindness not quite what it seems). Some editors prefer to render Q's 'Let no vnkinde, no faire beseechers kill' as 'Let no unkind no fair beseechers kill' (interpreted 'Let no unkindness kill any beseechers'); others, modifying the text printed here, give 'Let no unkind "no", fair beseechers kill' or (treating the refusal as an action rather than a word) 'Let no unkind No, fair beseechers kill'.
    fair beseechers (1) honest-dealing suitors; (2) courteous pleaders; (3) attractive wooers
14 *Think all but one* account all *beseechers* and their *wills* one (making a composite Lover and *one Will* out of lusty indifference)
    Will. All the available senses of the word here conspire.

Sonnet 136

1   *soul* (as the seat of premonition and sentient intelligence: see the quotation from *Hamlet* in the note to 107.1–2)
    check chastise (though *come so near*, with its image of movement, elicits 'stop, stay')
    I come so near (1) I am so forthright, I press you so hard in what I say (a

standard idiom in the period); (2) I come so close to your body (with evident sexual designs)

1, 3   *near . . . there.* Rhymed on long 'e' and closer in sound to modern '-ere' than '-ear'.

2   *blind* heedless, ignorant

3   *admitted there* (1) acknowledged in your *soul*; (2) allowed into your presence (or your bed, or even your body)

4   *for love* out of charity (a stock asseveration)
    sweet. Modernized punctuation marks this out as direct address, but without commas, as in Q, it can also modify *love-suit.*

4, 5, 6   *fulfil . . . fulfil . . . fill . . . full* (lecherously unfolding the word as though undressing it, exposing with seductive tardiness its sexual potential)

5   *treasure* treasury, vagina (see 20.14 and the note)

5, 7   *love . . . prove.* For the rhyme see the note to 25.13, 14.

6   *my will one.* A wittily reversed echo of 135.14.

7   *In things of great receipt* (1) in the case of treasure chests ('*things* holding valuable objects'); (2) in matters of importance; (3) in large *things* (sufficiently glossed by 135.5)
    with ease (1) easily; (2) with room to spare
    prove verify, demonstrate

8   *Among a number one is reckoned none.* See 8.14 and the note.
    reckoned. Both 'counted' and 'accounted'.

9   *number* total. With an implied 'crowd (of lovers, of *wills*)'.
    untold uncounted, unrecorded

10   *thy store's account* a list of your possessions, an inventory of your lovers

11   *For nothing hold me* think me worthless

11–12   *hold | That nothing me, a something* think that worthless I of some little value. Near-contradiction evokes a vague but evident play on *thing* as *will*; see the next note.

12   *sweet.* Even more ambiguous than the equivalent in line 4; the *sweet* lady is asked to *hold . . . something, sweet* (a male equivalent of the *sweet will* of 135.4), to herself. Q's spelling, 'some-thing', makes the bawdry unmistakable.

13   *Make but* only make, make just
    still (1) as before; (2) forever

14   *for* because (both 'since' and 'in that')
    my name is Will. And at the very point where the poetry seems autobiographically explicit, we are closest to the commonplace. Here is the fifty-first riddle in *The Book of Merry Riddles* (1629):

> My lover's will
> I am content for to fulfil;

> Within this rhyme his name is framed;
> Tell me then how he is named?

> *Solution.* – His name is William; for in the first line is *will*, and in
> the beginning of the second line is *I am*, and then put them
> together, and it maketh *William*.

According to J. O. Halliwell, who later made a connexion with the Sonnets, in 1851: 'The head-line of this excessively rare chap-book is *The Booke of Riddles*, and there can scarcely be a doubt that it is a later impression of the book which Master Slender lent "to Alice Short-cake upon Allhallowmas last, a fortnight afore Michaelmas" [*The Merry Wives of Windsor* I.1.188–90]'. Certainly, the echo of 'will . . . fulfil' in lines 4–6 of 136 suggests that Shakespeare knew the puzzle, while the popularity of the book – several times reprinted – supports the idea that he might have expected early readers to recognize at least the genre to which his self-revelation belonged. For the '*I am*' of 'William', see the note to 121.9.

Sonnet 137

Compare Sonnets 113–14.

1   *Thou blind fool, Love.* Referring to the heedless folly of love through its blindfold god, Cupid. That 'Love is blind' was proverbial.

2   *see not what they see* do not understand what they behold. An echo of Psalms 115.5: 'they have eyes and see not.'

3   *lies* resides (though line 4 makes 'deceives' relevant)

5–6   *eyes corrupt by over-partial looks | Be anchored* (1) eyes corrupted by *over-partial* gazing; (2) corrupt eyes be anchored by *over-partial* gazing. *Over-partial* means 'frankly prejudiced, favourably disposed, doting'.

6   *anchored in the bay where all men ride.* A standard image (compare *Cymbeline* V.5.393, where Posthumus 'anchors upon Imogen', or *Antony and Cleopatra* I.5.31–3, where Cleopatra claims that 'great Pompey | Would stand and make his eyes grow in my brow; | There would he anchor his aspect') turned to bawdy uses. Like *bay*, *anchored* works by innuendo, but *ride* carries – in addition to the nautical sense deployed at 80.10 – strong implications of sexual action.

7–8   *Why of . . . tied.* The grotesque couplings are completed as the *eyes*, already anchored to the lady by desire, hook the *heart* through *falsehood* and *judgement*. (Love's perverse ingenuity is particularly apparent in line 7, where he ignores sartorial norms and creates *hooks* from *eyes*.)

9   *that.* Demonstrative; *that* is the *place* of line 10, the woman and her vagina.

several plot patch of private ground, enclosed land

10   *common place* field, common pasture (on which every man's beast may graze. With a double quibble, *common* meaning 'sexually promiscuous' and a 'commonplace' being something which the *wide world* as well as the *heart knows*.)

11   *Or mine eyes seeing this* or why should my eyes, *seeing* (both 'beholding' and 'understanding') *this*

11–12 *say this is not,* | *To put* say that this is not so, in order to put. But the (editorial) comma is easily read through to give another twist to the self-deception: 'say that this is not to put, deny that this is an instance of putting'.

12   *To put ... face* (probably alluding to the proverbial notion that one should 'put a good face on things', bravely make the best of whatever may be)

fair truth lovely chastity, honest constancy, true beauty (the product of neither cosmetics nor the besotted beholder)

so foul a face features so hideous, such a vile visage. *Foul* carries both ethical and aesthetic implications.

13–14 *In things ... transferred.* This is the poet's answer to his accumulated questions, though it registers as a cry of despair. His *heart and eyes* have made mistakes *In* judging *things right true* ('chaste cunts' and 'honest women' as well as 'true acts and statements'), and love has enforced a deranged fixation on the dark lady as a punishment (*to this false plague ... now transferred* meaning both 'transformed into this self-deceiving disease, this affliction of misinterpretation' and 'shifted to this un*true* woman, this fever of mine').

Sonnet 138

Versions of Sonnets 138 and 144 were published ten years before the appearance of Q in *The Passionate Pilgrim*, a collection of twenty love poems published by William Jaggard under the inaccurate sub-title '*By W. Shakespeare*'. For the early texts and an estimate of their status, see pages 443 and 446–7 below.

1   *made of truth* fidelity itself, utterly honest. With perhaps a glancing quibble on 'maid of truth' in the sense 'truly virginal'; see the note to *A Lover's Complaint* 5.

2   *she lies.* Only on a first reading can 'she is deceitful' be kept free of the bawdy sense of *lie* exploited in line 13.

2, 4 *lies ... subtleties.* Rhymed like *die ... memory* at 1.2 and 4, though plural.

3   *That* so that
4   *false* deceiving
5   *Thus* (1) in that way; (2) therefore
        vainly (1) ineffectually; (2) flattering myself, full of my own conceit;
        (3) foolishly
7   *Simply.* 'Naively' as well as 'straightforwardly, unconditionally'.
8   *simple truth* (1) the plain facts; (2) candid honesty
9   *unjust* (1) unfaithful; (2) deceitful
11   *love's best habit is in seeming trust* (1) love looks best when clad in
        apparent faith (original readers would have heightened the irony of
        seeming by understanding 'seemly' as well as 'assumed'); (2) the best
        frame of behaviour for love (almost 'love's wisest policy') lies in
        seeming to *trust* (the beloved)
12   *age in love* (1) age when infatuated, an oldish person in love; (2) in
        matters of love an oldish person
        told (1) counted; (2) divulged. The ambiguities of 136.9 brought to
        the point of a pun.
13   *Therefore* that's why, on account of all that
        I lie with her (1) I make love with her; (2) I tell her lies
14   *in our faults* in respect of our shortcomings. The moral *faults* which
        make the lady promiscuous and the poet deceitful, and the failing (if
        not impotence) of the flesh in *age*.
        flattered pleasurably deceived. 'Caressed' may also contribute; see
        33.2 and the note.

Sonnet 139

Initially resisting convention – *to justify* a mistress's *wrong* was standard
sonneteering strategy – the poet succumbs to its pressure in the sestet (with a
lapse into the appropriate idiom), only to conclude with an image which,
despite its commonplace origins, is so violent that it carries a more than
conventional weight.

3   *Wound me . . . tongue* do not wound me by turning your eyes on others
        (this, it emerges, is what is implied, the opposite of what first reading
        suggests), but satisfy yourself with just telling me (about your *wrong*)
4   *Use power with power* use your strength strongly, powerfully exploit
        your *might. Power* is here monosyllabic.
        by art with cunning, artfully
5   *elsewhere* someone else (compare line 12)
        in my sight near me. *Glance* and *eye* (line 6) reactivate the metaphor in
        the idiom ('where I can see you'), so that the poet seems to seek eye
        contact but finds the gaze *elsewhere*.

6   *glance . . . aside* (in an œillade, or what 110.7 calls *blenches*)

7   *What* why

8   *o'erpressed* too hard-pressed
        bide endure, withstand

9–12   '*Ah, my love . . . injuries.*' In the Jacobean period, inverted commas
        were not in standard use to identify direct speech, and Q leaves this
        unmarked. Nevertheless, words like *pretty looks*, *enemies*, *my foes* (for
        eyes), *dart* – the common stock of poor sonneteering – set the lines
        apart as a consciously poetic utterance by a poet justifying a *wrong*.
        (Given that this is so, and that early readers, responsive to the shift in
        timbre, would have read the lines as direct speech, those editors who
        refuse inverted commas are misguided.)

10   *pretty* (with a glint of irony beneath the conventional compliment: see
        the note to 41.1, especially sense 3)
        looks (1) glances; (2) good looks, beauty

11   *therefore* that's why, on that account

12   *elsewhere.* In line 5 *elsewhere* implied a loved object; here its reference
        is vaguer, and the shift in sense points up the poet's success in
        justifying the mistress's *wrong*.

13   *near* (adverbial)

14   *Kill me outright with looks and rid my pain.* Though the likely source
        for this is *Astrophil and Stella* 48, 'Soul's joy, bend not those morning
        stars from me' (with its final line 'A kind of grace it is to slay with
        speed'), it evokes a host of Elizabethan love poems in which the
        mistress's eye is like Medusa's or the basilisk's. *Rid* here means
        'dispose of, do away with'.

Sonnet 140

1   *Be wise as thou art cruel* (1) be as wise as you are cruel; (2) be wise since
        you are cruel. *Cruel* is here two syllables.
        press (1) assail (compare 139.8); (2) oppress with melancholy; (3)
        torture with weights (using *peine forte et dure* to elicit a statement)

4   *pity-wanting* (1) unpitied (by *cruel* you); (2) pity-craving

5   *wit* practical wisdom

5–6   *better it were . . . to tell me so* it would be better for you, if not to love me
        (since you doubtless can't), then at least to tell me that you do

5, 7   *were . . . near.* Though 'weer . . . neer' is possible, the rhyme probably
        rested on a long 'e' sounding, in the period, like the 'ar' in modern
        'scarce', 'scares'.

6   *yet* nevertheless (with a touch of 'still, now as before')
        so (that you do *love* me)

7   *testy* fretful, peevish

10   *ill* (1) unkindly; (2) wrongs, evil. Recalling the state of the *sick men*.

11   *this ill-wresting world* this present day which twists everything to the
        bad (including things said about others. A hint of 'ill-resting'
        generates 'convalescent' and 'restive': in short, *testy sick men*.)

12   *mad ears* (listeners not sane enough to recognize that I'm raving)

13   *so* (a *Mad sland'rer* and, worse, *believèd*)
        belied be slandered

14   *Bear thine eyes straight, though thy proud heart go wide.* An image from
        archery strings the line together: 'direct (as in "bear left" or "take a
        bearing") your eyes straight (towards the target, *me*), though your
        proud heart shoots (or is shot) *wide* (of that aim)'. Ambiguity and
        connotation enrich it: *straight* is 'steadily, honestly' (see 121.11 and
        the note); *heart*, both 'desire' and 'thoughts'; *go wide*, 'go wrong,
        range widely'. The continuity with Sonnet 139, where the mistress's
        glance goes *aside*, is evident.

Sonnet 141

1   *In faith* truly, verily (though the context of surrounding sonnets,
        among which 141 clearly belongs, suggests an incurable fidelity, and
        so 'upon my faithfulness')

2   *errors* defects of beauty

4   *Who* which
        in despite of view regardless of what is seen, despite appearances
        is pleased to. 'Deigns to', modified by the context to a literal 'is glad
        to'.
        dote adore, love to distraction. See the second note to 131.3.

5   *thy tongue's tune* the sound of your voice. A standard, if ravishing,
        idiom (compare 'The tune of Imogen!' at *Cymbeline* V.5.238, and
        see *A Lover's Complaint* 4) here turned into a covert compliment
        (with its suggestion of melody) towards a lady whose charms are
        ostensibly dismissed.

6   *Nor tender feeling* nor is my keenly responsive sense of touch
        to base touches prone (1) susceptible to ignoble caresses; (2) liable to be
        marked by dishonourable taints. It is possible that *tune* enriches (1),
        an imagined hand delicately provoking the 'bass' string of a lute, viol,
        or harp.

8   *sensual* (two syllables)
        sensual feast. Alluding to the Banquet of Sense, a motif which during
        the 1590s bred a series of poems designed to provoke, and perhaps
        to purge, each of the reader's five senses through erotic indulgence.
        Compare *Venus and Adonis* 445–50 or, in greater detail, Berowne's
        account of love at *Love's Labour's Lost* IV.3.309–15:

It adds a precious seeing to the eye:
A lover's eyes will gaze an eagle blind.
A lover's ear will hear the lowest sound
When the suspicious head of theft is stopped.
Love's feeling is more soft and sensible
Than are the tender horns of cockled snails.
Love's tongue proves dainty Bacchus gross in taste . . .

alone exclusively, to the exclusion of other women (though 'in private' might also be intended, as an insinuation)

9 *But . . . nor* however, neither . . . nor

five wits. A standard division of the intellectual powers – 'four of his five wits went halting off', *Much Ado About Nothing* I.1.61, 'Bless thy five wits', *King Lear* III.4.55 – constructed by analogy with the *five senses* (too familiar to gloss) and usually reckoned thus: common wit, imagination, fantasy, estimation, memory.

10 *serving thee* (with a lover's devotion)

11–12 *Who leaves . . . to be* which *heart* leaves ungoverned what is (since it lacks a governing *heart*) the mere appearance, the husk, *of a man*, leaving its home to become your *heart's slave and vassal. Leaves* functions twice.

13 *Only . . . thus far* (1) however, to this extent; (2) thus far and no farther

my plague. Both the fever of love (compare 140.7–14) and the mistress herself (see 137.14).

count consider, take to be (though *my gain* quietly evokes an image from the soul's counting-house)

14 *awards me pain* (1) distresses me, inflicts pain on me; (2) rewards me with punishment (which will cut short or abolish my sufferings after death. *Pain* was often used in this second sense, evoked so strongly by *sin*.)

Sonnet 142

1–2 *Love is . . . loving.* The sonnet begins by glossing the last line of its predecessor, explaining that the poet's *sin* is only *love*. Chiasmus then delivers a harsh rebuke to the lady as 'your precious moral excellence' meets *hate* and becomes 'your inmost quality'. The rebuke softens in line 2 as the lady's *virtue* turns out to be *Hate of my sin* (though the reader is aware that this translates easily into the less laudable 'mislike of my love'); but the poet strikes again by deploying *sin* straightforwardly, complaining that the lady's *virtue* rests on *sinful loving* (the *sin* of adultery).

2, 4   *loving . . . reproving.* For the rhyme see the note to 25.13, 14.

3   *but* only
     mine (my *state*)

6   *scarlet ornaments* lips (resembling in redness and their power to clinch
     the seals of red wax which *sealed* and so authenticated documents)

7   *sealed* (with a kiss. Compare 'seal the bargain with a holy kiss', *The
     Two Gentlemen of Verona* II.2.7, or 'seal with a righteous kiss | A
     dateless bargain', *Romeo and Juliet* V.3.114–15.)
     false (1) insincere, faithless (to me); (2) unlawful

8   *Robbed others' beds' revenues of their rents.* The lady has *Robbed* other
     people's marriages of the sexual dues (the *rents*) which contribute to
     the emotional wealth, and the possibility of offspring (the *revenues*),
     in those relationships. Here, *rents* are 'fees paid by tenants' and
     revenues (accented on the second syllable) 'estates yielding income'.

9   *Be it lawful.* 'If it is permissible' tending towards 'let it be allowed'. A
     stock phrase enlivened by the legalistic *bonds*, *revenues*, and *rents*
     which precede it, and by the blatantly criminal conduct of the lady
     (adultery was illegal in the period). *Be it* elides into a single syllable.

11, 12   *pity.* The *pité* of the troubadours and their descendants; emotional
     grace and sexual favour, not just sympathy.

13   *what thou dost hide* (that is, *pity*)

14   *By self-example* by your own example, according to your own
     precedent
     mayst thou (1) may you, I hope that you; (2) it could be that you might
     denied refused (*pity*)

Sonnet 143

1   *careful.* Both 'prudent' and 'distressed'.
     housewife. The original pronunciation, 'hussif', is rhythmically
     preferable.

2   *One of her feathered creatures.* The poet's rival is charged, obliquely,
     with feathered foppery. He resembles that 'plume of feathers' Don
     Armado (*Love's Labour's Lost* IV.1.95) and the Ostricke (compare
     Ostrich) of the second Quarto of *Hamlet*, the absurd courtier with
     the fashionable hat. Feathered headgear was modish in the 1590s
     and 1600s.

4   *pursuit* (accented on the first syllable)

5   *holds her in chase* chases her. A standard idiom.

6   *Cries.* Both 'weeps' and 'yells'.
     busy care. Both 'earnest concern' and 'caring activity'.
     bent (1) single-mindedly directed; (2) turned aside (from the *child* to
     the bird)

7   *flies* flees (no doubt impotently flapping wings clipped of their flight feathers)

   flies before her face. Shakespeare mixes two stock idioms – 'flee from the face of' and 'before the face of' (meaning 'in the sight of') – to suggest the fowl's frustrating ability to stay in sight but out of reach. And a third – 'fly in the face of' (meaning 'oppose') – to point up the conflict implied by the separation.

8   *prizing* caring about

11   *catch.* 'Catch up with' and 'capture'.

   thy hope what you seek (note *thy Will* in line 13), the person you pursue

12   *be kind* (1) be generous; (2) behave naturally (treat me as a *mother* should her *babe*)

13–14   *So will . . . still.* The poet will pray that the lady will have what she wants (the *hope* of line 11, perhaps a youth named *Will*) if she will just *turn back* to *still* his *Cries.* Of course, if the lady turned back to *still* the poet, her *hope* would get away once and for all. But perhaps the poet means to imply that; certainly, if the lady turned back she would *have* her *Will* in the shape of the poet (that version of William Shakespeare). Here, as at 135.1, the proverb 'A woman will have her will' enriches the line.

Sonnet 144

On the text, see the headnote to Sonnet 138 and pages 443 and 447 below; for a critical account, see the Introduction, pages 59–60.

1   *Two . . . despair* I have two beloveds (that seem *Two* kinds of *love*), one bringing me comfort and the other despair

2   *suggest* prompt, tempt

   still continually

3   *right fair* (1) just, absolutely honest; (2) most beautiful (in a delicately pale, blond fashion). *Coloured ill* in line 4 makes the latter dominant by the end of the quatrain.

4   *spirit* (one syllable)

   coloured ill brunette (see Sonnets 127 and 132 and the notes. *Ill,* shadowed by the suggestion of devilry in *worser spirit,* prepares for the *hell* and *evil* of line 5.)

5–8   *To win . . . pride.* Like the hero of a Morality play or Marlowe's Dr Faustus, the poet is urged towards right and wrong by a pair of rival spirits; this drama takes an unexpected turn when the bad angel woos, not the susceptible poet, but her supposedly inviolable opponent.

5   *To win me soon to hell.* The metaphor translates: 'to make me utterly miserable, to throw me into *despair*'.

5, 7   *evil . . . devil.* Probably sounding 'eevil . . . deevil', though conceivably more like 'ivil . . . divil'.

7   *saint* (roughly equivalent to *angel* because opposed to *devil*)

8   *foul pride* (1) horrible allure (*pride* as a 'fine display of beauty' mingled with 'sexual readiness'); (2) ugly vanity (*pride* as the chief sin of seven deadlies, the one which made Lucifer fall from his angelic to his satanic state)

9   *whether that* whether it is true that

9, 11   *fiend . . . friend.* Rhymed on either long 'i' or short (Q spells 'finde' for *fiend*, which might just be a spelling variant), sounding 'feend . . . freend' or 'finnd . . . frind'.

10   *directly* (1) straightforwardly, by direct evidence; (2) entirely, completely ('This concurs directly with the letter', *Twelfth Night* III.4.66–7); (3) just now, immediately

11   *being both from me, both to each friend* since both are absent from me, and since each is the other's friend. *Both to each friend* also hints at the conclusion reached in line 12, 'and each friend gone to the other'.

12–14   *I guess . . . out.* For an explication of the intricate bawdry, see the Introduction, page 60.

Sonnet 145

A pretty trifle which has been much abused. Some have denied Shakespeare its authorship; but it has recently been argued, most plausibly, that *hate away* in line 13 puns on 'Hathaway', the surname of Shakespeare's Stratford wife. (See Further Reading, page 68.) In the period, 't' and 'th' were not exact, but were closer than now; compare the 'rhyme' at 20.10 and 12. That the sonnet uses *you* instead of the *thou* general in the dark lady series, and octosyllabics rather than pentameters (see the headnotes to Sonnets 13 and 99), supports the notion that 145 is a piece of juvenilia flanked by mature writing. Was it included for sentimental reasons? Did it find its way into Shakespeare's manuscript by mistake? Was it inserted by a scribe, by Thorpe, or by someone at Eld's printing shop? More than any other sonnet, 145 casts doubt on the authority and order of Q. Yet even here – it cannot be too strongly said – thematic links with what precedes and follows the poem in Q are evident: *fiend*, *heaven*, and *hell* in lines 11–12 help it blend into context. However aberrant 145 may be in form, whatever its date of composition, and despite its original tenor (apparently describing a wife rather than a mistress), it fits into the collection. More importantly, there is no other place where it could fit half so well; and whoever located it between 144 and 146 had a knowledge of the sequence superior to anything that the average scribe (who gets to know a text while copying) or compositor – who reads while printing, having already 'cast off' or allotted the material to particular pages (an arrangement not easily altered once printing begins) – might be likely to possess. Random shuffling can hardly explain the position of 145, and although intervention by Thorpe or an in-house editor of Eld's is possible, it seems less than probable. For the broad editorial context of these assertions, see the Account of the Text.

1   *Love's* (Venus's or Cupid's, presumably the former)

5   *Straight* immediately

6–7   *that ever sweet | Was used in giving gentle doom* which, always *sweet* (mild, plangent, generous – both tone and temper are involved), was accustomed to passing a mild sentence

8   *greet* address (me)

10–11   *day | Doth follow night.* A tritely commonplace example of inevitability ('After night comes the day' was proverbial); compare Polonius's 'And it must follow, as the night the day, | Thou canst not then be false to any man' (*Hamlet* I.3.79–80).

12   *is flown* has fled. Though the fallen angels did 'fly' (compare the ambivalence of flies at 143.9).

13   *'I hate' from hate away she threw* (flinging the words away from the feeling, freeing *'I hate'* from emotional reference. And see the headnote for a likely pun.)

Sonnet 146

Influenced by a long line of poems presenting dialogues between Soul and Body, by Sidney's famous sonnet 'Leave me, O Love, which reachest but to dust', by the dexterously serious style of the young John Donne, and, most immediately, by a weak poem in Bartholomew Griffin's *Fidessa* (1596):

Well may my soul, immortal and divine,
That is imprisoned in a lump of clay,
Breathe out laments until this body pine,
That from her takes her pleasures all away.
Pine then, thou loathèd prison of my life!
Untoward subject of the last aggrievance!
O, let me die! Mortality is rife! . . .

The sonnet has been widely discussed; see Further Reading, page 71.

1   *Poor soul, the centre of my sinful earth.* Resembling the *centre* attractive about which the *earth* spins, the *soul* lies at the centre of the body, giving stability and sustaining its action. Though the *soul* is a spiritual entity, it is here (as at 136.1 or 107.1) sensible and intellective – which makes it worth questioning, in line 2. *Earth* is the body as a microcosm, 'a little world made cunningly | Of elements', as Donne puts it, but it is also the substance of which the body is made. 'The

Lord God also did shape man, [even] dust from off the ground, and breathed into his nostrils the breath of life, and man was a living soul' (Genesis 2.7). Compare 32.2 and the headnote to Sonnet 74.

1–4   *Poor soul . . . gay*. Shakespeare conveys the confusion inherent in any struggle between the soul and body (the language being so inexact, and dualistic in contradictory ways). The body relies on its *centre*, but becomes rebellious; then the *rebel powers* clothe and mobilize (*array*) the *soul*; except that the *soul* stays *within* and starves; but then it also garrisons (by garnishing) the body's *walls* (allied again with its foe).

2   [   ] *these rebel powers that thee array*. A few scholars have found Q's 'My sinfull earth these rebbell powres that thee array' acceptable; most have not. Scores of emendations have been proposed for the phrase repeated from line 1, the most satisfactory (see the Collations, page 439) attending to the imagery of the sonnet, to warfare, hunger, service, architecture.

these rebel powers (the body and its passions. As Q's 'powres' indicates, *powers* is here one syllable.)

array (1) clothe, decorate; (2) marshal for war, line up for battle

3   *pine within* (1) sorrow inwardly; (2) waste away with hunger inside the body's walls (like a loyal population besieged by *rebel powers*)

suffer dearth endure deprivation, undergo the rigours of famine

4   *Painting thy outward walls so costly gay* adorning your body (thus) with (such) expensive display (cosmetics, fine attire, and the like. That Shakespeare should use *Painting* to cover the great variety of *outward* vanities seems significant; note the importance of the word in sonnets to the friend like 82–3. *Outward* is not only descriptive of the body but, in context (compare, for instance, 46.13, 69.5, 125.2), expressive of the kind of futile, morally dubious display that the line describes. On the specious gaudiness of *gay*, see the note to 68.8.)

5   *cost* expenditure. For some semantic complications, see the note to *A Lover's Complaint* 96 (the clothing and textile images being particularly relevant).

having so short a lease (and no one *spends* much money on a property soon to revert to the landlord)

5, 7   *lease . . . excess*. Rhymed on a short 'e', sounding nearer modern '-ess' than '-ease'.

6   *thy fading mansion* your increasingly decrepit body. The image, prepared by *walls* and *lease*, is ultimately biblical in origin. (Compare, especially, 2 Corinthians 5.1–10.)

7   *excess* superfluity, extravagance

8   *thy charge* (1) what you have spent so much on (in *cost*); (2) what has been entrusted to you (its *centre*)

end (1) fate, final end; (2) purpose

9   *live thou upon*. The body's *loss* is the soul's 'salary' and its 'food,

sustenance' (hence the imagery of line 12), both things which can be lived *upon*.

10   *that* (the body, *thy servant*)
     aggravate increase
     store stock, supply

11   *Buy terms divine* (1) purchase godly stretches of time (longer than *hours*, indeed eternal); (2) secure a deal with God (in which the contractual *terms* procured are godly, holy, spiritual)

12   *Within be fed.* Harking back to *pine within* (line 3) and *live thou upon* (line 9; see the note).
     without outside (on the body, the soul's outward walls)

13   *So shalt . . . men.* There may be, as in Sonnet 74 (see the headnote), an allusion to 1 Corinthians 15, 'Death is swallowed up into victory' (verse 54).

14   *And Death . . . then.* Compare 1 Corinthians 15.26, 'The last enemy that shall be destroyed [is] death', Isaiah 25.8, 'As for death He hath destroyed it for ever', and Revelations 21.4, 'there shall be no more death'. The subject of innumerable meditations, poems, and paradoxes, of which Donne's *Death be not proud* is only the most famous.

Sonnet 147

The sequence returns to the concerns of Sonnets 118–19 (and see the note to 129.7–8).

1   *still* incessantly

2   *For that* (with a secondary 'because of that, on account of that')
     nurseth fosters, nourishes (as a wet-nurse *nurseth*), tends (as a nurse tends a patient suffering from a *disease*)

3   *Feeding on that.* Parallelism with *longing . . . For that* makes the latter parenthetic and *love* and *fever* the more clearly joint antecedents of *Feeding*.
     ill (1) sickness; (2) evil

4   *uncertain* capricious, finicky, intermittent
     appetite (1) craving for food; (2) sexual desire; (3) whim. *Fever* and *love* elicit (1) and (2); though *appetite* for 'whim' was not common in the period (and is now obsolete), it was current enough to be discerned in the light of *uncertain*.

5   *reason, the physician to my love* (developing metaphorically the commonplace assumption that reason and appetite were at odds, the former attempting to govern, to 'diet' in Shakespeare's sense, the latter)

5, 7 *love . . . approve.* For the rhyme see the note to 25.13, 14.

6   *prescriptions are not kept* directions are not followed, restrictions

379

are not observed. Presumably the physician forbad the poet the tempting *that* of lines 2–3.

7   *left me* (at the mercy of my *fever*. And, since it is reason which departs, *left me* in a feverish madness.)

desperate (two syllables) frantic, restless, in despair

approve (1) find out from (bitter) experience; (2) exemplify, am clear proof that

8   *Desire is death, which physic did except* that appetite which Medicine proscribed – and which my physician and his course of *physic* forbad – leads to *death*. *Desire* is the antecedent of *which*. The phrase *Desire is death* recalls Romans 8.6: 'To be carnally minded, is death: But to be spiritually minded, is life and peace.'

9   *Past cure . . . past care.* While seeming to reproduce the saw 'Past cure, past care' (meaning 'It's no use crying over spilt milk'), Shakespeare effectively inverts it, saying that the case is *past cure* because the physician has ceased to *care*.

now since, now that

9, 11   *care . . . are.* For the rhyme see 48.5 and 7 and the note to 13.1, 3.

10   *frantic-mad with evermore unrest.* It was proverbial that 'Desire has no rest'. *Evermore* means both 'continual' and 'increasing' ('for *evermore*' and 'ever more').

11   *my discourse* what I say. The distinction between *thoughts* and *discourse* is sustained and elaborated in line 12 (the one proving false, the other poor in expression).

12   *At random from the truth* missing the point, wide of the mark
vainly idly, ineffectually, ineptly

13–14   *fair . . . bright . . . black . . . dark.* As the adjectives accumulate, their moral connotations gather.

14   *as black as hell, as dark as night.* Both comparisons were proverbial.

Sonnet 148

In this sonnet and the next, Shakespeare returns to the theme of 113–14: visual distortion and the mental trickery imposed by *love*.

1, 8, 9   *love.* There are strong but resistible reasons for giving the poet's *love* a capital letter. Blindfold in renaissance iconography to explain the random way in which his shafts of *love* are fired, Cupid is here (notably in line 13) associated with the lover's sensory delusion.

2   *have no correspondence with true sight* (1) have no likeness to *eyes* that see accurately; (2) do not see what is really to be seen, which are *blind* (line 13) to what really is. The ambiguity depends on *sight* as both seeing and what is seen.

380

4   *censures* judges (the modern implication 'unfavourably' was only emergent in the period)

      falsely (1) wrongly; (2) dishonestly

5   *fair* (1) beautiful; (2) honourable. The former links with 147.13–14 (and thus sonnets like 132), the latter – clearer on rereading (after line 14) – recalls the moral weight of *fair* in poems like 144.

      false (with a double implication matching the spread of senses in *falsely*)

      dote. See 141.4 and the note.

6   *What means* what reason has

      it is not so. Compare the negative judgement at 131.5–6.

7   *love doth well denote* my loving (with its kind of sight) clearly demonstrates that

8   *eye* (with a pun on 'ay', meaning 'yes', opposing *all men's 'no'*)

8, 9   *true* (like *falsely* and *false*, involving both accuracy and honesty)

8–9   *all men's 'no'. | How can it.* The Q punctuation 'all mens: no, | How can it?' indicates a syntactical ambiguity concealed by modern, logical punctuation.

9   *eye*. This time (as against line 8) the wordplay points to 'I' (a common spelling in the period, in any case, for 'ay'). As *love doth well denote* makes clear, the poet's self is compacted with its *eye* (which is *love's*).

10   *vexed* troubled (rather than, as now, angered)

      watching wakefulness, insomnia (compare 61.13)

11   *No marvel then though* so it is hardly surprising if

      I (with a pun on 'eye' prepared by *eye* in line 9. Compare 152.13.)

      mistake my view (1) see amiss (compare lines 1–2); (2) misunderstand what I see (compare lines 3–4). The former is supported by the *I/eye* pun.

13   *O cunning love, with tears thou keep'st me blind* O crafty infatuation, you make me *mistake my view* by filling my eyes *with tears*. The exclamation helps personify *love*, and that draws attention, in turn, to an odd parallel between the tearful poet and Cupid – both *blind*.

14   *foul faults*. Flaws both aesthetic (compare 141.1–2) and ethical (as in the previous sonnet).

Sonnet 149

In Sonnet 149 the implications of 148.14 are unravelled and unhappily resolved.

2, 3   *When . . . when*. Initially 'since', *When* becomes temporal once *when* is read.

2   *with thee partake* take your part, side with you

3   *think on thee* (1) think about you, recall you; (2) show consideration for you

3-4   *when I forgot | Am of myself, all tyrant.* Following Q's punctuation this means 'when I tyrannously forget myself (show myself little regard, indeed become slightly crazed)'. But *all* can be taken with *myself*, and *tyrant* interpreted as a vocative paralleling *O cruel*: 'when I, despotic mistress, forget myself (becoming alienated and distinctly touched, dotty, distrait)'. And *forget* can be attributed to the lady's amnesia (cut off by imagined commas), 'when I, forgotten by you, am tyrant over myself'.

4   *for thy sake.* 'On your behalf' or 'to think of you', according to one's interpretation of what precedes it (the weight allowed the ambiguities in lines 3-4).

5   *Who hateth . . . friend.* The echo of Psalm 139.21 is presumably unconscious: 'Do not I hate them, O God, that hate thee'.

6, 8 *upon . . . moan.* The rhyme may rest on long 'o' (sounding roughly 'uporn . . . morn') or a short vowel (resembling 'upon . . . mon'); either way, a full rhyme was available.

7   *spend* vent. The idea of expenditure combines with the notion of utterance (preparing *moan*).

8   *present moan* immediate suffering, instant lamentation

9   *respect* (1) discern; (2) consider worthwhile

10   *thy service* serving you, employment as your servant
      proud splendid (and so worthy *respect*), pride-inducing

11   *all my best* everything excellent in me
      defect (accented on the second syllable) imperfection (one flaw used to represent a general lack)

12   *motion* (1) movement (by glancing); (2) prompting, instruction (compare, for example, *The Merry Wives of Windsor* III.2.31-2, 'He gives her folly motion and advantage', *King John* IV.2.255, 'The dreadful motion of a murderous thought')

13   *love* beloved
      know thy mind (1) know what you have determined; (2) understand how your mind works

14   *Those that can see thou lov'st, and I am blind.* The lady loves those who see and admire her, but the poet so admires that he cannot really see (compare Sonnet 148); he is, because uncritical, *blind* (as at 148.13), and (in her mind at least) to that extent unlovable. The psychology of shallow loving.

Sonnet 150

1   *power . . . powerful might.* The line depends on a quibbling shift in sense from 'supernatural authority, temporal sway' (underwritten by 'faculty, capacity') to 'formidable capacity, mighty strength'. *Power* and *powerful* are contracted to one and two syllables.

2   *With insufficiency* through imperfection (the *defect* of 149.11), by means of weakness, through shortcomings
    sway move, persuade, govern

3   *give the lie to* flatly call a liar

4   *And swear . . . day.* The insufficiency of the lady seems so beautiful to the poet that he rejects everything fair, thinking only blackness an ornament to the day. Perhaps he even thinks, perversely, that since the day is lovely it must be dark, not bright.

5   *becoming of things ill* power to make vile things attractive (Enobarbus says of Cleopatra: 'vilest things | Become themselves in her, that the holy priests | Bless her when she is riggish' (II.2.243–5). As line 6 demonstrates, moral as well as physical ugliness is involved.)

6   *the very refuse of your deeds* (1) the least of your deeds (casual actions, slightest things done); (2) the most loathsome of your *deeds*

7   *warrantise of skill* assurance of expertise, evidence of ability

11, 12   *abhor.* Wordplay seems likely: in addition to 'despise', 'call a whore' in line 11 and 'make whorish' in line 12. Compare *Othello* IV.2.160–61, where Desdemona cries, 'I cannot say "whore": | It does abhor me now I speak the word' (because the word itself is so indelicate).

12   *With others.* If the last note is correct, 'with other lovers' as well as 'along with those who despise me'.

13–14   *If thy . . . thee.* Beneath the poet's claim that he deserves to be loved because he loves even the lady's faults lurks the insulting insinuation that by loving someone so unworthy as the lady the poet has shown himself unworthy enough to be worthy her love.

Sonnet 151

'*Penis erectus non habet conscientiam*' may have been proverbial in the period; 'It is impossible to love and be wise' and 'Love is without reason' certainly were.

1, 2   *Love . . . love* Cupid . . . the experience

1   *too young* (see 115.13 and the iconographical tradition which makes Love a *babe* or mischievous boy)

1, 2   *conscience . . . conscience* moral sense . . . sexual activity (*con-science*, 'knowing the *con*': the French word for cunt was often used bawdily in Elizabethan and Jacobean English)

1, 3   *is . . . amiss.* For the rhyme see the note to 59.1, 3.

2   *who knows not conscience is born of love.* The bawdy quibble remarked
         above deflates the renaissance notion that love exalts the lover,
         refining his sensibilities. *Love* may give him *conscience*, but of a less
         than moral kind.

2, 4   *love . . . prove.* For the rhyme see the note to 25.13, 14.

3   *gentle cheater* (carrying a range of oxymoronic senses, from 'kindly
         deceiver' to 'genteel fraud'. The infidelity is presumably that de-
         scribed in the next sonnet.)
         urge not my amiss do not invoke my fault, do not charge me with
         sinfulness (because if you do, I'll be tempted to make up for my lack
         of *conscience* (in the moral sense) by seizing it (in the sexual). This
         quibble is extended by lines 5–10 to mean, with hindsight, 'do not
         provoke my weakness to indulge itself'.)

4   *Lest guilty of my faults thy sweet self prove.* At first this means 'because if
         you *urge* my *faults* I can urge yours, *cheater*, and they are the same as
         mine'. The turn into line 4, however, with *For*, introduces the
         somewhat sophistical claim that for the lady to *urge* the poet's *amiss*
         (secondary sense) would be to *betray* him into *betraying* himself – and
         two betrayals of one kind (doubly leading to sexual *conscience*) would
         constitute identical *faults* on both sides.

5   *betraying me.* 'Revealing my moral flaws' follows from lines 3–4, but
         this is ousted by 'treacherously capturing my passion, *betraying me*
         into lust'. A third residual sense continues from *cheater*: the lady who
         reveals *faults* and precipitates desire is constantly *betraying* the poet
         with other men, and other men with him.

5–6   *I do . . . treason.* The *treason* discussed in Sonnet 146, simplified.
         Here the soul (*My nobler part*) is sacrificed directly to the *body's*
         appetites rather than to a decaying display which includes the
         passions as *rebel powers*.

8   *stays no farther reason* doesn't stop to argue, doesn't linger to hear
         more justification for its action. No doubt the *soul* means one thing
         by *love*, while the *body* and its *flesh* jump to quite another conclusion.

9   *rising at thy name, doth point out thee.* The stiffening penis is compared
         to a spirit conjured up by a magic word, its unerring response
         to the lady's *name* likened to a compass needle's tremblingly
         unfailing indication of the north and the determined probe
         of a censor pricking out a chosen *name* on a list (see the quo-
         tation from *Romeo and Juliet* in the note to 129.1–2 and the note to
         20.13).

10   *triumphant prize* spoils of victory, prize worth exulting over
         Proud of this pride glorying in this tumescence, lusty in this splendour
         (exploiting sexual senses standard in the period)

11   *He is contented thy poor drudge to be.* The poet ruefully undercuts the

victorious tone of line 10, conceding that the lady uses his *flesh* to *drudge* for her: he is his mistress's sexual slave.

12   *stand in thy affairs* be steadfast in business undertaken for you (describing the service offered in line 11), fight staunchly for your interests (anticipating the military implications of *fall*). With an obvious carnal innuendo.

    fall by thy side. Probably 'struggle beside you in battle until I die' (drawing on the stock imagery of love as war), *fall* describing detumescence after orgasm; but perhaps merely 'flop into bed next to you' (so that what stood proudly up is threateningly horizontal). *Fall* is one of the neutral words Shakespeare most liked to jest with; compare *Troilus and Cressida* III.1.96–7, 'Falling in, after falling out, may make them three', or the Nurse's repetitions of '"Yea," quoth he, "dost thou fall upon thy face? | Thou wilt fall backward when thou hast more wit . . ."' at *Romeo and Juliet* I.3.42–58. In a poem about the 'birth' of *conscience* as (quibblingly) the knowledge of good and evil, *fall* distantly suggests the *fall* of man and woman from Eden. *By thy side* supports this, since Adam fell with Eve after eating the forbidden fruit, plucked by her, 'through vehemence of love' – in one usual interpretation of Genesis, elaborated by Milton – 'Not deceived, | But fondly overcome with female charm' (*Paradise Lost* IX, 'Argument' and 998–9). The notion is further enforced by the idea of mutuality in sin at the heart of the sonnet (lines 3–10). Though nothing is easier to concoct than a 'lapsarian' reading of this or that text, the archetype surely makes its mark on this knowing poem about the dangers of knowing.

13   *No want of conscience hold it* do not think it shows a lack of *conscience* (in the sense employed in line 1, but fully aware of line 2 and what follows) in me

13–14   *call . . . fall.* The surface sense is so apparent (even allowing for the bawdy jest in *rise and fall*) that the reader feels tempted to interpret *'love'* and *for whose dear love*, on a secondary level, less as 'my love' and 'for heartfelt love of whom' than two modes of loving, double standards similar to those adumbrated in line 8. The mistress may be identified with *'love'* itself (wrongly no doubt), but the flesh rises and falls in a more sexual suit.

Sonnet 152

1   *am forsworn* break faith (with another lover. Perhaps the friend, to whom the poet has certainly sworn undying devotion. Some commentators prefer to invoke Anne Hathaway; if the poet is referring to

his wife, the broken oath might be not a lover's vow but a promise of fidelity made before God in the marriage service.)

2–4   *But thou . . . bearing.* Although a case can be made for excluding the friend from the count, the traditional interpretation of these lines – according to which the broken *bed-vow* was sworn to the dark lady's husband, the *new faith* sworn to the friend before being *torn*, and the *swearing* of line 2 made and repeated (or in the making) to the poet – seems very plausible. On the significance of our uncertainty, see the Introduction, pages 10–11.

3   *act* (as elsewhere in Shakespeare, suggesting 'the sexual act')
    torn. The image is of a written contract, *torn* and abandoned, but the verb more abstractly evokes the connective tissues of human feeling breached by the breaking of a *bed-vow*.

4   *new love bearing* entertaining new affection (affection for someone new. With a further quibble released by the sexual suggestions of *bearing*: the mistress bears the burden of a new lover in her bed.)

6, 8   *most . . . lost.* Probably rhymed on a variant pronunciation of *most* using short 'o' (so that the final effect would be '-ost' roughly as in modern *lost*)

7   *but to* to do nothing except, only to
    misuse. 'Revile', 'mistreat', 'slander', 'debauch', and 'deceive' all remain in play until the sestet fastens on 'lie about' in the benign sense 'favourably misrepresent'.

8   *And all my honest faith in thee is lost* and *In loving thee* I lose all my integrity (though the memory of lines 2–4 is strong enough to evoke a secondary 'and all the trust which I placed in your fidelity has vanished')

9   *deep oaths* solemn, heartfelt, profound, and altogether binding vows
    deep kindness. This time the adjective is hedged about with irony.

11   *enlighten thee* make you fair, qualify your blackness (but see the next note)
    gave eyes to blindness chose to become blind (to your faults), looked unseeingly. The intellectual implications of *blindness* (the *blindness* of ignorance, lack of 'insight') are elicited by *enlightened* – a word which would mean, in most contexts, 'intellectually illuminated'.

12   *Or . . . see* or made the eyes bear false witness about their perceptions. Compare Sonnets 114, 137, 148, and 149. The poet's contempt for the lady, explicit in the couplet, is communicated here by the dismissive *thing*.

13   *more perjured eye.* Echoing *I am perjured most* (line 6) through a quibble (compare 148.11).

Sonnet 153

When Shakespeare penned this poem and Sonnet 154, he was elaborating a conceit already at least a thousand years old. The Greek Anthology records a six-line epigram by Marianus Scholasticus, a fifth-century Byzantine poet, which has been translated thus:

> Beneath these plane trees, detained by gentle slumber, Love slept, having put his torch in the care of the Nymphs; but the Nymphs said one to another: 'Why wait? Would that together with this we could quench the fire in the hearts of men.' But the torch set fire even to the water, and with hot water thenceforth the Love-Nymphs fill the bath.

However, as James Hutton observes, in a carefully researched account (see Further Reading, page 71), there is no reason to think that Sonnets 153 and 154 rest on Marianus's Greek; Shakespeare could have found the epigram in one of several modern languages, or in Latin. For a discussion of the poems' place in the sequence – and their pervasive sterile bawdry – see the Introduction, pages 13–15 and 61–2.

1   *brand* torch. A standard piece of equipment for Cupid, representing passion. With an obvious phallic implication.

2   *A maid of Dian's* one of Diana's attendant virgins. The moon goddess, huntress, and queen of chastity, Diana, was said to be attended by a train of chaste nymphs.

4   *of that ground* nearby, in that vicinity

5   *Love.* Here Cupid becomes indistinguishable from the thing he represents, though typographical conventions require that either the god or the passion be judged primary.

5, 7   *love . . . prove.* For the rhyme see the note to 25.13, 14.

6   *dateless lively.* Some editors make *dateless* ('eternal') adverbial, hyphenating Q's two adjectives.
     still always, forever

7   *grew* became
     yet still, to this day
     prove find to be

7–8   *a seething bath . . . cure* (glancing wittily at the sweating tubs in which *men* were steamed as part of the treatment for venereal disease)

8   *sovereign* potent, excellent, certain

9   *new-fired* having been ignited afresh

10   *for trial needs would touch* needs must test it against
     trial (two syllables)

11   *withal* therefrom

11–12   *the help of bath desired, | And thither hied.* The suggestion that Shakespeare here alludes to a visit to the spa at Bath may be quietly ignored.

12   *hied* hurried

        sad distempered unhappy diseased (though *sad*, like *dateless* in line 6, might just be adverbial, producing the sense 'wretchedly ill')

13, 14 *my help lies . . . my mistress' eyes* (echoing the couplet rhyme of 152, and the opening words of 130, a link emphasized by *my mistress' eye* in line 9)

Sonnet 154

See the headnote to Sonnet 153.

1   *Love-god* Cupid

2   *by his side* (echoing the quibbling 151.12, in the context of *brand*, to heighten the sexual allusiveness, the slightly sordid frivolity)

5   *votary* one who has taken a vow

6   *legions* hosts (the hint of soldiery preparing *general* in line 7)

6, 8   *warmed . . . disarmed.* Probably rhymed on a short 'a' resembling the vowel in northern English 'bat', 'bad'.

7   *the general of hot desire* (Cupid, passion's commander)

9   *by* nearby

9, 11   *by . . . remedy.* A full rhyme, resembling 1.2 and 4.

10, 12 *perpetual . . . thrall.* The rhyme depends on a secondary stress in *perpetual* giving full weight to its final syllable, which would (like the '-all' of *thrall*) be closer to modern 'owl' than '-al'.

11   *Growing* becoming

12   *thrall* bondslave

13   *for cure* (from both love and slavery, and by implication venereal disease)

        this (the maxim of line 14)

        by that by virtue of my coming to the bath *for cure* (fruitlessly, as the next line reveals)

        prove (1) find to be (as at 153.7); (2) demonstrate

13, 14 *prove . . . love.* For the rhyme see the note to 25.13, 14.

14   *Love's fire heats water, water cools not love.* The first clause recapitulates the story retailed in lines 1–12, the second the poet's failure to be cured of love at the love-warmed *bath*. So, 'love may be able to heat water, but water can't cool love'. The wit of the line turns, in part, on the echo of the Song of Solomon 8.7: 'Her coals are coals of fire, and a very vehement flame [of the Lord]: so that many waters are not able to quench love, neither may the streams drown it: Yea, if a man would give all the good of his house for love, he should count it nothing.'

        The poem is followed in Q by 'FINIS.' in large capitals, a division between sequence and complaint which may or may not be authorial.

A LOVER'S COMPLAINT

This extreme, rewarding poem has been for many years marginalized in Shakespeare criticism. In part, this has stemmed from its aloofness: strange in diction, contorted in syntax, inventive but sometimes opaque in imagery, its central human situation is at once painful and presented with an artfulness which chills. It is, as Hamlet says of the Trojan play, 'caviary to the general'. Not that scholars have assisted 'the general'. Poorly edited because thought peripheral, the text has stayed peripheral because poorly edited. It has not been made accessible, nor become part of a larger debate about the nature of Shakespeare's achievement, and, while the Sonnets are difficult to gloss because so much work has already been done on them – making everything said implicitly an argument – the editor of *A Lover's Complaint* finds himself with no real tradition to draw on.

Some scholars have doubted Shakespeare's authorship. In 1912, noticing the coinages and archaisms which spatter the text, the 'tortuousness' and supposed 'cumbrousness' of its phrasing, J. W. Mackail influentially argued that the poem was not authorial, and had found its way more or less by accident 'into the same blank book as the Sonnets' from which Thorpe had printed Q. This hypothesis was given a further twist by J. M. Robertson when, in 1917, he identified Chapman as the poet of *A Lover's Complaint*. Though there were some dissenting voices, this view remained orthodox until the early 1960s. Then two independent studies were published, almost simultaneously, arguing, on the basis of parallel passages, recurring imagery, and distinctive items of vocabulary, that the poem was Shakespearian. Kenneth Muir and MacD. P. Jackson differed slightly over dating – the former preferring a date near 1600, the latter entertaining the idea that the text was Jacobean – but they agreed about authenticity. The web of Shakespearian echoes and anticipations which they discovered is not only fascinating as part of a piece of detection but critically illuminating, in that it points up the literary, wrought, self-conscious manner of the verse. Indeed, it is tempting to reproduce Muir's and Jackson's cross-references in the commentary – especially since Jackson's impressive pamphlet, barely circulated beyond New Zealand, has been little read – but, in accordance with the principles of the series, that temptation has been resisted. The notes below use quotation to clarify usage, not to demonstrate the authority of the text.

That, in any case, should need no urging. For the work of Professors Muir and Jackson has recently been complemented and confirmed by the research of Eliot Slater. After examining the text's vocabulary – against a statistical background provided by the plays and other poems – Slater concluded that *A Lover's Complaint* was 'an authentic work of Shakespeare' with a 'statistically highly significant association with the vocabulary of the third quarter [of Shakespeare's career] (*Hamlet, Troilus, All's Well* and possibly *Lear*), and also very definitely with *Cymbeline*.' While one might question the wisdom of an analysis so firmly based on statistics – and this editor would instinctively place the poem towards the middle and end of Slater's 'third quarter' rather than *c.* 1600 – the agreement with earlier inquiries is impressive. Moreover, in the year that Slater's article appeared, 1975, another, independent study by A. C. Partridge reached the same conclusion about authorship. Essentially a study of substantive grammar, Partridge's work moves inexorably from its assessment of vocabulary and syntax to the conclusion that *A Lover's Complaint* is Shakespearian. Detailed comparison with Chapman's *Caesar and Pompey*, *The Puritan*, and *Hero and Leander* III–VI (the sections added by Chapman to Marlowe's two sestiads) tends to confirm this, while disposing finally of Chapman as an alternative author. For Partridge, 'the poem was a belated experiment in Spenserian pastoral', but wholly Shakespeare's work.

Certainly, Spenser provided a model. In *The Ruines of Time* (published in his volume of *Complaints*, 1591), the poet describes his encounter with the spirit of the city of Verulam in terms close to those adopted by Shakespeare at the beginning of his own complaint:

> It chaunced me on day beside the shore
> Of siluer streaming *Thamesis* to bee,
> Nigh where the goodly *Verlame* stood of yore,
> Of which there now remains no memorie,
> Nor anie little moniment to see,
> By which the trauailer, that fares that way,
> This once was she, may warned be to say.
>
> There on the other side, I did behold
> A Woman sitting sorrowfullie wailing,
> Rending her yeolow locks, like wyrie golde,
> About her shoulders careleslie downe trailing,
> And streames of teares from her faire eyes forth railing.
> In her right hand a broken rod she held,
> Which towards heauen shee seemd on high to weld . . .
>
> Ah what delight (quoth she) in earthlie thing,
> Or comfort can I wretched creature haue?
> Whose happines the heauens enuying,
> From highest staire to lowest step me draue,
> And haue in mine owne bowels made my graue,
> That of all Nations now I am forlorne,
> The worlds sad spectacle, and fortunes scorne.

Much was I mooued at her piteous plaint,
· And felt my heart nigh riuen in my brest
With tender ruth to see her sore constraint,
That shedding teares awhile I still did rest,
And after did her name of her request.
Name haue I none (quoth she) nor anie being,
Bereft of both by Fates vniust decreeing.

I was that Citie, which the garland wore
Of *Britaines* pride, deliuered vnto me
By *Romane* Victors, which it wonne of yore;
Though nought at all but ruines now I bee,
And lye in mine owne ashes, as ye see:
Verlame I was; what bootes it that I was
Sith now I am but weedes and wastfull gras?

(lines 1–14, 22–42)

Though encounters of this kind are commonplace in late medieval and Tudor literature, and though further analogues for Shakespeare's fluvial setting can be identified (see pages 393–4 below, and the note to line 39), the overlap between Spenser's poem and the opening of *A Lover's Complaint* is unmistakable. There is the rhyme royal, the mysterious maiden sitting on the river-bank (line 39; and see the note to *set*), weeping tears which resemble the stream she borders (lines 40–42, 50), with her hair *untucked* (lines 29–39), lamenting her ruin (*passim*); and there is the suggestive notion of her namelessness. Moreover, the rest of Spenser's text comes close to Shakespeare in his Sonnets, emphasizing the transience of beauty, the violence of Time, and the importance of poetry as a means to immortality:

Thy Lord shall neuer die, the whiles this verse
Shall liue, and surely it shall liue for euer:
For ever it shall liue, and shall rehearse
His worthie praise, and vertues dying neuer,
Though death his soule doo from his bodie seuer.
And thou thy selfe herein shalt also liue:
Such grace the heauens doo to my verses giue.

(lines 253–9)

In his essay on 'The Genesis of Shakespeare's *Sonnets*', A. Kent Hieatt argues that Shakespeare found in Spenser's translation from Du Bellay, *Ruines of Rome* (also published in the 1591 volume), images of a city which became for him a metaphor for the lovely youth. Doubtless Spenser's depiction of another Roman city as a woman led Shakespeare towards *A Lover's Complaint*. Note the imagery of lines 176–7. In 1–126, Rome as the youth is a city ruined by time; in the complaint, by contrast, ruin is chiefly the correlative of unchastity.

Behind both Shakespeare and Spenser lie texts like Dorigen's sea-brink lament in Chaucer's 'Franklin's Tale' (V [F] 857–94) and the plaints which make up the *Mirror for Magistrates* (1559 etc.), especially Thomas Churchyard's 'Shore's wife' (1563 etc., revised 1593). The complaint genre, never unpopular, flowered afresh in the 1590s, in the work of Daniel and his followers. The influence of *The Complaint of Rosamond* has already been discussed (pages 13–17), but the author of *The Rape of Lucrece* – a poem which itself owes much to the complaint form – must have been aware of other exercises in the kind, and alert to the turn the tradition took in 1594 with the publication of *Willobie His Avisa*. With this extraordinary text, what has been called the 'democratization of the complaint form' began. Earlier complaints tend to be spoken by socially distinguished figures, of historical importance, or by personae like Spenser's Verulam. In Willobie's text, however, the heroine is a humble inn-keeper's wife, a lower-class Lucrece – virginal before marriage and loyal to her husband once wed. In social standing, if not in morality, Avisa anticipates the *fickle maid full pale* of Shakespeare's poem (see the note to line 8).

How deep did the influence of Willobie go? His book presents a series of dialogues and verse epistles between Avisa and her wooers: a wanton nobleman, a 'Cavaleiro', a Frenchman, one D.H. *'Anglo-Germanus'*, and her most persistent admirer *'Henrico Willobego. Italo-Hispalensis'*, assisted in his suit (which persists in written verses when it fails in speech) by a shadowy figure called W.S. The poem is not finally a true complaint, since, despite much woeful reflection on the nature of love and life, Avisa's impregnable virtue leaves her with nothing to regret. Yet, while Willobie's philosophical flights have not detained critics, his W.S. has – particularly in the context of H.W. Might these initials not represent William Shakespeare and Henry Wriothesley, Earl of Southampton, and a favoured candidate to be the friend of the Sonnets? Some circumstances in Willobie's story fit, but more do not. W.S. is called 'the old player', which gets the poet's occupation right, but was Shakespeare 'old' in 1594 (when just touching thirty)? He helps H.W. woo a woman he has himself sought; but Avisa is chaste, not promiscuous, and resists both wooers. 'Viewing afar off the course of this loving Comedy, he determined to see whether it would sort to a happier end for this new actor than it did for the old player. But at length this Comedy was like to have grown to a Tragedy, by the weak and feeble estate that H.W. was brought unto, by a desperate view of an impossibility of obtaining his purpose'. This may describe a triangular situation, with something of the dark comedy we find in the Sonnets – a triangle refracted in *A Lover's Complaint* – but, again, the anxiety of the poet in Shakespeare's collection is quite different from that of W.S. in *Willobie*, fearing as he does that the friend will be corrupted and probably diseased by too much access to the easy-going dark lady. As for

H.W.: why *Henry Wr*iothesley rather than *Henrico Wi*llobego (the presumed author, Willobie, in a modishly Italianate and Hispanic guise)? The whole issue of identification is so fraught – the current favourite for Avisa appears to be Queen Elizabeth – that no certainty is possible on the point.

A literary analogue, however, *Avisa* seems to be; and, since some of its devices (such as the use of written verse in wooing) recur in Shakespeare's sequence, it may even be thought a minor source. In this it takes its place alongside – though both are subordinate to *The Complaint of Rosamond* – the ballad which Desdemona sings in the Folio *Othello*. Known now to scholars as 'The Willow Song', this lament – widely circulated and set to music in the period – is entitled, in early black-letter printings included in the Pepys and Roxburghe collections, 'A Lover's Complaint, being forsaken of his Love' and 'The Complaint of a Lover forsaken of his Love'. This double and distinct testimony from the first half of the seventeenth century suggests that Shakespeare knew the text under a similar title, and that, in writing his complaint, he echoed or appropriated the title of the ballad. The debt perhaps goes deeper. Certainly, the ballad as Desdemona sings it recalls Shakespeare's poem. Folio *Othello* presents a dejected woman lamenting her abandonment, sitting on a river-bank, singing of willow:

> The poor soul sat sighing by a sycamore tree,
>   Sing all a green willow;
> Her hand on her bosom, her head on her knee,
>   Sing willow, willow, willow;
> The fresh streams ran by her and murmured her moans;
>   Sing willow, willow, willow;
> Her salt tears fell from her and softened the stones . . .
>
> IV.3.38–44

In Shakespeare's complaint, the same situation recurs, with the abandoned, apparently seated, *maid* weeping beside a river probably planted with willow. (For the 'salt' of her 'tears', see line 18 and the note; for her posture, line 39 and the note to *set*, and lines 65–6; for the willows along the river-bank, line 39 and the first note.) Significantly, in all the early manuscript and printed versions of Desdemona's song, the abandoned lover is male. This is evidence for, not against, some connexion between the complaint and the ballad, because the changes made for the tragedy would parallel or anticipate those made for the sake of the poem. Moreover, Shakespeare's complaint quibbles structurally with the term 'Lover' in ways which might follow from the word being inherited from another context; the poet surprises us with a female speaker, when 'Lover' was usually applied to a male, only to deliver what the title appeared to promise by including within the *maid*'s complaint the plaint of her treacherous male friend (see the Introduction, pages 15–16, on this embracing doubleness). The tragic context illuminates the complaint further, in that Desdemona recalls that the ballad was sung by her mother's

> maid called Barbary:
> She was in love: and he she loved proved mad
> And did forsake her.

> IV.3.25–7

Here we have, first, the idea of plaining by a socially lowly *maid*, and, secondly, a connexion with Ophelia – who loved a prince that 'proved mad' and drowned herself in a brook flanked by a willow, and whose predicament is echoed directly at *A Lover's Complaint* 39. On this textual nexus see the commentary at that point, and, more generally, consider the advice about chastity towards a socially superior suitor at *Hamlet* I.3.5–44, 115–31. Indeed, the burden of Ophelia's ballad at IV.5.48–67 – which has persuaded some scholars that Hamlet seduced her before the nunnery scene (when only her subconscious was seduced) – should also be borne in mind: the warnings of Laertes and Polonius are not in one sense idle; Ophelia could easily be the *fickle maid* deflowered, and the *fickle maid*, without assistance, the drowned Ophelia. (Compare also *The Two Noble Kinsmen* IV.1.52–103, especially lines 62–3, 79–82, 88–93, and 95–6.)

If these connexions with *Othello* and *Hamlet* are accepted, and if the congruence between the poem and *All's Well That Ends Well* is thought significant (see pages 12 and 17 and the essays by Roger Warren listed on page 70), a context for the composition of *A Lover's Complaint* is established which coincides with the dating produced by stylistic tests. Notice, too, the text's overlap with *Measure for Measure* through its interest in sexual irregularity, confessional utterance, problematic judgement, the cloistered life, worldly grace, and a fiend as angel. One can imagine Shakespeare, haunted by the ballad, using it in the tragedies and re-creating it – elaborated with a related narrative – in the poem, in 'the third quarter' of his writing life.

1   *concave womb*. Probably a steep and dished hillside rather than a cave, though Echo 'lives alone in . . . hollow caves' (*Metamorphoses* III.394, translated by Golding). The image of fertile potential provided by *womb* is productive, since the concavity yields the poet the complaint which his poem retails. Shakespeare claims for the word a complexity earned between 3.5 and 86.4, with the sequence's movement from breeding to art, underwritten by the commonplace that *poesis* was a kind of parturition (see, for instance, Holofernes on his verses at *Love's Labour's Lost* IV.2.69–71). Perhaps *womb* also alludes, obliquely, to the sexual nature of the *maid*'s predicament.

reworded echoed, repeated. This echoing from the *concave womb* recalls *Julius Caesar* I.43–7, where Marullus rebukes the citizens for forgetting Pompey:

> And when you saw his chariot but appear,
> Have you not made an universal shout,
> That Tiber trembled underneath her banks
> To hear the replication of your sounds
> Made in her concave shores?

Yet it is clear that, though the *Oxford English Dictionary* cites no unambiguous instance before the nineteenth century, *reworded* could imply for Shakespeare what it means to us – the telling over of something in new words. 'It is not madness | That I have uttered', Hamlet assures his mother in the closet scene: 'Bring me to the test, | And I the matter will re-word, which madness | Would gambol from' (III.4.142–5), his distinction between the 'matter' or 'substance' of his speech and its 'wording' being indicative. On the importance of this available extension of sense, supported by *womb*, with its creative implication, see the Introduction, pages 16–17, and the note on line 5 below.

1, 3   *reworded ... accorded.* Probably rhymed on a short 'o' (like the one we still use in *accorded*), but possibly on a longer sound, 'rewoorded ... accoorded'.

2   *sist'ring.* The *hill*'s and *vale*'s sonority depends on their contiguity, and on each defining the height and depth of the other. But *sist'ring* might also glance at the concavity which this *hill* shares with its adjacent *vale*.

3   *spirits* (one syllable)
   attend listen to (but with a hint of 'wait upon'. In the light of *spirits*, 53.2 seems relevant.)
   double (because echoed. But see the Introduction, pages 15–17.)
   accorded agreed

4   *laid* (probably an archaic form even for early readers)
   list hearken to
   sad-tuned (suggesting the mournful modulation of the maiden's plaint, but gesturing too at the general sense 'in a voice attuned to sorrow, adjusted to grief'. See 141.5 and the note.)

5   *fickle.* 'Full of changes, moody, agitated' must be primary, but the *maid*'s seduction by the youth makes 'capricious, morally unstable' available. Indeed, if the woman's emotional turbulence is felt to count against the objectivity of her *reworded* lover's *plaint*, so that she becomes herself implicated in the poem's bad 'doubleness', 'shifty, unreliable' and an (archaic) 'deceitful' can be registered. The word might then recede towards 'puzzling, teasing flattery' – old senses of *fickle*(ness), relevant here both in respect of the reader (the *maid*, much as she is none, puzzles yet pleases in being articulately *fickle*) and in respect of the *story*. For seduction is never

one-sided, least of all in Shakespeare, and through the *maid*'s confessed responsiveness to the young man's duplicity we might deduce, in a wary rereading, the kind of *fickle* 'flattery' addressed by Sonnet 138 (where *my love swears that she is made of truth*, though she is no *maid*, and *in our faults by lies we flattered be*).

6   *Tearing ... a-twain* (actions clarified in stanzas seven and eight)

7   *Storming ... rain.* The maiden's sighs and tears are (in a conventional image) like *wind and rain*, vexing her *world* like a storm. This *world* involves those things she sees and feels immediately – the *hill* and *vale* registered in her grief; but it is also her self, the human frame. For this latter sense of *world*, in the context of a psychic storm, see *King Lear* III.1.10–11: 'Strives in his little world of man to out-storm | The to-and-fro conflicting wind and rain.'

8   *platted hive of straw.* A heavy straw hat, resembling a miniature bee-hive. In the period, hives were usually made of rye or wheat straw, *platted* (a variant form of 'plaited' with an independent life well into the nineteenth century) into a domed or conical shape. Whether Shakespeare invented this image or inherited the *hive* from country speech is not clear. In *Henrietta* (1761), Charlotte Lennox describes a 'shepherdess ... with a straw hive on her head, and a tattered garment on', but this may derive from literary (and so Shakespearian) usage rather than archaic rural parlance. Though straw hats could be worn by aristocrats and gentlewomen, diverting themselves in gardens – and a lacy straw with a cherry silk lining, possibly worn by Queen Elizabeth, can still be seen at Hatfield House – the *hive* worn by the *fickle maid* is the simple, solid hat associated with country girls. In *The Tempest*, such 'rye-straw hats' are sported by 'sunburned sicklemen, of August weary' (IV.1.134–8); and in his tragedy *The Rape of Lucrece* (1606–8), Heywood includes a lyric which – connecting interestingly with line 9 – runs:

> O ye fine country lasses,
> That would for brooks change change crystal glasses,
> And be translapp'd from foot to crown ...
> Now your hawk-noses shall have hoods
> And billements with golden studs;
> Straw-hats shall be no more bongraces
> From the bright sun to hide your faces,
> For hempen smocks to help the itch,
> Have linen, sewed with silver stitch ...

Not till the reign of Queen Anne did pastoral attire become fashionable among gentlefolk; throughout the seventeenth century, straw hats were associated with rustic simplicity (one post-restoration rhyme goes, 'Give me a lass that's country bred | With paragon gown, straw hat on her head'). Nevertheless, despite this, and despite the reassurance of the scholarly M. Channing Linthicum that 'The straw hat does not seem to have been worn by any except country folk during Shakespeare's age' (*Costume in the Drama of Shakespeare and his Contemporaries*, Oxford, 1936, page 231), one can only be provisionally certain that Shakespeare's abandoned *maid* is an authentic country lass. All forms of dress are open to social inversion (note Jonson's Epigram CV to Lady Wroth, 'He, that but saw you wear the wheaten hat, | Would call you more than Ceres, if not that', where the context appears to be masque-like and courtly), and every wretched *maid* is entitled to conceal and declare her dejection under the cover of clothing belonging to a class less privileged than her own. That the *fickle maid* is not a courtier playing shepherdess (as, in a special sense, Perdita is), but a rustic girl – whether peasant or wealthy farmer's daughter – elevated by the semi-Spenserian idiom of the verse, must be inferred from the precedent set by *Willobie His Avisa* (see the headnote above), and from lines 148–51, where the *distance* adduced suggests a gap looked at from below rather than above. But perhaps Shakespeare presents sparse evidence of the girl's status because he wants it to remain more or less undistractingly inessential.

9   *fortifièd* protected, guarded
10   *Whereon* upon which *visage*
        the thought might think. A curious but thoroughly Shakespearian indication of uncertainty (justified by lines 71–4), with *thought* somewhere between the 'process of thinking' and 'mind', and *think* verging on 'fancy'. Compare *The Merchant of Venice* I.1.36–7, 'Shall I have the thought | To think on this . . . ?', or *Hamlet* IV.5.12–13, where it is said that Ophelia's raving 'would make one think there might be thought, | Though nothing sure, yet much unhappily.'
11   *carcass.* The maiden's *beauty* only survives as a 'lifeless remnant'.
        spent and done exhausted and finished
12   *Time had not scythèd all that youth begun.* A condensed, complex image, decipherable because so much in the Sonnets – see, for instance, 12.13, 60.12, 100.14, and 123.14 – lies behind it.
13   *all quit* left altogether, fled from every part
        heaven's (one syllable)
        heaven's fell rage. Here *heaven* is primarily the abode of God directing power in the *world, fell rage* its 'cruel anger' or 'vehement action against' the *maid* (anger expressed in the sorrows she is

subjected to); but the phrase is enriched by its association with lines 7 and 9, *heaven's fell rage* suggesting both the *maid*'s exposure to the elements (her being in the fields like a lesser Lear) and the storming grief which rages within her *world*.

14   *Some beauty peeped through lattice of seared age.* The image is of youthful beauty largely obscured by, but peeping through, the interstices of a lattice-work window, whose criss-cross pattern of wood or lead suggests, on some level, the wrinkles of *seared* ('dried-up, desiccated') *age*. (In so far as 'seared Age' emerges from Q's 'sear'd age', the *fickle maid*'s *beauty* peeps through its casement like a prisoner entrapped by Age.) Compare 3.11–12.

15   *heave* raise, lift. As at *Venus and Adonis* 351 ('With one fair hand she heaveth up his hat'), the implication 'with effort', invariable in modern usage, is absent.
     napkin handkerchief
     eyne eyes (an archaism, though used a dozen times in Shakespeare – usually, as here, under the pressure of rhyme)

16   *conceited characters* fanciful designs, emblematic devices, cunningly wrought mottos

16, 18,   *characters . . . tears . . . bears.* Probably rhymed on long 'e', sounding
19   like the 'ar' in 'scarce', 'scares', though *bears* may fit imperfectly, tending to an 'i' sound like the vowel in 'bit'.

17   *silken figures.* The *characters* of line 16, embroidered in silk.

18   *seasoned* (1) long-harboured, matured (like *seasoned* timber); (2) salted (suggested by the *brine* of the weeper's *tears*). This second association is characteristically Shakespearian. Compare *The Rape of Lucrece* 796, 'Seasoning the earth with showers of silver brine', or *All's Well That Ends Well* I.1.45–7, 'tears . . . the best brine a maiden can season her praise in.'
     pelleted. In the context of *seasoned* (sense 2), a bizarre culinary image emerges, since a 'pellet' was a meatball. Most prominent at the metaphoric level, though, is 'pellet' in the sense 'shot, gunstone, projectile' (note the imagery of lines 22–5). Significantly, the only other Shakespearian use of *pelleted* associates tears with a destructive bombardment. Accused of being cold-hearted towards Antony, Cleopatra protests that, if she is so, heaven should 'engender hail' from her tears and, in a 'pelleted storm' destroy herself, her heirs, and nation (III.13.158–67).

19   *And . . . bears.* Evidently, the *conceited characters* and *silken figures* recall the maid's false lover. Presumably the *napkin* is one of his now hurtful gifts.
     contents (accented on the second syllable)

20   *undistinguished.* 'Inarticulate' and 'confused' (leading towards line 21), with a hint of 'indiscriminate, heedless'.

21   *both high and low* (in volume, but with an inescapable suggestion of pitch, supported by the *sad-tuned tale* of line 4)

22–3   *Sometimes . . . intend.* The maiden's *eyes* resemble a cannon on a gun-*carriage*, aimed (*levelled*, as at 117.11, 121.9, and lines 282 and 309) at the planets (the *spheres*) as though they meant to barrage the heavens. *Intend* enriches the aiming imagery, implying (through the Latin idiom *intendere oculos*) 'strain towards, direct at' as well as 'purpose'.

23   *As* as if

24–5   *Sometime . . . earth.* When she stares fixedly at the ground, the despondent maiden's *eyes* seem attached to it. They seem *tied* to the *earth* (Hamlet's 'orbèd ground', III.2.165) like eye-*balls* connected to the head by means of the optic nerves, or, more distantly, like planets bound to and spinning about the *earth* in the conventional Ptolemaic cosmology outlined by (among others) Shakespeare's Ulysses (at *Troilus and Cressida* I.3.75–137). If this latter image is prompted by the *spheres* of line 23, *levelled*, *carriage*, and *batt'ry* make the maiden's *balls* gunstones to her *eyes*' cannon.

26   *right on* directly onwards
      anon at the next moment

26–7   *their gazes lend* | *To every place at once* (rolling wildly)

28   *The . . . commixed.* A sudden extension beyond visual disorder to the kind of perceptual confusion which exercises Shakespeare in Sonnets 114 and 148.
      distractedly wildly, crazily
      commixed mingled, confused

29   *nor . . . nor* neither . . . nor

30   *a careless hand of pride.* Though 'a hand whose pride showed itself in carelessness' is significantly not eclipsed, 'a hand indifferent to proud appearance' seems primary.

31   *descended* hung from
      sheaved woven with straw (as though a sheaf. See line 8 and the note.)

32   *pinèd* wasted with pining

33   *fillet* ribbon, hair-band

35   *slackly* loosely, laxly

36   *maund* basket

37   *beaded jet* jet beads. This assumes that Q's 'bedded' is a spelling variant, but it might mean 'embedded, inlaid'.

39   *Upon whose weeping margin she was set.* Obviously, *weeping* qualifies *she* ('Upon whose margin, weeping, she was set'), but it also modifies *margin*, the 'river-bank' being moist and muddy as though in sympathy with the tearful cheeks of the maiden (lines 7, 15–18, here and 40–42). Compare the 'weeping brook' which carries the

jilted Ophelia to 'muddy death' (and note *mud*, line 46) at *Hamlet* IV.7.166–83. That passage, 'There is a willow grows askant the brook . . .', raises a third possibility which, though imaginatively elliptical, cannot be excluded. *Weeping* suggests the dangling branches of willows along the river-bank – trees traditionally associated with *weeping* and lost love (see the headnote above). It is thus suggested that the maiden is *set* among *weeping* willows, *weeping*, or, like a metamorphosed figure in Ovid, is *set* beside the stream, like or as a *weeping* willow. *Set* is often used in Early Modern English to mean 'planted, rooted' (compare the *maiden gardens, yet unset* of 16.6), and the *reverend man* at line 66 is interestingly *sat*, not *set*. There would be nothing novel in Shakespeare using a willowy, river-bank setting for his encounter between the *fickle maid* and the *reverend man* who is to appear at line 57, overheard by the poet (the *I* of line 4). In Nicholas Breton's *Wit's Trenchmore, In a Conference had Betwixt a Scholar and an Angler* (1597), three figures are similarly disposed. The text – which Shakespeare perhaps knew – ends with the parting of the disputants and the emergence of an authorial persona:

> Thus with hearty thanks each to other, with a few good words of either side, taking a kind leave, the angler takes up his hook, and away they part from the riverside. From whence when they were gone in a manner out of sight, a certain odd Diogenes of the world, like a forlorn creature on the earth, thrown lately out of the fortune of his mistress' favour, getting a paper-book under his arm, and a pen and ink under his girdle, in a melancholic humour, meaning to trouble the Muses, with some doleful ballad, to the tune of all a green willow, sitting down on a little mole-hill, among a thick grown plot of osiers unseen, instead of his intended piece of poetry, writ as fast as he could this discourse that he heard betwixt this angler and the scholar.

set. In Elizabethan and Jacobean English, the sense 'seated' was strong as well as 'placed', and this is apparently primary here (compare the situation in Desdemona's ballad quoted in the headnote above). For the vegetative associations of *set*, see the previous note.

40   *Like usury* (which adds money to money, by charging interest)
40–42   *Like usury . . . all.* An odd but entirely Shakespearian notion. Compare *3 Henry VI* V.4.6–9, 'Is't meet that he | Should leave the helm and, like a fearful lad, | With tearful eyes add water to the sea, | And give more strength to that which hath too much . . . ?', or the river-bank scene described at *As You Like It* II.1.29–43, or Laertes

after 'There is a willow grows askant the brook . . .', anxious lest his 'tears' add *wet* to 'Too much of water' (IV.7.185–6).

41–2   *Or monarch's . . . all* or like the hands of a monarch who, ignoring the cries of the needy seeking some charity, gives plentifully to those who, already enjoying too much plenty, beg all the bounty there is to be had. Q's 'Monarches' is ambiguous, and it may be that, despite *lets* (which might refer to the single ruler behind the plural *hands*), 'monarchs'' should be read.

43   *schedules* sheets of paper containing writing (here, letters from the youth and/or poems: see lines 204–31)

43, 45   *one . . . bone.* Rhymed like *one . . . alone* at 36.2 and 4 on a long 'o' resembling the 'ar' in Scottish English 'ward'.

45   *Cracked many a ring* (see line 6)

posied inscribed with mottos. Presumably the *gold and bone* bore legends of love; rings were frequently so inscribed. 'Posy' in the sense 'bunch of flowers' was emergent but rare in the period, and is not relevant here. 'Poesy', however, ultimately is (since 'posy' meaning 'motto' is its contraction): the assault on artful language, announced in the tearing of *schedules*, continues in the breaking of rings.

bone ivory

47   *sadly.* 'Despondently', as in modern English, but 'gravely, seriously' too. The bloody ink seemed to show the writings sincere.

48   *sleided* separated into threads. A rare form of the never very common word 'sleaved' ('to sleave' being 'to ravel out a thread till it becomes floss'). Compare *Pericles* IV Chorus 21, 'Beet when they weaude the sleded silke', and *Troilus and Cressida* V.1.29–30, 'thou idle immaterial skeine of sleiue silke' (quoting from the quarto texts, both published in the same year as Thorpe's Q).

feat. The word – which was archaic by the end of the sixteenth century – fleetingly modifies *silk* in the sense 'delicate', but *affectedly* gives it the adverbial implication 'adroitly' and attaches it to *Enswathed and sealed.*

affectedly lovingly, with affection. But the implied care allows 'elaborately, archly' (the implication which survives in modern English) to register. Though the adjective was well-established and widely used, the adverb was not (it is first recorded in Chapman's translation of seven books of the *Iliad*, 1598).

49   *Enswathed and sealed to curious secrecy* wrapped about (*With sleided silk*) and sealed (with wax) into a state of intricate concealment. Letters were typically sealed with wax and silken thread. By using *to* rather than 'in', Shakespeare creates a paradox and (as it were) negative quibble: the reader expects 'to curious eyes', but *secrecy* retrospectively suppresses the primary sense of *curious* and allows

'complex, intricate' to emerge. *Enswathed* seems to be Shakespeare's coinage (based on 'swathed', with an archaizing prefix).

50　　*fluxive* apt to flow, weeping. Apparently minted by Shakespeare (from Latin *fluxivus*), and used sporadically until the eighteenth century.

51　　*'gan to tear.* Q's 'gaue to teare' might be retained if 'gaue to' could be read as 'devoted herself to' (making *tear* elliptical), but *often* tells against the former and there is no clear precedent for the latter. The eighteenth-century emendation 'gave a tear' bathetically undercuts line 50. Presumably Shakespeare's manuscript, or a transcriber's script, read 'gañe' – easily misreadable as 'gaue' in secretary hand.

51, 53,　*tear... bear... here.* A full rhyme, using long 'e' (sounding like the
54　　'ar' in 'scarce') rather than 'ee' in *here*.

52　　*O false blood* (with a glimmer of irony, since *blood* in the sense 'appetite, lust' has betrayed her, played her *false*)
　　　register record

53　　*unapprovèd* false, not confirmed (indeed, disproved) in practice. *Witness* and *bear* make the line allude to the Ninth Commandment: 'Thou shalt not bear false witness against thy neighbour' (Deuteronomy 5.20).

55　　*in top of rage* at the height of anger

56　　*Big* boisterous, mighty (in Shakespearian usage a judgement of vigour rather than scale)
　　　contents (stressed on the second syllable)

58　　*Sometime* once, formerly
　　　ruffle clamorous ostentation, hectic bustle

59–60　*had let... flew.* Though this *man* had *let go by*, almost carelessly, *The swiftest hours* of his life (the *hours* of his youth and prime), he had profited from their passage by observing what they showed him. For all their *ruffle*, the busy *court* and *city* made him a philosopher of life. Shakespeare draws here on a tradition of retirement poetry, founded by Horace and Virgil (in the *Georgics*). Enormously important in the later seventeenth and early eighteenth centuries, the theme was not much explored in English before Shakespeare composed his complaint. He will have known, however, the tale of Meliboe – the shepherd who, in *The Faerie Queene* VI.ix, tells Calidore how, as a youth, he went to work at court, but was quickly oppressed by its 'vainesse' and 'idle hopes', and returned to rustic life (the whole canto recalls Shakespeare's poem in timbre, situation, context). It is also likely that Shakespeare knew the 'Sonnet' on Sir Henry Lee's retirement from the office of 'Queen's Champion' at tournaments (*Polyhymnia*, 1590):

His golden locks time hath to silver turned,
O time too swift, O swiftness never ceasing:
His youth 'gainst time and age hath ever spurned
But spurned in vain; youth waneth by increasing.
   Beauty, strength, youth, are flowers, but fading seen;
   Duty, faith, love are roots, and ever green.

His helmet now shall make a hive for bees,
And lovers' sonnets, turned to holy psalms:
A man at arms must now serve on his knees,
And feed on prayers, which are age his alms.
   But though from court to cottage he depart,
   His saint is sure of his unspotted heart.

And when he saddest sits in homely cell
He'll teach his swains this carol for a song,
'Blest be the hearts that wish my sovereign well;
Cursed be the souls that think her any wrong.'
   Goddess, allow this aged man his right,
   To be your beadsman now, that was your knight.

The poem demands quotation in full since its anticipations of
Shakespeare's sonnet sequence – and 'youth waneth by increasing'
is only the clearest pre-echo (of 126.3–4) – serve to underline the
difficulty of disentangling the question of influence from a skein of
images and phrases current in the period. On the *Georgic* and
Horatian background, see the Further Reading, page 72.

61   *afflicted fancy*. In Shakespeare, fancy most often means 'amorous
passion'. Here the *afflicted* ('distressed' because 'love-sick', but
also, as it turns out, because 'cruelly treated') *maid* is summed up
by her feelings. Compare the metonymy at line 197, where the
women who have sought the young man's love are *wounded fancies*.
fastly (1) hastily (2) closely ('fast by')

63   *the grounds and motives of her woe*. A real distinction, *grounds* having
prompted the *woe*, *motives* giving it force and motion.

64   *So slides he down upon his grainèd bat*. Although the language allows
the reader to imagine the *reverend man* slipping and slithering down
the river-bank to where the maiden weeps, using the *grainèd bat* to
steady his uncertain progress, the dignity of the context prompts us
to take *slides* in the now obsolete sense 'passes smoothly', with *upon*
suggesting the support offered to the old man by his *grainèd*
('forked, pronged') *bat* ('staff'). A *bat*, as Spenser shows, was
associated at once with age ('a handsome bat he held, | On which
he leaned, as one farre in elde', *Mother Hubberds Tale* 216–17) and

the pastoral life: 'thus his carelesse time | This shepheard driues, vpleaning on his batt' (*Virgils Gnat* 154–5).

65 *comely distant* at a decorous distance

66 *again desires her* strongly urges her. *Again* is here an intensifier, with no strong suggestion of repetition. Compare, for example, *The Merchant of Venice* III.2.203, 'For wooing here until I sweat again' ('until I was positively dripping with sweat').
being sat (referring to the *reverend man*)

67 *Her grievance with his hearing to divide.* The *reverend man* invokes proverbial lore, 'Grief is lessened when imparted to others' (compare *The Passionate Pilgrim* XX.53–8), 'When shared, joy is doubled and sorrow halved', while the poet plays on *grievance* (both cause and, by extension, effect of 'grief') and emphasizes, once more, verbal 'doubleness' (*divide* as 'share even-handedly').

68 *applied.* As often in Shakespeare, used to suggest the application of a remedy to some hurt. Hence *assuage* in line 69. At 40–44 the link had been with *folded* (Latin *plicare*).

69 *suffering ecstasy* anguished frenzy, distressed derangement

71 *Father.* Not a melodramatic revelation of identity but – as at line 288 and, for instance, *Coriolanus* V.1.3 – a title of respect used of old and venerable men. Arguably, the *maid*'s predicament, the *reverend man*'s care, and the confessional nature of what is to follow make 'ghostly father, confessor' contribute to the vocative's ring.

72 *injury of* hurt inflicted by
blasting blighting

75 *spreading.* 'Opening its petals' rather than 'putting out stems and proliferating'.

76 *fresh to myself.* On this echo of Sonnet 94, see the Introduction, page 26.

78 *attended* listened to, heeded

79 *it was to gain my grace.* The *suit* (or 'request') was that the maid should grant her *grace* (her 'approval' or 'amorous favour') to her *youthful* suitor. The proleptic sense, 'this *suit* was, as it befell, to win my favour', is available, but hardly primary.

80 *O, one by nature's outwards so commended.* The Q ejaculation 'O' marks the point at which the young man, at first concealed behind his *youthful suit*, breaks into the maiden's thoughts, suddenly diverting the syntax. Most editors emend 'O' to 'Of', making *it was to gain my grace* a pointed parenthesis between *the youthful suit* and 'Of one . . .'
nature's outwards the appearance bestowed by Nature, natural good looks
commended recommended. The youth's good looks seemed to indicate good character.

81   *maidens' eyes stuck over all his face.* A grotesque but entirely
      Shakespearian way of describing the youth's sexual magnetism,
      with women gazing at his features, 'glued to' him. Compare
      Measure for Measure IV.1.59–60: 'O place and greatness, millions
      of false eyes | Are stuck upon thee', or *Timon of Athens* IV.3.262–5:
      'The mouths, the tongues, the eyes, and hearts of men . . . | That
      numberless upon me stuck, as leaves | Do on the oak'.

82   *Love* Venus
      Love . . . place. A commonplace of renaissance love poetry, but,
      interestingly, one usually applied to women, not men.

86   *every light occasion of the wind* each stirring in the breeze. *Light*
      means both 'unconsidered, merely chance' and 'gentle, not gust-
      ing', while *occasion* reaches beyond 'juncture, circumstance when
      something happens' to 'occurrence, action'.

86, 88,   *wind . . . find . . . mind.* For the diphthong on which this rhyme is
89   based, see the note to 14.6, 8.

87   *Upon . . . hurled.* The *wind* tossed the youth's *curls* against *his lips* in
      silky-fine bundles.

88   *What's . . . find* whatever deed is pleasant will readily find ways of
      being done (because people will as readily enable themselves to do
      it. Looking and falling in love seem to be in question here.)

89   *eye* (the 'I' pun of the late Sonnets seems merely latent here)

90–91 *For on . . . sawn.* The same topos is explored in Sonnet 68.

93   *phoenix* uniquely beautiful (like the *phoenix* invoked in Sonnet 19)

93, 95,   *appear . . . wear . . . dear.* For the basis of this rhyme see the note to
96   80.6, 8.

94   *termless.* This is often glossed 'untouched by time, youthful', but
      'beyond description, of inexpressible loveliness' seems more likely
      – especially in the light of *phraseless* at line 225. Was there,
      Shakespeare has us wonder, *fickle* 'flattery' on the maid's side too?
      See the Introduction, pages 15–17 and 59, and the note to line 5.

95   *Whose bare out-bragged the web it seemed to wear.* The youth's *bare* or
      'naked skin', around and under his *down*, surpassed in beauty the
      web (that beard regarded as 'woven stuff, tissue, fine cloth') which
      it *seemed to wear* (did in one sense *wear*, but did not since the beard
      was *down*, not clothing).

96   *Yet showed his visage by that cost more dear.* Though the *bare* was
      lovelier than the *web*, the *down*'s being there made the face, overall,
      more dear – presumably by contrasting with the *skin*. *Cost* works
      complexly, since both 'extrusion' and 'ornament' emerge from the
      initial 'outlay, expenditure', and since there is a pun on French *coste*
      or *côte*, 'silken floss'. (It seems less likely that *web* legitimates a pun
      on 'coat' – with a heraldic extension, as at line 236.) *Dear* is
      correspondingly ambiguous: 'loved, valued' and 'expensive, *costly*'.

97   *nice* fastidious, subtle, precise
      affections inclinations (of an amorously admiring kind), likings

98   *If best were as it was, or best without.* Discussion could not finally
      decide whether his *visage* was better with its *cost* (contrasting nicely
      with the *skin*) or better without (leaving more *skin* to be seen). The
      substitution of *best . . . best* for the grammatical 'better . . . better'
      adds a note of hyperbole.

99   *qualities* manner, accomplishments

100   *maiden-tongued.* Presumably both 'soft-spoken' and 'verbally
      blameless (speaking without sarcasm, scandal, obscenity)'. As at
      line 94, Shakespeare provokes a flicker of doubt – strengthened,
      Tom Morris and others persuade me, on second and subsequent
      readings. If the *maiden-tongued* youth proved deceitful, can we
      trust his *maiden-tongued* accuser?
      thereof (of his tongue)
      free liberal, eloquent

101   *moved him* roused him to anger

101–3 *such a storm . . . be.* On this time of year, and its not being as early as
      it might now seem, see 18.3 and the note. Citing *The Winter's Tale*
      IV.4.118–20 ('Daffodils, | That come before the swallow dares,
      and take | The winds of March with beauty'), Stanley Wells and
      Gary Taylor suggest to me that 'oft 'twixt March and April' might
      be read.

104–5 *His rudeness . . . truth* his boyish roughness (the blustery anger
      disclosed in lines 101–3) thus, 'justified' by his *youth* (though
      authorized, while meaning 'excused', also makes the youth's *youth*
      'indisputable'), dressed deceit (such as that discussed at lines
      52–4) in a fine display of integrity (so that it looked like *truth*'s
      servant, clad in the uniform of honesty)

104   *authorized* (accented on the second syllable, as at 35.6)

105   *livery* (two syllables)

107   *That horse . . . takes.* The horse and rider work together so well that
      the beast's *mettle* (its 'vigour, mettlesome spirit') cannot be disting-
      uished from its master's. Such skill was highly prized. See, for
      instance, Claudius's praise of Lamord, who 'grew unto his seat, |
      And to such wondrous doing brought his horse | As he had been
      incorpsed and demi-natured | With the brave beast' (*Hamlet*
      IV.7.84–7).

108   *noble by the sway* ennobled by his rider's control. The paradox is
      ultimately political, *subjection* to a *sway* not seeming *noble*.

109   *rounds* circuits (of a ring. The discipline is formal, as in dressage or
      a riding school.)
      bounds. 'Leaps' emerge from *bounds*' semantic and phonic overlap

with *rounds*. *Course* and *stop* equally refer to equestrian man-
oeuvres.

110   *controversy* (accented on the first and third syllables)
         controversy hence a question takes debate makes an issue of this (*hence*
         referring back to lines 106–9 and forward to the *question* posed at
         111–12).

111   *by him* because of (by virtue of) the young man's horsemanship
         became his deed. Between 'graced what he did' and 'acted becom-
         ingly', with 'turned into, was assimilated with' in the verb *became*.

112   *Or he his manage* or whether he *became* his *manage* ('formal ride,
         equestrian display'. The ellipsis is supplied by line 111.)
         by by virtue of, because of the mettlesome conduct of

113   *on this side* (of the *question*)

114   *real habitude*. Hard to characterize (since *real* is not recorded
         earlier in such a context, while *habitude* remains rare). 'Actual
         possessed quality', with an emphasis on *res* and *habere*, turned
         outward by *habitude* (accustomed behaviour as the self's attire).

115   *appertainings* belongings, appurtenances

116   *in* by virtue of
         case (1) situation, circumstances; (2) garb, trappings

117   *by their place* (that is, 'by their being about his person, being of
         him')

118   *Came for additions* offered themselves as improvements, advanced
         themselves as in some way supplementing the young man's *life and
         grace*. The Q reading 'Can for addicions' has its defenders, but
         even if 'Can' is taken in the archaic sense 'are effective (as)'
         (compare *Hamlet* IV.7.82–3, 'I have seen myself, and served
         against, the French, | And they can well on horseback'), its tense
         seems wrong (note *gave* in line 114 and *were . . . graced* at line 119).
         There is a similar 'Can' for *Came* error in the Folio text of *Macbeth*
         (I.3.97).
         their purposed trim. Because the *additions* did not piece out the
         young man's *grace*, 'the fine trimming they intended to provide'
         registers alongside the primary sense, 'the deliberate and decided
         finery they consisted in'.

119   *Pieced* patched, mended ('one girth six times pieced, and a woman's
         crupper of velure . . . here and there pieced with pack-thread', *The
         Taming of the Shrew* III.2.58–61), supplemented, extended ('I'll
         have five hundred voices of that sound. | FIRST CITIZEN I twice five
         hundred, and their friends to piece 'em', *Coriolanus* II.3.210–11)
         were (as though *aids* were the subject rather than *trim*)
         graced by him endowed with his grace by his graciously bearing
         them

120   *on the tip of his subduing tongue.* Alluding to the proverbial idea that
       words and phrases can be 'on the tip of one's tongue'. The
       available evidence suggests that, while this idiom and its equivalent
       'at one's tongue's end' could mean, as today, 'momentarily forgot-
       ten' ('when in striving to remember a name, men use to say, it is at
       their tongue's end', wrote Sir Kenelm Digby in 1644), early
       readers would have taken the phrase primarily in its now lost sense
       'readily put into words, verbally to hand' ('She had arguments at
       the tip of her tongue', declared Defoe in *Moll Flanders*, 1722).
       Thus, the proverbial cast of line 120 supports rather than playfully
       subverts what follows.

120, 122 *tongue ... strong.* Rhymed, though exactly how is uncertain – as at
       17.10 and 12.

121   *arguments* persuasions, discursive proofs (rather than 'wrangling
       contentions')
       question deep profound inquiry, weighty verbal examination of some
       doubtful point

122   *All* every kind of (parallel with *All kind of* in line 121)
       replication prompt ready reply
       reason strong powerful consideration, persuasive observation

123   *still did wake and sleep* (like servants matching their hours of activity
       to the convenience of their master)

125   *had the dialect and different skill* had a verbal knack and displayed a
       variety of gifts in variously deploying it. *Dialect* here suggests both
       'argot' and 'blarney'; *different* works twice, to describe the exercise
       of *skill* and its differentiating effect on the young man's speech (its
       making his discourse varied).

126   *Catching all passions* (1) snaring everyone's feelings, capturing the
       affections of all those who heard him; (2) enmeshing in his speech
       every kind of strongly moving emotion ('in his speech' emerging as
       much from the discursive overtones of *passions* as from the latent
       ellipsis after *Catching*. Compare Orsino at *Twelfth Night* I.4.24–8,
       'O, then unfold the passion of my love . . .', or Hamlet at III.2.8
       –10, 'O, it offends me to the soul to hear a robustious periwig-
       pated fellow tear a passion to tatters, to very rags, to split the ears of
       the groundlings'; and see the note to 20.2.)
       craft of will. Craft simultaneously suggests the young man's accom-
       plishment in general (as in 'the shoemaker's *craft*') and his 'skilful
       exercise' of this ('the shoe was a work of *craft*'). As so often in
       Shakespeare, *will* operates across a range of senses from 'purpose,
       powerful expression of volition' on the one hand to 'desire' in the
       sense 'affective emotion, lust' on the other. Enriched still further
       by its collocation with the ambiguous phrase *Catching all passions*,
       craft of will compromises several shades of significance, from

'cunning lust' to the 'crafting of language into persuasion' and 'verbal power' or 'discourse, the articulation of volition'.

127   *That* so that

in the general bosom (and so 'in everyone's hearts'). A very Shakespearian synecdoche; compare 'the general ear' at *Hamlet* II.2.560, 'the general tongue' at *Antony and Cleopatra* I.2.106, and, more generally, Sonnet 31.

128   *and sexes both enchanted*. Reading from line 127, *sexes both* seems strictly parallel to *young* and *old*, *enchanted* being a delayed adjectival qualifier of these two classes of admirer; but as the eye and voice pass to line 129, *enchanted* turns into a verb paralleling *did . . . reign* in 127. It is tempting to enforce what becomes the primary sense by deleting Q's comma after *enchanted*; but it does usefully serve to point the ambiguity. The youth's bisexual charm recalls, of course, the young man's double appeal in the Sonnets.

128, 130, *enchanted . . . haunted . . . granted*. Rhymed on a long vowel (be-
131   trayed by the frequent spellings 'enchaunted' and 'graunted'), sounding like 'o-u' or 'o' in modern English.

129   *To dwell with him in thoughts*. The unexpected preposition *with* (lovers usually *dwell* 'on' the beloved *in* their *thoughts*) enlivens a dying metaphor, to create a spatial image in which, after an initial suggestion that the admirers *dwell with* the young *in* his *thoughts* ('linger over' what he expresses in his *craft of will*), the admirers are said to cohabit mentally with the youth *in* their own *thoughts*.

remain. 'Lodge, dwell, abide' (as at *Cymbeline* IV.3.13–14, 'but for my mistress, │ I nothing know where she remains') in addition to 'stay, continue (with)' – the latter ousting the former, now obsolete, as the reader moves from *dwell with him* to *In personal duty*.

130   *In personal duty* (like a maid or page-boy. *Personal* suggests both close involvement and considerable intimacy, an attendance in person to the young man's person.)

personal . . . following (both bisyllabic in this line)

haunted. A suggestion of ghostly haunting can be discounted, though it arises naturally for modern readers from the post-Shakespearian restriction of the verb. In so far as there is an ambiguity here, it consists in the shadowing of one seventeenth-century sense of 'haunt' ('return habitually to one place or places, frequent') with another, elicited by the poet's placing of *following*, 'keep the company of, follow assiduously'. As the young man *haunted* his haunts, he was himself (at the level of wordplay) *haunted*.

131   *Consents bewitched, ere he desire, have granted* consenting persons (by metonymy), being *enchanted* with him, before he makes a request of them (with the evident erotic undertones of *desire*), have granted it

409

(succumbing, indeed, *in* their *thoughts*, to his *desire*). Only by an extreme ellipsis can the Q reading 'Consent's bewitcht, ere he desire haue granted' be construed: 'Consent is bewitched by him, and, before he requests, the *young* and *old* and *sexes both* of line 128, owners of this consent, have granted what he wants'.

132   *dialogued for him what he would say* invented dialogue for him to express what he wanted. The *enchanted* admirers not only succumb to the youth's merely incipient wants but – being so eager to be asked – imagine how he would put his *desire* to them, the more promptly to satisfy it.

133   *wills . . . wills* (the admirers' *Consents* are allowed a clearer erotic implication)

135   *To serve their eyes, and in it put their mind.* Intending only to look at the young man's portrait, to make it *serve* their gazing, the youth's admirers became fixated on his image. For a similar drama of *eyes* and *mind*, see Sonnets 113 and 114.

137   *objects.* Here, as often in Shakespeare, 'things perceived, perceptions presented to the *mind*'.
      abroad in the world at large

138   *theirs in thought assigned* formally made over to them as they fancy, in their imagination legally theirs

139–40   *And labouring . . . them.* Shakespeare describes the pleasant labours of those who, not possessing *lands and mansions*, nevertheless dispose and administer (that is, *bestow*) those rich estates in their imagination with greater satisfaction than the gout-ridden landlord who actually does own (*owe* in an obsolete sense) them.

141   *So many.* Simultaneously an intensified version of *Many*, at line 134, and 'thus, in that way, *many* . . .'.

142   *Sweetly supposed them* imagined themselves to be, and found the supposition sweet

144   *was my own fee-simple, not in part.* The maiden was in complete possession of herself, like the owner of 'land held in perpetuity'.

145   *art in youth, and youth in art.* Another of those doublings which ambiguate the text, here extending *art* into 'artfulness' and *youth* towards 'inexperience'.

146   *charmèd.* Essentially colourless at line 193, enough lingers here from *enchanted* at 128 to enforce the metaphor 'magical, casting a spell'.

147   *gave him all my flower.* Giving the youth her 'beauty', the 'best part' of her nature, she was 'deflowered'. Line 75 contributes crucially. In the movement of the line towards its sexual sense, the woman can be felt identifying her self with her virginity.

148   *some my equals* certain other maidens of my rank

149   *nor being desirèd yielded* nor did I yield up my virginity as soon as I

was requested to (or 'as soon as it was asked for', with the underlying implication 'when I was sexually desired')

151 *With safest distance I mine honour shielded.* The maiden protected her virtue (preserved her virginity) by keeping her *distance*. She found the greatest safety in 'cool reserve' and a 'deference' based on 'social distinction'. (For the latter see *All's Well That Ends Well* V.3.212, where Bertram describes how Diana, whom he thinks he has seduced, 'knew her distance and did angle for me'.)

153 *proofs new-bleeding* still-fresh evidences, or evidential instances, of injury. The process of seduction, already becoming concrete in *I mine honour shielded* (where *honour* is a maidenhead), is vividly so here, and the lost virginities seem to bleed, freshly deflowered.

153–4 *foil | Of this false jewel.* Initially *foil* operates with *shielded* and *bulwarks* as a quasi-military image of resistance to the youth's seductive charm. The *proofs new-bleeding*, that is, became the 'duelling sword' (Hamlet and Laertes fence with 'foils') with which the maid could *foil* – 'fend off, baffle', even 'defeat' (see 25.10) – her opponent. *Of this false jewel* modifies this ominously, however, by eliciting from *foil* the sense 'setting, dull material in which gems are fixed to heighten their allure' (hence Hamlet and Laertes again, at V.2.249–51, 'I'll be your foil, Laertes. In mine ignorance | Your skill shall, like a star i'th'darkest night, | Stick fiery off indeed'). Though this still works against the youth – especially since the alliteration *foil . . . false* implies that the 'setting' foregrounds the youth's duplicity – an image of active resistance is nevertheless replaced by passive regard, and the youth's allure is conceded by *jewel*. Indeed, *false jewel* can be read 'precious gem which played me false' as well as 'paste jewel, fake'. Thus Shakespeare shows the perverse way in which the young man's bad reputation heightened his appeal, breaking down the maid's resistance, evading her guard (in the duel of love).

154 *spoil* (1) plunder; (2) that which has been spoiled. The women reduced by the youth are his booty (the military imagery extended), but they are spoiled, damaged, in the taking.

155 *by precedent* because of some earlier instance

156 *assay* test (often used of metals and *foil*), try by experience

157 *forced examples, 'gainst her own content* who ever urged, or pressed upon herself, cautionary instances when she did not want to hear them (because they warned her against what it pleased her to do)

158 *by-past perils* dangers past (because finished with) and passed (because they afflicted other people)

159 *Counsel.* The *advice* of line 160.
     stop . . . stay (distinguishing between the outward obstacle and inner volition)

160   *rage* are passionate, sensual, wanton. Hence *Richard III* III.5.82,
       where 'lustfull eye' is Q's alternative to the usual, Folio-based
       'raging eye'.

160–61 *advice ... keen* when good *Counsel* takes the edge off our wanton-
       ness, our *wits*, newly sharpened (*keen*), find ways of evading or
       explaining away the *advice*, so that passion can *rage* once more

162   *blood* (as the seat of appetite. Here, as at line 184, sharply opposed
       to the rational powers.)

163   *proof.* As at line 153, the abstraction is made concrete by its context
       (the intensely physical *curb* doing the work of *new-bleeding*). This
       time, however, the balance of meaning within *proof* lies closer to
       'testing by trial, sexual experience' than 'evidence of sexual action'.

164   *forbod* forbidden (the form was unusual but current in the period)
       seems. Singular verbs for plural subjects are not uncommon in
       Shakespeare, but this one arguably points to the single centre of
       fascination behind the maiden's *sweets*: the youth.

165   *For ... behoof* lest we suffer the very misfortunes which offer moral
       Counsel for our benefit

166   *O appetite, from judgement stand aloof* (so that passion will not
       confuse the reason)

167   *The one* (that is, *appetite*)

167, 168 *taste ... last.* Rhymed on short 'a', 'tast ... last' (and *taste* was
       sometimes so spelled in the period).

168   *It is thy last* (because it will be your ruin, you will lose a virginity
       which can never be lost again)

169   *further I could say this man's untrue* I could say more about this man's
       faithlessness. The grammatical oddness of *untrue* is sometimes
       eased by reading 'further I could say "This man's untrue"': that is,
       'I could find even more ways of saying and proving "This man's
       untrue"'.

170   *the patterns of his foul beguiling.* Both 'the *examples* of those he had
       deceived' (other maidens as instances) and 'the strategies by which
       he beguiled'.

171   *his plants in others' orchards grew. Adulterate* in line 175 supports the
       suspicion that the youth was a weed in married men's gardens –
       begot, indeed, other men's children, by planting illegimate
       offspring in their wives' wombs.

172   *gilded in* goldenly glossed over with

173   *vows were ever brokers to defiling* oaths of fidelity have always been the
       agents of dishonour (if not 'pimps working for debauchery'.
       Pandarus is called 'broker' for his pains at *Troilus and Cressida*
       V.10.33.)

174   *characters and words* written and spoken language
       merely but art only artifice and nothing more

175   *bastards* (bred in immorality, and likely to deceive, as do the
bastards Edmund and Don John in *King Lear* and *Much Ado About
Nothing*)

adulterate (because the *heart* fathers verbal *bastards*, because it is
'corrupt, impure' within, and because, in the light of line 171,
adultery is being imputed. For the latter senses see 121.5 and the
note.)

176   *upon these terms.* 'In this way' is subverted by 'on these conditions'
as the reader realizes that the *city* is essentially in the attacker's
hands, is held *upon* his *terms.*

city (as elsewhere in Shakespeare, the chaste woman's body and its
chastity. See pages 391–2 and the article discussed there.)

177, 179, *maid ... afraid ... said.* Though *said* could be pronounced 'sed' in
180   the period, as now, an alternative, older pronunciation, with an 'a-i'
diphthong, is adopted here, to produce a full rhyme.

178   *suffering* (one syllable)

180   *That's to ye sworn to none was ever said* what is sworn to you has never
been said (never mind sworn) to anyone else

183   *abroad.* See the second note to line 137.

184   *blood ... mind.* See line 162 and the note.

185   *acture.* See the Introduction, page 16.

186   *nor ... nor* neither ... nor

188–9   *And so ... contains.* See the Introduction, pages 16–17, and the
note to 129.1–2.

191, 193, *warmèd ... charmèd ... harmèd.* Like *warmed ... disarmed* at 154.6
194   and 8, probably rhymed on a short 'a' resembling the vowel in
northern English 'bat', 'bad'.

192   *teen* trouble, sorrow. The word became a poeticism in the late
sixteenth century, being favoured especially by Spenser; since the
seventeenth century it has been obsolete except in Scottish dialect.

193   *leisures* times of leisure

195   *in liveries* as servants. Dependent (unlike the kingly heart of line
196), in servitude (unlike the *free* heart of 195), and, perhaps,
'wearing their master's colours' (almost literally, if they sport his
love favours). *Liveries* has two syllables.

197   *tributes.* Though the primary sense is 'payments made to a lord
or sovereign by subordinates under obligation' (developing the
regal imagery of line 196), the modern notion of 'voluntary
offerings made in recognition of some peculiar worth', emergent in
Elizabethan English, is also entertained.

wounded fancies doting women (*wounded* by love, shot perhaps by
Cupid's arrows. But the echo of *afflicted fancy* at line 61, and the
weight of what the maid has said about the youth, add an ironic
undertone: 'women *wounded* by mistreatment'.)

198   *pallid* (interpreting Q's 'palyd' as a spelling variant. It might, however, be the past participle of an unrecorded verb, 'paly', 'become pale'; certainly, 'palied' is found, with this implication, in a play performed about 1600, *The Return from Parnassus I*. Some editors prefer 'palèd', which sits easily with *grief* and *terror* in lines 200 and 202 – since pallor is usually ingrained, not emotional; but, arguably, this ease or anticipation obscures a crucial movement in the stanza from the static colouring of *pearls* and *rubies* to the interpretation of their colours in terms of paling and blushing.)

      red as blood (proverbial)

198, 200, *blood . . . understood . . . mood.* Rhymed on a long vowel, close to the
201   'oo' still found in *mood*.

199   *passions* demonstrations, displays. In Shakespearian English less inwardly emotional, and more discursive, than now. See the notes to line 126.

      they (the *wounded fancies* of line 197)

201   *mood* (1) mode, manner, form (as in the grammatical *mood* of a verb); (2) cast of mind, emotional state. The latter refers the ruby's crimson back to its blushing sender.

202   *Effects* manifestations, authentic indications

      dear (1) deeply felt, inward; (2) precious

203   *but fighting outwardly* only pretending to resist

204   *talents.* The primary sense extends from 'coins, plates of precious metal', as in the biblical 'parable of the talents' (Matthew 25.14–30), to 'riches' in general. The hair is seen as wealth, like the locks in Sonnet 68, paid as *tributes* to the youth. But the strong contemporary sense 'mental disposition' (narrowed to 'special aptitude' in modern English) makes the locks of hair, like the *pearls* and *rubies*, readily comprehensible as images of the senders' minds.

205   *amorously* (three syllables)

      empleached entwined, interwoven. A Shakespearian coinage from, or elaboration of, 'pleach', to 'interlace' or 'tangle'. On the archaic prefix, see the Account of the Text, pages 432–3.

205, 207, *empleached . . . beseeched . . . enriched.* Rhymed on a short vowel,
208   using variant pronunciations of -*pleached* and *beseeched* (thus 'emplichd . . . besichd . . . *enriched*').

206   *many a several fair* many different beautiful women

208   *annexions* adjuncts, things added. Another word not recorded before this poem, used occasionally until the eighteenth century. Gary Taylor has not persuaded me that, given the metrical irregularity of the line, *annexions* should be emended to 'annexation' (recorded by the lexicographer Cotgrave in 1611) and elided with *the*.

209   *amplify* hold forth about (and thus lend importance to. A rhetorical term widely current in the period.)

209, 210   *amplify . . . quality*. Rhymed on '-y' (with a secondary stress), sounding closer to the diphthong 'i-ee' than modern 'eye'.

210   *dear*. To the double implication registered at line 202 is added, perhaps, a third. 'Deeply felt' (by the viewer), 'inward, essential' (hence *quality*), 'precious' (hence *worth*).

212   *his* its

        invised hidden, invisible (presumably from Latin *invisus*, 'unseen'. The meaning is uncertain as the word is recorded nowhere else.)

        tend incline, lead towards

213–14   *in whose . . . amend*. The *em'rald* is re*fresh*ing to look at; indeed, because *regard* suggests 'looking at' as easily as 'being observed', its gaze is somehow felt to re*fresh*. *Fresh* is in turn ambiguous since the primary sense 'invigorating' overlaps with 'youthful, vigorous' – an implication elicited by the contrast with *Weak sights* (the penalty of age). Shakespeare often associates *fresh* and *green*, the connexion apparently running (as at 104.8) through the idea of sprouting vegetation. For *sickly radiance* as a description of failing sight see the note to 20.6, and, for the *em'rald* as a light-source, 27.11–12 and the note. Lapidaries regularly granted this stone, like the *opal*, a power to heal weak sight.

215   *heaven-hued* (because sky-blue)

215–16   *the opal blend | With objects manifold*. Either 'the opal blended with an eye-catching variety of colours, features, forms' (*object*, as often in Shakespeare, 'something offered to the sight'), or 'the blended opal, along with many other (and intricate) items'; probably the former.

216   *several* particular

217   *blazoned* glossed, described, catalogued (in the *deep-brained sonnets*)

218   *trophies* prizes, tributes, keepsakes (memorial objects). The word occurs elsewhere in the text, at 31.10, in a context closely resembling this phase of the complaint. Shakespeare shows himself preoccupied with the idea that *trophies* given to one lover can be passed to another with no loss of declared significance (since the *trophies* are signs), whatever their emotional impoverishment.

218–19   *affections hot . . . pensived and subdued desires* (reverting to the contrast between passionate *rubies* and modestly *pallid pearls*. *Pensived*, which means 'modified by thought, reduced by reflection', is not recorded before this poem.)

219   *tender* offering

220   *charged* commanded

221   *I myself must render* I must settle my account by making the payment

of myself. For the financial overtones of *render* see 126.12 and the note.

222   *my origin and ender* source of my life and death

223   *of force* perforce, necessarily
        oblations offerings (especially to God, or, here, an implied goddess)

224   *Since, I their altar, you enpatron me* since I am the altar on which the *oblations* are offered, and you are the patron saint to whom that altar is dedicated

225   *phraseless* indescribably beautiful

226   *weighs down the airy scale of praise* is beyond praise. The image is of a balance in which whiteness outweighs a set of eulogies which seem by comparison as 'light as air' and are indeed 'raised into the air' (by the balance). The association of *airy* and *praise* sets up an ironic undercurrent, characteristic of Shakespeare, in which the *praise* is dismissed as 'breezy, insubstantial' rhetoric.

227   *similes* (the likenesses figured in and between the *gems* and *deep-brained sonnets*. See the Introduction, pages 17–18. Two syllables.)

228   *burning* (with passion)

229–30   *What me . . . under you* whatever is at my command (*obeys* me) is at yours too, since I am your *minister* ('mercantile agent', looking forward to the *audit* of line 230, with perhaps a suggestion of 'religious representative on earth', recalling the imagery of lines 223–4), indeed it operates under your authority

230   *to your audit comes.* At first a statement about the *What* of line 229 and understood 'it' of line 230, the turn into line 231 makes the *distract parcels* (consisting of several 'it's) govern the phrase (with *comes*, as often in Shakespeare, an irregular plural).

231   *distract* distinct, separate. At the root of the word lies the Latin *distrahere*, 'to draw in different directions, tear asunder', and there seems to be a suggestion that these distinct tributes really always belonged together (devoted to the maiden), even when variously employed by others.
        parcels. A complex word, capable of opposed meanings, here (unlike line 87) operating across its full range. Primarily 'small items' (determined by *distract*), but also 'bundles of items' (still petty) and 'aggregates with a known value' (compare *sums*). Since it derives from the Latin *pars*, 'part', the word ultimately implies (like *distract*), even in its collective sense, some larger whole.
        sums. Just as *parcels* carries a financial sense, now obsolete, so *sums* meant 'aggregates of objects' as well as 'accumulations of wealth'.

232   *device* emblematic contrivance, quasi-heraldic figure

233   *sanctified* consecrated
        of holiest note noteworthy (and noted) for being most holy

234   *late* recently

noble (defining the woman's status, but also freeing her *suit* of base self-interest)

suit in attendance at

235   *havings* endowments

      blossoms young courtiers (in the spring of life)

236   *spirits* (one syllable) men (of spirit)

      richest coat the best extraction. Since *coat* is primarily heraldic ('coat of arms'), *richest* becomes a measure of breeding, inheritance (and so power) as well as wealth.

237   *remove* depart

237, 238   *remove . . . love.* For the rhyme see the note to 25.13, 14.

238   *living* life (with a quibble on 'property, wealth', elicited by *spend*)

      eternal (because religious, devoted to God)

239   *what labour is't to leave* what sort of labour is it to leave off (can it indeed be called a *labour* to abandon)

240   *mast'ring what not strives.* The clause is less inverted than elliptical: 'mastering what(ever) does not strive' rather than 'not mastering what strives', though 'mastering not what strives (but something else instead)' can of course be felt productively.

      strives resist (by struggling)

241   *Paling* enclosing, fencing off

      the place which did no form receive (the heart, on which no lover had made an impression, or 'which harboured no lover's image'. Compare 24.1–2 and 113.5.)

242   *Playing patient sports in unconstrainèd gyves* pretending to endure patiently (or 'play-acting at patience in') fetters which have not been imposed against one's will (or 'fetters which do not constrain, which are false, *sport*ive')

243   *that her fame so to herself contrives* who contrives to secure her own reputation (*to herself* suggesting both the dishonestly reflexive, indeed self-regarding, nature of such *fame* and its basis here in selfish enclosure. Though that is the young man's view.)

245   *makes her absence valiant, not her might* earns her reputation for coming through unscathed by fleeing, not by fighting staunchly

246   *in that* since. The youth asks to be forgiven for relating events which flatter him, *in that* they are true. Perhaps he also suggests that the sensual fault which he describes might be excused since he is honest about it.

247   *accident* incident, unfortunate event

248   *Upon the moment* instantly

249   *would the cagèd cloister fly* wanted to flee the barred nunnery. Seeing the youth and loving for the first time, she feels like a *cagèd* bird that wants to *fly* away.

250   *Religious love.* A tasteless quibble on the young man's part. Not the

eternal love of line 238 but secular love that is *Religious* in the sense 'devoted, committed, assiduous'. Perhaps a hint of 'the *love* of a *Religious* (one who was a *nun*)'.

put out religion's eye. Here religion is both the *nun* and the principles she had stood for. To *put out* the *eye* means, first, to 'gaze at amorously' ('At the first sight | They have changed eyes', *The Tempest* I.2.441–2) or 'gaze towards, stare, boggle at' (*Othello* II.1.36–8, 'Let's to the sea-side, ho! | As well to see the vessel that's come in, | As to throw out our eyes for brave Othello'), and, second, to 'be mutilated, spoiled' (here metaphoric, of course). There may be a complacently mocking echo of Matthew 18.9 and Mark 9.47, a text warning against the kind of fault the *nun* committed: 'if thine eye offend thee, pluck it out, and cast [it] from thee'.

251 *immured* enclosed behind walls (as at 84.3). Q's 'enur'd' might be right, as a form of 'inured' ('hardened, toughened'), but the contrast with *liberty* (established by *tempted* and *to tempt*) makes *immured* much more inviting.

252 *to tempt all liberty procured* to call on the whole of experience (with its attendant tempting evils) secured her freedom. *All* also modifies *liberty*, making it more licentious (no freedom is denied by *all*). Q's 'procure' makes perfect sense ('to tempt all *would she* procure all liberty'), but the demands of rhyme – whether 'enur'd', 'innured', or *immured* is read in line 251 – and the ease with which final 'd' can be taken as 'e' in secretary hand make emendation inevitable.

253 *mighty* (the echo of *might* in line 245 is flattering)

254 *bosoms* hearts (by synecdoche)

254, 256, *belong ... among ... strong.* The rhyme rests on short 'o', even in
257 *among*, where 'amung' is now the usual pronunciation.

256 *ocean* (an image of extensive worth, as at 80.5.–12)

257 *strong o'er* being stronger than, dominating

258 *Must for your victory us all congest* because of your triumphant dominance, *I* and *you* (from line 257) *Must* bring together (only use of *congest* in Shakespeare) my admirers and myself (*us all*, which cannot here include 'and you too').

259 *compound* composite (because made up of different loves. But *physic* enforces a quibble on the sense, new to English in the period, 'having the nature of compounded drugs'. See 76.4 and the notes, and compare 118.2.)

 cold unresponsive

260 *parts.* Not, as at line 83, simply 'limbs, parts of the body' but, as often in the Sonnets, 'accomplishments, good qualities' too.

261 *disciplined ... in grace* subjected to religious discipline (which

invites divine *grace*. The word *disciplined* was often applied to those who had, sometimes fiercely, mortified the flesh.)

dieted directed (in a way of life implicitly ordered and sparse)

262   *assail* assault (her heart, that is, with messages about the young man's beauty)

264–5   *O most . . . confine* in you (in your domain, under your control), O most powerful love, a *vow* has no *sting*, a *bond* is *knot*less, and *space* (as often in Shakespeare, suggesting limitation, not extent) does not *confine*. The immediate reference is to the nun's religious *vow*, the *bond* which tied her to God, the church, and the cloister; but line 266, with a blasphemous quibble, lends *love* Divinity.

267   *impressest*. Though the primary reference is to conscription (Henry IV is Christ's soldier, 'impressèd and engaged to fight', *Part 1*, I.1.21), the notion of love 'impressed' on the heart or mind – like printed text or the stamp on a coin (something evoked at *Love's Labour's Lost* II.1.222) – contributes too. (The sense 'affect strongly', primary for a modern reader meeting 'impress', is post-Shakespearian and only latent here.)

267–8   *precepts . . . Of stale example* apophthegmic injunctions based on old and musty instances

267, 269   *worth . . . forth*. For the rhyme see the note to 38.9, 11.

268   *wilt* (as often in Shakespeare, implying volition: 'when you choose to inflame')

269   *coldly* (opposed to the heat of *inflame*, but ineffectually opposed, since *coldly* can mean 'feebly, without power to move, influence')

270   *filial* (two syllables)

271   *are peace*. One of Shakespeare's dislocatingly proleptic images. *Love* is so *potential* that *rule*, *sense*, and *shame* cannot hope to overcome its *arms*. No sooner do these opponents war *'gainst* it than they are crushed by *Love*, and *peace* breaks out.

sense (here meaning 'reason, sensible faculties')

272   *sweetens*. The antecedent is *Love*.

bears endures

272, 273   *bears . . . fears*. The rhyme apparently rests on a long vowel sounding closer to the '-ears' of modern *bears* than *fears* ('bers . . . fers').

273   *aloes* bitterness. The herb known as *aloes* yields a sour purgative juice.

forces acts of force (such as armed *forces* inflict)

shocks encounters, clashes. Like the word *forces* strongly associated with military action in Shakespearian English.

274   *hearts* (as at 31.1, exploiting both the literal and synecdochic implication of the word)

275–6   *with bleeding groans . . . their sighs*. See 30.8 and the note.

276   *supplicant* (the first recorded use as an adjective)
       extend reach out (like imploring gestures)
277   *leave* abandon, leave off
       batt'ry assault with artillery
278   *Lending . . . audience* (alluding to the idiom 'give audience'. The
       youth's request is ostentatiously modest: he seeks a loan, not a gift.)
       design project, plan, purpose. Though not established until the late
       seventeenth century, the sense 'crafty contrivance, malevolent
       intent' is emergent in Shakespeare (see, for instance, *Macbeth*
       II.1.52–6, where 'Murder . . . With Tarquin's ravishing strides,
       towards his design | Moves like a ghost'). Here it adds a sinister
       undercurrent to the young man's plea.
279   *credent* believing, trustful. Apparently Shakespeare's coinage, not
       recorded before *Hamlet*. Its context there – 'If with too credent ear
       you list his songs . . .', says Laertes at I.3.30, warning Ophelia
       against Hamlet's advances – alerts us to a continued ominous
       undertone (*credent* as 'credulous') in the speech.
       strong-bonded firmly pledged and binding (like the 'bond' which
       Shylock makes with Antonio in *The Merchant of Venice*. The form
       bonded is not recorded before this poem, and may be Shakespeare's
       invention. Though the editorial hyphen, traditional since Malone,
       is no doubt justified, Q's paired adjectives 'strong bonded' make
       sense in themselves, and probably register in any reading of line
       279.)
280   *prefer* recommend, advance
       undertake (to see through, agree to conduct to its conclusion)
281   *wat'ry* (because weeping)
281–2 *dismount . . . sights . . . levelled on.* Images from gunnery, introduced
       to the poem at lines 22–3 and further developed at 277 and
       309–10, describe the way the youth cast down his eyes. *Dismount*
       means 'remove from its mountings', like a gun taken off its *carriage*
       (line 22); *sights* are 'gun-sights', 'glances', and, apparently (in
       Warwickshire dialect, still), 'pupils of the eyes'; *levelled on* means
       'aimed at'.
285   *the channel . . . the stream* (the young man's cheeks and tears)
286   *Who glazed with crystal gate the glowing roses* which (*stream* is the
       antecedent) sheened with a crystalline barrier the warmly lumi-
       nous roses (of the young man's cheeks). The image is presumably
       of a jewel or miniature, enclosed in crystal or glass. Malone's claim
       that '*Gate* is the ancient perfect tense of the verb *to get*' is usually
       spurned, but enough instances of its use survive from the fifteenth
       and early sixteenth centuries to make 'which *stream*, sheened with
       crystal, procured (or begat) the glowing roses in his cheeks'
       available.

287   *flame* (heightening to the point of paradox – fire burning under
      water – the suggestion of heat in *glowing*. If the image of a jewel is
      felt in line 286, it is sustained in 287, since gems were thought able
      to emit a *glowing* light; see lines 213–14 and the note.)
      hue. See the note to 20.7.

288   *father*. See line 71 and the note.

289   *particular* (four syllables functioning as three) single, distinct

289, 291, *tear . . . wear . . . here*. For an account of this full rhyme see the note
292   to lines 51, 53, 54.

290   *of* (both 'in' and 'from')

291   *What rocky heart to water will not wear*. This image of slow erosion is
      commonplace in Elizabethan poetry (compare line 7 of the Willow
      Song in the headnote above), and probably based on proverbial
      lore.

292   *What breast so cold . . .* The echo of the young man's words at line
      259 is telling.

293   *cleft* divided, twofold. Though this immediately qualifies *effect*,
      there is an underlying suggestion (elicited by *rocky heart* and *breast*)
      of the heart-break which is, in a sense, the *effect* of this *effect*.
      Compare, for instance, *Measure for Measure* III.1.66, 'To cleave a
      heart in twain', or Gertrude to her son at III.4.157, 'O Hamlet,
      thou hast cleft my heart in twain.'
      cleft effect. The poem's concern with doubleness in apparent
      singularity, announced in its opening stanzas (see the Introduc-
      tion, pages 15–17) and sustained through, for instance, the lines
      about *pearls* and *rubies* (197–203), recurs at the climax of the
      youth's persuasion. For a comparable, though not identical, crisis
      see the 'Bifold authority' forced on Troilus when Cressida betrays
      him with Diomedes (V.2.135–58).

294   *from hence* (presumably from the *inundation of the eye*, which is wet
      and chill, but fiery too, in its emotional *effect*)
      extincture extinguishing, extinction (with perhaps a play on 'ex-
      tincture', 'rob of colour', since the *chill* suppresses the *flame*-like
      colour of *fire*. Shakespeare's coinage, not recorded before this
      poem.)

295   *passion* emotional declaration (rather than 'ingrained powerful
      feeling'. See line 126 and its first note.)
      art of craft. Both *art* and *craft* show their worst sides here, the former
      (as at 139.4 and lines 145 and 174 of the complaint) implying
      deceitful artifice, and the latter (as at line 126, where it again
      overlaps with *passion*) suggesting sleight.

296   *Even* (one syllable)
      resolved transformed, dissolved, reduced. One of those 'discandy-
      ing' images of dissolution which preoccupied the Jacobean

Shakespeare; compare *Timon of Athens* IV.3.441–2, 'The sea's a thief, whose liquid surge resolves | The moon into salt tears.' Related, through the idea of deluding distilment, to 119.1–4 and, hence, the sestet of 147.

297   *daffed* took off, removed. Variant form, not recorded before Shakespeare, of 'doffed', from 'doff', 'do off'.

298   *guards* defences

      civil decorous, educated, socially-conditioned. As a description of conduct, new, much used, and (consequently) ill-defined in Elizabethan and Jacobean English.

299   *Appear ... appears*. By setting deceived against dissembling *appear*ance, Shakespeare adds to the verb – suddenly present tense – a suggestion of deceit barely available in his English. (Before about 1600, *appear* meant only 'be visible, be clearly seen'.)

300   *drops* (the tears of lines 281–7 and 296. Though the *Oxford English Dictionary* does not record *drops* in the medical sense 'drugs in liquid form' until the early eighteenth century, the contrast in line 301 between poisoning and restoration strongly suggests that it was current in Jacobean English. Compare 107.9 and, for the potent tears, 118.12–119.2, while the headnote to Sonnet 107 and the note to 118.14 are relevant. Shakespeare's interest in the ambivalence of drugs, and in the Platonic idea of the *pharmakon* (that which is interchangeably 'poison' and 'medicine'), can be followed from the philtres of *Romeo and Juliet* to those of *Cymbeline*. Indeed, the wrought perceptual mannerism of Imogen's IV.2. soliloquy – 'as small a drop of pity | As a wren's eye ... The drug he gave me, which he said was precious | And cordial to me, have I not found it | Murd'rous to the senses?' (296–333) – takes us close to the language of the *infected* and *fickle maid*, just as the variant 'poyson/medicine' at *King Lear* V.3.97, with its ramifications across the matrix of revision to the 'cordial' Cordelia's 'Restoration hang | Thy medicine on my lips' and Lear's 'mine own tears | Do scald ... Be your tears wet? Yes, faith! I pray, weep not. | If you have poison for me I will drink it' (IV.7.26–72), attests to the depth of Shakespeare's associating mutual *drops* with what, *poisoned*, can also *restore*.)

302–5   *In him ... paleness*. The image – which suggestively conforms to notions of creativity widely held in the renaissance – is of raw material found out and moulded into form. The youth includes vast quantities of this creative raw material (the *subtle matter* of line 302), shaped into or marked by *strange* ('novel' and 'remarkable') *forms* ('shapes, figures') and *Applied* or 'put into practice' ('found applicable') to 'tricks' and 'sleights' (*cautels*). The *forms* (and,

secondarily, *cautels*) in question involve blushing, tearfulness, and
fainting.

302, 304   *matter . . . water*. Rhymed on a short 'a', apparently not invariable in
the period (and now, of course, unknown); thus '*matter . . .* watter'.

305   *takes and leaves* uses this and shuns that (pleasing himself, accord-
ing to each sleight's effectiveness. Like *Troilus and Cressida* V.5.26,
where Hector 'leaves and takes' lives at will on the battlefield, this
plays on the phrase (used more directly by Lear at I.1.205, 'Take
her or leave her') 'Take it or leave it.' Probably there is also a
quibble on the idiom to 'take one's leave'.)

306   *either* (as sometimes, used of three alternatives)

307   *rank* gross, coarse

308   *white* (with *paleness*)

309   *That* so that, with the result that
level range and aim

310   *hail* shower, volley (not recorded in this sense before Shakespeare)

311   *Showing fair nature is both kind and true*. An essentially bland
parenthesis complicated by the context, and especially by *shows*
(line 308). 'Demonstrating that a truly *fair* (just, generous, attract-
ive) *nature* (disposition) is both *kind* and *true*' is the primary sense,
contrasting this *fair nature* with the youth's; but there is a hinted
interjection, 'to display *fair*ness of *nature* (which the youth does
not) is both *kind and true*', and also, in the light of *shows*, a note of
hypocrisy overwhelmed by *is*: 'pretending to a *fair nature* . . .'.

312   *them* (referring back to *blushes*, *weeping*, and *paleness* in the previous
stanza)

313   *would* wanted to, intended to

314   *heart-wished* desired-at-heart, deeply wanted
luxury lust

315   *pure maid* like a virginal girl (hence Rosalind's imperative at *As You
Like It* III.2.207–8, 'speak sad brow and true maid'). The troubling
likeness remarked at the first note to line 100 obliquely recurs.

316   *merely*. The word can, and here does, mean both 'only' and
'absolutely, totally'.
grace. Some editors read 'Grace', paralleling *fiend* (line 317), and, if
the youth can resemble a *maid* (line 315), he can doubtless be seen
as a goddess. Yet *grace* makes perfect sense ('charm, gracefulness
of manner'), *fiend* is arguably paired with *cherubin* (line 319), and
'Grace' makes the *garment* of line 316, suitably abstracted by *grace*,
potentially absurd.

317   *concealèd* (proleptic. The young man's fiendish nature, being
covered, was *concealèd*.)

317, 319,   *covered . . . hovered . . . lovered*. A feminine rhyme resting, almost
320   certainly, on a short 'u' sound: 'cuverd . . . huverd . . . luverd'.

318   *That* so that

th'unexperient those without experience (of the young man's wiles), the (generally) inexperienced. The word – which is not recorded before this – is arguably an early version of 'inexperient' and 'inexperienced' (both of which post-date Shakespeare), and it should, perhaps, be modernized to the latter. The effect of such a change on the music of the line urges caution, however, while the precedent set by words like 'empleacht' (see the Account of the Text, pages 432–3) encourages conservatism.

gave . . . place admitted, made room for, gave audience to

319   *like a cherubin, above them hovered.* Ostensibly a gesture of protection; see *Hamlet* III.4.104–5, 'Save me and hover o'er me with your wings, | You heavenly guards!' On the beauty of *cherubins* see 114.6.

320   *simple* naive (shading into 'foolish', the *simplicity* of 66.11)

lovered (always rare and not recorded before this poem)

321   *fell* (morally. Though the phrase 'a fallen woman' is post-Shakespearian, it points to the assumptions which lie behind this use of the verb.)

question make ask myself

322   *for such a sake* for the sake of falling in such a pleasant way (and, perhaps, 'for the sake of one such as that youth')

323   *infected moisture of his eye* (reverting to the imagery of line 300, though the *drops* here carry disease, not poison)

325   *forced* (with a suggestion of fakeness, 'not spontaneous')

thunder from his heart. For the connexion between sighing (this *thunder*) and the *heart*, see lines 275–6 and the note to 30.8. The ellipsis before *from* (and in line 326 before *his spongy*) is supplied by *which* (see line 324).

326   *spongy* (exactly descriptive rather than pejorative)

327   *motion* action of the body (as often in Shakespeare, implying rehearsal, enacted action)

owed owned

328   *yet* (echoing *yet* in line 321, but with a turn from 'nevertheless' to 'even now')

fore- already

329   *new* newly, afresh

reconcilèd maid. In the usual Shakespearian way, this conclusion raises as many problems as it solves. The *maid* may have been 'brought back to chastity, God, and the church' (an almost technical, religious sense of *reconcilèd*), but 'having atoned' for her offence (a second sense of the word) by regretting it, and suffering, it is not clear that she is so very 'penitent' (given the recognized risk of her fresh perversion), and she hardly seems *reconcilèd* in the sense – frequent in Shakespeare – 'acquiescent, calmed'. The distance measured between *fickle maid* (line 5) and this phrase thus becomes a problem of self-projection, of the kind found in the Sonnets. Are we to think that the *maid*'s finding an audience has helped purge her lapse, or should we conclude that line 329 shows her merely salving herself? Should we, correspondingly, think the word *fickle* diegetic – attractively antique but morally uncommitted – or the poet's in judgement, whether summarily, or as re-creating his sense of the *maid* before the complaint was overheard? On such questions the meaning of line 5 turns: its semantic depths are in large part stirred by the felt presence, in line 329, of the absent poet; and the issue is, ultimately, structural. For it is remarkable that the frame constructed in the opening stanzas – of landscape, poet, and *reverend* man – should not close. In Daniel's *Complaint of Rosamond* and Spenser's *Ruines of Time*, and generally in the complaint tradition, a lament is followed by the re-emergence of the poet, who describes the departure of the speaker and, on occasion, the emotional effect of the plaint. 'With dolefull shrikes shee vanished away,' writes Spenser, 'That I through inward sorrowe wexen faint . . . I felt such anguish wound my feeble heart, that frosen horror ran through euerie part' (lines 471–2, 482–3). The encounter may remain enigmatic – as it does indeed for Spenser ('deeplie muzing at her doubtful speach, | Whose meaning much I labored foorth to wreste', lines 485–6) – but the poet's reaction provides a measure for our own. Shakespeare, characteristically, unsettles our sense of the ending by omitting both the *maid*'s departure and the poet's re-emergence. A decade earlier, in *The Taming of the Shrew*, Shakespeare had – if the text can be trusted – opened a frame (Christopher Sly and the Players in the Lord's house) and not closed it. There, however, the inset comedy had developed a life, and conclusion, of its own. In *A Lover's Complaint*, the opening cannot close the text; line 5 remains intractable; and the heroine grows beyond the conventions which enclose her, developing an intense and human inconsistency which might be called dramatic. If the poem starts in the territory of Spenser and Daniel, it ends, like the problem plays, with the incorrigibility of passion. It makes us assent to and yet suspect the speaker, while bringing forward no Duke Vincentio or King of France to allot rough justice and focus our own responses.

AN ACCOUNT OF THE TEXT

SHAKESPEARE'S Sonnets and *A Lover's Complaint* were first published in 1609, in quarto, by Thomas Thorpe. Of the thirteen original copies extant, eleven have intact title-pages, all reading: 'SHAKE-SPEARES SONNETS. | Neuer before Imprinted. || AT LONDON | By *G. Eld* for *T.T.*'. While four add 'and are | to be solde by *William Aspley*. | 1609.', the other seven have 'and are | to be solde by *Iohn Wright*, dwelling | at Christ Church gate. | 1609.'. This division of Q between booksellers has seemed suspicious to some; it has even been suggested that Thorpe diverted copies to avoid the suppression of his volume by Shakespeare, angered by the publication of – it is alleged – private, compromising poems. In fact, the arrangement tells us nothing about the status of Thorpe's text, and it probably points to careful business dealing among the publisher's associates, to a spreading of risk and profit. Certainly, Thorpe dealt with Q in the usual way, placing an entry in the Register of the Stationers' Company to claim copyright (20 May 1609), and employing the well-established George Eld to print the book. As Leona Rostenberg, Katherine Duncan-Jones, and Michael Brennan have shown, Thorpe was a quality publisher: beginning his career with Marlowe's translation of Lucan (1600), he went on to handle plays and masques by Jonson, Chapman, and Marston, and, increasingly after 1610, theological treatises and translations. Eld, his printer, was similarly respectable, and capable of work to a high standard. The Thorpe–Eld quarto of *Sejanus*, for instance (1605), with its elaborate marginal annotation by Jonson, is formidably well done. Nothing in the process of Q's publication, or in the reputation of Thorpe and Eld, would lead one to postulate piracy.

The Sonnets and *A Lovers' Complaint* next appeared in 1640, published by John Benson and printed by Thomas Cotes. Showing scant respect for textual integrity, Benson selected, rearranged, and emended the poems (see page 46), mixed them with material from Heywood and other writers, and added a preface which, though shrewdly written, misrepresents the Sonnets' and the *Complaint*'s complexity: 'in your perusall you shall finde them *Seren*, cleere and eligantly plaine, such gentle straines as shall recreate and not perlexe your braine, no intricate or cloudy stuffe to puzzell intellect, but perfect eloquence'. Benson has been ably defended by Margreta de Grazia as an early Shakespeare editor, producing a commemorative volume (with tributes drawn from Milton, Jonson, and others), and adapting the poems to the anti-sonneteering taste of his generation. Certainly his work was influential; for most late-seventeenth-century and eighteenth-century readers, Shakespeare's poems were the text transmitted by Benson. But however interestingly the 1640 volume contributed to the history of

AN ACCOUNT OF THE TEXT

Shakespeare's reception, it does not alter the textual situation facing an editor of 1609. Though 1640 corrects some obvious 1609 misprints, none of its changes is editorially challenging. There is no evidence of independent manuscript authority, and no indication that Cotes's compositors were working with significantly variant pages which have not reached us in the extant copies of Q. (Within those thirteen quartos, indeed, only 'seife'/'selfe' at 47.10 and 'proface'/'prophane' at 89.11, and a few still less substantive variants, have been noted.)

A third authority is provided by *The Passionate Pilgrim*, a collection of short poems by Shakespeare and others published by Isaac Jaggard in 1599. Two of the Sonnets, 138 and 144, appear there in forms rather different from those printed in Thorpe's quarto. How far the variation stems from authorial revision, and how far from corruption is unclear, but it seems likely that the 1599 sonnets are at once corrupt and unrevised. Jaggard seems to have taken his texts from manuscripts in circulation, where memorial and copying errors are hardly avoidable, and there is increasing evidence that Shakespeare reworked his poems. The claim should be unsurprising: Daniel and Drayton revised their sonnets during the 1590s and 1600s, and Shakespeare, we know, rewrote a number of his plays, including *King Lear* after its first performance. The assumption that Jaggard poached from circulating manuscripts is supported by Meres's remarks about '*Shakespeare* . . . his sugred Sonnets among his priuate friends' in *Palladis Tamia, Wits Treasury* (1598). 'Sugred' may not seem quite the word for the cynical 138 and scabrous 144, but Meres goes on to judge the poet one of 'the most passionate among vs to bewaile and bemoane the perplexities of Loue', which offers a fair characterization of 127–52. In any case, enough Shakespearian sonnets survive in manuscript to make Meres's assertion supportable. From the extant miscellanies, that is, we can deduce that a number of poems circulated singly, or in small groups, before and after the publication of Thorpe's quarto. About a dozen of the sonnets are extant in manuscript – 1 (conflated with 2 and 54), 2, 8, 32, 33, 68, 71, 106, 107, 116 (as a lyric), 128, and 138 – and, though many of these texts patently derive from Q, Sonnets 2 (in eleven of its twelve or thirteen copies), 8 (one copy), 106 (two copies), and 128 (one copy) are possible 'sugred Sonnets', and both 2 and 128 likely. The miscellanies which include these poems apparently post-date Q, but their readings are often persuasively Shakespearian (and Elizabethan, where their 1609 equivalents feel later), and it is tempting to conclude that, despite an admixture of corruption, at least some of them preserve versions of the sonnets passed about at a stage preceding the poems' revision for, or at least before, publication by Thorpe. In preparing the present edition, the principle has been to allow Jaggard's and the manuscript texts their own integrity. Though the texts of 138 and 144 above admit two corrections and remove an elision on the basis of Jaggard's authority, the readings are essentially those of 1609. Similarly, the sonnets published in 1599 and the manuscript versions of 2, 8,

106, 116, and 128 are printed and collated in the appendix 'Variant and Further Sonnets'.

This raises the question of dating. On the basis of Meres and Jaggard, we can assume that numbers of the sonnets were written, or at least drafted, before 1598–9. Internal evidence supports this: theme, imagery, and idiom relate the early sonnets, and especially 1–19, to *Venus and Adonis* and *The Rape of Lucrece* (1593–4); Eliot Slater's vocabulary tests note a marked correlation between the Sonnets and the plays *c.* 1594–5 as well as *c.* 1598–9; and J. M. Nosworthy has established that a whole series of parallels places 138, at least in its Jaggard form, in the early 1590s. Moreover, Gary Taylor's detailed analysis of the manuscript versions of Sonnet 2 has placed the poem before 1596. Even without postulating the Earl of Southampton as the 'lovely boy' then, and Marlowe (who died in 1594) as the rival poet, there are strong arguments for dating some sonnets to the early and middle 1590s. Indeed, it seems likely that the basic configuration of the sequence was established by Shakespeare at this stage. Sonnet 2 gives us the gist of much in 1–126, Jaggard's 138 is equally representative of 127–54, and his 144 ('Two loues I have') characterizes the relationship between the poet and his contrasted lovers, bringing together dominant images from both sonnet groups. In these three indisputably early texts, the imaginative geography of the full sequence is already apparent. At the same time – and without concluding Chapman the rival and Herbert the friend – there are good reasons, internal and external, for thinking parts of Q relatively late, if not Jacobean. Evidence that *A Lover's Complaint* post-dates 1600, and that 107 topically alludes to 1603, has already been noted (pages 313–19 and 389–94); but the syntactical complexity, associative imagery, and bold enjambing of many late-numbered sonnets places them, on stylistic grounds, in the second half of Shakespeare's writing life. There is also the process of verbal echo and concentration to be considered. While one cannot be sure that 'certain o'er incertainty, | Crowning the present' (115.11–12) was written after the more straightforward and datable 'Incertainties now crown themselves assured' (107.7), or that 124 explores motifs from 116 rather than vice versa (see the Commentary) – as 107.10 precedes 108.9, and 109. 13 follows 107.1 (Introduction, pages 8–9) – it seems likely that the sonnets numbered higher than 107 post-date it, and are more chronologically ordered than not. This is not, however, a cautious way of suggesting that 1–126 and 127–52 were written in strict sequence: there must have been stages of reordering in the course of composition and revision, even if Q does represent Shakespeare's final preferred order.

But does it? That Thorpe was a responsible publisher working with a first-rate printer offers reassurance, yet it does not identify the nature of the copy which he secured. What kind of manuscript lies behind Q, our sole authority for *A Lover's Complaint* and all but a few of the Sonnets? In 'Punctuation and the Compositors of Shakespeare's *Sonnets*, 1609', MacD.

P. Jackson works his way towards answering that question by means of compositor analysis. Examining the accidentals of Q, he identifies two typesetters in Eld's shop – perhaps the pair who printed *Troilus and Cressida* for Eld in 1609 – whose very different styles of spelling and punctuation show up clearly in the quarto. Summarizing the differences, Jackson writes:

> A prefers the spellings *shalbe, wilbe, ritch, Oh, dost, gold, old, flowre, powre,*
> and *houre*, uses *eie* and *eye* indifferently, and strongly prefers colons to
> commas as an alternative to full stops at the ends of quatrains; B prefers
> the spellings *shall be, will be, rich, O, doost, eye, flower,* and *power,* is
> indifferent over *hower* and *houre*, uses *ould* and *gould* scarcely less often
> than *old* and *gold*, and slightly prefers commas to colons at the ends of
> quatrains; B places almost a quarter of the numbered sonnet-headings
> and about half of the signatures [symbols marking the position of gather-
> ings in the book] set by him further right than A ever places them.

Jackson's analysis might be extended: it is remarkable, for instance, that A should use 'time' where most modern editors have 'Time', while B uses 'time' and 'Time' indifferently (and more than once prints 'Time' where editors have 'time'), and significant that A should italicize more readily than B. Some of Jackson's ascriptions are necessarily tentative. Nevertheless, his division of the Sonnets between the two typesetters (twenty pages to A and forty-five to B) is persuasive. And it provides a solid foundation for the next stage in his inquiry: the definition of elements in Q which, cutting across compositorial stints, point up features of the underlying printer's copy. As Jackson summarily puts it:

> the number of internal commas – commas within the line, not at the end of
> it – bears no relation to the compositors' stints, but differs from one part of
> the sequence to another. In fact, if we count all the internal stops (the vast
> majority of which are commas), Sonnets 1–25 average 2.8 per sonnet,
> Sonnets 26–50 average 4.7, Sonnets 51–75 average 4.9, Sonnets 76–100
> average 5.5, Sonnets 101–26 average 5.4, and Sonnets 127–54 average
> 3.6.

These factors point, of course, to increased syntactical complexity from 1 to 126, and to the syntactical congruence of the dark lady sonnets with the relatively early friend poems, factors which support the general connexion between ordering and chronology proposed above. Jackson goes on:

> Dover Wilson thinks that the manuscript of Shakespeare's *Sonnets* which
> Thorpe handed to the printers was 'good' and that 'if not autograph it must
> have been a tolerably competent transcript, perhaps copied out by more
> than one transcriber.' As he points out, 'This contingency has seemed
> likely to many because of the error of *their* for *thy* first noticed by Malone,
> which occurs fourteen times between sonnets 26 and 70 and only once

later, in 128.' The other errors which Brooke [in his generally dull edition of 1936] classifies as misreadings tend to fall within roughly the same part of the text, and it is interesting that all but five of the forty-two parentheses in the *Sonnets* occur within numbers 26–98, and that two of the others occur within 126, which is close to 128 with its *their* error. This might be taken to support the theory that the printer's copy was in two hands.

Malone's and Dover Wilson's and Jackson's anxiety seems particularly just when it is realized that 'the error of *their* for *thy*' is recorded nowhere else in Shakespeare – including the several quartos set from authorial manuscript – and that, as the concordance suggests, the reverse error occurs only once, in the third Quarto of *Richard III*, where the mistake must stem from compositorial misremembering of printed copy, not misreading of a manuscript. It seems reasonable to assume that the manuscript behind 26–70 and 128 was formally distinctive, if not eccentric, and non-authorial. We seem to be dealing, then, with at least an admixture of scribal work. Indeed, given the absence of those features we have learned to associate with Shakespearian manuscript (particular spellings, kinds of misreading) elsewhere in Q, we are probably dealing with a mixed transcript. Yet that need not imply a pirated text, surreptitiously copied, nor the other unflattering conclusions about the manuscript behind Q which editors have jumped to. Transcription can be a sign of care; more than one Shakespeare play is well-printed from a transcript (Ralph Crane, the King's Men's scrivener, did loyal service for the Folio), and the fact that Q lacks the marks of holographic peculiarity does not mean that it wants authority. That the 1609 *Troilus and Cressida* was printed from authorial 'foul papers', and the Sonnets and *Complaint* from scribal copy, might simply point to the poet's and publisher's concern that the non-dramatic text should be cleanly printed. Fifteen years before, *Venus and Adonis* and *The Rape of Lucrece* had been seen through the press with even more care – no doubt because, since poems brought their author a social and literary prestige which plays (under the prejudices of the time) could not, it made sense to ensure their neat printing. Content that dramas like *Hamlet* and *King Lear* should reach readers in quartos set from not always legible 'foul papers', Shakespeare arguably sought to have all three non-dramatic quartos, of 1593, 1594 and 1609, well turned out.

The present edition follows New Penguin practice in taking full command of the punctuation (and, given the compositorial divergences in Q, it would be paradoxically unscholarly to follow the 1609 pointing), but it contracts and elides the verse more freely than is usual in the series, and is sometimes slow to modernize individual words, even within the Sonnets (see, for instance, the note on 'satire' at 100.11). The handling of Q's compounds of self, 'him selfe, thy selfe, my selfe, your selfe', presents peculiar difficulties in verse so much about selfhood. Occasionally, as in Sonnet 13 ('O That you were your selfe'), the temptation to echo or ignore Q's conventional spacing according to the state of the wordplay is almost irresistible. Many editors, for instance, read 'Yourself again after your self's decease' at 13.7, against Q's 'You[r] selfe again after your selfes decease'. In preparing this edition, however, it has been thought best to modernize consistently to 'himself, thyself, myself, yourself', answering a seventeenth-century convention with the modern one. To orchestrate the ambiguities by alternating 'yourself' and 'your self' is finally to weaken them, since the force of the wordplay registers in or stems from the breaking loose of 'self' from the constraints of a conventional verbal form.

Perhaps the most frustrating editorial problem is posed by *A Lover's Complaint*. This poem is highly neologistic; it includes a new coinage every twenty lines or so – an extraordinarily high figure, even for Shakespeare. But most of these words are, in A. C. Partridge's phrase, 'coined archaisms', words introduced to the language to look old. This conscious quaintness creates enormous difficulties in a modernized edition. At the simplest level is the question whether one should preserve words like 'moe' (for 'more'), in response to the archaizing impulse in the text, even though such forms, archaic now, were more or less current in 1609. Many modernizing editors preserve these forms, but it is the policy here to exclude them. Then there is the trickier category of words which were archaic or dialectal in the 1600s and part of the text's patina of archaism, but which have since lapsed into such obscurity that they strike modern readers as being opaquely antique. 'Margent' at line 39, for example, is Shakespeare's preferred form of 'margin', appearing several times in the first half of his career. Though the word possibly carried, by 1609, dialectal and (as later, in Milton and Gray) poetic overtones, it would have been readily comprehensible to early readers; yet to reproduce it now would baffle. No decision about modernizing 'margent' can be taken in isolation, however, since there are similar forms – like 'platted' in line 8 – which look appropriately quaint and cause no interpretative problem. In preparing this edition, the rule of thumb has been to accept the *Oxford English Dictionary*'s classification of such words as either variant or independent forms. Thus, 'margent' is taken to be an 'Altered form of MARGIN *sb*' and modernized, while 'platted' is preserved in its Q spelling, not 'emended' to 'plaited'. This is a rough and ready system, since the dictionary's practice is often questionable, and different from letter to letter; but it cuts the gordian. A third branch of the problem includes archaic coinages like 'empleacht' (line 205) which, partly because of Shakespeare's status, enjoyed a limited literary life, without becoming elements in standard speech, and were changed in use. The *OED* notes, for instance, uses of 'empleacht' by Tennyson and Swinburne, but in the form 'impleached'. For the *OED*, this makes 'impleached' the standard form, and 'empleacht' its variant. With such words, as with 'inhearce' at 86.3, the policy has been – inconsistently enough – to disregard the advice of the dictionary, however engagingly contradictory, and to modernize little, if at all (in this edition, line

205 has 'empleached'), on the principle that a few late literary echoes should not be allowed to obscure Shakespeare's intentions. This procedure, again, involves compromise, but it has seemed the most practicable option. Certainly, it cannot be argued from convenience that one should 'modernize' such words, since readers will need to check the meaning of 'impleached' as promptly as the more Shakespearian 'empleached'. Rhyme, finally, urges a further degree of pragmatism. At the end of line 297, for example, Q's 'daft' is clearly, as the *OED* says, a variant of 'doffed' (at IV.2.175, *Othello* Q and F employ both forms), but, despite the parallel with 'margent', 'daft' cannot be modernized, for the sake of consonance, and a word which would not have troubled early readers must, with no artistic gain, disturb modern ones.

The collations lists which follow are selective. They record the points at which this edition preserves Q readings which have been questioned or diverged from in the printed tradition, list its emendations of Q, and then provide a subsidiary list of interesting emendations, from Benson onwards, rejected where emending has been undertaken. Quotations from Thorpe's quarto and Jaggard's *Passionate Pilgrim* (*PP*) are in old spelling, with 'long s' (ſ) modernized. For a detailed collation of the manuscript texts of Sonnets 2, 8, 106, 116, 128, 138, and 144, supplementary to what follows, see pages 449–54.

COLLATIONS

I

Rejected emendations of Q – mostly nineteenth-century in origin – are listed below, to the right of the accepted Q reading (as given in this edition). The emendations are modernized; where several are listed, they are separated by semi-colons.

The Sonnets

7.9	car] care
11.11	the] thee
16.7	your] you
19.5	fleet'st] fleets
20.7	man in] maiden; woman's; native
20.13	women's] all men's
21.5	couplement] compliment; complement
22.4	expiate] expirate
23.9	books] looks
25.11	quite] forth
28.5	either's] other's (Q: ethers)
28.14	length] strength

433

34.8   heals] heles (Q: heales)
35.7   corrupting] corrupt in
35.9   in sense] incense (Q: in sence)
39.12   dost] do; doth
41.1   pretty] petty
41.9   seat] sweet
43.13   to see] to me
45.5   For] So; Forth
47.1   took] struck
47.10   are] art
51.11   neigh, no] need no; neigh to; wait no; weigh no
54.14   vade] fade
         by] my
55.9   oblivious] oblivion's
56.13   As] Or; Ah; Else
58.11   To] Do
59.11   Whether] Whe'er
59.12   revolution be the] by revolution both be
62.7   for] so
         do] so; to
62.10   Beated] Battered; Blasted; Bated
65.3   this] his
65.10   chest] guest; theft
69.14   soil is] toil is; solve is; sully's (Q: solye is)
70.1   are] art
70.6   wooed of time] wooed ofttime; wooed o'th'time; wood ofttime;
         void of crime
73.4   Bare ruined choirs] Barrened of quires (Q: Bare rn'wd quiers)
75.3   peace] price; prize; piece
75.8   bettered] better
75.14   or all away] or fall away
77.3   The] These
77.14   thy] my
83.2   fair] face
84.11   wit] writ
85.3   Reserve] Preserve; Rehearse; Deserve; Receive; Treasure;
         Re-serve; Refine
85.4   filed] filled
85.5   whilst] while
         other] others
86.13   filled] filed (Q: fild)
91.2   body's] bodies' (Q: bodies)
95.12   turns] turn
96.1   youth, some] youthsome; youth and

434

98.9   lily's] lilies' (Q: Lillies)
98.11   were but sweet, but] were, my sweet, but; were, best sweet, but;
          were but fleeting
99.13   eat] ate
99.15   sweet or] sweeter
100.14   prevene'st] prevent'st (Q: preuenst)
102.8   his] her
103.13   sit] fit
108.3   now] new
110.9   have what] save what
111.12   to] too
112.14   methinks they're dead] methinks are dead; methinks is dead;
          methinks y'are dead; you thinks me dead (Q: me thinkes y'are
          dead)
113.10   sweet-favour] sweet-favoured; sweet favour
114.10   kingly] kindly
118.5   ne'er-cloying] near cloying (Q: nere cloying)
119.7   fitted] flitted
119.14   ills] ill
120.13   that ... becomes] let ... become
123.7   born] bourn (Q: borne)
123.11   doth] do; both
124.9   fears] feres (Q: feares)
125.4   proves] prove
126.2   sickle] fickle; brittle; tickle
127.4   bastard] bastard's
127.10   and] as; that
128.4   wiry] witty
132.2   torment] torments
134.4   be] me
136.10   store's] stores' (Q: stores)
138.4   Unlearnèd ... subtleties] Vnskilful ... forgeries (PP)
138.6   she knows ... days] I know ... yeares (PP)
          are] be (PP)
138.7   Simply I] I smiling (PP)
138.8   On both sides thus is simple truth suppressed] Outfacing faults in
          loue, with loues ill rest (PP)
138.9   says she not she is unjust?] sayes my loue that she is young? (PP)
138.11   habit is in] habit's in a (PP ed. 1); habite is a (PP ed. 2)
          seeming trust] soothing toung (PP)
138.13   I lie with her, and she with me] I'le lye with Loue, and loue with me
          (PP)
138.14   And in our faults by lies we flattered be] Since that our faultes in
          loue thus smother'd be (PP)

141.5   tune] turn
141.14   awards me] awards my; rewards my
144.2   Which] That (*PP*)
144.3   The] (*PP*)
144.4   The] My (*PP*)
144.8   foul] faire (*PP*)
144.11   But . . . from me] For . . . to me (*PP*)
144.13   Yet this shall I ne'er know] The truth I shall not know (*PP*)
146.2   these] those
           array] warray
149.4   all tyrant] all truant
152.13   eye] I
153.8   strange] strong (Q: strang)

A Lover's Complaint

7   world] words
14   seared] sere
24   Sometime] Sometimes
26   lend] bend; tend
39   weeping margin] margent weeping (Q: weeping margent)
41   monarch's] monarchs' (Q: Monarches)
53   thou] him
54   here] ne'er
56   Big] By
61   fastly] softly
80   O] Of
87   hurls] purls
88   will] we'll
91   largeness thinks] large methinks
96   more] most
98   were] 'twere
102   oft] of
       May] March (*Wells and Taylor conj.*)
112   his manage] his, managed (Q: his mannad'g)
113   this] his
118   purposed] purpose
121   kind] kinds
       question] questions
137   goodly] goodliest
180   That's] What's
       ye] you
198   pallid] palèd; palied (Q: palyd)

208   the annexions] th'annexations (*Taylor conj.*)
233   Or] A
261   Who disciplined, ay, dieted] Tho' disciplined I dieted; Who disciplined and dieted (Q: Who disciplin'd I dieted)
265   sting] string
268   Of] Or
271   peace, 'gainst] proof 'gainst
321   Ay] Ah

2

Rejected Q readings are listed below, to the right of accepted emendations (mostly the work of Malone and his Victorian successors).

The Sonnets

12.4   all silvered o'er] or siluer'd ore
13.7   Yourself] You selfe
24.1   stelled] steeld
25.9   fight] worth
26.12   thy] their
27.10   thy] their
28.12   gild'st] guil'st
31.8   thee] there
34.12   cross] losse
35.8   thy . . . thy] their . . . their
37.7   thy] their
40.7   thyself] this selfe
41.8   she] he
43.11   thy] their
44.13   naught] naughts
45.12   thy] their
46.3, 8, 13, 14   thy] their
46.9   'cide] side
47.11   not] nor
50.6   dully] duly
51.10   perfect'st] perfects
55.1   monuments] monument
59.11   whe'er] where
65.12   spoil of beauty] spoile or beautie
67.6   seeming] seeing
67.12   'prived] proud
69.3   due] end

69.5   Thy] Their
70.6   Thy] Their
76.7   tell] fel
77.10   blanks] blacks
85.3   thy] their
90.11   shall] stall
99.9   One] Our
106.12   skill] (*manuscript reading*); still
111.1   with] wish
113.6   latch] lack
113.14   mak'th mine eye untrue] maketh mine vntrue
126.8   minutes] mynuit
126.12   (*Followed in Q by two sets of brackets marking 'missing' lines*)
127.9, 10   eyes . . . brows] eyes . . . eyes
128.11, 14   thy] their
129.9   Mad] Made
129.11   proved, a] proud and
132.9   mourning] morning
138.12   to have] *PP*; t'haue
144.6   side] *PP*; sight
144.9   fiend] *PP*; finde
146.2   ] My sinfull earth
153.14   eyes] eye

A Lover's Complaint

7   sorrow's wind and rain] sorrowes, wind and rain
51   'gan to tear] gaue to teare
118   Came] Can
131   Consents] Consent's
182   woo] vovv (*vow*)
228   Hallowed] Hollowed
241   Paling] Playing
251   immured] inured (Q: enur'd)
252   procured] procure
260   nun] Sunne
284   apace] a pace
293   O] Or

Emendations rejected not in favour of Q but for the sake of other emendations are listed below, to the right of the preferred readings. They are modernized and are separated by semi-colons when there is more than one.

The Sonnets

12.4   all silvered o'er] o'er-silvered all; are silvered o'er; ensilvered o'er (*Wells conj.*)

25.9   fight] might

35.8   thy . . . thy] thy . . . their; their . . . thy; thee . . . thy; thee . . . their

46.13, 14   thy] thine

47.11   not] no

51.10   perfect'st] perfect

59.11   whe'er] whether

65.12   spoil of beauty] spoil on beauty; spoil o'er beauty

67.12   'prived] proved; poore

69.5   Thy] Thine

76.7   tell] spell

113.14   mak'th mine eye untrue] maketh m'eyne untrue; maketh m'eye untrue; maketh mind untrue

127.9, 10   eyes . . . brows] eyes . . . hairs; eyes . . . brow; hairs . . . eyes; brows . . . eyes; hairs . . . brows

146.2   ] Foiled by; Spoiled by; Soiled by; Swayed by; Starved by; Thrall to; Yoked to; Prey to; Fooled by; Bound by; Grieved by; Galled by; Vexed by; Pressed with (*Booth conj.*); Served by; Ruled by; Feeding; Hemmed with; Leagued with

A Lover's Complaint

51   'gan to tear] gave a tear

241   Paling] Planing; Parting; Filling; Salving

VARIANT AND FURTHER SONNETS

In Volume I, part ii, of the *Index of English Literary Manuscripts* (London, 1980), Peter Beal catalogues twenty-five texts relevant to the sonnets in Thorpe's quarto. Although most of the manuscripts concerned date from the later Jacobean and Caroline periods, more than one seems to be an early witness, while even the latest texts might, in theory, have behind them Elizabethan versions of the poems as they were when circulated among Shakespeare's 'priuate friends' (above, pages 10 and 428–9). In practice, it is clear that many of the manuscript sonnets derive from printed texts. Folger MS V.a.148, for instance, includes several texts of no authority, in a verse anthology from *c.* 1660 once owned by a certain E.H.; Folger MS V.a.162 incorporates versions of Sonnets 32 and 71 apparently drawn from Q, 'in a miscellany compiled by an Oxford man and once owned by one Stephen Welden'; while Sonnet 138, first published in *The Passionate Pilgrim* (1599) and heavily variant in 1609, survives in Folger MS V.a.339 in a text which stems from Benson's edition of 1640. Of the clearly derivative texts, only one – Henry Lawes's lyric version of 116 – is printed below, as an indication of the kind of impact musical setting could have on a widely circulated sonnet.

Many of the manuscripts may therefore be dismissed, but about half of those listed by Beal are of considerable interest. Significantly, twelve of them reproduce a single poem: Sonnet 2, in the 1609 ordering. One of these twelve texts – in the St John's, Cambridge, MS S.23 – demonstrably derives from Q; but, as Mary Hobbs and Gary Taylor have argued, the other eleven appear to stem from manuscript copy circulating in the 1590s. The text printed below is modernized from the Westminster Abbey MS 41, which, as Jeremy Maule has demonstrated in unpublished research, offers the most authoritative version among the extant texts. Ample evidence for an early dating of '*Spes Altera*' – as the sonnet is entitled in several manuscripts – is provided by Taylor in 'Some Manuscripts of Shakespeare's Sonnets', *Bulletin of the John Rylands Library* 68 (1985–6), 210–46. Taylor identifies in the sonnet items of vocabulary favoured by Shakespeare before 1596, and notes a hardening of authorial opinion against the addressee between the manuscript version and 1609 consistent with the experience of disillusionment recorded in the sequence as a whole. Still more persuasively, he shows that the early text intimately relies on a passage generally accepted as a source for the equivalent poem in Q. In the text printed below, that is, the sestet is significantly closer to the Erasmian letter which lies behind the breeding sonnets (see the Commentary at 3.5–6) than the corresponding lines in 1609:

> what man can be grieved that he is old, when he seeth his own countenance . . . to appear lively in his son? You shall have a *pretty* little boy, running up and down your house, such a one as shall express your look, and your wife's look . . . by whom you shall seem *to be new born*.
>
> (my italics and modernization)

Such a drift away from source material in the process of revision is what common sense would lead us to expect, and it is what we find in Shakespeare's reworking of Q2 *Hamlet* (notably in the treatment of Rosencrantz and Guildenstern) and *King Lear* from Q to F (in, for example, the poet's handling of Cordelia's war against Gonerill and Regan).

Among the other manuscript texts, the one most likely to reflect an early version is 'how ouft when thow, deere' in Bodleian MS Rawl. poet. 152. While the variants in its opening line might be attributed to memorial contamination (and the text is marred at several points by obvious errors), the use of 'kies' for 'Iackes' in lines 5 and 13, and 'youre' for 'thy' in lines 11 and 14 is ponderable. Attempts have been made to account for the situation described in Sonnet 128 in terms of tuning rather than playing (see the Commentary at 128.5–6), yet it seems probable that Shakespeare used 'Iackes' loosely in Q, in an extended sense, to make room for his jokes about 'nimble' and 'sausie' fellows. It is easier to imagine Shakespeare's imagination being sparked verbally by the possibilities of 'nimble', and his taste affronted, in the couplet, by the too ready chiming of 'keyes . . . and kisse' (which unbalances the poise of 'fingers' against 'lipes') than it is to conceive of a reporter's weak memory dropping the stock phrase 'sausie Iackes' and substituting the musically less problematical 'keyes'. Moreover, if the Bodleian manuscript recorded elements of an early version, the gap between 'youre' and 'thy' would point to a shift in attitude paralleling that detected in the texts of Sonnet 2. In the manuscript, that is, 'how ouft when thow, deere' is a conventional tribute to the poet's mistress, playing the virginals, and 'youre' emerges naturally from the context. In Q, by contrast, the text is shaded with cynicism, as Shakespeare wrily remarks his mistress's liberality with her favours to every pert underling, and a corresponding movement into Q's strict 'thou' and 'thy' – the mode preferred throughout 127–52 in 1609, with the exception of the aberrant 145 (see the headnotes to 13 and 145 in the Commentary) – follows.

The popularity of Sonnet 2 in manuscript miscellanies is perhaps explained by its sub-title in Folger MS V.a.345, 'A Song'. Though it was rare for true sonnets to be set to music in the period, a handful of examples do survive, and Shakespeare's poem may have enjoyed that kind of currency. Certainly, it is no accident that the two sonnets dealing with music should have found their way into miscellanies – read, as they were, in gentle and aristocratic households where poetry offered entertainment on the same footing as performance on the lute or viols. Corresponding with the Bodleian version of 128 is the text of Sonnet 8 in British Library Add. MS 15226. Though its layout is distinctive, and lyrical, this text probably derives from Q; but its readings, while sometimes inferior to those of the quarto (as in line 8), are not inept, and might be Shakespearian. Of particular interest is 'Sweete wth. sweetes warre not' in line 2, compared with 'Sweets with sweets warre not' in Q. The 1609 text has the merit of balancing its line between equivalents – sweets and sweets, joy against joy – but the manuscript exploits the same ambiguous vocative as line 1 ('Musicke to heare, why hearest thou Musicke sadly'), while echoing the indubitably Shakespearian, and possibly proverbial, phrase 'Sweets to the sweet' (compare *Hamlet* V.1.239). Whether or not the manuscript derives from Q, its reading at this point must be attractive to editors of 1609.

While the manuscript title of Sonnet 2, '*Spes Altera*', may be, as Gary Taylor claims, authorial, and while the British Library heading for Sonnet 8, '*In laudem musice et opprobrium contemptorij eiusdem*', conceivably could be Shakespearian, the legend above the texts of 106 in the Holgate Commonplace Book and Rosenbach Museum and Library MS 1083/16, 'On his Mistris Beauty', hardly can be right. Apart from anything else, the compliment 'Eu'n such a beauty as you master now' would seem singularly ill-chosen in a sonnet written to a woman. A false title need not argue, however, a false text, and it may be that some authoritative early readings survive in the manuscripts. Certainly, there is nothing implausible in either (except the patent blunders 'mine' for 'rime' in Holgate and 'pleasant' for 'present' in Rosenbach), and the reading 'skill' in line 12 of both texts offers an alternative to Q's 'still' accepted by most editors since Tyrwhitt's conjectural emendation in the eighteenth century.

This selection ends with six texts from *The Passionate Pilgrim*. Despite its title-page '*By W. Shakespeare*', Jaggard's collection of twenty poems contains only five indisputably by Shakespeare, two of which are modernized below. Numbers I and II in the anthology are versions of Thorpe's 138 and 144. The former is markedly variant, and, since its 1599 readings are often plausibly Shakespearian, it has become the consensus view that – despite an overlay of error from memorial contamination or faulty copying in the early text – I and 138 substantially diverge because of revision. II and 144 are closer, and the 1599 readings less compelling. Presumably the sonnet neared its final form at an early stage. III, V, and XVI in Jaggard's quarto are versions of poems attributed to Berowne, Longaville, and Dumaine in *Love's Labour's Lost* IV.2 and IV.3. Though the pieces vary slightly from play to collection, Jaggard almost certainly took his texts from the 1598 quarto of the comedy, or from an earlier, lost, good edition. As all three poems, and the variants, can be consulted in the New Penguin *Love's Labour's Lost*, they are not reprinted here. *The Passionate Pilgrim* includes two or three more texts which have been

('Crabbed age and youth . . .') and still might be ('Sweet rose, fair flower . . .') thought Shakespearian, but only four further sonnets: IV, VI, IX, and XI. Since the poems are uneven in quality, yet connected as an erotic group devoted to Venus and Adonis, and since XI appears in Bartholomew Griffin's *Fidessa* (1596), the likelihood is that all four are not by Shakespeare. They are nevertheless included here without apology because they enforce, by poetic means, the critical claim implicit in the introduction to this edition – that the 1609 sonnets partly grew out of *Venus and Adonis*, with its emphasis on the narcissistic beauty of a young man, and the seductive power of vigorous female sexuality. Griffin's response to the long poem (if all the sonnets are indeed his) was more direct and less resourceful than Shakespeare's, but, like the dramatist, he sensed the validity of heightening and elaborating the emotional matter of the poem within the framework of the sonnet form.

All the poems reproduced below have been modernized in accordance with the principles of the series. Collations follow on pages 449–54.

Spes Altera [Sonnet 2]

When forty winters shall besiege thy brow,
And trench deep furrows in that lovely field,
Thy youth's fair liv'ry, so accounted now,
Shall be like rotten weeds of no worth held.   4
Then being asked where all thy beauty lies,
Where all the lustre of thy youthful days,
To say within these hollow sunken eyes
Were an all-eaten truth and worthless praise.   8
O, how much better were thy beauty's use
If thou couldst say 'This pretty child of mine
Saves my account and makes my old excuse,'
Making his beauty by succession thine.   12
    This were to be new born when thou art old,
    And see thy blood warm when thou feel'st it cold.

In laudem musicae et opprobrium contemptori[s] eiusdem [Sonnet 8]

I

Music to hear, why hear'st thou music sadly?
    Sweet with sweets war not, joy delights in joy;
Why lov'st thou that which thou receiv'st not gladly,
    Or else receiv'st with pleasure thine annoy?   4

2

If the true concord of well-tunèd sounds,
  By unions married, do offend thy ear,
They do but sweetly chide thee, who confounds
  In singleness a part which thou shouldst bear.   8

3

Mark how one string, sweet husband to another,
  Strikes each on each by mutual ordering;
Resembling child, and sire, and happy mother,
  Which, all in one, this single note doth sing;   12
    Whose speechless song, being many, seeming one,
    Sings this to thee: 'Thou single shalt prove none.'

On his Mistress' Beauty [Sonnet 106]

When in the annals of all-wasting Time
I see descriptions of the fairest wights,
And beauty making beautiful old rhyme
In praise of ladies dead and lovely knights;   4
Then, in the blazon of sweet beauty's best,
Of face, of hand, of lip, of eye or brow,
I see their antique pen would have expressed
Ev'n such a beauty as you master now.   8
So all their praises were but prophecies
Of these our days, all you prefiguring,
And, for they saw but with divining eyes,
They had not skill enough thy worth to sing: 12
  For we, which now behold these present days,
  Have eyes to wonder, but no tongues to praise.

[The Lawes version of Sonnet 116]

1

Self-blinding error seizeth all those minds
Who with false appellations call that 'love'
Which alters when it alteration finds,
Or with the mover hath a power to move –   4
Not much unlike the heretic's pretence,
That cites true scripture but prevents the sense.

2

O no, love is an ever-fixèd mark
That looks on tempests but is never shaken; 8
It is the star to every wand'ring bark,
Whose worth's unknown, although his height be taken:
No mountebank with eye-deluding flashes,
But flaming martyr in his holy ashes. 12

·3

Love's not Time's fool, though rosy lips and cheeks
Within his binding circle compass round;
Love alters not with his brief hours and weeks,
But holds it out even to the edge of doom. 16
If this be error and not truth approved,
Cupid's no god, nor man ne'er loved.

[The Bodleian version of Sonnet 128]

How oft, when thou, dear, dearest music play'st
Upon that blessèd wood whose motions sounds
With thy sweet fingers when thou gently sway'st
The wiry concord that mine ear confounds – 4
O, how I envy those keys that nimble leap
To kiss the tender inward of thy hand,
Whilst my poor lips, which should that harvest reap,
At the wood's boldness by thee blushing stand. 8
To be so touched, they fain would change their state
And situation with those dancing chips
O'er whom your fingers walk with gentle gait,
Making dead wood more blest than living lips. 12
    Since then those keys so happy are in this,
    Give them your fingers, me your lips to kiss.

The Passionate Pilgrim I [Sonnet 138]

When my love swears that she is made of truth
I do believe her, though I know she lies,
That she might think me some untutored youth,
Unskilful in the world's false forgeries. 4
Thus vainly thinking that she thinks me young,
Although I know my years be past the best,
I, smiling, credit her false-speaking tongue,
Outfacing faults in love with love's ill rest. 8

But wherefore says my love that she is young?
And wherefore say not I that I am old?
O, love's best habit's in a soothing tongue,
And age in love loves not to have years told. 12
   Therefore I'll lie with love, and love with me,
   Since that our faults in love thus smothered be.

The Passionate Pilgrim II [Sonnet 144]

Two loves I have, of comfort and despair,
That like two spirits do suggest me still;
My better angel is a man right fair,
My worser spirit a woman coloured ill. 4
To win me soon to hell, my female evil
Tempteth my better angel from my side,
And would corrupt my saint to be a devil,
Wooing his purity with her fair pride. 8
And whether that my angel be turned fiend
Suspect I may, yet not directly tell;
For being both to me, both to each friend,
I guess one angel in another's hell. 12
   The truth I shall not know, but live in doubt
   Till my bad angel fire my good one out.

The Passionate Pilgrim IV

Sweet Cytherea, sitting by a brook
With young Adonis, lovely, fresh, and green,
Did court the lad with many a lovely look,
Such looks as none could look but beauty's queen. 4
She told him stories to delight his ear;
She showed him favours to allure his eye;
To win his heart, she touched him here and there;
Touches so soft still conquer chastity. 8
But whether unripe years did want conceit,
Or he refused to take her figured proffer,
The tender nibbler would not touch the bait,
But smile and jest at every gentle offer. 12
   Then fell she on her back, fair queen, and toward:
   He rose and ran away – ah, fool too froward!

The Passionate Pilgrim VI

Scarce had the sun dried up the dewy morn,
And scarce the herd gone to the hedge for shade,
When Cytherea, all in love forlorn,
A longing tarriance for Adonis made   4
Under an osier growing by a brook,
A brook where Adon used to cool his spleen.
Hot was the day; she hotter that did look
For his approach, that often there had been.   8
Anon he comes, and throws his mantle by,
And stood stark naked on the brook's green brim:
The sun looked on the world with glorious eye,
Yet not so wistly as this queen on him.   12
   He, spying her, bounced in whereas he stood;
   'O Jove,' quoth she, 'why was not I a flood!'

The Passionate Pilgrim IX

Fair was the morn, when the fair queen of love,
     . . .
Paler for sorrow than her milk-white dove,
For Adon's sake, a youngster proud and wild,
Her stand she takes upon a steep-up hill.   4
Anon Adonis comes with horn and hounds;
She, silly queen, with more than love's good will,
Forbade the boy he should not pass those grounds.   8
'Once', quoth she, 'did I see a fair sweet youth
Here in these brakes deep-wounded with a boar,
Deep in the thigh, a spectacle of ruth!
See, in my thigh,' quoth she, 'here was the sore.'   12
   She showèd hers, he saw more wounds than one,
   And blushing fled, and left her all alone.

The Passionate Pilgrim XI

Venus with Adonis sitting by her
Under a myrtle shade began to woo him;
She told the youngling how god Mars did try her,
And as he fell to her, she fell to him.   4
'Even thus,' quoth she, 'the warlike god embraced me,'
And then she clipped Adonis in her arms;

'Even thus,' quoth she, 'the warlike god unlaced me,'
As if the boy should use like loving charms; 8
'Even thus,' quoth she, 'he seizèd on my lips,'
And with her lips on his did act the seizure;
And as she fetchèd breath, away he skips,
And would not take her meaning nor her pleasure. 12
    Ah, that I had my lady at this bay,
      To kiss and clip me till I run away!

COLLATIONS

Spes Altera [Sonnet 2]

In this collation, readings from the Westminster Abbey MS 41 are to the left of the brackets (except in the case of the title), while divergences from it are recorded to the right. BL1, 2, 3, 4, and 5 stand for British Library Add. MSS 10309, 21433, 25303, 30982 and Sloane MS 1792; FSL1, 2, and 3 are Folger Shakespeare Library MSS V.a.148, V.a.170, and V.a.345; N, R, W, and Y are University of Nottingham, Portland MS Pw V 37, Rosenbach Museum and Library, MS 1083/17, Westminster Abbey MS 41, and Yale University, Oxborn Collection, b. 205. Q indicates a reading from the quarto of 1609, and SJC stands for St John's College, Cambridge, MS S.23.

	Spes Altera] BL1, BL2, BL3; *Spes Altera* A song FSL3; To one y^t would dye a Mayd BL4, BL5, FSL2, W, Y; A Lover to his Mistres N; The Benefitt of Mariage. R; 2 Q; *untitled* SJC
1	forty] threscore BL1
	winters] yeares R
2	trench] drench R; digge Q, SJC
	furrows] trenches Q, SJC
	that lovely] thy beauties Q, SJC
	field] cheeke BL2, BL3
3	youth's] youth BL5, FSL3
	fair] fairer R; proud Q, SJC
	liv'ry] liuerie BL2, BL3, BL4, BL5, FSL2, FSL3, N, W; feild R
	accounted] accompted BL3; esteemed N; gaz'd on Q, SJC
4	Shall] Wil Q, SJC
	like] like like BL5; a Q, SJC
	rotten] totter'd Q, SJC ('tatterd')
	weeds] cloaths FSL2; weed Q, SJC
	no] smal Q, SJC
5	being asked] if we Ask BL2; if wee aske BL3; askt R
	lies] lye W (*cropped*)

6   Where] Where's BL1, BL2, BL3, FSL3, N, R
        lustre] treasure Q, SJC
        youthful] lusty Q, SJC
7   these] those Y; *not in* BL4; thine Q, SJC
        hollow sunken] hollow-sunken BL1; owne deepe Q, SJC
8   eaten] beaten FSL2; eating Q, SJC
        truth] shame Q, SJC
        worthless] thriftlesse Q, SJC
        praise] prays W (*cropped*); prayes BL4; pleasure BL5
9   O] *not in* BL5 *or* Q *or* SJC
        how] whow BL4
        much] far Y; *not in* BL5
        better were] more praise deseru'd Q; more prayse deserues SJC
        beauty's] bewtious Y
10   say] answere Q; say that SJC
        pretty] little BL2, BL3; faire Q, SJC
11   Saves] Saud Y; Shall sum Q, SJC
        my] mine N
        account] accompt BL3; count Q, SJC
        makes my old] makes me old BL4; makes no old FSL2; yeilds mee
        an N; makes the old R; make no old Y; make my old Q; make thy
        ould SJC
12   Making] Proouing Q
13   new born] made younge BL2, BL3; new made Q, SJC
14   feel'st] felst BL2, BL3, BL4

In laudem musicae et opprobrium contemptori[s] eiusdem [Sonnet 8]

This collation records, to the left of the brackets, readings from British
Library Add. MS 15226, and, to the right, variants from the quarto of 1609.

        In laudem musicae et opprobrium contemptori[s] eiusdem] 8
2   Sweet] Sweets
6   thy] thine
8   a part which] the parts that
10   on] in
11   child, and sire] sier, and child
12   Which] Who
        this single note doth] one pleasing note do
14   shalt] wilt

On his Mistress' Beauty [Sonnet 106]

In the following collation, R stands for Rosenbach Museum and Library MS 1083/16, H is the Holgate Commonplace Book (Pierpont Morgan Library, MA 1057), and Q Thorpe's quarto.

	On his Mistress' Beauty] R, H; 106 Q
1	annals of all-wasting] R; Annals of all wasting H; Chronicle of wasted Q
2	descriptions] R, Q; discription H
3	rhyme] R, Q; mine H (*with* 'rime' *written in the margin as a correction*)
6	Of face, of hand] R; Of face, of hands H; Of hand, of foote Q
	of eye] H, Q; or eye R
	or brow] R, H; of brow Q
8	Ev'n] H; Euen R, Q
9	their] H; these R
	were] R, H; are Q
10	these] R; those H; this Q
	days] R, H; time Q
11	saw] H; say R; look'd Q
	divining] H, Q; deceiving R
12	skill] R, H; still Q
	thy] R, H; your Q
13	we] H, Q; me R
	present] H, Q; pleasant R
14	no] R, H; lack Q
	tongues] H, Q; tongue R

[The Lawes version of Sonnet 116]

Henry Lawes's setting of 116 survives in a manuscript music book owned (at least in 1659) and partly compiled by the composer John Gamble. Readings from the text – Drexel MS 4251, No. 33, in the New York Public Library, Music Division – are given to the left of the brackets, with Q divergences to the right.

	untitled] 119 (*misprint for* '116')
1	Self-blinding error seizeth all those] Let me not to the marriage of true
2	Who with false appellations call that 'love'] Admit impediments, loue is not loue
4	with the mover hath a power to move] bends with the remouer to remoue
5–6	Not much unlike the heretic's pretence, | That cites true scripture but prevents the sense] *not in* Q

451

7   love] it
8   but] and
11–12   No mountebank with eye-deluding flashes, | But flaming martyr in
        his holy ashes] *not in* Q
14   binding circle] bending sickles
        round] come
16   holds] beares
17   not truth approved] vpon me proued
18   Cupid's no god] I never writ
        man ne'er loved] no man euer loued

[The Bodleian version of Sonnet 128]

In this collation, R stands for Bodleian MS Rawl. poet. 152, Q for Thorpe's
quarto.

        untitled] R; 128 Q
1   dear, dearest] R ('deere, deeist'); my musike Q
2   motions] R; motion Q
3   sway'st] Q; swaies R
4   confounds] Q; consoundes R
5   O, how] R; Do Q
        keys] R; Iackes Q
        leap] Q; leapes R
7   reap] Q; reped R
8   wood's] Q; wood R
9   touched, they fain] R (*reading* 'the' *for* 'they'); tikled they Q
11   O'er] Q; ouer R
        your] R; their Q
13   then those keys] R; sausie Iackes Q
14   your fingers] R; their fingers Q; thy fingers *this ed*.
        your lips] R; thy lips Q

Sonnets from *The Passionate Pilgrim*

'When my love swears', 'Two loves I have', and 'Sweet Cytherea' are
modernized from the fragmentary first edition of 1599, 'Scarce had the sun',
'Fair was the morn', and 'Venus with Adonis' from the intact second edition
(also 1599). Unidentified readings below are from the earliest extant Jaggard
text, while FSLX and Y refer to Folger Shakespeare Library MSS V.a.339
and V.b.43, G indicates Bartholomew Griffin's *Fidessa* (1596), and Q stands
for Thorpe's quarto. Benson's titles – 'False beleefe', 'A Temptation', 'A
sweet provocation', 'Cruell Deceit', 'Inhumanitie', and 'Foolish disdaine' –
are vivid but without authority. This edition follows the traditional practice of

marking the order of *The Passionate Pilgrim* with roman numerals. Versions of
I appear in Q and FSLX as well as in Jaggard's anthology; II recurs only in
Q, IV in FSLX and Y, and VI only in FSLX; IX is found nowhere else; XI
features in G and both FSLX and Y.

	untitled] I *eds.*; 138 Q
4	Unskilful . . . forgeries] Vnlearned . . . subtilties Q
6	I know . . . years] she knowes . . . dayes Q
	be] are FSLX, Q
7	I, smiling] Simply I Q
8	Outfacing faults in love with love's ill rest] On both sides thus is simple truth suprest Q
9	says my love that she is young?] sayes she not she is vniust? Q
11	habit's in a] habite is a (*ed.* 2); habit is in Q
	soothing] smoothinge FSLX, seeming Q
	tongue] trust Q
12	to have] t'haue Q
13	I'll lie with love, and love with me] I lye with her, and she with me Q
14	Since that our faults in love thus smothered be] And in our faults by lyes we flattered be Q

	untitled] II *eds.*; 144 Q
2	That] Which Q
3	My] The Q
4	My] The Q
6	side] sight Q
8	fair] fowle Q
9	fiend] finde Q
11	For . . . to me] But . . . from me Q
13	The truth I shall not know] Yet this shal I nere know Q

	untitled] IV *eds.*
1	Sweet] Faire FSLY
4	could] can FSLY
5	ear] FSLY; eares
8	soft] sought FSLX
10	refused] did scorne FSLY
	her] (*ed.* 2); his
11	touch] take FSLY
12	smile . . . jest] blusht . . . smild FSLY
13	queen] *not in* FSLY
14	rose] blusht FSLY
	ah] ô FSLY

	untitled] VI *eds.*
8	there] heare FSLX
12	this] the FSLX
14	O] ah FSLX

	untitled] IX *eds.*
2	. . .] *line missing in early editions*

	untitled] XI *eds.*
1	with] and G, FSLY
3	god] great FSLY
4	she fell] so fell she G, FSLY
5	warlike] wanton G
6	clipped] clasp'd G; tooke FSLY
7	Even] & FSLX
	warlike] lusty FSLY
9–12	'Even thus,' quoth she . . . her pleasure] But he a wayward boy refusde her offer | And ran away, the beautious Queene neglecting: | Shewing both folly to abuse her proffer, | And all his sex of cowardise detecting G
9	Even] Then FSLX
11	And] But FSLY
	fetchèd] tooke hir FSLY
13	Ah . . . this] Oh . . . that G, FSLY
	lady] mistris G, FSLX, FSLY
14	kiss and clip me] clipp and kiss hir FSLY
	run] ranne G, FSLY

INDEX OF SONNET FIRST LINES

READ MORE IN PENGUIN

BY THE SAME AUTHOR

These collections are accompanied by notes and an introduction to each text.

Four Tragedies
Hamlet • Othello • King Lear • Macbeth

The theme of the great Shakespearian tragedies is the fall from grace of a great man with a flaw in his nature. Whether it is the ruthless ambition of Macbeth or the folly of Lear, the irresolution of Hamlet or the suspicion of Othello, the cause of the tragedy – even the murder of a king – is trifling compared with the calamity it unleashes.

Four Comedies
The Taming of the Shrew • A Midsummer Night's Dream • As You Like It • Twelfth Night

Shakespearian comedy has as much to do with the structure and movement of the drama as the wit of its dialogue or the humour of its characters. In these four comedies there is a near-tragic crisis from which disaster or happiness may ensue, but the overriding force of goodwill and the power of understanding, love and generosity brings us through to a joyful conclusion.

Four Histories
Richard II • Henry IV • King Lear • Macbeth

This tetralogy of plays – written by Shakespeare *c.* 1595 to *c.* 1599 – inhabits the turbulent period of change from the usurpation of the throne of Richard II by Bolingbroke to the triumph – some would say triumphalism – of heroic kingship under Henry V. Walter Pater, in his famous essay, found the central ideas of the *Histories* to be 'the irony of kingship – average human nature, flung with wonderfully pathetic effect into the vortex of great events'.

Three Roman Plays
Julius Caesar • Antony and Cleopatra • Coriolanus

Each of these plays is profoundly concerned with political action, with the relation between the political and personal. Shakespeare, like Plutarch (his source for these plays), closely scrutinizes his heroes and compels us to question what sort of men they are.